AFTER KANT

After Kant

THE ROMANS, THE GERMANS, AND THE MODERNS IN THE HISTORY OF POLITICAL THOUGHT

MICHAEL SONENSCHER

PRINCETON UNIVERSITY PRESS

PRINCETON & OXFORD

Published by Princeton University Press
41 William Street, Princeton, New Jersey 08540
99 Banbury Road, Oxford OX2 6JX

press.princeton.edu

All Rights Reserved

Library of Congress Cataloging-in-Publication Data

Names: Sonenscher, Michael, author.
Title: After Kant : the Romans, the Germans, and the moderns in the history
    of political thought / Michael Sonenscher.
Description: Princeton, New Jersey : Princeton University Press, 2023. | Includes
    bibliographical references and index.
Identifiers: LCCN 2022032607 (print) | LCCN 2022032608 (ebook) |
    ISBN 9780691245621 (hardback) | ISBN 9780691245638 (paperback) |
    ISBN 9780691245645 (ebook)
Subjects: LCSH: Political science—Philosophy—History.
Classification: LCC JA71 .S64647 2023 (print) | LCC JA71 (ebook) |
    DDC 320.01—dc23/eng/20221101
LC record available at https://lccn.loc.gov/2022032607
LC ebook record available at https://lccn.loc.gov/2022032608

British Library Cataloging-in-Publication Data is available

Editorial: Ben Tate and Josh Drake
Production Editorial: Lauren Lepow
Cover Design: Hunter Finch
Production: Lauren Reese
Publicity: William Pagdatoon and Charlotte Coyne

Cover image: *The Oath of the Horatii by* Jacques-Louis David (1748–1825).
Purchased with funds from the Libbey Endowment, gift of Edward Drummond
Libbey. Courtesy of the Toledo Museum of Art.

This book has been composed in Arno

10 9 8 7 6 5 4 3 2 1

CONTENTS

DEMOCRACY, WE KNOW, began with the Greeks, just as the idea of a *res publica*, or republic, began with the Romans, and trials by jury began, it is said, with the Germans or, more specifically, with the trials by ordeal performed under oath a long time ago by several ancient Germanic peoples. Over time, however, all these local institutions and arrangements have become vectors of values that are, apparently, universal. Everything, it could be said, begins somewhere, but principles seem to apply everywhere. Reality, partiality, and ordinary historical scholarship seem to counter the claim, but the claim itself continues to command attention. This is because it is not really, or not only, a historical claim, but is also a moral claim; and something about morality, because it applies to many different peoples and many moments in time, seems to call for this additional, transhistorical, dimension. Sometimes this extra dimension has been called a state of nature, a veil of ignorance, or a thought experiment, but the name itself matters less than the aspiration to find an external, neutral or uncommitted starting point. The result is a well-known set of tensions about the relationship between facts and values, legality and morality, the time-bound and the timeless, the relative and the absolute, the local and the general, or the irrational and the rational.

As this brief but strongly signposted preface is intended to show, this is a book about how these tensions began to be described and discussed, mainly in France, but also in Germany, Switzerland, and Britain, and mainly between the late eighteenth and mid-nineteenth centuries. At its most straightforward it is a story about three successive sets of arguments—between the respective supporters of the Ancients and the Moderns,[1] the classics and the romantics, and the Romans and the Germans—and the impact that they have had on the history and the historiography of political thought. Its aim is to try to show that a great deal more of what is usually involved in thinking about politics was connected to the problem underlying these three sets of arguments. The

---

1. Capitalized in this preface as, along with "Romans" and "Germans," a reference to the subtitle, but lowercased thereafter.

problem in question was, and still is, how to connect the local to the general without falling either into circularity on the one side or partiality (and even imperialism) on the other. One solution was simply to drop the subject of origins and focus instead on outcomes. Origins, it could be said, are particular because they belong to the past, but outcomes can be universal because they belong to the future; and, since the future does not exist, it could, possibly, avoid the particularity of the past and, it could be added, the unavoidably local content of a veil of ignorance, a state of nature, or a thought experiment. Hence, and in keeping with the orientation of both the title and subtitle of this book, in place of the ancients and the Romans or the romantics and the Germans, the future could belong to the Moderns. But this apparent solution opened up another problem. If, almost by definition, the future belongs to the Moderns, then what about those left behind? They are, like all of us, obliged to live in the present. From the vantage point of the present, the prize promised by the idea of progress can look less like an achievement than an affront.

The book's title and subtitle are, therefore, a form of shorthand for a number of overlapping questions about the relationship between history and normativity, political institutions and individual freedom, social interdependence and moral choice that began to inform thinking about politics, initially after Rousseau, Kant, and Hegel, but also after the French Revolution and the British Industrial Revolution. The names of both the individuals and the periods mean that thinking about politics took place at the confluence of two distinct sets of arguments. One, by the late eighteenth century, was already known as the quarrel between the Ancients and the Moderns, while the other came to be known as the conflict between the supporters of the classics and the romantics. The subjects of the Romans, the Germans, and the Moderns were connected to both. Behind them lay a problem about time and a proliferating range of questions about identification, evaluation, and causation bound up with the subject of time because time, more than space, seems to bring out something genuinely unbridgeable in the problematic relationship between facts and norms, the relative and the absolute, and the particular and the general.[2] Time, it seems, is the medium that gave these divisions their unbridgeable quality. Space is not hard to traverse in several different directions. Time, however, seems to preclude the same range of choice because it does not house as many different directions of travel. It seems to go forward relentlessly, leaving no way back. It could, however, be infinity, or an endless succession of moments, and could also be eternity, or a moment that lasts forever. But whether

2. For a helpful way in, see M. F. Cleugh, *Time and Its Importance in Modern Thought* (London, Methuen, 1937).

it dissolves endlessly or crystallizes permanently, neither type of moment seems to be able to escape from the constraints of linearity.

One way of addressing this cluster of problems was to try to show that they could be disaggregated. The move applied most immediately to history because history could be said to be about both the past and knowledge of the past, and although the first might have gone, the second could still be alive and be available as a source of value. In this latter guise history could be combined with the human capacity for autonomy to symbolize a value, a goal, or a choice. Something about freedom, particularly if it was redefined as autonomy, seemed to form a link between causes and values. It also seemed to provide a way to close the gap between Kant and his critics because a value was something located somewhere between a fact and a norm. A value seemed to be a product of choice and choice in turn seemed to inject both an extra quality and a temporal specificity to the otherwise undifferentiated flow of events. Values were volatile, but something about the idea of freedom as autonomy, or as a value superimposed upon a condition, seemed to supply a kind of moral and historical compass that could point a way between the thickets of particularity and the emptiness of generality. Armed with the magical ingredient of autonomy, the apparently continuous sphere of human choice could, on this basis, be used to bridge the gap between facts and norms, the relative and the absolute, and the particular and the general and, consequently, bring the cluster of apparent antinomies into closer alignment. In this context, thinking about the Romans, the Germans, and the Moderns meant thinking not only about politics, whether retrospectively, prospectively, or simply cumulatively, but also about how, when, or whether these different historical and imaginative vantage points could be connected to something able to ignite the apparently timeless human capacity for autonomy and turn it into something more like practicality.

Thinking about autonomy also meant that thinking about politics began to include thinking about two further subjects that had not been as central to political thought as they have since become. One was money; the other was the law. Both appeared to make it possible to keep the value of freedom alive because both could be used either to impede and obstruct on one side or to enable and support on another. Thinking about money meant thinking about both the economy and the state, and, more particularly, about the bridge between the two formed by a state's capacity to borrow money and its concurrent power to create a currency. Thinking about the law also meant thinking about both the economy and the state because, as with money as either a currency, a commodity, a credit, or a capital, the law could equally well exist in several different guises and meet several different needs. It could be private or public, municipal or regional, as well as national or international, and could be made

as much by legal institutions, like courts, judges, or universities, as by legisla-
tures, governments, or peoples. Thinking about money and the law formed a
starting point for thinking about the passage of time in several new and different ways because the two subjects appeared to show how it might be possible
to add the human capacity for autonomy to the overlapping subjects of the
Romans, the Germans, and the Moderns.

They did so not only because they made judgment an unavoidable part of
political life but also because they gave a new significance to two long-
established terms. The first was the concept of civil society, while the second
was the much older concept of history. Adding money and the law to both
concepts created the possibility of giving a new conceptual framework to the
relationship between political society and civil society, with different sets of
institutions and arrangements taking responsibility for one side or the other
of the political and economic divide. Doing the same thing to history
amounted to giving a more firmly human direction to the interrelationship of
the past, the present, and the future because money and the law seemed to
have a built-in power to straddle them all. Together, they offered the prospect
of establishing a social and institutional setting that was able to provide a home
for both the idea of autonomy and the concept of a value. This is an exploration of the intellectual repercussions of adding this cluster of subjects to
established ways of thinking about states and governments, sovereignty and
democracy, justice and equality, morality and legality, the national and the
international—or, put differently, to the relationship between the political
and nonpolitical parts of human life. Together, they amounted to a protracted, and
now largely forgotten, set of discussions and arguments about the relationship
of the Romans and the Germans to the Moderns.

I first began to think about these subjects several years ago when I came
across the passage in the Swiss-French historian and political economist Jean-
Charles-Léonard Simonde de Sismondi's *Historical View of the Literature of the
South of Europe* that is described more fully at the beginning of chapter 3. In this
passage, Sismondi claimed that modern European civilization, as he called it,
had two origins rather than one. The first was Roman, while the second was
German. I began to get the point of the claim when, sometime later, I sat down
and really began to read Immanuel Kant's short essay entitled *Idea for a Universal History with a Cosmopolitan Aim* (or *from a Cosmopolitan Perspective*, as it is
also translated). The argument of Kant's essay is not really what its title now
usually suggests. Instead of an uplifting vision of history as progress and with
perpetual peace as its ultimate goal, Kant's essay disclosed a more morally disquieting discrepancy between the idea of progress and the length of a human
life. If, he argued, it was the case that there was such a thing as universal history
with a cosmopolitan aim, then it seemed to follow that history's benefits would

be available only to those living when history came to an end. It was not an uplifting claim. Nor, to many of Kant's early readers, did it look like one. Gradually, with more reading and more thought, it began to become clear that Sismondi's claim about the double origins of modern European civilization was a kind of indirect reply to Kant. It also became clear that a more careful examination of the full range of replies to Kant's argument had the effect of opening a window onto a surprisingly rich array of largely forgotten arguments about morality, history, economics, and politics. Explaining why these arguments mattered then, but have been forgotten now, began to reveal that many of the most fundamental concepts of modern politics had a more varied and a more recent array of origins and connotations than their names alone suggest.

It took some time to work out the connections between Kant and Sismondi because there was certainly nothing like a direct link between the two. Piecing the connections together has taken me into many different areas of eighteenth- and nineteenth-century European intellectual life, mainly at the interstices of history, politics, economics, religion, law, and morality. Its starting point, however, was a question about where modern political ideologies and the concepts ordinarily used in modern European and American political thought have come from. The answer that I began to see was that both had rather more to do with the thought of Immanuel Kant than is usually assumed because Kant invented a rather odd concept called "unsocial sociability" to explain some of the more familiar, conflict-driven, aspects of history and politics. The concept of unsocial sociability was in fact the other side of Kant's claim that historical progress favoured late arrivers rather than early starters. The argument that follows is that the concept actually played a bigger part than we usually assume in how we have come to think about politics because it had quite a lot to do with a number of subjects not usually associated with Kant, like the idea of the death of God (usually associated with Nietzsche) or the notion that history happens as either tragedy or farce (usually associated with Marx) or the concept of political theology (usually associated with Carl Schmitt). As will also be shown, the idea of the right to have rights (an idea usually associated with Hannah Arendt) actually began with Kant's critical follower, Johann Gottlieb Fichte. All these concepts play a part in the content of this book because all of them were responses to Kant's disturbing claim that any historical justification of political legitimacy was likely to be arbitrary, while any moral justification was likely to be viable only when history had run its course. After Kant, something extra was needed to bridge the gap between history and politics, or between the rival legacies of the Romans and the Germans to the values and arrangements of the Moderns.

What was extra turned out to be something less, rather than something more. Given a choice between an arbitrary past and an indeterminate—or, for most people, unattainable—future, it gradually became clear that the only available foundation of politics was politics itself. Unlike, for example, music, morality, economics, or mathematics, politics has no distinct subject matter, which means that any particular subject can become political. Much the same idea came, with Kant and his followers, to apply to the concept of freedom, but the concept of freedom is not so obviously bound up with other people as politics. Thinking about politics in the light of both the arbitrary quality of the past and the unattainable character of the future made politics, and a range of different and potentially competing evaluations of both the past and the future, the real foundation of modern politics. Since, it could be argued, politics had no distinct content, its content would then have to be determined at every moment, all the time. Thinking about politics now came to mean thinking not only about how to make politics manageable but also about why, from time to time, politics really did seem to have become manageable. I did not expect to find that the person who approached this problem with unusually illuminating insight was the German philosopher Georg Wilhelm Friedrich Hegel. The details of how he did so are set out in chapter 7. In the context of the line of thought running from Kant to Hegel and beyond, politics could be seen as something less than history, but also something more than the future, because politics could now be seen to be a matter of judgment not only over how and why to draw a line between apparently timeless truths and apparently local values but also over how to identify something (like the law, the state, the economy, or the constitution) capable of producing a switch from the latter to the former. Politics happened when values clashed with ideologies or, in the terms described in the final chapter of this book that became current towards the end of the nineteenth century, when things that were true and timeless clashed with things like atheism, realism, socialism, or conservatism and the many other highly charged words that (at least in English) all end in -ism. In this sense, although the phrase "the philosophy of history" began with Voltaire, the subject began with Kant, while its more comprehensive but still sometimes forgotten treatment began with Hegel.

As time has gone by, I have come to revise many of my initial assumptions about modern European history and historiography and to think more carefully and critically about a number of generally received ideas in the history and historiography of political thought. Modern scholarship did not lead me to expect the intensity of the debates that took place between Romanists and Germanists in the nineteenth century or the widespread early nineteenth-century hostility towards ancient Rome and, more specifically, Roman law that I first came across in the course of trying to find out about something called Krausism (which too is an aspect of European intellectual life that has largely disappeared from historical view). Nor did I expect to find a connection between subjects like these and the parallel distinctions between the general will and the will of all made by Jean-Jacques Rousseau, and between public law and private law made by Immanuel Kant. I did not know that there was once as much of a connection between the concept of palingenesis and the revolutions of 1848 as there was between the concept of democracy and the events of 1848, or that the word "historicism" (or *Historismus* in the original German) began as a dismissive comment on Kant's philosophy of history made by members of the literary and philosophical circles associated with romanticism and the Schlegel brothers, or that there were real and significant connections linking what palingenesis, historicism, and Kant were once taken to stand for. I was also unaware that the modern (as against the original) connotations of the word "ideology" began as a term of art in early nineteenth-century French legitimist thought, along with the phrase "the social question." Nor did I expect to find that the original French phrase *révolution industrielle*, or industrial revolution, began as a Saint-Simonian answer to the social question, which, in its turn, originated as a French royalist and legitimist question. In all these cases, there were surprising discoveries and significant connections that were all once usually better known. One indication of how well known they once were can be found in the contents of a letter written in 1861 by the future Regius Professor of Modern History at the University of Cambridge, Lord John Emmerich Edward Dalberg Acton, reproduced in part as an appendix to this book. I came across this letter some time after I had finished writing the book and it seemed, when I read it, to be rather like an executive summary of its subject matter. One of the aims of what follows is simply to describe the story that, in intellectual and historical terms, lay behind Acton's letter by setting out something more like the full version in this book. Together, both the letter and the story help to explain why, as several of my first teachers (Austin Gough, Gwynne Lewis, E. P. Thompson) told me, the period that straddles the French Revolution and the Industrial Revolution really does have as much to do with thinking about politics now as about finding out about history then.

In following up these subjects, I have had a great deal of help along the way, notably from Richard Bourke, Edward Castleton, Graham Clure, John Dunn, Lorna Finlayson, Ludovic Frobert, Peter Garnsey, Raymond Geuss, Joel Isaac, Duncan Kelly, Iain McDaniel, Robin Osborne, Anthony Pagden, Eva Piirimäe, Tom Pye, Sophus Reinert, John Robertson, Lucian Robinson, David Runciman, Paul Sagar, Ruth Scurr, Diana Siclovan, Damian Valdez, Hanna Weibye, Jim Whitman, Flora Willson, Waseem Yaqoob, and Sam Zeitlin, who have all given me helpful advice or generous and critical comments on earlier drafts of various chapters. Elizabeth Allen has reminded me of what I was meaning to say more frequently than anyone should be expected to do.

Charlotte Johann has been a considerate and constructive friend despite the fact that she has read more of my prose than anyone should. Béla Kapossy, Isaac Nakhimovsky, and Richard Whatmore have been ever-helpful sources of information and guides to what to think about next, too, or otherwise. More importantly, at least to me, they have kept me in good heart when my courage has flagged. I am more fully in debt to them all than they know. I am immensely grateful to Lauren Lepow not only for her skill, precision, and thoroughness in copyediting the typescript of this book but also for her forbearance in putting up with my erratic allegiance to both British and US English (sometimes in the same word). Thanks too to Ben Tate, Josh Drake, and their many colleagues at Princeton for bringing this book to a final conclusion. It is very unlikely that I would have embarked on this project without the sustained support I have received from a number of institutional sources. The first has been the Leverhulme Trust, which awarded me a senior research fellowship longer ago than it is probably wise to indicate publicly, and which has been a tactful and considerate monitor of my progress towards the completion of this book, together with an earlier examination of the thought of Jean-Jacques Rousseau, and a short essay on the word and the concept of capitalism. The second has been the Provost and Fellows of King's College and, more particularly, the college's research committee not only for their combined help and support but also for providing me with many opportunities to learn far more than I expected. The third has been the Institut des Etudes Avancées in Lyon both for awarding me a visiting research fellowship and for enabling me to use the small, but very well endowed, open-access library of the Ecole Normale Supérieure in Lyon where much of my initial reading was done. Finally, I have a large and irredeemable debt to librarians and archivists not only in King's College or the University of Cambridge but also in France, Switzerland, Germany, and the United States. My debt to them all is immense, and the content of this book is certainly a poor substitute for the knowledge, competence, and consideration that they have shown me.

1

Introduction

IT IS NOT WIDELY KNOWN, even among specialists in Kant studies, that the concept of freedom that Immanuel Kant called negative freedom applied in the first instance to God. This was not because God preferred shopping to civic virtue or favoured private life more than transcendental immanence, but simply because God was perfect in every way. Being perfect, as Kant explained in 1788 in his *Critique of Practical Reason*, God's will was axiomatically disinterested and universally applicable. This meant that the concept of a categorical imperative—or the idea of deciding to act only on the basis that your will could also be enacted as a universal law—was not really relevant to the divine will. A divine will did not have to make any comparison between an individual will and a universal law because it was, by definition, universal and could, therefore, identify and maintain the disinterested content of the moral law without having to obey a command, even from itself. A human will on the other hand was, categorically, a divided will, with a life that straddled both the spiritual and physical worlds and the separation of time into past, present, and future, and, since it was a divided will, it categorically required an imperative command, especially from itself. It could, however, sometimes be a pure will because it could use reason to set itself a goal that as Kant put it, at least in the rather literal rendition occasionally given in translations of his works, "could always hold at the same time as a principle in a giving of universal law."[1] The outcome of this capacity to imagine one's own will as a universal law was the condition that Kant called autonomy, or the distinctively human capacity for self-determination. The resulting coincidence between an individual will and a universal principle would, Kant explained, be just the same type of moral law that God could observe without any possibility of conflict. All this meant that the subject of autonomy did not really apply to God because God, not being

---

1. Immanuel Kant, *Critique of Practical Reason* [1788], in Immanuel Kant, *Practical Philosophy*, ed. Mary Gregor (Cambridge, CUP, 1996), bk. 1, sec. 7, p. 164.

bounded by time or space or any of the other conditions associated with human experience, did not have to deal with the choices or dilemmas involved in human life.

Where the subject of autonomy was concerned, what required effort by humanity was effortless for the divinity. This was why God's freedom was purely negative and why, from this perspective, it could be said that God was a kind of Epicurean. As Kant's favourite author, Jean-Jacques Rousseau, pointed out, being divine seemed to entail being entirely self-sufficient and fully at one with oneself.[2] The human condition, however, was different. It did, certainly, have some godlike features. "Pure reason," Kant wrote, "is practical of itself alone and gives (to the human being) a universal law which we call the *moral law*."[3] In this respect, human capabilities were comparable to the divine. But in other respects the two capabilities were radically different because the human will could also be determined "by needs and sensible motives," and this externally generated form of causation meant that further measures of both will and understanding were required to secure the human capacity for self-determination. "In the supremely self-sufficient intelligence," Kant explained, "choice is rightly represented as incapable of any maxim that could not at the same time be objectively a law and the concept of *holiness* which on that account belongs to it, puts it not indeed above all practically restrictive laws and so above obligation and duty."[4] But since humans have bodies and senses, with the needs and desires that accompany them, freedom for humans had to be positive as well as negative because this type of freedom had to involve choices and decisions, sometimes even in purely isolated circumstances. Being human meant, therefore, that autonomy called for positive freedom because autonomy for humans was predicated upon an initial capacity for choice. Humans, Kant concluded, were subject to heteronomy but were also capable of autonomy.[5] God, however, did not really have to try.

"*Autonomy* of the will," Kant continued in the next section of his book, "is the sole principle of all moral laws and of duties in keeping with them; *heter-*

2. On Rousseau, God, and Epicureanism, see Michael Sonenscher, *Jean-Jacques Rousseau: The Division of Labour, the Politics of the Imagination and the Concept of Federal Government* (Leiden, Brill, 2020), pp. 61, 90, 100, 144.

3. Kant, *Critique of Practical Reason*, bk. 1, sec. 7, corollary, p. 165. On the Kant-Rousseau relationship, and in addition to the works referred to in Sonenscher, *Jean-Jacques Rousseau*, see Claude Piché, "Rousseau et Kant: A propos de la genèse de la théorie kantienne des idées," *Revue philosophique de la France et de étranger* 180 (1990): 625–35.

4. Kant, *Critique of Practical Reason*, bk. 1, sec. 7, remark, p. 166.

5. On the centrality of choice in Kant, see Eric Nelson, *The Theology of Liberalism: Political Philosophy and the Justice of God* (Cambridge, MA, Belknap Press of Harvard UP, 2019), pp. 1–14.

onomy of choice, on the other hand, not only does not ground any obligation at all but is instead opposed to the principle of obligation and to the morality of the will." Autonomy presupposed a combination of "independence from all matter of the law (namely from a desired object)" and "a determination of choice" that could be compatible with the idea of making a maxim a universal law. "That *independence*, however," Kant explained, "is freedom in the *negative* sense, whereas this *lawgiving on its own* on the part of the pure and, as such, practical reason is freedom in the *positive* sense."[6] The wider historical and historiographical implications of this distinction will be spelled out more fully in the final chapter of this book because quite a lot of ground has to be covered to bring them out more clearly. Here, it is enough to note that for humans, at least on Kant's terms, the moral law presupposed a capacity for both negative and positive freedom, or, in other words, an initial ability to distinguish the form of a law from its matter, a capacity that could then be coupled with an imaginative ability to align the idea of a choice with the prospect of universalizing it. Putting the two capacities together, Kant claimed, would produce a

---

6. Kant, *Critique of Practical Reason*, bk. 1, sec. 8, theorem iv, p. 166. Curiously, the passage was not mentioned by Isaiah Berlin in his classic "Two Concepts of Liberty." For Berlin, Kant "came nearest to asserting the 'negative' idea of liberty" in a passage in his "Idea for a Universal History" of 1784 that describes the concept, but does not use the phrase: see Isaiah Berlin, "Two Concepts of Liberty," in *Liberty*, ed. Henry Hardy (Oxford, OUP, 2009), p. 199 n. 1. Kant, it should be stressed, actually wrote about "freedom" (*Freiheit*) rather than "liberty," and, although both terms can refer to either a condition or a capacity and also have somewhat different connotations in German, English, French, and Italian, Berlin's substitution of "liberty" for "freedom" (perhaps because of the resonances of John Stuart Mill's *On Liberty*) has had the effect of blurring the differences between freedom as a condition or capacity that is either there or not there and "liberty" as a condition or capacity that is distinct, different, outside, or separate from what is usual, normal, or standard (as in a *faubourg* or *métier libre* in eighteenth-century France or one of London's liberties in eighteenth-century England). "Franchise and liberty," wrote William Blackstone in 1768 in his *Commentaries on the Laws of England*, "are used as synonymous terms and their definition is a royal privilege, or branch of the King's prerogative, subsisting in the hand of a subject": Blackstone, *Commentaries*, ed. Thomas M. Cooley (Chicago, 1884), bk. 2, ch. 3, p. 37, cited in John R. Commons, *Legal Foundations of Capitalism* (New York, Macmillan, 1924), p. 48 (Commons's whole book is a very helpful guide to the differences between the concepts of liberty and freedom in the English language). The term "negative liberty" had the effect of turning a word originally associated with an exception into a norm, and, in Berlin's usage, this norm was then set against another norm, namely, "positive liberty," to form what then became more like a binary choice. Mill's text actually captures more of the original, English-language, sense of liberty as an exception rather than a norm because, as he argued, private life was something outside, rather than inside, the public sphere to which legal and moral rules apply.

maxim that could then be subjected to the two tests of formal coherence and universalizable content.

The question to Kant's critics, like the pastor Johann Gottfried Herder, the philosopher Moses Mendelssohn, and the theologian Friedrich Schleiermacher (all to be discussed later), was whether the resulting maxim had any particular real-world applicability, and, more fundamentally, whether any conceptual creation produced under the finite conditions that Kant described could transcend the limitations of time, place, culture, and belief in which human creation took place.[7] Another critic was an early nineteenth-century Alsatian law professor named Georges Frédéric (or Georg Friedrich) Schützenberger, mayor of the city of Strasbourg between 1837 and 1848 and deputy of the department of the Bas-Rhin from 1842 to 1845. In a book that he published in 1839, entitled *Études de droit public* (Studies of public law), Schützenberger quoted all the passages from Kant's *Critique of Practical Reason* that have been cited here and came to the depressing conclusion (depressing because he admired the ambition and precision of Kant's critical philosophy) that the answer to both questions was negative. "The doctrine to which Kant has given the name of the metaphysical principles of law (*droit*)," he wrote, "is no more than a summary of Roman legislation in abstract form, divested of arrangements bound up with national and historical particularities."[8] Kant's examination of positive and negative freedom, the moral law, the categorical imperative, and the concept of autonomy lead, disappointingly, to the conclusion that he had set out in his *Metaphysics of Morals* of 1797, namely, that the

7. As the twentieth-century French philosopher Raymond Polin put it in 1944, "On pourrait dire que, chez Kant, l'objectivité elle-même est relativiste" (It could be said that, with Kant, objectivity itself is relative). Raymond Polin, *La création des valeurs: recherches sur le fondement de l'objectivité axiologique* (Paris, 1944), p. 20. On Schleiermacher as a critic of Kant, see Ruth Jackson Ravenscroft, *The Veiled God: Friedrich Schleiermacher's Theology of Finitude* (Leiden, Brill, 2019), pp. 60–77.

8. "La doctrine à laquelle Kant a donné le nom de principes métaphysiques du droit n'est qu'un résumé de la législation romaine sous une forme abstraite et dégagée des dispositions qui tiennent à des particularités nationales et historiques." Georges Frédéric Schützenberger, *Etudes de droit public* (Paris and Strasbourg, 1839), p. 180. See also, helpfully, Mikhaïl Xifaras, "Droit rationnel et droit romain chez Kant. Note sur le Conflit des Facultés," in *Généalogies des savoirs juridiques contemporains. Le Carrefour des lumières*, ed. Mikhaïl Xifaras (Brussels, Bruylant, 2007), pp. 123–50. On Kant in France, see Laurent Fedi, *Kant, une passion française 1795–1940* (Hildesheim, Georg Olms, 2018), and Jean Bonnet, *Dékantations. Fonctions idéologiques du kantisme dans le xixe siècle française* (Berne, Peter Lang, 2011). For a further examination of reactions to Kant, see Michael Steinberg, *Enlightenment Interrupted: The Lost Moment of German Idealism and the Reactionary Present* (Alresford, Hants., John Hunt Publishing, 2014).

law could be defined as the set of conditions in which one person's freedom of action could be reconciled with the freedom of action of another. To Schützenberger, the description was true but trivial. It began with the individual will and ended with individual wills. "Kant's formula," he wrote, "exhausts the idea of the law in terms of its form, but the sterility of the formula is shocking as soon as one tries to deduce principles of law from it." Defining the law in terms of mutual freedom of external action amounted to using a purely negative criterion of what the law should *not* be, in place of a more positive indication of what it *should* be. "Between, for example, the formula of non-lesion for freedom of action," Schützenberger complained, "and the rights and duties that arise from marriage, conventions, etc., there is simply an unbridgeable gulf."[9]

This was not the only unbridgeable gulf (*abîme infranchissable*) that many of Kant's contemporaries found in his philosophy. In modern scholarship, the one referred to most frequently is the gulf between what Kant called the phenomenal and the noumenal worlds, meaning the world that, on the one side, was accessible to observation and could be understood in terms of natural causes and physical laws and, on the other, the world that lay beyond sensory experience and had to be conceptualized in terms of things that have no physical counterpart, such as morality, legality, rights, justice, or freedom. In one sense, of course, the gulf was as old as religion, philosophy, or Plato's cave, and, in recent Kant scholarship, the idea that Kant had a two-worlds view has given way to the idea that he had a two-perspectives view, meaning that, although there is only one world, it can still be thought about either independently of appearances or in the light of those appearances.[10] But what many of Kant's contemporaries found perplexing or disquieting about his version of the gulf was not only the bounded character of the human capabilities that he described in all his works but also the way in which the capabilities themselves seemed to be self-defeating. In this respect they were rather like Rousseau's concept of *perfectibilité*, in which human ingenuity was responsible not only

---

9. "La formule de Kant épuise l'idée du droit quant à sa forme; mais la stérilité en est choquante lorsqu'on essaie d'en déduire les principes mêmes du droit. Nous sommes encore à nous demander comment ce philosophe s'y est pris pour tirer de cette abstraction purement logique la règle des divers rapports tels qu'il les expose dans la métaphysique du droit. Le principe fondamental étant négatif, l'on conçoit la possibilité d'y trouver le *criterium* de ce que le droit ne doit point faire; mais l'on ne comprend plus de quelle manière il faut s'en servir pour y rattacher les principes positives de cette science. Entre la formule de la non-lésion de la liberté d'action, par exemple, et les droits et les obligations qui naissent du mariage, des conventions etc. se trouve un abîme infranchissable." Schützenberger, *Études*, pp. 179–80.

10. For a helpful recent way in to a large subject, see Dennis Schulting and Jacco Verburgt, eds., *Kant's Idealism: New Interpretations of a Controversial Doctrine* (Dordrecht, Springer, 2011).

for the discovery of metallurgy or the creation of agriculture, but also for the catastrophic consequences of the Lisbon earthquake of 1755 and the technological sophistication of war. Kant took the argument a step further by arguing that it was the human desire for justice and order that had given rise to the many different political societies that now dotted the globe. This, he argued, in the essay entitled "Idea for a Universal History with a Cosmopolitan Aim" that he published in 1784, was why sociability, or the human aptitude for society, was, paradoxically, unsocial, and why, as a result, what he called unsocial sociability (*ungesellige Geselligkeit*) was the underlying engine of human history.[11] The problem, as Kant presented it, was not that humans were unsociable by nature, but was rather that they were sociable too soon. Being prematurely sociable, human societies would have different interests, separate economies, particular cultures, dissimilar values, and partial requirements, and these unsociable propensities could sometimes collide, often in the name of freedom, justice, and rights. Reason, on Kant's terms, could supply reasons for violence as well as reasons for justice. Unsurprisingly, Kant had no hesitation in dismissing Grotius, Hobbes, and Pufendorf, the great seventeenth-century theorists of modern natural jurisprudence, as no more than "sorry comforters." Unsocial sociability was not simply a matter of the tension between reason and the passions, with reason, ultimately, having the trump card. It was, instead, the effect of having reasons for the passions. It ruled out the possibility of a global division of labour and entrenched the more dangerous and complicated reality of a world made up of many multiple divisions of labour all competing to survive. If, as many treatises of natural jurisprudence published in the seventeenth and eighteenth centuries often argued, values like freedom, rights, and justice were the goals, or *telos*, of human history, then on Kant's terms the *telos* of human history was a *telos* that was out of reach.

In this light, it could be said that the revealed mystery of Kant's impossible teleology was Friedrich Nietzsche's idea of eternal recurrence. It was not a consoling thought. "Thus, however much the world as a whole might benefit from this separated development of human powers," wrote the dramatist and philosopher Friedrich Schiller in 1795 in his *On the Aesthetic Education of Man*, "it cannot be denied that the individuals affected by it suffer under the curse of this cosmic purpose." Thinking about history on the basis of Kant's terms seemed to mean that real individuals "would have been the serfs of mankind,"

---

11. On the concept and its relationship to Rousseau's thought, see Raymond Polin, *La politique de la solitude. Essai sur Jean-Jacques Rousseau* (Paris, Sirey, 1971), notably pp. 1–34. Polin's interpretation of Rousseau was a development of his earlier work on the subject of values: see Polin, *La création des valeurs*, especially pp. 156–67.

doing "slaves' work for them" for "several millennia," to no other purpose than "that a future generation might in blissful ignorance attend to the care of its moral health and foster the free growth of humanity."[12] There was, it could be said, more than metaphorical hyperbole involved in Moses Mendelssohn's famous phrase, "the all destroying Kant," a phrase that he published in the preface to his *Morgenstuunden* (Morning hours) in 1785.[13] To Kant's former pupil Johann Gottfried Herder the "Idea for a Universal History" was an affront to humanity. What was particularly offensive, he wrote, was Kant's claim in the same essay that, since human progress necessarily had to occur in a setting formed by both the limited length of any individual life and the bounded quality of any particular set of individual capabilities, the benefits of progress would, logically, be available solely to those generations that came later, and only to collectivities rather than their individual members. On these terms, the appropriate subjects for evaluation would be things like the printing press, electrical power, or penicillin rather than musical skill, parental ability, or moral judgment. With this concept of progress, Herder wrote to his intellectual mentor Johann Georg Hamann soon after the publication of Kant's essay in 1784, it could only be concluded that "man was made solely for the whole species and—but only at the end of time—for the most perfect state-machine." Kant's concept of unsocial sociability, Herder wrote in a later letter, this time to the philosopher Friedrich Heinrich Jacobi, was not only absurd but morally repugnant because it attributed human improvement to nothing more than "political antagonism and the most perfect monarchy or, indeed, the co-existence of many, very perfect monarchies, ruled as a body by pure reason." The whole essay, Herder concluded, reeked of "wretched, ice-cold, slavish enthusiasm."[14] Much of the argument that supplied the content and

12. Friedrich Schiller, *On the Aesthetic Education of Man* [1795], ed. Elizabeth M. Wilkinson and L. A. Willoughby (Oxford, Clarendon Press, 1967), letter 6, p. 43. Subsequent citations of this work are to this edition. I have modified this version slightly in light of the later translation by Keith Tribe of Friedrich Schiller, *On the Aesthetic Education of Man*, ed. Alexander Schmidt (London, Penguin, 2016), p. 23.

13. On the phrase and its context, see Alexander Altmann, *Moses Mendelssohn: A Biographical Study* (London, Routledge, 1973), pp. 671–712 (particularly p. 673). See too Leo Freuler, "L'origine et la fonction de la metaphysica naturalis chez Kant," *Revue de métaphysique et de morale* 96 (1991): 371–94. On Mendelssohn's hostile assessment of Kant's essay, see George di Giovanni, *Freedom and Religion in Kant and His Immediate Successors: The Vocation of Humankind, 1774–1800* (Cambridge, CUP, 2005), p. 22 and n. 48.

14. I owe these quotations from the two letters to Eva Piirimäe, "State-Machines, Commerce and the Progress of *Humanität* in Europe: Herder's Response to Kant in *Ideas for the Philosophy of History of Mankind*," in *Commerce and Peace in the Enlightenment*, ed. Béla Kapossy, Isaak

shape of the huge, four-volume *Ideas on the History of Mankind* that Herder began to publish in 1784 was aimed directly at Kant. It would, he informed Hamann in 1785, "be very pleasant to see his idol of reason recoil in horror at the sight of its devastation."[15]

Even more than Schützenberger's disappointed assessment of the logical symmetry of Kant's concept of human freedom as no more than Roman law in a more abstract guise, Herder's reaction to Kant picked up something genuinely startling about his thought. This was the thought that human history and human life were, in a deep-seated sense, radically incompatible and, as with the distance between the principle of noninterference in human freedom and the real substance of marriage and other human conventions, there was an unbridgeable gulf between the two. The thought prompted the nineteenth-century Russian socialist Alexander Herzen to comment that Kant's treatment of human development seemed to have a kind of chronological unfairness built into it since those living later would benefit from the efforts of their predecessors but would not have to pay the same price. Earlier

---

Nakhimovsky, and Richard Whatmore (Cambridge, CUP, 2017), pp. 155–91 (p. 163 for the passages cited). See also her "Human Rights and Their Realisation in the World: Herder's Debate with Kant," in *Passions, Politics, and the Limits of Society*, ed. Heikki Haara, Koen Stapelbroek, and Mikko Immanen (Berlin, Walter De Gruyter, 2020), pp. 47–73 (pp. 59–60 for the passages in question). For a helpful compilation of quotations from Herder's *Ideas* centred on his hostility to Kant, see Noëlla Baraquin and Jacqueline Laffitte, eds., *Kant. Idée d'une histoire universelle au point de vue cosmopolitique. Réponse à la question 'Qu'est-ce que les lumières?'* (Paris, Editions Nathan, 1994). See too Lewis White Beck, *Kant on History* (New York, Macmillan, 1963), pp. viii–x, xxii–xxiii, 11–26. On the Kant-Herder relationship, see also Megumi Sakabe, "Freedom as a Regulative Principle: On Some Aspects of the Kant-Herder Controversy on the Philosophy of History," in *Kant's Practical Philosophy Reconsidered*, ed. Yirimiyahu Yovel (Dordrecht, Kluwer, 1989), pp. 183–95, and Allen Wood, "Herder and Kant on History: Their Enlightenment Faith," in *Metaphysics and the Good: Themes from the Philosophy of Robert Merrihew Adams*, ed. Samuel Newlands and Larry M. Jorgensen (Oxford, OUP, 2009), pp. 313–42, and the earlier literature cited there. For an intriguingly Straussian approach, see William A. Galston, *Kant and the Problem of History* (Chicago, U of Chicago Press, 1975), particularly pp. 205–68, and, for a pro-Herder and anarchist perspective, see Rudolf Rocker, *Nationalism and Culture* (Los Angeles, Rocker Publications Committee, 1937), pp. 151–55, 184–87. For further examples of Herder's assessment of Kant, see chapter 2 below. The polemical context generated by the Kant-Herder relationship is relevant to, but not particularly visible in, Frank Ankersmit, *Sublime Historical Experience* (Stanford, Stanford UP, 2005), pp. 69–75, 146–49, 210–17. See Herman Paul and Adriaan Van Veldhuizen, "A Retrieval of Historicism: Frank Ankersmit's Philosophy of History and Politics," *History and Theory* 57 (2018): 33–55.

15. The passage is quoted in Pierre Pénisson, "Kant et Herder: 'le recul d'effroi de la raison,'" *Revue Germanique Internationale* 6 (1996): 63–74 (see p. 67 for the passage in question).

generations would simply carry the load used to build the house that only the
final arrivals would occupy. "Do you truly wish to condemn the human beings
alive today to the sad role of caryatids [meaning an ancient Greek carving
used as an architectural pillar] supporting a floor for others someday to dance
on?" Herzen asked. "History is fond of her grandchildren," Herzen's contemporary Nicholas Chernyshevsky observed, "for it offers them the marrow
of the bones which the previous generation had hurt its hands in breaking."[16]
If, as Cicero had written, there was something poignant or heroic in the idea
of someone old planting a tree that would be available only to future generations, there was something more disorienting or absurd involved in applying
the same idea to the whole of human history. Discussion of the problem
continued well into the twentieth century, sometimes for and sometimes
against Kant. "With deep earnestness Kant takes up the thought that the development of civilization succeeds only at the cost of individual happiness,"
wrote the German neo-Kantian philosopher Wilhelm Windelband approvingly. "The more complicated relations become, the more the vital energy of
civilization grows, by so much the more do individual wants increase and the
less is the prospect of satisfying them. But just this refutes the opinion of the
Enlighteners, as if happiness were man's vocation." The political philosopher
Hannah Arendt disagreed, on the basis of the same concept of history. "In
Kant himself, there is this contradiction," she wrote. "Infinite progress is the
law of the human species; at the same time, man's dignity demands that he
be seen (every single one of us) in his particularity and, as such, be seen—but
without any comparison and independent of time—as reflecting mankind in
general. In other words, the very idea of progress—if it is more than a change
in circumstances and an improvement of the world—contradicts Kant's notion of human dignity. It is against human dignity to believe in progress." As
she wrote in her essay *On Violence* in 1970, even Kant himself had highlighted
the bewildering quality of the idea of progress.[17] Strangely, and although the
problem was also registered in a more muted way by Arendt's near contemporary Judith Shklar, the sense of perplexity or disorientation produced
by this temporal and moral gulf is no longer particularly apparent in Kant

16. The passages are quoted in Isaiah Berlin, *Russian Thinkers* (Harmondsworth, Penguin
Books, 1994), p. 92.

17. Hannah Arendt, *Lectures on Kant's Political Philosophy*, ed. Ronald Beinerweltan (Chicago, U of Chicago Press, 1975), p. 77, and her *On Violence* (New York, Harcourt Brace Jovanovich, 1970), p. 27, reprinted in her *Crises of the Republic* (New York, Harcourt, Brace & Company,
1972), p. 129. For the passage from Windelband, see Wilhelm Windelband, *A History of Philosophy* [2nd ed., Leipzig, 1899], 2 vols. (New York, Harper Torchbooks, 1958), 2:559.

studies.[18] To John Rawls, the most influential Kantian of more recent times, "these feelings while entirely natural are misplaced. For although the relation between generations is a special one, it gives rise to no insuperable difficulty." It was, Rawls continued, replying directly to Herzen's comment, "a natural fact that generations are spread out in time and actual exchanges between them take place only in one direction. We can do something for posterity, but it can do nothing for us. This situation is unalterable and so the question of justice does not arise."[19]

It was a confident statement but was predicated on a rather stylized characterization of the relationship between the generations. In real life, the members of various generations usually overlap and do not follow one another as a sequence of separate cohorts. If, as Rawls emphasized, savings are forward looking and desirable, this does not mean that the savings made by one generation will not affect levels of current consumption and, possibly, employment among other parts of the generational sequence.[20] Members of one part of the genera-

---

18. Judith Shklar, *After Utopia: The Decline of Political Faith* (Princeton, NJ, Princeton UP, 1957), pp. 67–69. Shklar, however, associated the problem rather too quickly with Hegel's concept of "the unhappy consciousness" rather than with Kant's philosophy of history, making it more difficult to see that what Hegel called "the unhappy consciousness" was a romantic reaction against Kant's philosophy of history, and that this placed Hegel's thought in alignment with Kant, against Kant's romantic critics. See too, more recently, the fascinating study by Michael Rosen, *The Shadow of God: Kant, Hegel, and the Passage from Heaven to History* (Cambridge, MA, Harvard UP, 2022), where the polemical response to Kant's philosophy of history is flattened out into a secular version of the rewards and punishments meted out in earlier conceptions of the afterlife.

19. John Rawls, *A Theory of Justice* (Cambridge, MA, Harvard UP, 1971), p. 291, referring to the remark by Herzen that was quoted by Isaiah Berlin in his introduction to Franco Venturi, *Roots of Revolution* (New York, Knopf, 1960), p. xx. The remark by Chernyshevsky was also quoted by Berlin on the same page. One of the few more recent scholars to have noticed this aspect of Kant's essay was Terence Ball, "'The Earth Belongs to the Living': Thomas Jefferson and The Problem of Intergenerational Relations," *Environmental Politics* 19 (2000): 61–77; see too his earlier "The Incoherence of Intergenerational Justice," *Inquiry* 28 (1985): 321–37. For an illuminating compilation of early nineteenth-century discussions of intergenerational justice and its relationship to questions of justice and distribution, see John Cunliffe and Guido Erreygers, *The Origins of Universal Grants: An Anthology of Historical Writings on Basic Capital and Basic Income* (Basingstoke, Macmillan, 2004), and, earlier, John Cunliffe, "Intergenerational Justice and Productive Resources: A Nineteenth-Century Socialist Debate," *History of European Ideas* 12 (1990): 227–38. To Rosen, *The Shadow of God*, pp. 7–8, the subject began with Diderot and the question of the judgments of posterity.

20. On the just savings principle in Rawls, see his *A Theory of Justice*, pp. 284–302, and on the broader framework of the argument, see, informatively, Stefan Eich, "The Theodicy of

tional continuum also sometimes make decisions with effects that go in more than a single linear direction. For David Hume, public debts were a way of drawing bills on posterity, and, despite its unpredictable retroactive effects, Kant, unusually, was publicly willing to endorse Hume's "heroic medicine" of a voluntary state bankruptcy if it ever came to a choice between keeping public faith and preserving the state.[21] Retroactive legislation—like the legislation abolishing previously legal feudal dues in France in 1789, or slavery in some parts of nineteenth-century Europe, or the American Supreme Court's endorsement of the Roosevelt administration's unilateral abolition of the gold clauses in contracts for public or private debt in 1936, or, more recently, the abolition of apartheid in South Africa and the reunification of Germany in 1990—can also have the same multidirectional distributional effects. As the nineteenth-century German socialist Ferdinand Lassalle explained in a large two-volume examination of the subject, there were identifiable reasons that could sometimes be found to establish intergenerational justice retroactively, just as there were similar reasons that could underlie intergenerational *injustice*.[22] Alongside public debt, at least on some interpretations, it is not hard to see why, in more recent times, the subject of climate change could give rise to similar sorts of questions about intergenerational justice and injustice, just as, from another perspective, the existence of money has sometimes been described as a means of intergenerational redress because, unlike credit, money can be used to pay off debts.[23] And, since states appear to have a capacity to create money as well as debt, the future sometimes seems to have an unusual ability to right past wrongs. In the context of climate change, posterity seems to be required very strongly to do something for us, just as in the context of slavery monetary compensation seems to be a way for posterity to atone for the past.

Growth: John Rawls, Political Economy and Reasonable Faith," *Modern Intellectual History* 18 (2021): 984–1009.

21. Immanuel Kant, *The Conflict of the Faculties* [1798], in Immanuel Kant, *Political Writings*, ed. Hans Reiss (Cambridge, CUP, 1991), p. 189. On Hume, Kant, and public debt, see Istvan Hont, "The Rhapsody of Public Debt: David Hume and Voluntary State Bankruptcy," in his *Jealousy of Trade: International Competition and the Nation-State in Historical Perspective* (Cambridge, MA, Harvard UP, 2005), pp. 325–53.

22. On these, see below, chapter 9.

23. As the early twentieth-century American political and economic thinker John R. Commons put it in his *Institutional Economics: Its Place in Political Economy* (New York, Macmillan, 1934), p. 513, "money, in its modern meaning, is the social institution of the creation, negotiability, and release of debts arising out of transactions." On this aspect of money, see the chapters on Hegel and Lorenz von Stein in Michael Sonenscher, *Capitalism: The Story behind the Word* (Princeton, NJ, Princeton UP, 2022).

It may well be true, as one recent scholar has put it, that "Kant in effect asks the question of how it is that a cosmopolitan world order (and thus a partially reconciled world) could and will come about by looking at it from the standpoint of a hypothetical future," as Kant undoubtedly did in his "Idea for a Universal History with a Cosmopolitan Aim." But, in contradistinction to Rawls, it is not clear that many of Kant's earlier readers thought that he had shown that it was a world within reach.[24] The point was made vividly by the early nineteenth-century Prussian writer Heinrich von Kleist in the short story entitled "On the Marionette Theatre" that he published nine years after his famous "Kant-Crisis" in 1801.[25] Puppets, Kleist wrote, can actually achieve real goals because they have both the physical ability to do what they were designed to do and the absence of any of the mental distractions that might get in the way. Humans, however, are enmeshed so deeply in layer upon layer of reflexive thought that it can seem quite impossible to identify any genuinely human capacity for purposive action located somewhere between the mechanical action of a puppet and the omnipotence of God. "Does that mean," asked the narrator of the story, "that we would have to eat again of the tree of knowledge to return once more to the state of innocence?" "Most certainly," his interlocutor replied. "That is the last chapter of the history of the world."[26] True innocence was omniscience. There was nowhere in between.

The gulf between individual lives and human history that Kant highlighted injected a real moral and political charge into the famous debate that took place between the two German philosophers Ernst Cassirer and Martin Heidegger at Davos in March 1929. It was, in certain respects, a replay of the earlier argument between Kant and Herder, with Cassirer cleaving to Kant's insistence on the foundational quality of human freedom, notwithstanding all the causal evidence to the contrary, and with Heidegger adopting a position more like Herder's, particularly in relation to the historically bounded character of human culture, language, and values.[27] There were, however, two major differ-

24. Terry Pinkard, *Does History Make Sense? Hegel on the Historical Shapes of Justice* (Cambridge, MA, Harvard UP, 2017), p. 46.

25. On Kleist's "Kant Crisis," see, recently, Tim Mehigan, "The Scepticism of Heinrich von Kleist," in *The Oxford Handbook of European Romanticism*, ed. Paul Hamilton (Oxford, OUP, 2016), pp. 256–74.

26. Heinrich von Kleist, "On the Marionette Theatre" [1810], trans. Thomas G. Neumiller, *Drama Review* 16 (1972): 22–26. I have modified the translation in the light of the later translation in *Essays on Dolls*, ed. Indris Parry (London, Penguin Books, 1974), pp. 1–12.

27. On the debate, see Michael Friedman, *A Parting of the Ways: Carnap, Cassirer, and Heidegger* (Chicago, Open Court, 2000); Peter Eli Gordon, *Continental Divide: Heidegger, Cassirer, Davos* (Cambridge, MA, Harvard UP, 2010) and his earlier *Rosenzweig and Heidegger: Between*

ences between the two pairs of protagonists because neither Kant nor Herder suggested that the concepts of time and temporality were as historically bounded as, certainly, Heidegger took them to be, while neither Cassirer nor Heidegger made any reference to God or introduced any comparison between divine qualities and human capabilities in the course of their debate. In that respect, however, each protagonist was rehearsing a position that Kant had also foreseen. As he wrote in his essay *Theory and Practice*, without some sort of assumption about God and some kind of initial belief in the intelligibility of history, human history would, at best, be something tragic or, at worst, no more than farce.

The opposition between history as tragedy and history as farce is now associated more usually with Karl Marx or, sometimes, Georg Wilhelm Friedrich Hegel. But, as with the distinction between positive and negative freedom (or positive and negative liberty, as the distinction came to be called by Isaiah Berlin in a version of the distinction that was somewhat different from Kant's), it was Kant who made it first. The details of how and why he made the distinction and the reasons why he argued that it mattered can be left to a later chapter.[28] But insisting on the purely chronological point about when the idea arose makes it hard to believe that nothing of substance occurred to thinking about the relationship between individual lives and human history between the time of the argument between Herder, Schiller, and Kant in the late eighteenth century and the debate at Davos between Heidegger and Cassirer in the third decade of the twentieth century. If the problems that Kant raised were registered at different times during the nineteenth century by Georges Frédéric Schützenberger in Strasbourg or Alexander Herzen in Paris and Nicholas Chernyshevsky in Russia (and, as will be shown, by many others too), it is hard to believe that the whole subject could have been dismissed as readily as might be suggested by Rawls's confident shrug. Looking back over the long nineteenth century from the vantage point of the debate between Heidegger and

Judaism and German Philosophy (Berkeley, U of California Press, 2003), pp. 277–304. See too Simon Truwant, *Cassirer and Heidegger in Davos: The Philosophical Arguments* (Cambridge, CUP, 2022); Daniel M. Herskowitz, *Heidegger and his Jewish Reception* (Cambridge, CUP, 2021), pp. 48–65, and, for Heidegger's contribution, Martin Heidegger, *Kant and the Problem of Metaphysics*, ed. and trans. Richard Taft (Bloomington, Indiana UP, 1997), pp. 191–207. For further indication of the continuities, see Kristin Gjesdal, "Literature, Prejudice and Historicity: The Philosophical Importance of Herder's Shakespeare Studies." in *The Insistence of Art*, ed. Paul A. Kottman (New York, Fordham UP, 2017), pp. 91–115. For a wide-ranging examination of the subject of time, see Simon Goldhill, *The Christian Invention of Time: Temporality and the Literature of Late Antiquity* (Cambridge, CUP, 2022).

28. See below, chapter 5.

Cassirer, it would seem that the gap which Kant had opened up between individual lives and human history had never been closed. This, in fact, was not the case. Behind the idea of the many possible types of unfairness that seemed to be built into the relationship between early starters and late arrivers, a range of now more familiar subjects came to be connected to the problem of how to think about the passage of time and how to identify those aspects of human morality, culture, or history that appeared to bridge the gap between something timeless, like a number, and something time-bound, perhaps also like a number but, more unequivocally, like a language, a value, or a culture.

This is a book about the many different attempts that were made to think about how this gap could be closed and, more broadly, about what the impact of these attempts to close the gap has been on thinking about morality, culture, history, and politics, mainly in Europe and mainly in the nineteenth century.[29] One, almost entirely forgotten, attempt was connected to the concept of palingenesis, or the idea of something being reborn, either suddenly or gradually. As will be shown in the next chapter, both versions of the concept came to be used surprisingly widely before and after the French Revolution, and among those who used these different versions were both Kant and Herder. This, in part, was because thinking about palingenesis as something sudden lent itself readily to the subjects of crisis and revolution, and this in turn meant that thinking about the three subjects together, in the order of crisis, revolution, and palingenesis, became the basis of the modern concept of revolution.[30] In part, however, it was also because thinking about palingenesis as something gradual lent itself just as readily to the subjects of history, culture, and civilization or, more specifically, to thinking about the differences between the ancients and the moderns and about the bearing of the assorted legacies of the Greeks, the Romans, and the Christians, particularly after the decline and fall of the Roman Empire, on modern social, economic, and political arrangements. Here, the concept of reform was more salient than the concept of revolution but, as with the concept of revolution, the idea of reform also began to acquire a new, more firmly future-oriented set of connotations. Instead of the more cyclical idea of going back to first principles or of reverting to the ideas or values of the founders, as had been the case earlier with the concepts of both

29. Compare to Frank Ankersmit, *Meaning, Truth and Reference in Historical Representation* (Leuven, Leuven UP; Ithaca, NY, Cornell UP, 2012). The one gap in Ankersmit's impressive oeuvre is his treatment of Kant's approach to history and its bearing on what became historicism.

30. On the concept, see John Dunn, *Modern Revolutions* [1972], 2nd ed. (Cambridge, CUP, 1989). For examples of the use of the concept of palingenesis before 1848, see Alan J. L. Busst, "Ballanche and Saint-Simonism," *Australian Journal of French Studies* 9 (1972): 290–307.

revolution and reform, both concepts began to look forwards rather than backwards.

The problem—and one of the points that Kant set out to make both in his essay on the idea of universal history and in several of his other publications— was that it was difficult to evaluate the significance of either reform or revolution (or any other type of putatively linear progress) without some measure of value against which the evaluation could be made. This, Kant explained, was one reason why the distinction between the divine and the human was worth making, and why some sort of suprahuman standard of value was worth trying to imagine. The claim forms part of the subject matter of the first chapter of this book because one of the aims of this chapter is to describe a number of early nineteenth-century arguments that were designed to show that the divinity, humanity, and history were more closely aligned with one another than was usually thought. The most intellectually economical way of doing this was to make a distinction between God's essence and God's existence. Since God's essence encompassed everything to do with the divinity, making a distinction between essence and existence usually meant not only that God's essence had to precede God's existence but also, in the light of this initial assumption, that the Creation had to involve creating something other than another essence (because two divine essences would, in fact, be indistinguishable, particularly to the Creator). This, it was claimed, was why, in the created world, existence had to precede essence rather than, as with the divinity itself, essence preceding existence. The Creation, in other words, called for something about God to exist in time, and, being time-bound, every aspect of the Creation could then be calibrated to have an existence that was distinct from the divine essence. The outcome was a new variation on the old idea of the Trinity. With the Creation, at least in this rendition of the concept, God became an incomplete God or, in more familiar terms, God became a Trinity because a Trinity, being more than a Unity, could exist in time and, incrementally, give an appropriate existence to various aspects of its essence.

This new variation on the idea of the Trinity was one reason why, after Kant, the subject of Spinoza and Spinozism became so prominent in nineteenth-century European intellectual life. In this context, the time-bound character of the Creation helped to neutralize the idea of the radically unfair quality of human history. It could, as Hegel argued, supply reasons that helped to explain why the reflexive side of human rationality made reason capable of correcting itself. From this perspective, reason was both the cause—and the potential solution—of the problem of unsocial sociability. Although it has recently become more usual to associate Spinoza with monism, materialism, and the eighteenth century, Spinoza's real intellectual heyday occurred in the nineteenth century.[31] It did so because his theology chimed readily both with the idea of an incomplete God and with the concept of the Creation as a process in which existence preceded essence. From this perspective, there was a significant overlap between the nineteenth-century Spinoza revival and the equivalent revival of the thought of the seventeenth-century Neapolitan theologian Giambattista Vico, particularly because of the distinction between divine creation and human making that was so prominent a feature of Vico's thought. The result, over a hundred years after their deaths, was that the thought of both Vico and Spinoza came to be associated with the concept of a philosophy of history and, more particularly, with the various political theologies of Kant's intellectual heirs and critics, the idealist philosophers Johann Gottlieb Fichte, Friedrich Wilhelm Joseph Schelling, and Georg Wilhelm Friedrich Hegel. To their critics, Fichte and, particularly, Schelling and Hegel were, simply, Spinozists. And, just as Kant's God was a kind of Epicurean, the concept of the divinity to be found not only in Fichte, Schelling, and Hegel but even in more orthodox theologians like Friedrich Schleiermacher was more radically historical than anything to be found in earlier Christian theology.[32] This new temporal aspect was used to inject a more moral but still Spinozist dimension into the idea of the Creation. "Can you not see?" as one of Spinoza's nineteenth-century French editors put it in a summary of what he took Spinozism to be, "that if God loves, he cannot be deprived of what he loves and, if creating is better than not creating, God cannot disobey the wisdom that shows him what is best or the holiness that forbids doing evil?" The Creation, in short, was necessary to the divinity because it was both an object of love and a fulfilment of duty. "God," as Spinoza's editor concluded in 1842, "without the world is an incomplete God."[33]

In itself, the claim could be used as an answer to Kant, but its existence also helps to indicate that the concept of political theology originated in the context of the speculations and discussions provoked by Kant. Ever since the con-

---

31. See Jonathan Israel, *The Radical Enlightenment* (Oxford, OUP, 2001) and its later sequels. For a helpful alternative approach, see Knox Peden, *Spinoza contra Phenomenology* (Stanford, Stanford UP, 2014). On Spinoza in the nineteenth century, see André Tosel, Pierre-François Moreau, and Jean Salem, eds., *Spinoza au xixe siècle* (Paris, Publications de la Sorbonne, 2007), particularly the chapter by Moreau on Emile Saisset.

32. See Jackson Ravenscroft, *The Veiled God*, pp. 116–24.

33. "Mais, sans parler de ce qu'il y a de visiblement humain dans ces images, ne voyez-vous pas que si Dieu aime, il ne peut pas ne pas être privé de ce qu'il aime, que si créer est mieux que de ne créer pas, Dieu ne peut pas ne pas obéir à sa sagesse qui lui montre le mieux, à sa sainteté qui lui défend le mal? Et alors le monde est nécessaire à Dieu, soit comme objet d'amour, soit comme devoir accompli; et alors Dieu sans le monde est un Dieu incomplet." Benedict Spinoza, *Œuvres*, ed. Emile Saisset [1842], 3 vols. (Paris, 1861), 1:348.

cept began to be used by the famous Nazi Carl Schmitt, the idea of political theology has become part of the intellectual repertoire of political theory and, by extension, the history of political thought. To Schmitt, the concept applied first and foremost to the state. "The juridic formulas of the omnipotence of the state," he announced in 1932, "are, in fact, only superficial secularizations of theological formulas of the omnipotence of God." The announcement echoed his assertion exactly a decade earlier that "all significant concepts of the modern theory of the state are secularized theological concepts."[34] But, as Schmitt's critic the Italian political philosopher Giorgio Agamben pointed out several decades later, the theological part of the concept was as important as its political part.[35] This was because far from containing "theological formulas of the omnipotence of God," the "secularized theological concepts" to be found in Fichte, Schelling, and Hegel had as much to do with multiplicity and particularity as with sovereignty and omnipotence and, as Agamben indicated in the subtitle of his book, were organized around what he called "a theological genealogy" of both the economy and government. Different theologies, in short, entailed different state theories. In this context, and in contradistinction to Schmitt, attributing theological concepts to the state meant moving quite a long way away from the idea of omnipotence as a load-bearing concept in either theology or politics. As Agamben went on to show, this made his own version of political theology rather like Michel Foucault's concept of biopolitics because both their respective political theories were designed to highlight the range of differentiated governmental and nongovernmental agencies and institutions that have come to be responsible for different aspects of human welfare.[36] For Agamben this process of institutional differentiation entailed

34. The two assertions are juxtaposed helpfully in Carl Schmitt, *The Concept of the Political*, trans. George Schwab, with a forward by Tracy B. Strong and notes by Leo Strauss (Chicago, U of Chicago Press, 2007), p. 42. For a concise and wide-ranging examination of the concept of political theology, see Ernst-Wolfgang Böckenförde, "Political Theory and Political Theology: Comments on Their Reciprocal Relationship" [1981], in Ernst-Wolfgang Böckenförde, *Religion, Law, and Democracy: Selected Writings*, ed. Mirjam Künkler and Tine Stein (Oxford, OUP, 2020), pp. 248–58.

35. Giorgio Agamben, *The Kingdom and the Glory: For a Theological Genealogy of Economy and Government* (Stanford, Stanford UP, 2011). On Agamben, see Claire Colebrook and Jason Maxwell, *Agamben* (Cambridge, Polity, 2016); Carlo Salzani, "Foucault and Agamben: Taking Life, Letting Live, or Making Survive," in *Reading Texts on Sovereignty*, ed. Stella Achilleos and Antonis Balasopoulos (London, Bloomsbury, 2021), pp. 171–78; Ian Hunter, "Giorgio Agamben's *Form of Life*," *Politics, Religion and Ideology* 18 (2017): 135–56, and his "Giorgio Agamben's Genealogy of Office," *European Journal of Cultural and Political Sociology* 4 (2017): 166–99.

36. On this aspect of Foucault's thought, see, helpfully, Keith Tribe, "The Political Economy of Modernity: Foucault's Collège de France Lectures of 1978 and 1979," *Economy and Society* 38

placing a stronger emphasis on what he called "the two paradigms" involved
in thinking about power and territoriality on the one hand and values and their
prerequisites on the other. In this, he explained, he was simply echoing what
he called "the eschatology of salvation . . . of which the philosophy of German
idealism was a conscious resumption." This philosophy, he continued, "was
nothing but an aspect of a vaster theological paradigm" made up of an initial
distinction "between the being of God and his activity," which formed the
basis of his theological genealogy of the economy and government.[37]

As Agamben went on to show, the concept of the Trinity was central to
the distinction between the being of God and the activity of God. But the
version of the Trinity that Agamben went on to describe was informed almost
entirely by an impressively detailed examination of medieval discussions of
the concept as the basis of showing how the combination of unity and variety
that it housed could be used as a counterconcept to Carl Schmitt's version of
political theology. The connections between these medieval discussions
of the Trinity and what Agamben, quoting Hegel, called "the real theodicy,
the justification of God in history," were less visible.[38] So too was the idea of
an incomplete God and the relationship of that concept not only to the long
afterlife of Spinoza's thought in nineteenth-century idealism but also, more
fundamentally, to the cluster of problems about political institutions, moral
values, and human history embedded in Kant's concept of unsocial sociability.
For Agamben, highlighting the theological part of the concept of political
theology turned the concept into a modern echo of medieval conceptions of
the Trinity and pushed the nineteenth-century significance of the concept
largely out of the picture. The result was another historical hiatus. As with the
apparently empty space between the debates between Kant, Schiller, and
Herder on the one side and Cassirer and Heidegger on the other, a similar
space continues to exist between early nineteenth-century German idealism
and its later echoes in the thought of Schmitt, Foucault, and Agamben. Much
the same type of problem applies to the parallel, and equally fascinating, examination of the concept of a person published by the Italian political philosopher Roberto Esposito, with its account of the idea of a rights-bearing

(2009): 679–98, and Michael C. Behrent, "Liberalism without Humanism: Michel Foucault
and the Free-Market Creed, 1976–1979," *Modern Intellectual History* 6 (2009): 539–68, together
with his "Foucault and France's Liberal Moment," in *In Search of the Liberal Moment: Democracy,
Anti-Totalitarianism and Intellectual Politics in France since 1950*, ed. Stephen W. Sawyer and Iain
Stewart (London, Palgrave, 2016), pp. 155–65, and Michael C. Behrent and Daniel Zamora, eds.,
Foucault's Neo-Liberalism (Cambridge, Polity, 2016).

37. Agamben, *The Kingdom and the Glory*, pp. 4–5.
38. Ibid., p. 5.

individual as a kind of palimpsest of Roman law and Christian theology and its interpretation of the idea of autonomy as one, later, part of the palimpsest issuing orders to the other, earlier, part.[39]

Part of the point of what follows is to try to fill these gaps. This, in the first instance, means getting rather more of the measure of Kant's concept of unsocial sociability. Although the details of the various ways in which Kant came to use the term are described more fully in the following chapters, it is important to see at the outset that it was a concept that applied in the first instance to sociability rather than unsociability. On Kant's terms, unsociability was an effect of sociability. This, he argued, was partly because humans form societies too soon. But it was also because, once in society, they were faced with problems of mutual comprehension, shared values, and collective decision making that, by definition, are largely beyond individual control. From this perspective, the concept of unsocial sociability could shade easily into a now more familiar set of problems associated with either of two related paradoxes. The first was Condorcet's paradox, meaning the idea that if several individuals are required to make a choice on the basis of their rank order of preferences, they will collectively choose something that is not actually anyone's first preference. The second, related paradox is associated with the thought of Vilfredo Pareto and with the idea that while individuals can opt for and achieve goals, collectivities will usually end up with compromises. Setting the concept of unsocial sociability against these two more familiar conundrums makes it possible to see the problems of collective choice and collective action not only as problems in their own right but also as the effects of the more deep-seated problem of unsocial sociability that Kant had highlighted.

Starting with Kant and the connection between the concept of unsocial sociability and the apparently intractable nature of the problems of collective choice and collective action that it brought in its wake also helps to throw fresh light on why the subjects of human history and the significance of the passage of time came to matter so much in nineteenth-century thought. These were the subjects that, in Kant's wake, brought the Trinity back to life as a real conceptual resource because, once it came to be seen as a sequence rather than a mystery, it was a concept that could be applied to the proliferating array of arrangements and institutions that lay somewhere between the length of an

39. See, initially, Roberto Esposito, *Third Person* [2007] (Cambridge, Polity Press, 2012), together with his "The *Dispositif* of the Person," *Law, Culture and the Humanities* 81 (2012): 17–30, and his "Totalitarianism or Biopolitics? Concerning a Philosophical Interpretation of the Twentieth Century," in *Biopower: Foucault and Beyond*, ed. Vernon W. Cisney and Nicolae Morar (Chicago, U of Chicago Press, 2016), pp. 348–59.

individual life on the one hand and the whole history of humanity on the other. In this variation on the idea of a political theology, it was not so much time that was speeded up, as, famously, was claimed by the great German historian Reinhart Koselleck, as it was God who was brought closer to the rhythms and patterns of ordinary human life.[40] Where Kant's concept of unsocial sociability seemed to push back the horizons of political possibility and social justice out of human reach, Kant's critics sought to pull forward those same horizons to within range of human grasp. By claiming that God's existence preceded God's essence, they could then claim that there was a real synchrony connecting individual history, human history, and sacred history and a corresponding significance and value in the arrangements, institutions, and continuity that, it could be claimed, straddled all three.

One strong candidate for continuity was the state, because the existence of its institutions and its territory was not limited to any single set of lives or generations. Here, the concept that came to matter was genuinely theological in origin because it was the concept of the general will. In this context, it was a concept that was given a more secular association with the somewhat counterintuitive idea of a state that could be sovereign but could also be compatible with individual autonomy.[41] As will be shown in the fifth chapter, Kant's distinction between public law and private law was based on this concept and, more particularly, the distinction made by Jean-Jacques Rousseau between the general will and the will of all (later, as will also be shown, the same distinction was carried through into Hegel's distinction between civil society and the state). This variation on the idea of political theology does not seem to have occurred to Carl Schmitt or his later critics, partly perhaps because by the early twentieth century Rousseau's distinction had been buried beneath a number of later neo-Kantian or neo-Hegelian versions of the idea of a dual rather than a unitary political system, made up of both a government and a sovereign or, in another idiom, civil society and the state or, more succinctly, the concept

40. On the quasi-eschatological idea of time speeding up, see Reinhart Koselleck, *Critique and Crisis: Enlightenment and the Pathogenesis of Modern Society* [1959] (Cambridge, MA, MIT Press, 1988). For an earlier examination of the same idea, see Daniel Halévy, *Essai sur l'accélération de l'histoire*, 2nd ed. (Paris, 1948).

41. On the theological origins of the concept of the general will, see Patrick Riley, *The General Will before Rousseau: The Transformation of the Divine into the Civic* (Princeton, NJ, Princeton UP, 1986), and, on its later significance in the dualism of Rousseau, Hegel, and Jellinek, see Sonenscher, *Jean-Jacques Rousseau*, pp. 141–77. See also Olivier Beaud, Catherine Colliot-Thélène, and Jean-François Kervégan, eds., *Droits subjectifs et citoyenneté* (Paris, Classiques Garnier, 2019), particularly the chapters by Olivier Jouanjan, pp. 49–74, and Jean-François Kervégan, pp. 75–96.

of a nation-state.[42] Another candidate for continuity was, for similar reasons, the law because it could be public or private, criminal or civil, and municipal or international. So too were things like money, industry, agriculture, trade, transport, music, architecture, or poetry. All of them seemed to offer the means to bring time, justice, and posterity into closer alignment. As the nineteenth-century French socialist Pierre-Joseph Proudhon noted in his diary, "the contradiction between work and the mind can never be entirely eliminated either in humanity or in individuals."[43] Individuals would always think of more than they can do because thoughts occur more quickly than work gets done. And, since humanity has no collective consciousness, it can think and act only as fast as its slowest individual members. This type of contradiction, Proudhon wrote, could not be eliminated. Industry was, therefore, built into the human condition, and, from this perspective, work was a kind of antidote to Kant. The contradiction that Proudhon highlighted helped to raise a question about the type—or types—of political and institutional arrangement that, on the one hand, could bring work and creativity into better and fuller alignment and, on the other, could form a bridge between the length of an individual life and the history of humanity as a whole. On Proudhon's terms, industry was the answer.

A far bleaker implication of the concept of unsocial sociability was that the answer to Kant's question was that there was no answer. Or, at best, that only time would tell. On Kant's terms, the direction of travel of human history was irretrievably ambiguous. It seemed to be either continuous or discontinuous, convergent or divergent, centrifugal or centripetal, and, in a more complicated sense, appeared to involve several different combinations of these binary possibilities. Since every actual human society was no more than a local and limited part of some more imaginatively generated kaleidoscope—or symphony—of human history, there were simply too many possible ways to connect what actually happened in real social and political time to anything more like a conceptually comprehensive history of humanity. From this perspective, the strange counterfactual history of Europe that was published under the title *Uchronie* (meaning another time, as against a utopia or another place) by the French philosopher Charles Renouvier in 1873 was, it could be said, a genuinely Kantian text because of the way that it made a mixture of imagined

---

42. See, however, Carl Schmitt, *The Value of the State and the Significance of the Individual* [1917], in *Carl Schmitt's Early Legal-Theoretical Writings*, ed. Lars Vinx and Samuel Garrett Zeitlin (Cambridge, CUP, 2021).

43. Daniel Halévy, *Proudhon d'après ses carnets inédits* (Paris, Sequana, 1944), p. 25. The whole passage as printed by Halévy should really be quoted in this note.

political decisions and real historical change the basis of a republican alternative to the history of imperial decline and fall that had once been the fate of ancient Rome (and was now, after Napoleon III, likely to be available to modern France).[44] History, in short, was always something more than causation because causation still had to accommodate freedom, however mysterious the process could seem. This, it is equally important to stress, was also the message of Kant's famous essay on the question of enlightenment. The more enlightenment there was, the less it was possible to rely on something outside or beyond human rationality, creativity, and ingenuity. But the greater the reliance on human rationality, creativity, and ingenuity, the less it looked possible to escape from their fundamentally bounded condition. Although Kant's essay is still sometimes taken to be the Enlightenment's manifesto, it was usually taken by his contemporaries to mark its limits, if not its end. From this perspective, keeping enlightenment alive meant finding a way to deal with Kant, or, more substantively, it meant developing an anthropology, a sociology, and a philosophy of history that could address the dilemmas that Kant had exposed (all three terms, it is worth emphasizing, were given much of their modern meaning in this context). From either a historical or a philosophical point of view, the effect of Kant's Copernican turn in philosophy was to generate a drive to establish an alternative.

One of the aims of what follows is to begin to describe the scale and the scope of the intellectual upheaval that this involved. In temporal terms, it straddled the period of the French Revolution and the Industrial Revolution. In spatial terms, it crisscrossed the boundaries of states and nations as new networks of argument, collaboration, or competition spread sporadically and unevenly between Paris, London, Berlin, Geneva, or Milan. Retrospectively, its outcome now seems to be the apparently modern distinction between historicity and normativity, or the idea that some values, beliefs, and arrangements belong very much to their time and place, while others are simply timeless. More historically, it was an upheaval that had the effect of turning a long-drawn-out seventeenth- and eighteenth-century argument usually known as the *querelle des anciens et des modernes*, or the quarrel of the ancients and the moderns, into a more ferocious early nineteenth-century argument between the supporters of the classics and the romantics. The difference

---

44. On the text, first published in 1857 but without the later title, see Alain Pons, "Charles Renouvier et l'*Uchronie*," *Commentaire*, 47 (1989): 573–82, and Catherine Gallagher, *Telling It Like It Wasn't: The Counterfactual Imagination in History and Fiction* (Chicago, U of Chicago Press, 2018), pp. 49, 58–66, 75–77. See also her earlier "What Would Napoleon Do? Historical, Fictional, and Counterfactual Characters," *New Literary History* 42 (2011): 315–36.

between the two sets of arguments can be taken as one measure of the scale of the intellectual upheaval that this book is about. As their respective names help to show, historical comparisons played a complicated part in both sets of arguments. In the earlier arguments, historical comparisons were centred on things (values, institutions, achievements, etc.) that were taken to be available to both the ancients and the moderns, but which were realized or achieved more fully and successfully on either one side or the other of the comparative divide.[45] In the second set of arguments, the comparisons were centred more fully on things that were taken to be *unavailable* to one side or the other of the comparative divide, such as Christianity or autonomy among the ancients, or slavery or, arguably, despotism and empire among the moderns. Here, history seemed either to rule some things in and others out or, finally, to reveal the true nature of what really could stand the test of time.

The difference between the two sets of arguments makes it possible to get rather more of the measure of the impact of Kant's unusual historical vision. In substantive terms, the quarrel between the ancients and moderns was an argument over whether the values, culture, civility, or grandeur of modern political societies such as the France of Louis XIV or the England of Charles II were like or unlike those of the ancients, particularly those of imperial Rome. The later argument between the supporters of the classics and romantics was more complicated because it was not only an argument over whether modern arrangements and values were superior or inferior to those of their ancient counterparts, but was also about whether, in a more comprehensive sense, some mainly ancient, but also sometimes modern or Christian, values were, simply, timeless. The difference was captured quite directly by the change in the meaning of the word "classic" in the early nineteenth century.[46] In earlier usage a classic was the name given to a text used in a class in Greek or Latin philosophy, rhetoric, and poetry because these were the subjects that, in early modern Europe, formed the basis of a humanist education. By the early nineteenth century, however, a classic had acquired a set of moral or aesthetic qualities that set it apart from the rest. Here, the putatively timeless quality of a classic was a foil to the putatively time-bound quality of a romantic.

45. On the *querelle*, see Larry F. Norman, *The Shock of the Ancient: Literature and History in Early Modern France* (Chicago, U of Chicago Press, 2011), the review of it by Marie-Pierre Harder, "Les anciens contre-attaquent, ou la querelle revisitée," *Acta fabula* 13 (2012): 1–11, and Norman's later chapter, "Ancients and Moderns," in *A History of Modern French Literature*, ed. Christopher Prendergast (Princeton, NJ, Princeton UP, 2017), pp. 269–90.

46. On this, see Christopher Prendergast, *The Classic: Sainte-Beuve and the Nineteenth-Century Culture Wars* (Oxford, OUP, 2007), and the further literature referred to in chapter 8 below.

A classic, in this rendition, was something like a symbol or incarnation of the values that it embodied. But it was also possible for the timeless or time-bound qualities of each side to be given radically different attributions and evaluations. From this latter perspective, a classic could be something that belonged very much to the language and culture of ancient Rome, while what was romantic could now be taken to be truly timeless, as it was sometimes said of the works of Shakespeare, Dante, or even Plato. "How apt we all are to look at the manners of ancient times through the false medium of our everyday associations," wrote a Cambridge scholar living in Munich in his introduction to a collection of essays on ancient Greek drama that was published in 1836. "How difficult we find it to strip our thoughts of their modern garb and to escape from the thick atmosphere of prejudice in which custom and habit have enveloped us."

> And yet, unless we take a comprehensive and extended view of the objects of archaeological speculation, unless we can look upon ancient customs with the eyes of the ancients, unless we can transport ourselves in spirit to other lands and other times, and sun ourselves in the clear light of bygone days, all our conceptions of what was done by the men who have long ceased to be must be dim, uncertain and unsatisfactory, and all our reproductions as soulless and uninstructive as the scattered fragments of a broken statue.[47]

It was perhaps appropriate that the editor of the collection was living in Germany because, as he acknowledged in a footnote to this passage, the text was in fact borrowed from a lecture on Roman history given in 1810 by the great German historian Barthold Georg Niebuhr.[48]

Importantly, however, both sides of the classic-romantic divide were alternatives to Kant. This, in turn, meant that both sides of the earlier quarrel between the ancients and moderns looked as if they could be folded into a broader, more comprehensively classic or romantic, anti- or post-Kantian alternative. Thinking about history as incremental and cumulative—with, for example, more Christianity but less slavery—amounted to cutting morality and culture free from their largely Greek and Roman pasts to open up more room to examine their putatively Germanic and medieval origins. Human

47. John William Donaldson, *The Theatre of the Greeks: A Series of Papers Relating to the History and Criticism of the Greek Drama*, 4th ed. (Cambridge, 1836), pp. 5–6.

48. The reference was to Barthold Georg Niebuhr, "Einleitung zu den Vorlesungen über die Römische Geschichte" [1810], in his *Kleine historische und philologische Schriften* (Bonn, 1828), pp. 92–93. On Niebuhr, see Peter Hanns Reill, "Barthold Georg Niebuhr and the Enlightenment Tradition," *German Studies Review* 3 (1980): 9–26.

history, from this perspective, could match the idea of the divine existence preceding the divine essence but on a more microhistorical scale. In this context, the idea of the jury, for example, could appear to have replaced the idea of the forum, and the idea of the rule of law could be taken to have superseded the idea of the living law, while what was romantic and Germanic in origin could also appear to trump—or perhaps absorb—what was classic and Latin. More saliently, this type of comparison appeared to underline the genuinely linear quality of history and, by doing so, to neutralize the concept of unsocial sociability by showing, as Rawls was later to do, that history had an unequivocally positive direction of travel. Equally, however, taking history to be the study of a medium responsible for transmitting significant concepts and values across time and space offered the alternative prospect of neutralizing the concept of unsocial sociability from a different direction. Here, what was linear and progressive would take second place to what was timeless and immutable, but, notwithstanding this still considerable difference, both points of view appeared to have the conceptual capacity to bridge the gap between human life and human history that Kant had opened up.

This, however, was where the real problems began. They did so because there was nothing to bridge the new gap between the mutable and the immutable or the time-bound and the timeless opened up by these two, apparently complementary, alternatives to Kant. Nor was it possible to identify something underlying either side of the divide that could make the distinctions secure. Something said to be classic could be shown to be relative and time-bound, just as something taken to be romantic could also be said to be absolute and timeless.[49] Nor, by definition, was there any robust set of criteria that could be used to adjudicate between the two types of evaluation because if the criteria were available, the problems would not have occurred. In themselves, the problems were moral or aesthetic, philosophical or sociological, economic or organizational, but their underlying intractability could ultimately make them political. Over the years, particularly as their original Kantian context has faded from historical view, many of these earlier problems have crystallized into a number of more recognizably discrete political ideologies. The best known are liberalism, nationalism, socialism, federalism, conservatism, and communism. More recently, there have been communitarianism, republicanism, feminism, and environmentalism. Part of the point of the argument that follows is to try to show why, as with any genealogy, they have both less and more in common

49. For a recent way in to the problem, see Martin Kusch, Katherina Kinzel, Johannes Steizinger, and Niels Wildschut, eds., *The Emergence of Relativism: German Thought from the Enlightenment to National Socialism* (London, Routledge, 2019).

than they seem, and why, therefore, it is not a good idea to take any single later term, like liberalism or civic humanism, as a starting point for thinking about politics. This is why this is a book about the history of political thought and, more specifically, about the long sequence of discussions generated by Kant's moral and historical vision. A surprisingly large number of apparently more recent political theories and concepts actually began from there.

The chapters that follow have been arranged to justify this claim. They are, accordingly, not so much a narrative as a cumulatively fuller reconstruction of a pattern or a half-buried mosaic. The next chapter is a development of this introduction and is a more detailed description of the relationship between the historical side of Kant's thought and a number of early nineteenth-century publications and artefacts that were informed by the concept of palingenesis. In 1848, as will be shown, it was a concept that came to be associated very directly with both the goals and the image of that revolutionary year. The following three chapters are an examination of the intellectual context in which both the image and the goals took shape. Their broad aim is to bring to light the scale of the hostility towards Rome and Roman law that developed in early nineteenth-century Europe, and the corresponding interest in the assorted legacies of the northern and Germanic peoples who had been responsible for the decline and fall of the Roman Empire. The intensity of that hostility has now been largely forgotten. "It was from Rome that we inherited the notion of rights," wrote the twentieth-century French moral and political thinker Simone Weil, "and like everything else that has come from ancient Rome, or the woman big with the names of blasphemy of the *Book of the Apocalypse*, it is pagan and unbaptizable. The Romans, like Hitler, understood that power is not fully effective unless it is clothed in a few ideas, and to this end they made use of the idea of rights, to which it is admirably suited." This, she explained, was because the Romans associated rights with property. "It is singularly shocking," she continued, here echoing Pierre-Joseph Proudhon's more famous claim that property is theft, "that ancient Rome should be praised for having bequeathed the notion of rights to us. If we examine Roman law in its cradle, to see to what species it belongs, we discover that property was defined by the *ius utendi et abutendi*. And, in fact, most of the things that any property owner had the right to use or abuse were really human beings."[50] As will be shown, this, to Simone Weil, was why, in substantive terms, the Nazis were actually Roman.

50. Simone Weil, "Human Personality" [1950], in Simone Weil, *An Anthology*, ed. Sian Miles (London, Virago Press, 1985; Penguin Classics, 2005), pp. 81–82. I have modified the translation slightly in the light of Simone Weil, *La personne et le sacré* (Paris, Editions Allia, 2020), pp. 33–34. On this aspect of Weil's thought, see Roberto Esposito, *Instituting Thought: Three Paradigms of Political Ontology* (Cambridge, Polity, 2021), pp. 59–60.

The countervailing interest in the Germanic peoples of the North was one that had arisen in sixteenth-century France, where it had been one of the features of monarchomach political thought, particularly the thought of François Hotman, at the time of the French Wars of Religion. It was given a more subtle and more durable expression in the political thought of Charles-Louis de Secondat, baron de Montesquieu, in the eighteenth century and, subsequently, acquired a more fiercely anti-Roman and anti-French orientation, not only in the German-speaking parts of Europe but also in Switzerland and France itself in the decades that followed the French Revolution and the establishment of the Napoleonic Empire. In these assessments, as is apparent in the passage quoted from Simone Weil, the political theory of possessive individualism was often said to have begun with Rome and Roman law rather than, as was said later, with the political thought of Thomas Hobbes and John Locke.[51] The initial focus of these Germanist-oriented chapters is on the Coppet group or the network of Swiss, French, German, Italian, and British literary, political, and economic thinkers associated most famously with Germaine de Staël and Benjamin Constant in the first two decades of the nineteenth century. Their more substantive aim is to describe the part played by members of that group in generating much of the early nineteenth-century European interest in developments in German-language moral and political thought, notably in the close and alarming relationship that came to be seen between Kant's concept of autonomy and the idea of the death of God.

As with the earlier occurrence of the distinction between history as tragedy and history as farce, this iteration of the idea of the death of God occurred far earlier in the nineteenth century than its better-known counterpart in the thought of Friedrich Nietzsche. The largely French and German repercussions of the idea, both in the form of what has come to be called recognition theory and in the distinction between civil society and the state made most famously by Georg Wilhelm Friedrich Hegel, form the subject matter of the sixth and seventh chapters. These two chapters are designed to form a bridge between intellectual developments in the German-speaking and the Francophone parts of Europe. The shift of focus that this involves was matched, historically, by a

---

51. On the phrase and its historiography, see C. B. Macpherson, *The Political Theory of Possessive Individualism* (Oxford, Clarendon Press, 1962). The claim was less pronounced in earlier Marxist evaluations. "Even Roman law," noted the Marxist scholar Georg Lukács in 1922, "which comes closest to these developments [meaning those underlying the capitalist phenomenon of reification] while remaining, in modern terms, within the framework of pre-capitalist legal patterns, does not in this respect go beyond the empirical, the concrete, and the traditional." Georg Lukács, *History and Class Consciousness* [1922], trans. Rodney Livingston (London, Merlin, 1971), pp. 96–97.

switch from a largely Germanic to a more firmly Roman subject matter in the years that preceded and followed the revolutions of 1848. The three chapters that follow are designed to convey something approximating to the real scale and scope of this now largely forgotten intellectual and evaluative transformation. Where, in the wake of Montesquieu and Hegel, it had once looked as if the arrangements and institutions of modern Europe were Germanic in origin, it now, with Jules Michelet and Edgar Quinet, began to look as if the opposite was the case. After 1848, it began to be clear that Rome was back. The final three chapters of the book examine the repercussions of this Roman revival, first in the long-drawn-out argument between Romanists and Germanists, mainly but not exclusively in the German-speaking parts of Europe, and second in the new evaluations given to arrangements and institutions that were once taken to be Germanic but were now said to be Roman. Gradually, as the scale of the transvaluation of values became more visible, the significance of Kant's concept of unsocial sociability began to become somewhat clearer. It was a concept that could encompass distinctions between states and governments, sovereignty and authority, unity and multiplicity, morality and legality, historicity and normativity, and, finally, between the real and the ideal. It ruled out much of the moral and political significance attached to historical legacies and binary choices. Sociability, from this perspective, was simply the clash of ideologies, while the impossible teleology that Kant set out in his "Idea for a Universal History with a Cosmopolitan Aim" could now be seen to be the modern framework of organized politics. Instead of the Romans or the Germans, there was no more than an empty future to be aimed for and filled, and endless argument over the competing components of the politics of dualism as the way to get there.

2

Palingenesis, History, and Politics

Paul Chenavard and the Panthéon

Few people have heard of the French painter Paul Chenavard (1807–1895) even though there is now a street named after him near the Museum of Fine Arts in his native city of Lyon. In 1848, however, Chenavard was almost as famous an artist as Eugene Delacroix and Dominique Ingres still are. In April of that year, Alexandre-Auguste Ledru-Rollin, the minister of the interior of the provisional government of the very recently established Second French Republic, commissioned Chenavard to redecorate the Panthéon, the imposing Parisian building that had started life in the eighteenth century as a refurbished church honouring the city's patron saint, Sainte-Geneviève, and, at the time of the French Revolution, had then been turned into a monument to great men. Chenavard's plan was different. Instead of being a monument to great men, the new incarnation of the Panthéon would be a monument to humanity itself.[1]

---

1. For recent studies of Chenavard's project, see David O'Brien, "Delacroix, Chenavard and the End of History," *Journal of Art Historiography* 9 (2013): 1–19; Marc J. Gotlieb, *The Plight of Emulation: Ernest Meissonier and French Salon Painting* (Princeton, NJ, Princeton UP, 1996), pp. 53–95; and Daniel Guernsey, *The Artist and the State, 1777–1855: The Politics of Universal History in British and French Painting* (Aldershot, Ashgate, 2007). The fullest description of the project is still to be found in Théophile Gautier, *L'art moderne* [1856], ed. Corinne Bayle and Olivier Schefer (Lyon, Editions Fage, 2011), pp. 26–93; see also Alexis Bertrand, "Art et sociologie d'après les lettres inédites de Paul Chenavard," *Archives d'anthropologie criminelle, de médecine légale et de psychologie normale et pathologique* 26 (1911): 525–49. For more information on both Chenavard and his project, see the catalogues of the exhibitions at the Musée des Beaux-Arts, Lyon, entitled, respectively, *Paul Chenavard et la décoration du Panthéon de Paris en 1848*, ed. Marie-Antoinette Grünewald (Lyon, 1977), and *Paul Chenavard, 1807–1895: le peintre et le prophète*, ed. Marie-Claude Chaudonneret (Lyon, 2000). See too Joseph C. Sloane, *Paul Marc Joseph Chenavard: Artist of 1848* (Chapel Hill, U of North Carolina Press, 1962); Jean Richer, *Une collaboration inconnue: la description du Panthéon de Paul Chenavard par Gautier et Nerval* (Paris, Lettres modernes, 1963); Thomas Schlesser, *Paul Chenavard: monuments de l'échec*

Its internal decorative scheme was to consist of three complementary sets of images representing the content and direction of human history. The lower part of the monument's interior wall would be made up of some sixty pictures designed to depict this vast historical process or, as Chenavard put it, "the march of the human race towards its future through the trials and alternations between ruin and renaissance that those trials involved."[2] The upper part was to be a frieze some 3 metres high and over 266 metres long that would be a visual image of the actions and events involved in giving the process its structure and shape. The centrepiece was to be a huge mosaic entitled either *The Social Palingenesis* or *The Philosophy of History* that was to be placed beneath the central dome to display humanity's past, present, and future. In it, in a small but significant reversal of actual chronology, the final moment of the present age was to be symbolized by Napoleon Bonaparte, while the first moment of humanity's future was to be represented by George Washington. This counterchronological switch followed the logic of ruin and renaissance underlying the whole decorative scheme. Accordingly, the end of the present age, along with the beginning of the transitional phase, was to be shown as an age in which humanity had been corrupted by money, machinery, and banking. In this sense, the modern age was a decadent age, in which both art and humanity had progressively declined (a diagnosis that earned Chenavard the qualified approval of his better-known contemporary Pierre-Joseph Proudhon).[3] Chenavard called it "the American Age" even though it had as much to do with Bonaparte as with Washington. Despite this bleak prognosis, which earned Chenavard the nickname of *Décourageateur le Grand* (the Great Discourager), the threat of impending ruin would, he claimed, provoke a further social renaissance, with both material and spiritual culture reaching a new and higher level. In this historical and philosophical setting, humanity would be reborn,

(Dijon, Les Presses du Réel, 2009); Eugene Vial, *Chenavard et Soulary. Discours de Réception, Académie des Sciences, Belles-Lettres et Arts de Lyon, 20 mai 1919* (Lyon, 1919); and Marie-Antoinette Grünewald, "La théologie de Paul Chenavard: palingénésie et régénération," in *Romantisme et religion: théologie des théologiens et théologie des écrivains*, ed. Michel Baude and Marc-Mathieu Münch (Paris, 1980), pp. 141–52. More generally, see Chantal Georgel, ed., *1848, La République et l'Art Vivant* (Paris, Fayard, 1998).

2. The passage—"la marche du genre humain vers son avenir à travers les épreuves et les alternatives de ruine et de renaissance"—is cited in Grünewald, *Paul Chenavard et la décoration du Panthéon de Paris*, p. 3.

3. Pierre-Joseph Proudhon, *Du principe de l'art et de sa destination sociale* (Paris, 1867), p. 166. See also Jean-G. Lossier, *Le rôle social de l'art selon Proudhon* (Paris, Vrin, 1937), pp. 25, 155. On Chenavard's bleak view of human history, see Henri Peyre, *Louis Menard* (New Haven, CT, Yale UP, 1928), pp. 28–29.

just like a phoenix. But, unlike a phoenix, humanity would also make the fire from which it would be reborn.

The project never happened because the coup d'état of 2 December 1851 that brought Napoleon III to imperial power also brought the Panthéon back its original function as the Church of Sainte-Geneviève and, over time, blotted out both Chenavard and the concept of palingenesis from historical memory. Although Chenavard still has a niche in art historical studies, the concept of palingenesis has fallen more firmly into the recesses of nineteenth-century historiography.[4] Once, however, it was possible to claim—as it was claimed by an early nineteenth-century French philosopher named Pierre-Simon Ballanche whose ideas were certainly well known to Chenavard—that "man is a palingenetic being."[5] For Balzac, the word was associated more grandly, but also more satirically, with "the palingenetic spectacle of the transformation of a spiritualized globe."[6] As time has gone by, the significance that this concept once had in European intellectual life has been largely forgotten. But its

4. For recent work on Chenavard, see David O'Brien, *Exiled in Modernity: Delacroix, Civilization, and Barbarism* (University Park, Pennsylvania State UP, 2018), pp. 32–38, 57–58. On palingenesis, see Laura Bessi, "Palingénésies: de Charles Bonnet à Chenavard," in *Romantisme et révolution(s)*, ed. Daniel Couty and Robert Kopp (Paris, Gallimard, 2008), pp. 375–94; Göran Blix, "La palingénésie romantique: histoire et immortalité de Charles Bonnet à Pierre Leroux," in *Les formes du temps. Rythme, histoire, temporalité*, ed. Paule Petitier and Gisèle Séginger (Strasbourg, PU de Strasbourg, 2007), pp. 225–40, and his *From Paris to Pompeii: French Romanticism and the Cultural Politics of Archaeology* (Philadelphia, U of Pennsylvania Press, 2009).

5. "L'homme dès cette vie est un être palingénésique." Pierre-Simon Ballanche, *Essais de palingénésie sociale* [1827–29], reprinted in Pierre-Simon Ballanche, *Œuvres*, 6 vols. (Paris, 1833), 4:137. On Ballanche, see Arthur McCalla, "*Palingénésie philosophique* to *Palingénésie sociale*: From a Scientific Ideology to a Historical Ideology," *Journal of the History of Ideas* 55 (1994): 421–39, and, particularly, his *A Romantic Historiosophy: The Philosophy of Pierre-Simon Ballanche* (Leiden, Brill, 1998); Jacques Rancière, *La mésentente. Politique et philosophie* (Paris, Galilée, 1995); Alan J. L. Busst, *La théorie du langage de Pierre-Simon Ballanche* (Lewiston, NY, Edwin Mellen Press, 2000); Lynn L. Sharp, *Secular Spirituality: Reincarnation and Spiritism in Nineteenth-Century France* (New York, Lexington Books, 2006), pp. 1–47, and her "Reincarnation: The Path to Progress," *Handbook of Spiritualism and Channelling* 9 (2015): 219–47; Martin Breaugh, *L'expérience plébéienne. Une histoire discontinue de la liberté politique* (Paris, Payot, 2006), pp. 119–30; and, recently, Pierre-Simon Ballanche, *Première sécession de la plèbe*, ed. Jacques Rancière (Rennes, Editions Pontcerq, 2017).

6. The description was used by Balzac in his *L'illustre Grandissart*: see Georges Matoré, *Le vocabulaire et la société sous Louis-Philippe* (Geneva, Slatkine, 1967), p. 40 (see also pp. 226–27 for other examples, this time from the novelist and art critic Théophile Gautier), and, in relation to the concept of a series, John Tresch, "The Order of the Prophets: Series in Early French Social Science and Socialism," *History of Science* 48 (2010): 315–42.

once-considerable currency helps to throw a different light not only on the moral and political thought of what, famously, has been called the age of revolution or the *Sattelzeit*, but also on a broader range of claims and counterclaims about history, culture, and politics that, between the middle of the eighteenth century and the middle of the nineteenth, were often associated with the concept of palingenesis.[7]

This chapter is about where these claims came from and what they were intended to do. Historians of political thought, from Leo Strauss to Quentin Skinner and Richard Tuck, have usually looked back to the age of Machiavelli, Bodin, Grotius, and Hobbes for the foundations of modern politics. Mainstream historians, however, have usually become more hesitant about maintaining that periodization.[8] Although their reluctance to maintain the older periodization now looks as if it was a result of the rise of social and cultural history, it is more accurate to think that the rise of social and cultural history was, in fact, a result of nineteenth-century criticism of the earlier emphasis on humanism, the Renaissance, and the age of Louis XIV as the initial sources of the transition to the politics of the modern era.[9] The concept of palingenesis played a significant part in giving this kind of criticism its content and shape because it was oriented towards the future rather than the past. It was also associated with the early nineteenth-century concept of romanticism and a cluster of claims about the values, culture, and historical legacies of the assorted northern and Germanic peoples responsible for the decline and fall of the Roman Empire. Putting both the concepts and the criticism into the picture makes it possible to see that the transition to modern politics and

---

7. See E. J. Hobsbawm, *The Age of Revolution: Europe 1789–1848* (London, Weidenfeld, 1972); Reinhart Koselleck, "Einleitung," in *Geschichtliche Grundbegriffe*, ed. Otto Brunner, Werner Conze, and Reinhart Koselleck, 8 vols. (Stuttgart, 1972–97), 1:xiii–xxvii, and, for commentary, Daniel Fulda, "Sattelzeit, Karriere und Problematik eines kulturwissenschaftlichen Zentralbegriffs," in *Sattelzeit. Historiographiegeschichtliche Revisionen*, ed. Elisabeth Décultot and Daniel Fulda (Berlin, De Gruyter, 2016), pp. 1–16, together with the collection of articles on Koselleck in *Revue Germanique Internationale* 25 (2017), ed. Jeffrey Andrew Barash and Servanne Jollivet, and Thomas Maissen, "Reinhart Koselleck, historien allemand de la guerre civile européenne," in *Historiens d'Europe, historiens de l'Europe* ed. Denis Crouzet (Ceyzérieu, Champ Vallon, 2017), pp. 99–120.

8. Compare, classically, Leo Strauss, *Natural Right and History* (Chicago, U of Chicago Press, 1953), and Quentin Skinner, *The Foundations of Modern Political Thought*, 2 vols. (Cambridge, CUP, 1978), to, for example, C. A. Bayly, *The Birth of the Modern World, 1780–1914* (Oxford, Blackwell, 2004); and, more recently, Richard J. Evans, *The Pursuit of Power: Europe 1815–1914* (London, Allen Lane, 2016).

9. For one example, see Roger Chickering, *Karl Lamprecht: A German Academic Life* (Atlantic Highlands, NJ, Humanities Press, 1993), especially pp. 117–39.

modern political ideologies had two turning points, not one. The first began with the humanism of the Renaissance and was the one that still dominates the history and historiography of political thought. The second was the one that has come to shape the history syllabus, with its focus on the period of the Enlightenment, the French Revolution, and the British Industrial Revolution as the real transition to the modern age. The aim of this chapter is to try to explain why both turning points matter, both historically and historiographically. Focusing on both these turning points helps to explain why thinking about politics has lost touch with culture, just as thinking about culture has lost touch with politics.

In keeping with the concept of palingenesis, the content of this chapter is arranged to look both backwards and forwards because it is designed, first, to provide a fuller account of the various questions and answers that formed the intellectual context of Immanuel Kant's unusual, and resolutely future-oriented, political vision, and, second, to show how some of the problems that Kant passed on to posterity became the starting point of a new set of attempts to establish an intellectually coherent relationship between history and politics. Its starting point is a story about political mutation and renaissance based upon several earlier descriptions of political mutation and renaissance that, together, were part of the famous *Persian Letters* published in the early eighteenth century by the French magistrate Charles-Louis de Secondat, baron de Montesquieu. This was the story that, in English translation, came to be called *The History of the Troglodytes*. It was a purely fictitious story, but it was based on two earlier versions of the story that Montesquieu certainly knew. The first was a story in the Bible about how God had resolved to punish the Hebrew people after they decided to give up their republican and patriarchal form of government and chose, instead, to entrust the government of their common affairs to the authority of a king, just as the Romans or the Etruscans were said to have done rather nearer to the time when the story was first recorded. The second was modelled on the scriptural story, but this time it made a more explicit endorsement of a mixed or republican form of government rather than one that was royal because it was centred on the historical legacy of the Germanic peoples who were responsible for the final decline and fall of the Roman Empire. In this, sixteenth-century French version of the story, having a king was not simply the price to be paid for establishing a single source of justice and authority, but was also a real threat to civil and political freedom. This meant, as this version of the story went to some lengths to show, that a monarch not only was accountable to part or all of the whole society but could, certainly, be rightfully resisted and, ultimately, overthrown. As Montesquieu knew, *The History of the Troglodytes* was a kind of palimpsest of a Hebrew story, a Roman story, a German story, and a monarchomach story.

The problem with the resulting maze was that it was difficult to reconcile the succession of stories with one another or to decide whether any one of them should be given a higher value than the others, or instead whether they were all designed to make a single cumulative point. This is why *The History of the Troglodytes* is a good starting point for thinking about the relationship between history and politics. A second reason, however, is that Montesquieu's story was used in the nineteenth century to illustrate a significant disagreement between the thought of the English utilitarian Jeremy Bentham and his later Anglo-Scottish critic Sir Henry Sumner Maine. This too was a disagreement about the relationship between history and politics. In this case, it arose because the several overlapping histories embedded in *The History of the Troglodytes* raised a question about anachronism and the extent to which any of the various fictional, scriptural, or historical aspects of the Troglodyte story had a significance outside the contexts in which they had been said to occur. The purpose of this chapter is to describe the ramifications of this cluster of problems as they were discussed between, roughly, 1748 and 1848, or between the time that Montesquieu published the much larger sequel to *The History of the Troglodytes* that he called *De l'esprit des lois* (or *The Spirit of Laws*, as the near-contemporary English translation was entitled) and the time, a hundred years later, when Paul Chenavard was invited to redecorate the Panthéon. Although the century between 1748 and 1848 has a somewhat misleading neatness, it also encompassed a series of intellectual developments generated by the problem that formed a link between the overlapping histories embedded in Montesquieu's Troglodyte history and the proliferating legal typologies underlying *The Spirit of Laws*. Part of the point of the first work was to claim that under certain conditions some historical precedents and parallels could be arbitrary or unsuitable, just as part of the point of the second work was to show that under certain conditions some types of law or legal entitlement could be inappropriate or misplaced. The problem with either claim was that each seemed to rely on some implicit norm that ruled some things in and others out, while the largely implicit presence of the shadowy norm simply failed to provide enough information about its own normative qualities to explain why it had this discriminatory power.

The problem was partly a problem about relativity but it was also a problem about normativity. In a deeper sense, however, it was really a problem about finding a way to reconcile the two. From this perspective, the real requirement was to identify what lay behind the precedents and the parallels, or what could form a link between the particular and the general or the facts and the norms. One solution was the concept of palingenesis and the mixture of change and continuity running from the past to the future that it implied. Another was Kant's with its apparently stronger orientation towards the future and its more urgent emphasis on decision making and choice. As Herder's outraged reaction to Kant helps to show, the two solutions clashed. In this respect, Herder's reaction to Kant in the 1780s was rather similar to his reaction to Montesquieu in the 1760s. Then, he described Montesquieu's *Spirit of Laws* as "metaphysics for a dead law-book." Subsequently, he described Kant's *Idea of Universal History* as "ice-cold, slavish enthusiasm,"[10] Both judgments were a reaction to the muted moral content of almost everything that Montesquieu published, beginning with his *History of the Troglodytes*. For all its brevity, the assortment of histories that it housed make it a very good initial example of the problematic relationship between history and politics.

The Troglodytes, the Hebrew Republic, and the Germanic Peoples

Montesquieu's decision to embed a scriptural story, a historical story, and a fictional story within *The History of the Troglodytes* is likely to have been deliberate. All three stories were connected to the problems of vacant thrones, disputed successions, and dynastic right that dominated European politics in the early eighteenth century and, by extension, gave rise to the various legal, moral, and religious questions bound up with attempts to find their solution. At the time when the *Persian Letters* was published, parallels between the ancients and the moderns, as well as arguments over the assorted legacies of the Hebrews, the Romans, and the Germans were staples of moral and political debate. Part of the background of *The Spirit of Laws* was an intense early eighteenth-century French argument between the partisans of what was called the *thèse royale*, or the view that the rights and powers of the French monarchy were a continuation of those exercised by the Roman emperors, and the supporters of the *thèse nobiliaire*, or the view that the rights and powers of the French monarchy derived from, and were limited by, the more fundamental rights and powers of the Germanic nobility who had been responsible for the conquest of Roman Gaul. During the first three decades of the eighteenth century both these approaches to the origins and nature of the French monarchy were matched in other parts of Europe by a number of related arguments

10. See the passages from Herder cited by Eva Piirimäe in her "State-Machines, Commerce and the Progress of *Humanität* in Europe," p. 163, and Johann Gottfried Herder, "Journal meiner Reise im Jahr 1769," in Johann Gottfried Herder, *Werke*, ed. Wolfgang Pross, 3 vols. (Munich and Vienna, 1984–2002), 1:355–465 (here, p. 470). On the scale of hostility towards *The Spirit of Laws* after its publication, see Michael Sonenscher, *Before the Deluge: Public Debt, Inequality and the Intellectual Origins of the French Revolution* (Princeton, NJ, Princeton UP, 2005), pp. 95–97.

over the Spanish Succession, the Hanoverian Succession, the Polish Succession, and the Austrian Succession. The ubiquity of the arguments and their recurrent connection to war meant that there was a considerable degree of analytical continuity between the various stories embedded in *The History of the Troglodytes* and Montesquieu's treatment of the law in *The Spirit of Laws*. As its title indicated, the book was about laws rather than any particular people or their history, and about laws not only in the context of human arrangements and institutions but also as they applied to God, the planets, nature, and physics. All of them had their laws, suggesting that the spirit of laws was rather like a multilayered legal equivalent of the palimpsest buried within *The History of the Troglodytes*.

The palimpsest itself was embedded in letters 11 to 14 of the *Persian Letters*, which Montesquieu published in 1721.[11] In a straightforward sense it was a story about a people known as Troglodytes who, after expelling their king, had been brought to the brink of extinction by their self-centred and thoughtless behaviour. They stole each other's property; they betrayed their wives and husbands; they preferred to profiteer rather than help others in adversity; and they paid a heavy price. Slowly, however, they were rescued by the virtuous conduct and moral example of two of their last surviving members. Although Montesquieu did not use the word, the story of ruin and recovery that he set out in *The History of the Troglodytes* made it something like an early example of social palingenesis and a potential archetype of every subsequent historical account that relied on the concept. As the story unfolded, the combination of pastoral farming, unselfish morality, and patriotic commitment promoted by the two virtuous patriarchs gave rise to a peaceful, prosperous, and industrious community, governed by the heads of the growing number of Troglodyte households. The scale of its resources and the virtue of its people meant that it could combine external stability with domestic social stability. But, as the demands of agriculture, trade, and industry grew, the Troglodytes began to think that the time and effort required for collective discussions and decisions were best left to a king, and implored one of the oldest and wisest members of their society to become their monarch. He wept as he accepted the office, not with gratitude, but with sadness.

11. Charles-Louis de Secondat, baron de Montesquieu, *The History of the Troglodytes* (Chelmsford, 1766), pp. i–ii (from which subsequent citations have been taken). The fullest scholarly edition is in Montesquieu, *Lettres persanes*, in Charles-Louis de Secondat, baron de Montesquieu, *Œuvres complètes*, vol. 1, ed. Jean Erhard and Catherine Volpilhac-Auger (Oxford, Voltaire Foundation, 2004), letters 11–14, pp. 161–72. Henceforth this edition of the *Lettres persanes* will be abbreviated to *LP*. Reference will also be made to the English translation of Montesquieu, *The Persian Letters*, trans. George R. Healy (Indianapolis, IN, Hackett, 1999).

Ambition, riches and pleasure begin to have charms for you; and you long to be placed in a situation in which you may court these vain delusions, in which you may aspire to be great, may pursue wealth or indulge in luxury, in which you may lay aside the solicitude after virtue, provided you are cautious to avoid open and dangerous crimes.[12]

What, he asked, his eyes streaming with tears, "is the nature of the office that you impose upon me? To command? Who or what shall I command? Am I to command a Troglodyte to be virtuous?"[13] But that, sadly, was the point. Ambition, riches, and pleasure had to be offset by royal power.

It is now generally recognized that Montesquieu's Troglodyte story was a reworking of a famous episode in the Old Testament that was described at 1 Samuel 8, where Samuel, in his old age, had made his sons judges over Israel.[14] The sons, however, lacked Samuel's moral qualities, and the elders of Israel turned to the Hebrew patriarch and pleaded with him, as the passage in scripture put it, to "give us a king, to judge us, like all other nations." God, however, was greatly displeased by the elders' appeal because it amounted to the end of divine authority over the Israelites' temporal affairs. God, accordingly, ordered Samuel to tell the people of Israel:

> These are the terms on which a king shall reign over you. Your sons he will take and make his charioteers and his horsemen and runners before his chariots. He will make of them captains over thousands, captains over hundreds, captains over fifties, and captains over tens. He will take of them to till his grounds and reap his harvests; to make his weapons of war and the furniture of his chariots. Your daughters he will take to be ointment-makers, cooks and bakers. The best of your fields, vineyards and olive-yards, he will take and give to his servants. The choicest and best of your men servants and of your maid servants, of your cattle and of your asses, he will take and put to his own work. Your very flocks he will tithe; and his servants you shall be.[15]

12. Montesquieu, *History of the Troglodytes*, p. 22; *Persian Letters*, letter 14, pp. 29–30.

13. Montesquieu, *History of the Troglodytes*, pp. 22–23; *Persian Letters*, letter 14, p. 30.

14. On the parallel between the Hebrews and the Troglodytes, see the editorial notes in Montesquieu, *LP*, pp. 161 n. 1, 162 n. 5, 164 n. 7, 165 n. 3, 170 n. 4, and 171 n. 1.

15. For the passage see *The Holy Bible*, ed. Alexander Geddes, 2 vols. (London, 1797), 2:58–59. On this episode, see Lea Campos Boralevi, introduction to Petrus Cunaeus, *De republica Hebraerorum libri tres* (Florence, Centro Editoriale Toscano, 1996); Gordon Schochet, Fania Oz-Salzberger, and Meirav Jones, eds., *Political Hebraism: Judaic Sources in Early Modern Political Thought* (Jerusalem and New York, Shalem Press, 2008), and, notably, Eric Nelson, *The Hebrew Republic: Jewish Sources and the Transformation of European Thought* (Cambridge, MA, Harvard

The price to be paid for monarchy would be human authority. Human authority, however, called not only for governments, states, and laws but also for the many resources of time, money, and personnel needed to make them work. It was, as Montesquieu wrote, alluding very clearly to the scriptural story, enough to make a Troglodyte weep.

Montesquieu did not explain why he wrote *The History of the Troglodytes*, and it is usually taken largely to be a story about the dangers of selfishness and the benefits of benevolence written in the context of the early eighteenth-century debates on the subject of luxury.[16] Although it was certainly this, because, as Montesquieu wrote, the Troglodyte history was intended to be an answer to the question about "whether men are made happier by the pleasure and satisfaction of the senses or by the practice of virtue" that Mirza had asked Uzbek in the tenth of the *Persian Letters*, the history was also a story about a people who had expelled their king.[17] This more directly political side of the story was connected to the fact that, by the time that Montesquieu came to write the tale, the scriptural story set out in 1 Samuel 8 had become a monarchomach story and, most saliently, was the centrepiece of a pamphlet published in 1689 entitled *Vindiciae contra Tyrannos: A Defence of Liberty against Tyrants or Of the Lawful power of the Prince over the People, and of the People over the Prince*.[18] The pamphlet in question was actually a translation of a much earlier and more famous tract published in 1579 during the French Wars of Religion and written either by François Hotman, Hubert Languet, Théodore de Bèze, or Philippe Duplessis-Mornay (at the time when Montesquieu was writing, the author was usually taken to be Hotman). It relied very heavily on the passages in 1 Samuel 8 that had earlier made that text the key source of the republican tradition in Hebrew thought. The translation published in 1689 was clearly designed to justify the Glorious Revolution of 1688, but it was also the fifth in a series of English translations published in 1622, 1631, 1648, 1660, and 1689 itself. As these dates suggest, monarchomach thought resurfaced at a

---

UP, 2010), pp. 26–35. Curiously, although Nelson refers to the parallel between the Troglodytes and the Hebrews in his *The Greek Tradition in Republican Thought* (Cambridge, CUP, 2004), pp. 156–58, he does not discuss it in his later *Hebrew Republic*.

16. See Alessandro S. Crissafuli, "Montesquieu's Story of the Troglodytes: Its Background, Meaning and Significance," *PMLA* 58 (1943): 372–92.

17. Montesquieu, *LP*, letter 10, p. 159; *Persian Letters*, letter 10, p. 22.

18. The pamphlet was edited by Harold Laski, *A Defence of Liberty against Tyrants: A Translation of the Vindiciae contra Tyrannos by Junius Brutus* (London, Bell, 1924); see pp. 73–74, 91, 119–20, 141–42, 148, 172–74 for Hotman's use of the passage of scripture. Note that the pamphlet is not attributed to Hotman in the most recent study of monarchomach thought: see Sophie Nichols, *Political Thought in the French Wars of Religion* (Cambridge, CUP, 2021).

number of moments of crisis in British politics, but the sequence of its appearances heralded a growing variety of different outcomes. With Hotman, the Hebrew story had become a Germanic story and one with a monarchomach point. By the time that it resurfaced in the *Persian Letters*, however, the point of the story had become far more ambiguous. Montesquieu himself seems to have been well aware of the ambiguity because he drafted a continuation of the story that he subsequently decided not to publish. Its content underlined the scale of the financial, fiscal, and, ultimately, political transformation involved in the switch from patriarchy to monarchy.[19]

Montesquieu was not a monarchomach. There is, however, good reason to think that he was well aware of how, over the years, monarchomach politics— or the politics justified by 1 Samuel 8—had come to have so many different outcomes that it was not possible to associate its moral, social, or institutional content with any determinate outcome at all. His transformation of the scriptural and monarchomach story into the Troglodyte story captured this indeterminacy very effectively. It was an allegory that offered as much, or as little, support as could be imagined to an impressively wide range of calls for regime change. It could appeal to the supporters of the Glorious Revolution of 1688, just as it could also appeal to the Jacobite supporters of a Stuart Restoration after 1715. Its very indeterminacy made *The History of the Troglodytes* a very sceptical approach to the subject of palingenesis. The same applied to the more elaborate treatment of history that informed *The Spirit of Laws*. There, as Montesquieu described it, modern Europe was heir to a Germanic legacy, but the legacy in question was either his famous description of the English system of government or his equally famous description of monarchy as a system of government in which, as he put it, "a single person governs by fundamental laws" together with a number of "intermediate, subordinate and dependent powers."[20] Both were Germanic in origin, but the two versions of the Germanic legacy that Montesquieu went on to describe were very different.

"In perusing the admirable treatise of Tacitus *On the Manners of the Germans*," he wrote famously, "we find it is from that nation that the English borrowed the idea of their political government. This beautiful system was invented first in the woods."[21] The same line of descent applied to modern monarchy, although here the evaluation relied more on the idea of unintended

19. On the sequel and the scale of the transformation that it implied, see Sonenscher, *Before the Deluge*, pp. 99–106.

20. Charles-Louis de Secondat, baron de Montesquieu, *The Spirit of Laws*, trans. Thomas Nugent (London, 1751), ed. Franz Neumann (New York, Hafner Publishing Company, 1949), bk. 2, ch. 4, p. 15.

21. Ibid., bk. 11, ch. 6, p. 161.

consequences than on the qualities of the original system. If it began with representation by way of estates, it ended with hereditary property, hereditary titles, and hereditary thrones. It was remarkable, Montesquieu wrote, still with an eye to moral ambiguity, "that the corruption of the government of a conquering people should have formed the best kind of government that men have been able to devise."[22] Here, the outcome was entirely unintentional and owed a great deal to the way that Roman law had come to be entangled with Germanic custom, particularly in the context of the trials by ordeal used to settle disputes in Germanic society. As a nineteenth-century French law professor put it, "lawyers are to Roman law what duelling is to Germanic law."[23] Together, their joint legacy gave rise to the combination of hereditary rule, judicial authority, and ostentatious social display that was the hallmark of modern monarchy.

For Montesquieu, monarchy in its modern guise was a fusion of Germanic and Roman elements. To Montesquieu's critics, however, monarchy was a corruption of either one side or the other of the fusion. The difference was emphasized forcefully by one of Montesquieu's relatively few eighteenth-century followers, the British historian Edward Gibbon at the beginning of the famous forty-fourth chapter of his *History of the Decline and Fall of the Roman Empire*. In it, Gibbon pointed out how the veneration in which the Roman emperor Justinian had come to be held because of his Code, Pandects, and Institutes had been matched by an equally powerful and hostile reaction. "The idolatry of love," Gibbon wrote, "has provoked, as it usually happens, the rancour of opposition. The character of Justinian has been exposed to the blind vehemence of flattery and invective, and the injustice of a sect (the *Anti-Tribonians*) has refused all praise and merit to the prince, his ministers, and his laws."[24] In a footnote, he referred to the work of "a learned and acute lawyer of the 16th century" whom he named as François Hotman as the originator of what he called the Anti-Tribonian sect. In place of the institutions and arrangements of the Romans that Justinian and generations of Roman lawyers had described, Hotman had extolled those associated with the Germans, particularly as they had been described by another Roman, Tacitus, in his *De moribus Germanorum* (On the manners and customs of the

22. Ibid., bk. 11, ch. 8, p. 163. On Montesquieu's two assessments of the Germanic legacy, compare Paul A Rahe, *Montesquieu and the Logic of Liberty* (New Haven, CT, Yale UP, 2008), to Sonenscher, *Before the Deluge*.

23. "Les juristes, c'est le droit romain; le duel, c'est le droit germanique." Alfred Bertauld, *La liberté civile. Nouvelle étude critique sur les publicistes contemporains*, 2nd ed. (Paris, 1864), p. clxxxv.

24. Edward Gibbon, *The History of the Decline and Fall of the Roman Empire* [1776–88], ed. David Womersley, 3 vols. (London, Allen Lane, 1994), vol. 2, ch. 44, pp. 778–79.

Germans) as the basis of another set of evaluations of a different set of institutions and another form of rule.

"All monarchies are not governed always and everywhere in the same way," Hotman had written in his *Anti-Tribonian*. "Some have a more absolute power, others more limited; some to a greater extent, others more restricted; some more military, others more civil offices." This, he concluded, meant "that the laws of a country should be accommodated to the state and not the state to the laws."[25] More or less the inverse of this thesis was carried over into *The Spirit of Laws* where Montesquieu argued that states and their internal or external arrangements actually had to be accommodated to the laws because of the many different types of law—some human, some natural, some divine— that they were required to address. From Hotman's point of view, states supplied norms or constraints and laws had to be adapted to them. From Montesquieu's point of view, laws supplied norms or constraints and states had to be adapted to *them*. Gibbon clearly sided with Montesquieu and, in the forty-fourth chapter of *The History of the Decline and Fall of the Roman Empire*, went on to explain why Roman law had outlived the Roman Empire and, because of its content, had become the basis of the legal systems of almost every modern European state. From this perspective, modern European history was a vivid refutation of the anti-Tribonian claim that laws should be accommodated to states. To Gibbon's readers, particularly in the German-speaking parts of Europe, Roman law belonged as firmly to modern economic and political arrangements as it had done to ancient Rome. The point was highlighted strikingly and schematically by the famous German jurist Rudolf Jhering in 1852. "Three times," he wrote at the beginning of the book to which he gave the Montesquieu-inspired title of *Geist des römischen Rechts auf den verschiedenen Stufen seiner Entwicklung* (The spirit of Roman law in the various phases of its development), "the laws of the world were dictated by Rome, three times it bound the nations together in unity: first, with the unity of the *state*, when the Roman people still stood at the fullness of its power; second, with the unity of the *church*, after the fall of the Roman Empire; and third, with the unity of the *law*, in the wake of the reception of Roman law in the Middle Ages."[26] The Roman Empire might have gone, but Roman law had lived on.

25. François Hotman, *Anti-Tribonian* [1567], cited in Donald R. Kelley, *François Hotman: A Revolutionary's Ordeal* (Princeton, NJ, Princeton UP, 1973), p. 195. For incisive summaries of Hotman's argument, see J.G.A. Pocock, *The Ancient Constitution and the Feudal Law* [1957] (Cambridge, CUP, 1987), pp. 11–15, 20–29.
26. See Rudolf von Jhering, *L'esprit du droit romain dans les diverses phases de son développement*, 3 vols. [1852–65] (Paris, 1886), 1:1. On Jhering, see Damiano Canale, Paolo Grossi, and

By the time, however, that Chenavard began to plan his project, Roman law and its legacy had come to be exposed to considerably more critical scrutiny.[27] Property, announced the Besançon printer and autodidact Pierre-Joseph Proudhon in 1840, "is theft." This, he explained, was because under Roman law property was the right to use or abuse a thing or, as he emphasized by quoting the Latin, "ius utendi et abutendi re sua, quatenus iuris ratio patitur." On the basis of this definition, Proudhon commented, use and abuse were just the same.[28] Property, he went on to argue, was an abstract legal concept superimposed upon the individual attributes of real physical things, like shoes or tomatoes. To the early nineteenth-century Swiss Catholic convert Karl Ludwig von Haller, Roman law was the largely unacknowledged source of the seventeenth- and eighteenth-century tradition of modern natural jurisprudence and the contractual theory of political society that was the basis of its concept of political obligation. As Haller went on to explain, what had once been a parochial set of Roman institutions and arrangements had, in the works of Hugo Grotius, Thomas Hobbes, and Samuel Pufendorf, followed by those of John Locke and Jean-Jacques Rousseau, been scaled up conceptually to become an untenable system of political obligation whose real consequences had been brought home, catastrophically, by the events of the French Revolution. "It cannot be disguised," Haller wrote, "that the exclusive study of Roman literature, the generally widespread use of Latin among scholars, and a measure of idolatrous respect for Roman law were the first, almost imperceptible cause

Hasso Hofmann, eds., *A History of the Philosophy of Law in the Civil Law World, 1600–1900* (Heidelberg, Springer, 2009), pp. 301–54.

27. For a once-classic, but now largely forgotten, overview of the subject, see Herbert Felix Jolowicz, "Political Implications of Roman Law," *Tulane Law Review* 22 (1947–48): 62–81, and, more recently, R. C. Van Caenegem, *European Law in the Past and the Future* (Cambridge, CUP, 2002), pp. 98–130. See too Peter Stein, *Legal Evolution: The Story of an Idea* (Cambridge, CUP, 1980); *The Character and Influence of the Roman Civil Law* (London, Hambledon Press, 1988); and his *Roman Law in European History* (Cambridge, CUP, 1999). On property in Rome and in Roman law, see Eric Nelson, "Republican Visions," in *The Oxford Handbook of Political Theory*, ed. John S. Dryzek, Bonnie Honig, and Anne Phillips (Oxford, OUP, 2008), pp. 193–210; Mathias Reimann, "Historical Jurisprudence," in *The Oxford Handbook of Legal History* ed. Markus D. Dubber and Christopher Tomlins (Oxford, OUP, 2018). See also Clifford Ando, ed., *Citizenship and Empire in Europe 200–1900* (Potsdam, Franz Steiner Verlag, 2016), as well as his earlier "A Dwelling beyond Violence: On the Uses and Disadvantages of History for Contemporary Republicans," *History of Political Thought* 31 (2010): 183–220; and Kaius Tuori and Heta Björklund, eds., *Roman Law and the Idea of Europe* (London, Bloomsbury, 2019).

28. Pierre-Joseph Proudhon, *Qu'est-ce que la propriété* [1840], ed. E. James (Paris, 1966), ch. 2, p. 85.

of the failure to recognize the essential difference between monarchies and republics (meaning lordships and communities) that gave rise to the idea of a social contract as the basis of every empire."

> Since Latin has virtually nothing in it other than republican names and terminology, at least where the subject of states is concerned, these were used frequently but applied subsequently to a range of objects and relationships of an entirely different nature. Thus, because Roman citizens were members of a corporation, belonged to a *bourgeoisie*, and formed a real *civil society*, it began to be imagined that every other human aggregation and every other set of reciprocal human relations were also *civil societies*. Soon every state, even monarchies, began to be called *civitates* or *respublicas* (commonwealths or republics).[29]

The result, as Haller put it, was that this Latinate republican vocabulary had seeped into relationships and activities that had nothing at all to do with republics. In keeping with the title of his book, these purely personal relationships formed a natural social state—as against the artificial civil state of social contract theory—whose internal arrangements and dynamics called for an entirely different conceptual vocabulary, oriented towards families, communities, kin, and service and emphasizing the ties of subordination, protection, and dependence that they housed. The task of restoring political science to its true vocation meant, therefore, breaking with both Roman law and the illegitimate offspring that it had spawned in modern natural jurisprudence by reinstating a conceptual vocabulary that was more attuned to the physical attributes, real differences, multiple hierarchies, and local particularities of the natural social state.

The problem with Haller's updated version of anti-Tribonianism was that it was as vulnerable to the charge of arbitrariness as its alternatives. The point was underlined in 1820 soon after the publication of the first volume of Haller's

---

29. Karl Ludwig von Haller, *Restauration de la science politique, ou théorie de l'état social naturel opposée à la fiction de l'état civil factice*, 6 vols. [1816–20] (Lyon and Paris, 1824–65), 1:98–99. I owe my knowledge of this passage to Béla Kapossy, "Karl Ludwig von Haller's Critique of Liberal Peace," in *Commerce and Peace in the Enlightenment* ed. Béla Kapossy, Isaac Nakhimovsky, and Richard Whatmore (Cambridge, CUP, 2017), pp. 244–71 (p. 256 for the passage cited). See too Béla Kapossy, "Words and Things: Languages of Reform in Wilhelm Traugott Krug and Karl Ludwig von Haller," in *Languages of Reform in the Eighteenth Century: When Europe Lost Its Fear of Change*, ed. Susan Richter, Thomas Maissen, and Manuela Albertone (London, Routledge, 2020), pp. 384–404. For an interesting earlier examination of Haller's thought, see Charles Edward Merriam, *History of the Theory of Sovereignty since Rousseau* (New York, Columbia UP, 1900), pp. 63–72.

book by the philosopher Georg Wilhelm Friedrich Hegel in a blistering passage of his *Philosophy of Right*. "For," Hegel complained, "since the sphere of contingency, rather than the substantial, is taken to be the essence of the state, the content of such a work is consistent precisely in the utter inconsistency of its thoughtlessness."[30] Although Haller was not alone in claiming that modern natural jurisprudence was simply Roman law in another guise, it was not easy, as Hegel pointed out, to see why his concept of a natural social state was any less arbitrary than Hotman's earlier endorsement of the customs of the ancient Germanic peoples as the real alternative to Roman law. From this perspective, giving the concept of a natural social state any specifiable content was as likely to be arbitrary as any other attempt to apply history or anthropology to morality and politics. With shortcomings like these, it is not hard to see why Haller's alternative to the legacy of Roman law never got far off the ground.

Immanuel Kant and the Future as History

Long before Hegel's attack on Haller and well before Chenavard began to plan his project, a new way of thinking about the relationship between history and politics had begun to emerge. Its author was Immanuel Kant. For Kant, politics had more to do with the future than with either the past or the present, and as much to do with time itself as with any particular period of human history. It is still quite difficult to get the full measure of Kant's historical and political vision, partly because many of his most unusual insights were protected by so dense a parapet of philosophical technicalities that their imaginative and creative side is sometimes quite hard to discern, but partly too because many of the insights themselves were not particularly attractive or appealing. In the case of the problematic relationship between history and politics, Kant's achievement was to transfer the solution to the problem from the past to the future. The move had the immediate effect of taking the largely imaginary and potentially arbitrary quality of historical origins out of social contract theory. Instead of a glaringly implausible historical document or any real past event, a social contract could be turned into a moral goal. In one respect, the move appeared to add a moral dimension to Kant's historical vision because it took history to be leading towards the idea of humanity as a single entity. In another respect, however, it also highlighted the scale of the injustice that was actually built into the passage of time. Kant explained why this was the case in the essay entitled "Idea for a Universal History with a Cosmopolitan Aim" (or "Perspec-

---

30. Georg Wilhelm Friedrich Hegel, *Elements of the Philosophy of Right* [1820], ed. Allen W. Wood (Cambridge, CUP, 1991), p. 278.

tive") that he published in November 1784, a month before he published his more famous essay, entitled "An Answer to the Question, What is Enlightenment?"[31] Although both the chronology and subject matter of the two essays suggest that their content was quite close, it is not usual, at least in recent Kant scholarship, to think about the two essays together. Taken together, however, the first essay throws a very bleak light upon the content of the second. This was something that many of Kant's early contemporary readers noticed quite quickly and, like Herder, reacted against quite strongly.

Kant's argument in his "Idea for a Universal History with a Cosmopolitan Aim" was that thinking about human history showed that it had the distressing power to deliver more future benefits than any real human being could actually benefit from. In the terms that Kant presented it: humans, on the one side, were radically shortchanged by human history but, on the other side, the discrepancy between the ideal goal and the real level of achievement was the reason why human history existed in the first place. As is well known, Kant was a great admirer of Jean-Jacques Rousseau, and the argument of his essay was a development of Rousseau's concept of perfectibility and, in particular, the

---

31. Immanuel Kant, *Idea for a Universal History from a Cosmopolitan Perspective* [1784], in Immanuel Kant, *Toward Perpetual Peace and Other Writings on Politics, Peace, and History*, ed. Pauline Kleingeld, trans. David L. Colclasure (New Haven, CT, Yale UP, 2006), pp. 3–16. The essay is organized around nine propositions, and, in citations in the following paragraphs, I refer to both the proposition and page numbers. For commentary on the text, see the various chapters in Amélie Oksenberg Rorty and James Schmidt, eds., Kant's Idea for a Universal History with a Cosmopolitan Aim: *A Critical Guide* (Cambridge, CUP, 2009), together with Blandine Kriegel, *La politique de la raison* (Paris, Payot, 1994), pp. 25–40, and Jean-François Kervégan, "Is There Any Philosophy of History?" in *Concepts of Normativity: Kant or Hegel?*, ed. Christian Krijnen (Leiden, Brill, 2019), pp. 216–34. See too John H. Zammito, "Philosophy of History: The German Tradition from Herder to Marx," in *The Cambridge History of Philosophy in the Nineteenth Century*, ed. Allen W. Wood and Songsuk Susan Hahn (Cambridge, CUP, 2012), pp. 817–65 (especially pp. 832–33), and his "Stealing Herder's Thunder: Kant's Debunking of Herder on History in 'Conjectural Beginning of the Human Race,'" in *Immanuel Kant*, ed. Günther Lottes and Uwe Steiner (Saarbrücken, Wehrhahn, 2007), pp. 43–72. For more general orientation, see Karl Ameriks, *Kant and the Historical Turn* (Oxford, Clarendon Press, 2006); Genevieve Lloyd, *Providence Lost* (Cambridge, MA, Harvard UP, 2008), pp. 287–98; Dalia Nassar, ed., *The Relevance of Romanticism: Essays on German Romantic Philosophy* (Oxford, OUP, 2014) and her *The Romantic Absolute: Being and Knowing in Early German Romantic Philosophy* (Chicago, U of Chicago Press, 2014), pp. 68–69, 96–97; and, recently, Paul T. Wilford and Samuel A. Stoner, eds., *Kant and the Possibility of Progress: From Modern Hopes to Postmodern Anxieties* (Philadelphia, U of Pennsylvania Press, 2021), particularly the chapters by Susan Meld Shell, pp. 115–34, and Karl Ameriks, pp. 137–51.

mixture of inventiveness and destructiveness that the concept implied.[32] The argument began with the recognition that no historical starting point could ever get out of the problem of arbitrariness. The Romans could be countered by the Germans, just as the West could be matched by the East. This meant that any viable starting point for thinking about the relationship between history and politics had to be single, and, by extension, that the only possible starting point had to be humanity as a whole. If this was the starting point, Kant argued, then the one quality that was common to humanity as a whole was rationality. Humans, he pointed out, are not like other animals because their behaviour is not purely instinctive. Nor, however, is it purely rational because, if it were, humans would simply follow the same rational plan. Human life, therefore, falls somewhere in between. This, Kant continued, meant that, although it is embedded in huge, largely self-made webs of values, beliefs, and arrangements, human reason is still recognizable as something rational across time and space. This was why the knowledge produced by, for example, Archimedes, Kepler, or Newton, could travel through the ages and, more significantly, could be used in settings that had nothing to do with the conditions in which the knowledge itself had arisen. Human reason could, therefore, cross the boundaries of belief and behaviour in which many other aspects of human life were enclosed.

But, as Kant pointed out, this meant that those who came later had the benefits of the rational knowledge produced much earlier. There was, therefore, an unpleasant paradox built into human history. From one side, the knowledge that could cross the boundaries of time and space could cumulatively improve the quality of human life and, by doing so, could also provide both a starting point and a framework for thinking about the relationship between history and politics. The general and durable quality of human rationality supported a claim that humanity could, in the future, attain a condition in which every individual would be able to be as fully and perfectly themselves as possible, but it also seemed to mean, from a second point of view, that the only individuals who really would be in a position to be as fully and as perfectly themselves as possible would be those who came last. The resulting discrepancy between the historically progressive character of human rationality and the historically static character of human biology was, Kant went on

---

32. On Rousseau and perfectibility, see Sonenscher, *Jean-Jacques Rousseau*, pp. xi, 62–68. On later use of the concept, notably by Tocqueville, see Gérard Gengembre, "De la perfectibilité en Amérique," *Littératures* 50 (2004): 39–54, and, on its origins, Florence Lotterie, "Chateaubriand contre Madame de Staël: la lettre sur la perfectibilité, ou du progrès hors des limites de la simple raison," *Revue des sciences humaines* 247 (1997): 89–105, and her "Les lumières contre le progrès? La naissance de l'idée de perfectibilité," *Dix-Huitième Siècle* 30 (1998): 383–96.

to explain, the real reason underlying his term "unsocial sociability."[33] In most interpretations, the emphasis falls on the unsociable, rather than the sociable, part of the phrase and the idea that unsocial sociability was synonymous with individualism, competitiveness, commercial society, or capitalism. Kant's point was rather the opposite because his aim was to show that partial, small-scale sociability was hard to reconcile with real sociability, or the kind of sociability that would arise within humanity as a whole if justice and the conditions for justice were fully aligned. Since, Kant pointed out, this was not the case, and since humans could see that they could not all benefit from human endeavour, they had what he described as a "a strong tendency to isolate themselves."[34] They would simply form their own societies with their own rules of justice. Sociability would still occur. But it would be the wrong kind of sociability because it would build divisions and the potential for conflict into human life. Paradoxically, however, it would also give authority real legitimacy because it was hard to see why a state that made justice available only to its last living members could have any ability at all to exercise legitimate authority.

It has often been said, both in the eighteenth century and more recently, that Kant was a member of an unusual (and very small) family of political thinkers whose two other most significant members were Thomas Hobbes and Jean-Jacques Rousseau.[35] Usually, the affinity has been explained in terms of a shared, minimalist, concept of sociability, meaning an initial rejection of the idea that humans are naturally sociable and, because of this, do not have any inbuilt ability to form societies irrespective of whether the initial sociable impetus might have been supplied by love, need, language, or rationality. There is certainly enough of this in both Hobbes and Rousseau to support a much thinner description of natural human capabilities. But it has usually been more difficult to identify an equally thin but powerful reason for explaining the opposite condition, meaning, in other words, something minimal but general

33. Kant, *Idea for Universal History* (proposition 4), p. 6.

34. Ibid., p. 7. For an example, see Paul Cheney, "Istvan Hont, the Cosmopolitan Theory of Commercial Globalization, and Twenty-First Century Capitalism," *Modern Intellectual History*, 2021, pp. 1–29: "At best 'commercial society' could, within individual polities, be understood as an example of Kant's 'unsocial sociability' (*ungesellige Geselligkeit*)" (p. 15).

35. See, for example, Richard Tuck, "The 'Modern' Theory of Natural Law," in *The Languages of Political Theory in Early Modern Europe*, ed. Anthony Pagden (Cambridge, CUP, 1987), pp. 99–119, and his *The Rights of War and Peace: Political Thought and the International Order from Grotius to Kant* (Oxford, OUP, 1999), pp. 12, 36–38, 197–200, 207–9, 218. See too Istvan Hont, *Jealousy of Trade: International Competition and the Nation-State in Historical Perspective* (Cambridge, MA, Harvard UP, 2005), pp. 37–51.

that has the effect of making sociability itself unsocial. On minimalist premises, it cannot be because humans are naturally wicked, selfish, or vainglorious.
To Hobbes scholars, the reason has usually been seen to be the absence of any
natural human ability to identify and establish a stable set of common moral
principles, caused most fundamentally by the unsettling effects of human desire and, as Hobbes himself put it, by the fact that "the object of man's desire
is not to enjoy once only, and for one instant of time, but to assure for ever, the
way of his future desire."[36] To Rousseau scholars, the same type of moral
cloudiness has usually been said to have been reinforced by the effects of
amour-propre, meaning a self-defeating human propensity to come to rely on
others for moral self-approval. To both sets of scholars, this seems to mean
that although humans have no reason to be sociable, the underlying reasons
for unsociability are more soluble and tractable. To Hobbes scholars, the problem of moral uncertainty could be addressed, if not eliminated, by the security
produced by a combination of democratic political sovereignty and effective
political accountability. To Rousseau scholars, the problem of amour-propre
could also be addressed, if not eliminated, by a comparable but more explicitly
egalitarian set of arrangements designed to prevent amour-propre from turning
into inflamed amour-propre or, more measurably, by establishing a fair and
reliable electoral system to make governments more accountable to their
electorates.[37] Kant's approach to the problem was equally minimal, but his
explanation of its initial causes and its ultimate solution was both more comprehensive and more powerful.

On Kant's premises, unsocial sociability was built into human history. If
one looked at human history from the vantage point of a single imagined
future that would encompass humanity as a whole, it was clear that unsocial
sociability was unavoidable. In this respect, the difference between Kant and,
for example, Herder on the unity of mankind was rather like the earlier difference between Rousseau and Diderot on the concept of the general will.[38] For

36. Thomas Hobbes, Leviathan [1651], ed. Richard Tuck (Cambridge, CUP, 1991), ch. 11, p.70.

37. See, particularly, Istvan Hont, Politics in Commercial Society: Adam Smith and Jean-Jacques
Rousseau (Cambridge, MA, Harvard UP, 2015), pp. 10–13; Richard Tuck, The Sleeping Sovereign:
The Invention of Modern Democracy (Cambridge, CUP, 2015), pp. 129–31; and Frederick Neuhouser,
Rousseau's Theodicy of Self-Love: Evil, Rationality and the Drive for Recognition (Oxford, OUP,
2008), as well as his later Rousseau's Critique of Inequality: Reconstructing the Second Discourse
(Cambridge, CUP, 2014).

38. On this aspect of the relationship between Rousseau and Diderot, see Alberto Postigliola, "De Malebranche à Rousseau: les apories de la volonté générale et la revanche du 'raisonneur violent,'" Annales de la société Jean-Jacques Rousseau 39 (1972–77): 123–38, and Robert
Wokler, "The Influence of Diderot on the Political Theory of Rousseau," Studies on Voltaire and

Diderot, the concept of the general will supplied a framework for thinking about the relationship between morality and politics because it was a concept that could be applied to the whole of humanity. For Rousseau, however, the concept of a general will presupposed the existence of a sovereign and a state. Neither, however, could be found within humanity as such. This meant, in reality, that the idea of a general will implied a multiplicity of states and a divided world. Kant, of course, did not know of the clash between Rousseau and Diderot. His argument, however, in the "Idea for a Universal History with a Cosmopolitan Aim" simply substituted time for space but still also rehearsed the problem of the unity of mankind that lay at the centre of the argument between Diderot and Rousseau. For Rousseau, the existence of a general will called for a state, and this meant that every general will was limited by the state's boundaries. For Kant, something comparable was an effect of the passage of time and the bounded quality of every individual life. On these terms, the solution to the problem of unsocial unsociability could not be found by means of more democracy and accountability on the one side or less *amour-propre* and inequality on the other. All of them might help, but none of them would be able to do so until the underlying cause of the problem came more clearly into view. This was that every human had good reason to be sociable but would be sociable on unsociable premises. They would form limited and partial societies, and these societies would, in turn, magnify the initial problem.

There was, in short, no single-state solution to the problem of unsocial sociability because the problem applied not just to individuals but to nations and states as well. Since the future was, by definition, out of range, but since every existing potential benefit could only be presently possessed, every individual and every nation had an incentive to make as much of the present as they possibly could. History, from this perspective, seemed to have a built-in free-rider problem but no corresponding game-theoretical solution.[39] This, Kant emphasized, was why the ultimate problem in human history was the problem of international relations, because the human propensity to establish partial societies—as the way to offset the contradiction between reason's human promise and reason's limited capacity for individual delivery—meant that the only genuine solution to the problem of unsocial sociability was to be found in relations between states. Kant called this solution "a federation of

---

the *Eighteenth Century* 132 (1975): 55–111, along with his *Rousseau on Society, Politics, Music and Language* (New York, Garland Press, 1987).

39. On the problem, but without Kant, see Richard Tuck, *Free Riding* (Cambridge, MA, Harvard UP, 2008).

peoples" or "this great federation of peoples."[40] He also emphasized that it would be a long time coming. It is more difficult, however, and more in keeping with the two-sided nature of the concept of unsocial sociability as a durable human predicament, to understand what Kant could have meant by the idea of a federation of peoples.

Although the phrase implies a certain level of social and political integration, it is still not clear what a "great federation of peoples" might be or how it might work. One reason for this uncertainty is that the type of federation that Kant envisaged was not like any actually existing federation because it was designed, from the outset, to address the problem of something like a state made up of states, or, it could be said, the problem of establishing an institutionalized form of unsocial sociability.[41] Usually this type of arrangement is called a confederation, rather than a federation (or a *Staatenbund* rather than a *Bundesstaat*), and is usually taken to be more exposed to the risk of dissolution than its federal counterpart because it is taken to be more likely to succumb to civil war on the one side or to default into a full-fledged state on the other. It is not clear whether there is anything distinct from either of these alternatives, and whether Kant's idea of a "great federation of peoples" was something that could meet its requirements. To his early readers, however, Kant's idea was the product of a process of moral and social improvement that applied more to the human race than to its individual members. This was how the idea was interpreted in 1798 by the first French translator of Kant's essay, a French émigré named Charles Villers then living in Hamburg who later became a close acquaintance of Germaine de Staël. Looking backwards for past precedents, Villers argued, was the procedure that had fuelled the ferocity of imperial conquerors, the pitilessness of republican fanatics, and the cruelty of religious enthusiasts. Kant's essay set out a comprehensive alternative. It presented human history as following "an ascending scale of gradation that stretches too far for the individual and can only be of value to the species." To Villers, the engine driving the process was human vanity or, as he put it, the emotion displayed by a child when it picked up a pebble to show it off with delight to its parent. "Vanity," Villers wrote, "is the means, but the end nonetheless is that people will communicate, learn, and improve. Guided by a powerful but invisible hand, they all play their part without knowing it."[42] It was a consoling thought, but it was not really Kant's thought.

---

40. Kant, *Idea for Universal History* (proposition 7), p. 10.

41. See, helpfully, Murray Forsyth, *Unions of States: The Theory and Practice of Confederation* (Leicester, Leicester UP, 1981), and Olivier Beaud, *Théorie de la fédération* (Paris, PUF, 2007).

42. Charles Villers, introduction to Immanuel Kant, *Idée de ce que pourrait être une histoire universelle dans les vues d'un citoyen du monde* (Hamburg, 1798), p. 40.

Kant's own approach was more state oriented. A start towards a solution to the problem of unsocial sociability, he wrote, was to address the problem at the level of individuals and groups by ensuring that states had the power to establish and maintain the rule of law. States, laws, and governments could prevent unsocial sociability from collapsing into predatory behaviour and could turn it, instead, into ingenuity, creativity, and competitive adaptability.[43] Scaled up to encompass nations and states, the benefits of internal peace and prosperity could be translated into cultural prestige and military power. From this perspective, unsocial sociability was, as Kant wrote repeatedly, the real engine of human history and the source of the huge range of material and cultural resources that the modern world now had available. But the fundamental gap between promise and delivery applied as much to nations as it did to individuals, and, on this international scale, it was the cause of the greatest risk to human culture and civilization that there could be. This, Kant emphasized, was the risk of war. Its existence brought home the magnitude of the problem. This was not only that, as Kant put it, "the human being is an *animal* which, when he lives among his own species, *needs a master*," but also that the masters responsible for exercising mastery were all too human themselves.[44] Unlike other humans, however, those in a position of mastery also had the power to respond to the unsocial incentive built into the human condition by trying to use their external power to close the gap between reason's promise and reason's delivery and, by one means or another, set out to take what they could get. As Kant warned, it was an incentive that carried the risk of the end of history itself.

Since the risk to humanity came from humans themselves, there was no perfect solution. As Kant wrote, "the supreme authority" in every state would have to be "just *in itself*" but would still nonetheless be "a *human being*." This meant that justice itself would be beyond human reach because, as Kant put it famously, "nothing entirely straight can be fashioned out of the crooked timber of which humanity is made."[45] Trees in a wood have a natural ability to grow up straight, but unsocial sociability rules this out from human life. Human societies could, however, be given a measure of institutional, or more than purely human, support. They could avoid dependence on purely human agency partly by relying on the procedures and distinctions of constitutional government, and partly, and more importantly, by establishing a more stable international system. Ultimately, Kant wrote, war and the threat of war would

---

43. On this theme, see Hont, *Politics in Commercial Society* and his earlier *Jealousy of Trade*.
44. Kant, *Idea for Universal History* (proposition 6), p. 9.
45. Ibid., p. 9.

"compel our species to discover a law of equilibrium with regard to the—in itself productive—resistance between many states which arises from their freedom and, in its wake, to introduce a united power which lends force to this law."[46] Although Kant is sometimes associated with the idea of a world beyond states, this was not really the case. Perpetual peace, he argued both in his *Idea of Universal History* and in his later *Towards Perpetual Peace*, was predicated upon a state-based world. But it also required a durable and powerful system of alliances (such as, it has begun to be shown, the idea of a Holy Alliance in its earliest incarnation) to maintain a stable balance of power. With this "great federation" in place, Kant claimed, there would be something analogous to a "civil commonwealth" because the resulting system would be able to "maintain itself automatically."[47]

Kant ended the essay by asking whether there was any evidence of the reality of this process. Without evidence, he wrote, his essay would not be history but a novel or an exercise in "political fortune-telling."[48] His own answer to the question singled out four developments. The first, he wrote, was the balance of power itself and the pressure on states that it imposed to avoid weakening their own internal culture and risk losing their capacity to compete with other states. This pressure was, second, a strong disincentive on governments to encroach upon civil liberties because the consequences of this type of encroachment were usually bad for industry and trade, and for external competitiveness. The same type of calculation applied, third, to religious freedom and public discussion. Here too, competition between states seemed to have had the effect of weakening the inclination to enforce and maintain conformity of worship, and this in turn had made it easier to tolerate a wider range of religious practices and beliefs. The final piece of evidence was the rising cost of warfare itself. The large standing armies, public debts, and tax burdens imposed by modern warfare on all the major powers were, Kant argued, both an incentive to governments to avoid wars and, at the same time, a potential cause of resistance by taxpayers to the prospect of having to pay for any more. There was, in short, limited—but real—historical evidence of the content and direction of human history.

Kant repeated the argument of the essay in his *Critique of Pure Reason* but gave it a more highly charged moral gloss. "The *Platonic republic*," he wrote

46. Kant, *Idea for Universal History* (proposition 7), p. 12.

47. Ibid., p. 11. On early versions of the idea of a "holy alliance," see the forthcoming work of Isaac Nakhimovsky.

48. Kant, *Idea for Universal History* (proposition 9), p. 16.

there, "has become proverbial as a supposedly striking example of a dream of perfection that can have its place only in the idle thinker's brain." But, he continued,

> we would do better to pursue this thought further and (at those points where the excellent man leaves us without help) shed light on it through new endeavours, rather than setting it aside as useless under the very wretched and harmful pretext of its impracticability. A constitution providing for the *greatest human freedom* according to laws that permit *the freedom of each to exist together with that of others* (not one providing for the greatest happiness, since that would follow of itself) is at least a necessary idea, which one must make the ground not merely of the primary plan of a state's constitution but of all the laws too; and in it we must initially abstract from the present obstacles, which may perhaps arise not so much from what is unavoidable in human nature as rather from the neglect of the true ideas in the giving of laws.

From this perspective, Kant continued, Plato was right.

> Even though this may never come to pass, the idea of this maximum is nevertheless wholly correct when it is set forth as an archetype in order to bring the legislative constitution of human beings ever nearer to a possible greatest perfection. For whatever might be the highest degree of perfection at which humanity must stop, and however great a gulf must remain between the idea and its execution, no one can or should try to determine this, simply because it is freedom that can go beyond every proposed boundary.

This too meant that "Plato was right to see clear proofs of an origin in ideas not only where human reason shows true causality, and where ideas become efficient causes (of actions and their objects), namely in morality, but also in regard to nature itself."[49] There was, however, a real line separating nature from morality. "For," Kant concluded, "when we consider nature, experience provides us with the rule and is the source of truth; but with respect to moral laws, experience is (alas!) the mother of illusion, and it is most reprehensible to derive the laws concerning what I *ought to do* from what *is done*, or to want to limit it to that."[50] Ultimately, history and politics were still far apart.

49. Immanuel Kant, *Critique of Pure Reason* [1785], ed. and trans. Paul Guyer and Allen W. Wood (Cambridge, CUP, 1998), pt. 2, div. 2, bk. 1 [A 316–17; B 371–72], p. 397.
50. Ibid. [A 318; B 374], p. 397.

Kant's Critics

To Kant's critics, however, the argument was not very convincing. The earliest and one of the most vocal was certainly Herder. "How, for instance," he wrote in his *Ideas on the Philosophy of History of Mankind* with Kant's essay clearly in his sights, "can it be that man as we know him here, should have been formed for an infinite improvement of his mental faculties, a progressive extension of his perceptions and actions? Nay, that he should have been made for the state as the end of his species, and all preceding generations made properly for the last alone which is to be enthroned on the ruined scaffolding of the happiness of the rest?" The claim, he asserted, was simply false. "The sight of our fellow creatures, nay even the experience of every individual life, contradicts this plan attributed to creative providence. Neither our head nor our heart is formed for an infinitely increasing store of thoughts and feelings; our hand is not made, our life is not calculated for it. Do not our finest mental powers decay as well as flourish? Do they not even fluctuate with years and circumstances and re- lieve one another in friendly contest or rather in a circular dance." Real life, Herder argued, was the work of real people, not an unrealizable journey to an impossible goal. "The savage," he asserted, "who loves himself, his wife and child with quiet joy and glows with limited activity for his tribe, as for his own life, is, in my opinion, a more real being than that cultivated shadow who is enraptured with the love of the shades of his whole species, that is of a name." Kant's most striking failure, however, was his infatuation with the state. "Still less comprehensible," Herder wrote, "is it, how man should be made for the state, so that his first true happiness must necessarily spring from its constitution."

> For how many people upon earth are entirely ignorant of all government and yet are happier than many who have sacrificed themselves for the good of the state. I will not enter upon the benefits or mischiefs which this arti- ficial form of society brings with it, but it may be observed, as every art is merely an instrument and the most complicated instrument necessarily requires the most prudence and delicacy in managing it, this is an obvious consequence, that with the greatness of a state and the intricate art of its constitution, the danger of rendering individuals miserable is infinitely aug- mented. In large states, hundreds must pine with hunger that one may feast and carouse; thousands are oppressed and hunted to death, that one crowned fool or philosopher may gratify his whims.[51]

51. Johann Gottfried Herder, *Ideas on the Philosophy of History of Mankind* [1784], trans. T. Churchill (London, 1800), bk. 8, ch. 5, pp. 222–23.

If the comment was designed to put Kant in his place, it also underlined the need for a clearer and fuller connection between history and politics.

Romanticism, it could be said, was designed to fill the void that Kant created. "The historian," wrote the romantic philosopher Friedrich Schlegel in 1798, "is a prophet facing backwards."[52] The aphorism looks as if it was inspired by Kant. But Kant's version of the relationship between history and politics was actually forward facing. It was also, because of the concept of unsocial sociability, state based. To many of his early readers, the combination appeared to be contradictory if only because it appeared to reduce the idea of a universal history from a cosmopolitan point of view to a more dispiriting account of the politics of the world as it was. As they described Kant's essay, beginning with a normative future and setting it against a factual present failed to provide any real explanation of how the two were connected. Schlegel called this failure *Historismus*—or, as the word has come to be known in the Anglophone world, historicism—meaning something that looked like history but was not really history.[53] Historicism, in other words, began as something that was more like the opposite of what it has come to mean. Instead of a way of thinking about history as an unfolding—or even inevitable—process of development, it seemed in its original meaning to place too much emphasis on chance, contingency, or some sort of purely arbitrary development to be real history. From this perspective, what has come to be called historicism was an indirect effect of trying to fill the gap between the past and the present that Kant had opened up with the concept of unsocial sociability. Kant's philosophy, wrote the French philosopher Victor Cousin, was condemned to lurch between scepticism and faith because his own epistemology lacked the historical insight that was needed to reveal that the categories of human knowledge had a historical quality that was incompatible with the timeless abstractions of his critical

52. Friedrich Schlegel, *Athenaeum Fragments* (fragment n. 80), in *Friedrich Schlegel's* Lucinde *and the* Fragments, ed. Peter Firchow (Minneapolis and London, U of Minnesota Press, 1971), p. 170.

53. On *Historismus* (or historicism) as Schlegel's coinage, see Georg G. Iggers, "Historicism: The History and Meaning of the Term," *Journal of the History of Ideas* 56 (1995): 129–52; Gunter Scholtz, "Zum Historismusstreit in der Hermeneutik," in *Historismus am Ende des 20. Jahrhunderts*, ed. Gunter Scholtz (Berlin, Akademie Verlag, 1997), pp. 192–214 (particularly p. 193 n. 9). This aspect of Schlegel's thought is, somewhat surprisingly, not visible in Michael N. Forster, "Philosophy, History of Philosophy, and Historicism," in *Doing Humanities in Nineteenth-Century Germany*, ed. Efraim Podoksik (Leiden, Brill, 2020), pp. 19–39. Herder's reaction to Kant is also absent from to Georg G. Iggers, *The German Conception of History: The National Tradition of Historical Thought from Herder to the Present* [1968], 2nd ed. (Hanover, NH, University Presses of New England, 1983).

philosophy. There was no reason to believe that concepts like time, space, or causation were any less historical than any other attribute of human reason. This, Cousin argued, was why, alongside the nature of human reason, there also had to be room for the type of examination of its origin and development that he called psychology.[54]

Kant, Schlegel complained, referring here to Kant's essay *Towards Perpetual Peace* rather than his *Idea of Universal History* (although in this context the arguments of the two texts were the same), relied too heavily on "the great artist, nature" to explain how perpetual peace could ever occur. Invoking nature simply turned the putative cause into a metaphor. It was one thing, Schlegel wrote, to indicate "the external occasions of destiny" that might make perpetual peace possible, but it was quite another thing to explain "whether the inner development of humanity leads to it." This was what Kant had failed to do. "The purposiveness of nature," Schlegel pointed out, "is here entirely indifferent; only the (actual) *necessary laws of experience* could accomplish a future success." The gap between the one and the other, Schlegel concluded, meant that Kant's idea of using history as an ideal rather than a real starting point had to be matched by the *"laws of political history* and the *principles of political education"* to make the ideal become an achievable task.[55] In light of this criticism, the historian really did have to be a backward-facing prophet. Some things, as Schlegel went on to claim, really could be pulled out of the past to become the basis of a new and better future. The resulting mixture of continuity and change, he argued, amounted to something like what would now be called a sequence of paradigms.[56] As Schlegel described them, these clusters of belief and behaviour would be held together by a mixture of truth and falsehood that, over time, would tilt too far to one side or the other to be durably stable, but, over further time, would acquire or revive a new array of stabilizing ingredients. One ingredient, as Schlegel's very public conversion

54. Victor Cousin, *Philosophie de Kant* [1820], 4th ed. (Paris, 1864), pp. 314–15.

55. For these passages from Schlegel, see Dalia Nassar, "Friedrich Schlegel (1772–1829)," in *The Oxford Handbook of German Philosophy in the Nineteenth Century*, ed. Michael N. Forster and Kristin Gjesdal (Oxford, OUP, 2015), pp. 68–93. Compare to Servanne Jollivet, *L'historisme en questions. Généalogie, débats et reception (1800–1930)* (Paris, Champion, 2013), pp. 31–33, and to Frederick Beiser, "Historicization and Historicism: Some Nineteenth-Century Perspectives," in *Historisierung: Begriff-Geschichte-Praxisfelder* ed. Moritz Baumstark and Robert Forkel (Stuttgart, J. B. Metzler Verlag, 2016), pp. 42–54.

56. The concept has been used particularly by J.G.A. Pocock, *The Machiavellian Moment: Florentine Political Thought and the Atlantic Republican Tradition* (Princeton, NJ, Princeton UP, 1975; 2nd ed., Princeton, NJ, Princeton UP, 2003; see too the further, 2016, Princeton edition, with an illuminating introduction by Richard Whatmore).

to Catholicism went on to highlight, was religion. Another was government, notably the decentralized governments of medieval society with its many municipalities, guilds, and corporations and its two different, but equally remote, papal and imperial heads. A third, which seemed to be a real conduit from the past to the present, was the law, particularly as this was illustrated by the way that Roman law had travelled down the ages from the Roman Empire to the modern German states. The idea appealed very strongly to Friedrich Carl von Savigny, the founder of the German historical school of law who, as a young man, was a very careful student of the works of Schlegel, Schiller, and Schelling through his friends at the University of Jena, Friedrich and Leonhard Creuzer.[57]

Criticism of Kant's "Idea for a Universal History" was not confined to the German-speaking world. The aim of the essay, wrote Count Jean-Etienne-Marie Portalis, one of the principal authors of the French Civil Code of 1801, "seems to be to prove that the individual is nothing within humanity and that perfection is not made for the individual but for the whole human race." Portalis was as appalled by Kant's historical vision as Herder had been.

> I would like to ask Immanuel Kant what we can learn from history if the play of human freedom is ruled by as invariable and imperious a law as the one that rules the physical world. I would like to ask if, in his system, history has any other purpose than to make us inconsolable for having been born too soon. Why does he tell us that individuals count for nothing and that only the species matters? What is the species if separated from the individuals who make it up? Is there anything other than the individual in nature? I would like to ask if there has been anything other than revolution among nations, either for good or ill, and whether the Greeks did not fall when the Romans rose. I would like, finally, to ask if there will ever be a day when people will be born without passions and will no longer be blind or subject to error and if climate, the soil, the sea, and distance will no longer have an eternal influence on the character and habits of peoples and the limits of empire. When the philosopher of Königsberg has solved all these problems satisfactorily, it will then be time to change the way to study and write history.[58]

57. See Frederick C. Beiser, *The German Historicist Tradition* (Oxford, OUP, 2015), pp. 214–52 (especially pp. 221–27). Compare to John Edward Toews, "The Immanent Genesis and Transcendent Goal of Law: Savigny, Stahl and the Ideology of the Christian German State," *American Journal of Comparative Law* 37 (1989): 139–69.

58. Jean-Etienne-Marie Portalis, *De l'usage et de l'abus de l'esprit philosophique durant le xviiie siècle* [1820], 3rd ed. 2 vols. (Paris, 1834), 2:24.

In broad terms, the content of Portalis's diatribe was similar to Herder's, and comparisons between Kant and Herder soon became one of the standard features of nineteenth-century discussions of the philosophy of history.

Few of these comparisons favoured Kant. One that did, by a philosophy professor from Orléans that was published in 1851, emphasized the future-oriented content of Kant's essay and the extent to which, in the light of Kant's own later assessment, it had been given "striking confirmation" by the events of the French Revolution.[59] Most, however, were less favourable. Kant's essay was published in an abridged translation in 1863 by the positivist philosopher and creator of the eponymous dictionary, Emile Littré, in his large and very sympathetic intellectual biography of positivism's founder, Auguste Comte. To Littré, Comte's three-stage theory of human history and culture, running from the theological to the metaphysical to the positive, was the solution to Kant's conundrum, and, since Comte had been given a translation of Kant's text in 1824, the existence of this link helped to show that Comte really was, as Littré wrote, Kant's intellectual heir. But, as Littré pointed out, Comte had revised and corrected Kant in two important respects. By dividing history into a sequence of culturally discrete stages, he had, Littré claimed, shown that it was possible to think of a way to close the gap between individual capabilities and the achievements of humanity. Unlike Kant, Littré emphasized, Comte had dropped "vicious passions and egotistical sentiments" from among the causes of human development and, instead, had shown that society and its development depended "above all" on what Comte, "happily, had called altruistic dispositions."[60] Comte had also, Littré claimed, substituted positive historical investigation for Kant's wishful thinking. In both respects, Comte's corrections aligned Kant with Herder. Altruism and historical stages, ultimately, trumped unsocial sociability.

Most comparisons, however, straightforwardly favoured Herder. According to a history of philosophy also published in the middle of the nineteenth century, Herder, unlike Kant, "did not believe that every human generation

59. Auguste Javary, *De l'idée du progrès* (Paris, 1851), p. 72.

60. Emile Littré, *Auguste Comte et la philosophie positive* [1863], 2nd ed. (Paris, 1864), pp. 53–54, 69–70. Kant's essay was described to Comte by Gustav d'Eichtal in a letter of 22 August 1824: see "Matériaux pour server à la biographie d'Auguste Comte: correspondance d'Auguste Comte et Gustave d'Eichtal," *Revue Occidentale*, 2nd ser., 12 (1896): 241, 244–45. On Comte and Kant, see Mary Pickering, "New Evidence of the Link between Comte and German Philosophy," *Journal of the History of Ideas* 50 (1989): 443–63, and, more broadly, her *Auguste Comte: An Intellectual Biography*, 3 vols. (Cambridge, CUP, 1993–2009). On Comte and altruism, see Thomas Dixon, *The Invention of Altruism: Making Moral Meanings in Victorian Britain* (Oxford, OUP, 2008).

was working for the prosperity of a single one that would emerge whenever it did" because, according to Herder, "every fraction of humanity would enjoy the perfection and happiness that matched its own moral conduct."[61] There was, in short, no absolute historical value, not even, according to the Scottish philosopher Robert Flint writing in 1874, "the particular final cause which Kant assigns to history," which was "the production of a perfect political constitution." The idea fitted Kant's account of the effects of unsocial sociability. Flint, however, disagreed. He took issue with the claim made by Kant's biographer and Hegel's disciple Karl Rosenkranz that Kant had been right to adopt this view of history. "The notion of the state," Rosenkranz had written, "alone supplies a firm foundation and renders possible organic development. Religion, art, science, can only be included in the philosophy of history in so far as they refer to political freedom, not as they are in and for themselves." Political freedom, Flint replied, was a means, not an end, which was why religion, art, and science were among the ends to which political freedom could be used. That had been Herder's point. "Hence," Flint concluded, "Professor Rosenkranz, instead of here making evident a merit in Kant's essay, has only brought into additional prominence its narrowness, its exclusiveness or, in other words, its deficiency in the excellences most characteristic of the conception and work of Herder."[62] For Herder every age had its own merits, and it was this, rather than Kant's bleak choice between an arbitrary past and an impossible future, that came to form the basis of the philosophies of history of the nineteenth century.

Ballanche, Quinet, and the End of History

The "excellences" that Flint identified in Herder's works formed the background to Chenavard's now-forgotten Panthéon project and the concept of palingenesis on which it relied. Although both the word and the concept of palingenesis were old—at least in the naturalistic sense of palingenesis as regeneration—the concept took on a new and somewhat different meaning when it began to be applied to the idea of a whole society. In this latter sense,

61. Gaetano Sanseverino, *I principali sistemi della filosofia sul criterio discussi con le dottrine de' santi padri e de' dottori del medio evo* [1850], 2nd ed. (Naples, 1858), p. 156.

62. Robert Flint, *The Philosophy of History in France and Germany* (Edinburgh, 1874), pp. 398–99. Compare to Frank Ankersmit, "History as the Science of the Individual," *Journal of the Philosophy of History* 7 (2013): 396–425, and his "Representationalist Logic," in *Other Logics: Alternatives to Formal Logic in the History of Thought and Contemporary Philosophy*, ed. Admir Skodo (Leiden, Brill, 2014), pp. 101–22. On Flint, see Stanley Ralph Obitts, "The Thought of Robert Flint" (unpublished PhD thesis, Edinburgh University, 1962).

palingenesis became a counterconcept to Kant's historical and political vision. Kant, in fact, had actually made use of the concept quite early in his publishing career, five years before the concept came into more general European circulation with the publication by the Genevan natural philosopher Charles Bonnet of his *Palingénésie philosophique* (Philosophical palingenesis) in 1769. Kant's use of the concept was, however, very much more limited than Bonnet's later, more extensive, usage. The concept itself was Greek in origin and meant being born again, sometimes in a physical sense—as in vegetation growing back after a forest fire—and sometimes in a more metaphorical sense—as in the idea of a revival of learning that, in the third decade of the nineteenth century, was to crystallize into the concept of the Renaissance.[63] It acquired a more particular theological and philosophical sense in the eighteenth century, mainly among the European followers of the early eighteenth-century German philosopher Gottfried Wilhelm Leibniz who, in this context, included Charles Bonnet. Leibniz's philosophy had a particular bearing on the concept of palingenesis because of his own interest in what he called "spontaneity."[64] In Leibniz's usage, spontaneity meant something more than directness, immediacy, improvisation, or creativity, as it now usually does. It was also a more technical property of the monads that he took to be the most basic units of creation. In this usage, monads lay beyond the world of matter, external causation, and materialism because they were self-directed and internally powered. They had, in short, something like the properties underlying the concept of palingenesis, and, as Leibniz's philosophy began to become better known over the course of the eighteenth century, the concept of spontaneity began to be incorporated into natural philosophy. This, put summarily, was Bonnet's achievement. The fusion that he established between the Leibnizian concept of spontaneity and the older idea of a great chain of being was what enabled Bonnet's book to push the subject of palingenesis into the mainstream of late eighteenth-century European intellectual life.[65]

63. The concept of the Renaissance began as a term of art in the history of architecture. For an early example, see the chapter headed "De l'art à l'époque appelée la renaissance," in Jean Antoine Coussin, *Du génie de l'architecture* (Paris, 1822), p. 135.

64. For a helpful examination of the concept in eighteenth-century thought, see Douglas Moggach, "Contextualising Fichte: Leibniz, Kant, and Perfectionist Ethics," *Fichte-Studien* 45 (2018): 133–53.

65. On Leibniz and Bonnet, see Olivier Rieppel, "The Reception of Leibniz's Philosophy in the Writings of Charles Bonnet," *Journal of the History of Biology* 21 (1988): 119–45; Marta Sukiennicka, "La palingénésie philosophique de Charles Bonnet: le pouvoir heuristique d'un imaginaire matérialiste des lumières," *Studi Romanica Posnaniensia* 44 (2017): 25–34; Michael Sonen-

The version of the concept that Bonnet began to describe was a product of a protracted discussion of a number of difficult subjects in Christian thought, like the relationship between the mind and the body, between the immortality of the soul and the resurrection of the body, and between human knowledge and human behaviour, on the one side, and the lives and behaviour of the many other types of being that, on the other side, were part of the whole creation. In Bonnet's usage the concept of palingenesis was bound up with a mixture of what would now be called theology, anthropology, philosophy, biology, chemistry, and physics, which meant, by extension, that it amounted to a more spiritually driven way of describing the great chain of being. The concept was used in this sense not only in Bonnet's own publications but also in those of his friend and contemporary, the Bernese natural philosopher Albrecht von Haller, and those of his Italian emulator, Lazzaro Spallanzani, as well as in the new, more highly spiritualized version of physiognomy developed by the Swiss theologian Johann Caspar Lavater.[66] As broader versions of the concept became current, it came to owe a great deal to developments in natural philosophy, particularly to research in electricity and magnetism, and the discovery that both these forces or powers relied on a combination of positive and negative poles for how they existed and worked. It seemed to follow that polarity and polarization were the keys to understanding both stability and change in natural and human life.[67] In this rendition, palingenesis amounted to a way of

---

scher, *Sans-Culottes: An Eighteenth-Century Emblem in the French Revolution* (Princeton, NJ, Princeton UP, 2007), pp. 119–27, and the further secondary literature referred to there.

66. On these subjects, see Fernand Baldensperger, "Les théories de Lavater dans la littérature française," in his *Etudes d'histoire littéraire*, 4 vols. (Paris, 1907–39), 2:51–91; Robert E. Norton, *The Beautiful Soul: Aesthetic Morality in the Eighteenth Century* (Ithaca, NY, Cornell UP, 1995), especially ch. 5; David Bindman, *Ape to Apollo: Aesthetics and the Idea of Race in the Eighteenth Century* (London, Reaktion Books, 2002), pp. 92–123; and, on some of their more tendentious features, Jeffrey Freedman, *A Poisoned Chalice* (Princeton, NJ, Princeton UP, 2002). More generally, see Jacques Roger, "The Living World," in *The Ferment of Knowledge: Studies in the Historiography of Eighteenth-Century Science*, ed. G. S. Rousseau and Roy Porter (Cambridge, CUP, 1980), pp. 255–83; Elizabeth A. Williams, *The Physical and the Moral: Anthropology, Physiology and Philosophical Medicine in France, 1750–1850* (Cambridge, CUP, 1994); Alan Richardson, *British Romanticism and the Science of the Mind* (Cambridge, CUP, 2001); Thomas Ahnert, "The Soul, Natural Religion and Moral Philosophy in the Scottish Enlightenment," in *Eighteenth-Century Thought*, ed. James G. Buickerood, vol. 2 (New York, AMS Press, 2004), pp. 233–53; Peter Hans Reill, *Vitalizing Nature in the Enlightenment* (Berkeley, U of California Press, 2005).

67. For a helpful, near-contemporary way in to this vast subject, see Georges Cuvier, *Histoire des sciences naturelles depuis leur origine jusqu'à nos jours*, 5 vols. (Paris, 1845), notably the chapter in the additional fifth volume of this edition by T. Magdeleine de Saint-Agy, entitled "De la philosophie de la nature en Allemagne et en France."

combining natural philosophy with a version of theology that, as *Naturphiloso-phie*, came to have a very wide appeal, particularly in the German-speaking parts of Europe, in the early nineteenth century.[68]

Life, it was claimed in these versions of nature-philosophy, was a product of powers or entities that were either positive or negative, generating myriads of real-life forms of existence made up of ever more complex syntheses of both. Subsequently, the usage was extended to the idea of artistic creativity and to the process of making something new and different out of an existing body of cultural, material, and technical resources, as in "the loom of palingenesis," the phrase used towards the middle of the nineteenth century by the English critic Thomas De Quincey to refer to what he took to be the vital power underlying both natural and cultural life.[69] As one early nineteenth-century reviewer noted, the term had become a synonym for the word "renaissance" and now referred to the idea that being was actually a continuous and cumulative pro-cess of self-transformation.[70] This broader redefinition extended the claim that all aspects of the creation were parts of an ascending hierarchy of being gener-ated by the drive of the spiritual to break free of the limitations of the physical. From this perspective, palingenesis meant replacing the idea that the body housed the soul with the more spiritually and socially dynamic idea that the soul shaped the body.

This was the claim underlying Herder's philosophy of history and the basis of the concept of palingenesis that Kant rejected. He gave the concept a quite positive and precise interpretation in his relatively early *Observations on the*

68. On this, see recently John H. Zammito, *The Gestation of German Biology: Philosophy and Physiology from Stahl to Schelling* (Chicago, U of Chicago Press, 2018).

69. On De Quincey's usage, see Frederick Burwick, "Nexus in De Quincey's Theory of Language," and Robert Lance Snyder, "'The Loom of *Palingenesis*': De Quincey's Cosmology in 'System of the Heavens,'" both in *Thomas De Quincey. Bicentenary Studies*, ed. Robert Lance Snyder (Norman and London, U of Oklahoma Press, 1985), pp. 263–78, 338–59, and Jonathan Smith, "De Quincey's Revisions of the 'System of the Heavens,'" *Victorian Periodicals Review* 26 (1993): 203–12.

70. "Le mot de *palingénésie* ou *renaissance* se trouve *consacré* par le divin auteur de notre croyance, qui s'en est servi: Matth. 19.28." [Anon.], "Quelques réflexions sur le plan total de la création et sur la palingénésie humaine de M. Nodier," *Annales de philosophie chrétienne* 7 (1833): 48 n. 1. See also the comment on the thought of Pierre-Simon Ballanche by Jean-Jacques Am-père, *Mélanges d'histoire littéraire et de la littérature*, 2 vols. (Paris, 1867), 2:129: "Le tout devait former comme un code de *Palingénésie sociale*. Par ce mot, qui veut dire *renaissance*, ou plutôt *génération renouvelée*, il désignait la loi de transformation qu'il regardait comme la loi de l'individu et de la société." For related discussion, see Julian Wright, *Socialism and the Experience of Time: Idealism and the Present in Modern France* (Oxford, OUP, 2017).

Feeling of the Beautiful and Sublime of 1764. There, towards the end of his essay, at the point at which he began a discussion "of national characters, so far as they rest upon the distinct feeling of the beautiful and of the sublime," Kant turned from making broadly national comparisons of the Italians, the French, the Germans, the Britons, and the Spanish to making a comparison between "the ancient times of the Greeks and Romans" and more recent times. In most respects, he went on to argue, it was a comparison that favoured the moderns. "At last," he wrote, "after the human genius has, by a sort of *palingenesis*, happily recovered itself from an almost total destruction, we see flourish in our days the just taste of the beautiful and noble as well in the arts and sciences as with regard to the moral and there is nothing more to be wished for than that the false glitter which so easily deceives may not insensibly lead us away from the noble simplicity."[71] Here, Kant continued, an antidote was at hand. This, as his late eighteenth-century translator put it, was because it was also to be wished "that the still undiscovered mystery of education can be rescued from the old fancy, in order to exalt at times the moral feeling in the breast of every young citizen of the world to an active sentiment, so that all fineness or delicacy may not tend to the merely fleeting idle pleasure, and instead to judge that which happens around us with more or less taste." It is tempting, particularly in the light of the respective dates of publication of their two works, to associate Kant's final remark with Rousseau and, particularly, with Rousseau's treatise on education, *Emile*, which had been published two years earlier in 1762.

On this occasion, Kant's use of the concept of palingenesis was more clearly limited in scale and scope than Bonnet's. Where Bonnet used the term to refer to the whole creation, Kant's usage was limited to matters of judgment and taste either in the arts and sciences or in morality because, even at his most speculative, he never endorsed the type of theory associated with Leibniz and his eighteenth-century followers. He made this clear in a two-part review of Herder's *Ideas on the Philosophy of History of Mankind* that was published in 1785. Herder, like Bonnet, was strongly attracted to Leibniz's philosophical and historical thought, while Kant was brusquely incredulous towards the idea of a spiritually generated chain of being and the part played by the concept of palingenesis in the intellectual architecture of Herder's philosophy of history. There was, he asserted flatly, nothing to indicate that anything like social palingenesis existed. "The reviewer," he wrote, "must confess that he does not

---

71. Immanuel Kant, *Observations on the Feeling of the Beautiful and Sublime* [1764], in Immanuel Kant, *Essays and Treatises on Moral, Political, Religious and Various Philosophical Subjects*, 2 vols. (London, 1799), 2:77–78.

comprehend this line of reasoning from the analogy of nature, even if he were prepared to accept that continuous gradation of natural creatures and its rule of a gradual approximation to man." Although, he acknowledged, it was true that a kind of palingenesis existed among "flying insects which develop from grubs or caterpillars," this type of palingenesis was "the sequel not of *death*, but merely of the *pupal phase*," and had nothing in common with the idea of a spiritual force rising, by way of palingenesis, up the scale of ever more spiritual forms of being. There was, Kant wrote, simply no evidence to suggest that anything like this could ever be found. The "whole hypothesis of invisible forces which give rise to organisation" and, subsequently, to higher and higher levels of organization was nothing more, he wrote dismissively, than an "attempt to explain *what is not understood* in terms of *what is understood even less*."[72]

Despite Kant's dismissal, the concept of palingenesis lived up to its name. It did so partly because Herder's ideas began to circulate widely all over Europe from the 1790s onwards. His *Ideas on the Philosophy of History of Mankind* appeared in an English translation in 1800, followed by a French translation in 1827.[73] Herder's translator, Edgar Quinet, went on to publish a huge epic poem, entitled *Ahasvérus* (the name given to the allegorical scriptural figure of the Wandering Jew), which supplied many of the intellectual resources involved in Chenavard's Panthéon project. It did so mainly, however, because between Herder and Quinet a third figure came to play a significant part in the formation of the conceptual edifice on which Chenavard's project was based. This was the writer and religious philosopher Pierre-Simon Ballanche. It was Ballanche, whose eponymous *Essais de palingénésie sociale* (Essays on social palingenesis) were published in 1827, the same year as Quinet published his translation of Herder, who turned Bonnet's concept of philosophical palingenesis into a Herder-inspired concept of social palingenesis. In doing so, he also made use of Herder's thought to explain why class struggle could be understood as the engine of human history. Here, it was not so much the social composition or the political aspirations of the classes themselves that were most significant, but the intensity of the conflict and the reasons for the durability of its legacy.

72. Immanuel Kant, "Reviews of Herder's *Ideas on the Philosophy of the History of Mankind* [1785], in Kant, *Political Writings*, pp. 208–9. See too, for a further dismissal of Bonnet's natural philosophy, Kant's later essay "On the Use of Teleological Principles in Philosophy" [1788], trans. J. Tissot, in Emmanuel Kant, *Mélanges de logique* (Paris, 1862), pp. 373–419 (especially pp. 409–13).

73. On Herder in France, see, above all, Henri Tronchon, *La fortune intellectuelle de Herder en France: la préparation* (Paris, Rieder, 1920) and, equally impressively, his *Allemagne-France-Angleterre. Le jeune Edgar Quinet ou l'aventure d'un enthousiaste* (Paris, Les Belles Lettres, 1937).

Ballanche relied quite strongly on an idea supplied by Herder as the basis of his concept of social palingenesis. This was the idea that abstract concepts, like justice or freedom, could be symbolized or personified so that the aesthetic or moral qualities of the symbols themselves would then become objects of allegiance in their own right. This, for Herder, was why history mattered. It was not only a record of events but was also a symbolic commentary on their moral significance. And, since the physical side of symbols was their least important part, the moral and emotional power of what they symbolized could be separated off from the spatial and temporal limits of their physical existence to become the sources of a second life. Just as plants come back to life when winter turns to spring, the emotional and aesthetic power of symbols made it possible to apply the same idea to a whole society. To Ballanche, history provided the evidence that palingenesis was real. Societies, he argued, were sometimes subject to huge catastrophes but did not always disappear from the face of the earth. There was, for example, a Jewish nation even though there was no kingdom of Israel. The Roman Empire was long gone, but Roman law and Roman institutions, including the idea of a *res publica* or republic, were still to be found in many parts of Europe and America. Ballanche, like several of his contemporaries, was also actively involved in the European campaign for Polish independence because, after three eighteenth-century partitions, there was still clearly a Polish people and a Polish nation even though there was no Polish state.[74] From this perspective, Greece, Italy, and even Germany could also look forward to a second coming because, as the metaphor itself suggests, several of the ways of describing this kind of life after death had, by the early nineteenth century, come to rely on a recognizably Christian framework of explanation. Ballanche himself made extensive use of the concepts of transgression, punishment, atonement, and expiation to provide much of the content and direction of his version of the idea of social palingenesis, which, with modifications, was also to become the basis of Chenavard's later project.[75]

As Ballanche presented them, the events of the French Revolution—from the fall of the Bastille to the execution of the king to the end of the first French Empire—could be fitted readily into a framework of atonement and expiation to form a story about transgression, retribution, remission, and regeneration

---

74. See the list provided by McCalla, *A Romantic Historiosophy*, pp. 436–37, of articles that Ballanche contributed in 1834 to a periodical entitled *Le Polonais, journal des intérêts de la Pologne*. See too Wacław Lednicki, "Mickiewicz at the Collège de France," in *Polish Civilization: Essays and Studies*, ed. Mieczysław Giergelewicz (New York, New York UP, 1979), pp. 182–97.

75. On the differences between Ballanche and Chenavard, see McCalla, *A Romantic Historiosophy*, pp. 404–6, and Herbert J. Hunt, *The Epic in Nineteenth-Century France* (Oxford, Blackwell, 1941), pp. 259–60.

that amounted to a long historical chain connecting Roman history to the events of the French Revolution because, he claimed, both were symbols of the fundamental content of human history as a whole. "As for me," Ballanche wrote, "my only wish is to show one thing: the universal struggle of plebeian-ism against the patriciate, that endlessly recurring struggle epitomized in so many civil mythologies, but made manifest among the Romans as a series of historical facts."[76] The point of this endlessly recurring pattern of class conflict, Ballanche emphasized, and the link between ancient Rome and modern France was the human price that it brought in its wake and the memory of human suffering that it left behind. Together, he explained, they meant that history was a kind of human initiation into humanity. Class conflict was humanity's way of coming to recognize and acknowledge itself in both a conceptual and an emotional sense. For Ballanche, the content of that historical and social recognition was provided by Christianity, underpinned by the natural human sense of justice. As Herder had shown in an essay on the Greek goddess Nemesis as a personification of the feeling of justice—an essay that was translated into French and cited by Ballanche in his very first publication (*Du sentiment*) in 1801—the sense of justice stood midway between the outrage produced by someone else's undeserved good fortune and the joy (or *Schadenfreude*) produced by their well-deserved ill-fortune. On the basis of this interpretation, Nemesis was a very good symbol of the reconciliation required for a postrevolutionary age.[77]

Chenavard's plan for the Panthéon lay at the confluence of these three historical visions. One came from Herder and another from Ballanche, while the third was supplied by the huge epic poem entitled *Ahasvérus* that was published in 1832 by the historian, poet, and philosopher Edgar Quinet. Chenavard knew both Quinet and Ballanche because all three lived in Lyon, and his decorative plan was something like a synthesis of Ballanche's *Essais de palingénésie*

---

76. "Quant à moi, je ne veux montrer qu'une chose, c'est cette lutte, sans cesse renouvelée, concentrée ailleurs dans les diverses mythologies civiles, et manifestée chez les Romains par une série de faits historiques, la lutte universelle du plébéianisme contre le patriciat, c'est-à-dire, comme nous l'avons vu, l'initiation même de l'humanité." Ballanche, *Essais de palingénésie sociale*, in *Œuvres*, 4:183–84. On the eighteenth-century French background to the subject, which seems to have escaped the attention of more specialized Ballanche scholars, see Michael Steinberg, "The Twelve Tables and Their Origins: An Eighteenth-Century Debate," *Journal of the History of Ideas* 43 (1982): 379–96.

77. Johann Gottfried Herder, "Némésis, symbole moral des anciens," in *Recueil de pièces intéressantes concernant les antiquités, les beaux-arts, les belles-lettres et la philosophie*, 6 vols. (Paris, 1796), 6:404–24. On the essay and Ballanche's use of it, see the unsurpassable Henri Tronchon, *La fortune intellectuelle*, pp. 136–37 and 395–403 in particular.

sociale and Quinet's *Ahasvérus* (Quinet, apparently, finished the poem in Rome in 1832 where one of his closest acquaintances was, in fact, Chenavard).[78] Where Ballanche's concept of social palingenesis was designed to show how history as class conflict could, ultimately, become the basis of humanity's capacity for social reconciliation, Quinet's epic ended more enigmatically. It reworked the story of the Wandering Jew as a symbol of human history and came to a somewhat opaque conclusion in a strange conversation between the figures of Eternity and Nothingness. In the end, the poem seemed to say, there was only Eternity. The point here was to show that humanity really was something complete or, in a sense, a full measure of itself, meaning, in more abstract terms, that the concept of eternity was able to illustrate this wholeness more effectively than could be done by the concept of nothingness. The reason was that the concept of nothingness presupposed a concept of being, or a concept of something other than itself, while the concept of eternity, Quinet claimed, could be both itself and its opposite. It could be either a single timeless moment or an endless sequence of particular moments but, in either guise, it would still be simply itself. Ultimately, according to *Ahasvérus*, humanity and eternity were fundamentally the same, with the same type of existence both inside and outside of time and, by extension, with the same capacity to become fully and entirely itself in both an individual and a generic sense. If unsocial sociability gave rise to a state-based world, Quinet's Herder-inspired alternative amounted to a world beyond states.

Industry and Individuality

From this cosmic perspective, there was no room for any of the more limited historical parallels that could be made with the Hebrews, the Romans, or the Germans. Quinet drove the point home some years after the publication of *Ahasvérus* by describing the catastrophic effects of the misplaced parallel between France's first absolute sovereign, Louis XIV, and the government of imperial Rome that had become current in the seventeenth and eighteenth centuries. It had arisen from the similarity between the reign of Louis XIV after the seventeenth-century French civil wars known as the Frondes and the rule of Augustus Caesar after the civil conflicts of the late Roman republic. "The standard way of doing this," Quinet wrote in an article on modern literature that he published in 1838, "was to isolate the age of Louis XIV, as if it were a solitary point in time. The stress fell on highlighting the differences between it and everything surrounding it because this made it seem all the greater.

---

78. Richard Heath, *Edgar Quinet: His Early Life and Writings* (London, 1881), p. 148.

By separating it from its natural origins, from the traditions of Christianity and feudalism, it was given a condition that set it apart from every other age."

> Thus, it became an age that seemed to be suspended or lost in time; or, to put the same thing differently, if the origins of the age of Louis XIV were to be sought anywhere, they could be found in the age of Augustus. Thus, however much they might really be separated by seventeen hundred years, the time-lapse seemed to be no more than an empty space, shaped on the same plane and from the same mould, in which the two ages could move closer and embrace one another without obstacle. The genius of Christianity, which formed the core of the seventeenth century, was neglected by critics who went on to set out, in endless profusion, the similarities between the poetics of that time and those of pagan times. Rome was imagined to be the site of an antiquity that was modern, just as Versailles was imagined to be the site of a France that was ancient and, on this imaginary terrain in which the distance separating Augustus from Louis XIV was truncated on both sides, the two civilizations were blended together to form a doubly impossible alliance.[79]

Quinet's version of the concept of palingenesis ruled out this type of parallel. Human beliefs and arrangements belonged fully to their time, but they also had a power to propel the jagged course of human history towards a goal that, ultimately, would enable humanity to acquire a quality of individuality that was never available at the beginning. As Quinet explained in a letter complaining about a hostile review of the poem in 1834, the point of the poem was to look towards the future rather than the past. Subjects like the Fall or the story

---

79. "Le moyen le plus ordinaire pour cela était de l'isoler, comme un point unique dans la durée. On s'efforçait d'en faire ressortir les différences d'avec tout ce qui l'entourait; par là on croyait le grandir. En le séparant de ses origines naturelles, des traditions du christianisme et de la féodalité, on lui faisait une condition différente de celle de tous les autres siècles. . . . Ainsi cette époque était comme suspendue et égarée dans le temps; ou ce qui revient au même, si l'on cherchait quelque part ses origines, on les trouvait toutes dans le siècle d'Auguste. En vain dix-sept ans les séparaient, cet intervalle semblait un espace vide à travers lequel ces deux époques jetées sur le même plan et, pour ainsi dire, dans le même moule, pouvaient sans obstacle se rapprocher et s'étreindre. Le génie chrétien, qui était au fond du dix-septième siècle, fut négligé par la critique, qui étala au contraire, à plaisir, les ressemblances de la poétique de ce temps avec la poétique païenne. On se figurait dans Rome une antiquité moderne, dans Versailles une France antique; et sur ce terrain imaginaire, abrégeant des deux côtes la distance qui séparait Auguste de Louis XIV, on confondait ces deux civilisations dans une alliance doublement impossible." Edgar Quinet, "De l'unité des littératures modernes," *Revue des Deux Mondes*, 4th ser., 15 (1838): 318–35 (here, p. 319).

of Cain and Abel were, therefore, beside the point. "One last word," he wrote in the letter. "I did not put either Adam or Cain back on the scene precisely because that poetry has been done and does not have to be redone and because humanity at its beginning appears to us today in the general form of races, empires, and various forms of worship, not yet in the individual state. My task was to begin with humanity and end with the individual."[80] To some of his later and more orthodox Christian critics, however, here including Tocqueville, modern individuality could be as uniform as ancient republicanism. Real diversity, almost by definition, had to be local and social, not individual or global, because generalized individuality could be readily redescribed as social conformity.[81]

Quinet did not explain in his poem how this individuality would be achieved, but, as he went on to argue in the article on the unity of modern literature in which he attacked the parallel between imperial Rome and the France of Louis XIV, the mechanism responsible for the process would be industry. It offered a way out of the "doubly impossible alliance" between different ages and civilizations because modern industry had the power to turn humanity into a single entity in which, as Quinet put it, the old set of moral and political concerns with superiority and inferiority would become irrelevant. "It seems today," Quinet wrote at the end of the article (which he recycled a year later as the introduction to a collection of his essays on Germany and Italy), "that matter, more intelligent than spirit, is germinating with the birth of a new world." The situation that it had brought about was, he continued, more similar than it seemed to the situation that had existed at the time of the invention of printing and the first use of gunpowder and the compass.

In France, people are usually persuaded that idealist philosophers ought to be the opponents of this type of revolution because it is usually supposed

---

80. "Encore un dernier mot. Je n'ai point remis en scène Adam ni Caïn, précisément parce que cette poésie a été faite et n'est pas à refaire, et parce que l'humanité nous apparaît aujourd'hui à son commencement sous la forme générale des races, des empires et des cultes, et non pas encore à l'état individuel. Je devais au contraire commencer par l'humanité et finir par l'individu." Edgar Quinet, "Lettre sur *Ahasvérus*," *Revue du progrès social* 1 (1834): 616–19. See also the helpful introduction by Ceri Crossley to the reprint of the 1834 edition of Edgar Quinet, *Ahasvérus* (Geneva, Slatkine, 1982), pp. i–xvi, as well as his earlier "Edgar Quinet: conscience de soi et mal du siècle," *Romantisme* 27 (1980): 47–58. See too Simone Bernard-Griffiths, "Lectures d'*Ahasvérus* d'Edgar Quinet: regards sur une palingénésie romantique du mythe du Juif errant," *Romantisme* 45 (1984): 79–104.

81. For an example of this type of criticism, see the chapter on Edgar Quinet in Alfred Michiels, *Histoire des idées littéraires en France au dix-neuvième siècle et de leurs origines dans les siècles antérieurs*, 2 vols. (Paris, 1842), 1:283–300.

that these extreme developments of the industrial world will destroy their
chimerical dreams. In fact, this is a thought that should be fought wherever
it appears. Those whom you call poets, presumably in order to avoid dealing
with them as rational people, would willingly accelerate these revolutions
in industry because they will hasten that explosion of unity in the civil
world which they have been pursuing by other means and which has indeed
been the subject of the whole of this preceding article.[82]

The real basis of palingenesis was, in short, industry. What Quinet called "revolutions in industry"—or what, at about the same time, was called the Industrial
Revolution—heralded a new age of human history.[83] He repeated this characterization of what an industrial revolution promised to do in his inaugural
lecture of 1839 as professor of foreign literature at the University of Lyon after
commending the establishment of the various chairs to which his own
belonged. They were, he said, "eminently liberal institutions, whose moral
objective is to enable nations to reveal to one another what they share most
intimately by tearing down the barriers raised by prejudice, provincialism, and
localism, thus constituting, in the true sense of the word, the fraternity of
modern peoples." Lyon, he added, was a particularly appropriate setting for
the literature chair that he now held because it housed both "the industrial arts

82. "Il semble qu'aujourd'hui la matière, plus intelligente que l'esprit, fermente pour enfanter
un nouveau monde. . . . Cette situation a plus d'analogie qu'il ne parait avec celle du monde au
moment de l'invention de l'imprimerie, et des premiers usages de la poudre à canon et de la
boussole. . . . On se persuade, en France, que les philosophes idéalistes doivent être les adversaires de ces sortes de révolutions, parce qu'on suppose leurs chimères détruites par les développements extrêmes du monde industriel. Or, c'est un pensée qu'il faut combattre partout où
elle se montre, car ceux que vous appelez poètes, apparemment pour vous dispenser de les
traiter en hommes raisonnables, hâteraient volontiers ces révolutions de l'industrie par
lesquelles doit justement éclater cette unité du monde civil qu'ils poursuivent sur d'autres voies,
et qui est le sujet de tout ce qui précède." Ibid., p. 334. See too Edgar Quinet, *Allemagne et Italie.
Philosophie et poésie* [1839], (Paris, 1846), pp. i–xlvi.

83. On the concept of an industrial revolution, see Gareth Stedman Jones, "Engels and the
Invention of the Catastrophist Conception of the Industrial Revolution," in *The New Hegelians:
Politics and Philosophy in the Hegelian School*, ed. Douglas Moggach (Cambridge, CUP, 2006),
pp. 200–219. "Cependant," wrote the French political economist Adolphe Blanqui in 1837,
"à peine éclose du cerveau de ces deux hommes de génie, Watt et Arkwright, la révolution industrielle se mit en possession de l'Angleterre." Adolphe Blanqui, *Histoire de l'économie politique
en Europe depuis les anciens jusqu'à nos jours*, 2 vols. (Paris, 1837), 2:209. For the classic study, see
Paul Mantoux, *La révolution industrielle au xviiie siècle* [1928], 2nd ed. (Paris, 1959). As will be
shown in chapter 8 below, the French phrase *révolution industrielle* actually had an earlier, Saint-
Simonian, provenance.

and the liberal arts" and could, therefore, rely on the former to stimulate the development of the latter. "It was and is animated by a double genius, that of industry and spirituality, geniuses personified eminently by the figures of Ballanche [the originator of the concept of social palingenesis] and Jacquard [the inventor of the eponymous loom]."[84] Irrespective of the rhetorical niceties and the gestures towards Lyon and its achievements that the occasion may have required, the combination of the essay and the lecture amounted to Quinet's own version of the idea of palingenesis.

Unusually, Quinet remained committed to this evaluation of industry all his life. The deliberate ambiguity of the title of his last major work, *La Création*, published in 1870 and meaning either creation or *the* Creation, was designed to emphasize the parallel, but also the discrepancy, between the productivity of nature and the productivity of industry. The parallel was underpinned by an argument that, equally unusually, relied for its content on a combination of Thomas Robert Malthus and Charles Darwin. As Malthus had shown, Quinet explained, the supply of the means of subsistence increased arithmetically, while population increased geometrically, and this imbalance, Quinet continued, was the basis of Darwin's principle of natural selection. But Darwin's principle, Quinet argued, helped to highlight the real difference between human beings and other species. Other species might evolve or mutate, but the division of labour meant that almost every aspect of human life was in a continuous state of mutation and evolution. The human capacity to manage the passage of time was, ultimately, the reason why Darwin's principle of natural selection could not apply to humans. Humanity could, simply, remake nature. It was a capacity that meant that the limitless process of innovation that accompanied the division of labour had the power to generate a potentially *endless* supply of new products, occupations, activities, machines, and procedures. As Darwin had shown, nature certainly evolved. But, as Malthus had earlier established, nature could not escape from the constraints of its own

84. "Institution éminemment libérale, dont le but morale est de révéler les nations les unes aux autres dans ce qu'elles ont de plus intime; de renverser les dernières barrières qu'ont élevées entre elles les préjugés, l'esprit de district, l'infatuation de la localité, et de constituer, dans la vraie acceptation du mot, la fraternité des peuples modernes.

"Une telle chaire à Lyon a-t-elle sa place? Oui. Lyon est et fut toujours animé d'un double génie, celui de l'industrie et celui de la spiritualité; génies hautement personnifiés tous deux, l'un dans Jacquard, l'autre dans Ballanche. Lyon assimile dans sa vie propre deux éléments, les uns dans leurs principes, les autres dans leurs buts ultérieurs: les arts industriels et les arts libéraux." The passage is taken from a summary of the lecture initially published in the *Revue du Lyonnais* 9 (1839): 445–71 and republished as an appendix to a lecture by Joseph Texte entitled *La jeunesse d'Edgar Quinet et son enseignement à Lyon* (Lyon, 1897), p. 19.

resources. Humanity, however, could. The protean character of the division of labour meant, as Quinet put it, that there was always the possibility of an extra place at the great banquet of life.[85] Humanity's most pressing problem was, therefore, not the problem of productivity, but the problem of equity and, more fundamentally, the problem of broadening and deepening the relationship linking human freedom, human creativity, and human individuality. As he had warned in 1857 in his *Révolution religieuse au xixe siècle* (The religious revolution of the nineteenth century), without this moral and political dimension, technical progress would simply replace enslavement to nature by enslavement to industry. On the evidence of *La Création*, Quinet retained his loyalty to the concept of palingenesis throughout his life.[86]

Quinet's evaluation of industry was unusual for someone with his moral and political allegiances (it was probably matched only by Marx). Even at the time that he gave his inaugural lecture in 1839, the concept of industry was associated more usually with two, essentially contested, concepts. One was the concept of the division of labour, while the other was that of civil society. The division of labour could be associated with industrial organization, occupational specialization, technical standardization, labour discipline, and routinized work or, in a broader sense, with capitalism, private property, competitive markets, the separation of urban from rural society, and the growth of the vast, complicated mechanisms of economic, social, and financial interdependence captured by the concept of globalization. It could also be associated with human diversity, social cooperation, flexible specialization, regional interdependence, local particularity, flourishing ability, personal talent, individual distinction, and growing self-realization.[87] But it was not clear how it could be associated with both, at least in the same world at the same time.

The same problem applied to the concept of civil society. In one sense, the concept of civil society was very old. It came from the Latin word *civitas*, meaning what in English would now be called a political society, or a state. In this usage, the opposite of a civil society was a religious society, and this, until the early nineteenth century, was how the two terms were standardly used. In

85. Edgar Quinet, *La création*, 2 vols. (Paris, 1870), vol. 2, bk. 10, ch. 6, pp. 253–61 and ch. 7, pp. 262–68.

86. On Quinet, humans, and nature, see Ceri Crossley, "Edgar Quinet et le monde animal: *La Création* et l'Esprit Nouveau," in *Histoire(s) et enchantements: Hommages offerts à Simone Bernard-Griffiths*, ed. Pascale Auraix-Jonchière et al. (Clermont-Ferrand, CELIS, 2009), pp. 403–13, and, for the warning about technology, see Serge Audier, *L'âge productiviste* (Paris, La Découverte, 2019), pp. 93–94.

87. For a wide-ranging recent essay, see Russell Jacoby, *On Diversity: The Eclipse of the Individual in a Global Era* (New York, Seven Stories Press, 2020), especially pp. 93–126.

the early nineteenth century, the term was given a different meaning, most famously by the German philosopher Georg Wilhelm Friedrich Hegel.[88] In this usage the concept of civil society was associated with clusters of intermediate institutions and associations and the many different types of collectivity and activity involved in nongovernmental organizations like businesses, trade unions, cooperative societies, limited companies, employers' associations, charities, trusts, interest groups, and particular societies of every kind, from choral, horticultural, literary, and philosophical societies to private libraries, football clubs, stamp collecting, pigeon fancying, and spiritualism. In this sense, civil society could be seen as both a bridge and a buffer, simultaneously reinforcing the relationship, but also forming a shield, between individuals and the state. Alternatively, however, civil society could also be seen as a barrier or an obstacle, separating communities, dividing regions, magnifying differences, promoting particularity, generating apathy, and producing a dangerously parochial and self-centred indifference to public life. In this evaluation, the growth of civil society threatened to transfer real power to an increasingly remote and unaccountable bureaucracy, leaving the state either in total command or at the mercy of an increasingly fractious and atomized civil society. Here too, it was not clear how both versions of civil society could exist, at least in the same world at the same time.

The two subjects were discussed long into the nineteenth century. This was because both were developments of the original argument that, in the late eighteenth century, set Kant against Herder, and the concept of unsocial sociability against the concept of palingenesis. In this context, the concepts matter more than the names. Unsocial sociability meant the premature formation of human societies and, being limited in scale and scope, their development on multiple moral, institutional, or economic foundations. Palingenesis meant the continuity of cultures and the durability of values notwithstanding the end of empires and the death of states. The difference between the two concepts was not enough, however, to ensure that one could entirely displace the other, because some of the attributes of the one seemed to be necessary to the other. The concept of unsocial sociability seemed to leave no room for the shared feelings and common objects of allegiance that gave the idea of social palingenesis its intuitive ability to explain the continuity of societies across space and time. Palingenesis appeared to lack the legal and institutional framework required to translate cultural particularity and local values into durable agencies of authority and power. The interdependence of the two concepts meant that they seemed to need each other as much as they threatened to

88. See below, chapter 7.

extinguish each other. The oscillations of the evaluations magnified the elasticity of the temporal horizons. Unsocial sociability could turn into eternal recurrence, just as palingenesis could turn into an endless quest, according to whether the future appeared to approach or recede. At different times and in different languages the tensions were registered by the coexistence of terms like "individuality" and "individualism," "nationality" and "nationalism," *Gemeinschaft* and *Gesellschaft*, or, in closer proximity to real life, the competing claims of states and markets, government and administration, charisma and bureaucracy, and the many different arrangements and activities that each implied.[89] Unsocial sociability, as Herder complained, substituted many goals for one goal but failed to explain how it was possible to get to any single goal. Palingenesis, as Kant complained, substituted linearity for causality but failed to explain how it was possible for social convergence and individual divergence to both be available at the journey's end. The uncertainties were deepseated and intractable and, as the next chapter will show, were central to the moral and political thought of the Coppet group.

89. On the oppositions, see, helpfully, Niall Bond, "'Gemeinschaft und Gesellschaft': The Reception of a Conceptual Dichotomy," *Contributions to the History of Concepts* 5 (2009): 162–86.

3

The Coppet Group and the Liberty of the Moderns

The Ancients, the Moderns, and the Concept of Perfectibility

"The civilization of the ancients had not, like ours, a double origin. All was there single and simple," wrote the Swiss-French historian and political economist Jean-Charles-Léonard Simonde de Sismondi in 1813 in his *De la littérature du Midi de l'Europe*, or *Historical View of the Literature of the South of Europe* as the contemporary English translation was entitled.[1] Ancient civilization and culture (both Sismondi and his translator used the two words interchangeably)

---

1. "La culture des anciens n'avait point, comme la nôtre, une double origine; tout y était plus un et plus simple." Jean-Charles-Léonard Simonde de Sismondi, *De la littérature du Midi de l'Europe*, 4 vols. (Paris, 1813), 2:156. For the English translation, see Sismondi, *Historical View of the Literature of the South of Europe*, 4 vols. (London, 1823), 2:158. On Sismondi's text, see the helpful collection of contemporary responses reprinted in Edmond Eggli, *Le débat romantique en France 1813–1816* (Paris, Les belles lettres, 1933), pp. 46–79, and Maria-Pia Casalena, "L'histoire à l'ombre de Coppet et de la Toscane: la découverte de l'individu et la marche des nations d'après Sismondi," *Cahiers Staëliens* 63 (2013): 157–79. For a further reply to Sismondi, see Jacques-Daniel Martine, *Examen des tragiques anciens et modernes, dans lequel le système classique et le système romantique sont jugés et comparés*, 3 vols. (Paris, 1834), 1:1–43. Generally and classically, but without Sismondi, see Claude Nicolet, *La fabrique d'une nation. La France entre Rome et les Germains* (Paris, Perrin, 2003) and, earlier, Jacques Barzun, *Romanticism and the Modern Ego* (Boston, Little, Brown & Co. 1944). On the broad subject of early nineteenth-century French historical writing, see Lionel Gossman, *Between History and Literature* (Cambridge, MA, Harvard UP, 1990), particularly pp. 83–151, together with the fascinating collection of texts edited by Marcel Gauchet, *Philosophie des sciences historiques. Le moment romantique* (Paris, Seuil, 2002), and the helpful guidance to secondary literature that it contains. More recently, see Matthew D'Auria, *The Shaping of French National Identity: Narrating the Nation's Past, 1715–1830* (Cambridge, CUP, 2020). For an initial way in to the protracted later argument between

began with the Greeks. Modern civilization and culture, on the other hand, began with the combined legacies of both the Romans and the Germans. This double origin, Sismondi went on to explain, was the reason why the name "romantic" had been given to the civilization of the moderns. "The name romantic," he wrote, "was taken from the Romance language, which owed its birth to the mixture of Latin with the ancient German. In a similar way, romantic manners (*mœurs romantiques*) were formed from the habits of the people of the north and the remnants of Roman civilization." Modern Germany, Sismondi continued, was also the source of the philosophical and historical theories underlying these distinctions. "The Germans," he wrote, "explain the difference between the ancients or classics, and the moderns or romantics, by the difference of religion. They assert that the first, with a material religion, address all their poetry to the senses; while the second, whose religion is wholly spiritual, place all their poetry in the emotions of the soul."[2]

The double origin of modern civilization was one answer to Kant. It supplied a blend of two different horizons of expectation, one inherited from the past and the other projected into the future. The resulting combination of continuity and change meant that while beliefs and values would vary, there was still something more fundamental accompanying the course of human history. Choices and values could be distinguished from their causes and content. Together, the two sides of the combination helped to rescue Kant's concept of enlightenment from some of the bleaker implications of Kant's own publications. It consigned some aspects of the past to arrangements and institutions whose time had passed. But it also claimed that other aspects of that past could be projected into the future and onto arrangements and institutions of later times. If history was incremental and cumulative, then adding the spiritual to the sensual, or the legacy of the Germans to the legacy of the Romans, helped to give humanity a range of cultural and material resources that had been absent at the start and, despite the decline and fall of the Roman Empire, meant that civilization had a second chance. The claim was redolent of the type of argument about the relationship

---

Romanists and Germanists, see David M. Rabban, *Law's History: American Legal Thought and the Transatlantic Turn to History* (Cambridge, CUP, 2013), pp. 63–149.

2. "Le nom de romantique a été emprunté de celui de la langue romane, qui était née du mélange du latin avec l'ancien allemand. De même les mœurs romantiques étaient composées des habitudes des peuples du Nord, et des restes de la civilisation romaine. . . . Les allemands expliquent la différence entre les anciens ou classiques, et les modernes ou romantiques, par la différence de religion. Ils disent que les premiers, avec une religion matérielle, mettaient toute leur poésie dans les sens; que les seconds, dont la religion est toute spirituelle, placent toute la poésie dans les émotions de l'âme." Sismondi, *De la littérature du Midi*, 2:156–57. I have slightly modified the translation in Sismondi, *Historical View*, 2:158.

between Christianity and the condition of the moderns made most powerfully in the early nineteenth century by the vicomte de Chateaubriand in his *Génie du Christianisme*, or *The Genius of Christianity* as the contemporary English translation was entitled, and, more subtly, by Germaine de Staël in her book on Germany, *De l'Allemagne*, which, after Napoleonic interruptions, was published in London in 1814. This aspect of early nineteenth-century intellectual life is relatively well known. What, however, is less well known is the concurrent hostility both to imperial Rome and Roman law and to the jarringly individuated set of Roman economic and social arrangements that accompanied them. If, as was claimed, Kant's moral philosophy was simply Roman law in a different guise, romanticism, in this context, was designed to rescue the concept of enlightenment from Kant's partiality towards Rome. Although Sismondi, who had a Protestant background, did not entirely accept the argument about the relationship between Christianity and the difference between the ancients and the moderns (the statues, rituals, and imagery of medieval Catholicism, he argued, had too much in common with ancient paganism to make the difference in religion a plausible explanation of the difference between the ancients and moderns), he was still willing to endorse the broader distinction between ancient unity and modern duality as the basis of a more detailed body of distinctions between the South and the North, the sensual and the spiritual, the classics and the romantics, the ancients and the moderns, and, finally, the respective legacies of the Romans and the Germans. Even if the difference in religion was not the real explanation, it was, he concluded, still the case "that the poets of the two epochs had different objects in view. Those of antiquity aimed at exciting admiration by beauty and by symmetry. Those of modern times wish to produce emotion by the feelings of the heart or by the unexpected issue of events."[3]

The part that these distinctions have played in the history of European and American political thought was considerably more substantial than we usually think. This, however, is not because there was once a body of thought that has since been forgotten and, once recovered, might now become the basis of a new and fresh way of thinking about states, governments, laws, and politics. It is, instead, because the range of subjects that, over the years, came to be entangled with the distinctions that Sismondi described has grown so large and diverse that what is now available to be recovered would amount not so much to an integrated body of thought as to a heterogeneous and proliferating body of conflict, argument, and polemic. This body of conflict, argument, and polemic was also considerably more substantial than we usually think. It is, in a sense,

---

3. Sismondi, *Historical View*, 2:159.

all around us. Thinking about politics today consists largely of fragments of forgotten arguments, propositions separated from earlier polemics, and concepts floating far from the conflicts in which they first arose. The aim of this chapter is, accordingly, not to try to reinstate or revive these earlier arguments, polemics, or conflicts but to try instead, by uncovering layer after layer of what now remains, to show what the disappearance of large parts of those earlier contexts has come to mean not only for thinking about the history and historiography of political thought but also, if less directly, for thinking about politics now.

Sismondi's claim about the double origins of the modern civilization or culture was shared by many of the other members of the large intellectual circle to which he belonged. This was the group of people that has come to be known as the Coppet group, named after the imposing house on Lake Geneva that Germaine de Staël—who, along with Benjamin Constant, was probably the group's most famous member—inherited from her father, the former French director general of finance, Jacques Necker, at the beginning of the nineteenth century. Their many publications—and the many assessments or responses that they provoked—add up to quite a comprehensive overview of European intellectual life in the first two decades of the nineteenth century. Adding in the publications of some of the group's other members—Prosper de Barante in France; Carl Victor von Bonstetten in Switzerland; Sismondi in Italy and Switzerland as well as in France; his brother-in-law Sir James Mackintosh in Britain; or the Schlegel brothers and Wilhelm von Humboldt in the German-speaking parts of Europe—allows the scale and detail of the subject matter to grow considerably. Other figures who, at one time or another, played a significant part in Germaine de Staël's intellectual life—like her English guide to German idealist philosophy, Henry Crabb Robinson, or the French émigré inhabitant of Hamburg Charles Villers, or the Danish aesthetic theorist Frederikke Brun, or Staël's first critical reviewer and future historian of Provençal poetry, Claude Fauriel, the lover of the widowed Sophie de Grouchy now better known as Mme Condorcet, as well as his Italian friend Alessandro Manzoni—are further testimony to the range of intellectual and cultural resources at the group's disposal. In one way or another, the Coppet group touched upon almost every aspect of European intellectual life in the first three decades of the nineteenth century. Although it was once usual to describe Marxism as a fusion of British political economy, German idealist philosophy, and French socialism, the first fusion could, with as much plausibility, be said to have taken place under the aegis of the Coppet group. Here, however, the key concept was not Marxism but romanticism. In other respects, however, the fusion was quite similar because, as was pointed out by a contributor to a debate organized by the

French provincial Academy of Rouen in 1824 on the respective merits of the
classics and the romantics, romanticism in France had taken its name from
England and its style from Germany.[4] This too is why the interests of the
Coppet group add up to a broad way in to the subject matter of this chapter.
It was something like a window on the changing architecture of early
nineteenth-century European intellectual life.

In one sense, the argument that gave rise to Sismondi's claim about the
double origins of modern civilization or modern culture is not hard to describe because many of its features are still well known. It was, as he wrote, an
argument between the respective supporters of the ancients or classics and the
moderns or romantics.[5] The two names that he gave to each side are also an
indication that this particular argument was also a kind of continuation of the
equally famous argument, usually known as the *querelle des anciens et des modernes*, that had begun in France in the second half of the seventeenth century
and had then been taken up and pursued, with different levels of intensity and
duration, in almost every European country and language throughout the

4. "La nouvelle école en France avait pris son nom de l'Angleterre et son style favori de
l'Allemagne." In [Anon.] *Du Classique et du Romantique. Recueil de discours pour et contre, lus à
l'Académie royale des sciences, belles lettres et des arts de Rouen, pendant l'année 1824* (Rouen, 1826),
p. 66. For a helpful overview, see Jean Quillien, ed., *La réception de la philosophie allemande en
France aux xixe et xxe siècles* (Lille, PU de Lille, 1994). Some of the most informative studies of
the interconnections of German, French, and British thought in the early nineteenth century
can be found in the work of two French scholars, Michel Espagne and Philippe Régnier: see,
for example, Philippe Régnier, "Les saint-simoniens et la philosophie allemande, ou la première
alliance intellectuelle franco-allemande," *Revue de Synthèse* 109 (1988): 231–45; "La question
romantique comme enjeu national: critique française et littérature allemande autour de 1830,"
Romantisme 73 (1991): 29–42; Michel Espagne and Michaël Werner, "La construction d'une
référence culturelle allemande en France: genèse et histoire (1750–1914)," *Annales. Histoire,
Sciences Sociales* 42 (1987): 969–92; Michel Espagne and Michaël Werner, eds., *Transferts. Relations interculturelles entre la France et l'Allemagne (18e et 19e siècles)* (Paris, 1988), pp. 447–64;
Michel Espagne and Michaël Werner, eds., *Contribution à l'histoire des disciplines littéraires en
France et en Allemagne au xixe siècle*, Philologiques, 1 (Paris, Editions de la Maisons des Sciences
de L'Homme, 1990); Michel Espagne, *En deçà du Rhin: l'Allemagne des philosophes français au
xixe siècle* (Paris, Cerf, 2004). For a suggestive case study, see Bonnie G. Smith, "The Rise and
Fall of Eugène Lerminier," *French Historical Studies* 12 (1982): 377–400.

5. See initially Hans Eichner, ed., *"Romantic" and Its Cognates: The European History of a
Word* (Manchester, Manchester UP, 1972); Eggli, *Le débat romantique en France 1813–1816*;
Frank Paul Bowman, "Religion, Politics and Utopia in French Romanticism," *Australian Jour-
nal of French Studies* 11 (1974): 307–24, together with his *French Romanticism: Intertextual and
Interdisciplinary Readings* (Baltimore, Johns Hopkins UP, 1990); and, helpfully, Prendergast,
The Classic.

eighteenth century.[6] But the addition of the two terms "classic" and "romantic" to the earlier distinction between the ancients and moderns also had the effect of changing the terms and orientation of the initial argument quite considerably, because they meant, in keeping with Sismondi's own usage, that the preferences and evaluations did not have to be binary. Something classic could be paired with something modern, just as something ancient could be equated with something romantic. This was the real point of the apparent tautologies in Sismondi's definition. They were designed, in a real sense, to highlight his insistence on the double origin of modern culture or civilization, and, by extension, to show that the combined legacies of the Romans and the Germans

6. The paradigmatic historical and analytical treatment of both the argument and its later reverberations can be found in a number of the publications of Hans Robert Jauss, starting with his essay "Ästhetische Normen und geschichtliche Reflexion in der 'Querelle des Anciens et des Modernes,'" introducing a reprint of Charles Perrault, *Parallèle des anciens et des modernes en ce qui regarde les arts et les sciences* [1688] (Munich, Eidos Verlag, 1964), pp. 8–64, and continuing with the essays published in Hans Robert Jauss, *Pour une esthétique de la réception* (Paris, 1978). See too his articles "Fr. Schlegels und Fr Schillers Replik auf die 'Querelle des Anciens et des Modernes,'" in *Europäische Aufklärung: Herbert Dieckmann zum 60 Geburtstag*, ed. Hugo Friedrich and Fritz Schalk (Munich, Wilhelm Fink Verlag, 1967), pp. 117–40; "The Idealist Embarrassment: Observations on Marxist Aesthetics," *New Literary History* 7 (1975): 191–208; "Tradition, Innovation and Aesthetic Experience," *Journal of Aesthetics and Art Criticism* 46 (1988): 375–88; "The Literary Process of Modernism from Rousseau to Adorno," *Cultural Critique* 11 (1988–89): 27–61; "The Theory of Reception: A Retrospective of Its Unrecognized Prehistory," in *Literary Theory Today*, ed. Peter Collier and Helger Geyer-Ryan (Ithaca, NY, Cornell UP, 1990), pp. 53–73. See also Walter Jaeschke, "Early German Idealist Reinterpretations of the Quarrel of the Ancients and Moderns," *Clio* 12 (1982–83): 313–33. More recently, see, helpfully, Norman, *The Shock of the Ancient*, the review of it by Harder, "Les anciens contre-attaquent, ou la querelle revisitée," and Norman's later chapter in *A History of Modern French Literature*, ed. Christopher Prendergast (Princeton, NJ, Princeton UP, 2017), pp. 269–90. On modernity, see Hans Ulrich Gumbrecht, "A History of the Concept 'Modern,'" in his *Making Sense of Life and Literature* (Minneapolis, U of Minnesota Press, 1992), pp. 79–110; François Hartog, *Anciens, modernes, sauvages* (Paris, Galaade Editions, 2005); Reginald Lilly, ed., *The Ancients and the Moderns* (Bloomington, Indiana UP, 1996); Ernst Behler, *Irony and the Discourse of Modernity* (Seattle, U of Washington Press, 1990); Alain Viala, *La France galante* (Paris, PUF, 2008); Anne-Marie Lecoq, ed., *La querelle des anciens et des modernes* (Paris, Gallimard, 2001); Luciano Guerci, *Libertà degli antichi e libertà dei moderni: Sparta, Atene e i «philosophes» nella Francia dei Settecento* (Naples, Guido, 1979); Luciano Canfora, "Dans la France des lumières: liberté des anciens, liberté des modernes," *Annales ESC* 38 (1983): 1075–83; Paddy Bullard and Alexis Tadié, eds., *Ancients and Moderns in Europe: Comparative Perspectives* (Oxford, Voltaire Foundation, 2016), and, for more recent variations on the theme of the modern, see Levent Yilmaz, *Le temps moderne. Variations sur les anciens et les contemporains* (Paris, Gallimard, 2004), and Josef Früchtl, *The Impertinent Self: A Heroic History of Modernity* (Stanford, Stanford UP, 2009).

amounted to a synthesis that was something like a chemical compound, meaning that the final product was qualitatively different from each of its constituent parts. The idea was taken a step further in a history of literary ideas in France in the nineteenth century published in 1842 by a Franco-Belgian critic and art historian named Alfred Michiels. To Michiels, who made a point of highlighting his respect for Sismondi, it was not only civilization that had a double origin, but each side of the classic-romantic pairing. The classical arts, he wrote, had come back from the tomb "as is shown clearly enough by the word *renaissance*." But the classical arts had then reinflicted their own earlier fate on "the Christian arts." In the end, however, the nexus of imagery and emotion that made the Christian arts "the representative of modern society triumphed comprehensively" because they too had come back—and on "a more general, eternal, and absolute" scale—as romanticism.[7]

The nature of the synthesis itself, however, is less easy to describe, particularly without the more Christian framework of Michiels's book. For Sismondi, at least in the context of his study of the literature of southern Europe, the synthesis was a product of a change in the nature and orientation of aesthetic and moral judgments. This type of judgment, he explained, had come to be guided more by evaluations of inner feelings and unforeseen events than by external patterns and forms of beauty in generating the motivation required for identifying and responding to what mattered. Here too the process of migration from North to South and the problems built into transposing some aspects of an original culture to a different setting supplied an explanation. Buildings, unlike languages and the more portable or imitative arts, were not movable from one setting to another, but the values that they had embodied or represented could still remain alive in a different setting. This, Sismondi explained, was why architecture was the first and most creative of all the arts. Its practitioners had to find ways to use different materials in unfamiliar settings to create buildings and environments that were still commensurate with recognized values. This was what had happened in Italy during the Middle Ages. It had been the architecture of the Italian city-states, and of Florence in particular, that had come to embody the synthesis of German and Roman culture now known as civic humanism.[8]

---

7. Alfred Michiels, *Histoire des idées littéraires en France au dix-neuvième siècle et de leurs origines dans les siècles antérieurs* [1842], 3rd ed. (Brussels, 1848), pp. 1–2. A comparable account can be found in Georg Gottfried Gervinus, *Introduction to the History of the Nineteenth Century* (London, 1853).

8. For a fuller presentation of Sismondi's argument see Michael Sonenscher, "Liberty, Autonomy, and Republican Historiography: Civic Humanism in Context," in *Markets, Moral, Politics: Jealousy of Trade and the History of Political Thought. Essays in Honor of Istvan Hont*, ed. Béla

To his friend and contemporary Benjamin Constant, however, much the same type of synthesis—which Constant publicly associated with Sismondi's vast and very recently completed *History of the Italian Republics in the Middle Ages*—had a more explicitly institutional and political character. Constant made this clear in the famous lecture entitled "The Liberty of the Ancients Compared with That of the Moderns" that he gave at the Parisian Athénée Royale in 1819, the same year as the publication of the final volume of Sismondi's history. There was, however, a substantial overlap between the two comparisons. "The liberty of the ancients, like their philosophy," Sismondi wrote at the end of the final volume of his *History*, "had virtue as its goal. The liberty of the moderns, like their philosophy, proposes no more than well-being (*bonheur*)." As the pronouncement implied, the obvious inference was to combine the two. This, Sismondi continued, was why "the legislator should no longer lose sight of the security of the citizen and those guarantees that the moderns have made into a system. But he should also remember that it is important to find ways to promote citizens' greater moral development." Peace and security could be reinforced by completing "the moral education of citizens" so that, "by multiplying their rights, by inviting them to share in sovereignty and to redouble their interest in public affairs, they would come to know their duties and acquire a desire and an ability to fulfil them."[9]

Kapossy, Isaac Nakhimovsky, Sophus Reinert, and Richard Whatmore (Cambridge, MA, Harvard UP, 2018), pp. 161–210. See too Ceri Crossley, "Some Attitudes towards Architecture during the July Monarchy," *French Forum* 8 (1983): 134–46.

9. "La liberté des anciens, comme leur philosophie, avait pour but la vertu; la liberté des modernes, comme leur philosophie, ne se propose que le bonheur. La meilleure leçon à tirer de la comparaison de ces systèmes seraient d'apprendre à les combiner l'un avec l'autre.

"Loin de devoir s'exclure mutuellement, ils sont faits pour se prêter un appui réciproque. L'une des espèces de liberté parait toujours être la route la plus courte et la plus sûre pour arriver à l'autre. Le législateur, désormais, ne doit plus perdre de vue la sécurité des citoyens, et les garanties que les modernes ont réduites en système; mais il doit se souvenir aussi qu'il faut chercher encore leur plus grand développement moral . . . et c'est en multipliant leurs droits, en les appelant au partage de la souveraineté, en redoublant leur intérêt pour la chose publique, qu'il leur apprendra aussi à connaitre leur devoirs, et qu'il leur donnera en même temps et le désir et la faculté de les remplir." Jean-Charles-Léonard Simonde de Sismondi, *Histoire des républiques italiennes du moyen âge*, 17 vols. (Paris, 1809–19), 16:405–6. On Sismondi's *Histoire*, see the introduction by Pierangelo Schiera to the Italian translation of Sismondi's *History of the Italian Republics, or The Origin, Progress, and Fall of Italian Freedom* (London, 1832), published as Jean-Charles-Léonard Simonde de Sismondi, *Storia delle Repubbliche italiane* (Turin, Bollati Boringhieri, 1996), pp. ix–xcvi.

The argument of Constant's more famous lecture was identical. "The aim of the ancients," he said midway through the lecture, "was the sharing of social power among the citizens of the same fatherland: this is what they called liberty. The aim of the moderns is the enjoyment of security in private pleasures; and they call liberty the guarantees to these pleasures accorded by institutions."[10] Ancient liberty subordinated the private to the public and set the concerns of the citizen above those of the individual. Modern liberty did the opposite, subordinating the public to the private and promoting the concerns of the individual above those of the citizen. As with Sismondi, the point of the lecture was to call for a new synthesis of the two types of liberty so that private liberty would be complemented by public liberty, while the freedom of the individual would be matched by the freedom of the citizen. Although the point has sometimes been missed, liberty on Constant's terms was, therefore, a synthesis of both the ancient and the modern. "It is not to happiness alone," he ended his lecture, "it is to self-development that our destiny calls us; and political liberty is the most powerful, the most effective means of self-development that heaven has given us."[11]

The French word that Constant actually used for what, in translation, has become "self-development" was *perfectionnement*.[12] It was a word that, at least in part, was redolent of the thought of Jean-Jacques Rousseau because it was Rousseau who first coined the neologism *perfectibilité* to describe the mixture of ingenuity and creativity (and, indeed, self-development) that, he claimed, distinguished humans from animals. The word, particularly in conjunction with the idea of human destiny to which Constant referred, was also loosely redolent of a protracted, largely German-language discussion of what was

10. Benjamin Constant, "The Liberty of the Ancients Compared with That of the Moderns" [1819], in Benjamin Constant, *Political Writings*, ed. Biancamaria Fontana (Cambridge, CUP, 1988), p. 317. On the lecture, but without Constant's Kantian emphasis on positive freedom, see the recent festschrift in honour of Biancamaria Fontana, *La liberté des Anciens et des Modernes, deux cents ans après Benjamin Constant*, ed. Antoine Chollet, *Annales Benjamin Constant* 45 (2020).

11. Constant, "Liberty," p. 327. The synthesis is described very clearly in Lucien Jaume, "Aux origines du libéralisme politique en France," *Esprit* 243 (1998): 37–60, and, later, in his "Germaine de Staël, une source jamais tariée pour notre temps," *Cahiers Staëliens* 67 (2017): 81–100. See too David Runciman, *Confronting Leviathan* (London, Profile Books, 2021), pp. 53–74. For amplification, see Maria Dimova-Cookson, ed., "Benjamin Constant: 200 Years of Ancient and Modern Liberty," *History of European Ideas* 48 (2022): 193–307, particularly the chapters by Alan Cromartie, Maria Dimova-Cookson, and Avital Simhony.

12. See the original version in Benjamin Constant, *Ecrits politiques*, ed. Marcel Gauchet (Paris, Gallimard, 1997), p. 617.

called the *Bestimmung des Menschheit*, meaning the vocation, destiny, purpose, objective, or goal of mankind.[13] Although Constant made a number of critical comments about Rousseau, he also made it clear, particularly in his lecture on ancient and modern liberty, that Rousseau's reputation as the inspiration of the Jacobin government of the Year II of the First French Republic had more to do with deliberate or inadvertent misinterpretation than with anything written by Rousseau himself (the real intellectual inspiration of the politics of the Terror, he asserted, had been the eighteenth-century French moralist Gabriel Bonnot de Mably).

Constant's knowledge of both the German language and German intellectual life was extensive, both by way of his marriage to Charlotte von Hardenberg in 1808 and, more fully, by way of his long relationship with Germaine de Staël. He knew therefore that there was a real connection between Rousseau's thought and the many German-language discussions of the vocation of mankind. The connection was supplied most fully and directly by the new version of the concept of autonomy that had been developed by Immanuel Kant and his many followers in the two final decades of the eighteenth century.[14] In earlier usage, autonomy was a largely legal concept that referred mainly to the right of something like a town, guild, corporation, province, or university to govern its own affairs. With Kant, echoing both Rousseau and the discussion of the vocation of mankind, autonomy turned into a largely moral concept that now referred to the individual (but possibly also collective) ability to be both the subject and object of a freely chosen objective or goal. In this version of the idea of self-determination, the emphasis fell as much on the concept of the self as on that of causation or determination. This was the concept that, for Constant, offered the basis of something more than the several existing versions of either ancient or modern liberty because it could be associated both with the goal of *perfectionnement*, or self-development, and

13. For helpful ways in, see Michael Printy, "The Determination of Man: Johann Joachim Spalding and the Protestant Enlightenment," *Journal of the History of Ideas* 74 (2013): 189–212, and Douglas Moggach, Nadine Mooren, and Michael Quante, eds., *Perfectionismus der Autonomie* (Paderborn, Wilhelm Fink/Brill, 2020). On the overlap between Rousseau's concept of perfectibility and German-language moral and political thought, see the very helpful collection of translated texts edited and introduced by Emmanuel Hourcade, Charlotte Morel, and Ayşe Yuva, *La perfectibilité de l'homme. Les lumières allemandes contre Rousseau?* 2 vols. (Paris, Classiques Garnier, 2022).

14. On autonomy, see initially Gerard Rosisch, *The Contested History of Autonomy* (London, Bloomsbury, 2019); Giovanni Cazzetta, ed., *Autonomia: Per un'Archeologia del Sapere Giuridico fra Otto e Novecento* (Milan, Giuffrè, 2014); and, for autonomy before Kant, Jerome B. Schneewind, *The Invention of Autonomy* (Cambridge, CUP, 1998).

with a concept of liberty that was compatible with the thought of Rousseau and with the content of the German-language discussion of the vocation of mankind.

The limitations of the concept of perfectibility were particularly visible in Kant's treatment of history. As Kant presented it, the benefits of progress seemed to be available only at history's end. Constant, in a late essay, unambiguously entitled *De la perfectibilité de l'espèce humaine* (On the perfectibility of the human race), disagreed. It was simply impossible, he pointed out, to describe the content of the future in any meaningful detail. Even the most farsighted of projections or speculations would still be limited by the knowledge, values, and beliefs associated with the conditions in which they were made. In this sense, every future goal was as time-bound and as exposed to the problem of arbitrariness as every claim about the past. Just as it was not possible to adjudicate among the rival claims of the Romans, the Germans, the Hebrews, and the Greeks as sources of political legitimacy, it was also not possible to identify a genuinely transhistorical goal of human history. The future, in short, was as relative as the past. All that could be said, Constant argued, was that the future had the power to motivate human action as much as either the present or the past. Unlike either the present or the past, however, the future had no fixed content. The trajectory of the human race, Constant wrote, could be divided into three parts: the given part; the debatable part, and the unknown part.[15] It was this, Constant emphasized, that was the real key to understanding human history. From this perspective, Kant's vision of the future was, simply, Kantian. Other possibilities and other alternatives were equally compatible with the concept of individual and general perfectibility. The indeterminate character of the goal meant that imagination, creativity, and rationality were the real foundations of perfectibility.

The Division of Labour and the Origin of Ideology

The many conceptual and practical implications of the concept of *perfectionnement,* and the question of how the idea of self-development could be connected to a form of freedom that was a synthesis of ancient and modern liberty, were central components of nineteenth-century moral, philosophical, and political thought. It is important at the outset, however, to indicate that all these subjects were also once connected to a further subject that is no longer associated very strongly either with the idea of self-development or the

---

15. Benjamin Constant, *De la perfectibilité de l'espèce humaine* [1829], ed. Pierre Deguise (Lausanne, Age d'Homme, 1967), p. 59.

relationship between ancient and modern liberty. This was the subject of the division of labour. Today, it is usual to associate both the subject and the concept of the division of labour with Adam Smith, productivity, and the history of economic thought. For both Sismondi and Constant, however, it was equally possible to associate the idea with the concept of *perfectionnement* because the idea of the division of labour could refer as much to the development of individual talents and abilities as to the increase of manufacturing capability and economic productivity. The word that originally captured the ambiguity was "individualism." It could be a synonym for egoism, but it could also refer to the distinctive attributes of every individual personality or the qualities that made all individuals uniquely themselves.[16]

In this version, individualism had a largely positive and a strongly spiritual set of connotations. Both could be counterposed to Kant's relentlessly inconclusive concept of history. The fullest description of what this implied and how it was connected to the idea of the division of labour was set out early in the nineteenth century by one of the more remote members of the intellectual circles in which both Sismondi and Constant moved, the Protestant theologian Friedrich Schleiermacher, in his *Monologen* (Soliloquies) of 1800.[17] Schleiermacher's assessment of the division of labour owed less to the subject of mechanization and far more to the older German Pietist discussion of the relationship between the vocation of mankind and the subject of human improvement. Here, the concept was incorporated into a broader discussion shaped by comparisons between divine capabilities and human limitations. For humans, so Schleiermacher's argument went, every choice carried an opportunity cost because the finite quality of human nature meant that doing one thing ruled out doing others. This was why the division of labour mattered. It could counter life's apparently relentless binary structure because it

16. For an illuminating examination of this latter concept of individualism, see Efraim Podoksik, "Georg Simmel: Three Forms of Individualism and Historical Understanding," *New German Critique* 10 (2010): 119–45. See too, classically, Koenraad W. Swart, "Individualism in the Mid-Nineteenth Century (1826–1860)," *Journal of the History of Ideas* 23 (1962): 77–90; Steven Lukes, "The Meanings of 'Individualism,'" *Journal of the History of Ideas* 32 (1971): 45–66; Gregory Claeys, "'Individualism', 'Socialism' and 'Social Science,'" *Journal of the History of Ideas* 47 (1986): 81–93, and, recently, Gregory Claeys, ed., *The Cambridge Companion to Nineteenth-Century Thought* (Cambridge, CUP, 2019), pp. 8–30, 72–94, 141–62. See too Marie-France Piguet, *Individualisme* (Paris, CNRS Editions, 2018).

17. See the editorial introduction to Friedrich Schleiermacher, *Der christliche Glaube* [1821–22], in Friedrich Schleiermacher, *Kritische Gesamtausgabe*, ed. Hans-Joachim Birkner, Gerhard Ebeling, Hermann Fischer, Heinz Kimmerle, and Kurt-Victor Selge, vol. 7 (Berlin and New York, Walter de Gruyter, 1980), pp. xli–xliii.

could be the basis of the idea that the development of each distinctively individual talent would enable humanity as a whole to have something like the capabilities of the divinity. Taken as far as they could go, the combined abilities and talents of every individual would amount to something like the divine capacity to escape the limitations of place and time. Moreover, since divinity lay beyond the limitations of time and place, only the existence of humanity made it possible for time and place to have a real existence, which, in turn, also made it possible for every individual to become aware of both these attributes of being. From either perspective, the development of the division of labour was the key to understanding not only the vocation of mankind—or the *Bestimmung des Menschen*—but also the concept of *perfectionnement* as, on Constant's terms, the basis of any future synthesis of ancient and modern liberty.

This insight into the real significance of human diversity, Schleiermacher wrote in his *Monologen*, had become his "highest intuition." Before it occurred, he went on to explain, he had subscribed simply to the conventional view that "humanity revealed itself as varied only in the manifold diversity of outward acts," and that individuals were not, as he put it, "uniquely fashioned" but were, instead, fundamentally "one substance and everywhere the same." The new insight entailed a radical change of perspective. Instead of each individual coming to represent the generic attributes of humanity, each individual would come uniquely to be—and represent—him- or herself. "I saw clearly," Schleiermacher wrote, "that each man is meant to represent humanity in his own way, combining its elements uniquely, so that it may reveal itself in every mode and that all that can issue from its womb can be made actual in the fullness of unending space and time."[18] In the light of this evaluation, promoting the development of the division of labour by way of further innovation and specialization became something like a duty (or possibly even a calling) because it now seemed to be the real vocation of mankind. To the nineteenth-century German Hegelians Karl Ludwig Michelet and Auguste Ott, Schleiermacher's vision was redolent of the vision of his friend, the idealist philosopher Johann Gottlieb Fichte. "He highlights the cult of particularity," Michelet explained, referring in the first instance to Fichte, but gesturing towards Schleiermacher as well. "Each individual is an expression of the absolute I, but as a special,

18. Friedrich Schleiermacher, *Soliloquies* [1800], ed. Horace Leland Friess (New York, Columbia UP, 1926), pp. 30–31. On this aspect of Schleiermacher's thought, see Frederick Beiser, "Schleiermacher's Ethics," in *The Cambridge Companion to Friedrich Schleiermacher*, ed. Jacqueline Mariña (Cambridge, CUP, 2005), pp. 53–71 (especially pp. 60–61), and, recently, Jackson Ravenscroft, *The Veiled God*, pp. 100–105.

determinate expression of it. Unity is the basis of the whole and each individual I has a duty to take care of and cultivate that particularity through which God is made manifest in each one. Each individual is obliged to maintain his or her own manner of being and individual character and particular feeling. Each individual thus represents an aspect of the whole of humanity and this is the precondition of liberty."[19] As the early twentieth-century German sociologist Georg Simmel put it more vividly, "the new individualism found its philosophical expression in Schleiermacher. For Schleiermacher, the moral task consists in each individual's *specific* representation of mankind. . . . The great world-historical idea that not only the equality of men but also that their differentiation represents a moral challenge, became the core of a new world view in Schleiermacher. The idea that the absolute only lives in the form of the individual, and that individuality is not a restriction of the infinite but its expression and mirror, makes the principle of the social division of labour part of the metaphysical ground of reality itself."[20]

Simmel's assessment of Schleiermacher could also have been applied to the early nineteenth-century German philosopher Ludwig Feuerbach, because Feuerbach's controversial *Essence of Christianity*, first published in 1841, contained the same substantive claim about the division of labour, without, however, relying on Schleiermacher's theology. As Feuerbach wrote, "the true sense of theology is anthropology and there is no distinction between the *predicates* of the divine and human nature, and, consequently, no distinction between the divine and human *subject*."[21] The predicates of the Christian God as omniscient, omnipotent, and omnipresent were equally applicable to humanity because, as Feuerbach went on to argue, the Christian version of history

---

19. "Schleiermacher fut encore, sous d'autres rapports, l'expression du système de Fichte. Il met en relief le culte de la particularité. Chacun est l'expression du moi absolu; chacun en est une expression spéciale, déterminée: l'unité est au fond de tous, et chaque moi a pour but de bien garder et de cultiver cette particularité par laquelle Dieu se manifeste en lui. Que chacun tienne donc à sa manière d'être, à son caractère personnel, à son sentiment particulier; chacun représentera ainsi un côté de toute l'humanité; la liberté n'est qu'à cette condition." Auguste Ott, *Hegel et la philosophie allemande* (Paris, 1844), p. 43, quoting, as indicated in a footnote, Karl Ludwig Michelet, *Histoire de la philosophie moderne*, vol. 2, ch. 1.

20. Georg Simmel, *Fundamental Problems of Sociology (Individual and Society)* [1917], in *The Sociology of Georg Simmel*, ed. Kurt H. Wolff (New York, Free Press, 1950), pp. 80–81. On this concept of individualism and its bearing on Simmel's thought, see Podoksik, "Georg Simmel," and, more recently, his *Georg Simmel and German Culture: Unity, Variety and Modern Discontents* (Cambridge, CUP, 2021), pp. 37–38, 103–21.

21. Ludwig Feuerbach, *The Essence of Christianity* [1841], trans. Marian Evans (New York, 1855), p. 7.

could be shown to contain all the component parts of the real historical anthropology. "Christianity," Feuerbach wrote, "has in fact long since vanished
not only from the reason, but from the life of mankind." It was "nothing more
than a *fixed idea*, in flagrant contradiction with our fire and life assurance companies, our railroads and steam carriages, our picture and sculpture galleries,
our military and industrial schools, our theatres and scientific museums."[22]
These, and the multiple forms of the division of labour on which they had
come to be based, were the real sources of humanity's new capabilities.

The overlap between Schleiermacher's theology and modern sociology was
also visible some time later in Emile Durkheim's distinction between mechanical and organic solidarity, which was his version of the parallel distinction
between a *Gemeinschaft* and a *Gesellschaft* made by the German sociologist
Ferdinand Tönnies.[23] "To him," reported one of Durkheim's closest associates, the sociologist Célestin Bouglé, in a wide-ranging review of the various
theories of the division of labour encompassed by the work of Durkheim,
Tönnies, and Simmel, "the true function of specialization is not to produce
more and more goods, but to bind individuals together in increasing intimacy."
This, as Durkheim had shown, was because the switch from mechanical to
organic solidarity was connected to a more fundamental displacement of the
axis of moral life from the outside to the inside. "Solidarity in its previous
form," wrote Bouglé, "extinguished individuality; solidarity in its new form
highlights the rights of individuality." As with Tönnies's distinction between
community and society, the division of labour gave rise to a new type of solidarity and a new type of individuality. "When," Bouglé wrote, "the similarities that
unite the members of a group are very numerous, collective sentiments are
very intense. They find expression in weighty traditions, with a religious character, and in strict prohibitions, with a repressive character. Collective consciousness suffocates individual consciousness. When, on the other hand, the
division of labour has been taken far, the authority of collective consciousness
gradually dissipates, allowing individuals to vary. The ability to differ comes
to be recognized, but however different they become, they are still seen to have
the same rights." Mechanical solidarity presupposed the primacy of what was
common; organic solidarity presupposed the variety and diversity of what
was individual. "The one common feeling," Bouglé concluded, "that develops
within this transformation is the cult of the human personality."[24]

22. Ibid., p. 16.

23. On the distinction and its dissemination, see Bond, "'Gemeinschaft und Gesellschaft.'"

24. Célestin Bouglé, "Revue générale des théories récentes sur la division du travail," *L'année
sociologique* 6 (1901–2): 73–122 (see pp. 99 and 102 for the passages summarizing Durkheim
translated here).

A more familiar, but also less positive, evaluation of the division of labour was published almost at the same time as Schleiermacher produced his *Monologen*. It first appeared in 1801 in a collection of essays by a now largely forgotten French writer named Pierre-Edouard Lemontey and, nearly a generation later, was given much greater prominence in a widely noticed discussion of Lemontey's essay and the concept of the division of labour that was initiated by the political economist Jean-Baptiste Say. Lemontey's essay, entitled "Influence morale de la division du travail, considérée sous le rapport de la conservation du gouvernement et de la stabilité des institutions sociales" (The moral influence of the division of labour considered in relation to the preservation of government and the stability of social institutions), took its cue from Adam Smith's description of a pin factory and, in keeping with its subtitle, proceeded to extrapolate the moral and political implications of the division of labour to modern political societies as a whole. "We are struck with admiration," Lemontey wrote, "when we see, among the ancients, the same person being at once, and to an eminent degree, a philosopher, poet, orator, historian, priest, administrator, and army general. Our souls take fright at so vast a domain. Each of us plants his hedge and shuts himself up in his enclosure."[25] This was what the division of labour had done. Once, Lemontey wrote, there had been hunters, trappers, or fishermen, and their way of life had called for "a combination of strength and skill" that equipped them with a substantial reservoir of sensory and imaginative knowledge. The same broad culture could be found later among those who cultivated the land, and among "those classes of workers in whom muscular strength was combined with some notions of design, calculation, and chemistry to form a very remarkable set of men." The most striking feature of their character, Lemontey wrote, was their "love of independence and that taste for a wandering life that took their industry to all the big towns of France and Europe." But the ongoing global war and the laws on emigration of the period of the French Revolution had brought an end to a way of life that could now be found only "by listening to workers conversing in the taverns of the industrious city of Geneva."[26] The division of labour, Lemontey

---

25. "Nous sommes frappés d'admiration en voyant parmi les anciens le même personnage être à la fois, dans un degré éminent, philosophe, poète, orateur, historien, prêtre, administrateur, général d'armée. Nos âmes s'épouvantent à l'aspect d'un si vaste domaine. Chacun plante sa haie et s'enferme dans son enclos." Pierre Edouard Lemontey, *Raison, folie, petit cours de morale mis à la porté des vieux enfants* [1801], 3rd ed. 2 vols. (Paris, 1816), 1:191 n. 1.

26. "Le sauvage, qui dispute sa vie aux éléments, et subsiste des produits de sa pêche ou de sa chasse, est un composé de force et de ruse, plein de sens et d'imagination. Le laboureur, que la variété des saisons, des sols, des cultures et des valeurs force à des combinaisons renaissantes, reste un être pensant malgré ses routines et ses débris d'astrologie. Ces classes d'ouvriers en qui

warned, would only make things worse because it would turn workers into appendages of machines, and this "worker-machine" (*ouvrier-machine*) would be "prodigiously ignorant, credulous, and superstitious." If, he concluded, the division of labour was ever to reach the level of development that cupidity aspired to achieve, it would "give rise to an impotent, degraded, and cowardly caste of men, incapable of undertaking anything to defend the fatherland and always on the verge of doing something whose excesses will be all the more harmful because it will be undertaken with all the gullibility of innocence and a profound inability to discern the absurd and unjust."[27] It is not hard to see the point of the warning, particularly in the militarized context of the late eighteenth-century Franco-British war for the world. There was, Lemontey concluded, a need to ensure that "property, which is indeed the basis of social organization, does not give rise to harsh and arid theories that substitute the spirit of interest for the spirit of fraternity and legitimate a sort of universal egoism which is worse than the necessity of the savage state."[28]

Lemontey's assessment of the division of labour is likely to have passed unnoticed if it had not been picked up for critical comment by the more famous French political economist Jean-Baptiste Say in his *Cours complet d'économie politique pratique* (Complete course of practical political economy) in 1828. Say, in his *Treatise of Political Economy* of 1803, had earlier made use, but without acknowledgement, of a satirical comment in Lemontey's essay about the skills involved in making the eighteenth part of a pin, something that Lemontey pointed out publicly and somewhat reproachfully when he reprinted his essay in 1816.[29] Say replied twelve years later in the published

l'emploi des forces musculaires se réunit à quelques notions de dessin, de calcul ou de chimie, formaient une espèce d'hommes très-remarquables. . . . Les lois sur l'émigration et la guerre qui a dévoré toute une génération ont rompu avec violence ces mœurs singulières et l'on ne saurait peut-être plus s'en retracer quelque idée qu'en écoutant converser dans les tavernes de Genève les ouvriers de cette ville industrieuse." Ibid., 1:178–79.

27. "On demeure convaincu que si ce fameux principe atteint le développement où la cupidité ne cessera de le pousser, il formera une race d'hommes lâche, dégradée, impuissant à rien entreprendre pour la défense de la patrie, et voisine d'excès d'autant plus funestes qu'elle s'y jettera avec la sécurité d'innocence, et la profonde incapacité de discerner l'absurde et l'injuste." Ibid., 1:182.

28. "Il faut prendre garde que la propriété, qui est bien la base de l'organisation sociale, n'introduise des théories dures et arides qui substituent partout l'esprit d'intérêt à l'esprit de fraternité, et consacrent en quelque sorte un égoïsme universel pire que la nécessite dans l'état sauvage." Ibid., 1:196.

29. On the debate and its background, see Ludovic Frobert, "Pierre Edouard Lemontey et la critique de la division du travail," *Economies et sociétés* 35 (2001): 1735–57; François Vatin,

version of his lecture course, arguing that Lemontey had conflated specialization with mechanization and had also presupposed that they both entailed a life of endlessly repetitive work and low-paid exploitation. Neither, Say argued, was necessarily the case because the causation was, in fact, more complicated, just as it was also not the case that workers in agriculture, where the division of labour was less pronounced, were any more open-minded, less gullible, and unsusceptible to frauds and charlatans than their urban and industrial counterparts. Although, Say concluded, there was no reason to dispute the occurrence of exploitation, low pay, and bad working conditions, the fact of their existence did not mean that Lemontey had been right to identify their prime cause as the division of labour.[30]

Say's refutation of Lemontey was noticed very widely because it fed into the developing discussion of social stability and political legitimacy that began at around the time of the French revolution of July 1830 and came to be centred on what was described, variously, as the *question sociale*, the social question, or the *soziale Frage*.[31] In this context, the earlier discussions of a type of liberty that would be a synthesis of both ancient and modern liberty acquired a new and more comprehensively political and institutional orientation. "The whole of the social question—all, absolutely all—consists of the question of sovereignty," announced the Belgian political reformer the baron de Colins at the beginning of the huge examination of the latter subject that he published in 1857.[32] The phrase itself began to become current in France shortly after the 1830 revolution when it was first used more by the revolution's legitimist opponents than by its republican critics. It made an initial appearance in an article by the disenchanted romantic literary critic Charles Nodier that was published in the *Revue de Paris* in May 1831. The title of the article—"On the Imminent End of the Human Race"—is an indication of its content. It was a

---

"Pierre-Edouard Lemontey, l'invention de la sociologie du travail et la question salariale," *Revue de MAUSS* 27 (2006): 398–420, and his "Romantisme économique et philosophie de la misère en France dans les années 1820–1840," *Romantisme* 133 (2006): 35–47.

30. Jean-Baptiste Say, *Cours complet d'économie politique pratique*, 6 vols. (Paris, 1826–28), vol. 1, ch. 17, pp. 370–76.

31. See, initially, Thomas Bremer, Wolfgang Fink, Françoise Knopper, and Thomas Nicklas, eds., *La question sociale du Vormärz/Vormärz und soziale Frage 1830–1848* (Reims, Epure, 2018); Holly Case, *The Age of Questions* (Princeton, NJ, Princeton UP, 2018), and, for a helpful late nineteenth-century overview, Thomas Ziegler, *La question sociale est une question morale* (Paris, 1893).

32. "Toute la question sociale, toute, absolument toute, consiste dans la question de la souveraineté." Jean-Guillaume-César-Alexandre Hippolyte, baron de Colins, *De la souveraineté*, 2 vols. (Paris, 1857), 1:3.

sharp attack on what Nodier presented as the materialism and selfishness of the modern age, which culminated in a backhanded recommendation of the new religion of Saint-Simon as a suitable doctrine for a world bereft of spirituality. Like several of his contemporaries, including the historian Jules Michelet, Nodier equated Saint-Simonianism with moral emptiness.[33] "To the world that time, perfectibility, and civilization have made, Saint Simon for God," Nodier proclaimed sardonically. "Therefore," he concluded, "I believe in Saint-Simon, the God of the nineteenth century, and I will firmly believe in him for as long as no other god of the same kind does not arrive to simplify the social question and reduce it to its ultimate terms. Let no one lose heart."[34] The same type of judgment, but couched in more directly political terms, appeared in an article published in November 1831, in a legitimist newspaper named *La Quotidienne*, attacking the Orleanist regime for its failure to win a broad body of popular support after a major insurrection by silk workers in the city of Lyon. "In the end," the newspaper commented, "it is necessary to understand that, beyond the parliamentary conditions on which the existence of power depends, there is a social question that still has to be answered. . . . A government is always wrong if it has no more than a flat refusal to listen as its reply to people calling for bread."[35] The alternative was spelled out repeatedly a few years later by the Catholic political writer Frédéric Ozanam. "The question that divides men of our day," he wrote in 1836, "is no longer a question of

33. On the analogous case of Michelet and Saint-Simonianism, see Philippe Régnier, "Michelet, les saint-simoniens et le saint-simonisme," in "Michelet et la «Question Sociale»," ed. Paule Petitier *Littérature et Nation* 18 (1997): 49–73.

34. "Au monde que la perfectibilité, la civilisation et le temps nous ont fait, Saint-Simon pour dieu. . . . Je crois donc en Saint-Simon, dieu du dix-neuvième siècle, et j'y croirai fermement, tant qu'un autre dieu de la même nature ne viendra pas simplifier la question sociale et la réduire à ses derniers termes." Charles Nodier, "De la fin prochaine du genre humain," *Revue de Paris* 26 (1831): 224–40. The article is reprinted in Charles Nodier, *Rêveries*, ed. Hubert Juin (Paris, Editions Plasma, 1979), pp. 191–210. See also Holly Case, "The 'Social Question,' 1820–1920," *Modern Intellectual History* 13 (2016): 747–55 (where the name of periodical in which the article was first published is slightly garbled), and, more recently, her *The Age of Questions*. For further studies, see Douglas Moggach and Paul Leduc Browne, eds., *The Social Question and the Democratic Revolution: Marx and the Legacy of 1848* (Ottawa, U of Ottawa Press, 2000).

35. "Il faudrait enfin comprendre qu'en dehors des conditions parlementaires d'un pouvoir, il y a une question sociale à laquelle il faut satisfaire. . . . Un gouvernement a toujours tort lorsqu'il n'a que des fins de non-recevoir à opposer à des gens qui demandent du pain." *La Quotidienne*, 28 November 1831, cited in Jean-Baptiste Duroselle, *Les débuts du catholicisme social en France (1822–1870)* (Paris, PUF, 1951), p. 201; see too Robert Castel, *Les métamorphoses de la question sociale* [1995] (Paris, Gallimard, 2013), p. 394.

political forms; it is a social question, i.e. whether the spirit of egoism or of sacrifice will prevail."[36]

Nodier's allusion to what he called the ultimate terms of the social question was spelled out more graphically in an article entitled "De l'individualisme et du socialisme" (On individualism and socialism) published by the unusual French political journalist Pierre Leroux in the *Revue Encyclopédique* in 1833.[37] In it, Leroux attacked both individualism and socialism. Individualism gave rise to inequality and social conflict, while socialism magnified state power and despotic authority. The indictment was repeated by a liberal-minded Catholic journalist named Ferdinand, baron d'Eckstein, in a review published in 1834 of the heterodox theologian Félicité de Lamennais's controversial *Paroles d'un croyant* (The words of a believer). There, Eckstein set Lamennais's volcanic attack on economic and political inequality against the equally fierce endorsement of power and authority made by Joseph de Maistre in his *Soirées de Saint-Pétersbourg* (Nights in Saint-Petersburg). It was right, Eckstein wrote, that both books had been published, "because they take the social question to its furthest extent."[38] In this context, the social question was, in the first

36. Ozanam to F. Lallier and L. Janmot, 13 November 1836, cited by Thomas O. Nitsch, in his introduction to Thomas O. Nitsch, Joseph M. Phillips Jr., and Edward L. Fitzsimmons, eds., *On the Condition of Labour and the Social Question One Hundred Years Later* (Lampeter, Edwin Mellen Press, 1994), pp. ix–xxi (here, pp. xvii–xviii n. 3).

37. On Leroux, see the doctoral thesis by Jean-Pierre Lacassagne, "Un mage romantique: Pierre Leroux (1791–1871)" (Université de Paris IV, 1989), and his two related publications, *Histoire d'une amitié. Pierre Leroux et George Sand* (Paris, Klincksieck, 1973) and Pierre Leroux, *La grève de Samarez: poème philosophique*, ed. Jean-Pierre Lacassagne (Paris, Klincksieck, 1979). For a particularly helpful way in to his thought, see Michael C. Behrent, "Pluralism's Political Conditions: Social Realism and the Revolutionary Tradition in Pierre Leroux, P-J Proudhon and Alfred Fouillée," in *Pluralism and the Idea of the Republic in France*, ed. Julian Wright and H. S. Jones (Basingstoke, Palgrave, 2012), pp. 99–121. See too Sharp, *Secular Spirituality*, pp. 4–24; Serge Audier, *La société écologique et ses ennemis* (Paris, La Découverte, 2017), pp. 125–33; and Georges Navet, *Pierre Leroux: Politique, socialisme et philosophie* (Besançon, Publications de la société P. J. Proudhon, 1994). On Leroux and Leibniz, see Lucie Rey, "Leibniz à l'appui de la doctrine de perfectibilité de Pierre Leroux," *Corpus* 68 (2015): 119–38; and on Leroux and Cousin, see Lucie Rey, "Les lumières comme enjeu philosophique et politique: Pierre Leroux face à Victor Cousin," *Dix-Huitième Siècle* 47 (2015): 501–28, as well as her earlier *Les enjeux de l'histoire de la philosophie en France au XIXe siècle. Pierre Leroux contre Victor Cousin* (Paris, L'Harmattan, 2012). More recently, see Lucie Rey, "Le 'sphinx de la révolution.' Pierre Leroux et la promesse révolutionnaire," *Archives de Philosophie* 80 (2017): 55–74.

38. "Tout bien considéré, ces deux livres ont dû être composés; ils ont posé la question sociale dans ses derniers termes: c'est pour l'instruction de tout le monde." Ferdinand d'Eckstein, "Jugement ou examen de l'ouvrage de M. de Lamennais," *La France Catholique* 2 (1834), re-

instance, a question about the relationship between poverty and inequality on the one side and legal equality and political sovereignty on the other. But it was also a question about ancient and modern liberty and the prospects for self-development offered by the modern age.

The subject was taken a step further with the publication in 1838 of a rhetorically overheated history of the working and bourgeois classes (*Histoire des classes ouvrières et des classes bourgeoises*) by a French nobleman named Adolphe Granier de Cassagnac. In it, Granier announced that "however general and extensive the working classes were in society," they were, in fact, a derivation of "an even more general and extensive social element." This "grand, simple, primordial historical fact, which preceded the working classes and of which they are no more than a fragment, subdivision, or branch," was, he asserted, "the *proletariat*."[39] Granier dedicated his history to François Guizot, by then one of France's most prominent public figures, perhaps because of the significance of class conflict in Guizot's own historical works, but he relied more fully on the thought of Vico and his French translator Jules Michelet for his own historical argument.[40] The argument itself, however, was somewhat similar to that of Karl Ludwig von Haller's *Restauration de la science politique*, but in this case it was centred on a claim about the gradual emancipation of individuals and households from an original condition of slavery. In the beginning, Granier argued, there were simply masters and slaves. Over time, this patriarchal relationship turned into a more elaborate combination of nobles and the ennobled on the one side and workers and the bourgeoisie on the other. Prior to both workers and burghers there was, therefore, the proletariat, meaning the previously enslaved members of households who had freed themselves piecemeal from the domination of their masters. While some parts of the proletariat had been able to establish guilds and corporations to form the nucleus of what would become an urban bourgeoisie, and while others had acquired land as the basis of what was to become the rural commune, those without property had turned either into the working classes or into an underclass that was forced to rely for its survival on prostitution, begging or crime. The modern condition was a product of this state of extreme social division.

For Granier de Cassagnac the way out called for the way back and a real reversion to the old hierarchies of the past. Since, he argued, the word

---

printed in Félicité de Lamennais, *Paroles d'un croyant* [1834], ed. Louis Le Guillou (Paris, Flammarion, 1973), p. 177.

39. Adolphe Granier de Cassagnac, *Histoire des classes ouvrières et des classes bourgeoises* (Brussels, 1838), p. 28. On the concept, see, helpfully, R. B. Rose, "*Prolétaires* and *Prolétariat*: Evolution of a Concept, 1789–1848," *Australian Journal of French Studies* 18 (1981): 282–99.

40. On Vico, see Cassagnac, *Histoire des classes ouvrières*, pp. 26, 75, 396–97, 404.

"proletarian"—now used by the French Saint-Simonians to designate "a free man possessing nothing"—was used originally in Roman law to mean "a serf of the glebe," reviving the old usage, but under modern conditions, held out the prospect of a restoration of corporate and communal paternalism.[41] It is not difficult to see why Granier's philologically based argument, with its Vico-inspired idea of using the meaning of words to identify underlying social conditions, earned an impressively long and hostile review in the *Revue des Deux Mondes* in 1839 or, later, was given an equally long, but far more favourable, endorsement by its pro-slavery, Confederate-supporting, American translator when it was published in English in 1871.[42]

More significantly, however, Granier used the same approach that he had given to the word "proletarian" to give the word "ideology" something like its modern meaning. Generic terms like "men" and "citizens," he argued, were logical but sterile, with no effective purchase outside the realm of "pure ideas." History, or the realm of "the complex and positive facts of politics," offered a better approach. This, Granier concluded, was why it was necessary "to learn from the mistakes of the ideologists by not taking men to be triangles, by not mixing up politics with geometry, and by distinguishing social questions from mathematical questions." Behind ideology, there were real people. "Thus, instead of saying that a worker is a citizen and a member of the sovereign, which is obvious and proper but leads to nothing useful, we need to find out from history what a worker really is, what is his origin, what causes produce him here, exclude him there, and multiply him elsewhere in order that, his social nature being known, his propensities being studied, it may become possible and easy to draw from the knowledge of his past and present the formula of his future." The study of history was, in short, the way to avoid the presuppositions of ideology. But, as Hegel had been quick to point out in attacking Karl Ludwig von Haller, this emphasis on the real relied upon a conflation of facts with values. The point was repeated more fully and clearly in the early twentieth century by the neo-Kantian philosopher Emil Lask in a brilliant characterization of the nature and origins of historicism. Hegel's point, he wrote, raised "the same complication as the confusion of the unique character of values with historicism. It is now understandable why historicism, which lives on confounding the empirically concrete with the concrete value, has become so seductive especially in the field of legal and social

41. Ibid., pp. 202–3.

42. The review was also published separately as Jean-Pierre Rossignol, *Examen critique de l'histoire des classes ouvrières et des classes bourgeoise de M. Granier de Cassagnac* (Paris, 1839). For the later endorsement, see Adolphe Granier de Cassagnac, *History of the Working and Burgher Classes*, trans. Ben E. Green (Philadelphia, 1871).

philosophy. What historism implies in an unreflecting way of evaluation was made explicit and dogmatized in the philosophy of the *Restauration*. In that philosophy, the forms of state organization which have empirically grown and become legitimate provide the unchangeable bars at which any criticism that measures by standards of absolute value must stand silent. The sharpest contrast with any such acceptance of given political facts as absolute may be found in the theory of Hegel, with its inexorable attack upon the vacuity of mere finiteness, upon the unreason of the single empirical 'this.'"[43]

Positive and Negative Liberty

The same, relatively unfamiliar, connotations of a now more familiar set of terms were once associated with the early nineteenth-century concepts of negative and positive liberty. The more familiar connotations of the terms were, for example, set out in an article published in Pierre Leroux's *Revue Indépendante* in 1845. "Even if I had to pass for the most intransigent adversary of freedom of commerce," its author, François Vidal, wrote, "I would still dispute its principles and its consequences." He was, he continued, "a partisan of freedom of commerce and a partisan of liberty in general" but "of positive liberty, not negative liberty; for real liberty, not a purely nominal liberty. I want a stable,

43. "Il faut donc aujourd'hui, pour être sage, profiter des fautes des idéologues, ne pas s'obstiner à prendre les hommes pour des triangles, ne pas mêler imprudemment la politique et la géométrie, distinguer les questions mathématiques des questions sociales." "C'est du reste au fond de mon esprit une conviction profonde que la politique ne cessera d'être un empirisme redoutable et ne deviendra une science calme et sereine que le jour où elle prendra l'histoire pour point de départ. Elle sent depuis un demi-siècle qu'il lui faut une base et elle en a cherché une dans des théories abstraites sur les droits de l'homme et autres entités métaphysiques qui n'ont rien de réel que dans la foi de ceux qui les acceptent, et que tout le monde peut nier. Ces théories sont aujourd'hui épuisées et sur les dents, sans avoir rien produit. On devait s'y attendre. Maintenant que l'expérience a amené la réflexion, il faut bien se dire que l'homme n'est ni un triangle, ni une idée, mais un être complexe qui a son histoire, laquelle il faut étudier et savoir pour apprécier sa nature sociale, son caractère et ses besoins. La première condition pour trouver les lois de l'avenir, c'est de connaitre celles du passé." Cassagnac, *Histoire des classes ouvrières*, pp. 28, 20–21. Here, I have largely followed Green's 1871 translation, p. 84. On the origins of the modern concept of ideology, see too Robert Derathé, "Quelques documents sur Chateaubriand, Napoléon et les Idéologues," *Revue européenne des sciences sociales* 17 (1979): 179–84, and Dan Edelstein, "The Birth of Ideology from the Spirit of Myth: Georges Sorel among the Idéologues," in *The Re-Enchantment of the World*, ed. Joshua Landy and Michael Saler (Stanford, Stanford UP, 2021), pp. 201–24. For the passage from Lask, see Emil Lask, "Legal Philosophy," in *The Legal Philosophies of Lask, Radbruch, and Dabin*, ed. Edwin W. Patterson and Kurt Wilk (Cambridge, MA, Harvard UP, 1950), p. 23.

permanent liberty, which is why I want liberty to be guaranteed and organized."[44] The same point was made by the French socialist or anarchist Pierre-Joseph Proudhon in a characteristic attack on what he described as the school of political economists represented by Adam Smith and Jean-Baptiste Say. "The theory of negative liberty," he wrote, "or of *laissez faire, laissez passer*, which amounts to the whole philosophy of the school, leads necessarily to a contradiction. It is clear, and the facts show it in front of our eyes, that if labour, or the whole organic economy, are released from their shackles and, as the followers of Smith and Say recommend, left to the attractions of nature, then work, after starting in freedom, will end in subjection."[45] From this perspective, negative liberty was the other side of the social question. This, according to the author of a philosophy of history published in 1840, was what Charles Fourier had shown. "Negative liberty, whether simple or physical, he [meaning Fourier] said, is the lot of the poor or someone with a very small revenue, meaning the strictly necessary or a military ration. Someone in this condition could have a very active physical liberty because he is not forced to go to work as is the case with a worker deprived of all revenue. He is, for example free to go to the opera, but to get in to the opera you have to have money and so he will have to stand at the opera door. For all his pride in the fact that he is a free man, he has no more than a mirage of social liberty. He is no more than a passive member of society."[46]

The tension between negative and positive liberty was also apparent in publications with a more Christian and legitimist orientation. In an article entitled "On Negative and Positive Liberty" ("Sur la liberté négative et positive") published in the *Revue Européenne* in 1831, the German Catholic Franz Baader argued that both types of liberty were prerequisites of the combination of centralization and decentralization that he hoped would be established in France after the revolution of July 1830. "It is not enough," he wrote, "if two citizens are negatively free in relation to one another, or if their spheres of activity do not collide and they do not *prevent* one another from existing or acting. It is also necessary that they mutually help and serve one another to support one another and reach an emancipated existence." The same thing, he

44. François Vidal, "Economie sociale—Les économistes de l'Institut—Monsieur Rossi," *Revue Indépendante* 10 (1845): 307–48 (p. 343 for the citation).

45. Pierre-Joseph Proudhon, *De la justice dans la révolution et dans l'église* (Paris, 1858), p. 150.

46. Jean-Jacques Altmeyer, *Cours de philosophie de l'histoire* (Brussels, 1840), pp. 159–60. For further variations on the subject, see David George Ritchie, "'Freedom'—Negative and Positive," in his *Principles of State Interference* (London, Swan Sonnenschein, 1891), pp. 145–51, and Thomas Hill Green, *Philosophical Works*, ed. Richard Lewis Nettleship, 3 vols. (London, Longmans, Green, and Co., 1885–88), 2:308–33.

continued, applied to the relationship between the government and the governed because, he wrote, "if negative liberty *unchains* men in society, positive liberty, which is the product of mutual services, *binds* men. One is not free unless one is strong and one is not strong if one is alone." This, he concluded, was why "religion extends and protects positive liberty by binding them with the ties of love and honour and, reciprocally, why all that binds men with these ties is religion." It followed that "religion is in essence antirevolutionary, just as it is also antiservile because it sows love, honour, and humility, while purely negative liberalism sows no more than hatred, pride, and baseness." "Negative liberalism" was no more than a fable whose morality was "servility."[47]

The slip from negative "liberty" to negative "liberalism" made by Franz Baader made it possible to switch the focus from liberty to liberalism and throw a more positive light on negative liberty. As the Dominican friar Henri-Dominique Lacordaire explained in a sermon given in the Cathedral of Notre Dame in 1835, the church too had a capacity for positive and negative liberty. In terms of the former, he said, "the spiritual action of the Church was free; she was free to spread truth by the word, grace by sacrifice and the sacraments, virtue by all the practices which are its source and confirmation: in this consists her positive liberty, her liberty of acting. But there is another liberty no less necessary and precious; this is negative liberty, the liberty of not acting, without which no sovereignty or dignity is possible." Negative liberty was the power of excommunication. Without it, Lacordaire asked rhetorically, "what should we be? Slaves. Whoever has not the liberty of refusing his service is a slave; whoever has the liberty of refusing it is master and lord."[48] It was a recognizable version of what, more recently, has been taken to be the neo-Roman idea of liberty as nondomination, but one given in a surprisingly different context and with the opposite set of evaluations to those now in use.

Roman Law and Its Legacy

The social question meant that the division of labour could be presented as either a catalyst of, or an obstacle to, self-development. The ambiguity played a major part in a now largely forgotten and Europe-wide argument over the

47. François Baader, "Sur la liberté négative et positive," *Revue Européenne* 2 (1831): 192–94.

48. Henri-Dominique Lacordaire, *Conférences de Notre Dame de Paris*, 4 vols. (Paris, 1853), 1:140. I have followed the English translation, *Conferences of the Rev. Pere Lacordaire*, trans. Henry Langdon (London, 1853), pp. 99–100. For a more familiar overview, see Quentin Skinner, "On Neo-Roman Liberty: A Conclusion and Reassessment," in *Rethinking Liberty before Liberalism*, ed. Hannah Dawson and Annelien De Dijn (Cambridge, CUP, 2022), pp. 233–66.

nature and content of Roman law and its cumulative impact both on the division of labour and on the relationship between property and political power. "There is a small sect," wrote an important Parisian lawyer named Claude Dupin in 1824, "that is trying to introduce *Germanism* into jurisprudence by following the example of that other school wanting to make *romanticism* dominant in our literature." It was, he stated, "a presumption that is as opposed to our good taste and national character as to the spirit and needs of the age in which we live."[49] The case against Roman law that Dupin is likely to have had in mind was set out fully and clearly by a lawyer named Etienne Aignan who was another member of the Coppet group, and one of Benjamin Constant's friends and political allies, two years after Constant gave his lecture on ancient and modern liberty. Aignan was one of the editors of Constant's periodical publication, *La Minerve française*, and was also the author of a history of the institution of the jury that he published in 1821. Its content throws a new, less familiar light on the intellectual and political concerns of the Coppet group, in contrast to many of the group's other, better-known publications, because its prime concern was with Roman law. When, Aignan wrote in his history of the jury, Rome began to turn from a republic into an empire, "the universe, having been enslaved and, as a result, having acquired the condition of a minor, had need of both protectors for its defence and tutors for its guidance, the Roman civil law was born."

> The civil law was the most powerful auxiliary of despotism because it was able to regulate despotism's actions and block its most monstrous deviations. Without its creation, the oppression of the human race would never have been more than momentary. Conquests and usurpations of power would have passed like rainstorms and calm would have been restored. It was the civil law that gave roots to absolute power. The Caesars would pass, but the Ulpians and Tribonians would remain.[50]

49. "Il existe une petite secte qui s'efforce d'introduire le *germanisme* dans la jurisprudence, à l'exemple de cette autre école qui voudrait faire dominer le *romantisme* dans notre littérature. Ces prétentions sont également opposées à notre bon gout, à notre génie national, à l'esprit comme aux besoins de l'époque où nous vivons." Claude Dupin, "Dissertation sur Pothier," in Robert-Joseph Pothier, *Œuvres* [1824], rev. ed., 11 vols. (Paris, 1827), 1:lxxvi. It is worth noting that this version of "Germanism" was very different from the type of Germanism described, famously, in Fritz Stern, *The Politics of Cultural Despair: A Study in the Rise of the Germanic Ideology* (Berkeley, U of California Press, 1961). An interesting story, however, could be told about the transformation of the one into the other.

50. "Cette grande et fatale époque de la déchéance du genre humain, a été merveilleusement observée dans ses causes [here a note referred to Bossuet, Montesquieu, and Gibbon], mais semble ne l'avoir pas été suffisamment dans ses effets. L'univers devenu esclave et par

They would remain, Aignan argued, because the civil law was—and had remained—the domain of the jurist and lawyer, not the citizen and public servant. Once the civil law was in existence, he wrote, "enlightened people" had come to fall into two broad classes. The most numerous were those who accepted the civil law because of its benefits, while the more philosophical minority was left to protest "at human degradation and servility," and to call for "the revival of human rights and dignity." This was the setting that gave rise to that "terrifying mass of laws brought together in the Code, the Digest, the Institutes, and the Novellas."[51]

Roman law, in these terms, was the real source of the truncated version of liberty that had become modern liberty. As with Constant, Aignan's evaluation of representative government was deeply coloured by this initial diagnosis. The final chapter of his book on the jury began with a question about how representative government could be defined. Taking issue with the threefold classification of governments into republics, monarchies, and despotisms that could be found in Montesquieu's famous *The Spirit of Laws*, Aignan argued that there were "really" only two forms of government, meaning "that of one, namely, the monarchic, and that of several, namely, the polyarchic or republican."[52] The vocabulary came from the individual sometimes taken to be the theoretical architect of the French Revolution of 1789, Emmanuel-Joseph Sieyès, and his public debate with the Anglo-American radical Tom Paine in 1791 about the attributes and merits of republics and monarchies, but Aignan gave the two terms a significantly different set of evaluations. For Sieyès, polyarchy was the form of government that could be coupled with Paine's concept of a republic, while monarchy went together with his own concept of a representative system or, as he also called it, a monarchical republic.[53] Unlike Sieyès, however, Aignan rejected monarchy and endorsed polyarchy. The initial, purely numerical, difference between the two meant, he argued, that

---

conséquent mineur, eut besoin tout à la fois de protecteurs pour se défendre et de tuteurs pour se conduire, et le droit civil romain fut créé; le droit civil, cet auxiliaire le plus puissant du despotisme, car il sut en régulariser l'action et en réprimer les plus monstrueux écarts. Sans cette création, l'oppression du genre humain n'aurait jamais été qu'instantanée. Les conquêtes, les envahissements de pouvoir auraient fui comme des orages, et le calme serait rétabli. Ce fut le droit civil qui donna des racines à la puissance absolue. Les Césars passent; les Ulpien et les Tribonien demeurent." Etienne Aignan, *Histoire du jury* (Paris, 1822), pp. 92–93.

51. Ibid., p. 93.

52. Ibid., p. 338.

53. On these distinctions, see Michael Sonenscher, "Revolution, Reform and the Political Thought of Emmanuel Joseph Sieyès," in *Revolutionary Moments*, ed. Rachel Hammersley (London, Bloomsbury, 2014), pp. 69–76.

they were as different from one another as night from day. "One," Aignan wrote, "has the authority of a name or a family as its unique principle, while the other has that of institutions and laws."[54] In reality, of course, the distinction was more blurred. Rules were required in a monarchy, just as laws were sometimes ignored or misapplied in republics. But monarchy was, ultimately, a personal form of rule, while polyarchy was, finally, impersonal. Obedience in a monarchy was ultimately obedience to "a magical name," even if the magic was sometimes lost, while obedience in a polyarchy called more prosaically for the ability of several individuals or families to move "immense multitudes" over extended periods of time, and this ability could only be the work of the law. "In a word," Aignan concluded, "unity of action, without which no state can live, resides either in the will of the prince, and there is a monarchy, or in the will of the law, and there is a republic."[55]

There was, however, a further difference between ancient and modern republics. Ancient republics, Aignan argued, relied on divisions, like those between aristocrats and democrats in Athens, or between patricians and plebeians in Rome, to produce the rivalry, rotation of office, and resources of patriotism that governed their political life. Conflict was, therefore, built into the political life of the ancient republics and was either a source of strength or, potentially, an ultimately fatal weakness. "Modern republics," Aignan continued, "and by this I mean any state moved by the impulse of the law, know better."[56] They made no formal distinctions between classes, castes, or tribes and, instead, attached more or less severe conditions to the single quality of citizenship. All those who met the relevant conditions formed a single entity that, given the size and changing social composition of most modern republics, had to rely on choosing delegates to fill the offices responsible for making them work. This, according to Aignan, made modern government "representative government," and, he continued, "whether it has a king or any other supreme figure as head of the executive power," representative government was "essentially republican because it derives from the law and the law is the sole motive force of its action."[57]

54. "Pour quiconque y veut bien réfléchir, quelle que soit son opinion sur la bonté absolue des gouvernements, il n'en existe que deux sortes: celui d'un seul, le monarchique; celui de plusieurs, le polyarchique ou républicain. . . . L'un a pour principe unique l'autorité d'un nom, d'une famille; l'autre, celle des lois et des institutions." Aignan, *Histoire du jury*, pp. 338–39.

55. Ibid., p. 340.

56. "Les modernes républiques (et j'appelle de ce nom tout état mû par l'impulsion de la loi), les modernes républiques, dis-je, en savent davantage." Ibid., p. 341.

57. Ibid., pp. 341–42. For a similar, slightly later, approach to Roman law by the law professor Denis Serrigny, see Dominique Hiebel, "Denis Serrigny, le droit administrative romain et la

Polyarchy, in Aignan's presentation, was the other side of the rule of law. The problem, however, was that most modern legal systems were often a derivation of Roman law, and, as Aignan emphasized, Roman law had more to do with monarchy than polyarchy and more in common with personal power than impersonal rule. In this sense, Aignan's description went with the grain of Constant's lecture of 1819, as well as with Constant's disenchanted analysis of the politics of reform from above in the long commentary on the works of the eighteenth-century Neapolitan reformer Gaetano Filangieri that he published in 1822.[58] This critical stance towards the combined effects of Roman law, civil law, and the primacy of civil, rather than political, liberty in modern social and political arrangements had already been highlighted four years earlier by another of Constant's friends, a lawyer named Jean-Pierre Pagès who was later to become Constant's literary executor. As Pagès put it in 1817, the "system of representative government" would be impracticable in "a nation that has the energy of youth, a consciousness of its manners, its strength, its love of country, and which seeks to enjoy the freedom to which it is entitled." But, he continued, "it is wonderful for peoples who have fallen into softness, corruption, avidity, and egoism because it denies them the possibility of completing the process of their depravation and of succumbing to anarchy through licentiousness. In states like these, representatives are harmful only to kings. With respect to the people, they are like viziers in whom its idleness can find repose from all political care."[59]

Representation, seen like this, took political liberty out of political society, leaving no more than civil liberty. To Pagès, like Sismondi, Constant, and Aignan, the separation was one of the legacies of Roman law. As one of its critics put it, Roman law was fine for its times, but was now no more than "the debris of a worn-out, artificial, and oppressive social state."[60] The same point was made by the liberal noble Jean Denis, comte Lanjuinais, the leading figure of the group of early nineteenth-century French advocates of constitutional

---

dénonciation du despotisme impérial," *Revue française d'histoire des idées politiques* 41 (2015): 123–60.

58. See Benjamin Constant, *Commentary on Filangieri's Work* [1822–24], ed. Alan S. Kahan (Indianapolis, IN, Liberty Fund, 2015).

59. Jean-Pierre Pagès, *Principes généraux du droit politique dans leur rapport avec l'esprit de l'Europe et avec la Monarchie constitutionnelle* (Paris, 1817), pp. 483–84. For further discussion of the Coppet group and this negative assessment of Rome, see Mouza Raskolnikoff, "Volney et les Idéologues: le refus de Rome," *Revue Historique* 267 (1982): 357–73—a far more wide-ranging article than its title suggests.

60. Pierre-Claude-Jean-Baptiste Bravard-Veyrières, *De l'étude et de l'enseignement du droit romain et des résultats qu'on peut en attendre* (Paris, 1836), p. 204.

government known as the *Doctrinaires*, in a note attached to an attack on Rousseau's concept of civil religion published in 1825. Roman law, he wrote, was a system "in which, alongside some fine axioms, can be found private slavery, public despotism, an abyss of disorderly substitutions, torture, religious inquisition, contradictory, incoherent, and uncertain texts." What Lanjuinais called that "chaos" had served to "combat, soften, complicate, support, and finally bring down the harmful aristocratic and feudal regime before becoming the pedestal on which the arbitrary power of monarchs was raised, and the source of the scaffolding on which the new civil codes were erected in Europe."[61] It was an evaluation that remained alive for many more years. "In keeping with its Roman archetype, Napoleon and his council of state gave us legislation in which everything was sacrificed to landed property," noted Louis Wolowski, a law professor at the Parisian Conservatoire des arts et métiers, in an introductory lecture to a course on industrial legislation that he gave in Paris in 1840. By the early twentieth century, this negative assessment of Roman law was even applied retrospectively—in a surprising reversal of perspective—to Guizot and the *Doctrinaires*. As one hostile commentator put it, "*L'état c'est moi*, said Louis XIV. 'The state is all,' said the *Doctrinaires*, those disciples of the Roman tradition. Where is the difference?"[62]

From the vantage point of Constant, Aignan, and many of the other members of the Coppet group, this type of evaluation of Roman law was a product of its imperial origins. Modern liberty was Roman and negative because it began and ended with the civil law and the tight correlation that it housed between the status of persons and the status of things. On the basis of the Roman-law principle that people were either free or slaves, and that their rights and entitlements were closely connected to these initial distinctions of status, the land had taken precedence over industry, while civil liberty had

61. "La bastonnade," he wrote, referring to the revival in Italy in 1822 of an old Roman practice, "n'est au fond qu'un retour au droit des codes romains et des Pandectes, à ce droit, où, à côté de quelques beaux axiomes, on trouve esclavage privé, despotisme public, substitutions abime de désordres, tortures, inquisition religieuse, textes incertains, incohérents, contradictoires. ... Ce chaos servit à combattre, adoucir, embrouiller, soutenir longtemps, abattre enfin le funeste régime aristocratique et féodal; il fut comme un piédestal sur lequel on érigea la puissance arbitraire des monarques; il a fourni des échafauds pour élever en Europe les nouveaux codes civils." Jean-Denis, comte Lanjuinais, *Examen du Huitième Chapitre du Contrat Social de J. J. Rousseau* (Paris, 1825), p. 35 n. 2.

62. "D'après le type romain, Napoléon et son conseil d'état nous ont donné une législation où tout est sacrifié à la propriété territoriale." Louis Wolowski, *Cours de législation industrielle* (Paris, 1840), p. 3. For the equation of Louis XIV, the *Doctrinaires*, and the Romans, see Noel Dolens, *Le socialisme fédéral* (Paris, 1904), p. 204.

prevailed over political liberty. From this perspective, what was once called "the political theory of possessive individualism" had in fact begun with Rome, just as the seventeenth-century advocates of modern natural jurisprudence, from Hugo Grotius to Thomas Hobbes and John Locke, could be described as the true intellectual heirs of Roman law. As an entry in the French *Encyclopédie nouvelle* put it in 1840, Grotius, Pufendorf, Barbeyrac, and Burlamaqui had all been members of that "family of scholarly jurists who built the jurisprudence of the human republic." For them, who were all Protestants, Roman law, "that Old Testament of ancient sociability, with its fatalistic realism, was what the Bible had been to the theologians of the Reformation."[63] From the perspective of these nineteenth-century assessments, and long before the Marxism of the twentieth century, "possessive individualism" began with Rome, rather than the seventeenth century and the bourgeoisie. As a hostile reviewer of a mid-nineteenth-century book on the principles of human society commented, the concept of utility "was indeed the principle of the old Italy of the Romans, a real race of Utilitarians."[64] The same evaluation applied to property, which, according to the nineteenth-century French socialist Benoît Malon, "only became entirely individual (as with the right to use or abuse) under the aegis of that odious Roman law which, to our misfortune, still governs us."[65] In the light of Aignan's book, twenty-first-century historiography has largely echoed its earlier nineteenth-century counterpart, but without incorporating its initial evaluations.[66]

63. Pierre Leroux and Jean Reynaud, eds., *Encyclopédie nouvelle*, 8 vols. (1839–43), 3:444 (entry on "Burlamaqui").

64. "C'est bien là le principe de l'antique Italie des Romains, vraie race d'utilitaires." Anonymous review of Vito d'Ondes Reggio, *Introduzione ai principi delle umane società*, in *La Libre Recherche* 7 (Brussels, 1857), p. 492.

65. "Sans remonter au communisme promiscue de l'origine des sociétés, nous voyons la propriété longtemps dépendante du droit social; elle ne devient entièrement individuelle (droit d'user et d'abuser) que sous l'odieux droit romain qui, pour notre malheur, nous régit encore." Benoît Malon, *Le socialisme intégral* (Paris, 1890), p. 36.

66. On Grotius and Roman law, see Benjamin Straumann, *Roman Law in the State of Nature* (Cambridge, CUP, 2015), and, more broadly, his *Crisis and Constitutionalism: Roman Political Thought from the Fall of the Republic to the Age of Revolution* (Oxford, OUP, 2016) and the discussion of that book in *Global Intellectual History* 4 (2019): 271–88. See too Theodore Christov, *Before Anarchy: Hobbes and His Critics in Modern International Thought* (Cambridge, CUP, 2015). More broadly, see Macpherson, *The Political Theory of Possessive Individualism*. For a helpful overview of the historiography of the legacy of Roman law, particularly in the context of international relations and property theory, see Ben Holland, "Sovereignty as Dominium? Reconstructing the Constructivist Roman Law Thesis," *International Studies Quarterly* 54 (2010): 449–80.

On these terms, Roman law appeared to favour civil, not political, liberty, and landed, not industrial or commercial, property. It was the real source of institutionalized egoism. As the gifted University of Strasbourg law professor Henri Klimrath put it in his doctoral thesis of 1833, "Roman legislation could never deny its fierce origin. Egoism was the basis of all its rights."[67] If this was true, then it was the legacy of Roman law that was largely responsible for the social question. By entrenching inequality while, at the same time, endorsing popular sovereignty and the idea of a republican form of government, Roman law appeared to have created the conditions that favoured the recurrent cycles of economic and social conflict that, from the vantage point of the early nineteenth century, had become the hallmark of politics after the French Revolution. And, to liberal critics of Roman law like Aignan, Pagès, and Constant, the cluster of moral, economic, and political problems encapsulated by the phrase "the social question" raised a further and more acute question about whether it could ever be given a liberal answer, or whether, as the royalist authors originally responsible for putting the phrase into circulation had implied, the right answer to the social question was one with a legitimist content.

This type of critical assessment of the legacy of Roman law was taken a step further in a book entitled *Philosophie de l'histoire de France* (The philosophy of the history of France) that was published in 1840 by a French jurist named Charles Guillaume Hello.[68] Its argument paralleled the earlier assessment of the relationship between modern liberty and Roman law made by Constant's collaborator Etienne Aignan. Hello's most immediate purpose in a work on the philosophy of history was to examine the relationship between agency and causation in politics and history or, more specifically, to explain how the apparently incompatible notions of freedom and necessity implied by the two concepts of agency and causation could be reconciled. His answer—which was similar to, but still different from, Constant's treatment of the same subject—centred on what he took to be a major difference between the ancients and the moderns. Ancient societies, Hello claimed, had founders and followers, like Moses and the Israelites, Romulus and the Romans, or Lycurgus and the Spartans. Ancient societies, accordingly, began with a determinate group of people and an identifiable set of actions. Their leaders were also their legislators because, as Prosper Enfantin, the self-proclaimed leader of the

67. "La législation romaine ne démentit jamais son origine farouche. L'égoïsme y était la base de tous les droits." Henri Klimrath, "Essai sur l'étude historique du droit et son utilité pour l'interprétation du Code Civil" [1833], reprinted in his *Travaux sur l'histoire du droit français*, 2 vols. (Paris, 1843), 1:37.

68. For a helpful recent discussion of the legacy of Roman law, see Ando, *Citizenship and Empire*, as well as his earlier "A Dwelling beyond Violence."

French Saint-Simonians had put it in the context of a far more recent dispute over his authority in the early 1830s, they were simply the living law, and, as the phrase went, their words were law. Ancient societies were, therefore, products of human design. Modern societies, however, just grew. Nobody had actually founded France or Spain, just as no initial criteria determined who or what was French or Spanish. This initial difference meant that ancient societies were the outcomes of agency in ways that were less easy to identify in modern societies. But the difference, Hello argued, had the paradoxical effect of making ancient societies more derivative of—and dependent on—an initial set of founding choices. Although they began freely, their long-term stability depended on their ability to preserve their original founding principles. Modern societies on the other hand were not only more fluid, but the very indeterminacy of their origins made them more able to accommodate diversity and, more significantly, also set no identifiable limits to their historical and political horizons. The modern world simply had the ability to go on and on.

The key to this difference, Hello argued, was that the moderns had something that was unavailable to the ancients. This was the concept of sovereignty. "Among the things," he wrote, "that man appropriates with the most ardour, but which actually belongs to him least, there is something that precedes all the social powers and, properly speaking, is not any one of them, even though it encompasses them all because it is almost a synonym for social existence. This is sovereignty, that terrifying word whose profound mystery sporadically releases the passions and darkness of which it is full."[69] The gothic imagery helped to highlight a more significant historical point. This was that "the ancient world was less familiar with sovereignty than with domination." The ancient city or *civitas* simply "dominated or was dominated." At home, its government stood for naked power, even if that power was applied in variously calibrated mixtures and combinations. Abroad, it was exposed solely to the vicissitudes of strength and weakness. The Greeks had tried to establish a place for something more than force above their assorted city-states in the shape of the Amphictyonic—or Ionic—League, but the Romans had remained more firmly committed to the original ancient principle and had simply incorporated a growing number

69. "Parmi celles que l'homme s'approprie avec le plus d'ardeur, et qui lui appartient le moins, il en est une qui précède les pouvoirs sociaux, qui n'est proprement d'aucun d'eux, mais qui les renferme tous, et qui est presque le synonyme de l'existence sociale; c'est la souveraineté: mot terrible, mystère profond d'où s'échappent confusément les passions et les ténèbres dont il est plein." Charles Guillaume Hello, *Philosophie de l'histoire de France* (Paris, 1840), p. 117. On Hello, see Christian Chêne, "L'histoire du droit par la biographie selon Charles Guillaume Hello et sa *Philosophie de l'histoire de France*," in *Histoire de l'histoire du droit*, ed. Jacques Poumarède (Toulouse, Presses de l'Université des Sciences Sociales de Toulouse, 2006), pp. 133–43.

of smaller dominations into their larger dominations until they had come to
rule much of the world. In doing so, Hello wrote, they established an empire
that might well have had the beneficial effect of preventing smaller dominations
from fighting one another to death. But neither the Greeks nor the Romans had
the one principle compatible with even the most humble of cities because it
could make it equal to the most powerful of empires. This was what the principle of sovereignty could do.

The idea that the concept of sovereignty was not coterminous with the
concept of the state has disappeared almost entirely from the history and historiography of political thought.[70] According to Hello, however, neither the
Greeks nor the Romans had a word for the concept. Although there was ample
evidence of their joint familiarity with the language of the law of nations, they
did not construe that language in terms of a concept of sovereignty or identify
its meaning as reciprocal national independence. For them, the law of nations
had only one source, and that source was usually Rome. "The Greek and
Roman languages," Hello observed, "abound in synonyms for the word 'empire' and, generally, for the actions of those who command on those who obey,
but they have no more than circumlocutions to express sovereignty. Antiquity
did not create a sign for an idea that it did not have. It was Italy in the Middle
Ages, the classical terrain of spiritual power, that, in the middle of the convulsions of its independence, gave modern politics this new word (*sovranezza*)
for a new idea."[71] In part, this was because papal power had none of the substance of Roman power. Since it was not simply de facto domination, it had,
instead, to be logically and conceptually coherent. Where the Romans were willing to leave peoples to get on with their own affairs, provided that they accepted
Roman domination, the papacy could afford no such latitude. Under papal authority, with its limited physical resources, the concept of sovereign power had
to be construed as an absolute power if it was to be morally and practically
viable. Sovereignty, from this perspective, began as something spiritual, not

---

70. It is absent, for example, from the otherwise wide-ranging Amnon Lev, *Sovereignty and
Liberty A Study of the Foundations of Power* (London, Routledge, 2014) and its more recent
French translation, *Souveraineté et liberté. Etude sur les fondements du pouvoir* (Paris, Garnier,
2020). See, however, Derek Croxton, "The Peace of Westphalia of 1648 and the Origins of Sovereignty," *International History Review* 21 (1999): 569–91.

71. "Les langues grecque et romaine abondent en synonymies pour exprimer l'empire, et en
général l'action de ceux qui commandent sur ceux qui obéissent, mais elles n'ont que des péri-
phrases pour exprimer la souveraineté. L'antiquité n'a point créé le signe d'une idée qu'elle
n'avait pas. C'est l'Italie du moyen âge, c'est la terre classique de la puissance spirituelle qui, au
milieu des convulsions de son indépendance, a donné à la politique moderne ce mot nouveau
(*sovranezza*) pour une idée nouvelle." Hello, *Philosophie de l'histoire*, pp. 120–21.

imperial. But, as "nations formed, populations established relationships, and social power began to emerge," this more purely spiritual side of the power of the church began to dissolve. Gradually, the balance between spiritual and temporal power tilted towards the latter, and the modern concept of sovereignty began to emerge.[72]

This, Hello emphasized, meant that the concept of sovereignty was far more recent in origin than was usually assumed. "We read in our books," he wrote, "that sovereignty is a generative, primary, idea and that its power is the greatest of all. It takes precedence over—and dominates—all others and, once it begins to act, all other powers shrink before it."[73] On this interpretation, bringing sovereignty into play was to introduce the possibility of reverting to ground zero. But if sovereignty was simply a result of the social state, it could never destroy anything essential without undermining the cause of its own existence and effectively condemning itself to commit suicide. There were, therefore, two ways of thinking about the concept of sovereignty. One was in terms of doctrine; the other was in terms of facts. To Hello, the correct approach was to follow the facts. As, he wrote, the political organization of the French monarchy had grown in scale and scope, it had become increasingly economically and socially integrated, and this in turn had added a further measure of legitimacy to the legality of royal legislation. Royal rights clashed with papal rights, with both invoking sovereign power and with each asserting that sovereign power had been sent from heaven to earth to either the one or the other. It was left, Hello argued, to an early sixteenth-century theologian named Jacques Almain to break the conceptual deadlock by showing that sovereignty was not an attribute of either monarchs or popes because it was something that travelled directly not only from heaven to earth but also, and more importantly, to nations, not to kings or popes. In making this move, Hello wrote, Almain had revived "the doctrine of the primitive church, motivated by a pure sentiment of the rights of man" (here Hello was referring not only to the authority of an assortment of Christian saints, but also to the more recent pronouncements of the controversial Catholic democrat Félicité de Lamennais). "Thus," he noted, "it was through theology that the notion of popular sovereignty entered into science."[74]

72. "Cependant les nations se formaient; les populations s'étaient mises en rapport; les territoires s'étaient réunis, et, par une conséquence nécessaire, le pouvoir social commençait à poindre." Ibid., p. 123.

73. "Nous lisons dans nos livres que la souveraineté est une idée primitive et génératrice, et que son pouvoir est le plus grand de tous; il précède et domine les autres; dès qu'il se met en action, ils s'anéantissent devant lui." Ibid., p. 140.

74. "C'était un retour à la doctrine de l'église primitive qu'animait un sentiment si pur des droits de l'homme. . . . Ainsi c'est par la théologie que la notion de la souveraineté populaire est

Almain's move, Hello continued, was reinforced by the early seventeenth-century founder of modern natural jurisprudence, Hugo Grotius, and, subsequently, by the combined political thought of the Swiss natural jurist Emer de Vattel and his Genevan contemporary Jean-Jacques Rousseau (Hello described the *Social Contract* as a reworking of Vattel under the aegis of Rousseau's "pitiless logic"). Its outcome, Hello announced, was an important truth. This was that sovereignty had to be seen as "a negative notion." But, he continued, "this negative notion can still be given a very real attribution because if a nation does not depend on anyone, on either the inside or the outside, then who or what does it depend on, if not on itself?"[75] Sovereignty was no more than the state of a nation that did not depend on anyone because it was, simply, independent. This, Hello insisted, was all that the word needed to mean. He drove the point home by telling a story about a hunter in the forests of Ceylon. One day, when out hunting, the hunter had suddenly lost almost all his freedom of movement. He turned to see an enormous snake hissing at him and realized that he was slowly becoming paralyzed by its venomous spray. In desperation, the hunter loaded his gun, shot the snake, and gradually began to recover his freedom of movement. The fable, Hello wrote, was "a symbol of the emancipation of nations. Once the Roman monster was dead, the poison began to lose its effects and nations began to recover their potential for sovereignty. Since antiquity was unaware of the gradual emancipation of human societies, the idea of sovereignty can only be modern."[76]

This negative conception of sovereignty, Hello concluded, was all that history showed. Doctrine (or dogma), however, implied something more. It made sovereignty not only "the simple negation of dependence, but an active

---

entrée dans la science." Ibid., p. 148. In a note on the same page, Hello indicated that he was referring to the "Réponse à la lettre du Père Ventura" that Lamennais published on 12 February 1831: see Félicité de Lamennais, *Œuvres*, 10 vols. (Paris, 1836–37), 10:249–68. On Almain, see Richard Tuck, *Natural Rights Theories* (Cambridge, CUP, 1979), pp. 28–30.

75. "L'enseignement de la souveraineté par l'histoire est d'une nature qu'il faut bien comprendre: il veut qu'on désapprenne, il supprime, il retranche, il démolit; c'est le contraire de la synthèse. . . . il s'arrête et semble nous inviter à ne voir dans la souveraineté qu'une notion négative. Cette notion négative renferme à la vérité une attribution très-réelle; car si une nation ne relève de personne ni au dehors ni au-dedans, de qui peut-elle relever sur la terre, si ce n'est d'elle-même?" Hello, *Philosophie de l'histoire*, pp. 159–60 (see p. 156 for Rousseau's "logique impitoyable").

76. "Cette fable est le symbole de l'affranchissement des nations. Le monstre romain une fois immolé, elles ont vu tomber le fluide et elles ont recouvré leur souveraineté virtuelle. L'antiquité ayant ignoré cet affranchissement successif des sociétés humaines, l'idée de la souveraineté ainsi entendue ne pouvait être que moderne." Hello, Ibid., , p. 161.

power that knows nothing that precedes it, nothing above it, which dies from being at rest and which society exercises constantly upon itself, like a fire that burns continually until it consumes its own source of life." From this perspective, sovereignty was "an all-powerful abstraction made manifest by human deliberations, but which somehow does not need them."[77] In this more extended sense, sovereignty was a radically incoherent concept because it seemed to be a power that somehow could precede and succeed the social state in which it was located. According to Hello this had been Rousseau's concept of sovereignty and, even more than the earlier, more limited versions of the concept, was far too dangerous to be applied positively. Sovereignty was not only modern and, therefore, not Roman; it also had to be negative.

The Federal Alternative

Hello's argument was soon picked up. The word "sovereignty," noted the author of a work entitled *Science des droits, ou idéologie politique* (The science of rights, or political ideology) published in 1844 but quoting an earlier political dictionary, was a derivation of the Italian word *sovranezza*.[78] This gave the word a medieval rather than an ancient origin and placed it firmly in the context of the competing imperial and papal claims to supreme authority. In this version, the modern quality of the concept of sovereignty was a product of the fact that neither the Greeks nor the Romans had used this type of concept because ancient polytheism ruled out the idea of a single, ultimate source of right and power. The point was made quite frequently in nineteenth-century discussions of Rome and its legacy but seems to have largely disappeared from later historical literature.[79] But the problem with the modern quality of the

77. "La doctrine en a fait, non pas la simple négation de la dépendance, mais une puissance active, qui ne connait rien avant elle, rien au-dessus d'elle, que le repos tue, et que la société exerce incessamment sur elle-même: feu qui brûle sans cesse, jusqu'à consumer son principe. . . . D'après les faits, une souveraineté qui préexiste et survit à l'état social ne serait pas intelligible, car un effet ne peut ni précéder sa cause ni durer plus qu'elle. D'après la doctrine, la souveraineté est une abstraction toute-puissante, qui se réalise par les délibérations humaines, mais qui n'a pas besoin d'elles." Ibid., pp. 161–62.

78. "Le mot *souveraineté*, qui n'a d'équivalent que dans le mot italien *sovranezza*, exprime dans son acception la plus étendue la toute-puissance humaine." F. Rittiez, *Science des droits, ou idéologie politique* (Paris, 1844), p. 71 n. 1, quoting J. A. Rogron, *Code politique* [1838] on the etymology of the word.

79. It is not a feature of the best two English-language monographs on, inter alia, the subject of Roman law in the early nineteenth century: see Donald R. Kelley, *Historians and the Law in Post-revolutionary France* (Princeton, NJ, Princeton UP, 1984); James Q. Whitman, *The Legacy*

concept of sovereignty was the fact that there now really was a single final source of right and power. This gave the problem of the relationship between ancient and modern liberty a new and sharper edge. If, as both Sismondi and Constant argued, modern civilization had two origins, the Romans and the Germans, and if modern liberty was supposed to be a synthesis of the public and private, the collective and individual, and, in the end, ancient and modern liberty, then the addition of sovereignty to these overlapping pairs made the problem more complicated. If, as Hello later claimed, sovereignty construed as independence was simply negative, it was not easy to see how to combine this concept of sovereignty with the idea that modern liberty also called for self-development or *perfectionnement*.

For both Constant and Sismondi, the solution to the problem was federal and was connected to the problematic nature of modern liberty. As Sismondi emphasized in all his publications, modern liberty had different origins and attributes from its ancient counterpart. "The first liberal institutions," Sismondi wrote, "were brought from the North to the degenerate Romans." But modern liberty had travelled in the opposite direction. The "liberal principles" on which it was based, Sismondi wrote, had moved as if under the aegis of "an invisible hand" from the South to the North, starting in Italy and Spain in the Middle Ages before proceeding to Switzerland and Germany in the fifteenth and sixteenth centuries and finally to England and France in more recent times. "This inverse movement," Sismondi added, "from the South to the North, in the development of the republican system is a very noticeable and constant phenomenon."[80] This was why the history of the Italian republics in

---

of Roman Law in the German Romantic Era (Princeton, NJ, Princeton UP, 1990). See, however, the study by Blandine Kriegel, *The State and the Rule of Law* [1989] (Princeton, NJ, Princeton UP, 1995), pp. 15–32, as well as her *La politique de la raison*, and, in parallel, J. K. Davies, "On the Non-usability of the Concept of Sovereignty in an Ancient Greek Context," in *Federazioni e federalismo nell' Europa antica*, ed. L. A. Foresti, et al. (Milan, Università Cattolico del Sacro Cuoro, 1994), pp. 51–65; Clifford Ando, *Law, Language and Empire in the Roman Tradition* (Philadelphia, U of Pennsylvania Press, 2011), pp. 69–72; Dean Hammer, *Roman Political Thought: from Cicero to Augustine* (Cambridge, CUP, 2014), pp. 9–10. I am grateful to my colleague Robin Osborne for these latter references. In the early twentieth century the French jurist Léon Michoud could still emphasize that "les jurisconsultes romaines n'ont jamais employé le nom de personne pour désigner l'état en tant que sujet des droits de souveraineté. Pour eux, être une personne, c'était seulement être capable de droits privés tels que les droits patrimoniaux et les droits de famille." Léon Michoud, *La théorie de la personnalité morale et son application au droit français* (Paris, LGDJ, 1906), pp. 21–22.

80. "Le premières institutions libérales avaient été apportées du Nord aux Romains dégénérés. Ce mouvement rétrograde, du midi au nord, est un phénomène constant et très remarquable.

the Middle Ages mattered to posterity. Modern liberty, on Sismondi's terms, had medieval, not ancient origins, just as its original, preclassical, template was not Roman, nor even Greek, but Etruscan. As Sismondi announced at the very beginning of his huge *History of the Italian Republics in the Middle Ages*, government was the primary cause of the character of peoples, and the Etruscan government had been federal. Unlike the Romans, he continued, the Etruscans valued liberty above power and glory. Their government promoted moderation and prized benevolence, not conquest. They were a "free nation" who relied on their "federal bond" both for defence against foreign aggression and as a "guarantee to their own passions from the distraction of ambition and the drunkenness of success."[81] It was a fairly transparent allusion to more recent French imperial policies and the neo-Roman aura used to burnish the image of Napoleon Bonaparte.

On Sismondi's terms, the foundations of modern politics were federal. In part this was because only a federal system was a viable alternative to the unitary territorial states whose rise was responsible both for the demise of the Italian republics of the Middle Ages and for the long cycle of territorial consolidation, state building, and imperial expansion that had culminated in the wars of the French Revolution and the age of Napoleon. In part, too, it was because only a federal system could be compatible with liberty and, at the same time, could accommodate the many different types of inequality that the modern age had inherited from its ancient, feudal, and republican pasts. Although, as Sismondi

---

En Italie, nous avons vu Naples, Gaète, Amalfi, et même Rome, précéder toutes les autres villes. . . . Cependant les villes de l'Allemagne et de la Suisse ne commencèrent à connaitre la liberté que dans les dernières années du douzième siècle, celles de la France et de l'Angleterre acquirent plus tard encore les droits des communautés." Sismondi, *Histoire*, 1:416–17.

81. Ibid., 1:ii–iv. For initial ways in to late eighteenth-century Etruscan studies, see Arnaldo Momigliano, "Ancient History and the Antiquarian," *Journal of the Warburg and Courtauld Institutes* 13 (1950): 285–315; Otto Wilhelm von Vacano, *The Etruscans in the Ancient World* (London, Edward Arnold, 1960), pp. 177–84; Melissa Calaresu, "Images of Ancient Rome in Late Eighteenth-Century Neapolitan Historiography," *Journal of the History of Ideas* 58 (1997): 641–61; and Axel Körner, *Politics of Culture in Liberal Italy* (London, Routledge, 2009), pp. 128–60. On the Etruscans in nineteenth-century thought, see the fascinating studies by Antonino De Francisco, *The Antiquity of the Italian Nation: The Cultural Origins of a Political Myth in Modern Italy, 1796–1943* (Oxford, OUP, 2013), and Katia Visconti, "Italian Celticisms: A Second (Unpublished) Version of Giovanni Fabbroni's *Antichi Abitatori d'Italia* (1803)," in *In Search of Pre-Classical Antiquity: Rediscovering Ancient Peoples in Mediterranean Europe (19th and 20th Centuries)*, ed. Antonino De Francesco (Leiden, Brill, 2017), pp. 19–40, together with the essays in William M. Calder III and Renate Schlesier, eds., *Zwischen Rationalismus und Romantik. Karl Otfried Müller und die Antike Kultur* (Hildesheim, Weidmann, 1998).

emphasized, the first Italian republics were federal in character, neither the Etruscan confederation nor later political associations like the Lombard League were truly federal systems of government. In a sense, the whole history of the Italian republics in the Middle Ages was a graphic illustration of the difficulties involved in establishing a genuinely federal constitution. This, Sismondi argued, was because "the concept of a federal constitution is one of the most refined and most abstract ideas that the study of political combinations has been able to produce." It was, therefore, hardly surprising that "peoples who were barely civilized"—as had been the case with the members of the Lombard League—had not been able to establish something corresponding to "the idea that we form of a federal republic, whose central government manages external relations and maintains dignity."[82]

It was this separation of external from internal affairs that Sismondi took to be the hallmark of a truly federal constitution. In this type of system, the initial properties of small-scale republics—their "democratic liberty," patriotism, and capacity for "enthusiasm" on the one side, and their proficiency in the arts and commercial resourcefulness on the other—would be reinforced by a permanent central government with sole responsibility for managing a purely defensive foreign policy. "If one follows the history of every federation," Sismondi observed, "there is not one that was not born when it was essential to repel an oppressor's attack and not one that did not triumph over an adversary equipped with infinitely superior numbers and strength. The kings of Macedonia were defeated by the Achaeans, the duke of Austria by the Swiss, Philip of Spain by the Dutch, and George III by the Americans." Federations were born when free peoples faced foreign invaders. "There, where liberty reigns, is love of country the great principle of strength. Never is this love more passionate; never does it move the soul more profoundly than when the fatherland is enclosed within tight limits and the boundaries of the same walls display the cradle of your childhood before your eyes." This was the setting in which "enthusiasm, whose power is far superior to that of a government, however strong it takes itself to be, unites separate states and supplies a centre of action, a centre of power, to a cluster of republics usually depicted as being so weak."[83]

82. Sismondi, *Histoire*, 2:187.

83. "C'est une circonstance singulièrement favorable pour constituer un gouvernement fédératif, que celle où une invasion redoutable menace un peuple libre. Là où règne la liberté, le grand principe de force, c'est l'amour de la patrie; et jamais cet amour n'est si passionnée, jamais il remue l'âme plus profondément, que lorsque la patrie elle-même est renfermée dans d'étroites limites. . . . Il faut se défendre, il faut vaincre, il faut repousser l'invasion, il faut briser le joug du despotisme; l'enthousiasme, dont la puissance est bien supérieur à celle d'un gouvernement, quelque forte qu'il prétende être, unit les états séparées, et donne un centre d'action, un centre

Sismondi repeated the claim a generation later in his *Etudes sur les constitutions des peuples libres*. On their own, he wrote, republics were "naturally bellicose." Federal states, on the other hand, usually lacked the potentially unlimited capacity for command associated with a powerful central authority because of the discussions and divisions among their members and the resulting weakness of their capacity for executive action. Federal systems were, therefore, primarily defensive.[84] The lack of unity at the centre, coupled with the intensity of local patriotic allegiance to their constituent parts, made them particularly suitable vehicles for self-preservation.

A federal state, and a matching federal system of government, limited the risks of both centralized and decentralized power. Centralized power, particularly if it involved a royal government and a capital city, magnified the dangers of political conflict and raised the level of risk associated with botched economic or social reform. If a centralized government were to fail, everything could fail. Decentralized government on the other hand, particularly when it was accompanied by democratic decision making, magnified the dangers of political division and increased the risk that economic and social inequalities would ossify into rigidly stratified, but still nominally democratic, majorities and minorities. If a decentralizedd government were to fail, democratic decision making could become civil war. A federal system, Sismondi argued, both in his early history of the Italian republics and in his late *Etudes sur les constitutions des peuples libres* of 1836, contained enough of a mixture of centralization and decentralization to limit both types of risk. As he wrote in the latter work, the most important constituent element of a federal system was a municipality or *commune* because it could become the type of intermediate agency that would establish the difference between a representative sovereign state on the one hand and a democracy on the other.[85]

---

de puissance à cet assemblage de républiques qu'on représente comme si faible. . . . Que l'on parcoure l'histoire de toutes les fédérations, on n'en trouve pas une qui ne soit née au moment où il fallait repousser l'attaque d'un oppresseur; pas une qui n'ait triomphé d'adversaires infiniment supérieurs en nombre et en forces. Les rois de Macédoine furent vaincus par les Achéens, le duc d'Autriche par les Suisses, Philippe d'Espagne par les Hollandais, George III par les Américains." Ibid., 2:184–86.

84. Jean-Charles-Léonard Simonde de Sismondi, *Etudes sur les constitutions des peuples libres* [Paris, 1836] (Brussels, 1839), pp. 292–93, 297.

85. "Qu'on ne cherche point dans les essais qui suivent, ces règles générales d'après lesquelles tant de jeunes gens, à peine sortis de l'université, se sont crus en état de donner à leur pays, à tous les pays, des constitutions. . . . Nous disons avant tout: Etudiez les faits, les circonstances, l'esprit du peuple et ses souvenirs; puis passant en revue l'élément démocratique, le monarchique, l'aristocratique, nous avons cherché ce qu'on pouvait attendre, ce qu'on pouvait craindre

As Sismondi described it, a federal system would be like an artificial version of Montesquieu's concept of monarchy, but with an elected, institutional hierarchy instead of a property-based, social hierarchy. A federal system would consist of a network of de facto political institutions whose relatively small size and social integration made them suitable settings for collective decision making and collective action. Inversely, however, a federal system would also contain a network of national or federal officials whose existence would give a local presence to the central government. Since these officials would be accountable to the central rather than the local government, they would give the network of municipalities a framework that would keep the network itself intact.[86] Part of the point of Sismondi's history of the Italian republics was that their internal and external arrangements had not been designed, either by a constitutional theorist or by a constituent assembly. From this perspective, republican history was also civic history because it could supply a broader and more varied range of examples and arrangements than any more considered process of constitutional design. "We have nothing to say," Sismondi wrote a generation later in his *Etudes sur les constitutions des peuples libres*, "about the constitutions of these federations; chance almost as much as necessity will lead them to be born and will dictate the conditions of the association."

> The social elements, the indestructible elements, will, as has been said, be the municipalities. But we should not conclude from this that confederations will consist only of towns or communes. Local interests, economic relationships, shared laws, religion, language, manners, and, above all, the history and memory of past glories give a gathering of men or population the feeling that they form a single people. That people can be large or small; it can be contained in a valley, like the Uri, or in a town, like Basel, or

de l'emploi de chacun. . . . C'est alors qu'une seule nous a paru sûre, la fédération; car lorsque l'ordre social a éprouvé une de ces convulsions violentes qui détruisent l'habitude de l'obéissance et du commandement, qui font disparaitre pour chacun l'idée du droit et de la légitimité du pouvoir, il y a guère que la commune qui recouvre sa vitalité, et ce n'est guère que les hommes qui se connaissent, et qui se confient les uns dans les autres, qui peuvent aussi poser les bases d'un nouveau pouvoir social." Ibid., pp. 31–32 (see too pp. 279–80, 290–91).

86. "Une des conséquences de la réunion d'un grand nombre de communes en une seule nation, c'est que la décision de ces communes ne peut plus être définitive. Au sein de chacune d'elles doit se trouver toujours le représentant de l'autorité centrale, pour que l'intérêt du tout national ne soit jamais sacrifié à celui de ses parties. Le maire du prince peut être ou ne pas être le même personnage que le maire du peuple; mais la présence du maire du prince, son autorité et l'intervention continuelle du pouvoir central dans le pouvoir communal, sont nécessaires pour qu'il y ait identité de législation, d'administration, de droits, d'une extrémité de l'empire a l'autre." Ibid., pp. 82–83.

occupy a powerful district, like Berne, or a duchy like the Italian states, or a kingdom, like Spain. All that it needs is life, unity, political organization, love of its independence, and individuality to be fit to become a member of a confederation. The tendency in every civilization is to unite and if there was to be a confederation today, it would be made up of states that are far more considerable than those that formed alliances in the Middle Ages. But this should still mean no symmetry, no rounding up of one state at the expense of another and no ambition to make states for the union rather than make the union for the states.[87]

Only later, once it had come into being, would the various members of the federation, "applying the principles of social science to themselves," begin to adjust their different internal arrangements and, as Sismondi put it, "try to balance its constitution in order to set the preservation of every interest in harmony with the rights of all."[88] In this sense, the initial, externally oriented, union that was the original feature of a federal system would gradually give way to something more integrated, even if the primary distinction between the external responsibilities of the federation and the internal responsibilities of its constituent parts would remain intact.

A further aspect of this type of system was its capacity to house both a government and an opposition. This aspect of modern politics was one of the most prominent features of the final, analytical, part of Germaine de Staël's *Considerations on the Principal Events of the French Revolution*, which was published a year after her death in 1817. The coexistence of government and opposition, she wrote

---

87. "Nous n'avons rien à dire sur la constitution de ces fédérations; le hasard presque autant que le besoin les fera naitre, et dictera les conditions de l'association. Les éléments sociaux, les éléments indestructibles, avons-nous dit, sont dans les municipalités; nous n'en concluons point cependant qu'il n'y ait de confédérations que celles des villes ou des communes. Des intérêts locaux, des rapports économiques, la communauté de lois, de religion, de langage, de mœurs, mais surtout l'histoire et ses souvenirs, et la gloire passée, donnent à un assemblage d'hommes ou de populations le sentiment qu'ils forment un seul peuple. Ce peuple peut être grand ou petit, il peut être contenu dans une vallée, comme celui d'Ury, ou dans une ville comme celui de Bâle, ou occuper un district puissant comme celui de Berne, ou un duché comme les états d'Italie, ou un royaume comme ceux de l'Espagne. Il suffit qu'il ait vie, unité, organisation politique, amour de son indépendance et de son individualité, pour qu'il soit propre à devenir membre d'une confédération. La tendance de toute civilisation est de réunir, et s'il se formait aujourd'hui une confédération, elle se composerait d'états bien plus considérables que ne l'étaient ceux qui s'alliaient au moyen âge. Seulement point de symétrie, point d'arrondissement des uns aux dépens des autres, point de prétention à faire les états pour l'union, au lieu de faire l'union pour les états." Ibid., pp. 297–98.

88. Ibid., p. 298.

there, helped to offset the otherwise centralized character of modern British politics. "Party loyalty," she explained, "is one of the virtues based on public spirit which give rise to the greatest advantages to English liberty." It was the source of both a stable government and a stable opposition because the moral pressures generated by party loyalty ruled out the more extravagant forms of political opportunism, quest for place, and factional intrigue associated with more centralized systems of rule. "Never do you hear the same mouth," Staël wrote, "give utterance to two opposite opinions; and yet in the existing state of things in England, the differences lie in shades, not colours. The Tories, it has been said, approve of liberty and love monarchy, while the Whigs approve of monarchy and love liberty. But between these two parties, no question could arise about a republican or regal form of government, about the old or the new dynasty, liberty or servitude or, in short, about any of those extremes and contrasts which we have seen professed by the same men in France, as if we ought to say of power as of love that the object is of no consequences provided one be always faithful to the sentiment, that is to devotion to power."[89] Party loyalty offset both the attractions of power and the rewards of power. On Staël's terms, it made decentralized power compatible with devotion to power.

These assessments of the compatibility between party politics and federal government were matched by Constant's. For Constant, as with Sismondi, the key component was the municipality or commune. "Even in those states that have been in existence for a long time," he wrote in 1814 in his anti-Napoleonic pamphlet *Of the Spirit of Conquest and Usurpation and Their Relation to European Civilization*, "and whose unification has lost the odium of violence and conquest, we can identify the patriotism that springs from local differences, the only genuine patriotism, reborn from its own ashes as soon as the hand of power loosens its grip for a moment."

> The magistrates of the smallest communes pride themselves on embellishing them. They keep up their ancient monuments with care. There is, in almost every village, some erudite man who likes to retell its rustic annals and who is listened to with respect. The inhabitants enjoy everything that gives them the appearance, even if deceptive, of forming a nation and of being united by particular ties.[90]

89. Germaine de Staël, *Considerations on the Principal Events of the French Revolution* [1818], ed. Aurelian Craiutu (Indianapolis, IN, Liberty Fund, 2008), pp. 666–67 (I have slightly modified the translation in the light of the 1983 French edition, edited by Jacques Godechot). On the broader subject of party politics, see William Selinger, *Parliamentarism: From Burke to Weber* (Cambridge, CUP, 2019).

90. Benjamin Constant, "Of the Spirit of Conquest and Usurpation and Their Relation to European Civilization," in Constant, *Political Writings*, p. 76.

As Constant had written in the larger, but unpublished, *Principles of Politics* from which he extracted this passage, patriotism of this kind had to be the basis of "the kind of federalism which seems to me useful and possible to establish among us."[91] Without this type of civic involvement, Constant warned, the combination of centralized government, individual self-interest, and the purely negative liberty of the moderns would lead individuals to "detach themselves from a fatherland they can nowhere see." Patriotism required a *patrie*, and it was this local and regional patriotism that had to be the basis of a new type of federal system. "Variety," Constant concluded flatly, "is what constitutes organization; uniformity is mere mechanism. Variety is life; uniformity death."[92]

On Constant's terms, keeping variety alive called for more than purely negative liberty. Over the years, a great deal of significance has come to be attributed both to the adjective and to the broader distinction between positive and negative liberty indicated by one or other of the two adjectives.[93] In English, however, either of the two adjectives could go together with the words "liberty" or "freedom." In French, however, there is only one word, *liberté*, to refer to the condition or capacity designated by the two English nouns. In English, free cities or free states could still have "liberties" because a liberty, as in one of the liberties of eighteenth-century London, lay outside the ordinary provisions of the law. In this light, any French-language distinction between different types of liberty seems to require a qualifying adjective, and, since Constant and Sismondi were, in very similar ways, making a case for the coexistence of what, in English, could be described by two different words, the case in question called for an initial distinction between *liberté négative* and *liberté positive*. In French (and German) putting together the negative and positive variants of liberty gave rise to something nominally different from either because the Kant-inspired name that came to be given to the resulting condition or capacity was "autonomy." As with the idea of a fusion of negative and positive liberty, autonomy presupposed self-direction, nondomination, and independent choice. But it also presupposed some sort of individual and collective ability to manage gendered distinctions, divisions of labour, economic inequality, public law, private law, financial institutions, and political power.

---

91. Constant, *Political Writings*, p. 254.

92. Ibid., pp. 76–77. See too the final part of Constant's lecture "Liberty," in ibid., p. 326: "The danger of modern liberty is that, absorbed in the enjoyment of our private independence, and in the pursuit of our particular interests, we should too easily surrender our right to share in political power."

93. For a helpful recent overview, see Alan Ryan, "Isaiah Berlin: Contested Conceptions of Liberty and Liberalism," in *The Cambridge Companion to Isaiah Berlin*, ed. Joshua L. Cherniss and Steven B. Smith (Cambridge, CUP, 2018), pp. 212–28.

From this perspective, thinking about the coexistence of a French-language (or Latinate) distinction between two adjectives was a rather less significant problem than thinking about the type of state that could accommodate the substantive economic, social, and political conditions associated with both. This was the real problem that lay at the centre of the Coppet group's moral and political concerns and, as the next chapter aims to show, was also the subject that lay at the heart of the long epistolary friendship between Germaine de Staël and Wilhelm von Humboldt.

4

Germaine de Staël
and Modern Politics

Germaine de Staël and Wilhelm von Humboldt

The problem of combining negative and positive liberty under modern conditions lay at the heart of the Coppet group's moral and political concerns. Just as the division of labour could be seen as either a springboard or an obstacle to self-development, or *perfectionnement*, the same type of problem applied to the idea of a federal system of government. The combination of the local and the national housed by a federal system could either provide the motivation for civic involvement or could simply magnify atomistic indifference. The two problems converged in a long epistolary conversation between Germaine de Staël, the Coppet group's most famous member, and one of her many German acquaintances and interlocutors, the founder of the University of Berlin, Wilhelm von Humboldt. That conversation began towards the end of the eighteenth century, when Humboldt, who was then living in Paris, published a French-language summary of an essay on Goethe's poetic drama *Hermann und Dorothea*, which he had earlier written in German. As Humboldt informed Goethe in 1800 soon after the essay appeared, it had been written especially for Germaine de Staël and "some others" to make them more aware of the discussions of morality, culture, and politics that had been taking place in the German-speaking parts of Europe during the previous two decades. Both its content and the date of its publication make the essay, published in the final issue of the Parisian *Magasin encyclopédique* of 1799 under the title of *Essais esthétiques de M. Guillaume de Humboldt* (Aesthetic essays of M. Guillaume von Humboldt), a helpful place to recapitulate the problems generated both by the combination of the division of labour, the social question, and the moral and institutional foundations of modern political societies, and by the question of how they could meet the challenge of Kant's philosophy of history.[1]

Humboldt's essay centred on the subject and concept of the imagination. It was, he began, "the domain of the poet," and, since it was distinct from both the senses and the analytical powers of the mind, it could not rely on either experience or analysis to communicate its content. Sights or sounds could be seen or heard, while analysis could follow the steps supplied by its own internal rational logic. The imagination, however, could not use any built-in sensory or analytical guidance. This, Humboldt explained, was why it had to rely on something else to make its content apparent. This was the emotion of enthusiasm. "Only enthusiasm," Humboldt wrote, "is able to awaken and master the imagination and this is what the poet has to inspire."[2] Enthusiasm, he also noted, could make the imagination spring to life more readily in

---

1. On the Staël-Humboldt relationship, see, most fully, the series of publications by Kurt Müller-Vollmer, starting with his *Poesie und Einbildungskraft. Zur Dichtungstheorie Wilhelm von Humboldts, Mit der zweisprachigen Ausgabe eines Aufsatzes Humboldts für Frau von Staël* (Stuttgart, J. B. Metzlersche Verlagsbuchhandlung, 1967), which reprints Humboldt's *Magasin encyclopédique* essay and, on p. 214, quotes Humboldt's letter to Goethe of 30 May 1800 describing the essay as a "French-language dissertation that I wrote to make the main ideas in my German book known to Madame de Staël and some others." See too his "Politique et esthétique: l'idéalisme concret de Constant, Humboldt et Madame de Staël," in *Benjamin Constant, Madame de Staël et le groupe de Coppet* (Oxford, Voltaire Foundation, 1982), pp. 453–73; "Guillaume de Humboldt, interprète de Madame de Staël: distances et affinités," *Cahiers Staëliens* 37 (1985–86): 80–96; "On Germany: Madame de Staël and the Internationalization of Romanticism," in *The Spirit of Poetry: Essays on Jewish and German Literature and Thought in Honor of Géza von Molnár*, ed. Richard Block and Peter Fenves (Evanston, IL, Northwestern UP, 2000), pp. 150–66. Curiously, neither Staël's correspondence with Humboldt nor Müller-Vollmer's pioneering research has been fully recognized by more recent Staël scholars, probably because the modern edition of her correspondence (Madame de Staël, *Correspondance générale*, ed. Beatrice W. Jasinski et al., 9 vols. [Paris and Geneva, 1962–2017]) contains the letters that she *sent*, but not those that she *received*. See, however, Axel Blaeschke, "Uber Individual- und Nationalcharakter, Zeitgeist und Poesie," in *Germaine de Staël und ihr erstes deutsches Publikum*, ed. Gerhard R. Kaiser and Olaf Müller (Heidelberg, Universitätsverlag Winter, 2008), pp. 145–61; Ian Allan Henning, *L'Allemagne de Mme de Staël et la polémique romantique* (Paris, Champion, 1929), pp. 239–40; and John Clairborne Isbell, *The Birth of European Romanticism: Truth and Propaganda in Staël's De l'Allemagne* (Cambridge, CUP, 1994), pp. 152–59. On Humboldt and his French connections, see Paul R. Sweet, "Wilhelm von Humboldt, Fichte, and the Ideologues (1794–1805): A Re-Examination," *Historiographia Linguistica* 15 (1988): 349–75. See too Sarah Bösch, *Wilhelm von Humboldt in Frankreich. Studien zur Rezeption (1797–2005)* (Paderborn, Ferdinand Schöningh, 2006), pp. 43–48.

2. Müller-Vollmer, *Poesie und Einbildungskraft*, pp. 120, 126.

circumstances in which a common language or shared way of life provided an initial level of familiarity. It was hard, Humboldt commented, to discover a new or interesting idea in another language, or find ways to express something in a different language in moments of strong emotion or pain. In this sense, the imagination was both responsive to the wider environment but, importantly, was also never entirely limited by it. It could turn general ideas into particular feelings and make something single and composite out of something multiple and separate. Its most "essential property," however, was its capacity "to push back the limits of space and time," either by transferring things to different times and places or, second, by rearranging their component parts to form different types of object or, third, by disassociating them from the limits and constraints to which they were usually subject. It could, in short, turn the real into the ideal by replacing an object of nature by an object of art. "Art," Humboldt wrote, "is a talent to represent nature by the free and independent action of the imagination alone."[3]

The primacy of the imagination meant the primacy of form in the objects it created. As Humboldt put it flatly, the "essential in art is form."[4] Since an art object has no real existence, its ideal existence depended almost entirely on the artist's skill in giving its component parts a distinct form. "In the tight mutual union that reigns in works of art," Humboldt explained, "each object depends on the other; the ideas of ends and means become blurred because both apply to each element; the parts constitute the whole and the details are connected to the totality."[5] Forms were either *plastic*, as in ancient sculpture, and were directly accessible to the senses, or were *musical* and, like music itself, could be both a sound and a sign of something more than the sound, like an image, a memory, or an emotion. This dual quality—a development of the distinction between the spatial properties of imagery and the temporal properties of sounds made by Jean-Jacques Rousseau in his *Essay on the Origin of Languages*—was the hallmark of the modern poetic art. Since musical form referred to two states rather than one, it gave this type of experience a reflexive quality that was not restricted to music. It enabled modern art to have an inward- rather than an outward-looking orientation, and this shift in orientation could then allow modern creativity to match the unity and power of its ancient counterparts despite the division and fragmentation of modern life. "If modern nations possess a real advantage over the ancients," Humboldt wrote, "it has been only by dividing their occupations more carefully and by increasingly

3. Ibid., pp. 128, 130, 164.
4. Ibid., p. 180.
5. Ibid., p. 170.

isolating the intellectual faculties that they have thus acquired."[6] Although depth had replaced breadth, with an attendant loss of wholeness, modern art could overcome this obstacle by focusing on particular subjects in close-wrought detail, as Goethe had done in his *Werther* with its dispassionate but humane examination of the sequence of psychological states that had led to its eponymous protagonist's suicide. The switch from the exterior to the interior that this examination required made it, like Goethe's later *Hermann und Dorothea*, the modern equivalent of Homer's epics. Instead of bringing art into alignment with nature, the "great poet" of the modern age had relied on his imagination to raise nature to the level of art.[7]

Humboldt repeated the claim that the switch from an externally generated unity to one that could be generated internally and imaginatively was one of the hallmarks of the modern age in an unpublished essay on the eighteenth century that he wrote during his time in Paris. "The sensitive student of antiquity," he wrote there, "filled with pleased and delighted astonishment at the harmonious development of every capacity, the noble freedom of thought, disdain for vile occupations, noble leisure, and the high esteem in which the Greeks held the human soul"—

> this same student would also observe, not without shame and sadness, that among us each individual is happy simply to develop his own dispositions without interesting himself in others; freedom of thought tolerates a multiplicity of chains; laborious occupations take up a large part of our lives; and often we subordinate the development of our internal capabilities to our external activities.

Faced with this reality, a "sensitive student" could be tempted to want to return to a happier age. But if, Humboldt pointed out, he was to examine how the human mind develops in stages, he would discover that the separate deployment of individual aptitudes allowed mankind to move from a unity of character deriving solely from the imagination and feeling to true perfection mediated by reason.[8] The essay was never published, perhaps because it added very little

6. Ibid., p. 200

7. Ibid., pp. 204, 206. On this aspect of Humboldt's essay, see Michel Espagne, "Humboldt à Paris, lecteur de Goethe," *Revue Germanique Internationale* 12 (1999): 195–209.

8. "Le connaisseur sensible de l'antiquité que remplissent d'un étonnement ravi et admiratif le développement harmonieux de toutes les forces, la noble liberté des esprits, le mépris de toutes les occupations viles, le noble loisir, la haute estime, enfin, dans laquelle les Grecs tenaient l'âme de l'homme, ce connaisseur remarquera, non sans en éprouver honte et tristesse, que, chez nous, chacun se content de développer ses propres dispositions sans s'intéresser à autrui, que la liberté de l'esprit tolère maintes chaines, que de laborieuses occupations re-

to what Humboldt's contemporary Friedrich Schiller had already said, or because, at least in this respect, it also covered much the same ground as Schleiermacher had done in his *Monologen*.

Humboldt's account of the unity of the ideal as an antidote to the divisions of the real paralleled, if it did not directly inspire, the analytical and historical framework of Germaine de Staël's first major publication, her *De la littérature* of 1800. The framework that she established had three major components. The first, which grew out of the ideal-real couple, was a version of Rousseau's concept of perfectibility that, Staël emphasized, was the basis of the whole argument of *De la littérature* and, later, formed the normative principle underlying Constant's lecture on ancient and modern liberty. For Germaine de Staël, the concept of perfectibility was the key to understanding the relationship between both ancient and modern and positive and negative liberty. Her version of the concept began with the idea of the double origin of modern culture that Sismondi was later to popularize and with the corresponding mixture of the ideal and the real that, as in Humboldt's essay, made it possible to measure the distance between the ancients and the moderns. Perfectibility itself, Staël emphasized, simply meant that "the mass of ideas of all kinds increases with the centuries." The "system of human perfectibility," she added, had been endorsed over the previous fifty years by philosophers living under every type of government: by Adam Ferguson under the "free monarchy" of Great Britain; by Immanuel Kant under the "still-feudal government" of Germany; by the French reforming minister Etienne Turgot under "the arbitrary, but moderate government" of Louis XVI; and by the Girondin political leader Nicolas Condorcet, even under the "bloody tyranny" that was the despair of the French republic.[9] What made it a system, however, was more than the growing mass

tranchent de nos vies une grande partie, que bien souvent, enfin, nous subordonnons le développement de nos capacités intérieures à notre activité extérieure. En proie aux emportements d'une noble ardeur, il maudira cette tendance propre à notre époque, et souhaitera le retour d'un âge plus heureux. Mais s'il examine comment l'esprit de l'homme se développé par étapes, il découvrira que l'éploiement particulier des forces individuelles permet à l'homme de passer d'une unité de caractère ne relevant que de l'imagination et du sentiment, à la vraie perfection que médiatise la raison." Wilhelm von Humboldt, *Le dix-huitième siècle*, ed. Jean Quillien, trans. Christophe Losfeld (Lille, PU de Lille, 1995), pp. 45–46.

9. "Premièrement, en parlant de la perfectibilité de l'esprit humain, je ne prétends pas dire que les modernes ont une puissance d'esprit plus grand que celle des anciens, mais seulement que la masse des idées en tout genre s'augmente avec les siècles." Germaine de Staël, *De la littérature* [1800], ed. Gérard Gengembre and Jean Goldzink (Paris, Flammarion, 1991), pp. 59 n.*, 60. On Staël, literature, and perfectibility, see Florence Lotterie, "L'année 1800—Perfectibilité, progrès et révolution dans *De la littérature* de Mme de Staël," *Romantisme*

of ideas. New ideas, particularly in the sciences, implied new powers, and new powers increased humanity's destructive capabilities. This, Staël argued, was why "progress in the sciences also makes moral progress necessary because the increase in man's powers makes it necessary to reinforce the brakes preventing him from abusing them." The same reflexive mechanism also applied to politics because the dynamics of international competition tended to force governments to pay more attention to public opinion when they began to compete with nations in which enlightenment was becoming more widespread. Without the concept of perfectibility, Staël argued, morality would not be able to trump moral relativism.[10]

Perfectibility, in this sense, was the other side of reflexivity and, by extension, the other side too of what Staël singled out as a peculiarly modern emotion, the feeling of melancholy.[11] It was her equivalent of Friedrich Schiller's distinction between naïve and sentimental poetry. Although, Staël wrote, melancholy could be found both in the ancient world and among the northern peoples responsible for the fall of the Roman Empire, the ancient emotion was still less complex than its modern counterpart. In its modern guise, melancholy was connected to feelings that were internally generated, and it was this internal dimension that set the modern version of the emotion apart from its ancient predecessors. Among the Greeks, Staël wrote, melancholy was bound up with the senses and, in particular, with an awareness that nothing can last forever. Summer turns to winter, just as youth gives way to age and beauty becomes frailty. Among the northern peoples too, melancholy was also externally generated, although it was now the uniformity and continuity of the dark northern environment rather than the variety and impermanence of its southern counterpart that were the initial sources of the emotion. Among the moderns, however, melancholy was connected most powerfully to what could be imagined rather than to what was real—to another life, another love, or another future. In moral terms, it could be associated with the glimpses of lost

---

108 (2000): 9–22, and her "Madame de Staël. La littérature comme 'philosophie sensible,'" *Romantisme* 124 (2004): 19–30.

10. "Je dirai plus, les progrès des sciences rendent nécessaires les progrès de la morale; car, en augmentant la puissance de l'homme, il faut fortifier le frein qui l'empêche d'en abuser. Les progrès de la science rendent nécessaires aussi les progrès de la politique. L'on a besoin d'un gouvernement plus éclairé, qui respecte davantage l'opinion publique au milieu des nations où les lumières s'étendent chaque jour." Staël, *De la littérature*, pp. 62, 410 (for the point about morality and moral relativism).

11. On melancholy in de Staël's thought, see Anne Amend-Sochting, *Zwischen 'Implosion' und 'Explosion': zur Dynamik der Melancholie im Werk der Germaine de Staël* (Trier, Wissenschaftlicher Verlag Trier, 1991).

opportunities and missed possibilities that were products of the ordinary capacity for choice, a capacity available to everyone, rather than with the more
humanly demanding and rare capacities involved in ancient Stoic courage and
endurance.[12] Melancholy, in short, supplied the motivation for the ordinary
heroism of the moderns. Much of the argument of De la littérature was a development of this idea. It meant that the emphasis in Staël's version of perfectibility fell as much on the qualitative as on the quantitative side of the concept
of perfectibility, with as much weight given to personality as to politics, and
as much significance afforded to individual and national character as to economic and political life. The concept was, in short, an earlier and similar version of Constant's notion of self-development or perfectionnement, with the
same emphasis on the relationship between modern liberty and the balance
between both the public and private and between sovereignty and government
that modern liberty required.

In this sense, the argument of De la littérature was designed to form a conceptual bridge between the old French distinction between the ancients and
the moderns and the new German distinction between the classics and the
romantics. The combination of similarities and differences made her book, as
the royalist literary critic Alexandre Vinet later put it, "the prospectus of
romanticism."[13] As much of its content was designed to show, the differences
between the two pairings arose directly from the normative premises that
formed the second major component of the book's broad framework. In the
seventeenth-century debates over the ancients and moderns, both sides of
the argument attributed normativity to the ancients (so that the arguments
were over whether modern arrangements were a realization of, or a deviation
from, ancient norms). But the argument of De la littérature began with an initial emphasis on the normativity of the moderns and, in particular, with a
strong claim about the primacy of the ideal and internal over the real and external in generating the imaginative material from which norms could be
made. The emphasis was not, of course, peculiar to Staël. As her friend Sismondi put it in 1809, love of one's country (patrie) meant binding oneself to
"that more than human entity that our imagination places between God and
man."[14] The idea of an imagined community was not, in short, a late twentieth-
century discovery. It lay at the heart of the large body of German thought that

12. Staël, De la littérature, pp. 402–3.

13. Alexandre Vinet, Etudes sur la littérature française au dix-neuvième siècle, 3 vols. (Paris,
1849–51), 1:76. On Vinet and Staël, see Jean-Marie Roulin, "Alexandre Vinet lecteur de Madame
de Staël," Annales Benjamin Constant 13 (1992): 129–41.

14. Among the virtues, wrote Sismondi, is "la révérence filiale et religieuse qui lie à la patrie,
cet être plus qu'humain, que notre imagination place entre Dieu et les hommes." Sismondi,

Staël's own work paralleled. But it also came to form the basis of the unusual historical vision that formed the third major component of the framework of *De la littérature*.

In many respects, this historical vision was the most original feature of the whole book. It enabled Staël to make two significant moves. The first was to integrate the claim about perfectibility and the normativity of the moderns into a detailed historical examination of the origins and course of the French Revolution. The second was to argue that this historical perspective explained why modern society required a new kind of politics, in which elections, publicity, and public opinion, together with the potentially unremitting questions about character and competence that they brought in their wake, were bound to play a larger part in modern life than had ever been the case in the past. This, Staël went on to argue, was not because modern governments were likely to revert to the democracies of the ancients, but because of the part played by the imagination in the life of the moderns. As Humboldt had explained, the content of the individual imagination was not directly communicable as sense experience. Nor, without an additional measure of understanding, could it be turned into common knowledge by way of a shared reliance on the analytical powers of the human mind. It had, therefore, to rely on enthusiasm to communicate its content, and this in turn meant that form, rather than substance, and conditions, rather than persons, were required to supply both the images and the appearances needed to give a real presence to what otherwise would remain an imperceptible cloud of qualities and abilities. "Enthusiasm," Staël wrote in *De l'Allemagne*, "gives life to what is invisible and interest to what has no immediate action on our comfort in this world."[15] Well before Max Weber adopted the word "charisma" to refer to the other, more emotionally compel-

Histoire, 1:419. For further examples of the same idea, see Geoffrey Cubitt, ed., *Imagining Nations* (Manchester, Manchester UP, 1998).

15. Germaine de Staël, *Germany*, 3 vols. (London, 1814), vol. 3, pt. 4, ch. 11, p. 395. The French original is slightly different: "L'enthousiasme prête à la vie ce qui est invisible et de l'intérêt à ce qui n'a point d'action immédiate sur notre bien-être dans ce monde." Here, and in all subsequent citations of the original, I have followed the variorum edition, namely, Germaine de Staël, *De l'Allemagne*, ed. Jeanne de Pange and Simone Balayé, 5 vols. (Paris, Hachette, 1958–60), 5:200. Henceforth, Staël, *De l'Allemagne*, followed by volume and page numbers. For contemporary responses to *De L'Allemagne*, see Henning, *L'Allemagne de Mme de Staël*, and Eggli, *Le débat romantique en France 1813–16*, pp. 138–240. For a recent examination of many of the same questions, see Richard Ned Lebow, *The Politics and Ethics of Identity: In Search of Ourselves* (Cambridge, CUP, 2012). On Staël and enthusiasm, see Gérard Gengembre, "Le romantisme de Madame de Staël, ou enthousiasme et politique," *Revue d'histoire littéraire de la France* 116 (2016): 69–78.

ling side of the rule-governed politics of modern industrial societies, Germaine de Staël used the concept of enthusiasm to mean much the same thing.

Enthusiasm, the Imagination, and the Nature of Modern Politics

De la littérature was not simply a study of literature, even in the broad, eighteenth-century sense of the word. In keeping with Staël's own description of the book as a study of the relationship between literature and society, its subject matter encompassed literature, philosophy, and history because its substantive aim was to specify the type of literature required—morally, aesthetically, and politically—by the modern age. Staël's starting point was the divisive character of private property. Echoing the ideas of her father, Jacques Necker, she highlighted the greater likelihood of the rotation of wealth under conditions dominated by manufacturing industry and the division of labour as an antidote to the more durably divisive effects of landed property and agriculture. But Staël also focused on the other effects of manufacturing industry and the division of labour and, in particular, the increasingly rigid occupational boundaries and narrowly specialized knowledge that they were likely to entail. The result, she argued, was a damaging interplay between the hopes of a better life that were associated with economic growth and rising prosperity and the real-life experience of daily work in manufacturing industry. The resulting tension between the ideal and the real, Staël argued, was an important prerequisite both to a fuller explanation of the French Revolution and, in the light of this explanation, to a clearer understanding of the nature of modern politics. The link between the two subjects, she went on to claim, was the imagination because it was the imagination that gave an emotional charge both to popular resentment of inequality and to the more positive popular interest in public figures.[16] Once this link was understood, Staël asserted, it was possible to see the French Revolution as a historical turning point of as much significance as the decline and fall of the Roman Empire. The Roman Empire, however, had fallen largely for external reasons, under the weight of the Germanic invasions from the north. Its fall had given rise to the close relationship between property and the right to rule that had been the hallmark

---

16. On this subject, but with less of a focus on these Rousseau-inspired discussions of the politics of the imagination, see Antoine Lilti, *The Invention of Celebrity* [2014] (Cambridge, Polity, 2017). On the imagination, see the secondary literature referred to in Sonenscher, *Jean-Jacques Rousseau*, pp. 86–114, and, for a helpful collection of essays, see Richard T. Gray et al., eds., *Inventions of the Imagination: Romanticism and Beyond* (Seattle, U of Washington Press, 2012).

of the old European regime. As Staël presented it, the French monarchy, on the other hand, had fallen largely for internal reasons, under the impact of the popular insurrections from within. Its fall now promised to break the old relationship between property and power by making personal qualities and electoral politics the hallmarks of the new regime.

The basis of this potential transformation, Staël argued, was the growing tension between the real and the ideal, particularly as they applied to the right to rule. Once, under the feudal system, property, authority, and morality had been fairly closely aligned. Property might really have originated in conquest, but the courage and strength that conquest required were also needed to enforce the rules of trials by combat and, more broadly, to reinforce the power and authority involved in maintaining stability in a warrior society. But once conspicuous consumption began to seep into social hierarchies based on a combination of physical force and inherited status, the nexus of property, authority, and morality began to break down. The rise of absolute government and the centralization of power and patronage magnified the growing discrepancy between ostentation and authority in the first place and between aspirations and experience in the second. As conspicuous consumption grew, so too did the range and number of specialized occupations required to service consumer demand. Knowledge and skill became increasingly narrow, while work itself became more repetitive and routine. Thus while the opportunities available to the propertied and powerful grew, the opposite applied to the growing number of specialized producers of the goods they consumed. These changes in society, Staël argued, were reflected by changes in the content and form of literature. Where the nexus of property, authority, and morality had once favoured either the epic or tragedy, the gradual disintegration of that nexus had come to favour either comedy or satire. Once, Staël wrote, European societies had been home to the works of a Tasso, a Shakespeare, or a Cervantes. France, however, was now home to the works of a Beaumarchais. Satire was particularly damaging to political authority because it arose from and, concurrently, helped to highlight the growing gulf between the real and the ideal. The gulf had opened up at all levels of society. It was visible at the top because of the multiple discrepancies between privilege, wealth, and power on the one side and real ability and talent on the other. It was visible too at the bottom because of the equally obvious discrepancies between the narrowness of ordinary individual life chances and the range of the resources available to society as a whole. The result was the moral and political void that came to be filled by the events of the French Revolution.

"Ridicule," Staël wrote in *De la littérature*, "is in many respects an aristocratic power. The more there are ranks in society, the more relations between them are supposed to be correct and the greater is the need to know and respect them. In the higher classes certain customs come to be established; certain laws of politeness and elegance serve, so to speak, as signs of allegiance, and to be ignorant of them seems to reveal different manners and membership of a different society. Those who form the upper classes, having at their disposal all the favours of the state, must necessarily have a great empire over public opinion because, apart from a very small number of occasions, power is usually held to be in good taste, credit is accepted with good grace, and those favoured by fortune are well loved."[17] This, she went on to explain, was why the culture of appearances and a disabused insight into its social and emotional demands were among the most prominent themes in French literature during the two previous centuries. It was also, she emphasized, one of the reasons why it had been so difficult to establish political stability in France after 1789. The same argument reappeared in an examination of French literature of the eighteenth century published by one of her protégés, Prosper de Barante, in 1810. "Whoever undertakes a history of vanity in France," he wrote, "would discover a large proportion of the causes of the revolution that France has experienced."[18] Once the moral basis of existing social distinctions began to look spurious, differences in rank became increasingly burdensome.

The comparison that she had made between the French Revolution and the fall of the Roman Empire might, Staël acknowledged, look like a conceit. But, even if it struck a false note, it still had the merit of highlighting the similarities and differences between ancient and modern politics. The most salient of these was the counterintuitive direction of travel of cultural exchange. Conquest, almost by definition, implied the domination of the conquerors over

---

17. "Le ridicule est, a beaucoup d'égards, une puissance aristocratique: plus il y a de rangs dans la société, plus il existe de rapports convenus entre ces rangs, et plus on est obligé de les connaitre et de les respecter. Il s'établit dans les premières classes de certains usages, de certaines règles de politesse et d'élégance, qui servent pour ainsi dire, de signe de ralliement, et dont l'ignorance trahirait des habitudes et des sociétés différentes. Les hommes qui composent ces premières classes, disposant de toutes les faveurs de l'état, exercent nécessairement un grand empire sur l'opinion publique; car, à l'exception de quelques circonstances très rares, la puissance est de bon gout, le crédit a de la grâce, et les heureux sont aimés." Staël, *De la littérature*, p. 276.

18. "Qui entreprendrait l'histoire de la vanité en France, découvrirait une grande portion des causes de la révolution que la France a éprouvée." Prosper de Barante, *De la littérature française pendant le dix-huitième siècle*, 2nd ed. (London, 1813), p. 104. See too the near contemporary English translation, *A Tableau of French Literature during the Eighteenth Century* (London, 1833), p. 79: "We might also observe the difference of rank becoming more and more insupportable because it had no longer a real foundation and seemed borne in falsehood. Those who study the history of pride in France will quickly discover a great portion of the causes of the revolution that France has proved."

the conquered. Although it was often partial (as, for example, was the case with British India), it did not usually lead to the culture of the conquered replacing that of the conquerors. But, Staël argued, it was this inversion that lay behind the parallel between the French Revolution and the fall of the Roman Empire. The latter event, she pointed out, had not led to the domination of the North over the South as might have been expected after the violent destruction of Rome's armies, and as had actually happened in the wake of the northwards expansion of Islam. Instead, the two very different cultures of northern and southern Europe had gradually merged. This, Staël claimed, was largely the effect of Christianity, either as a source of moral inspiration for the peoples of the North or as a medium of atonement for the peoples of the South. The two facets of Christianity complemented one another and had given rise to the slow cultural convergence between the North and the South.[19]

The point of the parallel emerged with Staël's treatment of the French Revolution. It revealed, she argued, the need for a similar cultural convergence, but this time between different social latitudes rather than different national longitudes. While the fall of the Roman Empire had led to an apparent translation of empire from the North to the South, but a real translation of culture from South to North, the fall of the old French regime had the potential to bring about a similarly inverted outcome, but this time from above to below rather than from below to above. "It will be a happy termination," Staël wrote, "if we shall discover, as at the epoch of the invasion of the northern peoples, a philosophical system, a virtuous enthusiasm, and a solid and equitable legislation that, just as the Christian religion was to the ancients, might be the sentiment in which the conqueror and the conquered were able to unite."[20] The combination would be like Christianity, but it would still be different from Christianity because its orientation would be secular rather than spiritual, and its primary components would be the three forms of understanding supplied by images, feelings, and ideas. The goal was to develop a culture in which all three complemented one another because this, Staël wrote, would be where "the harmony of creation" would be at its most pronounced.[21]

Staël did not give the combination a name, either in *De la littérature* or in its analytical successor, *De l'Allemagne* (On Germany). The letters that she

19. Staël, *De la littérature*, pp. 166–69.

20. "Heureux, si nous trouvions, comme à l'époque de l'invasion des peuples du nord, un système philosophique, un enthousiasme vertueux, une législation forte et juste, qui fût, comme la religion chrétienne l'a été, l'opinion dans laquelle les vainqueurs et les vaincus pourraient se réunir!" Ibid., p. 170 (I have followed, with modifications, the translation in Staël, *The Influence of Literature upon Society* [London, 1812], p. 216).

21. Staël, *De la littérature*, p. 381.

exchanged with Humboldt between the publication of *De la littérature* in 1800 and *De l'Allemagne* in 1813 continued to explore the same subject, focusing particularly on the relationship between the concept of perfectibility and the causes and forms of moral and social integration that were salient both to the afterlife of Rome and to the circumstances of postrevolutionary France. In keeping with the concept of perfectibility that she had presented in *De la littérature*, the emphasis fell mainly on the problem of combining unity with diversity both within and between states because to both Humboldt and Staël it was this combination that was the essential starting point for thinking about modern politics. "You know," Humboldt wrote to her on 7 June 1801, "that I attach a great value to the study of the nuances in the character of different nations, and I believe that it will be possible one day to show that unless we can achieve this, to the point of developing the character of each nation and even of each grouping according to its individual nuances, it will be pointless to be involved in either politics or morality."

> We take too little interest in man and too much interest in the things that he does and the institutions that are supposed to guide him, while failing above all to study him in his overall individuality. It seems to me that it is this, above all, that makes philosophy in France so vague and poetry there so cold and largely lacking in interest. Everything that consists only of abstract generalizations can neither go to the heart of, nor be applied fruitfully to, social life. This is also why the system of perfectibility has more opponents in France than in any other country. This system, which you have developed so well, is based on the idea that the development of human faculties has no limit other than those set upon its development by man himself. Human development can only be combated by binding it to the things or works that man produces. Beginning with a determinate and circumscribed idea of those works makes it easy to claim that it is impossible to go further. But it is easy to see the happy results produced by differences in the genius and the character of both individuals and nations. One has only to compare French and German literature to be convinced. But there still seems to be a desire to deprive ourselves of these same advantages and, instead of cultivating, developing, and differentiating character in society, there is a wish to put a stop to it and everywhere establish instead a single way of seeing, thinking, and speaking. The result is a failure to see how essential it is to search for new idioms because it is always possible to see no further than ideas that are already well-known and yet are still described no more than imperfectly.[22]

22. "Vous savez, Madame, que j'ajoute un grand prix à l'étude des nuances qu'il y a entre le caractère des différentes nations, et je crois pouvoir démontrer un jour qu'à moins de n'en venir

In a way that was paralleled by Friedrich Schleiermacher, human improvement, on Humboldt's terms, was a process of national and individual differentiation and diversification on the one side and, at the same time, a parallel
process of cultural and imaginative integration. Staël's version of this philosophy of history followed the same logic. As Humboldt put it to her in a letter of
6 February 1802,

> In studying ourselves, as you put it, we find within ourselves a faculty that
> is independent of sensations but which nonetheless needs them to develop,
> even though its power comes from another source. Is this not, Madame, the
> explanation of what you sometimes call the misfortune of human exis-
> tence? Does not this feeling come from our awareness of our independence
> and our dependence nonetheless on a mass of combinations and hazards, and
> our knowledge that, despite our awareness of a supernatural and divine
> force within ourselves, we cannot give it free rein?[23]

----

jusque là, jusqu'à développer le caractère de chaque nation, je dirais même de chaque peuplade
d'après ses nuances individuelles, on travaillera toujours en vain tant en morale, qu'en politique.
On s'occupe beaucoup trop peu de l'homme et beaucoup trop des ouvrages qu'il fait et des
institutions qui doivent le diriger, et on néglige surtout de l'étudier dans l'ensemble de son individu. C'est là surtout ce qui rend, ce me semble, la philosophie en France si vague et la poésie
pour la plupart aussi froide et peu intéressante. Tout ce qui ne consiste qu'en généralités, toujours abstraites, ne saurait all au cœur ni être appliqué avec fruit à la vie sociale. C'est encore là
pourquoi le système de la perfectibilité trouve plus d'adversaires en France qu'en nul autre pays.
Car ce système, comme vous l'avez si bien démontré, ne se fonde que sur ce que le développement des facultés de l'homme ne connait aucunes bornes que l'homme lui-même pût leur as-
signer. On ne peut le combattre qu'en s'attachant aux choses, aux ouvrages qu'il produit. On
part de l'idée déterminée et circonscrite qu'on s'est formé de ces ouvrages et il est aisé de dire
pour lors qu'il serait impossible d'aller plus loin. Il est si facile de voir les résultats heureux que
produit la différence entre le génie et le caractère des individus comme des nations; on n'a qu'à
comparer la littérature français et allemande pour s'en convaincre. Néanmoins on voudrait se
priver de ces mêmes avantages et au lieu de cultiver, de développer et de purifier la société des
caractères, on voudrait l'annuler, et n'établir partout qu'une même manière de voir, de penser
et de s'énoncer. On ne voit donc qu'il doit nécessairement chercher de nouveaux idiomes
puisqu'il entrevoit toujours des idées que ceux qu'il connait, n'expriment qu'imparfaitement."
Wilhelm von Humboldt to Germaine de Staël, 7 June 1801, in Albert Leitzmann, "Wilhelm von
Humboldt und Frau von Staël," *Deutsche Rundschau* 169 (1916): 95–112, 271–80, 431–42; 170
(1917): 95–108, 256–66, 425–35; 171 (1918): 82–95 (here, 169:278–79).

23. "En nous étudiant nous-mêmes, dites-vous, nous trouvons en nous une faculté indépendante des sensations qui a besoin d'elles pour se développer, mais dont la puissance vient d'une
autre source. Ne serait-ce pas là, Madame, l'explication de ce que vous nommiez quelquefois le
malheur de l'existence humaine? Ce sentiment ne nous viendrait-il pas de ce que nous sentant
indépendants en nous-mêmes, nous dépendons cependant d'une foule de combinaisons et de

Here, the stimulus was melancholy, or the feeling produced by the mixture of the limited and the limitless in human life. All great passions, Humboldt wrote, came from this source, and all the effects of poetry drew their strength from whatever happened to awaken its activity within us. Staël, he continued, had seen that this idea was specific to Kant's system, although, he noted, it was in fact generic to modern German philosophy and could be found "at its fullest and most sublime extent" in the thought of Friedrich Heinrich Jacobi. "As for myself," Humboldt added, "I am so persuaded of the existence of this internal faculty, this invisible force, that it seems to me that it alone constitutes what we call our individuality. It is the source of both the most sublime thought and the most intimate of inclinations. All that we ought to do is to develop it fully and allow it to shine in all its vigour and vivacity."[24]

The same idea featured prominently in a letter to Staël on national and individual character that Humboldt wrote on 1 October 1802. There were, he wrote there, two types of force involved in character. One was simply passive and produced the same effects from the same causes, while the other was "independent and free" and gave itself its own direction and purposes. Usually, however, character was taken to be a purely receptive faculty, and it was this misconception that was the source of "that mania to govern, oppress, or, so to speak, fashion men." In fact, however, every individual had what Humboldt called "an original and independent moral faculty" that was entirely distinct from sense experience and, as Schleiermacher also emphasized, was the part of every character that tended towards the ideal. If both forces were fully acknowledged, then government and politics would be more limited. The initial inertial force could be combined with the creative force to ensure that the progress made by the latter would be made more durable by the former.

This, Humboldt added, also explained why language mattered, because nothing had more of a bearing on human behaviour than the behaviour of other

---

hasards? De ce que connaissant en nous une force surnaturelle et divine, nous ne pouvons lui donner un essor libre et illimité?": Humboldt to Staël, 6 February 1802. Leitzmann, *Deutsche Rundschau* 169 (1916): 435.

24. "J'ai admiré, Madame, avec quelle profondeur de sagacité . . . vous avez distingué au premier coup d'œil que cette idée est particulière au système de Kant. Il est vrai qu'elle appartient encore plus à la philosophie allemande en général, mais vous n'avez pu vous apercevoir que de la différence entre cette philosophie et celle des anglais et des français. C'est surtout en Jacobi qu'elle existe dans toute son étendue et dans tout son sublime. . . . Quant à moi je suis si persuadé qu'elle existe, cette faculté intérieure, cette force invisible, qu'il me semble que c'est d'elle seule qui constitue ce que nous nommons notre individu. C'est d'elle que viennent les pensées les plus sublimes et les penchants les plus intimes; tout ce que nous avons à faire est de la développer entièrement et de la faire briller dans toute sa vigueur et sa vivacité." Ibid., p. 435.

humans. The part played by language as a force for both continuity and change meant, he claimed, that nothing was more significant than the division of mankind into nations because division was the source of both conflict and development. This version of the idea of unsocial sociability meant, Humboldt concluded, that no problem was more important than the problem of determining how far the character of nations and individuals should be limited by one another.[25] The idea was quite close to a further claim about the relationship between individuality and the division of labour, on the one side, and the

25. "Je m'occupe depuis longtemps d'un travail sur ce qu'on peut nommer caractère national et caractère des individus et je crois qu'il est possible de traiter cette question de manière à toucher ce qu'il y a de plus intime dans la nature humaine. Nous voyons évidemment même dans l'homme moral deux forces absolument différentes, l'une, une force d'inertie, pour ainsi dire, qui assimile toujours les mêmes effets aux mêmes causes, l'autre, indépendante et libre qui ne prend son essor et sa direction que d'elle-même. Quand cette dernière produit ce qu'on nomme caractères originaux, la première forme ceux des nations, et du résultat des deux dépendent les progrès et les destinées du genre humain. Cependant on n'influe ni sur l'une ni sur l'autre de la manière qu'on devrait, et cela uniquement parce qu'on méconnait ce qui devait être le dernier but de tout ce que l'on fait comme c'est la véritable cause de tout ce qui arrive—le caractère des hommes. On s'imagine communément qu'il n'est qu'un composé de toutes les impressions différentes que l'individu a reçu depuis sa naissance, on le croit factice et de là cette manie de gouverner, d'opprimer, de façonner pour ainsi dire les hommes. Quant à moi, il me parait décidé au contraire que chaque homme porte en lui une faculté morale indépendante et originaire qui tend, mais dans une direction particulière et différente de celle de tous les autres hommes, vers l'idéal, c'est-à-dire vers un perfectionnement indéfini. Il ne s'agit que de la développer cette force et de la débarrasser de tout ce qui nécessairement doit la paralyser, et il suffit de la supposer pour respecter l'humanité et aimer la liberté. De l'autre côté l'homme appartient à la nature; il est modifié par les impression qu'il reçoit; il dépend en même temps de la force d'inertie dont je viens de parler. Il est donc nécessaire de combiner l'action de ses deux forces différentes, de mettre celle qui est originaire et indépendante en état de donner à chaque individu la direction qui lui est propre, et de se servir de l'autre, pour rendre durables et permanents les progrès que celle-ci aura faits. Mais de toutes les choses qui influent sur l'homme il n'y en a aucune qui le modifie aussi puissamment que l'homme même, et puisque c'est par le langage que l'homme communique ses idées et même ses affections, que l'homme parlant le même idiome. Sous ce point de vue, rien n'est donc si intéressant que la division des hommes en différentes nations, division tout à la fois nécessaire et nuisible à leurs progrès. Si donc vous m'accordez, Madame, qu'il soit vrai qu'en dernier ressort tout dépende uniquement du caractère des hommes, le véritable problème sera de déterminer en combien le caractère des individus et celui des nations doivent se limiter réciproquement? Problème à la solution duquel l'expérience doit venir à l'aide du raisonnement." Humboldt to Staël, 1 October 1802. Leitzmann, *Deutsche Rundschau* 169 (1916): 441–42. On Humboldt and language, see Martin L. Manchester, *The Philosophical Foundations of Humboldt's Linguistic Doctrines* (Amsterdam, J. Benjamins, 1985).

romantic interest in originality, nationality, and creativity on the other. These were the subjects that formed the analytical core of Staël's *De l'Allemagne*.

There was a substantial degree of continuity between *De la littérature* and *De l'Allemagne*. The structure of both was supplied by the concept of perfectibility, with its emphasis on the similarities and differences between the ancients and the moderns in the first place and its commitment to careful investigation of the moral and political possibilities available to the moderns in the second place. By the time, however, that *De l'Allemagne* had completed its protracted publication, the idea of perfectibility had been buttressed by a number of other concepts that, together, helped to turn the old antithesis between the ancients and moderns into a new antithesis between classicism and romanticism. The names themselves are an initial clue to the reasons for their appearance. Classicism referred, in the first instance, to the languages of the classics, particularly to Latin, while romanticism referred initially to the Romance languages that had developed after the fall of the Roman Empire. The subject of language, in other words, was central to the transformation of the ancient-modern parallel into its classic-romantic counterpart, as this transformation began to appear in Humboldt's correspondence with Germaine de Staël. As is also apparent from Humboldt's correspondence, the reason why it was so central was not, in the first instance, because of the connection between language and nationality, originality, creativity, or any of the other romantic buzzwords, but because of its connection to the subject of the imagination.

Here, the initial problem was to explain how something imagined could be given a genuinely substantive existence and, by extension, how something imagined could be accessible to a whole community rather than simply to a single individual. This, as Humboldt had emphasized, was why enthusiasm mattered, and, if the emotional and cognitive effects of enthusiasm were to be significant, why some initial cultural familiarity was desirable. This familiarity was what a living language could supply. Since Latin and Greek were not living languages, their atrophied, purely written afterlives, Humboldt had argued, meant that the classics no longer had the ability to tap the power of the imagination in the ways that national languages, literatures, and cultures could do. It followed that, for the moderns, national languages were the means that allowed originality (rather than the imitation involved in using Latin) to be expressed. It also followed that creativity could be catered for more readily by a national language and literature than by the classics. The claim still has a historical and historiographical significance. It means that it is simply wrong to think of the early nineteenth-century preoccupation with nationality, originality, or creativity as a straightforward reaction against—or a crude alternative to—the putative cosmopolitanism, rationalism, materialism, or atheism of the Enlightenment. It makes more sense to think of the preoccupation with nationality, creativity, and the like as second-order implications of trying to solve the first-order problem of explaining how something imagined could be translated into something with a commonly identified emotional, rational, or simply intelligible content. This was the key problem, independently of the more familiar shibboleths of romantic historiography.[26] Dealing with it meant explaining how language and, more generally, the properties of whatever it was that gave aesthetics its content could transmit the enthusiasm generated by one imagination to the hearts and minds of others. The same problem applied to music, painting, or the plastic arts. Finding a way to solve it was, in a sense, the key to the politics of autonomy and the basis of the claim that the apparently timeless quality of human freedom really could find a modern home.

De l'Allemagne was an extended examination of these questions and themes. It consisted of four sections, beginning with a section on the Germans and their manners and customs, continuing with two sections on literature and the arts, followed by a third section on philosophy and morals, and ending with a fourth section on religion and enthusiasm. As Staël indicated, the four sections were designed to reinforce one another as they moved from the particular to the general to reveal more of the underlying system of perfectibility that gave the book its moral and political direction. As with De la littérature, the analytical and the historical sides of the book were developed in tandem. "It seems then," Staël wrote, "that the philosophical progress of the human race should be divided into four different periods: the heroic times which gave birth to civilization; patriotism, which constituted the glory of antiquity; chivalry, the warlike religion of Europe; and the love of liberty, the history of which dates its origin from the epoch of the Reformation."[27] "Henceforth," she added, "nothing great" was likely to be accomplished "except by the liberal impulse which, throughout Europe, has succeeded to chivalry."[28] The most significant

26. For a concise presentation of these shibboleths, see Tim Blanning, The Romantic Revolution (London, Weidenfeld, 2010), and, for some of the original versions, see Ernest Seillière, Le mal romantique (Paris, 1908); Irving Babbitt, Rousseau and Romanticism (New York, 1919), and Carl Schmitt, Political Romanticism [1919] (Cambridge, MA, MIT Press, 1991). For a memorably caustic dismissal of Seillière and Babbitt, see Shklar, After Utopia, p. 30 n. 11.

27. Staël, Germany, 1:46–47. "La marche philosophique du genre humain parait donc devoir se diviser en quatre ères différentes: les temps héroïques, qui fondèrent la civilisation; le patriotisme, qui fit la gloire de l'antiquité; la chevalerie, qui fut la religion guerrière de l'Europe; et l'amour de la liberté, dont l'histoire a commencé vers l'époque de la reformation." Staël, De l'Allemagne, 1:76–77. Interestingly, Staël's English translator substituted "the revolution" for "the reformation" as the time when the fourth period began.

28. Staël, Germany, 1:52. "Rien de grand ne s'y fera désormais que par l'impulsion libérale qui a succédé dans l'Europe à la chevalerie." Staël, De l'Allemagne, 1:85.

feature of this schematic progression, however, was the concept of liberty that Staël associated with the fourth period.

She set out this concept most fully in the third part of *De l'Allemagne*. "The ancient lawgivers," she wrote there in a chapter entitled "Of the Moral System, Founded upon National Interest," "made it a duty for citizens to be concerned with political interests. The Christian religion should have inspired a disposition of an entirely different nature, namely one of obeying authority but of keeping ourselves detached from the affairs of state when they might compromise our conscience." This difference, she went on to explain, was a product of the difference between ancient and modern governments.

> The political science of the ancients was intimately bound up with their religion and morals; the social state was a body full of life. Every individual considered himself to be one of its members. The smallness of states, the number of slaves which still further contracted that of the citizens, all made it a duty to act for a country which had need of every one of its children. Magistrates, warriors, artists, philosophers, almost the gods themselves, mingled together upon the public arena; and the same men by turns gained a battle, exhibited a masterpiece of art, gave laws to their country, or endeavoured to discover the laws of the universe.[29]

With the exception of "the very small number of free governments," these arrangements no longer applied. The "greatness of modern states," Staël continued, "and the concentration of monarchical power have, so to speak, rendered politics entirely negative." The prime purpose of modern politics was "to prevent one person from harming another so that government is charged with the high sort of police which permits everyone to enjoy the

---

29. Staël, *Germany*, 3:196. "Les législateurs anciens faisaient un devoir aux citoyens de se mêler des intérêts politiques. La religion chrétienne doit inspirer une disposition d'une toute autre nature, celle d'obéir à l'autorité, mais de se tenir éloigné des affaires de l'état, quand elles peuvent compromettre la conscience. La différence qui existe entre les gouvernements anciens et les gouvernements modernes explique cette opposition dans la manière de considérer les relations des hommes envers leur patrie.

"La science politique des anciens était intimement unie avec la religion et la morale; l'état social était un corps plein de vie. Chaque individu se considérait comme l'un de ses membres. La petitesse des états, le nombre des esclaves qui resserrait encore de beaucoup celui des citoyens, tout faisait un devoir d'agir pour une patrie qui avait besoin de chacun de ses fils. Les magistrats, les guerriers, les artistes, les philosophes et presque les dieux se mêlaient sur la place publique, et les mêmes hommes tour à tour gagnaient une bataille, exposaient un chef d'œuvre, donnaient des lois à leurs pays, ou cherchaient à découvrir celles de l'univers." Staël, *De l'Allemagne*, 4:308–9.

advantages of peace and social order by purchasing this security by reasonable sacrifices."[30]

Staël's two assertions were not obviously compatible with each other. On the one hand, she wrote, the principle underlying the modern age was "the love of liberty"; on the other hand, she also wrote, the size and centralization of modern states, had made modern politics "entirely negative." This was why the concept of autonomy mattered. It did so because it formed a link between the positive liberty of the ancients and the negative liberty of the moderns. This meant that negative liberty, as Staël, echoing Kant, conceived of it, called for strong moral foundations. It seemed to mean that modern liberty, which was largely negative, had to be aligned quite firmly with virtue, while ancient liberty, which was largely positive, could rely more readily on simple conformity.[31] The difference between virtue and conformity formed the basis of Staël's further claim that enthusiasm, or the intense compound of knowing, imagining, and feeling that, she claimed, was involved in altruistic behaviour, was also what was required to establish a stable relationship between the love of liberty and the entirely negative character of modern politics. Without enthusiasm, Staël argued repeatedly, there would be no capacity for duty, and without a capacity for duty, there would be no room for individual liberty. As with Sismondi and Constant, negative liberty called for positive liberty.

The initial problem was that modern politics, beginning with the politics of the old French monarchy, had become ancient in orientation. But, as almost every major eighteenth-century political theorist from Montesquieu and Rousseau to Adam Smith and Edmund Burke had warned, and as the events of the French Revolution had shown, combining ancient politics with a modern state—and with the financial resources available to a modern state—created a serious risk to the long-term survival of civil and political liberty.[32] From this perspective, Staël's point, in keeping with the progressive scheme of historical development implied by the concept of perfectibility, was not so much that prevailing economic and social arrangements meant that ancient politics had to give way to modern politics, but rather that the

30. Staël, *Germany*, 3:196–97. "Si l'on excepte le très-petit nombre des gouvernements libres, la grandeur des états chez les modernes et la concentration du pouvoir des monarques ont rendu pour ainsi dire la politique toute négative. Il s'agit de ne pas se nuire les uns aux autres, et le gouvernement est chargé de cette haute police qui doit permettre à chacun de jouir des avantages de la paix et de l'ordre social, en achetant cette sécurité par de justes sacrifices." Staël, *De l'Allemagne*, 4:309.

31. Compare to Berlin, "Two Concepts of Liberty"; Quentin Skinner, *Liberty before Liberalism* (Cambridge, CUP, 1998).

32. See Sonenscher, *Before the Deluge*, ch. 1.

real threat to liberty, whether positive or negative, was the poisonous mixture of both ancient and modern politics that had come to be joined together in theory and practice. This too was why the politics of autonomy were different from the politics of democracy. "Men who are ever desirous of theorizing their peculiar inclinations," Staël warned, "adroitly confound ancient and Christian morals."

> It is necessary, they say like the ancients, to serve our country and to be useful citizens in the state. It is necessary, they say like the Christians, to submit ourselves to power established by the will of God. It is thus that a mixture of the system of quietness with that of action produces a double immorality when, taken singly, they had both claims to respect. The activity of the Greek and Roman citizens, such as it could be exercised in a republic, was a noble virtue. The force of Christian quietness is also a virtue, and one of great power. . . . But the tricking selfishness of ambitious men teaches them the art of combining opposite arguments; so that they can meddle with everything like Pagans and submit to everything like Christians.[33]

The combination of state interference and a culture of civic passivity meant that both Robespierre and Napoleon were in fact the products of the same political pathology. This, Staël argued, was why modern politics called for different conceptions of political liberty and political obligation from its ancient counterpart. Ancient politics had allowed the impulse to duty to be externally supplied; modern politics, however, required the motivation to come from within.

Treating the present pathological mixture of the ancient and the modern was partly a matter of constitutional design, but with a particular emphasis on the properties of federal systems of government and the dual relationship between both sovereignty and government and the public and private that they were able to house. It was also a matter of morals and, more specifically, of the

---

33. Staël, *Germany*, 3:197–98. "Les hommes qui veulent toujours mettre en théorie leurs penchants individuels confondent habilement la morale antique et la morale chrétienne; il faut, disent-ils, comme les anciens, servir sa patrie, n'être pas un citoyen inutile dans l'état;—il faut, disent-ils, comme les chrétiens, se soumettre au pouvoir établi par la volonté de Dieu.—C'est ainsi que le mélange du système d'inertie et de celui de l'action produit une double immoralité, tandis que pris séparément l'un et l'autre avaient droit au respect. L'activité des citoyens grecs et romains, telle qu'elle pouvait s'exercer dans une république, était une noble vertu. La force d'inertie chrétienne est aussi une vertu, et d'une grande force. . . . Mais l'égoïsme patelin des hommes ambitieux leur enseigne l'art de combiner les raisonnements opposés afin de se mêler de tout comme un païen et de se soumettre à tout comme un chrétien." Staël, *De l'Allemagne*, 4:310–11.

capacity for self-abnegation or altruism that Staël called "enthusiasm" (in the French original she often coupled *enthousiasme* with the word *dévouement* or "devotion").[34] In keeping with the broader distinction between the ancients and moderns, enthusiasm centred on a range of historically specific objects. "At all the great periods of history," Staël noted, "men have embraced some sort of enthusiastic sentiment, as a universal principle of action."[35] In earlier ages, that sentiment had been associated with heroism, patriotism, or chivalry. In France, however, chivalry had disappeared after the rule of Cardinal Richelieu and the rise of absolute government in the seventeenth century. The result was that France was "without any sort of enthusiastic impulse whatever; and as such an impulse is necessary to prevent the corruption and dissolution of nations, it is doubtless that natural necessity which, in the middle of the last century, turned every mind towards the love of liberty."[36]

The love of liberty in question was, however, still something different from ancient patriotism. As Staël emphasized, its prime characteristic was respect for the liberty of others and recognition of something that gave value to other people's lives. This too was a form of selflessness, but it called for a type of enthusiasm that was different from the emotions involved in either medieval chivalry or the ancient virtues. Here, the emotion in question was internally generated because it had its source in the idea of free will. Since neither analysis nor experience could capture the full sense of what having a free will implied, that sense, as Kant had argued, was best captured initially by the imagination. It was also (again following Kant) best described in largely aesthetic terms because the idea of free will seemed to imply an empirically unverifiable imaginative ability to push back the limits of the here and now. Freedom, on these terms, seemed to be an ability to bring together and manage what, in ordinary circumstances, would be simply antithetical, like positive and negative or black and white. "The enthusiasm which the beautiful in idea makes us feel," Staël wrote, "that emotion, so full of agitation and of purity at the same time, is excited by the sentiment of infinity. We feel ourselves, as it were, disengaged by admiration from the shackles of human destiny and it seems as if some wondrous secret was revealed to us, to free the soul for ever from languor and

34. See, for example, Staël, *De l'Allemagne*, 1:109; 3:295 n. 1. Her English translator standardly turned *dévouement* into the now archaic, and hence misleading, "self-devotion."

35. Staël, *Germany*, 1:43. "A toutes les grandes époques de l'histoire les hommes ont eu pour principe universel d'action un enthousiasme quelconque." Staël, *De l'Allemagne*, 1:74.

36. Staël, *Germany*, 1:46. "La France se trouvait alors sans aucun genre d'enthousiasme; et comme il en faut un aux nations pour ne pas se corrompre et se dissoudre, c'est sans doute ce besoin naturel qui tourna vers le milieu du dernier siècle, tous les esprits vers l'amour de la liberté." Staël, *De l'Allemagne*, 1:76.

decline."[37] This, as she put it earlier, was why "all that is truly beautiful in man springs from what he experiences within himself, and every heroic action is inspired by moral liberty." The starting point of this "expectation of infinity," as Staël called it, was imaginative. But its conceptual components and internal logic were also not hard to grasp. Nature, she explained, had arranged "the infinite in symbols which may bring it down to us: light and darkness, storm and silence, pleasure and pain, all inspire man with this universal religion, of which his heart is his sanctuary." Without this ability to identify and respond imaginatively to opposites and, by doing so, to turn natural occurrences into symbols of infinity, "there would be nothing in man but physical instinct and calculation."[38]

In this sense, Staël concluded, enthusiasm, as the etymology of the Greek word from which it was drawn seemed to suggest, was best described as *God in us.*[39] But the god in question was also, in this context, a human creation. "What do we know," Staël asked rhetorically, "better than our feelings? And why should we pretend that they are inapplicable to the truths of religion? What can there be in man, but himself, and why, under the pretext of anthropomorphism, hinder him from forming an image of the Deity after his own soul. No other messenger, I believe, can bring him news from heaven."[40] If the

37. Staël, *Germany*, 3:269–70. "L'enthousiasme que le beau idéal nous fait éprouver, cette émotion pleine de trouble et de pureté tout ensemble, c'est le sentiment de l'infini qui l'excite. Nous nous sentons comme dégagés, par l'admiration, des entraves de la destinée humaine, et il nous semble qu'on nous révèle des secrets merveilleux, pour affranchir l'âme à jamais de la langueur et du déclin." Staël, *De l'Allemagne*, 5:12.

38. Staël, *Germany*, 3:29, 271, 272, 273. The French runs "tout ce qui est vraiment beau dans l'homme naît de ce qu'il éprouve intérieurement et spontanément; toute action héroïque est inspirée par la liberté morale": Staël, *De l'Allemagne*, 4:50. The French versions of the subsequent citations are as follows: "cette attente de l'infini," Staël, *De l'Allemagne*, 5:13; followed by "La nature a revêtu l'infini des divers symboles qui peuvent le faire arriver jusqu'à nous: la lumière et les ténèbres, l'orage et le silence, le plaisir et la douleur, tout inspire à l'homme cette religion universelle dont son cœur est le sanctuaire": Staël, *De l'Allemagne*, 5:15–16; and finally "le sentiment de l'infini est un fait de l'âme, un fait primitif, sans lequel il n'y aurait rien dans l'homme que de l'instinct physique et du calcul": Staël, *De l'Allemagne*, 5:18.

39. Staël, *Germany*, 3:388. "Le sens de ce mot chez les Grecs en est la plus noble définition: l'enthousiasme signifie *Dieu en nous.*" Staël, *De l'Allemagne*, 5:188. In an earlier draft, she called it "un dieu qui s'empare de nous": Staël, *De l'Allemagne*, 5:216.

40. Staël, *Germany*, 3:308–9. "que savons-nous de plus que nos sentiments, et pourquoi prétendrait-on qu'ils ne doivent point s'appliquer aux vérités de la foi? Que peut-il avoir dans l'homme que lui-même, et pourquoi, sous prétexte d'anthropomorphisme, l'empêcher de se former, d'après son âme, une image de la divinité? Nul autre messager ne saurait, je pense, lui en donner des nouvelles." Staël, *De l'Allemagne*, 5:75.

imagination gave rise both to the idea of infinity and to its attendant response in the emotion of enthusiasm, it also had to be the source of the human idea of the divine. It followed that there was a fundamental similarity linking or underlying religion, philosophy, and the creative arts. All three had the same imaginative source and the same affinity with the type of individual liberty required by what she had called the "entirely negative" politics of the modern age. "The philosophy of idealism, the Christianity of mysticism, and the poetry of nature have, in many respects, all the same end and the same origin," Staël concluded, memorably.

> These philosophers, these Christians, and these poets all unite in one common desire. They would wish to substitute for the factitious system of society, not the ignorance of barbarous times, but an intellectual culture, which leads us back to simplicity by the very perfection of knowledge. They would, in short, wish to make energetic and reflective, sincere and generous men out of all those characters without dignity, those minds without ideas, those jesters without gaiety, those Epicureans without imagination who, for want of a better word, are called the human race.[41]

It could have been written by Rousseau or Kant.

---

41. Staël, *Germany*, 3:334–35. "La philosophie idéaliste, le christianisme mystique, et la vraie poésie ont, à beaucoup d'égards, le même but et la même source; ces philosophes, ces chrétiens et ces poètes se réunissent tous dans un commun désir. Ils voudraient substituer au factice de la société, non l'ignorance des temps barbares, mais une culture intellectuelle qui ramène à la simplicité par la perfection même des lumières; ils voudraient enfin faire des hommes énergiques et réfléchis, sincères et généreux, de tous ces caractères sans élévation, de tous ces esprits sans idées, de tous ces moqueurs sans gaieté, de tous ces épicuriens sans imagination, qu'on appelle l'espèce humaine faute de mieux." Staël, *De l'Allemagne*, 5:111. (The English translation's "poetry of nature," rather than "true poetry," probably derives from the "littérature naturelle" of Staël's original edition.)

5

From the Concept of Palingenesis to the Concept of Enlightenment

THE ANTINOMIES ASSOCIATED with the idea of the division of labour and the concept of civil society were also applicable to the problem of the state. They were most visible in an expanding set of questions over whether, for example, states are singular or plural, unitary or composite, real or ideal, sources of peace or engines of war, instruments of justice or agents of empire. All these questions had arisen well before the nineteenth century, and all of them played a part in the various bodies of argument over the overlapping legacies of the Romans and the Germans, the ancients and the moderns, or the classics and the romantics. They were, however, given a new inflection in Kant's moral and political thought because it was Kant who first showed that the antinomies were not as radically incompatible as they seemed. In making this evaluation, he began by presenting a distinction between two different metaphors of social and political reform, and then went on to explain why the differences between them showed that the antinomies associated with the concept of the state also had a kind of self-cancelling quality. One of the metaphors was supplied by the concept of palingenesis, the concept that was to have so much ephemeral resonance in 1848, while the other was supplied by the concept of metamorphosis. As Kant presented them, the idea of palingenesis referred to something being born again, while metamorphosis referred to the same thing changing over time. Kant rejected the concept of palingenesis as incoherent but endorsed the concept of metamorphosis because, he argued, while the first concept was a purely metaphorical way of thinking about history, states, and politics, the second offered real intellectual purchase on all three.[1] One of the aims of this chapter is to try to explain what, in the first

1. On the distinction between metamorphosis and palingenesis in Kant's thought, see Howard Williams, "Metamorphosis or Palingenesis? Political Change in Kant," *Review of Politics*

place, Kant meant. Its broader aim is to establish a more general starting point for showing what, over the course of the nineteenth century, Kant's unusual ways of describing three ideas—the merits of metamorphosis over palingenesis, the relationship between public law and private law, and the significance of the distinction between the concepts of sovereignty and constituent power—came to mean for thinking about history, states, and politics.

Kant, Palingenesis, and Equality

Kant's concept of the state was clear, simple, and consistent. The state, on his interpretation, was the one thing that was the source and foundation of the only type of equality that was consistent with human society. In this, as in so much else, Kant's concept of the state was a clearer, more powerful, and more comprehensive rendition of the thought of Jean-Jacques Rousseau.[2] As Rousseau had argued, equality is a purely *relative* concept because its existence depends on a relationship. Freedom, he also argued, is an *absolute* concept because it can exist independently of any relationship (I can believe that I am free all by myself, but I cannot believe that I am equal without bringing someone or something else into the picture). Equality calls for comparison, but freedom calls only for introspection. Although both concepts are abstract, equality is other directed, while freedom is inner directed. This, Rousseau explained, was why the idea of equality began with comparison (and had the same origin as the feeling of *amour-propre*) and why, therefore, everything in nature, meaning everything identifiable by the senses, was best understood initially in terms of difference rather than equality. Everything, including humans, comes in the form of more or less of some or other quality. In themselves, Rousseau maintained, these different qualities would be unremarkable because, on their own, all things, including humans, could be said to have an existence that is recognizable in absolute terms. If humans really were the solitary, silent, sentient creatures that Rousseau claimed that they once might have been, the problematic relationship between equality and inequality would not have arisen.

For Kant, following Rousseau, the problematic relationship between equality and inequality began with society.[3] Neutralizing inequality had, therefore, to come from the one thing that could stand above society and, too, could be

---

63 (2001): 693–722. See also his earlier *Kant's Political Philosophy* (Oxford, Blackwell, 1983), pp. 4–5. On the broader subject, see John Edward Toews, *Becoming Historical: Cultural Reformation and Public Memory in Early Nineteenth-Century Berlin* (Cambridge, CUP, 2004).

2. On Kant and Rousseau, see Sonenscher, *Jean-Jacques Rousseau*, pp. 13–14, 20, 47, 94, 112, 134, 142, 144, 150–51, 163, 168, 176, and the further secondary literature referred to there.

3. For a summary of Rousseau's argument, see ibid., pp. 51–64.

armed with the authority and power to impose equality on society as a whole, meaning, in the first place, a single, sovereign state and, in the second place, a state equipped with the peculiar ability to establish and maintain equality before the law. States, as the phrase went, could act for reasons of state. On Kant's terms, the ultimate reason of state was equality before the law. Kant singled out this peculiar attribute of the state by giving it an unusual and obliquely historical justification. If, as he insisted repeatedly, the one thing that only a state can do is to establish and maintain equality, just as, inversely, the one thing able to establish and maintain equality in society is a single, sovereign state, then the obvious, evidence-based, way to justify the claim would have to be historical. The nexus formed by the state, equality, and this unusual way of thinking about history was, therefore, extremely tight. What Kant called the "uniform equality of human beings as subjects of a state" was a product of the state's capacity to establish and maintain equal rights. "For," he wrote, "all right consists merely in the restriction of the freedom of others, with the qualification that their freedom can coexist with my freedom in accordance with a universal law." Public right was simply this principle "backed up by power" and was designed to give rise to "a rightful condition as such (*status iuridicus*)," meaning, Kant explained, a condition "characterized by equality in the effects and counter-effects of freely willed actions which limit one another in accordance with the general law of freedom."[4] To avoid an argument that appeared to be circular, the justification of this kind of equality in "the effects and counter-effects of freely willed actions" had to be largely historical. Importantly, however, this was not a matter of empirical historical evidence but, instead, of comparing different conceptions of history.[5]

---

4. Immanuel Kant, *On the Common Saying: 'This May be True in Theory, but it does not Apply in Practice'*, in Immanuel Kant, *Political Writings*, pp. 61–92 (pp. 75–76 for the passages cited). Henceforth, Kant, *T&P*, followed by the page number(s). For commentary, see Ayşe Yuva, "La raison pure peut-elle être pratique? La figure du philosophe allemand au début du xixe siècle en France," in *France-Allemagne: figures de l'intellectuel entre révolution et réaction, 1780–1848*, ed. Anne Baillot and Ayşe Yuva (Lille, PU du Septentrion, 2014), pp. 115–33, and her *Transformer le monde? L'efficace de la philosophie en temps de révolution: France-Allemagne, 1794–1815* (Paris, Fondation Maison des Sciences de l'Homme 2016); Jean-Christophe Merle, "The Principle of Equality Governing Actions and Reactions in Kant's Practical Philosophy," *Con-Textos Kantianos* 2 (2015): 62–71; Agnes Heller, "Freedom, Equality and Fraternity in Kant's *Critique of Judgment*," *Critical Horizons* 19 (2018): 187–97; Howard Williams, "Liberty, Equality and Independence: Core Concepts in Kant's Political Philosophy," in *A Companion to Kant*, ed. Graham Bird (Oxford, Blackwell, 2006), pp. 364–82.

5. On the broader subject of history and politics in early nineteenth-century German thought, see Toews, *Becoming Historical*.

Kant, accordingly, went on to lay out his argument in an accessible way by making a comparison between history as tragedy and history as farce that, over the course of the nineteenth century, gradually came to eclipse the original claim about the significance of the nexus between the state and equality in which he made the initial comparison between tragedy and farce. The argument itself appeared in the final part of the essay that he published in September 1793, *On the Common Saying: 'This May be True in Theory, but it does not Apply in Practice'*. It was directed at an earlier work entitled *Jerusalem, oder über religiöse Macht und Judentum* (Jerusalem, or on religious power and Judaism) that had been published in 1783 by Kant's contemporary, the Jewish philosopher Moses Mendelssohn. Mendelssohn's work was part of the long-drawn-out eighteenth-century discussion of what, in German, was called the *Bestimmung des Menschen*, or the goal, end, purpose, vocation, or reason for the existence of mankind.[6] As its name indicates, this was a discussion of the relationship between human life, human misfortune, and human progress on the one hand and the ideas of justice, divine providence, and human purpose on the other. In this discussion, Mendelssohn's position was broadly sceptical and agnostic. As Kant commented in his reply, "he regards it as sheer fantasy to say that the whole of mankind here on earth must continually progress and become more perfect through the ages." Although Mendelssohn was quite willing to grant that individuals could progress, he still insisted that the weight of historical evidence indicated that "mankind constantly fluctuates between fixed limits." Regarded as a whole, he wrote, "mankind maintains roughly the same level of morality, the same degree of religion and irreligion, of virtue and vice, of happiness and misery."[7]

Kant disagreed. The sight of a virtuous individual "struggling against adversity and wicked temptation and yet managing to hold out against them" was, he wrote, a sight fit for a god. "But," he continued, "it is a sight quite unfit, not so much for a god but even for the most ordinary, though right-thinking man, to see the human race advancing over a period of time towards virtue, and then

6. For helpful ways in to this discussion, see George di Giovanni, "The Year 1786 and *Die Bestimmung des Menschen*, or *Popularphilosophie* in Crisis," in *Moses Mendelssohn's Metaphysics and Aesthetics*, ed. Reiner Munk, *Studies in German Idealism* 13 (2011): 217–34; and Philip Ajouri, "'The Vocation of Man'—'Die Bestimmung des Menschen': A Teleological Concept of the German Enlightenment and Its Aftermath in the Nineteenth Century," in *Historical Teleologies in the Modern World*, ed. Henning Trüper, Dipesh Chakrabarty, and Sanjay Subrahmanyan (London, Bloomsbury, 2015), pp. 49–70. On Mendelssohn, see Willi Goetschel, *Spinoza's Modernity: Mendelssohn, Lessing, and Heine* (Madison, U of Wisconsin Press, 2004), pp. 85–180; and Allan Arkush, *Moses Mendelssohn and the Enlightenment* (Albany, State U of New York Press, 1994).

7. Kant, *T&P*, pp. 87–88.

quickly relapsing the whole way back into vice and misery. It may perhaps be moving and instructive to watch such a tragic drama (*Trauerspiel*) for a while, but the curtain must eventually fall. For, in the long run, it becomes a farce."

> Even if the actors do not tire of it—because they are fools—the spectator does because even a single act will be enough for him if he can reasonably conclude that the never-ending drama will go on in the same way forever. If it is only a play, the final act will make up for the unpleasant feelings the spectator has felt. But, at least in my opinion, it cannot be reconciled with the morality of a wise creator and ruler of the world if countless vices, even with intermingled virtues, are in actual fact allowed to go on accumulating.[8]

Endorsing Mendelssohn's argument, Kant claimed, meant opting inadvertently either for hero-worship or for a kind of disabused cynicism. A fuller vision of human history called for an alternative to both and, by extension, for establishing a real analytical space for the idea of progress.

Over time, Kant's call for a progressive alternative to both history as tragedy and history as farce was given a heavily garbled rendition partly by Georg Wilhelm Friedrich Hegel, but mainly by Karl Marx. In fact, it was Marx who was really responsible for the distortion by associating a passage from Hegel's *Philosophy of History* with Kant's description of history as tragedy or farce without, however, referring to Kant. "Hegel," Marx wrote famously, "remarks somewhere that all the great events and personages in world history occur, as it were, twice. He forgot to mention: the first time as tragedy, the second as farce."[9] Although Marx was correct in pointing out that Hegel made no reference to the idea of history as either tragedy or farce, Hegel's remark was in fact much nearer in spirit to Kant's call to reinstate the idea of history as progress. Hegel made the remark as a comment on Julius Caesar's attempt to overturn the constitution of the Roman republic. "Caesar," he wrote, "judged by the great scope of history, did what was right." This, he continued, was because "only a *single* will could guide the Roman state and now the Romans were compelled to adopt that opinion because, in all periods of the world, a political revolution is sanctioned in men's opinions when it repeats itself. Thus Napoleon was twice defeated and the Bourbons were twice expelled. By repetition, that

---

8. Ibid., p. 88. It is worth noting that, in this English-language version, *Trauerspiel* is translated simply as drama rather than tragedy, as it is also frequently translated. I have compromised with "tragic drama."

9. Karl Marx, *The Eighteenth Brumaire of Louis Bonaparte* [1852], in *Marx: Later Political Writings*, ed. Terrell Carver (Cambridge, CUP, 1996), p. 31.

which at first appeared merely a matter of chance and contingency, becomes a real and ratified existence."[10]

As with Kant, the state was central to Hegel's historicist argument. The continuity produced by repetition, he argued, gave legitimacy to what, initially, seemed to be no more than contingent. Although the argument went back to the seventeenth-century English political theorist Thomas Hobbes, both Hegel and Kant gave the argument a more comprehensively historical orientation by focusing less on the state itself than on the causal and constitutional mechanisms responsible for giving the state and its institutions their capacity for combing continuity with change.[11] This focus on causation and on constitutional design meant, in the first instance, differentiating the concept of a sovereign general will more firmly from the figure of the sovereign, irrespective of whether the sovereign was one, few, or many or, in reality, a monarchy, an aristocracy, or a democracy. Adding something impersonal, like a general will, to something personal, like a monarch or a democracy, made it easier to distinguish the sovereign from the ruler. As Kant proceeded to show, none of the various forms of rule associated either with monarchy, aristocracy, or democracy was necessarily incompatible with the idea of a sovereign general will, provided that the one could be distinguished from the other. Once the distinctions were established and maintained, it would then be possible to combine the idea of sovereignty with the idea of a general will, leaving the actual human sovereign to be no more than the agent, vehicle, embodiment, or even representative of the general will, and the government to be responsible for its local and particular application. As this process of conceptual and constitutional differentiation developed, the growing number of different agencies and functions would, on the one hand, produce more possible occasions for division and conflict, but, on the other hand, would also produce a greater capacity to recognize the rule of law as the one thing that could transcend and unite them all. From this perspective, the rule of law, meaning equality before the law, was the one thing that could impose a recognizable

10. Georg Wilhelm Friedrich Hegel, *The Philosophy of History*, trans. J. Sibree (New York, 1900), pp. 312–13. I have taken the passage from the discussion of it by Bruce Mazlish, "The Tragic Farce of Marx, Hegel and Engels: A Note," *History and Theory* 11 (1972): 335–37. Mazlish, like Marx, does not refer to the relationship between tragedy and farce in Kant. The comparison is, however, mentioned by Arendt, *Lectures on Kant's Political Philosophy*, p. 51. For an illuminating discussion of the passage in Kant, see Robert B. Pippin, *Philosophy by Other Means* (Chicago, U of Chicago Press, 2021), pp. 19–38.

11. On Hobbes and the idea of de facto continuity as a source of political legitimacy, see, classically, Quentin Skinner, "Conquest and Consent: Hobbes and the Engagement Controversy" [1972], now in his *Visions of Politics*, 3 vols. (Cambridge, CUP, 2002), 3:287–307.

concept of equality on political society and, by doing so, could actually give the idea of equality some sort of real-world content. The possibility that this might actually occur in human history was the reason for Kant's fierce objection to the agnosticism of Moses Mendelssohn's *Jerusalem*. But the same historical and political possibility was also the reason for Kant's approval of the concept of metamorphosis as a real alternative to palingenesis.

Kant's position on the state was based on an unusual way of thinking about the problematic relationship between states and civil peace in both spatial and temporal terms. It amounted to a claim that the divisions built into a state-based world could be modified from within, not simply dissolved over time. States could keep the same form but acquire a different content. There was no reason, therefore, to imagine a world made up of either one state or no states as the ultimate solution to the problem of the state. This, put summarily, was why Kant called the process of historical and political change a metamorphosis rather than a palingenesis. He had already made his views of the concept of palingenesis very clear in 1785 in his reviews of Herder's *Ideas on the Philosophy of History*, and he repeated his hostile assessment in his *Metaphysics of Morals* in 1797. There, however, he also set out to explain why palingenesis was a concept that was particularly inappropriate in the context of politics.[12] Kant made this assessment in the section of his essay that he headed "The transition from what is mine or yours in a state of nature to what is mine or yours in a rightful condition generally." In this examination of the theory of property, Kant began by describing a rightful condition as one that enabled everyone to enjoy rights, meaning a condition in which the rule of law applied generally. It was, he wrote, a condition "in accordance with the idea of a will giving laws for everyone" concerning "either the possibility, or the actuality, or the necessity of the possession of objects."[13] Here, echoing Rousseau, Kant went on to argue that a rightful condition was one that enabled individual wills to coexist with a general will. As he went on to explain more fully, this coexistence was possible partly because individual wills were real because they were exercised by real people, while the general will was ideal because it belonged to an abstract concept, the state. More importantly, however, the same coexistence was also possible because the general will could be taken to be the agent responsible for establishing and maintaining

12. For commentary on the whole text, see Lara Denis, ed., *Kant's* Metaphysics of Morals: *A Critical Guide* (Cambridge, CUP, 2010).

13. Immanuel Kant, *The Metaphysics of Morals* [1797], in Immanuel Kant, *Practical Philosophy*, ed. Mary J. Gregor (Cambridge, CUP, 1996), §41, pp. 450–51 (henceforth Kant, *MM*, followed by the lemma and page numbers).

the reality and legitimacy of the arrangements and agreements made by many individual wills. In this sense, the general will, in Kant's rendition, was the basis of public law, while individual wills were the basis of private law. Here too the difference between the private and the public was also a difference between the real and the ideal. In private law, there were two or more real wills, and the law was the product of their agreement. In public law, however, there was only a single general will with no additional content because its own content was supplied solely by its constitutionally specified requirement to uphold the content of private law. Together, the two types of law amounted to what Kant called "a rightful condition generally," or what was later to be called a *Rechtsstaat*.

The absence of "a rightful condition generally," Kant wrote in the same passage, "is called a state of nature." But, as he also pointed out, the state of nature was not in fact radically presocial because it could also "contain societies compatible with rights (e.g. conjugal, paternal, domestic societies in general, as well as many others), but no law." On these terms, therefore, human life and human activity involved three types of condition. The first was simple individuality, which really was presocial. The second condition consisted of societies that could contain many sorts of rights. The third, however, would be a society with the addition of law, or civil society in the old, pre-Hegelian sense of a political society with a public law. "The first and second of these conditions," Kant wrote, "can be called the condition of *private right*, whereas the third and last can be called the condition of *public right*."

> The latter contains no further or other duties of human beings among themselves than can be conceived in the former state; the matter of private right is the same in both. The laws of the condition of public right, accordingly have to do only with the rightful form of their association (constitution), in view of which these laws must necessarily be conceived as public.[14]

Public law, on Kant's terms, had no distinct or substantive content of its own. It existed simply to maintain the content of private law. In this sense, the content of public law was largely negative, while that of private law was largely positive.

Public law, however, added law to rights. This was why it was the real basis of political society, or what Kant called a civil union. "The civil union," he explained, "is not so much a society but rather makes one."[15] It was founda-

14. Ibid., §41, pp. 450–51.
15. Ibid., §41, p. 451.

tional and irrevocable, because a civil union was the one single prerequisite of every political society, or every society based on the rule of law. Later, but in the same work, Kant made it clear that there could be no justification for the abolition or abrogation of this single prerequisite. To pursue such a course, he wrote, would not produce a "change in the civil constitution but its dissolution." Were this to occur, the apparent "transition to a better constitution" would not, in fact, be "a metamorphosis but a palingenesis, which requires a new social contract on which the previous one (now annulled) has no effect."[16] The idea of creating a new society out of the dissolution of the old was, therefore, simply incoherent because it amounted to removing the rule of law that had made it a society in the first place. It would, in fact, be just like adopting the idea of palingenesis that Herder had applied to the whole creation. Just as it was implausible to imagine that a new adult would come into being to replace the old one who had died, so it was equally implausible to imagine that a new society would come into being independently of the legal and constitutional foundations on which the old one had been based. Destroying a constitution, as Kant described it, amounted to destroying the one available provision for equality consistent with the existence of society, and this in turn meant eliminating the capacity to maintain any general acceptance of the many different types of economic, social, cultural, political, or institutional change that were likely to arise in a civil union. Removing the only criterion for equality from society itself amounted to exposing the civil union to the rule of the strong, the rich, the organized, the cunning, or the charismatic. Palingenesis would, in short, be radically self-defeating because, Kant emphasized, constitutional change was not only necessary but unavoidable, if only because of changes in circumstance and the passage of time. If palingenesis was impossible, metamorphosis was inescapable.

Kant did not actually spell out how constitutional change was supposed to occur. Instead, and immediately after making his distinction between metamorphosis and palingenesis, he wrote that "it must still be possible, if the existing constitution cannot well be reconciled with the idea of the original contract, for the sovereign to change it, so as to allow that form which is essentially required for the people to constitute a state to continue in existence."[17] But he then went on to emphasize that "this change cannot consist in a state's reorganizing itself from one of the three forms into another, as for, example, aristocrats agreeing to submit to autocracy or deciding to merge into a democracy or the reverse, as if it rested on the sovereign's free choice and discretion which kind

16. Ibid., §52, p. 480.
17. Ibid.

of constitution it would subject the people to." The change that mattered was one that, as Kant put it, made it possible "to continue in existence that form which is essentially required for the people to constitute a state." Here too Kant did not supply further precision but went on instead to introduce a further concept. This was the concept of a constituting power. Again, however, Kant did not specify what it was or where it was located. All that he went on to say was that "the *spirit* of the original contract (*anima pacti originarii*) involves an obligation on the part of the constituent power (*konstituierenden Gewalt*) to make the *kind of government* suited to the idea of the original contract."[18]

> Accordingly, even if this cannot be done all at once, it is under an obligation
> to change the kind of government gradually and continually so that it har-
> monizes *in its effect* with the only constitution which accords with right,
> that of a pure republic, in such a way that the *old* (empirical) statutory
> forms, which served merely to bring about the *submission* of the people, are
> replaced by the original (rational) form, the only form which makes *freedom*
> the principle and indeed the condition for any exercise of *coercion,* as is
> required by a rightful constitution of a state in the strict sense of the word.
> Only it will finally lead to what is literally a state—This is the only con-
> stitution of a state that lasts, the constitution in which *law* itself rules and
> depends on no particular person.[19]

The type of constitution in which only the law itself would rule and would, consequently, be independent of any particular person was, initially, a way of describing a social contract, but it was also, ultimately, a way of describing the real objective of political reform.

Constituent Power and the Politics of Reform

As Kant described it, the peculiar property of a constituent power was that it was a power that could not be exercised directly by a sovereign but could nonetheless change the nature of sovereignty itself. This concept of a power that could be applied to sovereignty but could not be exercised by the sovereign makes it possible to clarify not only what Rousseau could have meant by his assertion that sovereignty could not be represented, but also helps to explain what Kant meant by substituting the concept of metamorphosis for palingenesis as the metaphor that was most appropriate for thinking about the process of political reform and, more broadly, about the relationship between

18. Ibid., §52, p. 480.
19. Ibid., §52, pp. 480–81.

reform and revolution. If, Kant warned, here clarifying Rousseau, sovereignty *could* be represented, then the general will could not be sovereign because, in the light of how it was represented, the sovereign would be either an autocracy, an aristocracy, or a democracy. If, in a corresponding sense, Kant also pointed out, the sovereign was to call upon anything other than itself to represent it, then it would, effectively, have abdicated. Whatever it was, a constituent or constituting power was not the sovereign, because sovereignty was, ultimately, de facto power.[20] It was immediate and decisive, which meant that calling upon someone or something else to represent it was simply incompatible with the concept of sovereignty. This, Kant commented, was exactly what had happened in France in 1788 and 1789 and helped to explain why there had been a French Revolution. "It was," he wrote, "a great error of judgment on the part of a certain powerful ruler in our own times when he tried to relieve himself of the embarrassment of large national debts by leaving it to the people to assume and distribute this burden at their own discretion."

> It was thus natural that the people should acquire legislative powers not only in matters of taxation but also in matters of government, for they had to ensure that the government would incur no new debts by extravagance or by war. The monarch's ruling authority thus disappeared completely; for it was not merely suspended but actually passed over to the people, to whose legislative will the property of every subject was now submitted.[21]

On Kant's terms, the French Revolution was the real-life version of palingenesis, with all the incoherent properties of the concept.

The Metaphysics of Morals picked up many of the arguments that Kant had made earlier in his polemical essay *On the Common Saying: 'This May be True in Theory, but it does not Apply in Practice'*, which he published in September 1793, a little over a year after the proclamation of the First French republic. That earlier essay was an extended examination of the nature of political obligation, particularly in conditions of political conflict like those unfolding in France. The essay set out a clear set of criteria for distinguishing metamorphosis, which was necessary because it was unavoidable, from palingenesis, which was impossible, at least as a political concept, because it entailed replacing something that did exist by something that did not exist. But the initial aim of the essay, Kant emphasized, was to explain why political obligation could not be based on evaluations of individual or collective happiness, well-being,

---

20. On the concept of constituent power, although without Kant's version, see Lucia Rubinelli, *Constituent Power: A History* (Cambridge, CUP, 2020).

21. Kant, *MM*, §52, p. 481.

or welfare. This was not because these subjects were irrelevant to the subject of political obligation. Instead, he wrote, they had all too much to do with it, but in ways that involved so tangled a jumble of reasons, motives, values, judgments, and causal assessments that no stable answers or common goals were ever likely to be possible. Genuine common knowledge was simply not available in any moderately complicated society, and, in the absence of common knowledge, political obligation had to be based on something other than experience to have a chance of becoming binding. This, on Kant's terms, was why theory mattered. Used well, it could supply answers that were unavailable from experience.

Experience indicated that one way of answering the question about the grounds and extent of political obligation and its attendant duties was to focus on the self and its various physical and emotional states. In Jean-Jacques Rousseau's vocabulary, the self was an absolute entity (without a self, the subject of its duties would not arise), and if this was the case, there were good reasons to think that a duty was connected to those actions or arrangements that favoured individual well-being or happiness. In this sense, duty outside society was like Rousseau's concept of *amour de soi*, amounting to no more than a simple concern for one's own well-being. The problem, however, was that there was nowhere outside society and, consequently, no way to know whether, in the first place, two individuals' experiences of happiness were the same, and, second, what to do with possible discrepancies. In Rousseau's vocabulary again, trying to substitute someone else's happiness for one's own would open a door to the comparisons and assessments that gave rise to *amour-propre* or self-regard. This, Kant argued, was why the only genuine alternative to taking the self as a criterion for defining the grounds and extent of political obligation had to be something equally absolute, such as "the highest good possible on earth" and "the universal happiness of the whole world."[22] Like the idea of an isolated self, this alternative would also be absolute, and because it was, it would be a simple binary opposite to the self and its interests. It would also, however, be entirely out of reach as an individual goal. What, instead, it could supply was an imaginative equivalent of something like divine benevolence because an image of the highest possible good on earth would give the self an idea of a goal that was entirely disinterested and perfectly self-sufficient, leaving it, in addition, with no reason or motive to close itself off from others and, as a result, able, entirely freely, "to produce the highest good outside itself."[23] With this image of the universal happiness

22. Immanuel Kant, *T&P*, p. 65.
23. Ibid., p. 65 n.*.

of the whole world available, real choices could then be oriented towards an imagined goal that was the antithesis of the self, allowing the self to rely in turn for its moral guidance on what, in reality, was a self-generated goal. Duty was, therefore, the other side of what Kant, famously, called autonomy. It was self-generated and internally produced and, like virtue, was its own reward. "Happiness," Kant concluded, "embodies everything that nature gives us and nothing else. But virtue embodies that which no-one but man can give or take away from himself."[24]

Duty, in this rendition, was an ideal in both a moral and a substantive sense. This, Kant argued, was why it was grounded in theory, not practice, and why its moral foundations were imaginative and categorical, not empirical and prudential. The same applied to political obligation. Since a duty sometimes implied going against one's initial inclination, it presupposed a capacity to choose and the freedom to act. But, Kant pointed out in a note, there was simply no evidence of the existence of freedom that experience could supply. "It is," he wrote, "absolutely impossible to find a proof of its reality either in direct or indirect experience, and it cannot be accepted without any proof." Complicating things even further was the fact that the type of proof required was also not apparent. It could not, Kant wrote, be derived "from purely theoretical considerations." Nor could it be derived "from purely practical considerations of reason" or from "practical propositions in the technical sense" because these types of consideration relied ultimately on experience. Instead, the "only" considerations able to supply a proof were "moral-practical ones."[25] As Kant presented it, freedom was, therefore, something like the conceptual counterpart of a god or a state because evidence of its existence was supplied most vividly by the idea of an entity (like a state) or an image (like the happiness of the human race) that was able to hold different individuals, separated in time and space, accountable for obeying, or not obeying, a single prescription, like a law. In this sense, proof of human freedom was supplied by the possibilities of

24. Ibid., p. 68 n.*.

25. Ibid., p. 69 n.*. See also Immanuel Kant, *Groundwork of the Metaphysics of Morals* [1785], ed. H. J. Paton (London, 1948), p. 119: "We are unable to explain anything unless we can bring it under laws, which can have an object given in some possible experience. Freedom, however, is a mere idea: its objective validity can in no way be exhibited by reference to laws of nature and consequently cannot be exhibited in any possible experience. Thus the idea of freedom can never admit of full comprehension, or indeed of insight, since it can never by any analogy have an example falling under it. It holds only as a necessary presupposition of reason in a being who believes himself to be conscious of a will—that is, of a power distinct from mere appetition (a power, namely, of determining himself to act as intelligence and consequently to act in accordance with laws of reason independently of natural instincts)."

autonomy, morality, and sociability rather than by their actual existence. The fact that it was possible to think of ways that enabled them to exist was proof that they could actually exist.

Duty presupposed freedom. Freedom, additionally, presupposed political society because political society supplied equality under the law. Kant's indirect approach to the subject of freedom meant that the real possibility of its existence was predicated on the existence of a political society and, by extension, on the compatibility between individual autonomy and the rules establishing what he called "a civil state" or "commonwealth." For this to occur according to Kant's terms, both the state and its rules would have to be based on purely contractual principles. In addition, both had to have nothing to do with anything like an actual historical contract because the idea of a social contract was, essentially, "an idea of reason" whose sole purpose was to establish a political society as a union and end in itself, independently of any further goals.[26] In this sense, a civil state or commonwealth existed, in the first instance, simply to enable what Kant called autonomy to exist. The idea of a social contract would, therefore, have the effect of turning theory into practice by giving freedom practical existence as "the *right* of men under coercive public laws by which each can be given what is due to him and secured against attack from any others." A civil state had no other purpose. This, Kant wrote, was because "the whole concept of an external right is derived entirely from the concept of *freedom* in the mutual external relationships of human beings, and has nothing to do with the end which all men have by nature (the aim of achieving happiness) or with the recognised means of achieving this end." In other words, a commonwealth existed simply to enable all its members to enjoy the one good (freedom) that nature itself could not supply. To do this, it had to subject all its members to laws established by the general will because, as Kant put it, this "purely lawful state" gave every member of society an ability to enjoy freedom as a human being, equality as a subject, and independence as a citizen.[27]

As with the tight relationship between duty and freedom, so the relationship between the state and rights was equally tight. In one sense, Kant explained, freedom was a generic human quality because every human was capable of possessing rights. But the capacity to possess rights called for qualification. Rights, as Kant was reported to have said in his earlier lectures, were a "restriction of every particular freedom to the conditions under which universal freedom can exist." This meant that for rights to be exercised jointly and severally, they would have to be supplemented by a civil state because only a

26. Kant, *T&P*, p. 79.
27. Ibid., pp. 73–74.

civil state could enable its members to exercise rights equally. It could do this because the type of equality that the civil state could supply was what Kant called an equal "right of coercion" with respect to every other member of the state, with the single exception of the physical or moral person who was its head. Without that one exception, Kant emphasized, there would be no identifiable head of state, and since everyone would then have the same coercive right, "the hierarchy of subordination would ascend infinitely."[28] With the exception in place, however, there would be a "uniform equality of human beings as subjects of a state" because they would all be equal before laws that, Kant continued, again echoing Rousseau, "as the pronouncement of the general will, can only be single in form." This type of equality—and the general subordination to the law that it entailed—would mean that there would be no legal obstacle to equality of opportunity and no barrier to prevent anyone from rising to any position open to his (or her) talents, industry, and good fortune. To be born, Kant pointed out, was not an act by the person who was born. No right, therefore, could be acquired solely by the fact of birth, which left everyone to aspire to acquire any condition, possession, or fortune. Only the head of state, as the personification of the law itself, would be exempt from this general equality because only something outside the whole contractual system could enforce its provisions in the name of the law.

Kant made it clear that these provisions for careers open to talents were, as he put it, "perfectly consistent with the utmost inequality of the mass in the degree of its possessions." He also made it clear that this way of thinking about a contractual civil state ruled out any right of resistance.[29] Building a right of resistance into a constitution was, he argued, simply incoherent. Revolutions do not come with a built-in provision for a social contract. This, Kant explained, was why the concept of palingenesis had no bearing on the real-life events of a revolution even if it was one that still had a bearing on morality, culture, and the arts. To think, Kant argued, that there could be a right of resistance built into a civil constitution amounted to thinking that any particular part of society had the same type of legal exemptions as the head of state. But, he pointed out, turning an exemption into a general principle amounted to undermining the very idea of an exemption. This, in turn, not only undermined the special status of the head of state but also called into question the unitary concept of the civil state itself. There was, in short, no alternative between solitary individuals with

28. Ibid., p. 75.

29. On the widely debated subject of the right of resistance in Kant's political thought, see, initially, Christopher Meckstroth, *The Struggle for Democracy: Paradoxes of Progress and the Politics of Change* (Oxford, OUP, 2015), pp. 114–38.

real differences on the one side and legal equality under a civil union on the other. If the right to have rights began with political society, then overturning political society simply ruled out the right to have rights.

The irrevocable character of political society, Kant argued, not only ruled out palingenesis but also helped to justify the metaphor of metamorphosis. Although it could not be reborn, a political society would have to change and, in keeping with the metaphor of metamorphosis, would have to rely on its own resources to be able to change for the better. This latter imperative explained why it made sense to believe that humanity was capable of improvement, and too why it made sense, against Moses Mendelssohn, to think about human history in terms of what Kant called a "constant advance towards the good." Without this conception of history, he argued, a civil state would have no moral status. It would, instead, simply be one set of arrangements among others, with no special characteristics setting it apart from everything else in the ebb and flow of human history. Here, Kant turned Mendelssohn's agnosticism against itself. If the future was simply unknowable, this was still a good enough reason to subscribe to a belief about a future that, by definition, could not depend on anyone presently alive for its realization. In fact, Kant continued, the content of the future did not really depend on any individual at all. Just as "universal violence and the distress it produces must eventually make a people decide to submit to the coercion which reason itself prescribes (i.e. the coercion of public law) and to enter into a *civil* constitution," the same applied to states themselves, and this, Kant wrote, "must finally lead them, even against their will, to enter into a *cosmopolitan* constitution."[30]

The process, he predicted, would be driven by war and the growth of the public and private indebtedness produced both by war and by the never-ending preparation for war. In one scenario, the many possible effects of economic decay, fiscal disputes, tax strikes, war-weariness, debt defaults, or preemptive strikes might, initially, include "the most fearful despotism" or "a cosmopolitan commonwealth under a single ruler" because this, as Kant noted, "has indeed happened more than once with states that have grown too large." But another possible outcome could be "a lawful *federation* under a commonly accepted *international right.*"[31] Nothing, of course, could guarantee this outcome. But, Kant wrote, picking up the theme of the *Bestimmung des Menschen*, there were reasons to think that "the end of *man* as an entire species, i.e. that of fulfilling his ultimate appointed purpose by freely exercising his own powers, will be brought by providence to a successful issue, even though the ends of *men* as

30. Kant, *T&P*, p. 90.
31. Ibid.

individuals run in a diametrically opposite direction. For the very conflict of individual inclinations, which is the source of all evil, gives reason a free hand to master them all; it thus gives predominance not to evil, which destroys itself, but to good, which continues to maintain itself once it has been established."[32]

Kant and Enlightenment

Kant had already outlined the constitutional and institutional framework that was most compatible with his endorsement of the truth of theory over the experience of practice in one of his most famous works. This was the short essay that he published in 1784 and is now usually known as "What is Enlightenment?" The question in the title of Kant's essay was not actually rhetorical, because it had in fact had been asked originally by someone else. It had arisen in the context of a discussion of the ceremony of marriage, and whether, to be a valid and durable union, the ceremony had to be performed by a minister of the church. If, as the original questioner put it, marriage is a relationship between two adults who have chosen freely to live together in a state of union, the need for a minister to officiate at the ceremony seems to be redundant. If one was still required despite the obvious capabilities of the parties to the ceremony, then, asked the original questioner, "What is enlightenment?"

Kant's answer was predicated on at least some of the assumptions about personal freedom and responsibility motivating the initial question. Marriage was, certainly, voluntary and, equally certainly, involved adults. But marriages sometimes do not last, and death or divorce frequently gives rise to questions about property, responsibility, kinship, and inheritance. Marriage might well call for choice, but it also calls for rules that, because they apply to marriage and its consensual nature, still have to leave room for choice and, in addition, remain compatible with choices by others. There were, therefore, complicated questions about knowledge, causation, and consequences built into the subject of marriage, and, as Kant saw, these lent themselves very readily to a broader question about the nature and preconditions of enlightenment itself.

In one sense, Kant's answer to the question was a straightforward claim that the security provided by political stability would produce the conditions required for peaceful public debate, which, in turn, would favour a process of peaceful political and social reform. This type of process would therefore be a metamorphosis, not a palingenesis. Although Kant did not make use of the two terms in the essay itself, its argument prefigured the logic of his later insistence

32. Ibid., p. 91.

on the difference between the two concepts. The argument itself, however, was also rather more complicated than it can seem. It begins with a straightforward assertion. "Enlightenment," or "attaining enlightenment," Kant wrote (translations vary), "is humanity's exit from its self-incurred tutelage." This, he explained in the essay's first paragraph, was why the maxim "*Sapere aude!*—Have the courage to use your own understanding"—was "the motto of enlightenment."[33] But, as several of Kant's early critics, notably Johann Georg Hamann, also sometimes known as the "Magus of the North," were quick to point out, it is not easy to see how the absence of enlightenment can be *self-incurred*, just as it is hard to understand why an inability should be described as a fault, or how it can be possible to attain enlightenment simply by daring to know. To Hamann, Kant was simply "a Prussian Hume." Moses Mendelssohn picked up the complaint. As he commented, it is not clear why the use of one's own understanding calls for courage rather than, for example, culture, education, or, simply, more enlightenment.[34] The uncertainty is compounded by Kant's term *Unmündigkeit*, a term usually translated as immaturity or tutelage, but which his first English translator rendered in 1798 as "nonage," a word then used to describe the legal condition of being a minor.[35] In the light of this usage,

33. Immanuel Kant, "An Answer to the Question: 'What is Enlightenment'" [1784], in Kant, *Political Writings*, pp. 54–60 (henceforth cited as Kant, "What is Enlightenment"). I have also used the translation in Immanuel Kant, *Practical Philosophy*, ed. Mary Gregor (Cambridge, CUP, 1996), pp. 17–22.

34. The two assessments are described in the fine collection edited by James Schmidt, *What Is Enlightenment? Eighteenth-Century Answers and Twentieth-Century Questions* (Berkeley, U of California Press, 1996), pp. 53–57, 293–94 (the latter in the chapter by Garrett Green). For helpful descriptions of Hamann's hostility towards Kant, see Alexander Regier, *Exorbitant Enlightenment: Blake, Hamann and Anglo-German Constellations* (Oxford, OUP, 2018), pp. 11–12, 89–90, 112–15, 142–46. See too James Schmidt, "What Enlightenment Was: How Moses Mendelssohn and Immanuel Kant Answered the *Berlinische Monatsschrift*," *Journal of the History of Philosophy* 30 (1992): 77–101 (particularly p. 89), and his earlier "The Question of Enlightenment: Kant, Mendelssohn, and the *Mittwochgesellschaft*," *Journal of the History of Ideas* 50 (1989): 269–91. Hamman's description of Kant as a Prussian Hume is taken from Emile Boutroux, *Historical Studies in Philosophy* (London, Macmillan, 1912), p. 262.

35. As Kant's eighteenth-century translator put it: "*Enlightening is man's quitting the nonage occasioned by himself. Nonage* or minority is the inability of making use of one's own understanding without the guidance of another. This nonage is *occasioned by oneself*, when the cause of it is not from the want of understanding, but of resolution and courage to use one's own understanding without the guidance of another. *Sapere aude!* Have courage to make use of thy own understanding! is therefore the dictum of enlightening." Immanuel Kant, "An Answer to the Question, What is Enlightening," in Immanuel Kant, *Essays and Treatises on Moral, Political and Various Philosophical Subjects*, trans. A.F.M. Willich, 2 vols. (London, 1798), 1:3.

Kant seems to be saying that humanity had somehow made itself unfit to act for itself, or had made itself incapable of taking responsibility for its own actions, as would be the case with a minor. It is, in short, not immediately clear what Kant's essay was supposed to be about or what the point of his definition of enlightenment was intended to be.

An initial clue can be found in the second paragraph. It is, Kant wrote there, "so easy to be immature." This, he explained, had nothing to do with ignorance in the usual, largely negative, senses of a lack of knowledge or an absence of understanding, and far more, instead, to do with relying on information or judgments from other people. "If," Kant continued, "I have a book that has understanding for me, a pastor who has a conscience for me, a doctor who judges my diet for me, and so forth, I do not need to trouble myself. I have no need to think. If only I can pay; others will manage the tedious business for me."[36] As any reader of Rousseau is likely to see, Kant was not actually, or not only, writing about enlightenment, but was also writing about the division of labour, or, in the phrase standardly used to refer to the concept by Rousseau and his mid-eighteenth-century Francophone contemporaries, the separation of occupations and professions. Strangely, few of Kant's more recent readers have noticed this, even though Rousseau is often associated with this type of critical evaluation of the division of labour and, as is well known, was one of Kant's favourite authors.[37] Once seen, however, the presence of the subject of occupational specialization alongside the subject of enlightenment throws a different light on Kant's essay. In the most immediate sense, it makes the beginning of the essay look very Rousseauian. "Self-incurred tutelage," or nonage, begins to look rather like the course of human history if history is seen through the prism of the two *Discourses* (on the arts and sciences, and on the origin of inequality) that first made Rousseau famous.

"I hate books," Rousseau announced in *Emile* (the book that, according to the apocryphal story, caused Kant to drop his normally predictable midday walk and continue reading); "they only teach us to talk about what we do not

36. Kant, "What is Enlightenment," p. 54. On the problem of explaining the "self-incurred" quality of the condition, see also Tracy B. Strong, *Politics without Vision: Thinking without a Banister in the Twentieth Century* (Chicago, U of Chicago Press, 2012), pp. 24–39.

37. See, for example, Katerina Deligiorgi, *Kant and the Culture of Enlightenment* (New York, SUNY Press, 2005); Dan Edelstein, *The Enlightenment: A Genealogy* (Chicago, U of Chicago Press, 2011); Samuel Fleischacker, *What Is Enlightenment?* (London, Routledge, 2013); John Robertson, *The Enlightenment: A Very Short Introduction* (Oxford, OUP, 2015). For a modified view, see Sonenscher, *Jean-Jacques Rousseau.*

know."[38] One of the few exceptions to the rule, he went on to claim, was Daniel Defoe's *Robinson Crusoe* because it was, explicitly, a study of real utility and comprehensive self-reliance. Otherwise, however, less was more. Although, Rousseau wrote, also in *Emile*, there had been several claims to the contrary, "there is no real advance in human reason because all that is gained on one side, we lose on the other. All minds start from the same point and, since the time spent learning what others have thought amounts to so much time lost in learning to think for ourselves, we end up with more enlightenment and with less vigour of mind. Our minds, like our arms, are accustomed to use tools for everything and, as a result, they do nothing for themselves."[39] As he had put it earlier in the same book, "the more ingenious are our tools, the more our organs become clumsy and awkward. By dint of gathering machines around us, we can no longer find any within ourselves."[40] Although the phrases belong to Rousseau, the underlying idea meshes very readily with Kant's concept of self-incurred tutelage, or nonage. They suggest that the real nemesis of enlightenment was not ignorance, idleness, backwardness, superstition, or prejudice, but occupational specialization and the division of labour, and that the real problem motivating Kant's essay was the problem of knowing how to choose what to do, both individually and collectively, under conditions of economic, social, and epistemic interdependence.

Seen in this light, the condition of nonage meant that no single individual could have the knowledge or understanding disseminated widely among a plurality of individuals and would therefore have to rely on their collective expertise in order to access that knowledge or understanding. But nobody could simply rely on what others told them if they were to lead a self-determined life. This double bind, Kant continued, explained why it was particularly hard to escape from the condition of tutelage solely by relying on individual effort. This, he emphasized, was certainly required, but indi-

---

38. Jean-Jacques Rousseau, *Emile* [1762], in Jean-Jacques Rousseau, *Collected Writings*, 14 vols., ed. Allan Bloom, Christopher Kelly, Roger D. Masters, Philip Stewart, et al. (Hanover, NH, and London, University Presses of New England, 1987–2007), vol. 13, bk. 3, p. 331. For this translation see Jean-Jacques Rousseau, *Emilius, or an Essay on Education*, 2 vols. (London, 1763), 1:266.

39. Rousseau, *Emile*, bk. 4, p. 516.

40. "Plus nos outils sont ingénieux, plus nos organes deviennent grossiers et maladroits: à force de rassembler des machines autour de nous, nous n'en trouvons plus en nous-mêmes." Ibid., bk. 3, p. 322. See too Jean-Jacques Rousseau, *Les pensées de J. J. Rousseau* (Amsterdam, 1763), pp. 151–52, where, interestingly, the two passages have been merged. For this translation, see Jean-Jacques Rousseau, *Thoughts of Jean-Jacques Rousseau*, translated by Miss Henrietta Colebrooke, 2 vols. (London, 1788), 1:182.

vidual effort alone was never enough. "Rules and formulas," Kant explained, "these mechanical instruments for the rational use (or rather misuse) of humanity's natural gifts, are the ball and chain of an everlasting minority" because the point of a system of rules was that it was, by definition, uniformly applicable. "Hence," he concluded, "there are only a few who have managed to free themselves from immaturity through the exercise of their own minds and can yet proceed confidently" (Kant's eighteenth-century translator wrote "to emancipate themselves from nonage by their own labour").[41] There was, however, an alternative. Alongside individual effort, there could also be free public discussion. As Kant put it, "whether a public is able to enlighten itself is more likely; indeed it is nearly inevitable, if only it is granted freedom. For there will always be found some who think for themselves, even among the established guardians of the masses, and who, after they themselves have thrown off the yoke of immaturity, will spread among the herd the spirit of rational assessment of individual worth and the vocation of each man to think for himself."[42] From this perspective, there was a kind of causal process that did not depend entirely or exclusively on individual effort because the ebb and flow of free discussion would, in itself, produce the conditions that allowed the views of those who could think for themselves to circulate more widely. The onus for enlightenment would, therefore, fall less directly on individual effort and more on common involvement in free public debate.

There was, in addition, a further dimension to the process. As Kant began to describe it, the process of enlightenment ran, in the first instance, from public discussion to private judgment. But it also had a second side that, not entirely concurrently, ran from private judgment to public discussion. On the first side of the process, Kant wrote, there was "no danger even to his legislation" if a ruler was prepared to allow his subjects "to make *public* use of their own reason and put before the public their thoughts on better ways of drawing up laws, even if this entails forthright criticism of the current legislation." Here, the key word was the word *public* because it was used in conjunction with a concept of authority that Kant separated firmly from the public sphere. The public use of reason, he explained, was "that use which anyone may make of it *as a man of learning* addressing the entire reading public," while its private use was "that use which a person may make of it in a particular *civil* post or office with which he is

41. Kant, "What is Enlightening," p. 4; Kant, "What is Enlightenment," pp. 54–55.

42. As Kant's first translator put it, "it is sooner possible for a nation to enlighten itself; nay, when it has the liberty it is almost infallible": Kant, "What is Enlightening," p. 5; Kant, "What is Enlightenment," p. 55.

entrusted."[43] The public use of reason could be exercised by anyone. Its private use, however, was exercised by a member of an organization, a servant of the state, or what would now be called a civil servant, *Beamte*, or *fonctionnaire*. Using reason in this latter sense produced a second side of the process. It involved following the rules governing the institution, organization, or office in question because these were the rules that gave them their identity and function. In a church, the rules applied to the clergy and to the ritual, ceremonies, and dogma of the faith in question. In an army, they applied to the chain of command and the powers ascribed to each office in the hierarchy, and in a tax system the rules applied to the timing, proportions, and amounts of money to be collected or paid. While the public use of reason was, in most senses, free, its private or bureaucratic use was, by definition, firmly fixed. Importantly, however, in this second side of the process, the private use of reason took precedence over its public counterpart.

As Kant went on to argue, it was actually the private use of reason that made its public use effective. Here, as he put it with his usual, sometimes brutal, directness, "only a ruler who is himself enlightened and has no fear of phantoms, but at the same time has a well disciplined and numerous army ready to guarantee public security, may say what no republic or free state would dare to say: *Argue as much as you like and about whatever you like, but obey!*"[44] Here, the private use of reason was a rather euphemistic way of describing military, administrative, financial, or legal discipline. The public use of reason was supposed, therefore, to develop alongside an already-established, but still developing, rule-based system. The dual quality of the process has often been lost, particularly in the wake of the rather fuzzy international reception of the mid-twentieth-century debate between the two German political philosophers Reinhardt Koselleck and Jürgen Habermas (which, at bottom, was a debate about the historical and political implications of Kant's essay).[45] Kant's own argument could, in fact, accommodate both the Koselleckian and

43. Kant, "What is Enlightenment," p. 55.

44. Ibid., pp. 55, 59.

45. See Koselleck, *Critique and Crisis*, and Jürgen Habermas, *The Structural Transformation of the Public Sphere* [1962] (Cambridge, MA, MIT Press, 1989). Curiously, many historians in Britain, France, and the United States did not initially recognize the connection between the two works or register their rival engagement with the legacy of the Nazi legal and political thinker Carl Schmitt: compare, for example, Dena Goodman, "Public Sphere and Private Life: Toward a Synthesis of Current Historiographical Approaches to the Old Regime," *History and Theory* 31 (1992): 1–20, to T.C.W. Blanning, *The Culture of Power and the Power of Culture: Old Regime Europe 1660–1789* (Oxford, OUP, 2003). On the Koselleck-Habermas dialogue (and a great deal more), see, recently, the collection of articles on Koselleck in *Revue Germanique*

the Habermasian readings, and this, it could be said, helps to explain the fuzziness of the later reception. First, Kant emphasized, there was authority and then there was liberty. It was, he wrote, a causal process that revealed what he called "a strange and unexpected pattern in human affairs," in which a "high degree of civil freedom" seemed at first sight to favour intellectual freedom but would, in fact, give rise to "insurmountable barriers" to its actual existence, while, paradoxically, "a lesser degree of civil freedom" would give "intellectual freedom enough room to expand to its fullest extent."[46]

In the long term, Kant claimed, the two systems would develop in tandem. The private use of reason would change because the institutions of government would become more specialized and more differentiated from one another. Growing specialization would equip members of different branches of the administration with the knowledge and confidence to disseminate their views within the wider public. In this sense, the private use of reason would favour its public use, but the same outcome, Kant argued, would not apply if the public use of reason seeped into its private use. Rules had to be insulated from public discussion and the difficulties and dilemmas that public discussion could sometimes expose. Although, Kant noted, the pattern was "strange and unusual," it was, nonetheless, not untypical of human affairs because, he added, "nearly everything" considered in the widest sense was "paradoxical" in human affairs.[47] "When," he concluded, "nature, under this hard shell, has developed the seed for which she cares most tenderly—namely the inclination and the vocation for *free thinking*—this works back upon the character of the people (who thereby become more and more capable of *acting freely*) and, finally, on the principles of government, which finds it to its advantage to treat man, who is now *more than a machine*, in keeping with his dignity."[48]

The metaphorical association of a shell, a seed, and the process of enlightenment fitted Kant's later distinction between metamorphosis and palingenesis. Instead of the profusion of views generated by a single public sphere, the system that Kant envisaged had two distinct parts. The private part would be rules

---

Internationale 25 (2017), ed. Jeffrey Andrew Barash and Servanne Jollivet. See too Maissen, "Reinhart Koselleck."

46. As Kant's eighteenth-century translator put it, "Thus a strange unexpected course of human affairs presents itself here, so that when it is contemplated in the gross almost everything is paradoxical in it. A greater degree of civil liberty seems advantageous to the liberty of the *spirit of the nation*, and yet places insuperable barriers to it, whereas a degree less of that gives this full scope to extend to the utmost of its faculty." Kant, "What is Enlightening," p. 13; Kant, "What is Enlightenment," p. 59.

47. Kant, "What is Enlightenment," pp. 59–60.

48. Ibid., p. 60.

based and would also become increasingly specialized and differentiated as the range of government responsibilities grew in scale and scope. Public discussion, on its side, would take place within this composite setting and the many different viewpoints and evaluations that it was likely to generate. Enlightenment, Kant argued, lay at the junction of these two parts of political society, just as, in the context of the original discussion in which the question of enlightenment was raised, marriage lay at the junction of individual feelings and choices on the one side and rules, responsibility, and authority on the other.

Some of these distinctions, like the distinction between love and the law in the context of marriage, are not hard to see. It is more difficult to see how far, or even whether, distinctions appropriate to one context were suitable to, could be scaled up to, or could be transferred to other contexts. Many of Kant's claims, however, relied quite heavily on this type of conceptual acrobatics. There was, certainly, a clear difference between palingenesis, or the idea of something being born again, and metamorphosis, or the idea of the same thing changing over time. But, in the context of politics, history, and states, it was not clear why one of these concepts was any less metaphorical than the other. Although they certainly did describe change in different ways, neither offered much guidance about the mechanisms or causal agencies that were responsible for change. Unlike palingenesis, with its emphasis on one thing dying and being reborn, and, therefore, on the finitude of the body politic, metamorphosis was clearly dual, with continuity on the side of the body politic and with social and institutional change unfolding beneath it, but it was not clear what kept the two sides of the relationship between the state and society separate but connected. The problem was made more acute not only because the concept of metamorphosis was designed to capture Kant's initial distinction between history as progress and history as either tragedy or farce, but also because the combination of continuity and change built into the concept of metamorphosis was designed to secure Kant's further claim that the one type of equality available to every member of a political society was equality before the law. If the concept of metamorphosis was as much of a metaphor as the concept of palingenesis, then many other aspects of Kant's argument about the interrelationship of politics, history, and states could also begin to look questionable. The most immediate of these aspects centred on the concept of the state and the problem of identifying a less obviously metaphorical way of approaching the various combinations of continuity and change, causation and value, uniformity and variety, legitimacy and power embedded in the metaphor of metamorphosis. Alongside these questions there was, however, a further question, also raised by Kant's philosophy. This was the question of the death of God and its relationship to Kant's trademark concept of autonomy. Curiously, one of the answers to the question of the death of God and its relationship to Kant's concept of autonomy came to be supplied by the concept of the division of labour. Even more curiously, the concept of the division of labour gradually helped to push Kant's concept of history as progress out of the picture. As is shown by Paul Chenavard's plan for the Panthéon in 1848, in place of the metaphor of history as metamorphosis, the nineteenth century's metaphor had become history as palingenesis. The aim of the next chapter is to describe how this process began, first by describing the idea of the death of God and how it was connected to Kant's concept of autonomy, and second by showing how the idea of autonomy came to be bound up in turn with what, starting in France after the revolution of 1830, had come to be called the social question. By 1848, it was clear that thinking about equality involved the reinstatement of a metaphor that, according to Kant, had no place in politics.

6

The Death of God and the Problem of Autonomy

Germaine de Staël and the Death of God

The death of God was first announced in 1796. The announcement was provoked by Kant's philosophy and the combination of the concept of autonomy and the future-oriented vision of history that it housed. The announcement of the death of God was also, however, the starting point of a burgeoning array of attempts to fill the gap between future possibilities and present realities that Kant had opened up. The focus in this chapter is on aesthetics as one of the most significant and durable attempts to solve the Kant problem. The idea of the death of God is now associated with the thought of Friedrich Nietzsche and the late nineteenth century. In fact, however, it was an idea that had an older provenance because it first began to circulate in the German- and French-speaking parts of Europe soon after its appearance as a description of a dream in a late eighteenth-century novel entitled *Siebenkäs* by a German satirist and aesthetic theorist named Jean Paul Richter (usually called Jean Paul).[1] Jean Paul was a protégé of Herder and, like Herder, a critic of Kant.

---

1. Jean Paul Richter, *Siebenkäs* [1796], 2 vols. (Paris, Aubier, 1963), 1:448–56. For the Villers-Staël translation, see Staël, *De l'Allemagne*, 3:284–90, and, for a helpful examination of the respective parts played by Villers and Staël in the translation, see Byron R. Libhart, "Madame de Staël, Charles de Villers, and the Death of God," *Comparative Literature Studies* 9 (1972): 141–51. On the wider French reception, the best study remains Fernand Baldensperger, "Le songe de Jean Paul dans le romantisme français," *Revue universitaire* 18 (1909): 132–39, reprinted in his *Alfred de Vigny: Contribution à sa biographie intellectuelle* (Paris, 1912), pp. 159–76. A further French translation of Jean Paul's text was published under the title of "La dernière heure" in the *Revue de Paris* 16 (1830): 1–7. More generally, see Claude Pichois, *L'image de Jean Paul Richter dans les lettres françaises* (Paris, José Corti, 1963), pp. 254–93; Jean-Marie Paul, *Dieu est mort en Allemagne. Des Lumières à Nietzsche* (Paris, Payot, 1994), pp. 78–83, and Geneviève Espagne, *Les*

Like Herder too, he was also highly sympathetic to the concept of palingenesis. His account of the dream was translated into French and published in 1810 by Germaine de Staël in her hugely influential account of Germany and German thought, *De l'Allemagne* (the translation was actually by her friend Charles de Villers), and it was this version of the dream that came to be written about by almost every significant literary and philosophical figure in early nineteenth-century France, from Victor Hugo, Honoré de Balzac, Alfred de Vigny, Théophile Gautier, and Gérald de Nerval to Alphonse de Lamartine, Charles Nodier, Edgar Quinet, Pierre Leroux, and Ernest Renan. Jean Paul's dream was also translated into English, either with the help of Germaine de Staël's earlier French translation or more probably directly from the original German by one or other of the growing number of British students of German thought, including Thomas De Quincey and Thomas Carlyle. It soon travelled too to the United States of America where it was widely noticed, particularly in the transcendentalist circles associated with Ralph Waldo Emerson and Orestes Augustus Brownson.[2] By 1830, and almost anywhere within the European and North American reading publics, it would have been hard not to know of Jean Paul's claim that God was dead.

The dream itself was set in a graveyard where, in Jean Paul's description, the sequence of events started to unfold at midnight as the corpses housed in the cemetery slowly began to emerge from their tombs. These shades, or living dead, were querulous and irritable because they had no knowledge of where, beyond their present state of limbo, they would finally come to rest. They scuttled or shuffled around the graveyard, muttering and grumbling in muted,

---

années de voyage de Jean Paul Richter (Paris, Editions du Cerf, 2002), notably pp. 146, 169, but also more generally, because her book contains the fullest description of the relationship between Jean Paul and the Herder circle. See too Strong, *Politics without Vision*, pp. 16–56; Patrick Thériault and Jean-Jacques Hamm, eds., *Composer avec la mort de Dieu; littérature et athéisme au xixe siècle* (Paris, Hermann, 2014); and J. Hillis Miller, *The Disappearance of God: Five Nineteenth-Century Writers* (Cambridge, MA, Harvard UP, 1963). For a recent discussion of the subject (but without Jean Paul), see Terry Eagleton, *Culture and the Death of God* (New Haven, CT, Yale UP, 2014).

2. On the British and American receptions, see J. P. Vijn, *Carlyle and Jean Paul: Their Spiritual Optics* (Amsterdam, Utrecht Publications in General and Comparative Literature, 1982). An English translation was published in verse under the title "The Vision of Annihilation" and, it was said, with a verse pattern "chosen in imitation of Shelley's fine poem, *The Triumph of Life*, which the present poem also resembles in other respects": see [Anon.], "Chrestomathy: or Analects and Apologues," *Fraser's Magazine for Town and Country* 10 (1834): 439–42. For an earlier prose version, see [Anon.], "Jean Paul Richter," *New Monthly Magazine and Literary Journal* 38 (1833): 154–60.

quavering tones. "At this moment," Jean Paul wrote, "a tall majestic form with a countenance of imperishable anguish sank down from on high upon the altar; and all the dead cried: 'Christ! Is there no God?'"

And Christ answered, "There is none!"

The "shadows of every dead man" then began to tremble, and they trembled so hard that "one after another, their trembling dispersed them." And Christ then said:

> I have gone through the midst of the worlds. I mounted unto the suns, and flew with the milky way across the wilderness of heaven; but there is no God. I plunged down as far as Being flings its shadow and pried into the abyss and cried, 'Father, where art thou?' But I heard only the everlasting tempest, which no-one sways. And the glittering rainbow of beings was hanging, without a sun that had formed it, over the abyss, and trickling down into it. And, when I looked up towards the limitless world for the eye of God, the world stared back at me with an empty bottomless eye socket; and Eternity was lying upon chaos, and gnawing it to pieces, and chewing the cud of what it had devoured. Scream on, ye discords! Scatter these shades with your screaming. For He is not![3]

The conceit in Jean Paul's gothic fantasy was, daringly, to make Christ the bearer of the news that God was dead. It was this move, in sharp contrast to the orthodox image of the death of God as symbolized by Christ on the Cross, that gave his description its genuinely shocking impact.

The brilliance of Jean Paul's conceit horrified—and also captivated—his readers, including Germaine de Staël, whose own introduction to the translation in her *De l'Allemagne* (or *Germany*, as the contemporary English translation was called) made a point of suggesting the possibility that the dream could be a warning against materialism.[4] Other responses were less cautious. For Charles Nodier, one of the leading French critics of the generation after Staël, Jean Paul's vision amounted to "the boldest idea of the romantic genius," one to be set alongside Gottfried August Bürger's *Lenora* and Goethe's macabre, often erotic, short poems, "The Violet," "The Erl-King," and "The Bride of Corinth" as examples of what, to Nodier, gave romantic literature its transformative power. "The effort that I have made to focus on these singular objects," he wrote in 1818 in a review of the fifth (but first posthumous) edition of Staël's

---

3. I have used an early nineteenth-century English translation, entitled "The Vision of a Godless World," published in *The Atheneum; or the Spirit of the English Magazines*, 3rd ser., 2 (Boston, 1829): 83–86.

4. Staël, *De l'Allemagne*, 3:284–90.

book, "will not be entirely wasted if it leads some of our young poets to step out of the banal circle of salon poetry and seek more noble and abundant sources of inspiration in the sentiments and passions."[5]

In fact, it was Staël's interpretation of the dream that was the more accurate. Although she is often described as a literary dilettante whose knowledge of German and proficiency in philosophy were both open to question, much of the evidence suggests that she was, in fact, an unusually well-informed and reliable reader of her German sources (partly because of her initial tuition in German philosophy by the English literary critic Henry Crabb Robinson, but mainly because of her long epistolary friendship with Wilhelm von Humboldt).[6] In this case, she, more than Charles de Villers, the translator of Jean Paul's text (as too of Kant's *Idea of Universal History*), seems to have understood that Jean Paul's dream was actually a different kind of bravura performance from the one that it is now more usually taken to be. It was, in reality, an outcome of a protracted late eighteenth-century German argument over the related subjects of Spinoza and Spinozism in the first place and Kant and his critical philosophy in the second place. The key figure in this argument was another German philosopher, Friedrich Heinrich Jacobi, because the content of Jean Paul's dream was intended to be an endorsement of Jacobi's assessment of Kant and, by extension, a vivid illustration of what the moral and philosophical consequences of Kant's critical philosophy could be.[7]

5. "Je persiste à croire cependant que l'effort que j'ai fait pour la fixer [l'attention] sur ces singuliers objets ne sera pas tout à fait perdu, s'il porte quelques-uns de nos jeunes poètes à sortir du cercle banal de la poésie de salon et à chercher dans les sentiments et les passions une source d'inspirations plus nobles et plus abondantes." Charles Nodier, review of Germaine de Staël, *De l'Allemagne: Journal des débats politiques et littéraires*, 16 November 1818 (no pagination). The full, three-part review was reprinted in Charles Nodier, *Mélanges de littérature et de critique*, 2 vols. (Paris, 1820), 2:325–52. For further commentary on Nodier's long-drawn-out fascination with the dream, see Baldensperger, "Le songe de Jean Paul," in his *Alfred de Vigny*, pp. 164–65.

6. The correspondence is not in Staël, *Correspondance générale*. It was published by Leitzmann, "Wilhelm von Humboldt und Frau von Staël." On Staël's earlier tuition with Henry Crabb Robinson, see Henry Crabb Robinson, *Essays on Kant, Schelling and German Aesthetics*, ed. James Vigus (London, Modern Humanities Research Association, 2010).

7. For two helpful ways in to this argument and Jacobi's part in it, see Paul Franks, "'Nothing Comes from Nothing': Judaism, the Orient, and Kabbalah in Hegel's Reception of Spinoza," in *The Oxford Handbook of Spinoza*, ed. Michael Della Rocca (Oxford, OUP, 2017), pp. 512–42, and Richard H. Roberts, "God," in *The Oxford Handbook of Nineteenth-Century Christian Thought*, ed. Joel D. S. Rasmussen, Judith Wolfe, and Johannes Zachhuber (Oxford, OUP, 2019), pp. 573–91. See also Günter Zöller, "From Critique to Metacritique: Fichte's Transformation of Kant's Absolute Idealism," in *The Reception of Kant's Critical Philosophy*, ed. Sally Sedgwick (Cambridge, CUP, 2000), pp. 129–46 (notably p. 139).

Jacobi's assessment of Kant's philosophy can be summed up in a single word, "nihilism."[8] The assessment itself was based on a vision whose content and meaning were substantially the same as Jean Paul's later dream. Jacobi first mentioned this frightening prospect in his *Concerning the Doctrine of Spinoza*, which he published in 1785 as part of his *Letters to Moses Mendelssohn*, and described it more fully—as a vision of social annihilation and the complete disintegration of individual personality within the fathomless infinity of eternity—in later editions of his book. The reason for this attack was Kant's concept of autonomy and the idea of self-determination on which it was based. The concept, substantively, was designed to convey the content of Kant's essay on enlightenment and the watchword of *sapere aude* that announced the essay's broader message. For Jacobi, however, the idea of self-determination was offensively absurd because it seemed to mean that there was no identifiable difference between humanity and divinity, notably—and most damagingly—in terms of moral capability. As Jacobi objected, humans were not gods, and to imagine that they had the god-like power of self-determination was to open a door to nihilism and a vision of absolute social disintegration produced by trying to generalize the idea of individual autonomy across a real human society.[9] Jean Paul picked up the idea, describing the early nineteenth-century Jena romantics, notably the Schlegel brothers, as "aesthetic nihilists" whose thought, he wrote, was a product of "the lawless, capricious sprit of the present age, which would egoistically annihilate the world and the universe in order to clear a space merely for the free *play* of the void."[10] Like Jacobi too, Jean Paul associated "this lawless, capricious spirit" with Kant and the gap between the phenomenal and noumenal worlds embedded in Kant's philosophy. For them both, the death of God was a direct conceptual consequence of what they took to be the critical philosophy's groundless theory of self-determination.

As Jean Paul himself emphasized, the point of his dream was to shock his readers into seeing its truly horrifying implications. In his own German version, a part omitted from the French translation, the narrator wakes up to weep tears of joy when he sees the beauty of a setting sun and the evidence that it provides of God's continued existence.[11] This was the real message of the dream. In keep-

---

8. For a helpful way in, see Michael Gillespie, "Nihilism in the Nineteenth Century: From Absolute Subjectivity to Superhumanity," in *The Edinburgh Critical History of Nineteenth-Century Philosophy*, ed. Alison Stone (Edinburgh, Edinburgh UP, 2011), pp. 278–93, and his earlier *Nihilism before Nietzsche* (Chicago, U of Chicago Press, 1995).

9. For a clear summary, see Strong, *Politics without Vision*, pp. 21–22.

10. Gillespie, "Nihilism," p. 281.

11. This difference between the original and the translation is highlighted in Libhart, "Madame de Staël," p. 142.

ing with Jacobi's endorsement of faith, not reason, as the basis of both religious belief and moral judgment, Jean Paul's choice of Christ as the herald of the death of God was really designed to bring faith back to life. One of his aims, from this point of view, was to revive an older and still striking tradition of Lutheran imagery that was centred on the Crucifixion and was more obviously compatible with the traditional scriptural account of the death of God. This was the vision of the death of God that, complete with the colours of the setting sun—and possibly in the wake of Jean Paul's account—was to become a prominent feature of the work of the early nineteenth-century German painter Caspar David Friedrich. As Nietzsche himself noted later, announcing God's death was "an old-German word" (*ein alt-Germanisches Wort*).[12]

It was, however, a word that could mean several different things. As the collision of Jacobi, Jean Paul, and Kant's philosophy helps to show, it could mean that the critical philosophy amounted to the death of God. But it did not follow that actively endorsing the critical philosophy, as, almost by definition, Kant's followers went on to do, amounted to endorsing the idea of the death of God. If some of them—most famously the philosophers Johann Gottlieb Fichte, Friedrich Wilhelm Joseph Schelling, and Georg Wilhelm Friedrich Hegel—responded quite positively to the idea, they did so more to explore its imaginative and analytical possibilities than to assert its substantive material or doctrinal implications. Although the charge of atheism and materialism was levelled quite regularly at Fichte, Schelling, and Hegel, very little of their respective philosophies actually had anything to do with atheism or materialism. Much more, instead, had to do with the older question of the *Bestimmung des Menschheit*, or the question of the vocation, purpose, or goal of mankind that formed the broad background to Kant's protracted investigation of how the subjects of equality, freedom, and progress could be reconciled with the subjects of politics, history, and states. If the word "nihilism" summed up Jacobi's assessment of its results, Kant's own assessment could be summed up equally schematically by the word "autonomy."

The concept of autonomy was the conceptual lynchpin of the various types of dualism—between authority and liberty, the public and the private, and the noumenal and the phenomenal—that Kant outlined in his essay on enlightenment and, later, in his examination of the metaphysics of morals. In earlier usage, however, autonomy referred to something that was entitled—and

---

12. Quoted in Strong, *Politics without Vision*, p. 16 n. 1. On the overlap between the subjects addressed by Friedrich and Jean Paul, see, for example, Nina Amstutz, "Caspar David Friedrich and the Anatomy of Nature," *Art History* 37 (2014): 454–81, and, more recently, her *Caspar David Friedrich: Nature and the Self* (New Haven, CT, Yale UP, 2020).

able—to govern itself, like a municipality, province, university, guild, or corporation, under the aegis of a higher authority, like an empire, a church, or a
state.[13] Although his formulation echoed this usage, Kant turned the concept
into something that was intended to be compatible both with individual
agency and with the combination of public and private reason that he described in his essay on enlightenment. In this sense, the concept of autonomy
amounted to transferring and generalizing Leibniz's concept of spontaneity
from monads to humans. And, since Leibniz had many different types of follower in the German-speaking world, it opened a door to many different interpretations of what autonomy might be.

To Kant's critics, like Jacobi or Jean Paul, it was not clear how both the individual and the general parts of the concept could coexist. Autonomy, in the
first instance, was an individual capacity, based either on the idea that a present
self could bind a future self, or on the less time-bound idea that a noumenal self
could bind a phenomenal self. In either case, it implied a blend of a self-
generated choice, plus an ability to identify the right choice, plus an ability to
decide whether the right choice was a matter of reason or feeling (or both),
plus a further ability to produce the motivation required to keep to the aim or
goal of the initial choice. In addition, but in the second instance, autonomy
also had to be a collective choice or, at least, a product of the coordination, convergence, or sequence of an endlessly fluctuating number of individual choices.
As both Jacobi and Jean Paul were keen to emphasize, without this common
or collective dimension the idea of individual autonomy would turn out to be
radically self-defeating. If individual choices were to clash, or simply interfere
with one another, autonomy could turn into heteronomy, potentially producing
stasis, crisis, or worse. Together, these two aspects of the concept of autonomy
raised a number of questions about collective action, collective decision making, and the state that paralleled the questions generated by the opposition
between metamorphosis and palingenesis in Kant's thought. In both cases, the
question that really mattered was whether the concept in question, considered as either autonomy, metamorphosis, or palingenesis, was a real concept
or simply a metaphor. Finding an effective answer meant, above all, showing how and why states could be states while their members could still be
autonomous.

13. For a good example, see Alexandre Fauché-Prunelle, *Essai sur les anciennes institutions
autonomes ou populaires des Alpes Cottiennes-Briançonnaises*, 2 vols. (Grenoble and Paris, 1856),
1:49: "Les plus importantes des anciennes institutions, franchises ou libertés briançonnaises
sont d'origine ou de nature autonome; ce mot *autonome*, composé de deux mots grecs, signifie
loi de soi-même."

The Concept of Autonomy

The concept of autonomy that is now usually associated with Kant emerged from a series of attempts to come to terms with the moral and political implications of the thought of Jean-Jacques Rousseau, a series of attempts that became particularly rich and complex in the German-speaking parts of Europe mainly because of the substantial overlap between Rousseau's examination of the origin and nature of inequality and the parallel discussion of the vocation of mankind—or *Bestimmung des Menschheit*—that began to take place in the German-speaking parts of Europe several years before the publication of Rousseau's second *Discourse* and continued to inform German intellectual life long after Rousseau's death, most famously in Fichte's several early nineteenth-century variations on the subject. The most immediate reason for both the richness and the complexity of the discussion was Rousseau's concept of perfectibility. Although the word itself (*perfectibilité*) was Rousseau's own coinage, the concept could also be associated readily with long-established Aristotelian ways of thinking about political society, and, more specifically, with the idea that, unlike a household, a political society could be said to be self-sufficient or perfect. In a related sense, something like the same concept could also be associated with the moral and theological discussions of divine perfection and human imperfection to be found in the works of the German philosophers Gottfried Wilhelm Leibniz and Christian Wolff. The several different meanings of the concept of perfectibility—as both a condition and a capacity, and with both a moral and a historical dimension—gave the word a still further association with another, more or less concurrent, French neologism, *civilisation*, and, in the German-speaking world, with the related set of connotations of the word *Kultur*.[14] Rousseau's noun, *perfectibilité*, brought all these different connotations into closer, but cloudier, proximity, because he applied the concept directly to humans, rather than to states or to God.

Perfectibility, Rousseau wrote in 1755 in his *Discourse on the Origin of Inequality*, was the one faculty that distinguished humans from animals. It was, he asserted, "a faculty which, with the aid of circumstances, successively develops all the others, and resides among us as much in the species as in the individual." While humans could change and, over time, become different

---

14. For helpful ways into this family of related concepts, see Bertrand Binoche, ed., *L'homme perfectible* (Seyssel, Champ Vallon, 2004), and Bertrand Binoche, ed., *Les équivoques de la civilisation* (Seyssel, Champ Vallon, 2005); as well as his own *Les trois sources des philosophies de l'histoire (1764–1798)* (Paris, PUF, 1994) and *La raison sans l'histoire* (Paris, PUF, 2007). See also François Hartog, *Régimes d'historicité. Présentisme et expériences du temps* (Paris, Le Seuil, 2003) and, more recently, *Chronos. L'Occident aux prises avec le temps* (Paris, Gallimard, 2020).

types of human, an animal, Rousseau wrote, "is at the end of a few months what it will be all its life; and its species is at the end of a thousand years what it was at the first year of that thousand." Perfectibility was, therefore, the name that Rousseau gave to the mixture of individual inventiveness and collective innovation that enabled something new to be integrated into human culture in ways that, however ingenious an individual animal might be, were not visible in its species as a whole. However much they might vary in design, birds' nests would remain birds' nests, but human huts could become high-rise housing complexes, with all the attendant technical, material, and cultural acquisitions on which they relied. Perfectibility was, therefore, the faculty that "by dint of time, draws [man] out of that original condition in which he would pass tranquil and innocent days" and, by "bringing to flower over the centuries his enlightenment and his errors, his vices and virtues, in the long run makes him the tyrant of himself and of nature."[15]

Perfectibility, as Rousseau began to describe it, was a quality that was both positive and negative. It also had both quantitative and qualitative attributes. Initially, the term appeared to refer mainly to quantities—to more goods, more knowledge, more people, more civility, more morality, or, on Rousseau's terms, more vices and virtues. But this raised a further question about whether—or how—extra quantities could produce different qualities. It was a question that connected the idea of perfectibility to variety as well as quantity, and to a growing range of individual qualities and capabilities, like being an excellent musician, draughtsman, or cook—or, simply, to being Jean-Jacques rather than anyone else. In this sense, perfectibility seemed to go together with personality. Putting the two together meant that Rousseau's concept appeared to have several different dimensions, with perfection lying at a point in time at which the separate axes of material resources and human diversity intersected. But it was not clear whether it was possible to know whether these hypothetical axes would follow a measurable trajectory, and whether there really was a point at which they would actually converge. More material resources could mean more occupational and technical diversity, or vice versa, but, however the causation might work, there did not seem to be a way to know whether, over the course of time, the two trends would move towards or away from one another, or whether their effects would be visible at an individual level or at that of humanity as a whole, or perhaps at both.

15. Jean-Jacques Rousseau, *Discourse on the Origin and Foundations of Inequality among Men*, in Rousseau, *Collected Writings*, 3:26; Jean-Jacques Rousseau, *Oeuvres complètes*, ed. Bernard Gagnebin and Marcel Raymond, 5 vols. (Paris, Gallimard, 1959–95), 3:141–44, pp. 74–80 n. 7 (cross-references to the Pléiade edition are supplied in all volumes of Rousseau, *CW*).

These questions formed the intellectual setting in which the additional analytical precision given, respectively, by Moses Mendelssohn, Karl Phillip
Moritz, Immanuel Kant, and Friedrich Schiller to Rousseau's concept became
the basis of a new, aesthetically driven theory of individual and collective autonomy. As it did, the word "autonomy" itself began to acquire something like
its modern sense as its older, more narrowly legal and institutional connotations (as in an autonomous province or an autonomous professional body)
came, between the mid-1780s and the early 1810s, to be incorporated into the
more recent philosophical discussions generated by Rousseau's concept of
perfectibility. Two significant moves were involved in grafting the concept
of perfectibility onto the idea of autonomy. The first was a strong emphasis on
the relationship between freedom and moral self-determination, which was
Kant's move, while the second was an aesthetically generated explanation of
the imaginative and motivational capacities involved in Kant's version of moral
self-determination, which was Schiller's move.[16] The first move consisted of
giving the idea of self-determination something like the same sense as Rousseau's idea of a social contract, where the self in the guise of a private person
made a contract with itself as a public person. Kant, famously, repeated the
move by using the distinction between a noumenal and a phenomenal self to
produce the same self-binding outcome. The second move, by Schiller, added
an aesthetic dimension to the initial distinction. This addition, Schiller argued
in his *Letters on the Aesthetic Education of Man*, was connected to the human
ability to distinguish form from substance and appearance from reality. This
imaginative ability, he went on to claim, was the basis of the further human
ability to find likeness or resemblance in things that otherwise have nothing
in common, and to use the resulting patterns for decorative or ornamental
purposes. Schiller gave these abilities the rather unhelpful name of the *Spieltrieb*, or play-drive, as it is usually translated.[17] On his terms, the *Spieltrieb* was
actually the key to modern politics.

The combination of the ability to find resemblance and to use it decoratively
was, Schiller claimed, a sign of human freedom because it indicated that
there was something more to human nature than rationality and sensibility.

16. On the first of these moves and its relationship to the old heresy of Pelagianism, see
Nelson, *The Theology of Liberalism*.

17. On *Trieb* as instinct, appetite, force, impulse, or drive, see Myriam Bienenstock, ed.,
"Trieb: Tendance, instinct, pulsion," *Revue germanique internationale* 18 (2002): 12–13, as well as
the other articles in the whole issue. See also Fania Oz-Salzberger, "Schiller, Ferguson, and the
Politics of Play: An Exercise in Tracking the Itinerary of an Idea," in *In the Footsteps of Herodotus:
Towards European Political Thought*, ed. Janet Coleman and Paschalis M. Kitromilides (Florence,
Leo. S. Olschki, 2012), pp. 117–39.

Reason and sense obeyed logical or physical rules, but the rules involved in decoration and ornamentation were purely self-created, or autonomous. This difference, Schiller argued, revealed the deep historical interconnection of beauty, the arts, and the concept of moral autonomy. The connection formed the basis of his distinction between naïve and sentimental poetry as well as the further distinction that he went on to make between the spontaneous (or reactive) quality of the former and the autonomous (or reflective) quality of the latter. The combination of beauty and autonomy added up to what Schiller called an "aesthetic state." To some of his more philosophically informed contemporaries, Schiller's concept was an elaborate reworking of the argument of Kant's admirer and critic, the philosopher Johann Gottlieb Fichte in his *Wissenschaftslehre* (The science of knowledge). "Consider this," wrote a student at the University of Jena, where both men taught, "many well educated donkeys are willing to pretend that Schiller's *Letters* are nothing more than Fichte's system presented in a nicer fashion. They could not notice that those letters are based on it, but that they nevertheless go their own way. Instead of the play-drive, says Fichte, he (meaning Schiller) should rather have used 'imagination.'"[18] But whether it was a called a play-drive or, more simply, the imagination, it was the basis of the human ability to turn a vision into an achievement. "Truth," Schiller wrote in his *Letters on the Aesthetic Education of Man*, "lives on in the illusion of art, and it is from this copy, or afterimage, that the original image will once again be restored."[19] The absence of this shared image was the reason why the French Revolution had gone wrong, and was also confirmation that what Schiller called an aesthetic state was an essential precondition for what he described as "the construction of true political freedom" because, he added, "it is only through beauty that man makes his way to freedom."[20] As he added in a later letter, however much the cultivation of individual powers gave rise to the sacrifice of wholeness, "it must be open to us to restore by means of a higher art the totality of our nature which the arts themselves have destroyed."[21] Under certain conditions, Schiller claimed, freedom could repair the damage that it had itself created.

18. Daniel Veit to Rahel Levin, 23 April 1795, cited by Claude Piché, "The Place of Aesthetics in Fichte's Early System," in *New Essays on Fichte's Later Jena* Wissenschaftslehre, ed. Daniel Breazeale and Tom Rockmore (Evanston IL, Northwestern U Press, 2002), pp. 299–316 (p. 302 for the citation). I owe this reference to Isaac Nakhimovsky.

19. Schiller, *On the Aesthetic Education of Man*, letter 9, p. 57.

20. Ibid., letter 2, pp. 7, 9.

21. Ibid., letter 6, p. 43.

Rousseau, Mendelssohn, and Kant

The sequence of steps that eventuated in Schiller's concern with beauty and freedom began with Moses Mendelssohn's translation of Rousseau's *Discourse on the Origin of Inequality* in 1756 and the open letter on Rousseau's moral philosophy that Mendelssohn wrote to a friend, the Prussian dramatist and philosopher Gotthold Ephraim Lessing, in that year. In it, Mendelssohn claimed that Rousseau's bleak conjectural history was the outcome of a heavily one-sided view of the mind-body problem. It meant, he argued, that Rousseau had focused too strongly on the physical side of human nature and had placed too much weight on humanity's dependence on both the supply of subsistence goods and the social distribution of wealth. The result, he continued, was that Rousseau had failed to pay enough attention to the mind's ability to set prevailing economic and social injustices against a potentially large number of alternative visions of social and political order. Although he was entirely willing to endorse Rousseau's indictment of inequality, Mendelssohn was also committed to the idea that modern governments had a real capacity for reform. In this respect, he wrote, his own position was similar to that of the Swiss reformer Isaak Iselin, whose *Philosophical and Patriotic Dreams of a Friend of Humanity* (1755) he singled out as a model of how to criticize modern society without making Rousseau's mistakes.[22] "There are very few places in which I cannot be at one with Rousseau," Mendelssohn informed Lessing in a letter written while his translation was still in progress, "and nothing annoys me more than when I see political philosophy (*Staatskunst*) claim that everything as it now is must be in accord with reason. If only Rousseau had not denied all morality for civilized humanity! To this I am very much committed."[23] The problem with Rousseau was that he had not seen that humans really do have an individual capacity for improvement.

To deal with the problem, Mendelssohn turned to another of Rousseau's key concepts, the emotion of pity, to give the idea of perfectibility a more

22. See Altmann, *Moses Mendelssohn*, p. 101. For a fine discussion of Iselin's thought, see Béla Kapossy, *Iselin contra Rousseau: Sociable Patriotism and the History of Mankind* (Basel, Schwabe, 2006).

23. Mendelssohn to Lessing, 26 December 1755. Cited in Frederick C. Beiser, *Diotima's Children: German Aesthetic Rationalism from Leibniz to Lessing* (Oxford, OUP, 2009), p. 225. I have modified the translation slightly. Mendelssohn was, for example, prepared to compare the current situation of the Jews to the state of despotic oppression that Rousseau described at the end of his second *Discourse*: see David Sorkin, *Moses Mendelssohn and the Religious Enlightenment* (London, Peter Halban, 1996), p. 110. See too Matt Erlin, "Reluctant Modernism: Moses Mendelssohn's Philosophy of History," *Journal of the History of Ideas* 63 (2002): 83–104.

determinate meaning. In doing so, he gave it a content that brought it nearer to the older, Aristotelian idea of something self-sufficient (a *polis* rather than an *oikos*) and to the more recent discussions of the concept of perfection in the works of Leibniz and Wolff. Mendelssohn began the discussion by arguing, like several of Rousseau's other critics, that the Genevan's use of the emotion of pity to explain why humans (like animals) had no natural disposition to harm others was an explanation that began in midstream. Pity, Mendelssohn argued, presupposed an initial capacity to recognize order or harmony, and a further capacity to feel disturbed or upset when that order or harmony was itself disturbed. Before it was possible to feel pity, even in Rousseau's self-centred way, it was necessary, Mendelssohn argued, to have an initial ability to distinguish between perfection and imperfection to be able to make the further distinction between order and disorder that lay behind the emotion itself (we feel pity for the victims of injustice because their misfortune clashes with our sense of the underlying order or harmony that prevails in the world). This move brought Mendelssohn's argument onto the terrain explored over several generations by Leibniz and Wolf. In their usage, responding positively to order or harmony, and distinguishing between perfection and imperfection, were derivations of the human capacity to love. Here, love was a feeling generated by the pleasure produced by the beauty of something orderly or harmonious, because order and harmony could be connected to ideas of perfection and eternity. It was, Mendelssohn wrote, this capacity for what, earlier in the eighteenth century, was sometimes called rational love that was the basis of taste and discrimination on the one side and of the emotion of pity on the other.[24] If, he argued, the development of all the component parts of the world explained our love for its underlying harmony, so interference with that development violated the same harmony and helped to explain our pity for its victims. From this perspective, both pity and the concept of perfectibility had a basis in judgments that, because of the mixture of knowledge and feeling on which they were based, had come quite recently to be called "aesthetic" by one of Mendelssohn's contemporaries, Alexander Gottlieb Baumgarten.[25]

Mendelssohn's comments made it easier to see more of a connection between the quantitative and qualitative aspects of Rousseau's concept of perfectibility. More goods, more knowledge, and more of all the rest could be connected to more variety, diversity, and individuality if the combination

24. For an earlier example of this type of argument, see Isaac Nakhimovsky, "The Enlightened Epicureanism of Jacques Abbadie: *L'art de se connaître soi-même* and the Morality of Self-Interest," *History of European Ideas* 29 (2003): 1–14.

25. For a fuller account, see Beiser, *Diotima's Children*, pp. 196–243 (especially pp. 224–30). See also Altmann, *Moses Mendelssohn*, p. 70.

amounted to something self-sufficient because something self-sufficient could be perfect, just like God. Since it was self-sufficient, it would also display the kind of aesthetic qualities that gave rise to love. From this perspective, Rousseau's bleak assessment of the modern capacity for morality could be modified. Giving perfectibility both a quantitative and a qualitative content appeared to indicate that morality, or at least the possibility of morality, actually had more of a place in the modern world than had been the case in the past. Since, it could be claimed, the modern world housed both greater quantities and greater variety, it appeared to offer the prospect of a genuinely self-sufficient society, and, since something self-sufficient could also be something beautiful and hence loveable, it also appeared to offer the prospect of a genuinely disinterested morality. Even here, however, uncertainties remained. These centred on the fact that Mendelssohn's reply to Rousseau seemed to rely quite heavily on an initial set of assumptions about the underlying order and harmony in the world and about the human capacity to recognize and respond to these qualities with the mixture of knowing and feeling that was beginning to be called "aesthetic."

Several of Mendelssohn's contemporaries were, however, less confident. Among the most telling objections to his whole argument were those made by a young philosophy professor named Thomas Abbt who became famous at the age of twenty-three for a book entitled *Vom Tode fürs Vaterland* (On dying for the fatherland), which was published in 1761 at the height of the Seven Years' War and, as its title indicated, covered many of the questions about love, altruism, and patriotism that were central to Mendelssohn's criticisms of Rousseau. Abbt was sceptical about the case that Mendelssohn had made for perfectibility and its basis in the human ability to discern an underlying order and harmony in the world. "If it is the case," he asked Mendelssohn, "that all that must be developed must, up to a certain degree, be developed, why is it that on earth so many thousand capacities never come to be developed to the measure here possible?"[26] The question, as Abbt went on to show, was more than a question about injustice or the origin of evil because the usual answer to that type of question, with its emphasis on explaining misfortune in terms of a higher, but inscrutable, providential order, played into Mendelssohn's argument about perfectibility. Instead, Abbt raised a more radical question about the human capacity to discern any underlying order at all in the world. Imagine, he wrote, an army that was dispatched to carry out a secret

26. Cited by di Giovanni, "The Year 1786," p. 225. In this paragraph, I have followed di Giovanni's excellent description of Abbt's criticism. For a recent overview of the subject, see Ajouri, "'The Vocation of Man.'"

mission under the command of a general who was the only one to know its real nature and purpose. Then, he continued, imagine what would happen if the general disappeared, leaving the army knowing that it had been entrusted with a secret mission, but not knowing what the secret was. The result would be chaos because it was, by definition, impossible to know something secret (once the secret was out, it was not a secret). The same problem, Abbt argued, applied to Mendelssohn's justification of perfectibility. It might well be the case that there was an underlying order and harmony in the world, but it was also the case that no one could know what it actually was. Abbt's objections to Mendelssohn did not mean jettisoning the idea of perfectibility. Later, with Jacobi, the same type of objection could mean transferring the idea of perfectibility to God and reinstating the concept of faith. But it could equally mean concentrating on perfectibility in this life. Moral arguments, Abbt emphasized, could not rely on unverifiable claims about an underlying order and harmony in human affairs. They had, instead, to focus on human affairs themselves.

The same argument, coupled with a much fuller and richer set of claims about human capabilities, was made by another of Mendelssohn's critics, Johann Gottfried Herder.[27] Here too Rousseau's thought supplied the starting point. In this case, however, the outcome was a substantially different version of the idea of perfectibility. This version emerged in the course of the long-drawn-out argument between Herder and Kant over the content and direction of human history that complemented their dispute over the subject of palingenesis. Ostensibly, the argument between Herder and Kant was an argument about human nature that grew out of Herder's critical comments on Rousseau's discussion of the origin of language in his *Discourse on the Origin of Inequality*. Substantively, however, it was an argument that, as it unfolded, gave rise to Kant's distinction between "moral politics" and "political morality," or the difference between politics modified by moral considerations (Kant's position) and morality modified by political considerations (Herder's position). Both positions relied on different claims about perfectibility, with Kant's giving more weight to the systemic properties of a certain type of political constitution, and Herder's giving more weight to individual and collective moral capacities. Although Rousseau was not Herder's only target in his discussion of the origin of language (the French philosopher Etienne Bonnot de Condillac and the German divine Johann Peter Süssmilch were others), he was particularly exercised by the Genevan's minimalist description of human nature. "Condillac and Rousseau had to err in regard to the origin of language,"

27. On Mendelssohn and Herder, see especially Frederick C. Beiser, "Mendelssohn versus Herder on the Vocation of Man," in Munk, *Moses Mendelssohn*, pp. 235–44.

he wrote, "because they erred in so well known a way and yet so differently . . . in that the former turned animals into men (*Traité sur les animaux*) and the latter men into animals (*Sur l'origine de l'inégalité*)."[28] Both, he went on to argue, failed to pay enough attention to the properties of the human mind and, in particular, to the part played by the imagination in differentiating humans from animals.

Animals, Herder argued, could rely on instincts to perform the relatively limited range of actions required for their way of life. Humans had no instincts, but were capable of an immense array of actions and a huge variety of different ways of life. Language was the means that enabled people to perform or establish these tasks but was also what enabled them to invent new courses of action and devise new ways of life. It was, therefore, the medium that made human life historical in a sense that did not apply to animals or even to the idea of natural history itself. It equipped humans with a capacity for purposeful action that was broader and deeper than anything that instinct could supply. The basis of that capacity, Herder went on to claim, was the human imagination. It was the source of the conceptual power and inventiveness that language served to express. Here too the initial model was given by the animal-instinct pairing. Instincts were unerring but narrow in focus. Humans had no instincts and could focus on anything and everything. The imagination, however, enabled them to focus purposefully because it allowed them to cross the boundary between what Herder, following Leibniz, called perception and apperception, and to switch the focus of their attention from their perceptions to their perceptions of their perceptions. Language, Herder argued, was the product of this reflexive capability. It was a continuously changing system of signs that enabled humans to store and use information supplied by the imagination's reflexive power.

Rousseau's neologism "perfectibility," Herder noted, was simply another name for this specifically human capacity.[29] But since the capacity was built into human nature, the neologism was redundant. Humans, he asserted, have a natural capacity for apperception (or perceiving oneself perceiving), and this "new, self-made sense of the mind is, in its very origin, a means of contact!"

I cannot think the first human thought, I cannot align the first reflective argument without dialoguing in my soul or without striving to dialogue.

---

28. Johann Gottfried Herder, *Essay on the Origin of Language* [1772], in *Jean-Jacques Rousseau and Johann Gottfried Herder: Two Essays on the Origin of Language*, ed. Alexander Gode and John H. Moran (Chicago, U of Chicago Press, 1966), p. 103. On Herder, see R. G. Collingwood, *The Idea of History* (Oxford, OUP, 1946), pp. 88–93, and, recently, Kristin Gjesdal, *Herder's Hermeneutics: History, Poetry, Enlightenment* (Cambridge, CUP, 2017).

29. Herder, *Essay*, pp. 124–25.

The first human thought is hence in its very essence a preparation for the possibility of dialoguing with others. The first characteristic mark which I conceive is a characteristic word for me and a word of communication for others.[30]

From this perspective, the human capacity for society was generated outside of society by each individual's initial apperceptive relationship to him- or herself. Language, the imagination, and society were therefore seamlessly connected. Reflexion, or the mind's apperceptive capacity, enabled humans to give characteristic marks to particular things. These might be associated with a sound or a sight, but, since signs were not necessarily produced by physical needs or solely by an emotional response to something external, the character of the sign itself was determined purely by the active power of the human mind. Language worked like *Bildung*. It enabled individuals to transfer what was on the inside to the outside and, under the weight of this slow process of historical osmosis, to turn every language into the cement of society. In highlighting this feature of language, Herder was particularly willing to extend the argument about the original nexus of music, poetry, and society made by an English Anglican cleric named John Brown in his *Dissertation on the Rise, Union and Power, the Progressions, Separations and Corruptions of Poetry and Music* of 1761. "The philosophical Englishman [meaning John Brown]," Herder noted, "who in our century took up this matter of the origin of poetry and music would have been able to progress farthest if he had not excluded the spirit of language from his investigation and if, instead of concerning himself so much with his system of bringing poetry and music to a single focus (in which neither can show itself properly), he had concerned himself more with the origin of both from the full nature of man."[31] As this comment implied, there was no reason to try to guess the shape or content of an underlying order or harmony in human affairs, as Moses Mendelssohn had assumed.[32] Humans had a built-in capacity to perfect themselves without needing to rely for emotional or intellectual guidance on whatever lay beyond this life. The capacity for language itself might, in the final instance, be divine in origin but, Herder emphasized, its purpose and use could only be human.

It was left to Kant to suggest that, as with his endorsement of the concept of palingenesis, Herder had failed to see Rousseau's point about the relationship between human freedom and human evil. In a little essay entitled "Conjectures on the Beginning of Human History" that he published in the *Berlinische*

---

30. Ibid., p. 128.
31. Ibid., pp. 137–38.
32. The point is made clearly by Beiser, "Mendelssohn versus Herder."

Monatsschrift in 1786 and which he described as "no more than a pleasure trip," Kant presented the imagination as the problem, not the solution.[33] Although he did not mention Herder at all in the essay, he proceeded to recast Herder's argument about reason, the imagination, and human improvement as a para- phrase of the book of Genesis, 2–6, which, he emphasized, was also the template of Rousseau's *Discourse on the Origin of Inequality*. In Kant's version, Rousseau's second *Discourse* became scriptural history but without the scrip- ture, with the imagination producing both the Fall and, perhaps, humanity's redemption. Once the imagination had been awakened, Kant argued, its moral and political effects created a need to develop what he called a form of human culture that was compatible with humanity as a moral rather than a natural species. Only when art "once more becomes nature," Kant wrote, would the tension between the moral and the natural be resolved. History, he concluded, did not "begin with good and then proceed to evil." Instead, it "develops gradu- ally from the worse to the better."[34] As a rendition of Rousseau, it was entirely faithful to the double-edged character of Rousseau's neologism *perfectibilité* and the combination of improvement and depravity that it implied. In other works, Kant called the outcome unsocial sociability.

Both concepts formed the framework of Kant's *Conjectures*. In the begin- ning, he wrote, the first humans were "guided solely by instinct, that *voice of God* which all animals obey."[35] Like every other living creature, they were therefore guided absolutely by sense information, knowing, for example, that the sense of smell and its affinity with the sense of taste constituted a reliable indicator of the type of food that was fit for consumption. It was, in short, what Rousseau called *amour-de-soi*. The trouble began with the imagination and the human use of reason. It was, Kant observed, "a peculiarity of reason that it is able, with the help of the imagination, to invent desires which not only *lack* any corresponding natural impulse, but which are even *at variance* with the latter." These desires, Kant wrote puritanically, which were known primarily as "*lasciviousness*," might have been quite trivial (over an apple, for example), but their effects were still momentous. They led, he wrote, to a decision "to abandon natural impulses," and to a consciousness that reason was "a faculty which can extend beyond the limits to which all animals are confined." The result was "the first experiment in free choice," which did not turn out well. Once that choice was made, however, it was impossible "to return to a state of

---

33. Immanuel Kant, "Conjectures on the Beginning of Human History," in Kant, *Political Writings,*, pp. 221–34, and, on Herder as Kant's intended target, see Reiss's introduction, pp. 192–200.

34. Kant, "Conjectures," p. 234.

35. Ibid., p. 223.

servitude under the rule of instinct."[36] And, after the instinct for food had been upset by reason, the next to go was the sexual instinct. "Man soon discovered that the sexual stimulus, which in the case of animals is based merely on a transient and largely periodic urge, could in his case be prolonged and even increased by means of the imagination." This was where the fig leaf came in. By making the object of the sexual instinct inaccessible to the senses, the fig leaf allowed the imagination to make inclination more intense, so that animal desire could become love and "a feeling for the merely agreeable" turn into "a taste for beauty." It also produced a "*sense of decency*" or "an inclination to inspire respect in others by good manners (i.e. by concealing all that might invite contempt)," which, Kant noted, was "the first incentive for man's development as a moral being." The result was "a whole new direction of thought," not only because it brought thinking about others into the picture, but also because it led to thinking about the future.[37] This was the third step that reason took. The huge range of possibilities presented by this vista was both a source of anticipation, since it went along with an ability to make preparations, and a cause of apprehension, since it also went along with the knowledge that life would bring death. With this array of capacities, the fourth step could follow. This was the ability to differentiate human nature from animal nature and to see, first, that animals could be used to meet human purposes, but, second, that humans could not treat other humans as if they were animals.

The story of the Fall was, Kant concluded, "nothing other" than man's "transition from a rude and purely animal existence to a state of humanity, from the leading strings of instinct to the guidance of reason—in a word, from the guardianship of nature to the state of freedom."[38] Seen thus, it was also the way "to reconcile with each other and with reason the often misunderstood and apparently contradictory pronouncements of the celebrated *J. J. Rousseau*."

> In his essays *On the Influence of the Sciences* and *On the Inequality of Man*, he shows quite correctly that there is an inevitable conflict between culture and the nature of the human race as a *physical* species each of whose individual members is meant to fulfil his destiny completely. But in his *Emile*, his *Social Contract* and other writings, he attempts in turn to solve the more difficult problem of what course culture should take in order to ensure the proper development, in keeping with their destiny, of man's capacities as a *moral* species, so that this destiny will no longer conflict with his character as a natural species. Since culture has perhaps not yet really begun—let alone

36. Ibid., pp. 223–24.
37. Ibid., pp. 224–25.
38. Ibid., p. 226.

completed—its development in accordance with the true principles of man's *education* as a human being and citizen, the above conflict is the source of all the genuine evils which oppress human life, and of all the vices which dishonour it. At the same time, the very impulses which are blamed as the causes of vice are good in themselves, fulfilling their function as abilities implanted by nature. But since these abilities are adapted to the state of nature, they are undermined by the advance of culture and themselves undermine the latter in turn, until art, when it reaches perfection, once more becomes nature—and this is the ultimate goal of man's moral destiny.[39]

Kant did not provide an account of how the goal could be reached, at least in this essay. Instead, his speculations were entirely historical. The story that he laid out in the rest of his *Conjectures* began with the gulf that opened up between human and animal nature. It led, first, to the domestication of wild animals and then to the development of agriculture and, with it, the replacement of "the age of leisure and peace" by "the age of *labour and discord.*" "This epoch," Kant noted, "also saw the beginning of human *inequality*, that abundant source of so much evil, but also of everything good."[40] Inequality was, thus, the engine of history. Once there was inequality, there would be conflict, and, with conflict, there would be war. This was not just a matter of "actual wars in the past or present," but of the "unremitting, indeed ever-increasing *preparation* for war," and the massively wasteful consumption of resources that this involved. But it was still the case that war and freedom went hand in hand. "We need only look," Kant wrote, "at *China*, whose position may expose it to occasional unforeseen incursions but not to attack by a powerful enemy, and we shall find that, for this very reason, it has been stripped of every vestige of freedom." The grim conclusion was that "so long as human culture remains at its present state, war is therefore an indispensable means of advancing it further."[41]

This, in the second place, meant that there was no alternative to the jagged, often backward, course of human history. Although, Kant suggested, it might seem desirable for humanity to be equipped with a continuous collective memory of its own past existence, and a permanent store of experience to draw on to avoid its earlier mistakes, the price of this kind of agelessness was likely to be far too high. Every past wrong would remain permanently alive, leaving no room at all for time and forgetting to do their work. This too was the message of Genesis, where prediluvian humans had once lived for eight hundred years. "Fathers would live in mortal fear of their sons, brothers of

39. Ibid., pp. 227–28.
40. Ibid., pp. 229–30.
41. Ibid., pp. 231–32.

brothers, and friends of friends, and the vices of a human race of such longevity would necessarily reach such a pitch that it would deserve no better a fate than to be wiped from the face of the earth by a universal flood."[42] Nor, in the light of this version of the Deluge, was there any point in wishing for a reversion to some "*golden age*" in which "we are, supposedly, relieved of all those imaginary needs with which luxury encumbers us" and "are content with the bare necessities of nature and there is complete equality and perpetual peace among men."[43] The problem with the golden age was that there had actually been one, but those living in it had found it to be unsatisfactory when they had made the first discovery of choice. And even if it were possible to get back, it would simply be a new beginning, not the journey's end. There was, therefore, no alternative but to accept the fact that humans had got just the kind of history that they deserved.[44] And since it really was *their* history, it would also have to be their future.

Autonomy and the Imagination

Kant's position, laid out in 1784 in his "Idea for a Universal History with a Cosmopolitan Aim," was that the content of that future would involve a set of political arrangements consonant with both individual and general improvement. Moses Mendelssohn disagreed, again on the grounds of perfectibility. "Everything," he wrote in a comment on Kant's "Idea for a Universal History," "rests on the big question: *what is the vocation of man, and what is he to do here on earth?*"

> If his vocation is the progression to a higher perfection, then man is end, society means. Men will need various kinds of social ties for their advancement. . . . *The final end is not the advancement of society but of men.* . . . The progression of men can well coexist with the *standstill* or even the *regression* of humanity even though at the same time necessarily bound to either.[45]

The result of this exchange was that a generation after he had coined the word, Rousseau's concept of perfectibility could be associated with three possible permutations of the individual-species pairing. Individuals and humanity could either progress or regress together; humanity could progress, while individuals would regress; or individuals could progress, while humanity regressed. Kant's version, with its emphasis on individual moral choice and its

42. Ibid., p. 233.
43. Ibid., p. 233.
44. Ibid., p. 233.
45. Cited in di Giovanni, "The Year 1786," p. 231.

compatibility with what he called ambiguously a republican system of government, could be aligned most readily with the first scenario. Herder's version, with its focus on humanity's linguistically generated capacity for culture and the uneven distribution of individual and collective cultural resources and qualities, had more in common with the second possibility. Mendelssohn's version, with its basis in the Leibnizian idea of a preestablished harmony and the human ability to recognize and respond to its rational, but also orderly, properties, was nearest to the third. The permutations are certainly schematic, but they help to reveal the range of subjects encompassed by Rousseau's concept. The difficulty, in the face of these different characterizations of perfectibility, was not so much a matter of deciding which of them was right, but whether—or how—they could be connected.

Kant's "Copernican revolution" in philosophy, a transformation that began with the publication of the *Critique of Pure Reason* in 1781, opened up a number of ways to link the various meanings associated with Rousseau's term. As Kant himself emphasized, his initial distinction between the phenomenal and noumenal properties of the world also applied to the self, and, since the noumenal self lay as far beyond human understanding as any other part of the noumenal world, the distinction between a noumenal and a phenomenal self implied that many of the metaphysical concepts, like freedom, reason, justice, or goodness, that were often associated with the idea of perfectibility were simply out of analytical bounds. At the same time, however, Kant's insistence on the phenomenal world as the only resource available for measuring and evaluating changes in human capabilities gave a new value to the examination of the forms and appearances of human life rather than its irretrievably inaccessible essence. This shift of focus, from substance to form and from essence to appearance, opened up a variety of new ways to think about the interconnections of the aesthetic, cultural, and political dimensions of the concept of perfectibility and, by doing so, to explain why both the imagination and its emotional ramifications were more central to modern societies than they had been in the past.

The effects of Kant's scepticism towards metaphysical concepts like freedom were most immediately apparent in the new interest in beauty and aesthetics that developed after the appearance of the *Critique of Pure Reason*. Kant's system cut aesthetics free of its Leibnizian moorings because it ruled out the claim that beauty was related to something external, like a preestablished harmony or a rational order, rather than to something internal that could produce the effect of harmony and order. This initially left the concept in something of an analytical limbo. The first moves towards giving it a different content came from Mendelssohn's follower (and Goethe's companion in Rome in 1786 and 1787) Karl Phillip Moritz in a series of public lectures and essays that were published in Berlin during the decade before 1789.[46] In them, Moritz argued that beauty was an attribute of something complete in itself because only something complete in itself could be admired or loved solely for what it was, or for its own sake, in a way that was similar to the seventeenth-century Catholic idea of pure love, a theological current that was initially associated with the heterodox archbishop of Cambrai François de Salignac de la Mothe-Fénelon, but which was also widely endorsed in the German Pietist circles in which Moritz grew up. Beauty, on these terms, had nothing to do with utility, or even with something more exalted like a rational order or a preestablished harmony, because beauty, in the first instance, was entirely self-standing. As Benjamin Constant noted a generation later, this idea of beauty as something complete in itself meant that art existed, and could be valued, solely "for art's sake." "The impression made on us by the fine arts," echoed Germane de Staël in 1813, "has nothing whatever in common with the pleasure we feel from any imitation. . . . Of what is music, the first of all the arts, an imitation? . . . Music alone has a noble inutility, and it is for that reason that it affects us so deeply."[47] One model of this idea of self-sufficiency, Moritz himself went on to suggest, was a state. In this way of

46. On Moritz, see Elliott Schreiber, *The Topography of Modernity: Karl Philipp Moritz and the Space of Autonomy* (Ithaca, NY, Cornell UP, 2012); Jonathan Hess, *Reconstituting the Body Politic: Enlightenment, Public Culture and the Invention of Aesthetic Autonomy* (Detroit, Wayne State UP, 1999), pp. 15–18, 51–55, 155–79; Mark Boulby, *Karl Philipp Moritz: At the Fringe of Genius* (Toronto, U of Toronto Press, 1979); M. H. Abrams, "Kant and the Theology of Art," *Notre Dame English Journal* 13 (1981): 75–106 (especially pp. 91–95); Martha Woodmansee, "The Interests in Disinterestedness: Karl Philipp Moritz and the Emergence of the Theory of Aesthetic Autonomy in Eighteenth-Century Germany," *Modern Language Quarterly* 45 (1984): 22–47; Anne-Marie Baranowski, *Conquête du mouvement et recherche de soi. L'imaginaire de Karl Philipp Moritz* (Bern, Peter Lang, 1996); and Catherine J. Minter, *The Mind-Body Problem in German Literature 1770–1830: Wezel, Moritz and Jean Paul* (Oxford, Clarendon Press, 2002), pp. 101–12.

47. Staël, *Germany*, vol. 3, ch. 9, p. 140. On the phrase, see John Wilcox, "The Beginnings of *L'art pour l'art*," *Journal of Aesthetics and Art Criticism* 11 (1953): 360–77; W. Jay Reedy, "Art for Society's Sake: Louis de Bonald's Sociology of Aesthetics and the Theocratic Ideology," *Proceedings of the American Philosophical Society* 130 (1986): 101–29; Frederick Burwick, "Art for Art's Sake and the Politics of Prescinding: 1790s, 1890s, 1990s," *Pacific Coast Philology* 34 (1999): 117–26. For a useful bilingual collection of early nineteenth-century French texts dealing with the concept, see Roman Luckscheiter, ed., *L'art pour l'art. Der Beginn der modernen Kunstdebatte in französischen Quellen der Jahre 1818 bis 1847* (Bielefeld, Aisthesis, 2003), and, for a helpful recent overview of this aspect of eighteenth-century aesthetic theory and its resonances, see Timothy M. Costelloe, ed., *The Sublime: From Antiquity to the Present* (Cambridge, CUP, 2012). For a fascinating example of how ideas like these were developed and implemented in the early

thinking about the concept, he wrote, "each citizen of a state has a certain relationship to the state, or is useful to it; but the state itself, insofar as it forms itself into a whole, has no need of any relationship to anything outside of itself and has, therefore, no need to be useful."[48] Moritz was careful to add, however, that this did not mean that states themselves could be beautiful. If states and beauty shared the common attribute of self-sufficiency, there was still a fundamental difference. A state, Moritz pointed out, "neither falls under our external senses, nor can be embraced by the imagination, but can only be thought by our understanding."[49]

Moritz's distinction between something that "falls under our external senses" and something that could be "embraced by the imagination" pointed towards a further development of Kant's "Copernican revolution" in philosophy. This development paralleled Rousseau's earlier fascination with the imagination and centred, in particular, on the difference between the imagination as a repository of images and the imagination as a creative power.[50] This difference had already been registered analytically in the concept of *Dichtungskraft* (poetic power) used by the German philosopher Johann Nikolas Tetens in his *Philosophische Versuche über die menschliche Natur and ihre Entwicklung* (A philosophical inquiry into human nature and its development) of 1777.[51] Over the following two generations, it gradually became the basis of both the modern concept of literature and the broader distinction between creativity and knowledge that is still sometimes used to mark the difference between the artistic and academic ways of life. "All that is literature," wrote the critic and

---

nineteenth century, see Cordula Grewe, "Beyond Hegel's End of Art: Schadow's *Mignon* and the Religious Project of Late Romanticism," *Modern Intellectual History* 1 (2004): 185–217.

48. Karl Philipp Moritz, "Über die bildende Nachahmung des Schönen" [1788], translated as "Sur l'imitation formatrice du beau," in Karl Philipp Moritz, *Le concept d'achevé en soi et autres écrits (1785–1793)*, ed. Philippe Beck (Paris, PUF, 1995), p. 153. See also the English translation of Moritz's further essay, "An Attempt to Unify All the Fine Arts and Sciences under the Concept of *That Which Is Complete in Itself*," ed. Elliott Schreiber, *PMLA* 27 (2012): 94–100.

49. Moritz, "Über die bildende Nachahmung des Schönen," p. 154.

50. On this difference, see the classic article by Donald F. Bond, "The Neo-Classical Psychology of the Imagination," *ELH: A Journal of English Literary History* 4 (1937): 245–64.

51. On Tetens and the broader subject of the imagination, see particularly Thomas McFarland, *Originality and Imagination* (Baltimore, Johns Hopkins UP, 1985), pp. 100–119; Mary Warnock, *Imagination* (London, Faber, 1976); Rosemary Ashton, *The German Idea: Four English Writers and the Reception of German Thought 1800–1860* (Cambridge, CUP, 1980), pp. 1–66; James Engell, *The Creative Imagination: Enlightenment to Romanticism* (Cambridge, MA, Harvard UP, 1981); and Daniel Stempel, "Revelation on Mount Snowdon: Wordsworth, Coleridge and the Fichtean Imagination," *Journal of Aesthetics and Art Criticism* 29 (1971): 371–84.

student of German philosophy Thomas de Quincey in 1828, "seeks to communicate power; all that is not literature, to communicate knowledge."[52]

The power-knowledge distinction underlying de Quincey's concept of literature (a distinction now more frequently associated with the thought of Michel Foucault) actually originated independently of Kant's critical philosophy and, in its early form, owed more to the widespread late eighteenth-century interest in what has come to be called vitalist natural philosophy, with its emphasis on explaining many of the nonmechanical aspects of life, like sexual reproduction, reflex actions, organic growth, or binary vision, in terms of something like the type of force putatively responsible for natural phenomena like electricity, combustion, or magnetism. This type of natural philosophy also had a substantial bearing on the late eighteenth-century interest in the concept of palingenesis, because it made it easier to give a new content to the old idea of a great chain of being and to superimpose a more theologically inspired progression from the physical to the spiritual upon the old hierarchy of minerals, vegetables, animals, and humans.[53] In this context, the imagination could be associated with a spiritually oriented progression from nature to culture, and with a strong emphasis on its creative or poetic power as the force driving humanity's ascent from the physical to the spiritual.

In Germany, this type of claim about the imagination was made particularly vigorously by Johann Gottlieb Herder. "Of all the powers of the human mind," he wrote in 1784 in the section of his *Ideen* (Ideas for a philosophy of the history of mankind) that was directly aimed at Kant, "the imagination has been least explored, probably because it is the most difficult to explore. Being connected with the general structure of the body, and with that of the brain and nerves in particular—as many diseases remarkably reveal—it seems to be not only the basic and connecting link of all the finer mental powers, but, indeed, the knot that ties body and mind together."[54] In Anglophone culture, a similar

52. Thomas de Quincey, "Letters to a Young Man," in Thomas de Quincey, *Essays* (London, Ward, Lock and Co., no date, but c. 1870), p. 269. It is worth remembering, therefore, that the *pouvoir-savoir* pairing began as an antonym before, in the wake of Michel Foucault's Nietzsche-inspired scepticism, turning into a synonym. On the concept of literature, see Jean-Marie Schaeffer, *Art of the Modern Age: Philosophy of Art from Kant to Heidegger* [1992] (Princeton, NJ, Princeton UP, 2000), pp. 96–134.

53. On vitalism in late eighteenth-century intellectual life and its bearing on Herder's thought, see Sonenscher, *Sans-Culottes*, pp. 119–26, and, more generally, Jean Starobinski, *Action and Reaction: The Life and Adventures of a Couple* [1999], trans. Sophie Hawkes (New York, Zone Books, 2003), chs. 2 and 3.

54. Cited in F. M. Barnard, *Herder on Social and Political Culture* (Cambridge, CUP, 1969), p. 301. See also McFarland, *Originality and Imagination*, p. xiii.

claim was made a generation later by Samuel Taylor Coleridge, just as it was Coleridge too who was responsible for the now rather opaque distinction between what he called fancy and the imagination. Here, "fancy" referred to the mind's ability to classify and arrange information, or to associate ideas in the eighteenth-century sense of the phrase, while the imagination, as Coleridge put it in his *Biographia Literaria*, was "essentially vital, even as all objects (*as* objects) are essentially fixed and dead." The difference amounted to a more analytical version of Rousseau's insight into the imagination's ability to turn general ideas into particular sensations. Elsewhere, in terminology redolent of Emmanuel-Joseph Sieyès and the French Revolution, Coleridge called the imagination the "co-adunating faculty," or the faculty responsible for turning the many into one (here meaning both one concept and one person), with fancy defined as simply "the aggregating faculty of the mind."[55] But while the terminology might have been French, the concepts themselves were, like so much else in Coleridge's thought, recognizably German.

Kant, famously, was reluctant to endorse this type of claim about the imagination. "Only this much seems to be necessary by way of anticipation or introduction," he wrote at the beginning the *Critique of Pure Reason*, "namely that there are two stems of human knowledge, *sensibility* and *understanding*, which perhaps spring forth from a common, but to us unknown, root. Through the former, objects are given to us; through the latter they are thought." Later, he referred to "the point where the general root of our cognitive power divides and branches out into two stems, one of which is *reason*," while the other, he added a sentence later, was "the empirical."[56] On both occasions, he made no attempt to give this "common root" a name. One recurrent suggestion is that Kant must have meant the imagination, although it is not obvious how the imagination could be said to be "unknown."[57] The statement makes more

<hr />

55. Samuel Taylor Coleridge, *Biographia Literaria* [1817], ed. James Engell and W. Jackson Bate, 2 vols. (Princeton, NJ, Princeton UP, 1983), 1:304–5, and, for Coleridge on the "co-adunating faculty," McFarland, *Originality and Imagination*, p. 106. For William Hazlitt, on the other hand (as cited by Laurence S. Lockridge. *The Ethics of Romanticism* [Cambridge, CUP, 1989], pp. 362–63), the power of the imagination made it "an exaggerating and exclusive faculty," "a monopolising faculty which seeks the greatest quantity of present excitement by inequality and disproportion." On the distinction between "fancy" and the imagination, see, helpfully, John Spencer Hill, ed., *The Romantic Imagination* (London, Macmillan, 1977), and the editorial guidance in Coleridge, *Biographia Literaria*, , pp. lxxxi–civ. For an overview, see Theresa M. Kelley, *Reinventing Allegory* (Cambridge, CUP, 1997), especially pp. 6, 15, 121–24.

56. Kant, *Critique of Pure Reason*, pp. 135, 693.

57. The claim has come to be associated with Heidegger, *Kant and the Problem of Metaphysics*, p. 110.

sense in the context of the claims about vital powers widely made in late eighteenth-century natural philosophy and, most saliently in this context, by Herder in relation to palingenesis and to Kant's suspicion of both vitalism and Herder. On Kant's terms, whatever it was that lay at the root of sensibility and understanding had to be different from both, and, if it was, it had by definition to be unknown.

If Kant's reluctance to give a name to whatever lay at the root of sensibility and understanding was connected to vitalist claims about the imagination rather to than the imagination itself, there is good reason to assume that exploring its properties and powers was as central to his concerns as it had been to Rousseau.[58] The process of exploration was particularly salient to the subject of morality and its putatively self-sufficient character. In one sense, Kant's insistence on thinking about morality and autonomy as two sides of the same coin went with the grain of Moritz's idea of beauty as something complete in itself, and, because of this, as something that could be associated with the idea of an entirely disinterested principle. In another sense, however, Kant's distinction between the noumenal and the phenomenal played into treating morality in a more differentiated way, with as much emphasis on its appearance as on its content and on the imagination's ability to apply a range of different qualities to the same person or being. Justice for a parent, for example, could look quite different from justice for a judge, even if both still conformed to an underlying concept of justice. From this perspective, the appearance of an action could matter as much as its underlying motive.

Friedrich Schiller and the Idea of Aesthetic Education

The link between these two facets of morality was supplied by Kant's younger contemporary Friedrich Schiller, rather than by Kant himself. Its outcome was a broader concept of autonomy in which Kant's initial version of the concept was given a more comprehensively aesthetic dimension. Schiller made the move in three long essays, beginning with his *On Grace and Dignity* of 1793, continuing with the *Letters on the Aesthetic Education of Man* of 1795 and concluding with the two shorter essays "On Naïve and Sentimental Poetry" that he published in the winter of 1795–96. The first of the essays, however, set out the framework of the whole extended argument. Schiller began it by describing

---

58. On Kant and the imagination, see, particularly, Sarah L. Gibbons, *Kant's Theory of Imagination: Bridging Gaps in Judgment and Experience* (Oxford, Clarendon Press, 1994), and Jane Kneller, *Kant and the Power of Imagination* (Cambridge, CUP, 2007). On Rousseau's earlier exploration of its properties and powers, see Sonenscher, *Jean-Jacques Rousseau*, pp. 86–114.

a symbol, the girdle or belt worn in Greek mythology by Venus or Aphrodite, the goddess of love. The belt had the power to confer grace on its wearer and, as Juno found, to win the love of someone else. Schiller used the symbol to explain, in a development of Kant's moral theory, why morality was connected both to the idea of freedom and to that of beauty. Freedom presupposed a range of abilities, like making choices, recognizing values, or acting disinterestedly, that were suprasensible or noumenal in origin, while beauty belonged firmly to the world of sensations and appearances. Morality, Schiller argued, was connected to both. This was the point of the Greek and Roman mythological symbol. Venus remained beautiful even after giving the belt or girdle to someone else, like Juno, to wear because she was still able to believe in what its power had enabled her to do. The girdle itself did not confer beauty but endowed its wearer with an ability to do things gracefully, and it was this beautiful addition to the action itself that gave it an extra quality called "moral."

In this respect grace was different from beauty. Where beauty was essential to an object, grace was something additional. Like the girdle, it could be put on or taken off without altering the physical constitution of its wearer, even though it did alter something about the quality of its wearer's actions. Doing something moral could be a matter of doing something that feels fine just as much as it could be a matter of something that feels right. Importantly, because this extra quality could be added or removed, it was not part of nature. Nor, however, was it simply an appearance. Instead, like the imagination in Rousseau's *Pygmalion*, grace had the magical power (the phrase was Schiller's) of being able to add something to an action by giving it an aesthetic quality.[59] This addition, Schiller went on to argue in more detail, was what gave morality its dual character, as something that could be either attractive or imposing but, in either guise, would still remain recognizably moral. In this sense, the aesthetic dimension of morality was the outward sign of free human choice. Like art, morality consisted of rules that were self-generated. But while the rules of morality were supplied by human reason, the rules of art were supplied by the human capacity for play, or the ability to separate semblance from substance and create links between things without any substantive connection. Since beauty was sensible, while reason was suprasensible, the former could be used to symbolize the latter.[60] The play-drive, Schiller wrote later, or "the

59. On Rousseau and *Pygmalion*, see Sonenscher, *Jean-Jacques Rousseau*, pp. 108–10, as well as the further literature cited there. For a helpful examination of Schiller on grace and dignity, see Michael Rosen, *Dignity: Its History and Meaning* (Cambridge, MA, Harvard UP, 2012), pp. 31–38.

60. As one of his early translators explained, Schiller's concept of "the play-drive" (*Spieltrieb*) referred to something more than "the desire for amusement" or "the faculty of humour"

union of reality with form, contingency with necessity, passivity with freedom, makes the concept of human nature complete."[61] Without its aesthetic guise, he argued, morality would be no more than obedience, and, if this was the case, it would not be morality at all.

Schiller illustrated the idea by an image. If, he wrote, a monarchical state was governed in such a way that an ordinary citizen could believe that he could do as he pleased and obey no more than his own inclinations, even though everything was actually subject to the will of one person, this would be "what is called a liberal government."[62] But the name would not be appropriate either if the sovereign gave precedence to his own will over the citizen's inclinations or if the citizen's inclinations took precedence over the sovereign's will. In the first case, Schiller wrote, "the government would not be *liberal*, while in the second it would not even be a *government*." Here, what mattered was the restraint shown by the sovereign towards the citizen. "It is certainly possible," he continued, "to *leave* liberty, but it cannot be *given*." The same idea applied to human development under the rule of the mind. Just as it was inappropriate to say that the sovereign created liberty, so it was wrong to say that the mind produces beauty. If, Schiller wrote, "the mind was to externalize itself in sensible nature in such a way that nature were to carry out the mind's will as faithfully as possible and to express its sensations in the most eloquent fashion, without clashing with the requirements that the senses make of nature as a totality of phenomena, then nature itself would display grace." But the term could not be applied either if the mind used force on sensibility or if the expressions of the mind were deprived of the free effect of sensibility. In the first case there would be no beauty, while in the second case it would not be the beauty of a free-flowing game.[63]

The same balance between control and contingency applied to the idea of autonomy. Pure autonomy implied mastering every external sensation, while pure sensibility implied abandoning all autonomy. Neither condition was com-

---

(although it could refer to them too). In its broadest sense, it indicated "all that is neither internally nor externally contingent or constrained" or "a nature whose two tendencies [matter and spirit; perception and reflection] are poised and have a mutual and harmonious operation." Friedrich Schiller, *The Philosophical and Aesthetic Letters and Essays*, ed. J. Weiss (London, 1845), p. 13. For an example of the fate of the concept, see Jacques Rancière, "The Aesthetic Revolution and Its Outcomes," *New Left Review* 14 (2002): 133–51.

61. Schiller, *On the Aesthetic Education of Man*, letter 15, p. 103.

62. Friedrich Schiller, *Grace et dignité et autres textes*, ed. Nicolas Briand (Paris, Vrin, 1998), p. 35.

63. Ibid., pp. 35–37.

patible with autonomy in a proper sense.[64] "The first of these relations between man's two natures," Schiller observed, "is reminiscent of *monarchy*, where the strict control of the sovereign represses all free movement, while the second is reminiscent of a wild *ochlocracy*, where the citizen, by refusing to obey a legal government, is instead as unfree on its side as a human formation will be embellished by subjecting itself to moral autonomy."[65] Autonomy called for a combination of reason and feeling, not the subordination of the latter to the former, which, Schiller suggested, was the case with Kant's version of the concept. Establishing a balance between the two, he argued, was why autonomy had to have an aesthetic dimension. "Thus," he wrote, "if *neither reason ruling over sensibility, nor sensibility ruling over reason* is compatible with the beauty of the term, then (since there is no fourth case) the state of the mind in which *reason and sensibility*—duty and inclination—are in *concord* will be the condition that allows the beauty of free play to occur." This, he added, implied recognizing "the demands of sensibility that, in the field of pure reason and the framework of moral legislation, were *totally* rejected."[66]

Schiller's concern with giving the concept of autonomy a closer relationship to the reality of human sensibility was developed more fully two years later in his *Letters on the Aesthetic Education of Man*. Its outcome, it should be noted, was not only a fuller version of the concept of autonomy but also a radically new theory of property. Its initial emphasis, however, fell on the aesthetic as the means available to the moderns to recover imaginatively the unity of sensibility and reason that, Schiller claimed, had once been the hallmark of the ancients. For them, he wrote, "sense and intellect did not as yet rule over strictly separate domains." This was not because the one was indistinguishable from the other, but rather because both were integrated into the various images of human qualities represented by the Greek gods. Among the moderns, however, there was no equivalent means to keep sense and intellect together. "With us too," Schiller pointed out, "the image of the

64. On this concern with autonomy as balance, see, helpfully, Frederick Beiser, *Schiller as Philosopher* (Oxford, OUP, 2005), pp. 168–90 (pp. 187–89 in particular). See also Katerina Deligiorgi, *The Scope of Autonomy: Kant and the Morality of Freedom* (Oxford, OUP, 2012), pp. 142–72, and her earlier "The Convergence of Ethics and Aesthetics: Schiller's Concept of the 'Naive' and Objects of Distant Antiquity," in *Critical Exchange: Art Criticism of the Eighteenth and Nineteenth Centuries in Russia and Western Europe*, ed. Carol Adlam and Juliet Simpson (Bern, Peter Lang, 2009), pp. 63–78.

65. Schiller, *Grace et dignité*, p. 37.

66. Ibid., pp. 37, 38. See too the famous comment: "In Kantian moral philosophy, the idea of *duty* is set out with a rigour capable of terrifying all the Graces, one that might easily tempt a feeble mind to seek moral perfection along the road of a dark monastic asceticism." Ibid., p. 39.

human species is projected in magnified form into separate individuals, but as fragments, not in different combinations, with the result that one has to go the rounds from one individual to another to piece together a complete image of the species." The intellectual, occupational, and administrative specialization that was both the cause and the effect of *Kultur* meant that "little by little the concrete life of the individual is destroyed in order that the abstract idea of the whole may drag out its sorry existence, and the state remains forever a stranger to its citizens, since at no point does it ever make contact with their feelings." This, Schiller argued, was why aesthetics mattered. On his terms, the aesthetic capabilities of the moderns made it possible to reproduce the moral capabilities of the ancients, but in a way that was consonant with the Kantian idea of autonomy.

The overlap between their respective moral and aesthetic theories was particularly marked in Schiller's account of the emergence of human aesthetic capabilities. As in Kant's "Conjectures on the Beginning of Human History," the first move consisted of using a sense for a purpose other than its own (like taking an apple's colour to be a sign of its taste). Something like this move, Schiller conjectured, must have occurred among "savages." "Once," he wrote, "he does begin to enjoy through the eye, and seeing acquires for him a value of its own, he is already aesthetically free and the play-drive has started to develop." What had happened was the emergence of an ability to distinguish "semblance from reality, form from content," and, with this, a capacity for "imitative art" or a "capacity for form." Semblance, Schiller continued, was not a natural property, like existence. "The reality of things," he noted, "is the work of things themselves; the semblance of things is the work of man." Since "all semblance originates in man considered as perceiving subject," it followed that "he is only availing himself of the undisputed rights of ownership when he reclaims semblance from substance and deals with it according to laws of his own."[67] Property, in keeping with the same logic, belonged to the world of semblance, rather than that of things. "This sovereign human right," Schiller concluded, "he exercises in the art of semblance; and the more strictly he here distinguishes between mine and thine, the more scrupulously he separates form from substance, and the more complete the autonomy he is able to give to the former, then the more he will not only extend the realm of beauty, but actually preserve intact the frontiers of truth."[68] The imagination, in other words, had the power to re-create the unity and diversity of the ancients, but in a genuinely divided world.

67. Schiller, *On the Aesthetic Education of Man*, letter 26, pp. 193, 195, 197.
68. Ibid., letter 26, pp. 195, 197.

"In whatever individual or whole people we find this honest and autonomous kind of semblance," Schiller noted, "we may assume both understanding and taste, and every kindred excellence."

There we shall see actual life governed by the ideal, honour triumphant over possessions, thought over enjoyment, dreams of immortality over existence. There, public opinion will be the only thing to be feared, and an olive branch will bestow greater honour than a purple robe.[69]

Schiller had already made the point in 1791 in a description of the effects of the division of labour that he incorporated into a critical review of the poems of Gottfried Auguste Bürger, the writer whose poem *Lenora* was later compared by Charles Nodier to Jean Paul's dream.

With the isolation and fragmentation of our mental faculties, necessitated by the expansion of knowledge and the division of labour, it is poetry almost alone that reunites the separate faculties of the soul, that employs head and heart, shrewdness and ingenuity, reason and imagination in a harmonious alliance that, so to speak, restores the *whole person* in us.[70]

Much the same argument also informed Schiller's Rousseau-inspired poem about landscape, "Der Spaziergang" (The promenade).[71] Once, so the poem's argument ran, there was land and the natural objects that it housed. Time and human cultivation, however, had turned the land into fields, woods, parks,

69. Ibid., letter 26, pp. 197, 199.

70. Friedrich Schiller, "Über Bürger's Gedichte," in *Schillers Werke*, Nationalausgabe, 22, ed. Herbert Meyer (Weimar, 1958), cited by Martha Woodmansee, *The Author, Art, and the Market: Rereading the History of Aesthetics* (New York, Columbia UP, 1994), p. 72. On Woodmansee's own interpretation of Schiller's thought, see the comments in Beiser, *Schiller as Philosopher*, p. 201 n. 25. For earlier discussion of these themes, see Roy Pascal, "'Bildung' and the Division of Labour," in *German Studies Presented to Walter Horace Bruford*, [ed. Anon.] (London, Harrap, 1962), pp. 14–28, and Philip J. Kain, *Schiller, Hegel and Marx* (Kingston and Montreal, McGill-Queen's UP, 1982), pp. 13–25.

71. On Rousseau's thought in the poem, see Wolfgang Riedel, *Der Spaziergang: Ästhetik der Landschaft und Geschichtsphilosophie der Natur bei Schiller* (Würzburg, Königshausen & Neumann, 1989), especially p. 58. On the broader subject of the interrelationship of history, landscape, and the imagination, see, classically, Joachim Ritter, *Paysage. Fonction de l'esthétique dans la société moderne* (Paris, Editions de l'Imprimeur, 1997), and, earlier, Georg Simmel, "Philosophie du paysage" [1913], translated in his *La tragédie de la culture* (Paris, Rivages, 1988), pp. 231–45. See too François Walter, *Les figures paysagères de la nation. Territoire et paysage en Europe (16–20 siècle)* (Paris, Editions de l' EHESS, 2004), and, recently, Jeff Malpas, ed., *The Place of Landscape: Concepts, Contexts, Studies* (Cambridge, MA, MIT Press, 2011).

meadows, lawns, orchards, and gardens. Once, the land and the goods it supplied were immediately knowable. Now, with time and human cultivation, the land had turned into landscape, and its natural constitution had become a mass of more varied functions and forms of property. The shift from land to landscape was, however, as much of a gain as a loss because the idea of landscape implied the existence of a human capacity to re-create nature's original unity in imaginative terms. The point of Schiller's poem, therefore, was not only that walking out from a city was a journey in time as well as space, but also that the direction of travel was forwards rather than backwards.

For Schiller, this temporal direction and its underlying basis in the play-drive and aesthetics were what was missing from Rousseau's thought. He made the point forcefully in his "On Naïve and Sentimental Poetry" in 1794–95. "Caught in the straights of passion at one time, of abstraction at another," he wrote, "he seldom or never brings it to the sort of aesthetic freedom that the poet must assert over his material and communicate to his reader." This was more than a matter of style. "Thus too," Schiller continued, "in the idea of humanity that he sets up, too much attention is paid to the limitations of humanity and too little to its capability. Everywhere in this ideal a need for physical *peace* is more visible than a need for moral *harmony*."

> His passionate sensitivity is responsible for the fact that, simply in order to be rid of the conflict in humanity as soon as possible, he would rather see it led back to the spiritually empty uniformity of its original condition than see the battle ended in the spiritually rich harmony of a thoroughly developed culture. He would rather not let art begin at all than wait for its completion; in short he wants to set the goal lower and to scale down the ideal simply in order to attain it all the more quickly and certainly.[72]

The verdict matched Kant's description of Rousseau as "that subtle Diogenes."[73]

Schiller set out the most detailed description of differences between "spiritually empty uniformity" and "spiritually rich harmony" in the two essays "On Naïve and Sentimental Poetry" that he published in 1794–95. "There are moments in our lives," he began, "when we extend a kind of love and tender respect toward nature in plants, minerals, animals, and landscapes, as well as to

72. Friedrich Schiller, "On Naïve and Sentimental Poetry," in Friedrich Schiller, *Essays*, ed. Walter Hinderer and Daniel O. Dahlstrom (New York, Continuum, 1993), pp. 213–14. See too E. L. Stahl, "Schiller on Poetry," in *German Studies Presented to Walter Horace Bruford* (London, Harrap, 1962), pp. 140–52.

73. On the label, see Sonenscher, *Sans-Culottes*, pp. 195–201.

human nature in children, in the customs of country folk, and the primitive world." The feelings arose when something seemed to be entirely natural and to belong to a world that was no longer our own. "They *are* what we *were*; they are what we *should become* once more. We were nature like them, and our culture should lead us along the path of reason and freedom back to nature." The difference, Schiller continued, was a product of human freedom.

> What constitutes their character is exactly what ours lacks to be perfect. What distinguishes us from them is exactly what they lack to be divine-like. We are free and what they are is necessary; we alter, they remain one. Yet only if both are combined with one another—only if the will freely adheres to the law of necessity and reason maintains its rule in the face of every change in the imagination, only then does the divine or the idea emerge. Hence in *them* we forever see what eludes us, something we must struggle for and can hope to approach in an endless progress, even though we never attain it. *In ourselves* we see an advantage that they lack, something that they either could never participate in at all, as in the case of being devoid of reason, or can participate in only inasmuch as they proceed down the same path that *we* did, as in the case of children.[74]

What was naïve was spontaneously moral, but what was sentimental called for the addition of something reflexive to make morality appear. "As long as the human being is still part of nature that is pure (which, of course, is not to say 'unrefined')," Schiller explained, "he operates as an undivided sensuous unity and as a harmonizing whole."

> Sense and reason, receptive and spontaneous faculties, have not yet divided the tasks between them; still less do they contradict one another. His feelings are not the formless play of chance; his thoughts are not the empty play of imagination. The former proceed from the law of *necessity*, the latter from the law of *actuality*. Once the human being has entered into the condition characteristic of culture and art has laid its hands on him, that *sensuous* harmony within him is overcome and he can only express himself as a *moral* unity, that is to say, as someone striving for unity. The agreement between his feeling and his thinking, something that *actually* took place in the original condition, now exists only *ideally*. It is no longer in him but rather outside him, as a thought that must first be realized, and no longer as a fact of his life.[75]

74. Schiller, "On Naïve and Sentimental Poetry," pp. 179, 180–81.
75. Ibid., pp. 200–201.

The distinction was a development of Schiller's earlier argument about the relationship of grace and dignity to morality. Neither grace nor dignity was actually morality itself but, for the moderns, both were required to make morality part of life.

In this sense, aesthetics and autonomy were different sides of the same coin. Both relied on the human capacity for reflexivity, or, as Germaine de Staël was to call it in her *De la littérature*, on the type of reflexive emotion that distinguished sentimental from naïve poetry. From this perspective, there was not much difference between describing the modern capacity for morality in terms of a combination of the naïve and the sentimental and the later calls by Sismondi, Constant, and the Coppet group for a combination of positive and negative liberty as the basis of modern freedom. "The road taken by the modern poets," Schiller wrote, "is the same road humans in general must travel, both as individuals and as a whole. Nature makes a human being one with himself, art separates and divides him; by means of the ideal he returns to the unity."[76] Modern culture, in short, allowed art to complete nature. From this perspective, what Schiller called the "aesthetic state" (meaning, in the first instance, a condition, rather than a political society) was designed to describe a condition that was both a cultural acquisition and, in a sense, a work of art.[77] Form, not substance, and conditions, not persons, were its key features. Both relied as much on the imagination as on perception or understanding to be what they were. And, since forms and conditions could change in ways that substances and persons could not, it was also possible to claim that the modern world had acquired a plasticity and capacity for change that earlier ages had lacked. Thanks, in large measure, to its *appearance*, it offered an unprecedented prospect for individual and collective choice. Much of Schiller's claim relied on Kant for its initial conceptual impetus. Equally, many of the objections to its apparently benign vision relied on Kant's critics, Jacobi and Jean Paul. As they saw it, the other side of the human capacity to recognize and respond to the sentimental was, it seemed, the death of God.

76. Ibid., p. 202.

77. For a more directly institutional interpretation of Schiller's concept of an aesthetic state, see Josef Chytry, *The Aesthetic State: A Quest in Modern German Thought* (Berkeley, U of California Press, 1989). More generally, see also Dushan Bresky, "Schiller's Debt to Montesquieu and Adam Ferguson," *Comparative Literature* 13 (1961): 239–53; Douglas Moggach, "Schiller's Aesthetic Republicanism," *History of Political Thought* 28 (2007): 520–41; Alexander Schmidt, "The Liberty of the Ancients? Friedrich Schiller and Aesthetic Republicanism," *History of Political Thought* 30 (2009): 286–314.

7

The Idea of Autonomy and the Concept of Civil Society

Disciplining the Uncontrolled Natural Will

To many of his early readers, Kant's philosophy of history appeared to house a number of gaps, or missing links. More distressingly still, it appeared to present a set of insoluble antinomies. As Kant himself emphasized, reason, justice, and freedom were, in principle, universal values. But any examination of their content seemed to indicate that they were, in reality, the values and arrangements of particular peoples at particular times and places. Irrationality seemed to be built into rationality, just as unsocial sociability was built into sociability. As many of Kant's more critical early readers concluded, Kant had not shown how it was possible to build a bridge between, for example, freedom and causation or between the noumenal and the phenomenal; nor, by extension, had he explained how it was possible to find a link between a global and cosmopolitan ideal located somewhere near the outer edge of the horizon of political expectations and the many different sets of arrangements that were simply locally and partially real. The problem was not so much that any of these subjects or concepts were cloudy or indistinct but rather that—irrespective of whether they were general or particular—they were all delineated so clearly and distinctly that it was almost impossible to explain how they could be connected, or to see how the heterogeneous ingredients of Kant's bleak philosophy of history could ever have any recognizable human applicability. As a philosophy of history, it was, as Friedrich Schlegel complained, no more than *Historismus* or "historicism."[1]

Paradoxically, the solution came from Kant himself. It came in the form of the concept of a *Weltanschauung*, or a worldview.[2] The concept made a modest

---

1. On the complaint, see above, chapter 2.

2. On the concept and its history, see David Keith Naugle, *Worldview: The History of a Concept* (Grand Rapids, MI, William B. Eerdmans, 2002) and his earlier PhD thesis, "A History and

initial appearance in Kant's 1790 *Critique of Judgment* in a passage in which he began to discuss the human capacity to conceive of the infinite. It was, he pointed out, a highly unusual capacity because it was not clear how the idea of infinity could refer to something singular when the combination of singularity and infinity has no identifiable counterpart in any human experience. "If the human mind is nonetheless to be able even to think the given infinite without contradiction," Kant wrote, "it must have within itself a power that it is supersensible, whose idea of the noumenon cannot be intuited but can yet be regarded as the substrate underlying what is mere appearance, namely, our intuition of the world (*Weltanschauung*). For only by means of this power and its idea do we, in a purely intellectual estimation of magnitude, comprehend the infinite in the world of sense entirely under a concept, even though in a mathematical estimation of magnitude by means of numerical concepts we can never think it in its entirety."[3] Something about this "intuition of the world" made the unthinkable thinkable.

Kant himself did not address the problem of how this intuition of the world could straddle both the natural and the supernatural or blend the sensible with the supersensible. But the question of how it could was quickly taken up by Kant's early admirer Johann Gottlieb Fichte in his first major publication, entitled *Attempt at a Critique of All Revelation*, in 1792. He did so in the course of setting out to explain how a natural law, which worked by way of causes and consequences, and a moral law, which worked by way of freedom and choice, could both coexist in a world bounded by sense. It was, Fichte wrote, certainly clear that they did, but it was less clear how they could.

> Their effects in the world of sense do, however, meet and must not contradict each other if either natural knowledge, on the one hand, or the causality of freedom required by practical reason in the world of sense, on the other, are not to be impossible. Now the possibility of this agreement of two legislations entirely independent of one another can be conceived in no other way than by their common dependence on a higher legislation that underlies them both but which is entirely inaccessible to us. If we were to take the principle of this higher legislation as a basis for a world view (*Welt Anschauung*), then according to this principle one and the same effect

Theory of the Concept of Weltanschauung (Worldview)" (University of Texas at Arlington, 1998). See too Hans-Georg Gadamer, *Truth and Method* (London, Continuum, 2004), pp. 85, 194–201, 336, 438–39, 443–45, and Martin Heidegger, "L'époque des 'conceptions du monde,'" in his *Chemins qui ne mènent nulle part* [1949 and 1962] (Paris, Gallimard, 1980), pp. 99–146.

3. Immanuel Kant, *Critique of Judgment*, trans. Werner S. Pluhar (Indianapolis, IN, Hackett, 1987), pp. 111–12.

would be cognized as fully necessary—an effect which appears to us as *free* in relation to the world of sense according to the moral law and as *contingent* in nature when it is associated with the causality of reason. But since we are not able to do so, it plainly follows that as soon as we take into consideration a causality through freedom, we must assume that not all appearances in the world of sense are necessary solely according to natural laws, but rather that many of them are only contingent. Accordingly we should not explain them all *from* the laws of nature, but rather some merely *according to* natural laws. *To explain something merely according to natural laws* means, however, to assume the causality of the matter of the effect to be outside of nature, but the causality of the form of the effect to be within nature. All the phenomena of the sensible world must be capable of explanation *according to* the laws of nature because they could never otherwise become an object of knowledge.[4]

Underlying the distinction between an explanation *from* the laws of nature and an explanation *according to* the laws of nature was a distinction between matter and form, or, in the later more technical language in which Fichte's distinction came to be described towards the end of the nineteenth century, between things that are historical, or idiographic, and are simply one of a kind, and things that are natural, or nomothetic, and are subject to general causal laws. Since, Fichte claimed, both qualities could be attributes of the same thing, it followed that both could coexist, and that an accessible form would be a guide to an inaccessible matter.

The form, in short, was a clue to the matter. But forms, by definition, are variable and can be identified and evaluated in many possible ways. To God, Fichte explained, the difference between form and matter did not exist. But the same did not apply to humans. Humans could not avoid having to face the distinction that Kant, echoing Plato, had underlined. Some, dogmatically, would deny it. Others, equally arbitrarily, would affirm it. But since neither position was based on anything more than individual temperament and disposition, humanity seemed to be condemned to the existence of many worldviews, and, since the principle underlying different worldviews was inaccessible, no final authority was available to settle the differences between incompatible worldviews. All that could be established initially, as Fichte went on to show, was an awareness of subjectivity and, on reflection, of the variety

4. Johann Gottlieb Fichte, *Attempt at a Critique of All Revelation* [1792], ed. Garrett Green (Cambridge, CUP, 1978), §9, p. 119. I have modified the translation in the light of that given in J. G. Fichte, *Essai d'une critique de toute révélation (1792–1793)*, ed. Jean-Christophe Godard (Paris, Vrin, 1988), §9, p. 134.

of worldviews that different individual subjectivities could house. Although some worldviews and their attendant concepts were general and extensive, while other worldviews were particular and intensive, both still belonged to the same mysterious underlying concept of a worldview. It was this concept of a worldview, or *Weltanschauung*, that made it possible for Fichte, followed by Schelling and, finally, Hegel, to add a more firmly historical dimension to Kant's distinctions between creativity and causality, the noumenal and the phenomenal, and the separate spheres of freedom and necessity.

Ultimately, the solution to the problem of many worldviews was history. But, if it was a solution, this was also because history was, initially, the fundamental cause of the problem. Fichte coined a rather recondite technical term, *facticity*, to give the problem a name. Usually the term has been taken to refer mainly to how things are and how things appear, and to the related cluster of problems involved in working out the relationship between subject and object, categories and concepts, or, in short, to everything involved in applying Kant's critical philosophy to the putatively brute facts of experience. Fichte's usage, however, also had a further point because his use of the concept applied to some of the assumptions embedded not only in Kant's distinction between the phenomenal and the noumenal, but also in his approach to history. To Fichte, facticity encompassed them both because history, on inspection, was very real evidence of the coincidence of the phenomenal and causal with the noumenal and singular. Every historical event was, in a sense, a thing in itself, but every historical event had also been caused. The problem was how to explain this apparently contradictory compatibility built into human history. As Fichte put it, there was what he called a *hiatus irrationalis*—or a gap that reason could not close—lying between a concept and its content. Something about a concept seemed to fall short of the matter or substance of the very thing that it was supposed to be a concept of. This, Fichte went on to claim, was more than an epistemological problem because it was a problem that seemed to apply to things that were real because they had happened but still seemed to be impervious to the sort of exhaustive analysis that applied to the natural world. Facticity, in this sense, seemed to apply particularly to things that occurred in time, such as the Reformation or the Seven Years' War or the French Revolution, but, on closer inspection, it seemed, in fact, to apply to human events in general.

Every human event was, in fact, a complex compound that was as deeply embedded in value as in space and time, which was why Fichte applied the word "facticity" to them. Even in ordinary language, value made something stand out from all the rest. Facticity made things look factual but their very facticity covered up something more complicated, because they were made up as much of what they were *not* as of what they were. This rather odd combination arose from Fichte's initial examination of the elusive quality of the self. No amount of analysis, he pointed out, could find a positive predicate that could be applied to the idea of subjectivity because, as soon as a subject was defined or described, it turned into an object. Facticity, on Fichte's terms, applied as much to the self as to any other, more general, but still somehow singular historical phenomenon, like a coronation, a war, or a revolution. It was a product of what he called *Tathandlung*, meaning something like "a fact as deed," that was the basis of his famous claim that the idea of the self actually began with a deed.[5] It did so, Fichte argued, because a deed or an act had a quality of specificity produced by a combination of what it was and what it was not, performed by an agent who was both a self and a not-self. This—apparently impossible—union of opposites was, Fichte explained, a product of the one thing that gave humanity its capacity for creativity. As was also the case with his earlier explanation of how something higher made it possible to see how natural causation and moral choice could both genuinely coexist, the one thing that in this case enabled the self and the not-self to coexist was freedom. It was the condition, capacity, or quality that imparted singularity or substance to what was otherwise simply causality. Freedom could do this because it had no substance or content of its own. If it really had a positive content, it would not be free. But, because its content was indeterminate, the existence of freedom meant that the positive content of the self and the equally positive content of the not-self could be kept separate. Freedom was the thing that could enable something that is, like a real individual, to coexist with something that is not, like a goal or an aim or even another life. Freedom, in short, was a limiting concept. It imposed a limit on both the self and the not-self, and, because it could do this, it enabled them to exist alongside one another.

---

5. On this aspect of Fichte's thought, see, recently, George di Giovanni, *Hegel and the Challenge of Spinoza: A Study in German Idealism, 1801–1831* (Cambridge, CUP, 2021), pp. 17–24. The significance of the concept of facticity in Fichte's thought was first highlighted by the neo-Kantian German philosopher Emil Lask and documented more recently by Theodore Kisiel. See Theodore Kisiel, "Das Entstehen des Begriffsfeldes 'Faktizität' im Frühwerk Heideggers," *Dilthey Jahrbuch* 4 (1986–87): 91–120; "Heidegger, Lask, Fichte," in *Heidegger, German Idealism, and Neo-Kantianism*, ed. Tom Rockmore (New York, Humanity Books, 2000), pp. 239–70 (plus the chapters by Claude Piché and Marion Heinz in the same book); *Heidegger's Way of Thought* (New York and London, Continuum, 2002), pp. 101–36; and "On the Genesis of Heidegger's Formally Indicative Hermeneutics of Facticity," in *Rethinking Facticity*, ed. François Raffoul and Eric Sean Nelson (New York, State University of New York Press, 2008), pp. 41–67. This concept of facticity is different from the one used by Jean-Paul Sartre in his *Being and Nothingness* [1943]. Sartre used the concept to mean something more like a contingent fact and as a straightforward antonym of freedom in ways that were consonant with his later version of Marxism.

From this perspective, Kant's distinction between the world of appearance and things in themselves could be seen in a different light. In human terms, the veil that seemed to separate the noumenal world from the phenomenal world could be redescribed as something analogous to a landscape at night, with dark or deep patterns of causality forming a backdrop to bright but contingent flashes of creativity. On Fichte's terms, facticity was what straddled the noumenal and phenomenal worlds because human freedom was the thing that enabled them to coexist. There was, in short, a real point to the idea of a worldview, particularly if it was predicated on all the implications of the initial distinction between a subject and an object. In this light, Kant's coinage "unsocial sociability" was a particularly vivid illustration of what both facticity and the concept of a worldview actually implied. The phrase captured the way that historicity was built into human life because human life was an endless process of individual and collective self-creation generated both by the facticity of the self and by the kaleidoscopic quality of the worldviews that it brought in its wake. Behind the feelings of identification and alienation, belonging and exclusion, allegiance and abhorrence, anger and loss built into the endlessly changing islands of human association, there was a more fundamental process of causation and creation that came with the passage of time. History, here, went together with a worldview or, more fully, with the many worldviews that time came to house. Fichte himself drove home the point by inventing the concept of what he called a *Normalvolk*.[6] They were a people who had norms but no history. Real people had both. This, according to Fichte, was why human association was a problem. But if this was the problem, then the solution had to be to find a way to get out of history or, less drastically, to think about whether history itself could supply an alternative to the apparently finite quality of every worldview.

Fichte's own solution supplied one of the links connecting the dispute between Herder and Kant to the later Davos dispute between Ernst Cassirer and Martin Heidegger. A more immediate link was supplied rather nearer to the time of the Davos dispute by the early twentieth-century German philosopher Emil Lask. Lask was the author of a doctoral thesis, published in 1902 and reissued in 1923 (eight years after his death during the First World War), on Fichte's idealism and history, written under the influence, or supervision, of two more famous German students of Kant and history, Wilhelm Windelband and Heinrich Rickert, as well, more remotely, of the now relatively little known

6. On this concept in Fichte's thought, see George Armstrong Kelly, "Notes on Hegel's 'Lordship and Bondage,'" *Review of Metaphysics* 19 (1966): 780–802, and Xavier Léon, "Fichte contre Schelling," *Revue de Métaphysique et de Morale* 12 (1904): 949–76.

German philosopher Hermann Lotze.[7] As Lask, echoing Lotze, described Fichte's thought, it contained something like the range of conceptions of history that is now more usually associated with Heidegger. History could consist simply of a sequence of undifferentiated events. In this sense, it would be the temporal backcloth to the life of a *Normalvolk*, doing today what they had done yesterday and as they would go on to do tomorrow. Sometimes, however, there

---

7. On Fichte, Lask, and Heidegger, see initially Emil Lask, *Fichtes Idealismus und die Geschichte* (Tübingen, J.C.B. Mohr, 1902), and the commentary on it by George Lichtheim, *The Origins of Socialism* [1968] (London, Weidenfeld & Nicolson, 1969), pp. 270–71. On Lotze and Lask, see Lask's many positive assessments of his legacy in Emil Lask, *La logique de la philosophie et la doctrine des catégories: étude sur la forme logique et sa souveraineté* [1911] (Paris, Vrin, 2002), notably pp. 41–42. On Lotze, see William R. Woodward, *Hermann Lotze: An Intellectual Biography* (Cambridge, CUP, 2015), and, more directly, Frederick Beiser, *Late German Idealism: Trendelenburg & Lotze* (Oxford, OUP, 2013). On facticity as defined by Heidegger, see Robert Nichols, *The World of Freedom: Heidegger, Foucault, and the Politics of Historical Ontology* (Stanford, Stanford UP, 2014), p. 38, for two illuminating quotations from Heidegger's works. See too Guy Oakes, "Weber and the Southwest German School: The Genesis of the Concept of the Historical Individual," in *Max Weber and His Contemporaries*, ed. Wolfgang Mommsen and Jürgen Osterhammel (London, Allen & Unwin, 1987), pp. 434–46; Lucien Pelletier, "L'influence d'Emil Lask sur le jeune Ernst Bloch," *Revue philosophique de Louvain* 110 (2012): 23–49, and his "Les sources de la philosophie de l'histoire d'Ernst Bloch," *Revue internationale de philosophie* 3 (2019): 261–77. For a helpful broader presentation, see Beiser, *The German Historicist Tradition*, pp. 443–67 (particularly pp. 446–47, 456), together with his earlier "Historicism and Neo-Kantianism," *Studies in History and Philosophy of Science* 39 (2008): 554–64, and "Normativity in Neo-Kantianism: Its Rise and Fall," *International Journal of Philosophical Studies* 17 (2009): 9–27, and, more recently, his "Neo-Kantianism as Neo-Fichteanism," *Fichte Studien* 45 (2018): 307–27. See also Georges Gurvitch, *Les tendances actuelles de la philosophie allemande: E. Husserl, M. Scheler, E. Lask, M. Heidegger* [1930] (Paris, Vrin, 1949), particularly pp. 207–34; Tom Rockmore, *Irrationalism: Lukacs and the Marxist View of Reason* (Philadelphia, Temple UP, 1992), pp. 59–75; and Claudio Tuozzolo, *Emil Lask e la Logica della Storia* (Milan, Franco Angeli, 2004), pp. 20–25, as well as Agostino Carrino, "Law and Social Theory in Emil Lask," in *Rechtsnorm und Rechtswirklichkeit. Festschrift für Werner Krawietz zum 60. Geburtstag*, ed. Aulis Aarnio, Stanley L. Paulson, Ota Weinberger, Georg Henrik von Wright, and Dieter Wyduckel (Berlin, Duncker & Humblot, 1993), pp. 209–31. As Beiser has pointed out, there is a particularly clear examination of the thought of both Fichte and Lask in vol. 3, ch. 2, of Ernst Cassirer, *Le problème de la connaissance dans la philosophie et la science des temps modernes* [1911–23], 4 vols. (Paris, Editions du Cerf, 1999–2005), where Cassirer set out to show (notably in the long footnote at 3:146 of the French translation) that Fichte's treatment of the related problems of irrationality, historicity, and causality was more consistent than Lask had claimed because, almost from the beginning, it was already compatible with Lask's interpretation of the later Fichte. For a further interpretation, see G. Anthony Bruno, "*Hiatus Irrationalis*: Lask's Fateful Misreading of Fichte," *European Journal of Philosophy*, 2021, 1–19, DOI: 10.1111/ejop.12719.

were surprising and unforeseen events, bringing great and unheralded changes in their wake. With events like these, time could take on a new, more value-laden character. It could look backwards to a founding deed or moment, or forwards towards a new and different future. Temporality would be overlain by different types of periodization with all the various moral or political orientations that these evaluations entailed. On the basis of Fichte's presentation, history could supply a vantage point for thinking about history from outside of history because it also offered a value-laden perspective. It could do this because the ingredients of history, like wars, revolutions, or even apparently simple events like a harvest or a market day, actually had the same qualities of facticity, such as singularity, locality, or temporality, as those that Fichte singled out to address the more problematic parts of Kant's philosophy. Events were clearly real entities, but like everything else after Kant's Copernican revolution, they were knowable only on human terms. This made it hard to know how to differentiate one event from another without either collapsing into circularity or, to avoid circularity, by exploring the additional ingredients involved in Fichte's concept of facticity, as Lask began to do. In the light of facticity, the content of categories like the past, present, and future was far less determinate than Kant's rendition of them had made them seem. Instead of being categories that were mutually exclusive, they could all be alive, all the time.

History, in this light, could be seen as something that could supply the means to overcome the division between the local and partial and the general and universal that, deliberately or inadvertently, Kant had gone to some lengths to highlight. What came to be called historicism began, it could be said, as a reply, or as a correction, to what Friedrich Schlegel had called the historicism of Kant's disquieting concept of history. Culture and the arts that it contained now took on a further sense both as symbols of something suprasensual and as evidence of a more morally acceptable fusion of many worldviews.

The discussion of the concept that began with Kant and Fichte took a different direction with Hegel. For Hegel, history showed that there was also the possibility of a step beyond a worldview towards a real synthesis of matter and form. Beyond art or religion there was rationality, or something more than a *Weltanschauung*. "The history of the world," Hegel announced famously, "is the disciplining of the uncontrolled natural will, bringing it into obedience to a universal principle and conferring subjective freedom. The East knew—and to the present day knows—only that *one* is free; the Greek and Roman world, that *some* are free; the Germanic world knows that *all* are free."[8]

---

8. Hegel, *The Philosophy of History*, p. 104 (like Friedrich, I have modified the original translation). On nineteenth-century philosophies of history, see Ayşe Yuva, "Effets politiques et fron-

As with Fichte, something about freedom and, more specifically, about the fact that, by definition, freedom had no determinate content so that its existence set limits on the content of concepts that did, made it possible to use the concept of freedom as a means to think about history from a position outside of history. Freedom made it possible to bring together several different world-views and show how they could be reconciled or incorporated into the type of higher level of rationality that allowed things that looked to be incompatible to coexist. From this perspective, reason could correct its own propensity to partiality. Hegel's assertion was matched, at about the same time and also in a public lecture, by a comparable assertion by the French historian and politician François Guizot. "You are aware," he announced in a lecture published in 1828, "that the essential, fundamental elements of modern civilization in general, and of French civilization in particular, reduce themselves to three: the Roman world, the Christian world and the Germanic world; antiquity, Christianity, and barbarism."[9] The overlap was not complete, partly because of Hegel's broader comparative range, but mainly because of the difference between the related subjects of freedom and civilization as the respective focal points of the two statements. It is, however, sufficiently visible to suggest a common set of historical and political concerns. Guizot's examination of the relationship between modern civilization and the combination of antiquity, Christianity, and barbarism can be left to the next chapter because it was, in most respects, a product of his long, but largely overlooked, intellectual engagement with the moral, historical, and political thought of the German-speaking world. In this respect, and as several of his critics and admirers emphasized, his vison of history and politics paralleled the thought of Hegel. When, in 1844, his lectures on the history of European civilization were given a German translation, his translator made a point of highlighting their similarity to Hegel's *Lectures on the Philosophy of History*.[10]

Hegel's description of history as "the disciplining of the uncontrolled natural will" looks at first sight like the kind of pronouncement that is probably best left to a lecture. It was, however, based on a comprehensive examination

tières culturelles de l'histoire de la philosophie au xixe siècle," in *Faire de l'histoire de la philosophie, ou les présents du passé*, ed. Chantal Jaquet (Paris, Garnier, 2020), pp. 61–75.

9. François Guizot, *The History of Civilization in France* [1828–30] in François Guizot, *Historical Essays and Lectures*, ed. Stanley Mellon (Chicago, U of Chicago Press, 1972), lecture 30, p. 337.

10. François Guizot, *Allgemeine Geschichte der europäischen Civilisation in vierzehn akademischen Vorlesungen*, trans. Karl Sachs (Stuttgart, 1844), p. iv. See also the assessment of Guizot made by Flint, *The Philosophy of History in France and Germany*, p. 240 and the comparison between Guizot and Eichhorn made by Albion Small, *Origins of Sociology* (Chicago, U of Chicago Press, 1924), p. 78.

of the concept of autonomy not only by Hegel himself, but also by his many political, philosophical, or theological contemporaries thinking and writing in Kant's wake. There was, however, a real irony in the subsequent fate of Hegel's pronouncement. What began as a claim about "subjective freedom" and its association with a "Germanic world" that was indisputably modern turned, over a century later, into a series of claims about "civic republicanism" and "neo-Roman liberty" and *their* association with a concept of freedom that, it was now claimed, was indisputably ancient.[11] The aim of the next part of this chapter is to begin to describe how this switch occurred, and to examine the bifurcation in the content and direction of political thought that it began to produce. Here, the initial focus is on how this process unfolded during the nineteenth century in the German-speaking parts of Europe. In the next two chapters the process is followed in Francophone Europe. On one pathway, it gave rise to a new vision of ancient politics that was oriented towards republican Rome and its historically unusual amalgamation of the condition of being free with the capacity to be free. On the other pathway, however, it gave rise to a new vision of modern politics that also presupposed freedom as both a condition and a capacity, but was now oriented towards a concept of civil society located somewhere between individuals, families, and households on the one side and sovereignty, the state, and the rule of law on the other. The starting point of this process of bifurcation was the problematic concept of autonomy. Although the *concept* of autonomy was given its modern meaning only towards the end of the eighteenth century, this does not mean that the *capacity* for autonomy was, or was taken to be, similarly restricted in time or place. Autonomy as a capacity could be found anywhere, from ancient Greece to modern Europe. This was one reason why it came to be possible, also in the twentieth century, to describe the late eighteenth-century German fascination with autonomy as "the tyranny of Greece over Germany."[12] What actually made the concept problematic was not so much the capacity itself but the question of whether exercising the capacity over a whole society called for the existence of a new type of state and a different set of social arrangements and legal institutions.

This, as Jacobi and Jean Paul had both stressed, was because the concept of autonomy had a built-in double bind. It began with the idea of self-

11. See, most saliently, Pocock, *The Machiavellian Moment*, together with Philip Pettit, *Republicanism: A Theory of Freedom and Government* (Oxford, OUP, 1997), and Skinner, *Liberty before Liberalism*. For a range of recent assessments of the latter, see Hannah Dawson and Annelien De Dijn, eds., *Rethinking Liberty before Liberalism* (Cambridge, CUP, 2022).

12. See, famously, Eliza Marian Butler, *The Tyranny of Greece over Germany* (Cambridge, CUP, 1935).

determination and a focus on the self that seemed to leave no room for determination by others. But without coordination between the self and others, more autonomy could, counterproductively, produce more heteronomy, meaning that the more effort that was put into self-determination the more probable external society would push back. Autonomy, in short, would be impossible because, from this perspective, it was simply a misleadingly positive name for selfishness, or for what, more recently and politely, has been called the "unencumbered self."[13] Since almost any self was embedded in a more or less dense array of economic, social, or emotional encumbrances, scaling up autonomy to encompass a whole society looked likely, Jacobi emphasized, to default into either anarchy or despotism, or both. There was, as Jean Paul announced, a very close connection between the concept of autonomy and the idea of the death of God.

Fichte and the Problem of Autonomy

In the face of this problem, one response was to show that it was, in fact, possible to find a way out of the double bind that seemed to be built into autonomy by focusing on the imaginative and epistemological dynamics of its initially self-centred starting point. The outcome was a new twist on the concept of perfectibility. In this version of perfectibility, the one thing that humans had in common, namely, their capacity for autonomy, was also shown to be the one thing that made them individually different and, consequently, able to be fully—or perfectly—themselves. This was the move that gave rise, in the twentieth century, to what came to be called recognition theory. In its original guise, however, the move was made by Johann Gottlieb Fichte, and was centred on the idea that self-determination was predicated upon an imaginative interactive encounter between the self and an other.[14] Fichte's initial insight

13. Michael J. Sandel, "The Procedural Republic and the Unencumbered Self," *Political Theory* 12 (1984): 81–96. For a comparable, and far less polite, assault on the uses to which the Kantian philosophy could be put, see the energetic attack by Schelling on Germaine de Staël's friend Charles Villers's efforts to make Kant's philosophy better known in France, recently edited and translated by Patrick Cerutti as "FWJ Schelling, 'Notice sur les tentatives de Monsieur Villers pour introduire la philosophie kantienne en France,'" *Revue Germanique Internationale* 18 (2013): 7–26.

14. On Fichte and recognition theory, see, notably, Axel Honneth, *The Struggle for Recognition: The Moral Grammar of Social Conflicts* (Cambridge, MA, MIT Press, 1996), and, helpfully, Isaac Nakhimovsky, *The Closed Commercial State: Perpetual Peace and Commercial Society from Rousseau to Fichte* (Princeton, NJ, Princeton UP, 2011), especially pp. 49–51. See too Luc Ferry, *Political Philosophy* [1984], 3 vols. (Chicago, U of Chicago Press, 1990–92), notably vol. 2, *The*

was to see that, in this type of encounter, the self would always appear as something other to itself. This meant that the initial encounter between the self and an other could take place within a single mind because it would begin to occur as soon as the mind saw the difference between itself and something external, like a wall. The really significant move would be what happened next, when the thinking subject began to notice that thinking of its awareness of its own awareness made it see itself as an identifiable object. This was the point of Fichte's otherwise enigmatic formulation I = I. However much it tried, the subjective self would always see itself as an object. The effortless and almost imperceptible quality of this switch from subjectivity to objectivity had two important implications. First, it seemed to mean that the reflecting self had no determinate or settled content because the self that was the subject would always turn into an object to itself, leaving the underlying subject with no determinate attributes other than its awareness that it was equipped with the freedom to determine itself, or to be autonomous. But if this attribute of the self could be found in any single self, it could also be an attribute of every other self. This was the second implication of Fichte's examination of autonomy. It made it possible to broaden and deepen the idea of natural rights by showing why the mind's reflexive powers made human freedom as foundational to a political society as any of the other criteria minimally specified in earlier theories of the political state (such as indigence, need, rationality, or language).[15] Fichte, in short, turned natural rights theory into recognition theory.

He did so by highlighting a significant difference between something natural, like a tree, and someone human, like a real individual named, for example, Clara. Trees change from season to season and can, over time, become entirely unrecognizable. In purely physical terms, individuals can change even more but will still somehow remain recognizable as themselves. This, Fichte argued, was because the one thing that makes them recognizable in a more than purely physical sense is the one thing that can also be recognized in oneself, namely, the ability to feel free produced by the quicksilver relationship between subjectivity and objectivity. This was the feeling that was the basis of autonomy, or the idea of a subjective self giving rules or orders to an objective self. The existence of this idea meant that the self that was recognizable in

System of Philosophies of History; David James, Fichte's Social and Political Philosophy: Property and Virtue (Cambridge, CUP, 2011) and his Fichte's Republic: Idealism, History and Nationalism (Cambridge, CUP, 2015), together with Gabriel Gottlieb, ed., Fichte's Foundations of Natural Right: A Critical Guide (Cambridge, CUP, 2016).

15. On the idea of a natural right as something minimal, meaning something without which human existence would not be possible, see, particularly, Richard Tuck, Philosophy and Government 1572–1651 (Cambridge, CUP, 1993).

another person was, in some not entirely clear sense, actually a self-made self. This was because behind the physical changes causing changes to someone's appearance, there was still a recognizably identifiable person equipped with a capacity for autonomy.

Recognition of this capacity in someone else had two further and equally important implications. If, in the first place, it established the reality and continuity of another personality, it also made it possible to corroborate the existence of the same capacity within oneself. But it also, in the second place, showed that while the capacity was the same, the effects that it would produce were actually quite different because autonomy, by definition, amounted to *self*-determination. Recognition was, therefore, a kind of amalgamation of similarity and difference. It meant that it was actually the other who was responsible for corroborating the subjective self's capacity for self-determination because the combination of change and continuity that it revealed was evidence that the same capacity for self-determination was, simultaneously, what made each of them different. But the idea of *self*-determination also meant not being subject to someone else's will. If this was the case, then the only possible relationship between two autonomous individuals had to be a relationship of equality. The interplay between subjectivity and objectivity meant, therefore, that the foundational relationship of human society was one of equality because only equality could enable both of them to be fully themselves.

The combination of autonomy and what Fichte called "formability" meant, as his students at the University of Jena noticed, that this part of his thought was quite close to Schiller's.[16] "Removed alike from uniformity and from confusion," Schiller wrote in his *Aesthetic Education of Man*, "there abides the triumph of form," meaning the combination of the real and the ideal that made up what he called "the aesthetic state."[17] In this usage, the idea underlying the loosely Platonic phrase "the triumph of form" was the human ability to distinguish form from substance and, as Fichte also claimed, to use this ability to act autonomously. Its existence, Schiller claimed, meant that, unlike animals or the weather, humans had the ability to decide on future, particularly moral, courses of action and, accordingly, to subject themselves to freely chosen goals. It also meant that the sources of motivation underlying political obligation and civic virtue could be as much internal and ideal as external and real.

16. On the overlap, see the comment on Schiller described in the previous chapter.

17. Schiller, *On the Aesthetic Education of Man*, letter 4, p. 23. As this passage indicates, Schiller's usage was closely connected to the subject of reform. In this sense, the concept of "the aesthetic state" was considerably less substantive than it has become in, for example, Gilles Lipovetsky and Jean Serroy, *L'esthétisation du monde. Vivre à l'âge du capitalisme artiste* (Paris, Gallimard, 2013).

"If," Schiller wrote by way of illustration, "the Trojan host storms on to the battlefield with piercing shrieks like a flock of cranes, the Greek army approaches it in silence, with noble and measured tread. In the former case we see only the exuberance of blind forces; in the latter the triumph of form and the simple majesty of law."[18] Although, as the description implied, both sets of people were involved in warfare and killing, the Trojans were driven by their emotions, while the Greeks were the authors of their own actions.

The concept of "formability" repeated the same distinction but gave it a more egalitarian inflection. After Fichte, recognition and its dynamics could be construed as the real foundation of equality. If, as is usually thought, recognition requires reciprocity, Fichte insisted that the relationship actually worked the other way round because it was actually reciprocity that, in the first place, requires recognition. "Nature completed all her works," he wrote in his *Foundations of Natural Right* in 1796.

> Only from the human being did she withdraw her hand and, precisely by doing so, she gave him over to himself. Formability as such is the character of humanity. Since it is impossible to superimpose upon a human shape any other concept than that of oneself, every human being is inwardly compelled to regard every other human being as his equal.[19]

Since every human being could recognize a self underlying or accompanying the changes that occurred to a physical self, the same ability required them each to recognize freedom's hidden presence in others and see that it made them autonomous as well. "Surely," Fichte continued, "there is no human being who, upon first seeing another human being, would immediately take flight (as one would in the presence of a rapacious animal) or prepare to kill and eat him (as one might do to a beast), rather than immediately expect reciprocal communication. This is the case, not through habituation and learning, but through nature and reason, and we have just derived the law that makes it the case."[20] As with natural rights theory, autonomy in Fichte's interpretation did not call for any initial assumptions about human benevolence or altruism. All that it required was the idea of a self that could determine itself and, as Fichte put it in a phrase now usually associated with the twentieth-century German, Jewish, and American political thinker Hannah Arendt, was equipped correspondingly with "the one true human right that belongs to

18. Schiller, *On the Aesthetic Education of Man*, letter 27, p. 213.

19. Johann Gottlieb Fichte, *Foundations of Natural Right* [1796–97] (Cambridge, CUP, 2000), p. 74.

20. Ibid., p. 75.

every human being as such: the right to be able to acquire rights."[21] The idea of the right to have rights began, in other words, with Fichte's version of recognition theory. With it, recognition was inseparable from reciprocity and equality, and with reciprocity and equality the nightmare vision of social disintegration imagined by Jacobi and Jean Paul could be pushed to one side. In addition, by showing that recognition was predicated upon an individual capacity for autonomy, and that the capacity for autonomy was in turn predicated upon a joint recognition of freedom, Fichte began to show that there could be a way to reconcile Kant's future-oriented vision of history with Herder's historically bounded concept of culture. However time-bound culture might be, it could still be compatible with human freedom and its capacity to create new and different ways of separating form from substance.

Schelling and Subjectivity

Despite its ingenuity, Fichte's philosophy displayed a continuing tension between autonomy and equality. To its critics, its emphasis on subjectivity as the key to the recognition of similarity and difference that was the basis of equality still left a gap between individual autonomy and social coordination that only a state seemed able to fill. Fichte himself appeared to acknowledge the problem by envisaging an energetically interventionist state. He described its features most fully and powerfully in his *Closed Commercial State* of 1800, and he continued to maintain his commitment to its implications until his death in 1812. The most prominent of these features was a state-generated fiat currency created, Fichte argued, because a free state could have no place for any medium of international payments like gold or silver and the unequal distribution of economic and social resources that, in the longer term, they were likely to produce. The state would also be responsible for the provision of education and training and, as a result, would also be in a position to administer the

---

21. Ibid., p. 333. As Arendt wrote later (probably without knowing of Fichte's phrase), "We became aware of a right to have rights (and that means to live in a framework where one is judged by one's actions and opinions) and a right to belong to some organized community, only when millions of people emerged who had lost and could not regain these rights because of the new global political situation." See Hannah Arendt, *The Origins of Totalitarianism* [1951] (2nd ed. Cleveland and New York, Meridian Books, 1958), pp. 296–97. For recent commentary, see Stephanie DeGooyer, Samuel Moyn, et al. *The Right to Have Rights* (London, Verso, 2018), and Hannah Arendt, *Il n'y a qu'un seul droit de l'homme*, ed. Emmanuel Alloa (Paris, Payot, 2021). After completing this book, I now see that the point was also made by Eric D. Weitz, *A World Divided: The Global Struggle for Human Rights in the Age of Nation-States* (Princeton, NJ, Princeton UP, 2019), pp. 2 and 431 n. 3.

distribution of occupations and activities within the economy as a whole. Together, state control of the money supply and state provision of education and training meant that there would be substantial limits on private property.[22] Given the consistency and clarity of Fichte's views, it is not surprising that part of his posthumously published *Die Staatslehre* (Doctrine of the state) was picked up and translated into French in 1831 under the title *De l'idée d'une guerre légitime* (On the idea of a just war) by Louis-Pierre Babeuf, the son of the better-known French revolutionary conspirator Gracchus Babeuf, whose views on property as the source of the distinction between "the order of egoism" and "the order of equality" had been commemorated publicly in 1828 by the Franco-Italian socialist Filippo Buonarotti.[23] In this rendition of Fichte, legal and political equality were to be matched by economic and social equality, buttressed ambiguously by state power.

The alternative to Fichte's transformation of natural rights theory into recognition theory came from something like the opposite direction, in the thought of Friedrich Wilhelm Joseph Schelling. Where Fichte had highlighted the feeling of nothingness produced by the subjective self's efforts to define itself, Schelling began by highlighting the being of nothingness itself. Fichte's starting point was the radical indeterminacy of subjectivity and the freedom that it housed. Since it had no determinate content, individual subjectivity was, by definition, free to determine itself. Schelling's starting point was equally indeterminate, but its initial focus was on objectivity rather than subjectivity, or, more specifically, on the nature of whatever it was that enabled the verb "to be" to be a link between a subject and a predicate. The grass might well be green, but something seemed to be needed to form a link between the grass and the greenness. This implied that behind the grass and the greenness there was simply being, and before it had any determinate attributes, being was simply being. "In its innocence," Schelling explained in his lectures *On the History of Modern Philosophy*, "being is always simply what does not know itself. As soon as it becomes an object for itself it loses its innocence. The subject

---

22. For a helpful way in to these aspects of Fichte's thought and its legacy, see Beiser, "Neo-Kantianism as Neo-Fichteanism." More broadly, see Nakhimovsky, *The Closed Commercial State.*

23. On this aspect of Fichte's legacy, see Johann Gottlieb Fichte, *La doctrine de l'état* [1813], ed. Jean-Christophe Goddard and Grégoire Lacaze (Paris, Vrin, 2006), pp. 12–13. On "the order of egoism" versus "the order of equality," see Filippo Michele Buonarotti, *Conspiration pour l'égalité dite de Babeuf*, 2 vols. (Brussels, 1828), 1:9, and, more recently, John Dunn, *Setting the People Free: The Story of Democracy* (London, Atlantic Books, 2005), p. 124. On Babeuf, see Michael Sonenscher, "Property, Community and Citizenship," in *The Cambridge History of Eighteenth-Century Political Thought*, ed. Mark Goldie and Robert Wokler (Cambridge, CUP, 2006), pp. 465–94.

can never possess itself *as* it is, because in trying to do so it turns entirely into its other. This is the fundamental contradiction or, it could be said, the misfortune of all being. . . . It experiences its existence as something that it has contracted and, therefore, as something accidental. In this sense, and this should be noted, the first being (*primum existens*) is at the same time, the first contingency, the original chance."[24] On Schelling's terms, objectivity, not subjectivity, was the real ground of human freedom.

Schelling set out to explain the point of this move from radical subjectivity to radical objectivity in an allegorical story entitled *Clara, or On Nature's Connection to the Spirit World*, a work published only posthumously but which Schelling probably wrote in 1810, not long after the death of his own wife, Caroline. As he put it in his introduction to the story, philosophy after Kant had been marked by "a lively effort to attain the spiritual, matched by a corresponding failure to do so in any real sense."[25] The demise of the old, pre-Kantian distinction between physics and metaphysics had, he argued, not only made it harder for philosophy to have any real purchase on nature but also, paradoxically, made it equally hard for philosophy to deal with the spiritual itself. This was because the new focus on subjectivity made everything look spiritual, and this in turn seemed to rule out identifying any of the distinctive attributes of the spiritual as such. Schelling's switch from subjectivity to objectivity was, therefore, designed to reinstate the spiritual by starting first with the being of being.

The initial problem built into this move was to find a way to inject consciousness into being. For Fichte, with his focus on subjectivity, the problem did not arise. For Schelling, however, it was a real problem that gave rise to an abiding interest in the many intermediate states between consciousness and the unconscious, at least as these could be described in the light of phenomena like fantasy,

24. Friedrich Wilhelm Joseph Schelling, *On the History of Modern Philosophy* [1856–61], trans. Andrew Bowie (Cambridge, CUP, 1994), pp. 114–16. I have modified the translation in the light of that given in Schelling, *Contribution à l'histoire de la philosophie moderne*, trans. J. F. Marquet (Paris, PUF, 1983), pp. 118 et seq.

25. Friedrich Wilhelm Joseph Schelling, *Clara, or On Nature's Connection to the Spirit World* [1810], ed. and trans. Fiona Steinkamp (Albany, State U of New York Press, 2002), pp. 3–4. I have used the more recent French translation and its helpful accompanying essays published in Alexandra Roux, ed., *Schelling, philosophe de la mort et de l'immortalité: études sur* Clara (Rennes, PU de Rennes, 2014), abbreviated here as Schelling, *Clara*, p. 183. As Roux notes in her introduction (Schelling, *Clara*, pp. 9, 11), commentary on *Clara* is not as considerable as on Schelling's other works. See, however, Daniel Whistler, "Schelling's Politics of Sympathy: Reflections on *Clara* and Related Texts," *International Yearbook of German Idealism* 15 (2017): 245–68, and Susanna Lindberg, "Les hantises de Clara," *Revue Germanique Internationale* 18 (2013): 235–53.

dreaming, somnambulism, hallucination, or hypnotism, as well as the various types of mental activity associated with mesmerism, or the study and application of what the doctrine's eponymous founder, Franz Anton Mesmer, called animal magnetism (as against physical magnetism) in treating various forms of psychic disturbance.[26] Topics like these brought Schelling's philosophy quite close to the subject matter of palingenesis, particularly as it had been used in the work of Charles Bonnet and Johann Gottfried Herder, to describe an increasingly spiritualized hierarchy of beings stretching from inanimate matter to the immaterial souls of the afterlife. But Schelling used the idea in a different and more sophisticated way by focusing on consciousness as the key to understanding how being as such had come to be differentiated into an immense range and variety of individual beings. Here, the key move was to focus on the distinction between being in itself and being in time, or being as a succession or sequence of forms, states, modes, mutations, or conditions. If the variety and particularity of the latter could be thought of as a kind of subtraction from something more general or uniform, then the link between the two could be established by something artificial, like a sign, a symbol, or a microcosm of a macrocosm. On this basis, the combination of similarity and difference that was the hallmark of Fichte's system no longer needed to rely on reciprocal recognition of an internal capacity for autonomy. It could, instead, rely on recognition of something common, but external, like a symbol, a flag, or a song. They too were types of being, but their attributes and significance belonged to the world of the arts and not to that of nature. From this perspective, symbols rather than states could supply an alternative solution to the problem of reconciling autonomy with society. Symbols could be recognized more readily than the individual capacity for self-determination because they were made manifest externally, not internally, and, since their external existence meant that they could be recognized collectively, joint recognition could give rise to shared identities, a common culture, and a national spirit or *Volksgeist*. On Schelling's terms, starting with being rather than consciousness, as Fichte had done, made it possible to see how to combine human similarity with individual difference without having to fall back on the power of the state.

Schelling showed how this could be done in *Clara*. Since, he wrote, starting with the self amounted to trying to understand the spiritual by way of the spiritual, the first move had to be to start with nature. This was the real point

26. For an initial way in to these subjects, see David E. Leary, "German Idealism and the Development of Psychology in the Nineteenth Century," *Journal of the History of Ideas* 18 (1980): 299–317, and Angus Nicholls and Martin Liebscher, eds., *Thinking the Unconscious. Nineteenth-Century German Thought* (Cambridge, CUP, 2010).

of *Naturphilosophie*. Identifying something knowable, or spiritual (in the sense of ideal or conceptual), in nature would make it possible in turn to identify the specific attributes of subjectivity. This, in the first instance, would show that "nature was simply one aspect of the whole and that the spiritual world was its other, opposite, aspect."[27] The spiritual world was, more or less by definition, inaccessible, but knowing nature could help to establish a bridge between the natural and the spiritual. This was one reason why Schelling's philosophy also came to be known as a positive philosophy. The label was not intended to refer simply or mainly to the positive study of what was empirically observable but was used instead to justify the positive knowledge of what was *not* observable in the light of a careful study of those things that were. In this sense, there was a real overlap between Schelling's philosophy and the now better-known positive philosophy of the nineteenth-century French moral and political theorist Auguste Comte. "No-one." according to a British commentator writing in 1856, "who compares the philosophic method of Schelling with the *philosophie positive* of Auguste Comte, can have the slightest hesitation as to the source from which the latter virtually sprang. The fundamental idea is indeed precisely the same as that of Schelling, with this difference only, that the idealistic language of the German speculator is here translated into the more ordinary language of physical science."

> That Comte borrowed his views from Schelling we can by no means affirm. But that the whole conception of the affiliation of the sciences in the order of their relative simplicity and the expansion of the same law of development so as to include the exposition of human nature and the courses of social progress is all to be found there, no one in the smallest degree acquainted with Schelling's writings can seriously doubt.[28]

Comte's prime concern was with the origins and nature of what he was the first to call "altruism," or the capacity for self-sacrifice that he associated emblematically with the figure of the strikingly young Jacobin leader Louis-Antoine Saint-Just and, more generally, with the heroism of the French republican *levée en masse* of 1793.[29] In its original guise, positive philosophy was designed to identify and explain this other-oriented human quality. As its subtitle indicated, *Clara* was designed to be an allegory of what this involves.

27. Schelling, *Clara*, p. 184.

28. John Daniel Morell, "German Philosophy in the Nineteenth Century," originally published in *Manchester Papers* (1856), and reprinted in his *Philosophical Fragments Written during Intervals of Business* (London, Longmans, 1878), p. 101.

29. On Comte and altruism, see particularly Dixon, *The Invention of Altruism*.

The story begins on All Saints' Day with a conversation between Clara, the recently widowed wife of a grocer, and a number of other witnesses to the events taking place on that ceremonial day of the Christian year, including a priest, a doctor, and the narrator himself. From the start, therefore, it is a conversation about the relationship between the living and the dead, the physical and the spiritual, and the real and the ideal. It is also, as Schiller intended, a conversation that takes place not only on a day, but on a symbolic day, or a day that exists to mark the multiple and timeless bonds between the communities of the living and the dead at a determinate moment in time. The initial focus of the story is on the gulf between these various conditions, and on how certain types of emotion, like love, can somehow bridge the divide. As Clara points out in reply to the priest, who had claimed that as part of the spiritual world her husband now belongs to God, it is not entirely true to think that the separation is complete. She would, she says, still feel love for her children even if, like her husband, they were to die. Some sort of capacity, in the light of this feeling, seems able to bridge the divide between the two realms. Once, as the narrator then goes on observe, monasteries were a setting for cultivating this capacity. Now, however, it has come to belong to science because science has the same type of ability to produce a bridge between the physical and the spiritual by adding a potentially rich conceptual overlay to simple physical experience. But, as Schelling himself went on to argue in the persona of the narrator, the real source of the connection is the peculiarly human capacity to capture something spiritual by *making* something physical, like a work of art considered in the broadest sense.

In itself, Schelling claimed, nature is full of things that die. But awareness that this is the case cannot be the work of nature itself because nature is synonymous with life. Equally, the same kind of knowledge of death cannot be the work of God, not only because God is eternal and spiritual, but also because God is not actually the cause of death. It follows that awareness of death and the impermanence of natural things has to be the work of humanity, which, Schelling went on to claim, explained why this distinctively human type of knowledge was the bridge between life and death. Knowledge of death was, for humans, the key to understanding the being of being. It was finite and could be created. Humans give life to the external world by creating things that are perishable, and without this injection of the perishable into the material, all life would be purely physical and endlessly uniform. In this sense, the other side of the process of bringing death into life was what Schelling called the "magical relationship" between humanity and nature.[30] It was magical because it was predicated on an initial awareness of

30. Schelling, *Clara*, p. 206.

being as otherness, and, by extension, on the peculiar effect on human capabilities that this awareness entailed. Awareness of being as otherness meant that being had a beginning and an end. Something other existed in space and time, and because of this it was, by definition, finite. The discovery of the finite quality of being was, Schelling argued, the basis of the human capacity to produce the new type of being involved in the arts. Something finite could be replicated, imitated, or created. From this perspective, humanity's discovery of the otherness of being was responsible for shattering the original unity that was once the being of being. By injecting its own creativity into the primary fusion of matter and spirit, human consciousness was then responsible for causing the original unity of the creation to break apart as things, including God, proceeded to contract into themselves.[31] The differentiated being of nature was therefore, and in a more than purely metaphorical sense, a human creation, and if this was the case, humanity also had the capacity to bring back unity to variety. "History," Schelling wrote, "is an epic poem emanating from the spirit of God. Its two principal parts are the one that represents the departure of humanity from its centre and its progression towards the furthest point away from it, while the other part represents its return to that centre from the furthest point."[32] As one of his admirers, the French spiritualist philosopher Félix Ravaisson, noted in 1840, "Schelling establishes the basis of any future metaphysics in action, personality, and liberty." His insistence, Ravaisson wrote many years later, on "the absolute freedom of the will, as against Hegel's logical mechanics," was both "the foundation and the pinnacle of his system."[33] In this sense, Schelling's examination of the transformation of the otherwise inexorable

31. This is the theme of a famous article by Jürgen Habermas, "Dialectical Idealism in Transition to Materialism: Schelling's Idea of a Contraction of God and Its Consequences for the Philosophy of History" [1969], in *The New Schelling*, ed. Judith Norman and Alistair Welchmann (London, Continuum, 2004), pp. 49–89. On the subject of death in *Clara*, see too Amstutz, *Caspar David Friedrich*, pp. 191–93.

32. Friedrich Wilhelm Joseph Schelling, *Essais*, trans. S. Jankélévitch (Paris, Aubier, 1946), pp. 212–13.

33. "M. Schelling place dans l'action, dans la personnalité, dans la liberté, la base de la métaphysique future." Later, Ravaisson singled out the "système par l'achèvement duquel Schelling a terminé sa glorieuse carrière, et dont la liberté absolue du vouloir, par opposition au mécanisme logique de Hegel, forme à la fois et la base et le couronnement." Cited by Andrea Bellantone, "De la persévérance à la donation: la décision métaphysique de Ravaisson," *Revue philosophique de la France et de l'étranger* 144 (2019): 49–62 (p. 58 for the passages cited). See too Andrea Bellantone, "L'expérience de l'ego dans le spiritualisme français: de l'objet à l'œuvre," in *Le renouveau de l'idéalisme*, ed. Giovanni Dotoli and Louis Ucciani (Paris, L'Harmattan, 2018),

processes of life and death into the humanly created processes of nature and art picked up many of the themes of the old German question of the vocation of mankind, or the *Bestimmung des Menschheit*. As *Clara* was designed to show, the ultimate answer to the vocational question was that the arts had the power to restore the lost unity of matter and spirit. This, in the final analysis, was why their creation and development constituted the real vocation of mankind. And, as Schelling went on to show, this meant explaining how the unavoidably individuated capabilities involved not only in the arts but also in the broader capacity for autonomy could be scaled up to encompass a whole society and, ultimately, humanity as a whole.

If, as Schelling was well aware, Fichte's version of autonomy veered too far to the side of subjectivity and gave rise to the problem of the unencumbered self, his own version of autonomy ran the risk of veering too far in the opposite direction, raising a problem about a self that was all too obviously encumbered because it was enmeshed so deeply in a web of creation, both by itself and by others, that it was impossible to identify how it could be accountable or could be held to be responsible for values and arrangements that were not obviously its own. The world as it is, says Clara, is a necessary world. Its only contingent part is mankind. But what could begin as contingency would turn, once enacted, into "terrifying necessity" because the initial sense of inner freedom could not be insulated from the tangle of exteriority.[34] This was the real reason why the arts mattered. Liberty, Schelling went on to explain—and, with it, the human capacity for accountability and responsibility—was "unconditioned" and, because of this, was beyond the world of causation. But this meant that liberty was not of this world. Art, however, was its this-world equivalent because it was an external surrogate for the internal and, in this guise, was able to supply a number of related ways of turning the internal and inaccessible into something external and motivational. The first was simply the feeling of euphoria, bliss, or simple sense of achievement that art can sometimes produce. The second was the ordinary activity of daily life and its intermittent connection to the first set of feelings. The intense quality of the emotional response to art could be a goal or motivation for ordinary activity, while the work involved in daily life could, in an important sense, be a solution to the problem of accountability and responsibility built into an extended network of social interdependence.

---

pp. 149–63. On Schelling and Ravaisson, see helpfully Dominique Janicaud, *Une Généalogie du Spiritualisme Français* (The Hague, Martinus Nijhoff, 1969), pp. 95–100.

34. Schelling, *Clara*, pp. 207–8.

But the bridge between the physical and the spiritual supplied by art also had a third effect. Art was the work of the mind and body, but the author of the art was also a person. This added a third component to the analysis. As Schelling described it, personality was not quite the equivalent of Fichte's subjective I because, as he put it, it was "the unifying consciousness" of both body and mind. Another word for this unifying entity was the soul.[35] In this life, Schelling continued, souls are quite hard to describe because they have to coexist, first, with the body and, second, with the mind. There is therefore an initial triad consisting of a body, a mind, and a soul. Although, Schelling went on to explain, the same triad continues to exist in the afterlife, the hierarchical arrangement of its component parts will now be different because the triad will now consist of a soul, a mind, and, last, a body. The difference between the two triads helps to clarify two important facts, first about death and second about being. It shows, first, that it is death that is responsible for the existence of the two different triads, and, second, that this in turn makes it possible to conceive of two different forms of being. The first form of being is simple existence, like the existence of a stone, but the second form of existence is being in time, or being that is aware of being.[36] It is this form of being that can posit being as such or give being a being as simple existence. Death, particularly in the light of the disorienting thought of imagining how you would be after you have died, shows that the two forms of being cannot both exist simultaneously. If they could both be simultaneously present, then the internal and the external would be identical, and humans would be like gods with no need to rely on experience for the interior to be guided, stimulated, provoked, or misled by the exterior. Being existed in time and, paradoxically, it was being in time that, first, made it possible to identify the underlying character of being as being and, second, made it possible to explain how the two forms of being could coexist. Understanding the human awareness of death was, therefore, the key to understanding the human capacity for life.

Examining being enabled Schelling to give autonomy a new foundation. If, as the argument of *Clara* was designed to show, existence preceded essence, then a being that was aware of being could determine the being of being as such and, by doing so, establish a new version of the relationship between subject and object that was the hallmark of autonomy. It could do so if, as the narrator put it in the final part of *Clara*, "God's sole final aim is that the interior is made as fully manifest on the exterior so that the two extremities—the one in which the interior is preserved in all its purity and the other in which it is embodied and

---

35. Ibid., p. 216.
36. Ibid., pp. 223–24.

externalised most completely both acquire an equal importance."[37] Achieving this balance between the spiritual and the physical was, Schelling wrote, the ultimate destination (*Bestimmung*) of mankind. In one sense, the concept of self-determination was the same as Fichte's. But it differed from it in one important respect. It did not rely as heavily on the interpersonal dynamics of recognition as Fichte's system had done because it could rely instead on common recognition of the value of a symbol, including a day like All Saints' Day. Symbols like these were the foundation of a distinctive culture or, in Schelling's German term, a *Volksgeist* or national spirit. Here, the most important feature of a symbol was its synthetic quality. As Schelling described it, a symbol was something that combined the general with the particular as a single vivid experience. A symbol was not a metaphor or an allegory because, like a work of art, it was complete in itself. And, although it might be individually produced, it could be commonly and immediately recognized.[38] Symbols removed much of the need for interpersonal recognition and the emphasis on equality entailed by Fichte's version of the process. And this, by extension, removed much of the need for a state. Schelling's abiding hostility to the state is well-enough known. On his terms, most of life's requirements could—or at least should—be captured and maintained symbolically. One very powerful symbol of what these requirements usually involve, from marriage, birth, and death to work, property, and the economy, was the law. There was, as a result, a close relationship between Schelling's thought, with its focus on the significance of symbols in giving the concept of a *Volksgeist* its affective force, and the idea of the law as something that could develop and change under the auspices of a judicial authority, but without the presence of a legislator, that was one of the features of the thought of Friedrich Carl von Savigny and the historical school of law.[39]

37. Ibid., p. 262.

38. For a very clear presentation, see Patrick Cerutti, *La philosophie de Schelling: Repères* (Paris, Vrin, 2019), particularly pp. 33–133. See too Warren Breckman, *The Adventures of the Symbolic: Post-Marxism and Radical Democracy* (New York, Columbia UP, 2013), pp. 27, 29–34, 36–37.

39. The relationship was highlighted by Franz Rosenzweig, drawing upon a number of more detailed early twentieth-century studies, in his brilliant *Hegel et l'état* [1920], ed. and trans. Paul-Laurent Assoun and Gerard Bensussan (Paris, PUF, 1991). On Savigny and Schelling, see Whitman, *The Legacy of Roman Law in the German Romantic Era*, p. 92 n. 5 and, earlier, S. Brie, "Der Volksgeist bei Hegel und in der historischen Rechtsschule," *Archiv für Rechts- und Wirtschaftsphilosophie* 2 (1908/1909): 1–10 (thanks to Charlotte Johann for this latter reference and, more generally, for many helpful discussions of Savigny and German legal history).

From Autonomy to Civic Humanism

There is a noticeable, but bleaker, echo of Schelling's interest in the symbolic
in the powerful and imaginative essay by Hannah Arendt "On the Concept of
History: Ancient and Modern," which she published in full for the first time
in her *Between Past and Future* in 1961. As she presented it, the human ability
to create symbols was the cause of both the human emancipation from nature
and the human enslavement to technology. "In the beginning of Western history," she wrote, "the distinction between the mortality of men and the immortality of nature, between man-made things and things which come into
being by themselves, was the tacit assumption of historiography. All things that
owe their existence to men, such as works, deeds and words, are perishable,
infected, as it were, by the mortality of their authors." In modern culture, however, the antithesis was reversed. The idea of mortality, Arendt wrote, quoting
a poem by the early twentieth-century German poet Rainer Maria Rilke, had
now come to be associated with what is natural, while immortality was associated instead with what is human. In Rilke's poem, "even the mountains only
seem to rest under the light of the stars; they are slowly, secretly devoured by
time; nothing is forever; immortality has fled the world to find an uncertain
abode in the darkness of the human heart that still has the capacity to remember and to say: forever."[40] Here, the emphasis fell on the word "seem" and its
bearing on even the most apparently timeless parts of nature. As the timelessness of nature slowly receded, human artifice became the new foundation of
immortality. This new sense of the meaning of the passage of time, Arendt
went to claim, had given rise to the modern concept of history as an endless
process of creation and destruction. Although this might look like a secularized version of Christianity, it had, in fact, nothing to do with Christianity.
"What at first sight," she wrote, "looks like a Christianization of world history
in fact eliminates all religious time-speculations from secular history. So far as
secular history is concerned we live in a process which knows no beginning
and no end and which thus does not permit us to entertain eschatological
expectations. Nothing could be more alien to Christian thought than this concept of an earthly immortality of mankind."[41]

Although, in an immediate sense, this echo of Schelling is likely to have
owed more to Arendt's familiarity with the thought of Martin Heidegger than
to any more direct engagement of Schelling's own views of nature, art, and

40. Hannah Arendt, "The Concept of History: Ancient and Modern," in her *Between Past
and Future* [1961], ed. Jerome Kohn (London, Penguin, 2006), pp. 43–44.
41. Ibid., p. 74.

history (although she did actually own all of Schelling's works), it still captures an aspect of the now less well-known early nineteenth-century discussion of autonomy that has continued to resonate well into the twenty-first century. As Arendt put it graphically in the final paragraph of her essay, the concept of autonomy was, ultimately, self-defeating. "In the situation of radical world-alienation," she wrote, "neither history nor nature is at all conceivable."

> This twofold loss of the world—the loss of nature and the loss of human artifice in the widest sense, which would include all history—has left behind it a society of men who, without a common world which would at once relate and separate them, either live in a desperate lonely separation or are pressed together in a mass. For a mass society is nothing more than that kind of organized living which automatically establishes itself among human beings who are still related to one another but have lost the world once common to them all.[42]

Autonomy, in short, had turned into atomization. It was an assertion that could have been written as much by Jacobi or Jean Paul as by David Riesman (author of *The Lonely Crowd*) or C. Wright Mills (author of *The Power Elite*).

The early nineteenth-century discussion of autonomy also had a further resonance in the two, related, late twentieth-century concepts of civic humanism and republicanism.[43] Here, it was Arendt herself who was the intermediary. "In terms borrowed from or suggested by the language of Hannah Arendt," wrote J.G.A. Pocock in the first, 1975, edition of his pathbreaking book *The Machiavellian Moment*, "this book has told part of the story of the revival in the early modern West of the ancient idea of *homo politicus* (the *zoon politikon* of Aristotle) who affirms his being and his virtue by the medium of political action, whose closest kinsman is *homo rhetor* and whose antithesis is the *homo credens* of Christian faith."

> Following this debate into the beginnings of modern historicist sociology, we have been led to study the complex eighteenth-century controversy between *homo politicus* and *homo mercator*, whom we saw to be an offshoot and not a progenitor—at least as regards the history of social perception—of *homo creditor*. The latter figure was defined and to a large degree discredited by his failure to meet the standards set by *homo politicus*, and eighteenth-

42. Ibid., pp. 89–90.

43. For recent overviews, see Olivier Christin, ed., *Demain La République* (Lormont, Le Bord de l'Eau, 2018); Olivier Christin, ed., *Républiques et Républicanismes: Les Cheminements de la Liberté* (Lormont, Le Bord de l'Eau, 2019); and Yiftah Elazar and Geneviève Rousselière, eds. *Republicanism and the Future of Democracy* (Cambridge, CUP, 2019).

century attempts to construct a bourgeois ideology contended none too successfully with the primacy already enjoyed by a civic ideology; even in America a liberal work ethic has historically suffered from the guilt imposed on it by its inability to define for itself a virtue that saves itself from corruption; the descent from Daniel Boone to Willy Loman is seen as steady and uninterrupted. But one figure from the Arendtian gallery is missing, curiously enough, from the history even of the American work ethic: the *homo faber* of the European idealist and socialist traditions, who served to bridge the gap between the myths of the bourgeoisie and the proletariat. It is not yet as clear as it might be how the emergence of this figure is related to the European debate between virtue and commerce; but because industrial labor in America conquered a wilderness rather than transforming an ancient agrarian landscape, *homo faber* in this continent is seen as conquering space rather than transforming history, and the American work force has been even less willing than the European to see itself as a true proletariat. The ethos of historicist socialism has consequently been an importation of transplanted intellectuals (even the martyr Joe Hill left word that he "had lived as an artist and would die as an artist"), and has remained in many ways subject to the messianic populisms of the westward movement."[44]

Behind the ornate typology—*homo politicus, homo rhetor, homo credens, homo mercator, homo creditor, homo faber*—and its bearing on European politics and American exceptionalism, lay an adaptation of Arendt's moral and political thought. Its prime concern was with the divided character of modern humanity, not only among nations, states, or cultures, but, more poisonously, among the multiple obligations imposed upon modern individuals, along with their equally poisonous twentieth-century outcomes. As Pocock explained in the second (2003) edition of his book, he had been "preoccupied as a historian with the dialogue between ancient and modern liberty," which meant, he continued, that it was "unsurprising that the recent political philosopher whose work has the greatest resonance for me should be the late Hannah Arendt." This, he wrote, was why they had both written accounts of what he described as "the history of a phenomenon" that had occurred in the eighteenth century when, as Arendt had put it in her most influential book, *The Human Condition*, in 1958, "the social rose up against the political, and the image of human action

44. Pocock, *The Machiavellian Moment*, pp. 550–51. For a fine account of the process of its gestation see the introduction by Richard Whatmore to the Princeton Classics edition, pp. vii–xxii. Henceforth, references to the first or second editions will be abbreviated as Pocock, *MM1* or Pocock, *MM2*. A fuller version of this section is in Sonenscher, "Liberty, Autonomy and Republican Historiography."

was replaced by that of human behavior." For Pocock, this meant that the analytical core of *The Machiavellian Moment* was an examination of what, historically, had been involved in this switch from an "image of human action" to an image of "human behavior." "This formula," he commented, "is deeply illuminating," although, he added, it did not mean that he had "selected Arendt's as a philosophy whose work I may convert into history; the life of the mind is neither as simple nor as muddled as that."[45]

Pocock's description of the analytical core of *The Machiavellian Moment* as an adaptation of what Arendt had called a switch from an image of action to an image of behaviour was put more directly in *The Human Condition* by Arendt herself. The subject of her book, she wrote, was simply what Aristotle had called a political way of life, or, she explained, "an autonomous and authentically human way of life," because, in contradistinction to the activities associated with labour or work, it was "independent of human needs or wants."[46] On this interpretation, and unlike labour or work, a political way of life was one that was freely chosen. As Arendt went to some lengths to explain, it could be freely chosen not primarily because of the relative absence of external constraints, but also, or mainly, because of the *presence* of a type of individual personality that made a choice a deliberate act. Ancient slavery might have had something to do with the idea of a political way of life, but slavery itself was not peculiar to ancient Athens in anything like the sense that, according to Arendt, a political way of life had been. Autonomy, or what Arendt called "an authentically human way of life," presupposed a capacity to choose rather than a simple opportunity to choose. On her terms, this was why autonomy was not simply freedom, or even liberty, but something that could be associated with "an image of human action." Here, the image mattered as much as the action. As with the radically different but equally disinterested approaches to the subject of autonomy to be found in Fichte and Schelling, the key to this version of the idea of autonomy was that the quality of the action could be separated from the motivation of the agent, so that the action itself could be evaluated in its own right, or, as Arendt put it, independently of human needs or wants. This was the concept of liberty as autonomy that was grafted onto the idea of a civic tradition.

Arendt's conceptual vocabulary allowed Pocock to integrate the concept of civic humanism, a concept coined by the great historian of Renaissance Florence Hans Baron, into a broader narrative centred on the idea of a republic as

---

45. Pocock, *MM2*, p. 573.

46. Hannah Arendt, *The Human Condition* [1958], 2nd ed. (Chicago, U of Chicago Press, 1998), p. 13.

the locus of a distinctive combination of citizenship and autonomy. Here, it was the civic quality that turned both the word and the concept of a republic into something more than a simple English translation of the Latin *res publica*, or its various French, Italian, or German equivalents.[47] As Pocock later indicated, Baron's intellectual formation was quite similar to Arendt's. He was, Pocock wrote, "among the last great exponents of the German historical school, for whom history was the movement towards the freedom of the individual in the life of the state." This meant, as with Arendt, that freedom was virtually synonymous with autonomy, and, as Pocock later put it, that this version of freedom presupposed "a move into history, itself defined as the self-determining existence of states and their citizens in secular time."[48] On this premise, civic humanism was Baron's version of autonomy, but one that seemed to entail a far closer relationship between states and their citizens than Kant's original concept of autonomy had implied.

It was this relationship between states and their citizens that gave the relationship between autonomy and civic humanism a more actively republican hue. Republics, Pocock argued, did not fit into the various theological and legal cultures—or their attendant idioms of political legitimation—that had developed in Europe after the fall of the Roman Empire. This meant that the old Christian or Stoic concepts of natural law had no real purchase on what made a republic distinctively republican. Unlike a monarchy or an empire, Pocock claimed, a republic like Florence "was not timeless, because it did not reflect by simple correspondence the eternal order of nature; it was differently organized and a mind which accepted republics and citizenship as prime realities might be committed to implicitly separating the political from the natural order." Politics, in a republic, took their legitimation from the republic, not from nature, God, or any other putatively timeless entity. This, Pocock wrote, in a passage as redolent of Arendt as of Baron, meant

47. Compare to David Wootton, "The True Origins of Republicanism: The Disciples of Baron and the Counter-Example of Venturi," in *Il repubblicanismo moderno: l'idea de Repubblica nella riflessione storica de Franco Venturi*, ed. Manuela Albertone (Naples, Bibliopolis, 2006), pp. 271–304. On Baron, see Martin A. Ruehl, *The Italian Renaissance in the German Historical Imagination, 1860–1930* (Cambridge, CUP, 2015), pp. 34–37, 49–51, 224–52, 254–60. For related discussion, see Rocco Rubini, *The Other Renaissance: Italian Humanism between Hegel and Heidegger* (Chicago, U of Chicago Press, 2014), pp. 272–85, and, more recently, David Weinstein and Avihu Zakai, *Jewish Exiles and European Thought in the Shadow of the Third Reich; Baron, Popper, Strauss, Auerbach* (Cambridge, CUP, 2017), pp. 20–70.

48. J.G.A. Pocock, *Barbarism and Religion*, 6 vols. (Cambridge, CUP, 1999–2015), vol. 3, *The First Decline and Fall*, p. 154. See, however, Pocock's own reservations about Baron's thesis in ibid., pp. 179–80.

that a republic or, in this case, the Florentine republic "was more political than it was hierarchical; it was so organized as to assert its sovereignty and autonomy, and therefore its individuality and particularity."[49] Republican civic life, as a result, was grounded on a level of historicity that, in this late medieval setting, was simply unavailable elsewhere. From this perspective, Baron's account of the Florentine republic's struggle for survival in *The Crisis of the Early Italian Renaissance* not only provided an elegantly economical account of how historicity, civic humanism, and republicanism came to be connected, but also supplied an explanation of how the components of a distinctively republican language of politics, with its concerns with citizenship, virtue, and patriotism, were able to travel from Florence to England and then, at the end of the eighteenth century, to the United States of America.[50] Florence was not simply a republic; it was a republic that was forced to rely on a mixture of civic commitment and military prowess to maintain its political and territorial integrity. These were the ingredients that became the key components of a tradition that, as Pocock described it, came to span centuries and continents.

The early nineteenth-century discussion of the concept of autonomy also anticipated some of the features of the late twentieth-century concept of republicanism. Autonomy, especially in Fichte's rendition, meant nondomination, or the type of liberty produced by not being subject to someone else's will. This emphasis on nondomination has usually also been taken to be one of the hallmarks of late twentieth-century versions of republicanism. But there are still significant differences between the two types of republicanism. Early nineteenth-century discussions of autonomy focused on the problematic relationship between the individual capacity for autonomy and its general exercise. The need to address the problems of coordination and compatibility built into the relationship between individual autonomy and society, especially in the light of the criticism by Jacobi and Jean Paul, motivated both Fichte's version of recognition theory and Schelling's version of positivism. Both set out to show how it was possible to give the individual capacity a general existence and, by doing so, describe the types of arrangement that would make autonomy compatible with social cohesion and political stability. Both also emphasized that the arrangements in question would be peculiarly modern, either because, with Fichte, they were associated with a certain type of state and the limitations on private property that it entailed, or, with Schelling, because

49. Pocock, *MM1*, p. 53.

50. Hans Baron, *The Crisis of the Early Italian Renaissance: Civic Humanism and Republican Liberty in an Age of Classicism and Tyranny*, 2 vols. (Princeton, NJ, Princeton UP, 1955).

the arrangements in question were associated with a certain type of culture and the limitations on state power that *it* would entail.

In more recent versions of republicanism, however, the emphasis has switched from a capacity to a condition, and, either deliberately or inadvertently, the problematic relationship between individual and general autonomy has disappeared from sight. The most significant effect of this switch has been that republicanism has turned from being modern into being ancient and, more specifically, Roman, because it has now come to be said to be based on a concept of liberty that was part of Roman law. In this neo-Roman concept of liberty, liberty has come to mean nondomination in a more formal and legal sense than it did with Fichte because it referred, in the first instance, to the difference between being free and being a slave, and, consequently, to a difference in a condition rather than a capacity. It was this difference in status, rather than anything more reflexively subjective, which, in the first place, has come to mean that liberty could be defined as nondomination and, in the second place, could be associated with a way of thinking about politics that came to be called "neo-Roman."

The range of interpretations that can now be applied to republicanism, here meaning a more actively civic-minded concept of a republic, has become bewildering. Autonomy, for Kant, Fichte, and Schelling, was modern. It was a personal capacity rather than an attributed status. It came from within, not from without. For these reasons, autonomy called either (with Fichte) for the existence of a certain type of state or (with Schelling) for the *absence* of a certain type of state before it could be generalized across a whole society. For Arendt and, with qualifications, Pocock, the capacity had become ancient, while its disappearance was modern. More recently still, however, the capacity has become a condition and, in this guise, has again become ancient but is now Roman as well, although, as with Arendt, it has also been associated with Greece. In a further complication, and considered as a condition rather than a capacity, having the status of being free and not being subject to someone else's will is also said to be compatible with modern economic and social conditions. This, however, raises a further question. If liberty has come back to being a condition rather than a capacity, it is not clear why its existence should call for the altruism, virtue, or civic commitment usually associated with the concept of republicanism, rather than, for example, the arrangements described by Kant in his essay on enlightenment or even by Thomas Hobbes in his *Leviathan*. But if freedom is also a capacity as well as a condition, it is not clear whether the types of arrangement now usually associated with republicanism and the concept of nondomination can deal with the problems of compatibility and coordination any more fully or successfully than the types of arrangement described by Fichte and Schelling. There is, however, a third way.

Between the versions of autonomy produced by Fichte and Schelling and those now associated with more recent versions of republicanism, there was also the version produced by Georg Wilhelm Friedrich Hegel. Describing this version makes it possible to begin to see what happened to the concept of autonomy after Hegel's death, and, by extension, why Kant's idea of a political metamorphosis began to turn into the idea of a political palingenesis.

Hegel and Civil Society

The concept of autonomy ran from one end to the other of Hegel's many lectures, publications, and drafts of publications on political theory.[51] In his early epistemological epic, *The Phenomenology of Spirit*, it was the key to understanding his dramatization of Fichte's concept of recognition as, in his own rendition, a conflict between a master and a slave. In his late lectures on the philosophy of history, it was the key to understanding history itself. Between the two works, however, Hegel established a third concept, first, to go alongside Fichte's examination of the dialectics of similarity and difference as the basis of a viable combination of autonomy and equality, and, second, to go alongside Schelling's examination of the arts as the basis of the idea of a law-governed society without a law-generating state. This was the concept of civil society. With it, Hegel was able to distance himself from the radically egalitarian implications of Fichte's version of recognition theory by relegating the dynamics of recognition to the ordinary activities of everyday life. With it too, Hegel was also able to relegate Schelling's concept of a *Volksgeist* to the sphere of civil society, turning the concept into something more like the equivalent of the French term *moeurs* or the English term "custom." With this move, which involved explaining why the *Volksgeist* was part of civil society and, by extension, part of a law-governed state, Hegel was also able to explain why it existed within, rather than instead of, the concept of a state, and, equally significantly, why government was as much a part of civil society as of the state.[52]

51. On Hegel and autonomy, see Axel Honneth, *The Pathologies of Individual Freedom* (Princeton, NJ, Princeton UP, 2010) and his *Ce que social veut dire*, 2 vols. (Paris, Gallimard, 2013), especially1:36–127. See too Beaud, Colliot-Thélène, and Kervégan, *Droits subjectifs et citoyenneté*, particularly the chapters by Olivier Jouanjan, pp. 49–74, and Jean-François Kervégan, pp.75–96.

52. For helpful discussion (although without Schelling), see Shlomo Avineri, "Hegel and Nationalism," *Review of Politics* 24 (1962): 461–84. See also his "The Problem of War in Hegel's Thought," *Journal of the History of Ideas* 22 (1961): 463–74, and, particularly, his *Hegel's Theory of the Modern State* (Cambridge, CUP, 1972), pp. 16, 20–24, 222–29.

Before Hegel, the term "civil society" was used mainly as a translation of the Latin term *civitas*. In the works of the early nineteenth-century French royalist political thinker Louis de Bonald, for example, a civil society was something that complemented a religious society and a political society. By this, Bonald meant that a civil society would combine the spirituality of a religious society with the materiality of a political society to form a powerful and integrated synthesis of the two. Each of the two initial types of society could, as Bonald put it, be "constituted," and when each was constituted in ways that complemented the other, civil society as a whole would be properly constituted. History, from this perspective, was a product of the variable levels of assonance or dissonance between the two underlying components of civil society, while civil society itself would be properly constituted when both its spiritual and material components were endowed, respectively, with a single head on each side and with mutually compatible religious and legal doctrines on the other.[53] Although the terminology was loosely redolent of Rousseau and Sieyès (Bonald frequently gave his publications an epigraph from Rousseau), the broader conceptual framework underlying this version of civil society was supplied by Aristotle and the concept of perfectibility associated with Aristotle's distinction between a household, or *oikos*, and a *polis*, or state. With Bonald, civil society was religious and political society perfected.

With Hegel, the relationship of the three components was reversed. Political society was civil and religious society perfected. For the first time, at least in political language, civil society turned into the name given to a subordinate sphere of social activity. Hegel's own term, *bürgerliche Gesellschaft*, captured the difference directly. In English, the term is now usually translated as "civil society," but in French it was translated as *société bourgeoise*, or bourgeois society. This latter translation, with its evocation of burghs, boroughs, and urban society, actually captures rather more of what was original in Hegel's usage because it referred to those things that were economic and social, or generally nonpolitical, in human life, like production, distribution, exchange, and consumption,

---

53. Louis de Bonald, *Théorie du pouvoir politique et religieux dans la société civile* [1796], 2 vols. (Paris, 1843), 2:47, 176, 237–38, 310–11, 318, 441. On Bonald's thought, see Gérard Gengembre, "Entre archaïsme et modernité: Bonald, la contre-révolution et la littérature," *Revue d'histoire littéraire de la France* 90 (1990): 705–14, and his "Bonald ou l'esthétique sociale de la littérature," in *Romantismes: l'esthétisme en acte*, ed. Jean-Louis Cabanès (Paris, PU de Paris Ouest, 2009), pp. 143–54, as well as Flavien Bertran de Balanda, "Contre-révolution ou contre-subversion? Le sens rétabli selon Louis de Bonald, une métaphysique sémantique de la régénération sociale," in *Les mots du politique 1815–1848*, ed. Aude Déruelle and Corinne Legoy (Paris, Classiques Garnier, 2021), pp. 31–46. See also Louis de Bonald, *Œuvres choisies. Ecrits sur la littérature*, ed. Gérard Gengembre and Jean-Yves Pranchère (Paris, Classiques Garnier, 2010), pp. 7–62.

together with the array of activities, arrangements, and institutions with which they were associated.[54] Civil society was bourgeois society. It was urban and plural because it housed a differentiated array of interdependent occupations, professions, and activities. In the nineteenth century, Hegel's term was sometimes translated into English as "the social community." "In this community," as an essay on Hegel's *Philosophy of Right* put it in 1855, "everyone is to be looked on as striving for himself. All else is nothing to him; but without entering into relations with others he cannot attain his own ends. Other persons are thus means by which the desired end is attained, but still this reference to others introduces something of an universal."[55] This version of the idea of a "social community" captures something of the similarity between Hegel's concept of civil society and Kant's concept of unsocial sociability. It also helps to explain why Kant's earlier, more historical concept came to be conflated with Hegel's later, more moral concept. Hegel's concept had an analytical and causal dimension that, on his terms, explained why civil society—or the social community—was the real foundation of the state. This, as the author of the essay published in 1855 recognized, was because civil society, because of the emotional resources generated within the bourgeois family, was inadvertently other-oriented but was also the source of the human and material resources that enabled every state to exist and act.

It was once claimed, mainly in the late nineteenth and early twentieth centuries, that this concept of civil society began with Jean-Jacques Rousseau. In this respect, the continuity from Rousseau to Hegel was documented quite fully by the French political philosopher Paul Janet in the history of political science and morality that he began to publish in 1858 and continued to revise until his death in 1899. In a note that he added to the third edition of his history, Janet (a follower of France's best-known early nineteenth-century philosopher Victor Cousin and, like Cousin, a critical but sympathetic reader of Hegel) picked out seven passages from Rousseau's *Social Contract* that, he

54. On the concept, but without referring to either Schlözer or Rousseau, see Z. A. Pelczynski, ed., *The State and Civil Society: Studies in Hegel's Political Philosophy* (Cambridge, CUP, 1984); Adam B. Seligman, *The Idea of Civil Society* (Princeton, NJ, Princeton UP, 1992); Frank Trentman, ed., *Paradoxes of Civil Society: New Perspectives on Modern German and British History*, 2nd ed. (New York, Berghahn Books, 2003). On Schlözer's terms, see too Norbert Bobbio, *Democracy and Dictatorship: The Nature and Limits of State Power* (Cambridge, Polity Press, 1989), p. 22.

55. Thomas Collett Sandars, "Hegel's Philosophy of Right," in *Oxford Essays, Contributed by Members of the University, 1855* (London, 1855), pp. 213–50 (here, p. 238; see too p. 239). For a further example, see J. MacBride Sterrett, ed., *The Ethics of Hegel: Translated Selections from his 'Rechtsphilosophie'* (Boston, 1893), p. 15.

claimed, supplied a link between Rousseau's concepts of the general will and the will of all and the concepts of freedom, civil society, and the state that, according to Hegel, had emerged with Rousseau and formed the transition to the Kantian philosophy.[56] One of the fullest examples of the claim was set out subsequently in the *Allgemeine Staatslehre* published in 1900 by the Austrian jurist Georg Jellinek.[57] It is worth describing in some detail because it helps to throw light on how Hegel envisaged the mechanics of the relationship between civil society and the state. In his account of the origins of the concept, Jellinek initially associated Rousseau with the thought of a late eighteenth-century Göttingen University lawyer, historian, and statistician named August Ludwig von Schlözer and then went on to identify both Rousseau and Schlözer with the concept of civil society now usually associated with Hegel. The term "civil society," Jellinek wrote, originated with a distinction that Schlözer had made between what he had called a *societas civilis sine imperio* and a *societas civilis cum imperio*, meaning a civil society with or without an empire, where empire, or *imperium*, meant not territory but the power to command (as in being imperious or having the quality of imperiousness), so that the two phrases meant, substantively, civil society without a sovereign state and civil society with one. According to Schlözer the best example of a civil society without a state was Switzerland, and as he went on to show, the difference between a civil society with or without a state was connected to a further difference between what he called *Metapolitik* and *Politik*, or between metapolitics and politics. In this pairing, metapolitics had the same conceptual and practical relationship to politics as metaphysics had once had to physics. Just as metaphysics referred to concepts like being, time, and space as prerequisites

56. Paul Janet, *Histoire de la science politique dans ses rapports avec la morale* [1858], 3rd ed. 2 vols. (Paris, 1887), 2:584–85. On Janet's views of Hegel, see his review in *Le Temps* of 11 August 1876 of the translation by Augusto Véra of Hegel's lectures on the philosophy of religion, reprinted in Paul Janet, *La philosophie française contemporaine* (Paris,1879), pp. 261–77, and the reply by Véra in his forward to vol. 2 of *Philosophie de religion de Hegel*, 2 vols. (Paris, 1878), 2:i–lxxxiv.

57. On this aspect of Rousseau's intellectual legacy, see Sonenscher, *Jean-Jacques Rousseau*, pp. 141–77. On Jellinek, see Sara Lagi, *Georg Jellinek: storico del pensiero politico 1883–1905* (Florence, Centro Editoriale Toscano, 2009), and her edition of a further selection of texts in Sara Lagi, ed., *Georg Jellinek: 'Il Tutto' e 'l'Individuo'* (Rubbettino, Catanzaro, 2015), as well as her "The Formation of a Liberal Thinker: Georg Jellinek and His Early Writings," *Res Publica* 19 (2016): 59–76. More broadly, see Duncan Kelly, *The State of the Political: Conceptions of Politics and the State in the Thought of Max Weber, Carl Schmitt and Franz Neumann* (Oxford, OUP, 2003) and his "Revisiting the Rights of Man: Georg Jellinek on Rights and the State," *Law and History Review* 22 (2004): 493–529.

of physics, so metapolitics referred to subjects like population, agriculture, industry, and trade as prerequisites of politics.

For a time, the term seems to have circulated quite widely. It was picked up in 1814 and translated with much the same meaning as *métapolitique* by the French royalist political thinker Joseph de Maistre.[58] By then, however, it had been superseded by Hegel's concept of *bürgerliche Gesellschaft*, a term that echoed Schlözer's distinction between a *societas civilis sine imperio* and a *societas civilis cum imperio*, but gave the concept a clearer content. It made civil society the basis of the state, but it also raised a question about how the two were related. This, for Jellinek, was why the real source of this new way of describing the relationship between civil society and the state was not Schlözer, but Rousseau. The key to understanding the relationship was to be found in Rousseau's distinction between the will of all and the general will. This, Jellinek explained, was why, although Schlözer had been responsible for the term, it was Rousseau who had established the concept. Right from the outset, Jellinek wrote, and over a long period of time, Schlözer had failed to establish a school. "On a different path from his, but with far more success," he continued, "an autonomous concept of society had taken shape in France."

> Like Schlözer's concept, it too had its basis in natural jurisprudence. In this school, Rousseau was the first to counterpose society to the state, even if, in his terminology, the distinction did not appear in all its precision. This terminological uncertainty makes it possible, without much difficulty, to explain why even those who have done the most to establish a deeper

---

58. "J'entends dire que les philosophes allemands ont inventé le mot *métapolitique* pour être à celui de *politique* ce que le mot *métaphysique* est à celui de *physique*." Joseph de Maistre, *Essai sur le principe générateur des constitutions politiques* [Saint-Petersburg, 1814] (Lyon, 1833), p. vi. For later, and different, usages, see Charles Edward Merriam, *American Political Ideas* (New York, Macmillan, 1920), p. 373; and Peter Viereck, *Metapolitics* [1941] (New Brunswick, NJ, Transaction Books, 2004). On metapolitics, palingenesis, and fascism, see Roger Griffin, *The Nature of Fascism* [1991] (Abingdon, Routledge, 2006), pp. 33–38. This cluster of usages seem to have originated with a passage in Coleridge's *The Friend*, essay 3, and its assertion "so might the philosophy of Rousseau and his followers not inaptly be entitled metapolitics and the doctors of this school, metapoliticians." Samuel Taylor Coleridge, *The Friend* [1809] (London, Pickering, 1844), p. 243, n.*. This version of the concept of metapolitics continued well into the nineteenth century. Thus, in an essay on the political philosophy of Herbert Spencer published in 1890, the French political theorist Henry Michel wrote that, although Spencer was "un individualiste intransigeant," he had, in fact, reconstituted "toute la métapolitique du xviiie siècle" by connecting his sociological and biological givens to natural rights theory, the idea of a social contract, and the theory of progress: see [Anon.] in *Bulletin de la société historique d'Auteuil et de Passy* 1 (1892–94): 39–40. On Michel, see chapter 12, below.

understanding of the history of the doctrine of the state have failed to understand the scale of the developments that Rousseau brought to this subject.[59]

In saying this, Jellinek was referring quite specifically to the work on the history of state theory by one of his Heidelberg predecessors, a law professor named Robert von Mohl, because it had been von Mohl who had claimed that Rousseau had no self-standing concept of society. Jellinek, however, disagreed. To support his assertion, he quoted a long passage from Rousseau's *Discourse on Political Economy* which announced that "every political society is made up of several different types of smaller ones, each with its own interests and maxims," and that "every individual united by a common interest amounts to so many other, passing or permanent associations, whose strength is no less real for being less apparent."[60] This insight, Jellinek claimed, was the real basis of the fundamental distinction between the general will and the will of all that Rousseau had made in the *Social Contract*. The general will, Jellinek wrote, referred to the will of the state, while the concept of the will of all referred to "the will of society divided by conflicts of interest."[61] The implications of the distinction were considerable, not only for understanding Rousseau but also for understanding the idea of the modern state. It meant, as Rousseau showed, that any partial association would have its own general will, at least as it applied to its own members, even if, from the standpoint of society as a whole, all these localized general wills would still be no more than a proliferation of particular wills. The resulting proliferation of local and particular wills meant, as Jellinek went on to emphasize, that the general will of the state would be different from the multiple general wills housed by the various components of civil society.

59. Georg Jellinek, *L'état moderne et son droit*, 2 vols. [Paris, 1904 and 2013], ed. Olivier Jouanjan (Paris, Editions Panthéon Assas, 2005), 1:150–51. For a concurrent examination of Rousseau's two-sided state theory, which appeared in the same issue of the journal in which Jellinek's examination of the intellectual origins of the French Declaration of the Rights of Man was published, see Achille Mestre, "La notion de personnalité morale chez Rousseau," *Revue du droit public et de la science politique* 18 (1902): 447–68, and the use to which it was put in Michoud, *La théorie de la personnalité morale*, pp. 82–85. Both were probably inspired by Maurice Hauriou, "L'alternance des moyen-âges et des renaissances et ses conséquences sociales," *Revue de métaphysique et morale* 3 (1895): 527–49 (especially pp. 548–49). See too Julia Schmitz, "Hauriou versus Rousseau, Duguit et Kelsen," in *Mélanges en l'honneur du professeur Christian Lavialle*, ed. Nathalie Bettio et al. (Toulouse, Presses de l'Université de Toulouse 1 Capitole, 2020), pp. 645–62. I did not know of these publications when I wrote my book on Rousseau.

60. Jean-Jacques Rousseau, *Discourse on Political Economy*, in Jean-Jacques Rousseau, *Collected Writings*, 3:142–44; Rousseau, *Oeuvres complètes*, 3:245–46.

61. Jellinek, *L'état moderne et son droit*, 1:151–53.

If these latter were to coexist alongside the will of the state, then the state, peculiarly, would have to have a will that would be compatible with all the other general, but particular, wills scattered over civil society. It would, in short, have to be a *Rechtsstaat* and, possibly, a *Bundesstaat*. The general will would be the one will that allowed or enabled many particular wills to coexist. It would be permissive rather than prescriptive because its content underpinned the content of its component parts.

"It seems certain," Jellinek concluded, "that these developments by Rousseau inspired Hegel to establish his concept of civil society."[62] Between the two, however, lay the thought of Immanuel Kant, and, as Hegel noted, it was actually Kant's distinction between public and private law that established the link between Rousseau and his own formulation of the relationship between civil society and the state.[63] Kant himself did not describe civil society as distinct from a state. But the distinction that he made in his *Metaphysics of Morals* of 1797 between the respective attributes of public and private law formed the basis of the same conceptual distinction. As has been shown, Kant described its implications most fully in the section of his *Metaphysics of Morals* that he headed "Transition from what is mine or yours in a state of nature to what is mine or yours in a rightful condition generally." As Kant presented it, a rightful condition was one that enables everyone to enjoy rights. This, he wrote, was a condition "in accordance with the idea of a will giving laws for everyone" with reference to "either the possibility, or the actuality or the necessity of the possession of objects."[64] On this basis, a rightful condition was one that enabled individual wills to coexist with a general will. They could do so partly because individual wills were real, while the general will was ideal. But they could also do so because the general will existed to uphold the reality and legitimacy of a large, but indeterminate, number of individual wills. The general will, in other words, formed the basis of public law, while individual wills formed the basis of private law. Together, the two types of law amounted to what Kant called a *Rechtsstaat*, or a rightful condition, with a will that was able give laws for everyone.

It was this combination of private law and public law that, on Kant's terms, made it possible for a people both to constitute a state and, more importantly,

62. "Il parait bien certain que ces développements de Rousseau ont inspiré Hegel dans sa conception de la société civile." Ibid., 1:153.

63. See the passage from Hegel's lectures on the history of philosophy cited by Janet, *Histoire de la science politique*, 2:584 n. 1. The note was already in place on the same page in the 3rd, 1887, edition, of Janet's book.

64. Kant, *MM*, §41, pp. 450–51. See chapter 5 above for the earlier description of this passage.

to reform a state. The process of change would, therefore, not be an act of public law, or an act of sovereignty, or the general will. It would, instead, be an effect of actions by government and the many different types of government encompassed both by a number of subordinate, dependent, and intermediate powers and by the provisions of a constitution that was capable of change. As Kant put it, "the *spirit* of the original contract (*anima pacti originarii*) involves an obligation on the part of the constituting authority to make the *kind of government* suited to the idea of the original contract."

> Accordingly even if this cannot be done all at once, it is under obligation to change the kind of government gradually and continually so that it harmonizes *in its effect* with the only constitution which accords with right, that of a pure republic, in such a way that the *old* (empirical) statutory forms, which served merely to bring about the *submission* of the people, are replaced by the original (rational) form, the only form which makes *freedom* the principle and indeed the condition for any exercise of *coercion*, as is required by a rightful constitution of a state in the strict sense of the word. Only it will finally lead to what is literally a state—This is the only constitution of a state that lasts, the constitution in which *law* itself rules and depends on no particular person.[65]

There would, in short, always be governments and laws. But the type of constitution in which only the law itself would rule and which would, consequently, be independent of any particular person was, on the one hand, a way of describing a social contract, and, on the other hand, a way of indicating the distance between this radically impersonal conception of the rule of law and the various types of sovereignty embodied in what Kant called autocracy, aristocracy, or democracy.

The number of steps from Kant to Hegel was, in one sense, quite small. But between Kant and Hegel were Fichte and Schelling, and Hegel's concept of a political society was designed to integrate their concepts of recognition theory and symbolic power into a broader conception of the relationship between the state and civil society. Hegel made it clear, in his *Philosophy of Right*, that the concept of *bürgerliche Gesellschaft* encompassed partial associations of every kind. Guilds, corporations, companies, and partnerships clearly belonged to civil society. So too did municipalities, provinces, districts, or departments because they too had multiple memberships and single identities. In this respect, both types of institution had the common attribute of a personality. They could do many of the things that real people could do, like own property, make

65. Ibid., §52, pp. 480–81.

contracts, bring actions, or take legal responsibility. In this sense, they were the constituent parts of societies made up of other societies, with general wills when seen from within, and particular wills when seen from without, just as Rousseau had described them nearly two generations earlier. Most importantly, however, the administrative system formed a bridge between civil society and the state because it was part of them both and, by extension, meant that government straddled both civil society and the state. Its members and resources were drawn from civil society, but its rules and structure were supplied by the state. With Hegel, the administration would be the mechanism responsible for giving the modern state its dual character, and, as a result, for giving autonomy a home.

Hegel, notoriously, called the administration a "universal estate." It was, he wrote in his *Philosophy of Right* of 1821, part of the state and the system of estates that it housed. Unlike the various other estates, however, it was funded by the state itself out of the tax revenue supplied by civil society. It is well known that Hegel was fascinated by the thought of the eighteenth-century Scottish political economist Sir James Steuart, and, in particular, by Steuart's unusually positive evaluation of public debt.[66] Hegel's treatment of the state bureaucracy or universal estate was, on the financial side, a development of the logic of Steuart's theory of public debt as a key component of a state. "The *universal estate*," Hegel explained, "has the *universal interests* of society as its business. It must therefore be exempted from work for the direct satisfaction of its needs, either by having private resources, or by receiving an indemnity from the state which calls upon its services, so that the private interest is satisfied by working for the universal."[67] This conflation of the private interest with the universal gave the estate its particular character. It was, Hegel added later, "integral to the definition of the *universal* estate—or more precisely, the estate which devotes itself to the service of the government—that the universal is the end of its essential activity."[68] It is important here to see what Hegel meant. What he did *not* mean was that the universal estate was an equivalent of Plato's guardians or China's mandarins. This was because Hegel's universal estate did not have to be equipped with a personal quality like knowledge, wisdom, or judgment, as was the case with a mandarin or guardian. It could,

66. On Hegel and Steuart, see Paul Chamley, "Les origines de la pensée économique de Hegel," *Hegel Studien* 3 (1965): 225–61, and his "Notes de lectures relatives à Smith, Steuart et Hegel," *Revue d'économie politique* 77 (1967): 857–78. On Steuart and public debt, see Ramón Tortajada, ed., *The Economics of Sir James Steuart* (London, Routledge, 1999), and Sonenscher, *Before the Deluge*, pp. 24–26, 58–64, 256–58.

67. Hegel, *Elements of the Philosophy of Right*, §205, p. 237.

68. Ibid., §303, p. 343.

instead, rely on money, either to buy in services or to pay for the provision of public goods, and, equally importantly, on the law for providing a framework of rules to guide public and private life. Both, Hegel emphasized, have an intrinsically universal quality that obviates the need for any equivalent personal, or subjective, quality. "It is implicit in the organic unity of the powers of the state itself," he wrote, "that *one* and the same spirit decrees the universal and brings it to determinate actuality in implementing it."

> It may at first seem remarkable that the state requires no direct services from the numerous skills, possessions, activities and talents [of its citizens] and from the infinitely varied living *resources* which these embody and which are at the same time associated with the disposition [of those who possess them], but lays claim only to the *one* resource which assumes the shape of *money.* . . . But money is not in fact one *particular* resource among others; on the contrary it is the universal aspect of all of them, in so far as they express themselves in an external existence in which they can be apprehended as *things.* Only at this extreme point of externality is it possible to determine services *quantitatively* and so in a just and equitable manner.[69]

The same quality belonged to the law, a subject that Hegel discussed alongside the subject of money in the same lemma. It was universal because it was rational, and this rationality meant, almost by definition, that a law was something less than a pure command (like "Thou shalt not kill"), but was also something more than a purely factual description because it could also entail a permission or prohibition.[70] Its relationship to the state meant that the law was also more general than a command, but less particular than a fact. Together, the combination of money and the law added up to both a fiscal state and a *Rechtsstaat*.

Hegel also addressed the more fundamental problem of the tension inherent in the coexistence of justice, progress, and the passage of time that Kant had laid out so provocatively. He did so in a way that established a recognizable connection between the early nineteenth-century reception of Kant's thought and the twentieth-century debate at Davos between Cassirer and Heidegger. This is because he began to examine the future-oriented quality of the concept of autonomy more carefully and precisely. Autonomy, as Kant had shown, was literally unthinkable without a concept of the future. The past could well house different models, examples, or precedents for future action, but if these were to be reconciled with the idea of autonomy or self-determination, they still had to be selected and projected into the future. Without this, autonomy would give

69. Ibid., §299, p. 338.
70. Ibid., §299, pp. 337–39.

way to heteronomy. As Hegel began to show, this meant that something about the future was connected to the concept of autonomy but was connected to it in ways that were different from Kant's unsettling presentation of the connection between the two subjects in his essays on universal history and on enlightenment. In these essays, and in contradistinction to his treatment of time in his more analytical philosophical publications, Kant presented time as a succession or sequence of moments, with the benefits of progress reserved for the later moments. Hegel's treatment was different, and the difference had a considerable bearing on his broader treatment of politics.

At any moment, Hegel pointed out, the future was simply not the present, but would at the next moment turn into the present. As he went on to show, examining what was involved in this switch helped to explain how it was possible to reconcile the idea of autonomy both with the idea of many different worldviews succeeding one another in time or space and with the idea of history as progress, development, or improvement. As he also began to show, most graphically in his *Phenomenology of Spirit*, the orientation towards the future built into the concept of autonomy made it possible to overcome the tension between justice and progress involved in Kant's concept of unsocial sociability. Unsocial sociability presupposed an idea of the future as a goal or a target that was attainable only over the passage of time. To Hegel, the future did not have to be seen as a moment in time that formed a standard to be used to measure earlier achievements and resources. The future had a substantive existence only in the present because it had no positive or determinate existence as such. The future was simply not the present. As it became present, however, it lost its negative quality and became whatever it was. The same type of mutability could not apply to the past because, even in the present, the past was already what it was. While the past was not the present, but still the past from the vantage point of the present, the future was both not the present and not the future when it became the present. The switch from the future to the present was, therefore, a negation of a negation and, Hegel claimed, the real basis of human freedom.

The indeterminacy of the future was central to an understanding of autonomy. As several recent Hegel scholars have shown, Hegel's argument relied on an initial comparison between ancient and modern scepticism and a strong endorsement of the former over the latter.[71] Modern scepticism, he argued,

---

71. Michael N. Forster, "Friedrich Schlegel and Hegel," in *Idealismus und Romantik in Jena. Figuren und Konzepte zwischen 1794 und 1807*, ed. Michael N. Forster, Johannes Korngiebel, and Klaus Vieweg (Jena, Wilhelm Fink, 2018), pp. 139–80. See also Forster's earlier publications, *Hegel and Skepticism* (Cambridge, MA, Harvard UP, 1989), pp. 9–43; *Kant and Skepticism* (Princeton, NJ, Princeton UP, 2008); and, more directly, "The History of Philosophy," in *The*

meaning mainly the scepticism of Locke, Berkeley, and Hume, but also, though in a modified sense, the scepticism of Kant, was radically limited because it began and ended with claims about the deceptive quality of the information supplied by the senses (about, for example, distance, size, location, or duration, as well as the many abstractions, generalizations, and causal assertions that they brought along with them). The claims themselves could well be true or false, but, unlike ancient scepticism, they still presupposed the availability of truth over and beyond the initial claim about the deceptive quality of sense-based information. Ancient scepticism, Hegel argued, was less dogmatic and more open-ended because its presuppositions were negative as well as positive. The senses might produce illusions, but they might also produce truth because in any evaluation of this sort the negative was as relevant as the positive. To Hegel, this negative side of an evaluation had dropped out of modern scepticism, to the real detriment of thought. Negation, he argued, mattered because it brought a more finely grained analytical attention to bear not only on what happened in thought but also on the myriads of subjects that, in different times and places, thought was required, or able, to think about.

The subject of time provided unusually strong evidence of the existence and importance of the negative side of thought, on both an individual and a human level. It did so partly because the existence of temporality as something measurable depended initially upon its binary quality. The future was not present, just as the present was not past. But the future became positive when it became present, whereas the present became negative when it was past. But the switch from the future to the present produced a different type of moment from the one produced by the switch from the present to the past. As a moment, the future was a negation of the present. But when it turned into the present, it became a negation of itself. When the present turned into the past, however, both types of moment kept both types of status. The present was not the past, but the past could still be present because it could be remembered or commemorated in ways that were not available to the future. The future was open, but the past was closed. The future had no particular content, but the past had as many different contents as the present was able to identify, excavate, or

---

Cambridge History of Philosophy in the Nineteenth Century, ed. Allen W. Wood and Songsuk Susan Hahn (Cambridge, CUP, 2012), pp. 866–904, together with his "Philosophy, History of Philosophy, and Historicism." In addition, see Peter Trawny, "The Future of Time: Reflections on the Concept of Time in Hegel and Heidegger," *Research in Phenomenology* 30 (2000): 12–39; Johannes Korngiebel, "Friedrich Schlegel's Sceptical Interpretation of Plato," in *Hegel and Scepticism: On Klaus Vieweg's Interpretation*, ed. Jannis Kotzatsas et al. (Berlin, Walter de Gruyter, 2017), pp. 65–84, and Klaus Vieweg, *The Idealism of Freedom: For a Hegelian Turn in Philosophy* (Leiden, Brill, 2020), pp. 27–30.

commemorate. Keeping the future alive was, therefore, the key to keeping freedom alive and in a more than trivial sense.

Hegel also pointed out that part of the content of the division of time into past, present, or future seemed able to transcend these temporal units because the parts in question were simply true. Time does not seem to matter to things like triangles or tripods because their qualities are either timeless or eternal. A future triangle would be like any triangle past or present. Truth, in other words, seems either to eradicate time or, at least, to take the temporality out of time. In the terms that Hegel began to establish, Kant's disquieting claim about the injustice built into time, history, and progress began to look more surmountable. On one side, there was a world made up of moments, some present, some past, some future. The future would turn into the present and negate itself. The present would turn into the past but could still be available in the present. The passage of time and the endless stream of negations of negations built into the human ability to make choices and decisions would give rise to many different values, arrangements, and worldviews. Some, however, might turn out to be true. This was the hallmark of the other side of human history. If something was true, it would fall out of time and become, simply, timeless. On Kant's terms, time and history were the problem. On Hegel's terms, they were the solution.

This did not mean, however, that history would end because, as the metaphor of the Owl of Minerva was designed to show, only history could establish the timelessness of truth. In this sense, Schiller's phrase *Weltgeschichte als Weltgerichte* had a point. The history of the world really was the judgment of the world. On Hegel's terms, however, his version of Schiller's point was a more structured point than it now seems. It began with a multiplicity of worldviews. These certainly changed under the aegis of the complicated dynamics of collective decision making and choice. As they changed, new ideas and values came into being. Some were true; others were not. Some were timeless; others were time-bound. From this perspective, history was not really a continuum but an endless process of bifurcation. It was also, however, an endless process of assimilation and inclusion. This process too was supplied by time, but in this case by consciousness of time rather than the division of time. As with the relationship between temporality and durability, Hegel set out to show that appearances were deceptive.[72] In this case, however, the deception applied to

---

72. In this and the next two paragraphs, I have relied heavily on the still-fascinating description of Hegel's thought in Josiah Royce, *The Spirit of Modern Philosophy* [1892] (Boston, 1901), pp, 190–227. On Royce, see Gladys Bournique, *La Philosophie de Josiah Royce* (Paris, Vrin, 1988), and Bruce Kuklick, *Josiah Royce: An Intellectual Biography* (Indianapolis, IN, Hackett, 1985).

consciousness of time rather than the division of time. While the division of time into past, present, and future seems to be objective and external, consciousness of time seems to be subjective and internal. Hegel, however, switched the predicates. Just as he had shown that the apparently objective and external quality of the division of time actually had a radically subjective basis, so he also went on to show that consciousness of time had, inversely, an unavoidably objective content.

To explain why this was the case, Hegel reversed Fichte's insight into the elusive character of the self. For Fichte, the discrepancy between the subjective self and the self that it could imagine or posit was the first step towards showing how human freedom could be established and secured across a whole society. For Hegel, however, an elusive self was either an empty self or a uniform self. Time made this clear. Self-knowledge, Hegel argued, is knowledge of the moment at which the knowing self gives way to the known self, making every moment of consciousness part of an infinite regress of past moments. From this perspective, the subjectivity built into self-consciousness simply imposed an empty self upon an empty self, leaving behind an unbroken chain of blank uniformity. Subjectivity, in short, created no more than a precipice over a void. As Hegel described it, the negativity built into subjectivity was an immediate, personal, and existential version of the negativity that separated the future from the present. On these terms, Martin Heidegger did not have to look far for his concept of a *Dasein*. Temporality, as Hegel described it, forced the empty self to become an identifiable and identified self by pushing it into relationships with others. Otherness broke the endless circle of self-reflection by injecting being into time. Self-consciousness, paradoxically, called for a nonself in order to be conscious of itself. In this sense, consciousness was to self-consciousness as the present was to the future. Both were negations of a negation, and, paradoxically, both types of negation were the real basis of human society and, by extension, a vindication of ancient scepticism over its modern counterpart. This was the insight that, in a real sense, allowed Hegel to build on Kant more fully than either Fichte or Schelling was able to do. History, on Hegel's terms, was not simply a matter of the putative goals, targets, or destinations involved in Kant's concept of the future. It was, instead, the endless product of, first, turning unknown futures into known pasts, then, second, of adding new otherness to familiar sameness, and, finally, of integrating temporal and cultural diversity into richer, more complicated, versions of the present. History was the medium in which the differences between the goals, targets, or destinations and the mirages, blind alleys, or wrong turnings were established. It was, in short, human life, but human life charged with the possibility of living life self-consciously. Hegel's philosophy of history was not so much an alternative to Kant as a very thorough and sympathetic version of Kant.

The endless process of discrimination and assimilation built into Hegel's philosophy of history was also an endless argument about where and when the lines could be drawn. In this version of history, relativity would be built into the many worldviews generated by the process of bifurcation, but some truths could encompass them all. Diversity would also be built into the endless interaction between selves and others, but some values could be compatible with, or could accommodate, them all. From this perspective, the real content of history was either logic or politics, or, possibly, something with the ability to turn the latter into the former, as has sometimes appeared to be offered by the idea of a legal system. This, for Hegel, was why autonomy mattered. Without autonomy, the future was fate. Inversely, without the future, autonomy was heteronomy. On these terms, freedom secured autonomy, just as autonomy secured freedom. Together, they meant that Hegel's concept of a philosophy of right and the arrangements and institutions involved in the concept of a *Rechtsstaat* had a very precise content. They fitted his endorsement of the open-ended, or two-sided, character of ancient scepticism as exemplified by the paradigmatic case of the subject of time. They also helped to rescue the idea of autonomy from Kant's many critics.

Hegelian Political Economy: Stein and Dietzel

There was a firmly modern orientation to the nexus of the state, civil society, and the administration that Hegel began to present as the one setting in which the requirements of autonomy could be made to fit the intricacies of a whole society. It was a nexus that presupposed private property, a market economy, and a sophisticated division of labour. It also presupposed permanent taxation, a permanent public administration, and a permanent legal system. Finally, and more controversially, it presupposed—or concluded—that both these initial presuppositions were the real foundation of a rights-based system. The argument was made considerably more explicit some two decades after Hegel's death in 1831, at the end of the great cycle of revolutions that swept across Europe in 1848, by the Austro-German legal and political thinker Lorenz von Stein, whose influential study of the social movement in France before and after 1848 relied very heavily on Hegel's state–civil society distinction.[73] Stein's

73. For a helpful introduction to Stein's thought, see Felix Gilbert, *History: Choice and Commitment* (Cambridge, MA, Harvard UP, 1977), pp. 411–21. More generally, see Othmar Spann, *Types of Economic Theory* [1930] (Abingdon, Oxon, Routledge, 2000), pp. 247–49; Pasquale

version of the nexus formed by the state, civil society, and the administration centred on money, credit, and public debt. He set out this version most fully in 1850 in the long introduction to his most famous book, *The History of the Social Movement in France*. Its title—"The Concept of Society and Its Laws of Motion"—was, as Stein went on to show, designed to indicate that the concept of the state had to be matched by a concept of society.[74] Putting the two together, Stein claimed, would become the basis of a theory of state action that really would be compatible with, but also distinct from, society.

The starting point of Stein's theory of state action was the problematic relationship between individual autonomy and social interdependence. As with Hegel, it was a problem generated by the initial tension between individual needs and desires, on the one hand, and the limited amount of individual time and ability available to meet them. The obvious solution to this tension, Stein wrote, was the division of labour. But the development of the division of labour gave rise to a further array of problems about information, coordination, and rules. Something more than interpersonal reciprocity was needed to provide a common will to meet these common needs. This, Stein argued, was what a state could do. It was also why it made sense to define the state as simply "a community manifesting its actions and will through its personality."[75] Personality, according to Stein, was, thus, the principle of the state. It was the name that could be given to the state's ability to unite and coordinate individual wills in ways that could enable them to realize all that was best in each and every individual personality. The claim was redolent of the long-drawn-out eighteenth-century discussion of the *Bestimmung des Menschen*, or the

---

Pasquino, "Introduction to Lorenz von Stein," *Economy and Society* 10 (1981): 1–6; Olivier Jouanjan, "Lorenz von Stein et les contradictions du mouvement constitutionnel révolutionnaire (1789–1794)," *Annales historiques de la révolution française* 328 (2002): 171–91; Peter Koslowski, ed., *The Theory of Ethical Economy in the Historical School* (Berlin, Springer Verlag, 1995); and Norbert Waszek, "L'état de droit social chez Lorenz von Stein," in *Figures de l'état de droit: Le Rechtsstaat dans l'histoire intellectuelle et constitutionnelle de l'Allemagne*, ed. Olivier Jouanjan (Strasbourg, PU de Strasbourg, 2001), pp. 193–217, as well as his earlier "Lorenz von Stein: Propagateur du droit français en Allemagne, 'ambassadeur' officieux de la recherche juridique allemande en France," in *Influences et réceptions mutuelles du droit et de la philosophie en France et en Allemagne*, ed. Jean-François Kervégan and Heinz Mohnhaupt (Frankfurt, Vittorio Klostermann, 2001), pp. 379–403.

74. Lorenz Stein, *Le concept de société*, trans. Marc Béghin, ed. Norbert Waszek (Grenoble, ELLUG, 2003). Originally published as *Geschichte der sozialen Bewegung in Frankreich, von 1789 bis auf unsere Tage* (1850). Reference in what follows is to the Waszek edition, here indicated simply by "Stein" and the page number, as in this case, Stein, p. 63.

75. Stein, pp. 79–80.

vocation or purpose of mankind. As in the original discussion, Stein's version of the answer had a clear moral and historical goal. Given, he wrote, that the state was made up of individuals, it followed that "the measure of development of every individual is the measure of development of the state itself."[76]

Stein's initial argument appeared to lead towards two apparently incompatible conclusions. If, on the one hand, the state's development was based on every aspect of individual material, cultural, and spiritual development, it followed that its constitution had to make as much provision as possible for all its members to be as fully involved as possible in the life of both the state and its government. From another point of view, however, the same emphasis on the symbiotic relationship between individual personality and the personality of the state seemed to mean that the state-person would be radically dependent on its members' resources. If, as the locus of the division of labour, civil society was subordinate to the state, the reality, in fact, was the opposite. "The state," as Stein put it, "has no real existence outside of society."[77] But society was, by definition, an acquisitive society (a phrase that Stein was one of the first to use) because, in an important sense, it was predicated on the aspirations and ambitions of a multitude of increasingly differentiated individual personalities, while the identity of the state was predicated on a single common personality. In a state, individual personality was combined with the unitary personality of the state, but in society individual personality was differentiated from every other individual personality. The combination of the drive for unity and the drive for individual acquisition meant that the state-society relationship was based on a radical contradiction. As Stein went on to show, this meant that while personality, or a single will made up of an integrated combination of unity and multiplicity, was the underlying principle of the state, the underlying principle of society was actually interest, or a centrifugal combination of diversity and difference generated by the division of labour.[78] The two principles were not only radically at odds with one another but also locked into a power relationship in which the state would, in effect, be little more than a target waiting to be captured by one or other of its predatory components.

Not only did the contradiction supply a framework for explaining why, as Stein went on to describe it, the history of the social movement in France was a history of class struggle; it also seemed to show, more generally, why any claim about the compatibility between individual personality and the personality of

76. Ibid., pp. 101–2.
77. Ibid., pp. 80–81, 145.
78. Ibid., pp. 107–10; see pp. 190 and 196 for the phrase "acquisitive society."

the state was condemned to end in a double bind.[79] If the personality of the state supplied the means to manage the division of labour, the division of labour was, inversely, the source of the individual drives and inequalities of property, capital, time, and money that ruled out the idea of a state-personality. The dilemma soon gave rise to a number of putative solutions. One solution, usually associated with Marx and his followers, was to try to eliminate the state, while another, associated with Chenavard and the concept of palingenesis, was to try to dissolve the state into as many self-governing institutions as possible. Stein's solution was to remain closer to Hegel's concept of the state, but to combine it with a radically different theory of state power and state action.

Stein's theory of state power and state action was fiscal and financial in character. It was fiscal because a functioning fiscal system called for a comprehensive administrative system, made up not only of a body of tax officials, but also of further clusters of legal, financial, and property-related offices to supply the information and procedures required by the functional ramifications of the fiscal system itself. This meant that a bureaucratically organized administrative system, comparable to Hegel's own idea of a universal estate, would have to be the other side of what, as Stein emphasized, would be a highly inclusive political constitution. While a constitution was the means by which individual personalities could have a real relationship to the personality of the state, an administrative system was the means to ensure that the two types of personality would be kept distinct. Without a constitution and with no proper administration, Stein argued, individuals would simply turn towards monarchy as the most obvious embodiment of the idea of the state.[80] Trying to maintain the same distinction between individual and state personalities under the aegis of a genuinely democratic regime would be even more difficult, because the separation of the public from the private built into a bureaucracy would dissolve into a reiterated and more morally demanding game of role switching. Representative government, from this point of view, required a bureaucratic state.

Importantly, however, the core of Stein's theory of state power and state action was more financial than fiscal and relied as much on monetary as on administrative or bureaucratic means. This, Stein claimed, was because the one self-evident sign of a sovereign state was its ability to create money and, by extension, to manage and preserve a stable currency. The claim meant that public debt was the key to reconciling the state and civil society because the financial resources that the state could generate had the potential to overcome the

79. Ibid., pp. 121–225.
80. Ibid., pp. 106–7.

contradiction between multiple individual personalities and its own single personality. They would do so, Stein argued, because the funds borrowed by the state could be added to the pool of private capital both by means of a decentralized system of interest-free loans and, more generally, because borrowing funds would remove smaller amounts of capital from society than would taxation, while payments of interest on debt would ensure that some of the borrowed funds would go back into circulation. The state-backed flows of income and expenditure generated by public debt would be managed by the bureaucracy, but the resources themselves would be allocated by means of decisions within a constitutionally specified institutional network. Monetary and financial policy could be used, therefore, to offset the divisions generated by private property to enable the propertyless to acquire the education, skills, and capital required for economic survival in an acquisitive society. "A state without a debt," Stein famously observed, "either cares too little for its future or demands too much from its present."[81] Trade without credit, he wrote elsewhere, was "like a bird without wings," while credit itself was rather like the clothes that parents would buy for their children: the right measure had to be several sizes too large.[82] Seen thus, Stein claimed, public debt went together with "social democracy." In his usage, there was a real significance to both parts of the phrase. The democratic side applied to the constitution and its arrangements, while the social side applied to the bureaucracy and its provisions. "The principle of social democracy," Stein concluded, "is therefore *universal suffrage* inasmuch as it has to do with the constitution and the *abolition of social dependence* in the working class and inasmuch as it has to do with the administration. In social democracy, the constitution is the democratic element, while the administration is the social element." The combination, he added, was the "natural and unavoidable outcome of the liberal movement."[83]

As with Hegel, credit was the key to the nexus formed by the state, civil society, and the administration. As with Hegel too, the administration formed

---

81. The passage (from the 1871 edition of Stein's textbook on public finance, *Lehrbuch der Finanzwissenschaft*, p. 666) is quoted by Carl-Ludwig Holtfrerich, "Government Debt in the Economic Thought of the Long 19th Century" (Discussion Paper 2013/4, School of Business and Economics, Freie Universität, Berlin, 2013), pp. 17–18. See also his "Public Debt in Post-1850 German Economic Thought vis-à-vis the Pre-1850 British Classical School," *German Economic Review* 15 (2013): 62–83. For the broader context, but without Stein, see Stefan Eich, *The Currency of Politics: The Political Theory of Money from Aristotle to Keynes* (Princeton, NJ, Princeton UP, 2022).

82. The phrases are quoted in Maurice Block, *Les progrès de la science économique depuis Adam Smith*, 2 vols. (Paris, Guillaumin, 1890), 1:403.

83. Stein, p. 202.

the bridge between the two because it was responsible for managing taxation and expenditure, but was not itself involved either in the production of resources or in political decision making. The more elaborate the administration and the more extensive the range of its responsibilities, the more public debt would come to be built into the whole system because of the proliferating number of leads and lags between income and expenditure generated by its many different parts. The idea was given a more technically precise and carefully calibrated formulation soon after the publication of Stein's book with the publication in 1855 of Carl Dietzel's *Das System der Staatsanleihen im Zusammenhang der Volkswirtschaft Betrachtet* (The system of state loans considered in the context of the national economy). Its appearance gave rise to a public dispute between Stein and Dietzel over who had first made their jointly positive evaluations of debt finance. Although it is clear that it was the combative Stein who supplied the inspiration, it is also clear that it was Dietzel who, as he put it, showed how the component parts of "public credit in its application as a system" and "as a necessary feature of higher economic development" could be put together to form an analytically coherent system of debt-based state finance.[84]

Dietzel's chief insight was to see that the relationship between state expenditure and private expenditure could be used to generate many different types of information to guide economic policy. The relationship between the two types of expenditure would be complex, and this complexity would be both an advantage and a disadvantage. On the plus side, distinguishing current

84. Carl Dietzel, *Das System der Staatsanleihen im Zusammenhang der Volkswirtschaft Betrachtet* (Heidelberg, 1855), p. 20. On Dietzel, see particularly Walter F. Stettner, "Nineteenth-Century Public Debt Theories in Great Britain and Germany and Their Relevance for Modern Analysis," (PhD thesis, Harvard University, 1944); and his "Carl Dietzel, Public Expenditure and Public Debt," in *Income, Employment and Public Policy: Essays in Honor of Alvin H. Hansen*, ed. A. M. Lloyd (New York, Norton, 1948), pp. 276–99. Stettner, who began his career as law student in Vienna before moving to the United States to escape the Nazis, had no hesitation in associating Dietzel's thought with his own training as a Keynesian economist under the supervision of the Harvard economist Alvin H. Hansen: see his posthumously published autobiography, *Witness to a Changing World* (Huntingdon, WV, University Editions, 1999), pp. 121–22. See, more recently, Rolf Glaeser, "Carl Dietzel (1829–1884): A Pioneering and Unorthodox Thinker on Public Debt and Fiscal Policy," in *European Economists of the Early 20th Century*, ed. Warren J. Samuels, 2 vols. (Cheltenham, Edward Elgar, 2003), 2:81–103; Richard M. Salsman, *The Political Economy of Public Debt: Three Centuries of Theory and Evidence* (Cheltenham, Edward Elgar, 2017), pp. 117–18; and Richard Sturn, "Public Credit, Capital and State Agency: Fiscal Responsibility in German-Language Finanzwissenschschaft," Graz Schumpeter Centre, Discussion Paper Series, Paper 19 (Graz, 2019).

expenditure, like paying wages or salaries, from capital expenditure, like building roads or canals, would make it easier to decide whether to rely on loans or
taxes for public funds. Adding to the number of variables by including, for
example, public and private expenditure, local, regional, and national expenditure, expenditure on capital goods and consumer goods, or on fixed and
circulating capital, would make it possible not only to target different types of
fiscal and financial resources for different purposes but also to set the different
components of public expenditure against one another as components of
larger wholes, like total national income or gross national product. Policy
could then be guided by a tracking of the shifts in these various proportions
of the larger whole, with the resulting ratios functioning as a kind of financial
gyroscope to navigate the ebbs and flows of income, expenditure, monetary
creation, trade, and payments balances and local, national, and international
rates of interest. Dietzel made a point of emphasizing the continuity between
this concept of debt-based public finance and the thought of the eighteenth-
century political economists Isaac de Pinto and Sir James Steuart. He also
emphasized its compatibility with the thought of John Stuart Mill. But the
analytical framework of debt management that he, more than Stein, began to
establish also had a logic of its own. As, from the early twentieth century, the
subject of debt management merged with economics and moved, more
broadly, towards models and mathematics, both its Hegelian origins and its
broader orientation towards the problematic relationship between individual
and collective autonomy disappeared gradually from view. In place of autonomy, Hegel's legacy turned into social democracy, the economics of John
Maynard Keynes, and the proliferating range of arguments generated by the
politics of public expenditure all over the world.

Rudolf von Jhering and the Rule of Law

While Stein's version of the state–civil society distinction relied, in the last
instance, on public debt and the state's ability to create money to limit the level
of conflict in civil society, a second version of the same type of dual system
relied more directly on the concept of law and the idea of law as a combination
of a legal right and a legal rule. The composite nature of this mixture of rights
and rules is more apparent in the overlapping connotations of the German or
French words *Recht* and *droit* than in the less ambiguous English-language
distinction between a law and a right. The most significant initial move in
explaining how the law could have this dual quality was an insistence on the
historical and analytical priority of assertions of rights generated from below
over prescriptions of rules issued from above. This was the move made by
another Austro-German law professor, Rudolf von Jhering, in two books

entitled, respectively, *Der Kampf ums Recht* (The struggle for law) of 1872 and *Der Zweck im Recht* (Law as a means to an end) of 1877 and 1883. For Jhering, the idea of the law as a product of conflict was the key to understanding how the combination of a legal right and a legal rule could make a law something more than a written formula. It was also the basis of his insistence on the need for a further programme of legal and political reform designed to bring back what he called the combination of subjective and objective rights into a viable and robust working order.

In the Kantian and Hegelian language that became the lingua franca of nineteenth-century German legal and political thought, legal rights were subjective rights, while legal rules were objective rights. At first, as Jhering presented them, subjective rights were all that any society had housed. These were straightforward assertions of entitlement either to this fish, that riverbank, or those trees, in order to meet a physical need, a common interest, or a collective activity. Their basis and justification was, therefore, utility (this was one reason why Jhering was sometimes labelled the German Bentham). But utilities could clash, and the resulting conflict could give rise to various mechanisms or procedures for dispute settlement, like trials by combat, pronouncements by oracles, or rulings by elders. Here two developments came to have a durable significance. The first, Jhering argued, was the concept of a fault, which arose when a largely shame-based culture gave way to a largely guilt-based culture. The second, which mattered more in a guilt- than in a shame-based culture, was the concept of evidence that began to arise when it became usual to establish different degrees of responsibility and different measures of punishment for some particular act. Together, the combination of finding fault and using evidence came to give the law an objective dimension. Alongside rights, there were now also rules. This meant that subjective rights, or rights that could be exercised by individuals or groups, now went together with objective rights, or rights that could be exercised only by states or other agents of authority. Together, the combination of subjective and objective rights amounted to laws.

For Jhering, what he called the struggle for law began, in an anticipation of the better-known definition by Max Weber, as a struggle to exercise a monopoly of legitimate violence in a given territory. It amounted to the imposition of a rule-based system upon a rights-based system by adding a system of objective rights to a heterogeneous cluster of subjective rights. In this setting, both the positive and negative aspects of the idea of the rule of law were visible. In a positive sense, adding a system of rules to a system of rights injected a new type of moral evaluation into what, at bottom, was still an interest-based claim. Once a right was sanctioned by a rule, it acquired a quality of legality and legitimacy that formed a real link between the subjective and objective sides of the law. In this sense, the law was the medium that could turn a subjective interest into an objective rule and, by doing so, could have the further ability to turn a claim about interest and utility into a more highly motivating claim about status, process, and personality. The resulting alignment between the subjective and objective dimensions of the law meant that a struggle over something real was also, more importantly, a struggle over something ideal, and it was this additional quality that, ultimately, gave the law its force. "This connection between the law and the person," Jhering wrote, "gives all rights, whatever their nature, that incommensurable value which I call *ideal* to distinguish it from the purely material value that it has in terms of interest."

> The law, which on one side seems to tie people to the lower regions of egoism and calculation, raises them up to an ideal above the level of subtlety and calculation that they have learned on the scale of utility and enables them to fight fully and purely for an idea. Although it will be prose in the sphere of purely material things, the law becomes poetry in the personal sphere and in the struggle to defend personality. The struggle for law is the poetry of character.[85]

Just as a state's ability to create money was a real measure of its autonomy, so its ability to fuse rights with rules was a real measure of its power. As Jhering described it, what began as a simple assertion of an interest took on a new lease of life once it had been given the further quality of a subjective right. In this sense, the interplay between subjective and objective rights supplied the motivation to turn subjective claims about rights into publicly recognized legal rights. Jhering called this reflexive motivation a "feeling of legal right" or a "sense of justice." Whether, he wrote, the sense in question was individual or collective, it was "the root" of the whole legal system.[86] On his terms, the struggle for law began from below.

Later, in his *Der Zweck im Recht*, Jhering pointed out the similarity between this way of thinking about the law and Rousseau's concept of the general will. The "opposition," he wrote, between "the *particular* and the *common* interest" had been what Rousseau had also emphasized in book 1, chapter 7, of his *Social Contract*. "Indeed," Jhering added, quoting Rousseau's own words, "each indi-

---

85. Rudolf von Jhering, *La lutte pour le droit* [1872], ed. Olivier Jouanjan (Paris, Dalloz, 2006), pp. 46–47. On the impact of Jhering's thought in France, see Mikhaïl Xifaras, "La *Veritas Juris* selon Raymond Saleilles. Remarques sur un projet de restauration du juridisme," *Droits* 47 (2008): 77–148.

86. Jhering, *Lutte*, p. 81.

vidual can, as a man, have a private will contrary to, or differing from, the general will he has as a citizen."

> His private interest can speak to him quite differently from the common interest. His absolute and naturally independent existence can make him think that what he owes the common cause is a voluntary contribution whose loss will be less harmful to others than its payment is to him. And, considering the moral person of the state to be a figment of the imagination because it is not a man, he will seek to enjoy the rights of a citizen without fulfilling the duties of a subject, an injustice whose progress would cause the ruin of the political body.[87]

What was important, in the context of this opposition, was the need for a third term to bridge the gap between the particular and the general. For Jhering, the missing third term was the law.

Georg Jellinek and the Concept of Sovereignty

A further sequences of moves was made towards the end of the nineteenth century by a third Austro-German law professor, Georg Jellinek. Jellinek added a further concept to the combination of financial autonomy and legal authority that he took over from the thought of Stein, Dietzel, and Jhering. This was the concept of sovereignty. As Jellinek presented it, the concept of sovereignty was the key to a state's capacity for self-limitation.[88] In itself, he argued, a state was simply organized force. In this sense, states were simply a generic feature of human history. They were as widespread and powerful, at least on their own terms, among the ancients as among the moderns, and among republics as among despotisms. In this respect, they were straightforward engines of power. Paradoxically, Jellinek argued, it was the concept of sovereignty, with its emphasis upon supremacy, immediacy, and finality, that added the further qualities of legitimacy and authority to the idea of a state. It did so because these, importantly, were qualities that required the initial existence of a relationship, like the relationship between one large association and many smaller associations that Hegel, echoing Rousseau, had identified as the key to the combination of the state and civil society, and that Kant had

---

87. Rudolf von Jhering, *Law as a Means to an End* [1877] (Boston, The Boston Book Company, 1913), pp. 420–21, and n. 122, quoting Jean-Jacques Rousseau, *Social Contract*, bk. 1, ch. 7, in Rousseau, *Collected Writings*, 4:140–41.

88. The idea was foreshadowed in the talk that Jellinek gave in 1891, entitled (in the modern Italian edition that I have used) "La politica dell assolutismo e quella del radicalismo. Hobbes e Rousseau," in Lagi, *Georg Jellinek: storico del pensiero politico*, pp. 53–69.

highlighted as the basis of the difference between public and private law. Adding sovereignty to a state meant, on the one hand, emphasizing the one quality that distinguished the state from every other type of association while, on the other hand, predicating that quality on the continued existence of exactly those other types of association. From this perspective, sovereignty had a built-in capacity for self-limitation that was unavailable to states themselves. It was the extra ingredient that turned force into law while, at the same time, adding force to the law.

As Jellinek himself described his conceptual move, "in order to supply a foundation to public law, I transferred the central idea of modern ethics, ethical autonomy, by analogy, to the state."[89] Just as autonomy called for limiting present freedom in order to maintain future freedom, so sovereignty called for limiting present superiority in order to maintain future superiority. Adding autonomy to force meant that, despite appearances to the contrary, sovereignty was the key to the overlapping distinctions between the state and civil society, and between public law and private law. Without it, the distinctions would collapse, leaving the state either in total command or at the mercy of an increasingly fragmented civil society. In making his argument Jellinek established a position that combined important aspects of the old Roman-law concern with the state, status, and the *res publica* with a new emphasis on sovereignty as a peculiarly modern concept with origins that went back no further than the Middle Ages because it grew out of the doctrinal fallout of the long-drawn-out struggle for power between Europe's medieval emperors and popes, together with their respective clients and vassals. "The Greeks and the Romans," Jellinek asserted at the beginning of a historical examination of the concept of sovereignty that he included in his *Allgemeine Staatsrecht*, "were equally unaware of the notion of a sovereign state." The Greek states were too small and too similar for any single state to stand out above the rest, while the Roman state was too large and too powerful to be described in terms of the type of comparative conceptual vocabulary to which the concept of sovereignty belonged. The ancient world, Jellinek claimed, "lacked the one single thing that could have given rise to the concept of a sovereign state, namely the opposition between political power and other powers."[90] This, instead, was the legacy of the Middle Ages and the reason why the three-sided struggle embroiling the various forms of religious, legal, and military power claimed by Europe's popes and emperors,

89. The passage is cited in Peter Ghosh, "Max Weber and Georg Jellinek: Two Divergent Conceptions of Law," *Saeculum* 59 (2008): 299–347 (p. 312 for the passage in question).

90. Jellinek, *L'état moderne et son droit*, 1:78–79.

and their urban or rural retainers, had eventuated in the modern concept of a sovereign state.

Jellinek's concept of sovereignty relied on an initial distinction between political power and other forms of power. In this sense, sovereignty was to the state as Rousseau's concept of the general will was to the will of all or, more directly, to Hegel's state-civil society-administration nexus. It supplied the additional level of legality and legitimacy that turned power into authority and decisions into rules. Sovereignty was singular, not plural, but still had the ability to maintain institutional and social pluralism. However contradictory it appeared to be, sovereignty was simultaneously law-generated and law-based, but was still somehow sovereign. The mechanism responsible for this fluidity of status was, Jellinek argued, the law itself. Importantly, however, this was not because the law functioned in a positive way, but, especially in conditions of social and institutional complexity, because the law functioned negatively. It was responsible for maintaining the positive rights, entitlements, and attributes of the various individual and collective arrangements that fell under its aegis. It was, at least in Jellinek's rendition, both a bridge between the state and civil society and, more fundamentally, politics conducted in a different, rule-based idiom. The rule of law could add the authority of a command to the utility of a contract and, by doing so, could impose a minimal set of legal obligations upon the divisions and arguments of civil society. Where politics itself had no determinate content, the concept of sovereignty endowed the law with a peculiarly modern ability to give politics a relatively stable content. Sovereignty, in short, made the law the other side of politics.

8

From Romanticism to Classicism

"A TRUE CLASSIC, as I would like to hear it defined," wrote the French literary critic Charles Augustin Sainte-Beuve in 1850,

> is an author who has enriched the human mind, who has really added to the store of its treasures and caused it to advance an extra step; who has discovered some unequivocal moral truth, or reawakened some eternal passion in a heart to which all seemed to be known and to have been discovered; who has expressed his thought, observation or invention in no matter what form, provided only that it is broad and great, refined and sensible, sane and beautiful in itself; who has spoken to all in his own distinctive style, a style which also happens to be the style of the whole world, a style which is novel but without neologism, which is both ancient and new, or readily contemporary with every age.
>
> Such a classic might for a moment have been revolutionary, or might at least have seemed so. But it is not. At first it seized hold only of what was around it and only overturned what was obstructing it to restore that balance which benefits order and beauty.[1]

---

1. Charles Augustin Sainte-Beuve, "What Is a Classic?" in Sainte-Beuve, *Essays*, trans. Elizabeth Lee (London, 1890), pp. 3–4. "Un vrai classique, comme j'aimerais à l'entendre définir, c'est un auteur qui a enrichi l'esprit humain, qui en a réellement augmenté le trésor, qui lui a fait faire un pas de plus, qui a découvert quelque vérité morale non équivoque, ou ressaisi quelque passion éternelle dans ce cœur ou tout semblait connu et exploré; qui a rendu sa pensée, son observation ou son invention, sous une forme n'importe laquelle, mais large et grande, fine et sensée, saine et belle en soi; qui a parlé à tous dans un style à lui et qui se trouve aussi celui de tout le monde, dans un style nouveau sans néologisme, nouveau et antique, aisément contemporaine des tous les âges.

"Un tel classique a pu être un moment révolutionnaire; il a pu paraitre du moins, mais il ne l'est pas; il n'a fait main basse d'abord autour de lui; il n'a renversé ce qui le gênait que pour rétablir bien vite l'équilibre au profit de l'ordre et du beau." Charles Augustin Sainte-Beuve,

It was an unusual definition of a classic because, on closer inspection, it could just as well have been a definition of a romantic. The same ambivalence—or sleight of hand—can also be found in the assortment of figures selected by Sainte-Beuve to illustrate the qualities of a classic. These included the two former romantic icons, Dante and Shakespeare, together with Molière and Lafontaine, alongside, but in a lower key, the earlier classic staples, Corneille and Racine. The reversal is intriguing, even if this type of unannounced evaluative switch was not unknown in French literature at the time.[2] Usually, the reasons given to explain Sainte-Beuve's indifference to the older definitions of a classic—and his reluctance to engage with the earlier emphasis on drama and, particularly, the neo-Aristotelian unities of time, place, and action that lay at the heart of the rival evaluations of a classic made by supporters of the classics and romantics during the period of the Restoration—have been largely biographical. From this perspective, the strange content of Sainte-Beuve's endorsement of a classic has usually taken second place to an account of a political trajectory running from disenchantment to apostasy and a sequence of shifts of allegiance that took Sainte-Beuve from political opposition in the period before the revolution of 1830, to the political caution of the years around the revolution of 1848, and, finally, to the endorsement of the coup d'état that brought Louis Napoleon Bonaparte to imperial power in 1851.[3] There is no reason to call the trajectory itself into question, but the curious transposition of the content of what was earlier taken to be romantic to what was now described as classic raises a number of further questions both about what these shifts of allegiance were intended to do, and who, if anyone, Sainte-Beuve hoped to associate with the new content that he gave to the idea of a classic.

"Qu'est-ce qu'un classique," in Sainte-Beuve, *Causeries de lundi*, 3rd ed. 16 vols. (Paris, 1852–62), 3:42. I have modified the English translation slightly.

2. Flaubert, for example, is said to have done something similar to Balzac by turning Goriot's morally impressive funeral at the end of *Le père Goriot* into the far less morally impressive funeral of Monsieur Dambreuse in his own *L'éducation sentimentale*: see Richard Burton, "The Death of Politics: The Significance of Dambreuse's Funeral in *L'éducation sentimentale*," *French Studies* 50 (1996): 157–60. Flaubert's *Tentation de Saint-Antoine* also originated as something like a parody of Quinet's *Ahasvérus*: see Mary Orr, *Flaubert's* Tentation (Oxford, OUP, 2008), p. 1.

3. See particularly Prendergast, *The Classic*. The broader theme is probably best known in an Anglophone context from the essay on Wordsworth and Coleridge by E. P. Thompson, "Disenchantment or Default? A Lay Sermon" [1969], in his *The Romantics: England in a Revolutionary Age* (New York, The New Press, 1997), pp. 33–74. For a range of essays on Sainte-Beuve, see *Romantisme* 109 (2000), "Sainte-Beuve, ou l'invention de la critique."

Humanitarianism, Hegelianism, and Saint Simonianism

In a narrow sense, the answers have a great deal to do with a word that Sainte-Beuve was one of the first to use, namely, *humanitarisme*, a word that was coined to mean something rather different from its apparent English equivalent, humanitarianism.[4] In a more general sense, the answers also have to do with the parallel careers of the two most prominent French politicians and public intellectuals of the early nineteenth century, François Guizot and Victor Cousin (Guizot, born in 1787, was five years older than Cousin, born in 1792, while both were over a decade older than Sainte-Beuve, who was born in 1804). Substantively, however, the answers had most to do with the question of thinking about politics in commercial society and, more particularly, with the struggle to establish a common object of political allegiance under the combined pressures of the problems of restitution and retribution that divided French politics after the restoration of the monarchy in 1815.[5] Of all the many legacies of the French Revolution, these two subjects were among the most difficult to deal with because, in an almost literal sense, they brought back the related problems of public debt, fiscal privilege, and political representation and accountability that had produced the revolution in the first place. Of the two, the subject of retribution—whether for the execution of the king and queen or for the many insurrections, murders, massacres, or mutinies that had occurred after the Bastille fell—was the more manageable. The scale and variety of potential offenses provided many opportunities to offset punishment with magnanimity or, inversely, to appease anger with severity, while the relatively limited number of candidates for retribution—as against the larger number of potential victims of restitution—meant that the two subjects could be largely separated. In this sense, the subject of retribution lent itself more readily to the politics of Restoration France than the subject of restitution because the latter pitted the current owners against the former owners of what had been church property, émigré property, or colonial property in direct and durable ways. Restoring this property to its former owners not only amounted

---

4. On the concept of humanitarianism, see Naomi J. Andrews, "The Romantic Socialist Origins of Humanitarianism," *Modern Intellectual History* 17 (2019): 737–68, although her approach is different from the one set out here. On the background to the term and its relationship to the Saint-Simonianism of Sainte-Beuve's time, see A. G. Lehmann, *Sainte-Beuve: A Portrait of a Critic 1804–1842* (Oxford, Clarendon Press, 1962), pp. 114–33.

5. See Hont, *Politics in Commercial Society*, a book that is as compatible with the thought of Guizot and Hegel as it is with Rousseau and Smith. On the still-understudied issues of restitution and retribution in the politics of Restoration France, see Sonenscher, *Before the Deluge*, pp. 349–71.

to dispossessing hundreds of thousands of their present owners but also threatened to destroy large amounts of the capital invested in former ecclesiastical buildings or landed estates that had been turned to commercial or manufacturing purposes after 1789. Faced with a choice between damaging one group of property owners or another, the easier solution was to choose to compromise and opt for compensation rather than confiscation, which entailed turning to the capital markets to borrow the relatively large sums of money required to circumvent the political and economic hazards likely to come with a full-blooded policy of restitution.

The compromise brought back the problem of public debt, which, in turn, made it more difficult to keep the issues of retribution and restitution separate. Compensating the former owners of different types of property meant increasing the tax burden on the new owners while, at the same time, adding to the pressure on the costs and competitiveness of the manufacturing and commercial sectors of society. Alongside these pressures, there was the further pressure generated by the need to raise revenue to pay off the war debt imposed on France by the victorious allied powers at the Vienna Settlement of 1815. Together, they meant that any restored French government would have to rely quite heavily on economic growth to reinforce the process of reconciliation but would still have to face the potentially divisive distributional effects of economic growth before reconciliation took hold. In these conditions, Hegel's distinction between civil society and the state had a real salience. It built debt into the financial relationship between the different levels of the whole political and administrative system, and, by making government part of both civil society and the state, it produced a need to establish a constitutional framework that could form a bridge between the several different types of private association of civil society on the one side and the several different levels of public office and administration of political society on the other. The resulting combination favoured the coexistence of the market and the state because civil society, at least on Hegel's terms, was global and, ultimately, market driven, while states were local and, ultimately, value driven. Together, they formed the basis of an economy that was open, but a polity that was closed. The combination amounted to taking the state—and the politics of reason of state—out of economics in much the same way that nationally bounded citizenship and state-based elections had done to politics. Just as substituting election to office for the inheritance of thrones removed much of the need for dynastic politics, so substituting the natural liberty of civil society for the bounded quality of political society removed much of the need for mercantilist politics. From this perspective, Hegel's political theory was the right solution, but for the wrong country. Its origins and outcomes were not so much a *Sonderweg* as an accident of history.

It was, however, less than a complete accident partly because Rousseau's thought, which meant so much to Hegel, was associated more readily in France with Robespierre than with Kant, but mainly because Hegel's own thought came to be entangled in nineteenth-century France not only with the careers and thought of Guizot and Cousin but also with the overlapping subjects of Saint-Simonianism and *humanitarisme*. Here, it is important to point out initially that *humanitarisme* began as something different from humanitarianism. It did so partly because the British equivalent of Saint-Simonianism was Chartism, and, as will be shown in a later chapter, the subject of Chartism was connected not so much to humanitarianism as to a broader European discussion of reform and revolution, along with the differences between British political stability and French political *instability* before and after 1848.[6] Chartism had a clear, six-point, political programme, but Saint-Simonianism— with its striking announcement that the golden age lay ahead, not behind, and that the government of men would give way to the administration of things—had the more poetic political vision and, as both its supporters and its critics agreed, many more considerable similarities to the philosophy and politics of German idealism, even if these were not those of Hegel himself. The main reason, however, was that the English-language version of humanitarianism was already in existence long before the appearance of Saint-Simonianism, because England was a Protestant country, while France remained Catholic. In this earlier incarnation, humanitarianism was used to refer, usually dismissively, to the claim that Christ was human, not divine, so that a humanitarian was someone like, for example, the English Unitarian Joseph Priestley, who rejected the concept of the Trinity and, accordingly, the divinity of Christ. The French word was also used initially as a term of disparagement, but here the initial target was Saint-Simonianism rather than Unitarianism. Later, it was applied to the subject of romanticism and also to evaluations of the moral stance adopted by the romantic poet Alphonse de Lamartine towards the Saint-Simonians. To Sainte-Beuve, *humanitarisme* encompassed them all. Opting for what it stood for amounted to opting for the politics of romanticism. Opting *against* what it stood for amounted to opting for the politics of Hegelianism, with all the tensions and contradictions that, particularly in a French context, Hegelianism came to entail.

6. On this later discussion, see chapter 11 below. Comparisons between Saint-Simonianism and Chartism are surprisingly scarce, despite the well-documented interest of figures like Thomas Carlisle, John Stuart Mill, and Alexis de Tocqueville in both. For a helpful comparative study, see Thomas Hopkins, "Liberal Economists and Owenism: Blanqui and Reybaud," *History of European Ideas* (2020), DOI: 10.1080/01916599.2020.1798622.

The word *humanitarisme* seems to have been coined in 1836 by the literary critic Alexandre Vinet in a courteous, but hostile, review of Lamartine's *Jocelyn*, a poetic drama about a Catholic priest's search for a form of religion that could overcome the conflict between clerical celibacy and human sexuality.[7] This, notoriously, was one of the aims of the Saint-Simonian movement and, ultimately, one of the reasons for its disintegration after the French revolution of July 1830. Saint-Simonianism (named after Claude-Henri de Rouvroy, comte de Saint-Simon) began to gather pace in France after the death of Louis XVIII in 1824 and the coronation of his very reactionary brother, Charles X. Its slogan about replacing the government of men by the administration of things was designed, more substantively, to turn the government of Restoration France into a form of rule that could combine the interests of industry, the sciences, and the arts under the aegis of a single but differentiated political and administrative system that was quite similar in structure to Hegel's.[8] In the years that immediately preceded and followed the revolution of July 1830, Saint-Simonianism became a real political force but it disintegrated noisily and comprehensively under the combined effects of spiralling internal argument over its doctrinal content, disagreement about the status of women, failure to respond to strikes by workers, splits among its leaders, and a growing exodus of many of its earlier supporters. By 1836, it was a spent force.

For Vinet, humanitarianism was a concept that had been created by Lamartine to describe Saint-Simonianism's moral and religious content. This, in fact, was a fairly accurate description of the assessment of Saint-Simonianism that Lamartine had made in a pamphlet entitled *Sur la politique rationnelle* (Rational politics) that he published in 1831. Saint-Simonianism, he wrote there, was an encouraging symptom of the new type of politics that was being adopted by the younger generation. It was "a bold plagiarism taken from the Gospel that will one day revert to it." It had "already wrested some enthusiastic spirits away from the vile doctrines of political and industrial materialism" and placed them on "the firm and solid ground of humanity," meaning "respect for every right, recognition of every duty, and the reform, not the destruction, of the

7. Alexandre Vinet's review appeared in *Le Semeur* 5, no. 12 (23 March 1836): 89–94. On Vinet, see Ernest Seillière, *Alexandre Vinet, Historien de la Pensée Française* (Paris, Payot, 1925). On the concept of humanitarianism in Lamartine and its broader context, see Henri Guillemin, *Le Jocelyn de Lamartine* (Paris, 1936), pp. 96–138.

8. For a brief and clear overview, organized around an illuminating initial quotation, see Neil McWilliam, "How to Change the World: Claude-Henri de Rouvroy, comte de Saint-Simon," in *Utopian Moments*, ed. Miguel A. Ramiro Avilés and J. C. Davis (London, Bloomsbury, 2012), pp. 106–12. See, more fully, his earlier *Dreams of Happiness: Social Art and the French Left:1830–1850* (Princeton, NJ, Princeton UP, 1993).

only basis given by God to the family and society, namely, property." It was "a religion minus a god" or "Christianity minus the faith that is its life."[9] He repeated the assessment three years later in his *Voyage en Orient* (Travels in the East) when it had already become clear that the days of Saint-Simonianism were over. Despite its eclipse, Lamartine wrote, Saint-Simonianism still had "something in it of what is true and great and fertile," meaning, he continued, "Christianity applied to political society and legislation adapted to human fraternity." In this respect, he concluded, "I am a Saint-Simonian."[10]

Vinet's evaluation was not entirely different. Saint-Simonianism's fate, he argued, helped to show that real humanitarianism was Christianity. "It is not the case," he wrote, "that those who invented that grand word 'humanitarianism,' or those to whom M. de Lamartine has given the honour of using it, should feel entitled to believe that they have invented charity." Charity began with Christ, as too had humanitarianism. "He," Vinet proclaimed, "who in the midst of Hebrew nationalism, in the face of Roman egoism, and at the height of the usurpations carried out by the individual and political *me* (*moi*), proclaimed . . . the principle of human fraternity," had also removed the need "for any further discoveries or conquests in the moral world."[11] From this perspective, both Saint-Simonianism and any alternative to Saint-Simonianism were redundant. Christ had done enough. Vinet made much the same point, but with a stronger allusion to Saint-Simonianism, several months later in a review of a very successful book entitled *Riche et Pauvre* (Rich and poor) by a writer from Nantes named Emile Souvestre. Like Lamartine, Vinet wrote, Souvestre was sympathetic towards Saint-Simonianism, and it was well known, he added, that a number of men of distinction had once been Saint-Simonians. Although they had now parted company with the movement, they were, like Souvestre, still prepared to remain loyal to some of its principles. "Stripped of its theocratic apparatus," Vinet explained, Saint-Simonianism "left nothing to be seen but its *humanitarisme*." This was the version of humanitarianism that Souvestre had adopted. As Vinet put it nastily, it was "philanthropy delivered wholesale and hope written out in capital letters." It also came in two guises. There was a humanitarianism of the

9. Alphonse de Lamartine, *Sur la politique rationnelle* (Paris, 1831), pp. 107–10. See now the most recent edition of *Sur la politique rationnelle*, ed. Romain Jalabert (Paris, 2020), p. 68.

10. Alphonse de Lamartine, *Voyage en Orient (1832–1833)* in Lamartine, *Œuvres* (Brussels, 1836), p. 208.

11. "Celui qui, du sein du nationalisme hébreu, en face de l'égoïsme romain, au fort des usurpations du *moi* individuel et politique, proclama de sa bouche, réalisa dans sa vie, consacra par sa mort le principe de la fraternité en Dieu." Alexandre Vinet, review of *Jocelyn*, in *Le Semeur* 5, no. 12 (23 March 1836): 93. The review was reprinted in Vinet, *Etudes*, 2:200–201

head, which was no substitute for Christianity, but there was also "a humanitarianism of the heart that deserves all our respect."[12]

Sainte-Beuve gave Vinet's coinage a somewhat more positive inflection. He also, however, associated humanitarianism with romanticism rather than, as Vinet had done, with Saint-Simonianism. Ultimately, as Sainte-Beuve went on to explain, none of them could deliver what they promised. It was this diagnosis that helps to explain Sainte-Beuve's willingness to ignore—or override—the usual range of recognized distinctions between a classic and a romantic. It also helps to explain the convergence, after 1848, between Sainte-Beuve's political views and the historical research of one of his oldest friends, a man named Hippolyte Fortoul who became minister of primary education under Napoleon III, into the life and ideas of Emmanuel-Joseph Sieyès, the individual who in 1799 had played a major part in organizing the coup d'état that brought Napoleon Bonaparte to power. In this political and intellectual context, both the indifference towards the classic-romantic split and the convergence between Sainte-Beuve and Bonapartism were connected to the subjects of Saint-Simonianism, humanitarianism, and romanticism and, more substantively, to the growing number of moral and political dilemmas that they began to represent. In a small way, Sainte-Beuve's identification of a classic as a romantic was his solution to the increasingly untenable implications of these dilemmas.

The first dilemma arose from the Saint-Simonian vision of a form of rule designed to combine industry, the sciences, and the arts under the aegis of a single but differentiated legislative and administrative system. As a vision of the future, and as several of Sainte-Beuve's contemporaries pointed out, it looked surprisingly like Hegel's combination of civil society and the state. From this perspective, Saint-Simonianism could be redescribed as a French version of Hegelianism.[13] But the association between Saint-Simonianism

12. "L'humanitarisme est de la philanthropie en masse et de l'espérance en grand": Alexandre Vinet, review of Emile Souvestre, Riche et Pauvre, in Le Semeur 5, no. 49 (7 December 1836): 385, reprinted in Vinet, Etudes, 3:315. On Souvestre, see David Steel, ed., Lettres d'Emile Souvestre à Edouard Turquéty (Rennes, PU de Rennes, 2012), and David Steel, Emile Souvestre: Un Breton des Lettres, 1806–1854 (Rennes, PU de Rennes, 2013).

13. For different characterizations of the relationship between Saint-Simonianism and Hegelianism, see Hans-Christoph Schmidt am Busch, Hegel et le saint-simonisme. Etudes de philosophie sociale (Toulouse, PU du Mirail, 2012); Hans-Christoph Schmidt am Busch, Ludwig Siep, Hans Ulrich Thamer, and Norbert Waszek, eds., Hegelianismus und Saint-Simonismus (Paderborn, Mentis, 2007); Douglas Moggach, ed., The New Hegelians: Politics and Philosophy in the Hegelian School (Cambridge, CUP, 2006); Warren Breckman, Marx, the Young Hegelians and the Origins of Radical Social Theory (Cambridge, CUP, 1990).

and Hegelianism seemed to indicate that Saint-Simonianism was also disturb-
ingly similar to the philosophy and politics of Victor Cousin and François
Guizot, because they, far more than their Saint-Simonian counterparts, were
quite explicit about their interest in, and endorsement of, many of the ideas
associated with Hegel and Hegelianism. The incongruities built into this initial
juxtaposition were compounded by the fact that several of the critics of Hegel
and Hegelianism, not only in France but also in the German-speaking parts of
Europe, also described themselves as romantics, mainly because they subscribed to philosophies of history that were even more strongly oriented
towards the future than Hegel's. This further juxtaposition seemed to mean
that the supporters of Saint-Simonianism could also be described as supporters of both Hegelianism and eclecticism and, like Hegel himself, as critics of
romanticism, while the critics of Guizot and Cousin could also be described
as critics of Saint-Simonianism and supporters of romanticism. In the light
of these discordant alignments, Sainte-Beuve's choice of Vinet's coinage *humanitarisme* as a symbol of his own allegiances looked initially like a way to avoid
these accumulating incompatibilities.

Sainte-Beuve used the word in a book review, published in the *Revue des
Deux Mondes* in 1838, of a novel written by Hippolyte Fortoul, who, like Sainte-
Beuve himself, was once a supporter of the Saint-Simonians. "The French
Revolution," Fortoul had written in 1833, "was an era of universal palingenesis.
All over the world it has sown the seeds of a social revolution."[14] The combination of revolution and palingenesis was a subject that remained with him all
his life, although it is not clear what kind of social revolution he thought that
the French Revolution would entail. His novel, entitled *Grandeurs de la vie
privée* (The grandeurs of private life), dealt with some of the themes, like the
tension between the public and the private, or between the life of world and
the life of the mind, that Lamartine had written about in *Jocelyn*. Fortoul's version, as Sainte-Beuve discreetly suggested, was not a masterpiece (its high
point was a walk-on part for a yet to be famous Jean-Jacques Rousseau as an
illustration of what could happen when private integrity gives way to public
celebrity).[15] Fortoul, according to Sainte-Beuve, was one of those standing "at
the head of those most affected by *humanitarisme*." This, he wrote, was a name

14. "La révolution française est une ère de palingénésie universelle; elle a fait éclore par tout
le monde les semences d'une révolution sociale": Hippolyte Fortoul, "De l'art actuel," *Revue
Encyclopédique* 59 (1833): 151–52.

15. For one of the few studies of the novel, see Claudine Lacoste, "*Grandeur de la vie privée
de H. Fortoul*," in *Rousseau et Voltaire en 1978* (Geneva, Slatkine, 1981), pp. 118–26.

sometimes given to a very precise and subtle thinker, meaning, he went on to explain, someone who would look for a symbol in a painting by the romantic painter Alexandre-Gabriel Decamps, or a synthesis in a song by the popular singer Pierre-Jean Béranger, or a formula that could encompass Béranger's songs and a philosophical poem by Herder's translator, Edgar Quinet. The three names—Decamps, Béranger, and Quinet—were a kind of shorthand for an amalgamation of three different subjects. Decamps stood for orientalism and the French (and Saint-Simonian) interest in Egypt, Algeria, and Tunisia. Béranger stood for everyday life and ordinary culture, and for a partly Bonapartist and partly socialist version of popular politics. Quinet stood for history and the idea of history as palingenesis. Humanitarianism, Sainte-Beuve implied, was a doomed attempt to combine them all.

If, Saint-Beuve wrote, humanitarianism was a weakness or a failing in criticism, this was because it was a product of another failing, which was romanticism. The shortcomings of romanticism, he claimed, had produced humanitarianism as its antithesis. In the first, the only thing to be valued in any work was "the condition of *pure art.*" This had led its critics to take the opposite path by valuing nothing else but "the social idea and the motivation for the good, magnified to the level of the grandiose." In this formulation, humanitarianism was romanticism revised and corrected by Saint-Simonianism, which, it could be said, was quite an accurate description of Lamartine's own position.[16] As Sainte-Beuve later wrote in a portrait of the poet that he published at the time of the banquet campaign that preceded the French revolution of 1848, "*humanitarisme* has become so dear a preoccupation to the poet that he introduces it on every occasion, even in the toast delivered to the Breton and Gaulois banquet held to commemorate the peoples (*races*) of old, with their tribes, their families, and their distinctive language." Humanitarianism was, in short, "humanity personified" or "*cosmopolitanism* in poetic verse."[17]

Saint-Simonianism, however, could also be associated with Hegel and Hegelianism. This meant that it could be associated, to the growing discomfort of both sides, with the political thought and political visions of Victor Cousin and François Guizot and their long, relatively unrecognized, engagement with German philosophy from the time of Kant to the years that followed

16. On Saint-Simonian concepts of art and the avant-garde, see Marie-Claude Genet-Delacroix, "Académisme et avant-garde dans la peinture française du xix siècle," in *Avenirs et avant-gardes en France: xix–xx siècles,* ed. Vincent Duclert, Rémi Fabre, and Patrick Fridenson (Paris, La Découverte, 1999), pp. 115–27; McWilliam, *Dreams of Happiness.*

17. Charles Augustin Sainte-Beuve, *Portraits contemporains,* 2 vols. (Paris, 1847), 1:269.

Hegel's death in 1831.[18] Both, it could be said, were France's first Hegelians, although the point was made more usually by their critics than by their admirers. To Cousin's Catholic critics, like Henri Maret, Auguste Barchou de Penhouen, or the abbé Louis Bautin, the version of philosophy that Cousin called eclecticism was, in fact, no more than Hegelianism, and both led to pantheism or Spinozism.[19] To his supporters, the opposite was the case because both Hegelianism and eclecticism were the alternatives to the materialism of the eighteenth century. The arguments made by both sides echoed the earlier German-language arguments generated by Kant's concept of autonomy and the efforts by Fichte, Schelling, and Hegel to explain how a multiplicity of autonomous agents could all coexist. If we set Sainte-Beuve's conflation of a classic with a romantic in this transnational context, his redefinition of the first as the second can be seen to be part of a larger, more complicated story made up of a comprehensive rearrangement of almost all the pairings and oppositions that informed the pattern of intellectual and political alignments between 1815 and 1848. Tracking this early Weimar-style rearrangement means, initially, examining the dialogue between French and German philosophy in the early years of the Restoration and assessing the impact of the thought of Hegel and Schelling in France before and after the July Revolution of 1830, especially as this was registered by Victor Cousin. It also involves following the long intellectual and political career of François Guizot, who, between 1830 and 1848, became France's most influential politician. It calls, finally, for examining the convergence between Hegel's thought and French Saint-Simonianism and the growing body of criticism directed at both. The starting point of the whole sequence, however, was Cousin's discovery of Hegel.

18. The lack of recognition applies more to Guizot than to Cousin, although it was actually Guizot, rather than Cousin, who was the more proficient in German. On Cousin and Hegel, see helpfully Andrea Bellantone, *Hegel en France*, 2 vols. (Paris, Hermann, 2011), 1:19–156, and, particularly, Michel Espagne and Michael Werner, *Lettres d'Allemagne. Victor Cousin et les hégéliens* (Tusson, Charente, Du Lérot, 1990). The absence of an examination of the German side of Guizot's thought, particularly of a comparison between the political thought of Guizot and Hegel, is the one flaw of the classic study by Pierre Rosanvallon, *Le moment Guizot* (Paris, Gallimard, 1985). In it, the preference (pp. 51–54) goes to a somewhat anachronistic (and Franco-French) comparison between Guizot and Tocqueville.

19. The two key texts that conflated eclecticism, Hegelianism, and pantheism were Louis Bautain, *De l'enseignement de la philosophie en France au xixe siècle* (Strasbourg, 1833), and Henri Maret, *Essai sur le panthéisme dans les sociétés modernes* (Paris, 1840). More generally, see Michel Despland, *L'émergence des sciences de la religion. La monarchie de juillet: un moment fondateur* (Paris, L'Harmattan, 1999).

Victor Cousin and the Impersonality of Reason

For Cousin, Hegel was the Plato of the modern age.[20] He made this clear in the dedication of his translation of Plato's *Gorgias* to Hegel. The dedication, he wrote, was "due homage to the one who was the first to reinstate with all due honour the maxims contained in this ancient monument to their rightful place among the eternal principles of the philosophy of right (*philosophie du droit*)."[21] The equivalence was justified because, like Plato, Hegel had shown that it was possible to bridge the divide between the world of forms and the world of things, and close the gap that Kant had opened up between the noumenal and the phenomenal, the ideal and the real, the spiritual and the physical, and, ultimately, individual lives and human history. This was the point of the metaphor of the rose in the cross or the symbol of love and suffering that Hegel used at the beginning of his *Philosophy of Right*.[22] To Cousin, Hegel had shown, most fully in his *Encyclopaedia*, that human reason could straddle the subjectivity of consciousness, as Fichte had described it, and the objectivity of being, as Schelling had described it. Reason, on Hegel's terms, was both subjective and objective because it was both a capability and a condition. The link between the capability and the condition was formed by history because it was history that was at once the source and the setting of the growing body of conceptual resources that allowed human reason to override the distinction between subjectivity and objectivity and, after their initial estrangement, begin to find itself at home again in the world. Historical understanding might come late, but it was matched by the fact—and by the emotion—that it was real understanding.

This, it could be said, was Hegel's version of Schleiermacher's insight into the division of labour. Individual rationality was scalable into a rational system. As Cousin described it, the most vivid illustration of the underlying power of human reason was the cry of "Eureka" that Archimedes had issued when he had

20. On the combination of Platonism and Hegelianism in Cousin's philosophy, see, helpfully, Bellantone, *Hegel en France*, 1:43–47, 60–66, 73–86. On Hegel and Plato, see Hegel, *Leçons sur Platon*, ed. Jean-Louis Vieillard-Baron (Paris, Aubier-Montaigne, 1976), especially pp. 71–77. On Hegelianism in France, see Amaury Catel, *Le traducteur et le demiurge. Hermann Ewerbeck, un communiste allemand à Paris (1841–1860)* (Nancy, Editions de l'Arbre Bleu, 2019), pp. 131–39, and the earlier studies referred to there.

21. "Je viens, mon cher Hegel, vous prier d'accepter l'hommage de cette traduction du *Gorgias*. Il était du sans doute à celui qui le premier replaça avec honneur, parmi les principes éternels du droit, les maximes contenus dans cet antique monument." *Œuvres de Platon*, trans. Victor Cousin, vol. 3 (Paris, 1826), unnumbered dedicatory page.

22. Hegel, *Elements of the Philosophy of Right*, p. 22.

seen how to calculate something's density by measuring the volume of water that it displaced, and, by doing so, to work out how much gold there was in the king of Syracuse's crown. As Cousin also emphasized, Archimedes's excitement showed that the discovery had an emotional as well as a rational dimension, and had as much to do with intuition, the imagination, and enthusiasm as with identifiable causes and measurable consequences. The combination meant, Cousin wrote, that philosophy had something in common not only with reason and rationality but also with romanticism and religion because enthusiasm played a part in all four. "It is enthusiasm," Cousin wrote in 1829, "which gives birth to religions; for every religion supposes two things; namely, that the truths which it proclaims are absolute truths, and that it proclaims them in the name of God himself by whom they are revealed."[23] As was the case with the moment of revelation that led Archimedes to exclaim "Eureka," enthusiasm was the feeling generated by reason's recognition of its own rationality and of the power that it had at its disposal. While the feeling was personal and subjective, rationality was impersonal and objective. For Cousin, by showing how to understand both, Hegel had produced a real reply both to the scepticism of the seventeenth and eighteenth centuries and to Kant's romantic critics from Herder into the early nineteenth century.

Cousin visited Germany in 1817 and 1818 where, somewhat fortuitously, he met Hegel. He revisited Germany in 1828 and continued to correspond with members of Hegel's circle long after Hegel's death in 1831. As he later wrote, they got on personally and politically, even if their respective philosophies were not fully aligned. Hegel's strong endorsement of the principles of the French Revolution, most visible in the content of his lectures on the history of philosophy that his students passed on to Cousin, chimed readily with his own views. "Monsieur Hegel liked France," Cousin recalled. "He liked the revolution of 1789. He was, as he often reminded me, a *Bleu*, to use an expression of the emperor Napoleon [meaning the opposite of a White, the colour of a legitimist]. He was at one and the same time a strong liberal and a strong monarchist, and both these sentiments are also lodged to the highest degree

---

23. Victor Cousin, "Philosophy of Enthusiasm," in *Specimens of Foreign Standard Literature*, ed. George Ripley 2 vols. (Boston, 1838), 1:213–22 (p. 215). The extract was translated from Cousin's *Cours de l'histoire de la philosophie: philosophie du xviiie siècle*, 2 vols. (Paris, 1829), 2:478–85. Cousin's treatment of religion paralleled Benjamin Constant's distinction between religious feeling and religious forms in his *De la religion* [1824–31], ed. Tzvetan Todorov and Etienne Hofmann (Arles, Actes Sud, 1999). See, particularly, Constant's long note on Lamennais, pp. 587–96, with its aim of justifying his claim that the strength of the feeling usually overrode the frequently immoral appearance of many of the forms of religious belief.

in my own heart and head."[24] It was a very apt summing up of the convergence of their political views and, at the same time, an indication of its basis in their joint endorsement of the idea of the impersonality of reason. This, as with Hegel, was to be found in the mind's capacity to identify and understand its own capacity for logical inquiry. "Observation," Cousin wrote in the printed version of the lecture course that he gave in 1818, soon after his return from Germany, "immediately registers principles that, as soon as they make themselves apparent to the observer, seem to be independent of, as well as prior, posterior, and superior to, observation itself."[25] They were, in an intuitive sense, knowledge of knowledge and recognition of the rationality of reason itself. This, as with Hegel, meant that the fundamental property of reason was its impersonality.

Cousin's version of the impersonality of reason was somewhat different from Hegel's, with rather less emphasis on the intricacies of consciousness, culture, and history that Hegel had developed so powerfully in the wake of Kant, Fichte, and Schelling. "Hegel," Cousin wrote in 1833, "begins with abstractions that, for him, are the foundation and archetype of all reality, but nowhere does he indicate or describe the procedure that gave rise to these abstractions."[26] By 1836, his reservations had come to include Plato as well as Hegel. "Plato's ideas are exclusively general; Aristotle's principles combine both generality and particularity," he wrote in a report on a prize competition on Aristotle's metaphysics organized by the Academy of Moral and Political Sciences (won, however, by one of Hegel's former students, Karl Ludwig Michelet).[27] Modern philosophy called for a synthesis of the general and the particular, the ideal and the real, or, metaphorically, the joint legacies of Plato and Aristotle. By then, Cousin had already given the new synthesis the name of eclecticism, and he now began to use the new name to argue repeatedly that eclecticism required a more positive and empirical examination of the workings of the human mind than, he

24. Victor Cousin, *Fragments et souvenirs* (Paris, 1857), p. 79. On this characterization of liberalism, compare Helena Rosenblatt, *The Lost History of Liberalism: From Ancient Rome to the Twenty-First Century* (Princeton, NJ, Princeton UP, 2018), to William Selinger and Gregory Conti, "The Lost History of *Political* Liberalism," *History of European Ideas* 46 (2020): 341–54. For Hegel's endorsement of the French Revolution, see George Wilhelm Friedrich Hegel, *Lectures on the History of Philosophy* [1840], 3 vols. (Oxford, 1892–96), Special Combined Edition (Lector House, 2020), p. 750.

25. Victor Cousin, *Cours de philosophie, professé à la faculté des lettres pendant l'année 1818 sur le fondement des idées du vrais, du beau, du bien* (Paris, 1836), p. 286.

26. Victor Cousin, "Préface" to his *Fragments philosophiques* (Paris, 1833), p. xliii.

27. See Cousin's "Avant-Propos" to Karl Ludwig Michelet, *Examen critique de l'ouvrage d'Aristote intitulé Métaphysique* (Paris, 1836), p. xxii for the passage cited here.

claimed, had become usual in German philosophy.[28] Cousin used the term "psychology" to describe this type of examination but emphasized that it was still compatible with the idea of the impersonality of reason. In his usage, however, the idea of the impersonality of reason was as redolent of the rationalism of the great French philosophers of the seventeenth century as of German philosophy of the nineteenth century. The point was not lost on some of his readers. "Monsieur Cousin," wrote one of his admirers, "speaks of reason as did Malebranche," the seventeenth-century French theologian best known for his book *De la recherche de la vérité* (The search after truth). Reason, Cousin had written, "is impersonal by nature. It is not us who make it. There is so little in it that is individual that its character is exactly the opposite of individuality because it is, instead, universality and necessity." It was, therefore, "a necessary and universal revelation that has never failed anyone and enlightens everyone on its appearance in the world."[29] Although it has recently become usual to associate the idea of enlightenment with the monism of Spinoza, it was once just as usual to associate the idea with Malebranche or the influential early eighteenth-century German philosopher Christian Wolff. Cousin's version of enlightenment was a kind of synthesis of Malebranche and Hegel.

François Guizot and the History of Civilization

Like Cousin's philosophy, Guizot's political thought also had seventeenth-century undertones. In his case, however, they came not so much from Malebranche but from the seventeenth-century Jansenist and mathematician Blaise Pascal. "A multitude which cannot be reduced to unity is confusion," Pascal had written in one of his aphoristic, posthumously published, *Pensées*. "Unity," he continued, "which is not a multitude is tyranny." This, Guizot wrote some two centuries later, "was the finest and most precise definition of representative government."[30] The definition chimed readily both with

28. Michelet, Cousin wrote in his foreword to the prize-winning work, was "a fervent disciple" of Hegel but, without giving up on his allegiance to "his famous master's system," could have raised the level of his language to "that simplicity and universality which, without distorting them, is to be found in the systems of every country and every time." Ibid., p. xxxviii.

29. Francisque Bouillier, "Raison," in *Dictionnaire des sciences philosophiques*, 5 vols. (Paris, 1844–51), 5:344–45, which summarizes his earlier *Théorie de la raison impersonnelle* (Paris, 1844).

30. The passage can be found in Blaise Pascal, *Pensées*, ed. Léon Brunschvicg, introduced by Charles Marc Des Granges (Paris, Garnier, 1958), *pensée* 871, p. 317, and in the translation of the Lafuma edition of the *Pensées* by John Warrington, ed. H. T. Barnwell (London, Everyman, 1960), *pensée* 848, p. 243. The same passage is in François Guizot, *Histoire des origines du gouvernement représentatif en Europe*, 2 vols. (Paris, 1851), 1:93–4, and *The History of the Origins of Repre-*

Cousin's concept of the impersonality of reason and with the concept of government best suited to maintain it. "Royalty," Guizot wrote in the version of his lecture course on the history of civilization in Europe that was published in 1828, "is something quite other than the will of a single individual, although it appears to have exactly that form. It is instead, the personification of the sovereignty of law and of that essentially reasonable, enlightened, just, impartial will that is foreign to—and higher than—every individual will and is, for this reason, entitled to rule them all."[31] The ultimate source of legitimate authority was what Guizot called *le souverain de droit*, a term probably best translated as "sovereign law" rather than either "the rule of law" or, more menacingly, "the sovereign *of* the law." In substance, it was Guizot's version of the impersonality of reason.

Sovereign law, Guizot explained, was something "that cannot belong to anyone" so that "any attribution of sovereign law to any kind of human force whatsoever is radically dangerous and false." Maintaining its impersonal quality called for "the necessity of limiting every sort of power whatever its name or form," and for recognizing "the radical illegitimacy of every form of absolute power irrespective of whether it originated in conquest, inheritance, or

---

sentative Government in Europe, trans. Andrew R. Scoble, introduced by Aurelian Craiutu (Indianapolis, IN, Liberty Fund, 2002), p. 52 (I have modified the translation to restore the antithesis between "unity" and "multitude" in Pascal's phrase). See too Thomas Hare, *The Machinery of Representation* (London, 1857), pp. 37–38, and his *A Treatise on the Election of Representatives, Parliamentary and Municipal*, new ed. (London 1861), p. 257 (both citing Guizot on Pascal). See also Frank Ankersmit, "Sovereignty and Political Representation," *Redescriptions* 17 (2014): 10–43; Federico Tomasello, "Il governo della storia. La dottrina delle capacita politiche nel pensiero di François Guizot," in *Libertà, uguaglianza, democrazia nel pensiero politico europea (xvi–xxi secolo)*, ed. Rossella Bufano (Milella, Lecce, 2018), pp. 131–48.

31. "La royauté est toute autre chose que la volonté d'un homme, quoiqu'elle se présente sous cette forme. Elle est la personnification de la souveraineté de droit, de cette volonté essentiellement raisonnable, éclairée, juste, impartiale, étrangère et supérieure à toutes les volontés individuelles, et qui, à ce titre, a droit de les gouverner." François Guizot, *Histoire générale de la civilisation en Europe* (Paris, 1828), 9th lecture, p. 10. On the concept of *souveraineté de droit* and its analogues, although without Hegel, see Pierre Rosanvallon, *Democracy Past and Future*, ed. Samuel Moyn (New York, Columbia UP, 2006), pp. 117–26, and his introduction to a previously unpublished essay by Guizot of 1822 entitled "De la souveraineté" and published in François Guizot, *Histoire de la civilisation en Europe*, ed. Pierre Rosanvallon (Paris, Hachette, 1985), pp. 307–18, followed, pp. 319–89, by Guizot's text. On the broader intellectual setting, see Corinne Doria, *Pierre Paul Royer-Collard (1763–1845). Un philosophe entre deux révolutions* (Rennes, PU de Rennes, 2018); Aurelian Craiutu, *Liberalism under Siege: The Political Thought of the French Doctrinaires* (Lanham, MD, Lexington Books, 2003); Rosenblatt, *The Lost History of Liberalism*.

election."[32] It also, however, called for a strong endorsement of a constitutionally limited royal government because, as Guizot emphasized, monarchy was
the form of government that best fitted the concept of sovereign law. Like the
idea of sovereign law itself, monarchy was unitary and continuous. And, like
the concepts of truth and justice, it was also singular and timeless because even
the most limited of limited monarchies could be renewed by indivisible hereditary succession. The "rational and natural character" of sovereign law was,
therefore, best represented most fully and visibly in the image of a single royal
ruler. Here, as Guizot went on to show, Benjamin Constant could be set alongside Pascal. "Open the work," he wrote, "in which Benjamin Constant has
presented royalty so skilfully as a neutral and moderating power, placed high
above the accidents and struggles of society, only intervening in great crises.
Is this not the position to be adopted by sovereign law in the government of
human affairs?"[33] Like Hegel, at least in Cousin's description of the philosopher he had once called "the man for me," Guizot was also a strong liberal and
a strong monarchist.

Guizot's version of how it was possible to be both a strong liberal and a
strong monarchist was also surprisingly similar to Hegel's. There is no evidence
that Guizot ever read Hegel, but the relatively large number of references to
German-language publications in his footnotes indicates that, at least by contemporary French standards, he was unusually proficient in German (and too
in English, as the translator of both Shakespeare and Gibbon).[34] In 1816 he
published a translation of an essay on sovereignty and forms of government by

32. Guizot, *Histoire générale de la civilisation en Europe*, p. 13.

33. "Messieurs, ces caractères rationnels, naturels, du souverain de droit, c'est la royauté qui
les reproduit extérieurement sous la forme la plus sensible, qui en parait la plus fidèle image.
Ouvrez l'ouvrage où M. Benjamin Constant a si ingénieusement représenté la royauté comme
un pouvoir neutre, un pouvoir modérateur, élevé au-dessus des accidents, des luttes de la société, et n'intervenant que dans les grandes crises. N'est-ce pas là, pour ainsi dire, l'attitude du
souverain de droit dans le gouvernement des choses humaines?" Ibid., p. 15. On Constant's
concept of monarchy as a "neutral power," see Selinger, *Parliamentarism*, pp. 11–13, 115–16, 120–26,
133–39, 182.

34. See, for example, his bibliographical advice in his *Histoire de la civilisation en France depuis
la chute de l'empire romain*, 3rd ed. (Paris, 1840), p. 40, to "ceux d'entre vous, Messieurs, qui savent
l'allemand," recommending Savigny on the history of Roman law in the Middle Ages, Henke
on the history of the Christian church, and Gieseler on ecclesiastical history, and, in the same
work, pp. 313–20, his well-informed discussion of Savigny. A comparable parallel has been drawn
between Hegel and Guizot's political mentor, Pierre Paul Royer-Collard: see George Armstrong
Kelly, *Hegel's Retreat from Eleusis: Studies in Political Thought* (Princeton, NJ, Princeton UP,
1978), pp. 146–51. I am grateful to Lucian Robinson for pointing this out to me.

a German political commentator named Friedrich Ancillon, with an extensive set of critical comments of his own.[35] His later account of the origins and development of the form of limited royal government that was compatible with the idea of the sovereignty of law was unusually similar to Hegel's. For Guizot, the key ingredient of this form of government and the key to the difference between the ancients and the moderns, in terms of both the sovereignty of law and of the activities and arrangements underpinning the idea of impersonal rationality, was the nuclear family. Guizot was adamant that this type of family had no counterpart either in ancient society or in any of those to be found outside of western and central Europe. The nuclear family was, therefore, a product of Europe's Middle Ages and, more specifically, of a gradual fusion of the domestic values of feudal society with the economic values of urban, or bourgeois, society after the fall of the Roman Empire.[36] Guizot did not use the term "civil society" in anything like Hegel's sense. But his own account of the origins and significance of bourgeois society was, at least in conceptual terms, surprisingly similar to Hegel's idea of *bürgerliche Gesellschaft*.

Guizot may or may not have read Hegel, but he certainly translated Gibbon, whom Hegel also read. As Guizot described it, the decline and fall of the Roman Empire was the product of the absence of an economically and politically independent bourgeoisie. "The great fact," he wrote in 1823 in his *Essais sur l'histoire de France*, "that the system of imperial despotism brought in its wake and the one that alone explains the phenomenon under review is the dissolution, destruction, and disappearance of the middle class (*classe moyenne*) from the Roman world. When the barbarians arrived, that class no longer existed. This is why there was no longer a nation."[37] The underlying cause of "this annihilation of the middle class" was the growth of a municipal regime that had turned the middle class into both an instrument and a victim of imperial despotism. The process had occurred because the old republican system of election had been replaced by a centralized system of administration and appointment, and this in turn had generated a lethal combination of privilege, patronage, and corruption. The imperial state had hollowed out the whole social hierarchy, leaving "the lower classes brutalized, the middle classes ruined, and the upper

35. Frédéric Ancillon, *De la souveraineté et des formes du gouvernement* (Paris, 1816).

36. Guizot's examination of the nuclear family as the basis of bourgeois society adds a further dimension to Sara Maza, *The Myth of the French Bourgeoisie: An Essay on the Social Imaginary* (Cambridge, MA, Harvard UP, 2003). On the intellectual background to Guizot's examination of the origins of modern social, economic, and political arrangements, see Istvan Hont, "Adam Smith's History of Law and Government as Political Theory," in *Political Judgment: Essays for John Dunn*, ed. Richard Bourke and Raymond Geuss (Cambridge CUP, 2009), pp. 131–71.

37. François Guizot, *Essais sur l'histoire de France* (Paris, 1823), p. 4.

classes enervated, with no public spirit, no magistrates, and no citizens," and, by extension, turning the whole Roman Empire into ready prey for the waves of northern invaders.[38]

The way back was a product of the reversal of the causal mechanisms that were responsible for the decline and fall of imperial Rome. The key to the process of decline, Guizot claimed in a moment of historical illumination that was later to be picked up and used by Alexis de Tocqueville, was the growing disintegration and atomization of the Roman Empire as the multiple imaginative, economic, legal, and administrative links between its subjects were gradually and progressively eroded. It was a mistake, Guizot argued in his eighth lecture, to think of the barbarian invasions in terms of dramatic metaphors like a flood, an earthquake, or a conflagration. The real process consisted of events that were "essentially partial, local, and momentary." Their cumulative effect, however, was to break down all the invisible ties that bound together households, regions, occupations, and classes. Human social life, Guizot asserted, "is not confined to the material space or fleeting moments that are its theatre. It extends not only over all those relationships that are contracted over a whole territory, but also over all those that it can contract or conceive of contracting. It extends over the future as much as the present. People draw life from a thousand and one places that they do not inhabit and from a thousand and one moments that have not yet happened. If this living process of development is cut back; if people are forced to live within the narrow confines of their present material conditions of existence and isolate themselves in space and time, then social life is mutilated. Social life is no longer there."[39]

Recovery was a gradual process of reintegration. As Guizot presented it, the epicentre of the whole process was France. "Gaul was situated at the limits of the Roman and Germanic worlds. The south of Gaul was essentially Roman; the north essentially Germanic." Modern France was, therefore, heir to them both. "The civilization of England and Germany is above all Germanic; that of Italy and Spain, above all Roman. Only the civilization of France has had an equal share of both origins and, from the beginning, has reproduced the complexity and variety of the elements of modern society."[40] The assertion was an amplification of Sismondi's earlier claim about the dual origins of modern civilization. Guizot's account of how it had occurred was also similar to Sis-

---

38. Ibid., p. 373.

39. François Guizot, *Cours d'histoire moderne. Histoire de la civilisation en France depuis la chute de l'empire romain jusqu' en 1789* (Paris 1829), 8th lecture, pp. 298–99. For Tocqueville's use of the argument, see below, chapter 11.

40. Guizot, *Histoire de la civilisation en France*, 3rd ed., p. 37.

mondi's, but its focus fell less on the Italian republics of the Middle Ages and more instead on the relationship, also in the Middle Ages, between the feudal system and the emancipation of the communes. This was the relationship that produced the institutions and arrangements that enabled the towns to govern themselves.

Part of the process was caused by the decapitation of the upper echelons of the imperial system of administration and the elimination of the mechanisms of fiscal extraction that had previously been used to turn local resources into imperial patronage. The disappearance of the governors of the Roman provinces, together with the elimination of the *praesides, consulares,* and *correctores* of the imperial administration, left local rule in the hands of either the Germanic counts or the municipal magistrates. Although fiscal extraction continued, it now went to the local warlord rather than the imperial capital. For as long as their fiscal requirements were met, the Germanic counts tended to leave local affairs to the local *curia* or municipal magistrates. The resulting decentralization then helped to change the nature of municipal government itself. The disappearance of the upper echelons of the imperial administration meant that the combination of personal authority and appointment from above that was the hallmark of the old system of municipal government began to disappear, and this opened up room for the emergence of a combination of delegated authority and election from below. As municipal magistrates began to be elected rather than appointed, it became easier to see that their powers were delegated, not personal, and, under the aegis of these procedural and conceptual changes, the Roman municipality began to turn into the medieval commune.[41]

The process was magnified by the collapse of imperial authority on the one side and the culture of the Germanic invaders on the other. What Guizot called "the empire of personality" (*l'empire de la personnalité*)—meaning, he explained, "individual independence, that characteristic feature of modern civilization"—was Germanic in origin.[42] He went to some lengths to describe its attributes and qualities because, he argued, the impact on European history of what he also called "this characteristic of barbarism" had been considerable. Only the historian Augustin Thierry, in his *History of the Conquest of England by the Normans,* and the American writer James Fenimore Cooper in his accounts of the indigenous peoples of North America, personified by the figure of Leatherstocking, had come close to capturing the mixture of brutality, materialism, blind egoism, and individual independence that, appearances

41. Ibid., pp. 324–26.
42. Ibid., p. 334.

notwithstanding, made the resulting amalgam "a noble and moral sentiment." It was one that drew its power from "man's moral nature, from the pleasure of feeling human, from the feeling of personality, of human spontaneity in its free development." The prominence of this distinctively Germanic version of barbarism, Guizot emphasized, lay at the heart of the difference between the ancients and the moderns.

> It was by way of the Germanic barbarians that this sentiment was introduced to European civilization. It was unknown to the Roman world, unknown to the Christian church, unknown to almost all the ancient civilizations. When, in ancient civilizations, you find liberty, you find political liberty, the liberty of the citizen. A man was not concerned there with his liberty as a man, but with his liberty as a citizen. He belonged to an association, was devoted to that association, and was prepared to sacrifice himself to that association. The same applied to the Christian church, where there was either a great attachment to the Christian corporation, a devotion to its laws, and a lively need to expand its empire or there was a reaction by the individual upon himself and his soul and an inward effort to subdue his freedom and to subject himself to the requirements of his faith. The feeling of personal independence, the taste for unlimited freedom, with no other objective than its own satisfaction, was a feeling that was unknown to both Roman and Christian society.[43]

The strength of this taste for unlimited freedom meant, however, that it was implausible to claim, as several recent historians of the German nation had done, that the Germanic peoples really had been self-governing communities. Here, Guizot made a point of singling out a work entitled *Über das Gerichtswesen der Germanen* (An essay on the judicial system of the Germans) published in 1820 by a young legal scholar named Karl August Rögge. In it, Rögge had described the old system of trial by ordeal as a real system of self-government, based upon the "noble character" and "unlimited truthfulness" of the Germanic peoples. The modern jury system, he had claimed, was a pale shadow of this once-vibrant form of government. Guizot disagreed. Anyone, he commented, who had read the story of the *Nibelung* with its many episodes of treachery, betrayal, and brutality was unlikely to think that Rögge's description was a particularly accurate picture of ancient Germanic behaviour.[44] Barbarism was, ultimately, a system based upon force.

---

43. Guizot, *Histoire générale de la civilisation en Europe*, pp. 35–36.

44. Guizot, *Histoire de la civilisation en France*, 6th ed. (Paris, 1851), pp. 250, 254–55. On this aspect of Guizot's historical work, see Jean-Marie Moeglin, "François Guizot historien: à propos

As well as relishing their personal freedom, the Germanic peoples were also migrant warriors. In this aspect of their culture, personal freedom was combined with voluntary fidelity, which together gave rise to a system of military patronage that formed the nucleus of what became the feudal system. Here too, Guizot emphasized, the Germans were different from the Romans. For the Germans, allegiance was a relationship between individuals. In the ancient republics, on the other hand, "you would never find anyone freely and particularly attached to another man; they were all attached to the city-state (*cité*)."[45] The modern world had, therefore, a more varied set of origins than its ancient counterpart. It was a compound of municipal society, Christian society, and barbarian society. None of these elements was able to dominate the others, and, Guizot argued, it was this absence of uniformity that was the real source of the distinctive character of European civilization. It meant, in the first place, that European history after the fall of the Roman Empire was a history of conflict. The frequency and intensity of conflict had the effect of throwing a spotlight on the idea and principle of political legitimacy. Standardly, Guizot explained, the principal criterion for political legitimacy was simply durability and the passage of time. Age gave legitimacy to what was originally established by force. It did so because the mere fact of continuity could be taken as a sign that a government also had other attributes, like justice, reason, and truth, and these in turn could give a further and fuller content to the idea of political legitimacy. In Europe, the recurrent and protracted conflicts between the different components of the post-Roman world meant that the question of political legitimacy was both durably salient and never finally settled.

The resulting moral and political indeterminacy applied to the status of both persons and institutions. It meant that there were no fixed boundaries between freemen, bondsmen, slaves, and freed slaves, just as there were also no stable distinctions between different forms of ownership and types of property. These absences gave barbarism a longer life than might otherwise have been expected, a condition reinforced by the brutal individualism of

---

de la réfutation des thèses de Karl August Rögge dans l'*Histoire de la civilisation en France*," in *Des économies et des hommes. Mélanges offerts à Albert Broder*, ed. Florence Bourillon, Philippe Boutry, André Encrevé, and Béatrice Touchelay (Paris, Editions Bière, 2006), pp. 475–86; and his "Le 'droit de vengeance' chez les historiens du droit au moyen âge (xix–xx siècles)," in *La Vengeance*, ed. Dominique Barthélemy, François Bougard, and Régine Le Jan (Rome, Ecole Française de Rome, 2006), pp. 101–48. For a parallel, and fascinating, modern history, see James Q. Whitman, *The Origins of Reasonable Doubt* (New Haven, CT, Yale UP, 2008).

45. "Vous ne verrez dans les républiques anciennes aucun homme attaché spécialement et librement à un autre homme; ils étaient tous attaches à la cité." Guizot, *Histoire générale de la civilisation* [1828], p. 37.

Germanic culture. This was the setting in which "the empire of personality" was most influential and pronounced. As Guizot put it, "it presided over laws as well as actions." It meant that "the individuality of peoples, even when subject to the same political domination, was proclaimed as if it was the same as real individuality. Centuries were to pass before the notion of territoriality could displace the notion of race, and before legislation that was personal could once again become real and lead to the emergence of a new national unity from the slow, painful fusion of such disparate components."[46] Gradually, however, the human aspiration for a better life, the memories of Rome's former grandeur, and the order and discipline of the medieval church began to work in different ways to create the conditions for recovery. In many parts of Europe, the Germanic peoples started to keep legal records and draft legal codes. In Italy and southern France, vestiges of the Roman system of municipal government were revived or restored. In Spain, where the church had a strong presence among the Visigoths, legislation ceased to be personal and became territorial, making the same laws applicable to everyone, irrespective of whether they were Spanish, Roman, or Goth. In France, recovery began with the leadership of Charlemagne and the powerful obstacle to invasion represented by the immense empire that he formed. Slowly, the endless migration of peoples came to a stop. As it did, populations became more settled, and property more clearly defined. "On the one side, every man of standing established himself in his domains, alone with his family and servants. On the other, a certain hierarchy of services and rights began to be established among all those warlike proprietors dispersed over the territory."[47] Barbarism began to give way to feudalism.

Feudalism marked the apogee of "the empire of personality." It did so partly because it cemented the position of the great feudal lords as powers that were independent of both the church and the crown. It did so too because it inflated the independence and individual freedom that were already the hallmarks of barbarian society. A feudal lord was not only a warrior but was also a landowner, a head of a family, and master of a household. He had, Guizot commented, a far higher level of independence and standing than a Roman patrician. He was also a member of a smaller family with a more limited body of kin than any other family unit. He was not a biblical patriarch, nor the head of a clan. He had nothing in common with his servants or followers. "The population living alongside the owner of a fief was entirely alien to him. It did

---

46. Guizot, *The History of Civilization in France* [1828–30], in François Guizot, *Historical Essays and Lectures*, ed. Stanley Mellon (Chicago: U of Chicago Press, 1972), p. 334.

47. Guizot, *Histoire générale de la civilisation en Europe*, lecture 3, p. 32.

not bear his name. Between it and him there was no kinship, no family connection, no moral or historical tie."[48] The feudal family lived apart from the
rest of the population, alone in its château. "It was bound, obviously, to acquire
a distinctive character. It was enclosed, concentrated, called on ceaselessly to
defend itself, to be suspicious and at a minimum to isolate itself, even from its
servants. Domestic manners and its inner family life were bound to become
preponderant."[49] This, rather than the German woods, was the real setting
in which the influence of women began to grow, just as it was also the setting in
which the complex system of inheritance based upon the idea of primogeni-
ture began to take hold.

Feudalism was a system based on force. In it, force was embodied directly
in the person of the feudal lord. A priest could invoke the authority of god; a
despot could rely on his acolytes and clients. Nothing like them was available
to a feudal lord. His power was direct and personal, and this, Guizot explained,
was why feudal lords were hated so widely and so fiercely. But feudalism was
also a system of loyalty and fidelity based on strong personal obligations and
ties. The problem was that there was no stable or durable way to resolve the
deep-seated tension between these two aspects of the feudal system. "There
are," Guizot asserted, "no more than two possible systems of political guarantees." Either there had to be "the despotism of a single individual or body," or
there had to be "a free government." But neither the one nor the other could
exist under feudal conditions. Despotic power was simply too precarious to
maintain. Rights were simply too personal to be generally applicable. "When,"
Guizot argued, "we talk today about public power or what we call the rights of
sovereignty, the right to impose laws, to tax, and to punish, we believe and
think that these rights belong to no one, and that no one has a personal right
to punish others or impose a tax or law. These are rights that belong to society
as a whole, are exercised in its name, and are maintained not for itself but
for a higher purpose."[50] A free government, in short, presupposed an impersonal authority and an impersonal rationality.

48. Ibid., lecture 4, p. 15.

49. Ibid., lecture 4, p. 16.

50. "L'autre système, celui du gouvernement libre, d'un pouvoir public, d'une force publique,
était également impraticable; il n'a jamais pu naitre au sein de la féodalité. La cause en est simple.
Quand nous parlons aujourd'hui d'un pouvoir public, de ce que nous appelons les droits de la
souveraineté, le droit de donner les lois, de taxer, de punir, nous savons, nous pensons tous que
ces droits n'appartiennent à personne, que personne n'a pour son propre compte, le droit de
punir les autres, de leur imposer une charge, une loi. Ce sont là des droits qui n'appartiennent
qu'à la société en masse, qui sont exercés en son nom, qu'elle ne tient pas d'elle-même, qu'elle
reçoit de plus haut." Ibid., lecture 4, pp. 22–27 (pp. 26–27 for the passage cited).

Neither was available under feudal conditions. This meant that there was no political guarantee of social stability. Power was too local to become despotic but too personal for government to become free. The one remaining alternative was to federate. But, Guizot pointed out, "of all systems of government and political guarantees, the most difficult to establish and maintain is certainly the federal system (*système fédératif*)."

> This system involves leaving each locality, each particular society, with as large a portion of government as can remain, taking only the portion that is indispensable for maintaining society in general and moving it to the centre to constitute it as a central government. A federal system, which is logically the most simple, is, in fact, the most complex. Reconciling the degree of independence and local liberty that is allowed to remain with the degree of general order and general submission that in certain cases must also be presupposed and required calls for a very advanced civilization where, more than in any other system, human will and individual liberty both contribute to the establishment and maintenance of the system because coercive resources are far less available than anywhere else.[51]

In one sense, the feudal system contained all that was needed for a federal system. There had, after all, been many attempts by groups of barons or other feudal magnates to establish general procedures for conflict resolution and dispute settlement. "Generalized feudalism," Guizot wrote, "was a real federation. It was based on the same principles that, for example, have founded the federation of the United States of America."[52] But feudal power was ultimately too local and too personal to become federal.

The impasse gave rise to Guizot's most famous pronouncement. "Modern Europe," he announced in his seventh lecture, "was born of the struggle between the various classes of society."[53] It was the product of class struggle because, in a negative sense, impersonal authority could not be established in feudal society, and, more positively, because class struggle entailed the emancipation of the communes and the rise of the bourgeoisie. The two processes were connected because the instability of feudal society left urban society continuously exposed to conflict and plunder, and, at the same time, gave rise to a convergence of fiscal interests between royal authority and the urban bourgeoisie. Class struggle began with endemic conflict between feudal lords and the

51. Ibid., p. 29.
52. Ibid., pp. 29–30.
53. "L'Europe moderne est née de la lutte des divers classes de la société."Ibid., lecture 7, p. 29.

inhabitants of towns. In this context, the rebellious character of feudal society became a model for the rebellious character of urban society. Fortified châteaux were matched by fortified towns filled in turn by fortified houses. Communes rebelled against their feudal lords spontaneously and intermittently throughout the eleventh century, sealing victory with charters whose terms sometimes gave rise to further disputes. The legal character of enfranchisement and the convergence of interests between monarchs and municipalities meant that the emancipation of the commons was sometimes carried out under the aegis of royal power. But disputes over charters and privileges could also induce feudal lords to appeal to royal authority to support their claims. Monarchs, in keeping with the way that Constant was to describe them, began to hold the political balance in conflicts between the commons and their feudal lords. The real winners of the class struggle were Europe's monarchs.

The process had the effect of enhancing the status and authority of the royal courts and of supplying new sources of tax revenue to the royal government. The emancipation of the commons went hand in hand not only with the erosion of feudal privilege but also with the growth and consolidation of royal power. In this context, something like the opposite of the process that had caused the decline and fall of the Roman Empire took place. Instead of the hollowing out of imperial Rome under a centralized system of patronage and power, the hollowing out of feudal Europe enabled the towns to recover their capacity to govern themselves. In place of the fortified towns of the Middle Ages, Europe began to be dotted by the commercial towns of the modern age. The outcome was a further series of transformations as centralized royal government grew up alongside decentralized municipal government. The long-term effect of the process was that a "great social class, the bourgeoisie, was the necessary result of local bourgeois enfranchisement."[54] It was a process that had occurred most fully in Britain but was now also possible in France. In the Middle Ages, "the bourgeois nation was nothing and the commune everything." By the eighteenth century, "the bourgeois nation was everything and the commune nothing." The scene was now set for Sieyès's memorable question, "What is the Third Estate?" The answer, Guizot reminded his audience, was "everything."[55]

The transformation of the bourgeoisie was matched, finally, by the transformation of monarchy. This began to occur in the twelfth century and, in France under the aegis of Louis the Fat and Abbot Suger, with the gradual substitution of public power for personal power. "For the first time," Guizot announced, "it

54. Ibid., lecture 7, p. 27.
55. Ibid., lecture 7, pp. 9 and 5.

was possible to see, in a confused, incomplete, and feeble sense, a recognition of the idea of a public power, foreign to the local powers that society possessed, called upon to dispense justice to those unable to obtain it by ordinary means and, at the same time, able to impose order or, at least, to command it." It was this "great magistracy" with its judicial function that was "the real origin of modern royalty" because it was "the repository and protector of public order, general justice, and the common interest." With the emancipation of the bourgeoisie on the one side and the emergence of monarchy as a public power on the other, Guizot concluded, European societies had acquired their modern character, with the reduction of all the elements of society to their two most fundamental components: the government and the country (here, the word that Guizot used was *pays* with its undertones of something ordinary, popular, and general).[56] The first, in a sense, was already in place with the transformation of monarchy during the long century made up of the reigns of Louis XIV and Louis XV. That process had turned the fortified towns, privileged enclaves, and gated communities of medieval Europe into an open economic and social space. The burghers of the Middle Ages had become the *bourgeois* of the age of Louis XIV. But, as Sieyès's pamphlet showed, the power of government now had to be matched by the moral and political presence of the *pays* before a real combination of unity and multiplicity could be established. This, as Hegel had recognized, was the legacy of 1789, and this, for Guizot, was also the goal of the restored French monarchy.

There was, however, a further component of Guizot's story. This was the positive reevaluation of democracy that was so strong a feature of the modern age. Here, Guizot's explanation looked something like an anticipation of Nietzsche although it was more probably indebted to his translation of Gibbon many years earlier. Christianity, he argued in a long review essay on democracy in modern societies published in 1837, had been a religion for outcasts, among both the Hebrews and, later, the Romans.[57] Its early supporters had been the poor, the oppressed, and the marginal, or, as Guizot emphasized, all those usually associated with the stream of negative evaluations of democracy that were predominant in ancient philosophy from Plato to Aristotle and the Roman Stoics. Christianity, because of the disreputable status of its early followers, was almost the only religion to have developed entirely independently of the state and the institutions of political society. It was democratic but its collective cohesiveness was a product of the strongly spiritual values of the poor and outcast.

56. Ibid., lecture 9, pp. 31–34.

57. François Guizot, "De la démocratie dans les sociétés modernes," *Revue française* 3 (1837): 193–225.

Modern democracy grew out of the gradual and contingent imbrication of these values with the affairs of states, starting with the Romans and continuing with the origins and development of papal power. The addition of this secular dimension to Christianity made its commitment to equality and fraternity highly suitable as an ideology to legitimate resistance to inequality, injustice, and oppression. In this secular setting, Christianity intermittently became a religion of revolt and the source of all those movements that, over the past millennium, had been responsible for building individual liberty into modern life. This, Guizot claimed, had been the positive effect of Christianity. Its negative effects, however, still had to be addressed, first by restoring the purely private quality of religious belief and life, and, second, by superimposing the institutions and arrangements of representative government upon the resistance theories that were the original core of modern democratic politics. To his critics, Guizot's vision of politics amounted to pantheism for some, Hegelianism for others, and, possibly, bad things for all.

Hegelians and Saint-Simonians

Guizot may or may not have read Hegel. Whether or not he actually did, there was a recognizable similarity between their respective specifications of the family, civil society, and the state as the fundamental nexus of modern politics. The similarity extended beyond the reciprocities of domestic life or the liberty of economic life because it also applied to the state and to the fundamentally impersonal character of its legitimacy and authority. It extended too to the strongly historical orientation of their moral and political thought. For both, irrespective of whether there was any genuine conceptual common ground—meaning, substantively, whether or not Guizot's concept of the bourgeoisie was a deliberately chosen conceptual equivalent of Hegel's concept of *bürgerliche Gesellschaft*, which is what, in most respects, it appears to be—modern political arrangements appeared to owe as much to history as to rationality. This, however, was both a strength and a weakness. If, on the one side, their common historical orientation helped to explain the gulf that existed between the values, arrangements, and possibilities available, respectively, to the ancients and the moderns, it also, on the other side, exposed them both to the claim that other values, arrangements, and possibilities could also become available from history's capacious resources.

This, it could be said, is where the problem of historicism began because this was the context in which, in the 1840s, the word itself began to be given a more positive sense. Earlier, with Herder, Jacobi, Novalis, and the Schlegel brothers, *Historismus* was a term that was used to refer to what they took to be Kant's failure to supply any historical justification of his unusual claims about

autonomy as one of history's goals. This criticism was countered, notably by
Fichte and Hegel, by the claim that there was real evidence to show that autonomy was a personal capacity that still, however, called for special historical
conditions to be compatible with human society. It was more difficult, however, to try to do the same thing to the concept of impersonal rationality,
because it was, by definition, *impersonal*, and since it could not be personal, it
had to be either logical or historical. The next, but fatal, step, was to equate the
logical with the historical and to argue, not that humans were like gods as Jacobi had complained about Kant, but that history really was. Hegel certainly
played a part in the process by picking up a phrase, *Die Weltgeschichte ist das
Weltgericht*, meaning "the history of the world is the judgment of the world,"
from Friedrich Schiller's poem "Resignation," and by going on to turn it into
something different from what Schiller had intended it to mean. When, in
1784, Schiller gave the poem its bleak title, it was designed to raise a question
mark against the Christian doctrine of rewards and punishments. This life, the
poem announced, was for enjoyment, while the next life was for hope, but
there was nothing to link the one to the other. This was why the only conceivable judgment of the merits of any individual life was the judgment of posterity or of world history.[58] The subject of the poem was, therefore, very similar
to the one that, at very much the same time, separated Herder from Kant over
the philosophy of history. As Schiller's first French translator, Prosper de Barante (another member of the Coppet group), noted, the poem meant that
"what has been, has been, and that is the end of the matter," a verdict, Barante
commented, that was "certainly to deny Providence and morality." But, as Barante then went on to point out, to persist in endorsing disinterested virtue in
the face of this bleak assessment was to seek, if it was possible, to combine
what he called "faith with scepticism," or "the revolt of a religious heart against
a harmful error of the mind."[59] From this perspective, the poem was some-

58. For an English version of the poem, see *Schiller's Poems and Plays*, ed. Frederick Morley
(London, Routledge, 1890), pp. 156–58, and, for a bilingual German-French version, see Schiller,
Poèmes philosophiques, ed. Robert d'Harcourt (Paris, Aubier, 1954), pp. 64–71. For helpful interpretations of its content, see Beiser, *Schiller as Philosopher*, 2:20, and Reinhart Koselleck,
Sediments of Time: On Possible Histories (Stanford, Stanford UP, 2018), p. 124. Thanks to Charlotte Johann for guidance with the German original. On the connection between the phrase
and the idea of the verdict of posterity, see Rosen, *The Shadow of God*.

59. "Dire 'l'histoire du monde, voilà le jugement du monde' ou, en d'autres termes, 'ce qui a
été a été, et tout est fini par là' c'est assurément nier la Providence et la morale. Mais professer
en même temps le culte désintéressé de la vertu, c'est rapprocher s'il est possible le scepticisme
de la foi; c'est la révolte d'un cœur religieux contre une funeste erreur de l'esprit." Prosper de
Barante, "Vie de Schiller," in Schiller, *Œuvres dramatiques* (Paris, 1834), p. 50. See also the en-

thing like Schiller's version of Jean-Jacques Rousseau's *Profession of Faith of a Savoyard Vicar*. On its terms, there were choices, not goals, because the only goal that mattered was to hope for further choice. Although it is not clear whether this was Schiller's intention, it was, in its way, a poetic rendition of Kant's *Idea of Universal History*.

Hegel switched the focus of the poem from its original subject (resignation) to its palliative (history). Several of his followers went one step further and turned the palliative into the subject. Some came to be known as "Young Hegelians," and this is usually taken to mean that they were critics of Hegel. Others, however, were the French Saint-Simonians, and it is not entirely clear whether they were critics or supporters of Hegel.[60] According to several of their contemporaries, the intellectual origins of Saint-Simonianism were as much German as French because almost all of its important ideas were an outcome of the way that Rousseau's thought had been picked up, first by Kant, and then more fully by Fichte, before coming back to France in this Fichtean, but also Hegelian, guise. The result, particularly in the immediate aftermath of the revolution of July 1830, was that France came to house two versions of Hegelianism. One was the version associated with Cousin and Guizot, with its emphasis on representative government, bourgeois society, and the impersonality of reason. The other was the version of Saint-Simon and the Saint-Simonians, with its emphasis on representative government, industrial society, and the impersonality of science. Although they had a great deal in common, they were not obviously compatible. "They believed," wrote one hostile critic of the Saint-Simonians, "that having arrived at a palingenetic epoch, they were the agents of the regeneration that God had provided for humanity."[61] It is unlikely that comments like this were directed at Guizot or Cousin.

The overlap between German philosophy and Saint-Simonian political economy was described quite fully in a number of issues of a royalist periodical entitled *Le Catholique* that began to appear in January 1826. Its editor, and the author of much of its content, was a rather unusual man of letters named

---

dorsement of Barante's reading of the poem in *The Minor Poems of Schiller*, ed. John Herman Merivale (London, 1844), pp. 12, 371–72.

60. For examinations of the question, see Michel Espagne, "Le saint-simonisme est-il jeune hégélien?" in *Regards sur le saint-simonisme et les saint-simoniens*, ed. Jean-René Derré (Lyon, 1986), pp. 45–71; Régnier, "Les saint-simoniens et la philosophie allemande" and his "La question romantique." For indications of an overlap between Hegel and the Saint-Simonians on the subject of aesthetics, see Philippe Régnier, "Saint-Simon, les saint-simoniens et les siècles dits 'classiques,'" in *Les âges classiques du dix-neuvième siècle*, ed. Delphine Antoine-Mahut and Stéphane Zékian (Paris, Editions des archives contemporaines, 2018), pp. 215–39.

61. H. Cavel, *Epitaphe des partis; celui dit du juste-milieu, son avenir* (Paris, 1833), p. 34.

Ferdinand, baron d'Eckstein (1790–1861). He was both a native German
speaker and also quite well acquainted with recent developments in German
philosophy.[62] It is not clear whether he really was a baron or even whether his
name was actually Eckstein. He was a member of a German Jewish family who
grew up in Denmark and converted, first to Lutheranism, then to Catholicism,
before settling in France after a tumultuous involvement in royalist politics in
Belgium and Austria during the final years of Napoleon's rule. In later life he
came to be known as Baron Buddha, partly because of his sustained and sophisticated interest in comparative religion and Buddhism in particular, and
partly, it should be added, because only Heinrich Heine could have thought
of a name like that. His consistent intellectual curiosity meant that Eckstein's
views were usually regarded with suspicion both by dogmatic Catholics and
by more secularly minded positivists. In later life, particularly after 1848, he
became part of the circle of reform-minded Catholics associated with the
comte de Montalembert and the periodical *Le Correspondant*.[63] But, as Eck-

62. On Eckstein, see François Berthiot, *Le baron d'Eckstein, journaliste et critique littéraire*
(Paris, Editions des Ecrivains, 1998); Nicolas Burtin, *Le baron d'Eckstein. Un semeur d'idées au
temps de la Restauration* (Paris, 1931); Louis Le Guillou (ed.), *Lettres inédites du baron d'Eckstein:
société et littérature à Paris en 1838–40* (Paris, PU de France, 1984); and Louis Le Guillou, ed., *Le
'baron' d'Eckstein et ses contemporains: Lamennais, Lacordaire, Montalembert, Foisset, Michelet,
Renan, Hugo, etc.: correspondances avec un choix de ses articles* (Paris, Champion, 2003). See also
Arthur McCalla, "Paganism in Restoration France: Eckstein's Traditionalist Orientalism," *Journal of the History of Ideas* 76 (2015): 563–85; Joseph Lecler, "Montalembert et le baron d'Eckstein.
En suivant leur correspondance inédite," *Revue d'histoire de l'Eglise de France* 56 (1970): 47–70;
Christian Maréchal, "L'abbé de La Mennais, le comte de Montlosier et le baron d'Eckstein: un
probleme d'influence," *Revue d'histoire litteraire de la France* 50 (1950): 16–26; Giovanni Bonacina, "Hegel, il barone d'Eckstein e 'L'ala erudite della Congrégation,'" *Rivista di Storia della
Filosofia* 60 (2005): 409–41; Régnier, "La question romantique"; and Paul Rowe, *A Mirror on
the Rhine? The Nouvelle Revue Germanique, Strasbourg 1829–1837* (Bern, Peter Lang, 2000), p. 17.
Further information on Eckstein can be found in Franz Liszt, Marie d'Agoult, *Correspondance*,
ed. Serge Gut and Jacqueline Bellas (Paris, Fayard, 2001), and his correspondence with the
comtesse d'Agoult (aka Daniel Stern), published in Marie de Flavigny, comtesse d'Agoult, *Correspondance générale*, 12 vols. (Paris, Champion, 2003–22).

63. On this circle, see Louis de Carné, *Souvenirs de ma jeunesse au temps de la Restauration*
(Paris, 1872), pp. 38, 162–66, 170, 340; Charles de Lacombe, "Le comte de Serre," *Le Correspondant* 75 (1878): 257–60; Jean des Cognets, "Lamartine et le comte de Carné d'après des documents inédits," *Le Correspondant* 273 (1925): 830–52, and his "Autour du vieux roi Lamartine,"
Le Correspondant 275 (1927): 481–517. See too Eckstein's four-part "Essai d'une philosophie de
l'histoire," published in *Le Correspondant* of 25 February, 25 April, 25 July, and 25 November 1854.
It was followed by further articles in the same periodical on 25 August 1857, 25 November 1858,
and 25 June 1860.

stein himself recognized, his philosophical and theological interests owed a great deal to the ideas of his intellectual idols, the German philosophers Wilhelm von Humboldt and, more particularly, the Catholic convert and philosopher of romanticism Friedrich Schlegel.[64] Eckstein's intellectual debt to Humboldt and Schlegel was not, however, limited to the study of comparative religion. It also gave him the reasons for his identification of Rousseau as the inadvertent source of the Saint-Simonian concept of industrialism. Here, he was drawing on an approach to Rousseau's thought that was once well known in the German-speaking parts of Europe because, with different degrees of emphasis, it was shared by Kant, Schiller, Fichte, and Hegel as well as by Humboldt and Schlegel.[65]

Eckstein began to describe the linkage of Rousseau, Fichte, and the concept of industrialism in a survey of French political alignments and divisions that he published as an introduction to the very first issue of *Le Catholique* in January 1826. The survey presented a summary of how Rousseau's thought had been picked up in the German-speaking parts of Europe, particularly by Fichte, and had then come back to France in the guise of industrialism. Alongside the group known as the *Doctrinaires*, whose ranks Eckstein noted included "all that is most honourable and most worthy of esteem that liberal France possesses" (the allusions here were to Cousin and Guizot, along with their older mentor Pierre-Paul Royer-Collard), there were also three other varieties of "liberalism," adding up to what Eckstein had no hesitation in calling "the left." These latter three types of liberalism, he wrote, were variously "Voltairian," sentimental, and industrial (*voltairien, sentimental et industriel*). The first took its largely anticlerical cue from Voltaire's intellectual allies, the eighteenth-century French Encyclopaedists, while the two others followed the system of what Eckstein called "the economists" insofar as they agreed with, or diverged from, the opinions of Jean-Jacques Rousseau.[66] These latter two strands of liberalism, Eckstein continued, "divided into a productive and industrial

64. "Citer M. de Humboldt, c'est s'engager à ne rien ajouter à ce nom justement célèbre: je ne connais personne que l'on puisse placer au-dessus de lui pour l'instruction riche et variée, pour l'érudition profonde. A Vienne, surtout, M. de Schlegel (Fréderic) m'attira, et son amitié m'honorait. Il aimait mon enthousiasme et jusqu'aux derniers moments de sa vie, il prit un vif intérêt à mes travaux." Eckstein, "De ma carrière politique et littéraire en France et dans les Pays-Bas," *Le Catholique* 14 (1829): 338. For further indications, particularly of Eckstein's admiration of Schlegel, see Burtin, *Eckstein*, pp. 10 n. 2, 16–17, 33, 70, 118, 125–26, 215, 255, 340, 351–52, 355, 364 n. 2, 388.

65. On this aspect of Rousseau's legacy, see Sonenscher, *Jean-Jacques Rousseau*, pp. 141–77.

66. On this argument, see Michael Sonenscher, "Jean-Jacques Rousseau and the Foundations of Modern Political Thought," *Modern Intellectual History* 14 (2017): 311–37.

school on the one hand and a *sentimental* school that takes pride in its *religiosity* on the other, sometimes fall into quite entertaining disputes, but, at the least sign of danger, are always ready to unite and place their Rousseauesque theory (*théorie à la Jean-Jacques*) under the auspices of their doctrine of industrialism."[67] On Eckstein's terms, although the word "industrialism" was not available in Rousseau's works, the "doctrine of industrialism" was still compatible with Rousseau's thought.

Industrialism, Eckstein wrote in a later article published in *Le Catholique* in February 1827, was a new name for what had previously been called "luxury." To pretend that it was the basis of the prosperity of states, he added disdainfully, was "a shameful doctrine, if ever there was one."[68] Industry, he conceded, was certainly useful because it maintained a taste for elegance and helped to develop the genius of the arts. This, he acknowledged, had to be recognized, just as it was also right to recognize that it was a mistake to make landed property the sole basis of the well-being and security of states. But to turn acknowledgement of industry into a dogma named industrialism was, Eckstein stated flatly, "to turn the social order into a republic of beavers, ants, or bees."[69] This drift into dogma had occurred, he argued, because, after the failed republicanism of the revolution and the subsequent despotism of Napoleon, nothing else was available as a value that could be an object of political allegiance for the supporters of the revolution's original principles. "Liberalism's present-day tribunes and pamphleteers," Eckstein wrote, "are obliged to preach industrialism as the sole guarantee of what remains of the revolution's last breath." In one version, industrialism had become the "new industrial

---

67. Ferdinand, baron d'Eckstein, "Introduction," *Le Catholique* 1 (1826): 6–8: "La France libérale suit deux bannières différentes qui furent, au siècle de Louis XV, arborées par les coryphées de ses doctrines. Elle adhère, d'une part, aux systèmes des Encyclopédistes, de l'autre, à celui des Economistes, en tant que ces derniers se rapprochent ou diffèrent des opinions de Jean-Jacques Rousseau. . . . Tandis que les successeurs des Encyclopédistes nient, persiflent, et métamorphosent leurs raisons, bonnes ou mauvaises, en sarcasmes amers, les Economistes du jour sont les meilleurs gens du monde. Divisés en une école productive et industrielle, et en une école *sentimentale* qui s'enorgueillit de sa religiosité, ils se livrent parfois entre eux des combats assez plaisants; mais, au moindre signe de danger, ils sont toujours prêts à se réunir pour placer leur théorie à la Jean-Jacques sous les auspices de leur doctrine d'*industrialisme*." For a recent examination of the divisions within French liberalism, see Lucien Jaume, "The Unity, Diversity, and Paradoxes of French Liberalism," in *French Liberalism from Montesquieu to the Present Day*, ed. Raf Geenens and Helena Rosenblatt (Cambridge, CUP, 2012), pp. 36–54.

68. "Parer le luxe du nom d'industrialisme, et prétendre fonder sur lui la prospérité des états, est une doctrine méprisable, s'il en fut jamais." *Le Catholique* 5 (1827): 233.

69. Ibid., p. 234.

religion" of the comte de Saint-Simon and the Saint-Simonian movement whose periodical, *Le Producteur*, began to appear in 1826, the same year as the inaugural issue of *Le Catholique*. This type of industrialism, Eckstein wrote, was "the industrialism of the ell and the yard (*industrialisme de l'aune et de la toise*)."[70] But there was also another version of industrialism. This second version was what Eckstein called the "transcendental industrialism" of Fichte's book *Der geschlossen Handelstaat*, a title that is usually translated as "The closed commercial state" but which Eckstein translated as "The completed social order, such that industry serves as its base."[71]

Saint-Simon, Eckstein reported, had been trying to realize a sort of "industrial Catholicism" that had won the support of some liberals, to the alarm of some others, headed by Benjamin Constant. The latter, however, had no reason to be alarmed because, Eckstein predicted confidently, there was no prospect that the "mandarinate of chemists, geometricians, and naturalists" of Saint-Simon's dreams would ever produce any noticeable results. The same applied to Fichte's "transcendental industrialism." His followers had not really understood his system, and their attempts to apply his ideas had eventuated in a type of "ridiculous and barbaric Teutonism" before it had died away to become a more restrained and dull German liberalism.[72] Eckstein's verdict was matched by a parallel assessment of Saint-Simonianism and its putative sources. In this assessment the source was to be found in the thought of a now far less famous German philosopher named Karl Christian Friedrich Krause. Krause was a contemporary of Hegel's but had a far less successful academic career. Shortly before he died, in the year after Hegel's death, he had given the Saint-Simonians his broad approval. Their doctrine, he wrote in a letter in 1831, amounted to a combination of "*German* thought

70. Ibid., p. 233.

71. "l'ordre social achevé, tel que l'industrie lui sert de base": *Le Catholique* 5 (1827): 241. For the earlier citation, see ibid., p. 236: "Les tribuns et les pamphlétaires actuels du libéralisme, sont obligés de prêcher l'industrialisme, comme unique garantie qui reste à la révolution expirante." For a helpful discussion of this aspect of Fichte's thought, see Nakhimovsky, *The Closed Commercial State*, notably p. 164 for an illuminating comparison between Rousseau and Fichte made by the early nineteenth-century German critic and *salonnière* Rahel Varnhagen. For parallel discussions in the circle around Auguste Comte (who began as a follower of Saint-Simon), see Régnier, "Les Saint-simoniens et la philosophie allemande." As Comte's disciple Gustave d'Eichtal wrote of Rousseau in 1825: "C'est le seul de nos philosophes dont les Allemands tiennent encore compte, et c'est une chose très connue que c'est Rousseau qui a développé Kant" (cited by Régnier, p. 234).

72. Eckstein, in *Le Catholique* 5 (1827): 242.

coupled with *French* feeling for life (*Lebensinn*)."[73] He also made it clear that he took Saint-Simonianism to be a less sophisticated version of his own moral and political thought. The same assessment was made in an article published in the French *Revue Encyclopédique* in 1831, which noted that Krause was close to, but critical of, Saint-Simon and the Saint-Simonians. "In recent times," the article stated, "the religious and political ideas of the disciples of Saint-Simon began to penetrate Germany, and it then began to be remembered that Krause had already expounded a doctrine which has the most numerous analogies to the Saint-Simonian doctrine."[74]

The possible common ground was also apparent to Krause's critics who, in the course of a series of bitter arguments between different strands of Belgian Catholicism towards the end of the same decade over the putatively pantheistic character of Krause's philosophy, accused Krause's Belgian followers of actually being followers of Saint-Simon. But the overlap was described more sympathetically in a three-part article headed "Contemporary Socialist Philosophers" that was published in 1844 in the *Revue Indépendante*, a periodical published by the socialist philosopher Pierre Leroux together with his now far better known friend, George Sand.[75] According to its author, a man named Pascal

73. Karl Christian Friedrich Krause, *Briefwechsel*, ed. Paul Hohlfeld and Auguste Wünsche, 2 vols. (Leipzig, 1903–7), 2:246. For further comments on the Saint-Simonians, see 2:206, 224, 236–37, 246, 270–72, 625–28.

74. "Dans ces derniers temps, les idées politiques et religieuses des disciples de Saint-Simon pénètrent en Allemagne, et alors on s'est souvenu que Krause avait déjà exposé une doctrine qui a les plus nombreuses analogies avec la doctrine saint-simonienne." Heinrich Ahrens, "Tendance sociale et religieuse de la philosophie allemande," *Revue Encyclopédique* 52 (1831): 686–95 (p. 687). Ahrens, in a note on the same page, added that the parallel had also been made by Friedrich Wilhelm Carové in his *Der Saint-Simonismus und die Philosophie des 19ten Jahrhunderts in Frankreich* in 1831 and in the *Blätter für literarische Unterhaltung*. Ahrens highlighted the similarity a second time in an article entitled "Uber den Saint-Simonismus in seiner letsten religiosen, moralischen und politischen Entwicklung," which was published in *Das Ausland* 190 (8 July 1832): 757–58; 191 (9 July 1832): 761–62; 192 (10 July 1832): 766–67. For a helpful overview, see John Bartier, *Naissance du socialisme en Belgique. Les Saint-Simoniens* (Brussels, Présence et Action Culturelles, 1985), pp. 124–31.

75. Pascal Duprat, "Les philosophes socialistes contemporains," *Revue Indépendante* 12 (1844): 35–55; 13 (1844): 465–500; 14 (1844): 5–35. As Duprat noted in a further article, published at the same time in the same periodical, "Il y a dans les ouvrages de Krause une critique approfondie de Hegel, que l'école hégélienne n'a pas encore réfutée." On this see Jacques Grandjonc, *Marx et les communistes allemands à Paris* (Paris, Maspero, 1974), p. 115 n. 6. Duprat's involvement with the philosophy of Krause continued into his exile in Brussels after 1848 when he edited a periodical entitled *La Libre Recherche*. For an overview, see [Anon.], "Le mouvement philosophique en Belgique apprécié par l'Allemagne," *La Libre Recherche* 9 (1858): 132–37, and,

Duprat, Krause, Leroux, and Sand were all socialists, but still not the same type of socialist as the Saint-Simonians. Duprat, according to one hostile commentator, had been able to make Krause look like a socialist just as he would have made Goethe look like a republican. But, according to another student of German philosophy writing at the same time, "Krause is a socialist philosopher in the purest sense of the word, as too was Kant, and as is the case with all philosophers who combine knowledge of human nature with love of humanity."[76]

The parallels between Saint-Simonianism and the thought of Fichte and Krause was subsequently extended to a further parallel between the Hegelians and the Saint-Simonians. It was made by a Polish exile living in Paris named August Cieszkowski, whose publications formed a link between German-language discussions of Hegel after his death in 1831 and those produced after 1830 by the Saint-Simonians.[77] The best-known of these was a book entitled *Prolegomena zur Historiosophie* (Prolegomena to historiosophy) that was published in Berlin in 1838. It was followed, less than a year later, by the work that helps to explain why, in 1850, Cieszkowski was offered the position of Prussian

more generally, see Pierre Viaud, *Une humanité affranchie de Dieu au xix siècle* (Paris, Cerf, 1994), pp. 171–96.

76. The parallel between making Krause a socialist and making Goethe a republican was articulated by Karl Grün, *Die soziale Bewegung in Frankreich und Belgien* (Darmstadt, 1845), p. 317. "Krause est un philosophe socialiste, dans la plus pure acception de ce mot, comme le fut Kant, et dans le même sens que celui-ci, comme le sont nécessairement tous les philosophes, qui à l'amour de l'humanité unissent la connaissance des hommes." Joseph Willm, *Histoire de la philosophie allemande depuis Kant jusqu'à Hegel*, 4 vols. (Paris, 1846–49), 4:443. Willm also quoted a passage from Krause's *Philosophie der Geschichte* pointing out that the Saint-Simonians objected to constitutional government because, they claimed, it was based upon suspicion, although they themselves expected blind and unconditional trust in their own hierarchical organization. Trust, Krause wrote, has to be deserved and cannot be given to promises of what is impossible. Ibid., p. 444.

77. On Cieszkowski, see the fine study by André Liebich, *Between Ideology and Utopia* (Dordrecht, 1979), and, helpfully, Laurence Dickey, "Saint-Simonian Industrialism as the End of History: August Cieszkowski and the Teleology of Universal History," in *Apocalypse Theory and the Ends of the World*, ed. Malcolm Bull (Oxford, Blackwell, 1995), pp. 159–99. See too Lichtheim, *The Origins of Socialism*, pp. 271–72; Christophe Bouton, "L'histoire de l'avenir. Cieszkowski lecteur de Hegel," *Revue Germanique Internationale* 8 (2008): 77–92; Andrej Walicki, *Philosophy and Romantic Nationalism: The Case of Poland* (Oxford, OUP, 1982), pp. 127–51, 295–307, and his *Russia, Poland, and Universal Regeneration* (Notre Dame, IN, U of Notre Dame Press, 1991), pp. 73–106; as well as Leszek Kolakowski, *Main Currents of Marxism*, 3 vols. (Oxford, Clarendon Press, 1978), 1:85–88. For English translations of Cieszkowski's works, see August Cieszkowski, *Selected Writings*, ed. André Liebich (Cambridge, CUP, 1979), and Lawrence S. Stepelevich, ed., *The Young Hegelians: An Anthology* (Cambridge, CUP, 1983), pp. 55–89.

minister of finance. This was a book, this time published in Paris, entitled *Du crédit et de la circulation* (On credit and circulation). Although the titles of the two books were very different, their content was actually very similar because the first of the two laid out the Hegelian theory of history (historiosophy) that the second book was designed to implement. As Cieszkowski presented it, public debt was the engine of modern history and the means to bring human history and human agency into the kind of self-conscious alignment that would enable humanity to become the subject and object of its own choices.

Autonomy, from this perspective, would become a collective rather than a purely individual capacity. The move meant that, just as there was a strong similarity between Hegel and Guizot, so there was also a strong similarity between Cieszkowski and the thought of the French Saint-Simonians. Both subscribed to the idea of history as a purposeful process that, one day, would be guided by a real human subject. Both also subscribed to the idea of using the financial resources of the modern state to become the basis of a less gradual and more centrally directed programme of economic and social redistribution and reform than anything that Hegel or Guizot envisaged. Cieszkowski, in addition, made it very clear that this combination of history, public credit, and social reform was the real meaning of romanticism. In this version of the connection between public debt and political romanticism, the link was based on a philosophy of history (Cieszkowski called it a historiosophy) that was somewhat different from Hegel's, because Cieszkowski's vision of history culminated in the idea that humanity would take charge of its own destiny. There was no room for the Owl of Minerva in Cieszkowski's historiosophy.

Cieszkowski divided this philosophy of history into three broad epochs. "Before Christianity," he wrote, "there was an age of exteriority and immediate objectivity." In subjective terms, it was an age of sensibility and physical beauty. In objective terms, it was an age of abstract principle symbolized by the severity and formalism of Roman law. In both, the outside ruled the inside. In the second epoch, and with the emergence of the Christian-Germanic world, the value of truth was added to the value of beauty. In it, the Christian emphasis on "interiority, reflexion, and subjectivity" enabled sensibility to become "internal consciousness in general," and "law to reach the level of morality." Here, the inside ruled the outside. These were the two epochs that had brought the history of the modern age up to the present. Cieszkowski called the first epoch "the classical edifice" or the "classical architectonic" of his historiosophy, while the second was its "Gothic construction" or its "romantic architectonic."[78] If

---

78. August Cieszkowski, *Prolégomènes à l'historiosophie*, trans. Michel Jacob (Paris, Editions Champ Libre, 1973), p. 72.

the hallmark of the first epoch was beauty (or what was external to consciousness because it was on the outside), while that of the second was truth (or what
was internal to consciousness because it was on the inside), then the hallmark
of the third epoch would be "absolute goodness" and "absolute teleology" (or
the creative activity involved in transferring what was inside to the outside). The
transition from the first to the second epoch, he explained, had been produced
by the barbarian invasions that precipitated the decline and fall of imperial
Rome. The third epoch, Cieszkowski announced, was presently beginning, and
it too would be the product of migration and invasion. Unlike the transition
from the first to the second epoch, this third epoch would be inaugurated by
a reversal of the great migrations that had brought the Roman Empire to an
end. Instead of the barbarian invasions that had inaugurated the second epoch,
the new migrations would involve "civilized nations submerging peoples who
are still barbarous." Where the earlier invasions were the work of "brute force,"
their modern counterparts would be the work of "spiritual force," bringing
backward societies up to the level of advanced societies. "Consequently,"
Cieszkowski wrote, "raising up natural peoples to the more spiritual levels
reached here will raise us up too and will renovate those aspects of nature that
have been corrupted in us. This revenge of the universal spirit, with the second
great wave of reverse migration that it entails, will be the inevitable transition
to the third period."[79] It was an unusually sanguine, but not entirely fanciful,
prediction of the great settler empires that were to dominate Europe's history
for much of the rest of the century.

To Cieszkowski, the third epoch also offered the prospect of the general
emancipation of humanity. The basis of his claim, however, was a real deviation from Hegel's philosophy. Hegel, he wrote, had been right to show how consciousness gave the mind an extra dimension, but had failed to see that
consciousness itself could also have an extra dimension by willing to enact
what it had come to think. The will, in short, was not simply a derivation of
an idea but was instead a more dynamic synthesis of theory and practice.
"According to Hegel," Cieszkowski wrote, "the will is a particular mode of
thought, which is the wrong way to conceive of it. Instead, thought is simply
a constituent element of the will because will and action are nothing more
than thought that reverts to being."[80] The will, in short, could give being a
new being. The three attributes of the mind—as perception, consciousness,
and will—corresponded to the three attributes of history—as beauty, truth,

79. Ibid., pp. 28–29, 31–33. Compare to Andrews, "The Romantic Socialist Origins of Humanitarianism," although Cieszkowski is not mentioned in her article.

80. Cieszkowski, *Prolégomènes*, p. 109.

and goodness—to promise a new age of human association in which an institutionalized synthesis of all these principles would enable humanity to
remake itself. Unsurprisingly, Cieszkowski subscribed very strongly to the idea
of palingenesis.[81] Hegel, Cieszkowski argued, had been misled by the distinction between theory and practice, with theory appearing to belong to the
realm of ideas and practice to the realm of reality. But the real distinction, he
claimed, was between the ideal and the material. Enacting an idea was not
simply a matter of translating theory into practice, but also a matter of turning
something ideal into something real. The will, in other words, could create a
radically different real world from the world as it was. It could do so, subjec-
tively, by means of "the adequate perfecting of the will," but also objectively,
by means of the "adequate perfecting of political life."[82] The process would
be entirely similar to the transition from "classical art" to "romantic art." In
that case, art had remained art, even though it had lost its broader moral and
epistemological status. In the transition from the second to the third epoch,
philosophy would remain philosophy, but it too would lose its broader moral
and epistemological status. In place of philosophy, there would now be the
new combination of thought and action that would effectively enable humanity to make itself. Cieszkowski did not describe the long-term goal of this
process in any detail. Instead, he gestured towards what he called "the system
of Fourier," meaning the thought of the early nineteenth-century French socialist Charles Fourier. Fourier's system, he wrote, was "an important step"
towards the development of "organic truth within reality." It amounted to "a
direct reconciliation of the principle of Plato and that of Rousseau" and, for
this reason, had an "immense bearing on the future."[83] Plato's principle was
classical; Rousseau's was romantic. A real synthesis of the two was what the
third historical epoch had the potential to deliver.

Much of the substance of how that synthesis was to be achieved was set out
in Cieszkowski's *Du credit et de la circulation*. He illustrated its main idea by
quoting a statement made by the early eighteenth-century Scottish financier
John Law. "It is the responsibility of the sovereign to give credit, not to be
given it," Law was reported to have said. This, Cieszkowski wrote, was undoubtedly "one of the most fruitful ideas ever to be issued in political economy." It was, he continued, "almost incomprehensible that, having succeeding
in organizing a *single, centralized, guaranteed* monetary system, states should
voluntarily surrender the analogous attribute in the organization of circulation

81. He was in fact the author of a work entitled *Gott und Palingenesie* (Berlin, 1842).
82. Cieszkowski, *Prolégomènes*, p. 110.
83. Ibid., pp. 130–31.

and general credit. A government's right to mint money is one that has never been reasonably disputed, but the entirely analogous right to issue circulating assets is one that governments have never claimed."[84] It was now time, he argued, to develop and improve upon Law's fundamental idea by creating a centralized system of public and private credit to be managed by a state-owned public bank. The way to do this was to use credit to turn fixed assets into circulating assets and, inversely, to use taxes to turn circulating assets into fixed assets. The value of the fixed assets could be made to circulate by the issuing of interest-bearing stocks and shares underpinned by a fiat currency, while the value of the circulating assets could be fixed by the use of the tax system to generate enough income to cover the interest payments on the circulating currency. Private credit would, therefore, be reinforced by public credit, while more capital would circulate within the economy, and the state, rather than private capital, would be the real beneficiary of the profits generated by the rising level of economic activity. "If," according to a summary of his system published some years later, "Ricardo could say that circulation will never reach its highest level of development until it is carried out entirely on paper, Cieszkowski has gone further by asserting that the normal medium-term level of circulation should be made increasingly ideal and become a *relationship*, measured by an *interest rate*"[85]

The system would work like a giant development bank based, ultimately, on the state's ability to create and manage a fiat currency. In many respects, Cieszkowski's theory of public credit was similar to the one set out a decade or so later by Lorenz von Stein. It also appealed very strongly to the French political reformer Pierre-Joseph Proudhon, whose own, controversial, views on property overlapped with Cieszkowski's. "Will M. Cieszkowski's system be put into practice?" he asked rhetorically in 1848 in his *Système des contradictions économiques*. His answer was unequivocally positive. "All ideas in France revolve around mortgage reform and the organization of land credit, two things that in a more or less acknowledged form necessarily imply the application of this system. M. Cieszkowski, like a true artist, has traced the idea

84. August Cieszkowski, *Du crédit et de la circulation* (Paris, 1839), p. 99. On the still-understudied afterlife of Law's monetary and financial theories, see Sonenscher, *Sans-Culottes*, pp. 39–45, 129, 260–73, 315–23.

85. "Si déjà Ricardo a pu dire que la circulation n'arrivera à son développement suprême que lorsqu'elle se trouvera à l'état du papier, M. Cieszkowski croit devoir aller plus loin en affirmant que le moyen terme normal de la circulation doit s'idéaliser encore davantage et devenir un *rapport*, exprimé par une *rente*." Report of a discussion in the *Journal des économistes* 17 (1858): 155. Liebich's description in his *Between Ideology and Utopia*, pp. 132–37, is very clear.

of this project."[86] Proudhon never entirely explained why he found Ciesz-kowski's project so significant, partly perhaps because he never spelled out his own alternative to the existing system of private property. It is well known that he emphasized the difference between possession and property, and highlighted the fact that possession implied the use of a thing while the con-cept of property also included its abuse. From one perspective, this could mean that Proudhon associated Cieszkowski with the idea of using public credit to reinstate possession and push back the entitlements of property. From another perspective, however, it could mean that Proudhon began to see that credit and money were a rather special type of property. Property, he wrote repeatedly, was different from possession because it could be abused as well as used.[87] But, as Law's system had demonstrated and the experience of the *assignats* had confirmed, the abuse of money actually undermined the use of property. This meant that, since money was a form of property that, experience showed, had to be used rather than abused, it was not necessary to promote a real reversion to possession because a state-backed currency would impose a set of imperatives that would be powerful enough to generate those forms of behaviour that would do much the same thing. The effects of the abuse of money would block the effects of the abuse of property.

If Cieszkowski was willing to associate his ideas with Law's widely discred-ited system, he was also prepared to identify them with the financial theories of the French Saint-Simonians. He made a point of signalling the similarity between his own views and those of the former Saint-Simonian political econ-omist Michel Chevalier, not only because Chevalier was a strong advocate of the economic and social benefits of public credit but also because the idea of capitalizing the fiscal system had been a prominent feature of Saint-Simonian financial theory before the movement disintegrated after 1832. The

86. Pierre-Joseph Proudhon, *Système des contradictions économiques*, p. 113, cited by Liebich, *Between Ideology and Utopia*, p. 145. On Proudhon on credit, see Marc Aucuy, *Les systèmes so-cialistes d'échange* (Paris, 1908); William Oualid, "Proudhon banquier," in *Proudhon et notre temps*, ed. Célestin Bouglé et al. (Paris, Chiron, 1920), pp. 131–55, and, more recently, Olivier Chaïbi, "Entre credit public et credit mutuel: un aperçu des théories du crédit au xix siècle," *Romantisme* 151 (2011): 53–66, and Andrea Lanzi, "Démocratie et propriété chez les premiers socialistes républicains français: les enjeux politiques de l'organisation du crédit," *Histoire, Economie et Société* 30 (2011): 81–94. For a helpful recent compilation of Proudhon's publications on credit, see Pierre-Joseph Proudhon, *Solution du problème social et autres textes (mars–juillet 1848)*, ed. Marc Lauder (Paris, Classiques Garnier, 2021).

87. See the various passages from Proudhon's publications dealing with the subject of prop-erty in Stewart Edwards and Elizabeth Fraser, eds., *Selected Writings of Pierre-Joseph Proudhon* (London, Macmillan, 1969), pp. 124–43.

need to do so was underlined by a Swiss supporter of Saint-Simonianism named James Fazy in a book entitled *Principes d'organisation industrielle pour le développement des richessse en France* (Principles of industrial organization for the development of wealth in France). As Fazy argued in a chapter headed "Necessity of an Industrial Revolution to Avoid a New Political Revolution," the growth of public credit was the way to neutralize class conflict and prevent a local eruption of what he called the "apostolic sans-culottisme" that was presently exemplified by events in Portugal and Brazil.[88] Although Fazy's strong endorsement of public credit earned him a rebuke from the political economist Jean-Baptiste Say, it was an evaluation that was echoed by many of his own supporters among the Saint-Simonians.[89] One of its leaders, Prosper Enfantin, a banker himself, called in 1831 for something similar in nature to Cieszkowski's later plan, recommending the establishment of a state bank to be funded by capitalizing the income from a progressive tax on inherited property.[90] If Cieszkowski's plan was more ambitious in scale and scope, the goal of Saint-Simonian development strategy was, fundamentally, the same. In both, the combination of credit and taxation would simultaneously level up and level down. It is also well known that Cieszkowski's call for exporting the spiritual power of European science, technology, and finance to the less developed parts of the world was matched—and implemented—by the Saint-Simonians, particularly in the Mediterranean, from Tunisia and Algeria to the Suez Canal.

The convergence between Cieszkowski and the Saint-Simonians was highlighted in a hostile entry on the subject of government borrowing published in 1843 in the French *Encyclopédie nouvelle*, edited by the socialists Pierre

---

88. Jean-Jacques (James) Fazy, *Principes d'organisation industrielle pour le développement des richesses en France* (Paris, 1830), pp. 271–82: "Nécessité d'une révolution industrielle pour échapper à une nouvelle révolution politique."

89. For Say's assessment, see his review of Fazy's book in *Revue Encyclopédique* 46 (1830): 625–30.

90. On the affinity between Saint-Simonianism and public credit, see Jean-Baptiste Vergeot, *Le crédit comme stimulant et régulateur de l'industrie: la conception saint-simonienne* (Paris, 1918), and, more recently, Gilles Jacoud, ed., *Political Economy and Industrialism: Banks in Saint-Simonian Thought* (London, Routledge, 2010), which reprints, in translation, the articles on banks, credit, and taxation by Prosper Enfantin. See also Franck Yonnet, "De l'utopie politique à la pratique bancaire: les frères Pereire, le Crédit mobilier et la construction du système bancaire moderne sous le Second Empire," in *Les traditions économiques françaises 1848–1939*, ed. Pierre Dockès et al. (Paris, CNRS Editions, 2000), pp. 203–16, and Clément Coste, "L'économique contre le politique: la dette, son amortissement et son financement chez les jeunes et les vieux Saint-Simoniens (1825–1880)," *Cahiers d'économie politique* 70 (2016): 7–44.

Leroux and Jean Reynaud. The article, written by Leroux's brother, Jules Leroux, attacked both Cieszkowski and the Saint-Simonians, not so much for their positive endorsements of public credit as for their failure to identify the underlying social and political conditions on which modern evaluations of public credit were based. In the hands of orthodox political economists, Leroux wrote, public debt was usually said to be a necessary evil, something that was used to fund the costs of emergencies or to offset the fluctuations of employment produced by trade and business cycles, but was not taken to have a more durable or significant place in modern political societies. Both Cieszkowski and the Saint-Simonians appeared to have made the opposite case by emphasizing the part that it could play both in promoting economic growth and as an agent of distributive justice. But, Leroux argued, their strong endorsement of public debt flew in the face of the realities of the divided societies of the modern world. The fundamental fact of the modern world was the fact of separation: of producers from products, of productive instruments from legal ownership, of physical capabilities from social benefits. Unleashing the power of public debt onto already-divided societies was, Leroux argued, a formula for war, not peace. "The more active the industrial and commercial free-for-all," he wrote, "the greater will be the social free-for-all."[91] Class war between the bourgeoisie and the proletariat would be the unforeseen effect of Cieszkowski's and the Saint-Simonians' misguided proposals. The problem, Leroux wrote in a complementary entry on "credit," was more deep-seated than either had seen because it was, in fact, an effect of private property. "For reasons that cannot now be addressed," he stated, "only a single mode of possession has been put into effect by mankind, and this is the individual mode. Except for monastic societies, no other mode of possession has yet to be seen. We are, of course, well aware of the existence of state forests, palaces, or monuments that do not have any individual owners, and of public gardens and establishments that belong to all, but the right of all to any of these establishments, gardens, palaces, forests, or monuments is an illusory right. Like any other domain, they are all exploited by, and for, particular individuals."[92]

There was a technical point to Leroux's claim that was more apparent in his entry on borrowing. This was that the subject of public credit was inseparable not only from the subject of taxation—because every type of public debt would have to be funded—but also from the subject of property. This, Leroux

91. Leroux and Reynaud, *Encyclopédie nouvelle*, 4:755 (entry on "Emprunts"). On Jules Leroux, see *Jules Leroux. D'une philosophie économique barbare*, ed. Ludovic Frobert and Michael Drolet (Lormont, Le Bord de l'Eau, 2022).

92. Ibid., 4:96 (entry on "Crédit").

argued, meant that any system of public debt would have to be accompanied by a far more comprehensive programme of reform than anything that Ciesz-kowski and the Saint Simonians had envisaged. It would have to mean that the agency responsible for public expenditure would be the same as the one re-sponsible for raising public revenue. It would, in short, mean that the owner-ship of property and the collection and expenditure of tax revenue would have to be managed by a far more integrated set of institutions than Cieszkowski and the Saint-Simonians had been prepared to contemplate. The "essence of sovereign authority is to be *one*," Leroux wrote, "not multiple or fragmented," The same applied to property. Spending was impossible without property, which meant that to be a "proprietor" was to be the "*absolute master*" or the "*king* of the things that one possesses."[93] Real property, by implication, was collective, not individual, in nature, just as real sovereignty was unitary, not plural, in its nature. The alternative to Cieszkowski and the Saint-Simonians—and, by extension, to Cousin and Guizot—was, therefore, a sovereign republic with real ownership of its property. It was a claim that converged very di-rectly with the republicanism of Edgar Quinet and Jules Michelet.

The explosive potential of the overlapping concerns of Hegelianism and Saint-Simonianism—or, in a more narrowly Franco-French context, of the parallel but conflicting concerns of romanticism, humanitarianism, eclecti-cism, and socialism—were readily identifiable. They had already been high-lighted in 1832, the year after Hegel's death, with the publication of a series of articles entitled *Lettres philosophiques adressées à un Berlinois* (Philosophical letters addressed to a resident of Berlin) by a student of German legal and philosophical thought named Eugène Lerminier. The main aim of the series was to explain why conditions in both France and Prussia after the French revolution of 1830 favoured a closer relationship between the two powers than had been possible after the revolution of 1789. In this sense, the articles com-plemented Cousin and Guizot's views. But, Lerminier warned, much would depend on calibrating the pace of reform in both states to ensure that the ex-tremes on one side had no opportunity to promote extreme responses on the other. From the vantage point of the French, he wrote, one extreme was rep-resented by Saint-Simon and the Saint-Simonians, and the possibility that the Prussian admirers of Saint-Simon would provoke a repressive reaction in Prus-sia. From the vantage point of Prussia, the opposite danger was represented by Hegel and his followers, and the possibility that Hegel's French disciples, notably the followers of Victor Cousin, would provoke an equally hostile reac-tion against Hegelianism there. As Lerminier presented them, Cousin and

93. Ibid., 4:756–57 (entry on "Emprunts").

Hegel were twin symptoms of the same pathology, so that eclecticism, the official name of Cousin's philosophy, was simply a French version of Hegelianism, with the same deep-seated endorsement of the social and political status quo that, according to his critics, Hegel had baked into his own philosophy of history. In this sense, Hegelianism according to Lerminier was a new version of "optimism," or, echoing Leibniz, the realist claim that the best of all possible worlds was, simply, the world as it is.

According to Lerminier, Cousin's moral and political philosophy was a product of an incident that had happened when he had been arrested as a political conspirator when travelling in Germany in 1824. He owed his release to Hegel's intercession with the Prussian authorities in Berlin, where he had also been befriended by Hegel's pupils Edouard Gans and Karl Ludwig Michelet. This exposure to the "Hegelian school," Lerminier wrote nastily, allowed Cousin to pick up "the principles and consequences of an eclectic, optimistic realism that flattered itself in its ability to explain everything, understand everything, and accept everything."[94] The results of what he had assimilated, Lerminier continued, were on display in the course of lectures that Cousin went on to publish in 1828. Although he presented these lectures as a course that he had given in 1818, they were in fact entirely indebted to Hegelian philosophy. "From the heights of a dogmatism of which he alone had the secret," Lerminier wrote, "he laid out for inspection history, philosophers, great men, war and its laws, along with Providence and its decrees. He professed the legitimacy of a universal optimism and, in the name of philosophy, pronounced the absolution of history."[95] When, according to Lerminier, Hegel and his followers read the lectures, they reacted with surprise and amusement because they looked remarkably like plagiarism. Although, Lerminier added, this had not been his intention, Cousin "in his improvisations managed to forget his borrowings, and it was with the best will in the world that he was able to persuade himself that he had created something with his amalgamation of Kant and Hegel."[96] At the end of this performance, Lerminier concluded, Cousin went back to the history of philosophy, declaring that philosophy itself had no more to do because its task was essentially complete. All that remained was to bring its components together, which was why, for Cousin, modern philosophy and eclecticism were, in fact, synonymous. It was a cruelly dismissive performance but one that was echoed repeatedly over the following fifteen years. It played its part not only in

94. Eugène Lerminier, *Lettres philosophiques adressées à un Berlinois* [1832], lettre 3, (Paris, Association Corpus/EUD, 2011), p. 57.

95. Ibid., p. 58.

96. Ibid., p. 59.

eroding the authority that Guizot and Cousin had earlier acquired, but also in undermining the cluster of related ideas about the Romans and the Germans that, for the generation of Germaine de Staël, Sismondi, and Constant, appeared to herald a new fusion of ancient and modern liberty. With Quinet and Michelet, autonomy began to give way to democracy.

Fortoul, Sainte-Beuve, and Sieyès

The ways in which it was done are described in the following chapter. These were all largely in place before the revolution of 1848, and, as the events of that year began to unfold, they were summed up vividly and brilliantly by Edgar Quinet in his *Révolutions d'Italie*. By then, Sainte-Beuve had found a new interest in the historical research of his friend Hippolyte Fortoul and Fortoul's plan for a political and intellectual biography of Emmanuel-Joseph Sieyès, the chief theoretical architect of the French Revolution of 1789 and one of the main organizers of the coup d'état that brought Napoleon Bonaparte to power in 1799. It is tempting to think that, to Fortoul and Sainte-Beuve, Sieyès appeared to offer what, both jointly and severally, Saint-Simonianism, romanticism, and humanitarianism had failed to deliver. It was more like Hegelianism without Hegel.

Hippolyte Fortoul was not a good novelist, although, as Sainte-Beuve recognized, he could write fluently and evocatively about landscape. He was, however, an unusually thorough and imaginative historical researcher. He never completed his biography of Sieyès, although his papers (now in the French Archives nationales) show that he made many attempts to plan and draft it. It is not clear when or how he got to know Sieyès's nephews, Ange and Paul (possibly, however, as a professor and administrator at the University of Aix-en-Provence), but by the mid-1840s he had acquired all of Sieyès's surviving papers. His notes, both on the papers themselves and on an impressive range of other sources, are a treasure trove of tiny items of information that, taken together, add up to an absorbingly detailed and effective picture of both Sieyès and his thought on the one side and of Fortoul, Sainte-Beuve, and the reasons for their fascination with Sieyès on the other. For Fortoul, the nearest counterpart to Sieyès that he could think of was Félicité de Lamennais, the ultra-Catholic, then former Catholic, cleric who abandoned theocracy for democracy. There was, he wrote, "a connection" (*rapport*) between the logic of Sieyès and that of Lamennais. "Both were products of the seminary, and both were intolerant."[97] For Lamennais intolerance was verbal and volcanic; for Sieyès it was discreet

---

97. Archives nationales de France (hereafter "AN"), 246 AP 35, fol. 46.

and disdainful. For both, however, its target was the same. It was the cascade of real or moral affronts inflicted by the injustice, inequality, idleness, and indifference of the modern world.

Fortoul picked out these aspects of Sieyès's character very well. He noticed the similarity between what Sieyès had written about the formation of a *classe morale*—or "moral class"—and what the "Scottish school," particularly Adam Ferguson, had written about the same subject.[98] He was also quick to see how much of Sieyès's political and economic system had been foreshadowed in a passage of Condorcet's *Vie de Turgot* (Life of Turgot) that was published in 1787. "In a nation in which the greatest number is truly enlightened and free from prejudice," Condorcet had written, "there would be laws that are simply wise and just."

> Similarly, a nation whose laws are due to the genius of someone with superior ability will not remain in ignorance for long. Most people, doubtless, will not have much time for learning because they will be required, in order to live, to follow a profession that occupies all their time. But it is still easy to see that if the laws are good, if they do not condemn any class of citizens to humiliation, and if they favour the division of property and wealth, the number of the poor would be lower and the time allocated to education in each family would be less limited.[99]

To Fortoul, the passage was "the basis of Sieyès's ideal constitution."[100] Accordingly, he made extensive notes on what Sieyès had written about taxation and citizenship, the idea of graduated promotion, ministerial accountability and royal unaccountability, and the relationship between the division of labour and the idea of a representative system. He was careful to note the similarity between Saint Simonianism and Sieyès's conception of a social system as a compound of three loosely industrial, administrative, and artistic parts (Fichte and Hegel, however, were largely off his conceptual map). He twice copied out the title of Sieyès's never-written *Traité du socialisme* as well as Sieyès's description of what he meant by *onéologie* and why the concept (meaning the study of origins and increase of wealth) lay behind his claim that he, rather than Adam Smith, had first thought of the relationship between the division of labour and

98. AN 246 AP 34, fol. 160.

99. There were two editions of Jean-Antoine-Nicolas de Caritat, marquis de Condorcet, *Vie de M. Turgot*, one published in 1786 and the other in 1787, with London as their fictitious place of publication. This quotation is from the 1787 edition, p. 224. Thanks to Graham Clure for supplying this information.

100. AN 246 AP 34, fol. 29.

a representative system.[101] Most of all, however, Fortoul was fascinated by the many elaborate schemes that Sieyès devised for using public credit to redistribute resources, and to bring about something like what August Cieszkowski and the Saint-Simonians had also speculated about being able to achieve for much the same developmental and redistributive reasons.

"It is certain that common property cultivated not by helots, but by citizens themselves, for several hours a day," Sieyès wrote, "would entail, beyond a moderate amount of work, an obligation to be content with simple physical enjoyment and consumption, two things that are particularly essential for a good constitution." But, he continued, "there are no means available to make the nations of the present, based as they are on exclusive property and endlessly seeking the mirage of ever-greater prosperity and wealth, do anything other than give moralists an opportunity to rehearse their complaints and regrets."[102] At some stage in his career, however, Sieyès clearly contemplated the possibility of something more. In Fortoul's rendition of the various schemes that he devised, the basic idea was that the 648 communes into which France had come to be divided after 1789 would be the real owners of the territory. They would lease off units of this communal property to life tenants who, in turn, would sublet their tenures to other tenants for specified periods of time. Some forms of property would be rural, others urban, but individual ownership would always be conditional. The combination of absolute communal ownership and conditional individual tenure would then become the basis of a system of debt-based public finance, with a mixture of taxes and rent generating a revenue stream that would fund the payment of interest on the bonds and shares that would be issued by the state, the communes, and private corporations and would be denominated in a state-backed currency. It was, Fortoul noted, "a system of finance that was not readily reconcilable with the right of property" because, with Sieyès, legal titles rather than physical possession would be the basis of the complex and usually multiple forms of ownership of the modern world.[103]

Sainte-Beuve paid considerable attention to Fortoul's research and made quite extensive use of Fortoul's notes in the essay on Sieyès that he published in 1851. The timing was carefully chosen. Its aim was to highlight the continuity between Sieyès, 1799, and Napoleon I and Sieyès, 1851, and Napoleon III.

101. AN 246 AP 35, fols. 152 and 220–23.

102. The passage is contained in a manuscript entitled "Simplification morale et politique" published in *Des manuscrits de Sieyès*, ed. Christine Fauré, Jacques Guilhaumou, and Jacques Vallier, 2 vols. (Paris, Champion, 1999–2007), 2:439–40.

103. AN 246 AP 36, fol. 199. See too 246 AP 35, fol. 235.

"If," Sainte-Beuve wrote at the time, "there is anything left of democracy in France, or in our institutions, it is to the government of a single individual that it should be owed."[104] It was, in one sense, an obituary. In another sense, however, it was also a revival. But the identity of what was buried or revived is still somewhat surprising. On the side of the first were the republican policies of Jules Michelet, Edgar Quinet, and Victor Hugo. On the side of the second were the financial and economic policies of the Saint-Simonians. Sainte-Beuve's final published work continued to keep the uncertainty alive. It was a sympathetic, but incomplete, biography of Cieszkowski's now better-known admirer, Pierre-Joseph Proudhon.

104. Charles Augustin Sainte-Beuve, *Nouveaux lundis*, 13 vols. (Paris, 1875–78), 10:328–29. For his essay on Sieyès, see his *Causeries du lundi*, 16 vols. (Paris, 1857–70), 5:189–216.

9

The Return of Rome

Symbols, Enthusiasm, and Culture

August Cieszkowski had an attentive reader in the French poet, historian, and philosopher Edgar Quinet.[1] Quinet probably came to know of his publications because of his friendship with the Polish exile Adam Mickiewicz, who, like Quinet himself, taught at the Collège de France in Paris in the early 1840s. Mickiewicz knew Cieszkowski and referred to his books quite frequently in the lectures on Slav literature that he gave at the Collège de France. In addition, however, there was also a real intellectual convergence based on their respective treatments of the subject of palingenesis, first in Quinet's philosophical poem *Ahasvérus*, published in 1832, and then in Cieszkowski's *Prolegomena to Historiosophy*, published six years later. Quinet read German and had first made his name in 1827 by publishing a French translation of Herder's *Ideen*, or *Ideas on the History of Humanity*, together with a long introduction to Herder's thought.[2] Like Cieszkowski, he was a critic of Hegel, and, although it is not usual to do so, he could be described as a kind of French Young Hegelian. He was also a more radical critic of Hegel and Hegelianism than most of his political and intellectual peers. This was not simply a matter of the ferocity and intensity of his recurrent attacks on Hegel, German philosophy, and French eclecticism— all represented, as Quinet presented them, by Victor Cousin and François Guizot. It was also, more fundamentally, a product of his determination to apply the values and concepts of German philosophy to the neo-Roman history of Italy and Spain, and to transfer the Germanic cultural and institutional legacy

---

1. Z. L. Zaleski, "Edgar Quinet et Auguste Cieszkowski," in *Mélanges d'histoire littéraire générale et comparée offerts à Fernand Baldensperger*, [ed. Anon.] 2 vols. (Paris, Champion, 1930), 2:361–71.

2. On Quinet and Herder, see Tronchon, *La fortune intellectuelle* and his *Allemagne-France-Angleterre*. See too, helpfully, Willy Aeschimann, *La pensée d'Edgar Quinet: étude sur la formation de ses idées avec essais de jeunesse et documents inédits* (Paris, Anthropos, 1986).

of the North to the Latin legacy of the South. This meant reassigning the cultural, moral, and political values that, a generation earlier, Germaine de Staël had associated with the North to the new concept of the Renaissance that Quinet's close friend and intellectual collaborator, the historian Jules Michelet, took over and amplified from the history of Italian architecture. The modern concept of the Renaissance transferred the attributes of romanticism from the North to the South. In a superficial sense, Quinet's concept of palingenesis overlapped with Cieszkowski's. In reality, the content and conclusions of their respective philosophies of history were radically different.

The difference was a product of their respective responses to Kant's intellectual legacy and, in particular, the grim philosophy of history implied by Kant's concept of unsocial sociability. On its premises, justice for humans always came too soon because justice for humanity always came too late. Justice was partial and limited because the human struggle for justice was the source of a world of states. Justice in one state was, accordingly, different from justice in others. In this context, and despite his criticisms of Hegel, Cieszkowski remained a Hegelian (as too, it could be said, did his admirer Pierre-Joseph Proudhon). Quinet never was. Although his thought was as deeply engaged with German philosophy as Cieszkowski's, its main points of reference came from Kant's critics and opponents, from Herder and Jacobi to Fichte, Schelling, Görres, and Creuzer. Its starting point was, therefore, the problem of partiality and the difficulty of identifying something that could be used to make reliable and durable moral distinctions between the local and contingent and the general and obligatory. With this in place, it would then be possible to deal with what Friedrich Schlegel called Kant's "historicism," or the problem of the absence, outside of empty generalizations like nature, providence, or history, of anything able to indicate a way out of humanity's state-centred condition and the partiality that it brought in its wake. Kant's concept of autonomy appeared to avoid these problems, but its individualistic orientation also seemed to entail a general indifference to anything more substantive than a categorical imperative, and anything more precise than a broad distinction between republican and despotic forms of rule. This was the context in which the early nineteenth-century revival of the thought of the late seventeenth-century Neapolitan theologian, historian, and political thinker Giambattista Vico took place. Vico was a critic of the natural jurisprudence of Grotius, Hobbes, Pufendorf, and Locke. The content of his *New Science*, particularly in its concern with mythology, allegory, and symbols, was similar to the later publications of Herder, Brown, or Klopstock. In this context, both the subject matter of the *New Science* and the recognizably Christian progression of its argument about the Fall and recovery from the Fall gave a new impetus to the study of the symbolic, the allegorical, and the mythological as the means to escape from the otherwise intractable problem of unsocial sociability. Empires could swallow up nations and Latin had become the lingua franca of the ancient world, but nations could be reborn from empire and national languages could escape the uniformity of imperial rule. Culture, in short, was the solution to the problem of historicism that Kant had created, just as, and in a similar sense, democracy could be described as a precondition of autonomy.

Quinet's achievement was highlighted in a review of *Ahasvérus* by the French literary critic Charles Magnin, a review that Quinet subsequently used as an introduction to further editions of his poem. "We should," Magnin wrote, "congratulate present-day art for finally coming to understand that so-called works of the *imagination*, as they have been called very improperly up to now, ought to be composed to please the imagination."

> This happy change in art dates from the first years of the nineteenth century. In the aftermath of the great social commotions that shook Europe between 1792 and 1816, we have finally come to see that man, even under our temperate skies, is not only endowed with reason and sensibility, but also has another faculty within him that is quite distinct from these two companions, a faculty whose analysis was almost entirely forgotten by Scottish and Kantian philosophy, a faculty that is certainly more energetic and demanding under other climates, but still needs exercise and nourishment even under ours.[3]

Whether or not it really was a faculty, Magnin insisted that there was a real connection between the imagination and the events of the French Revolution. Something about that connection, he wrote, meant that "a new era of enthusiasm had to open, and it has."[4] One sign of its arrival, he claimed, was *Ahasvérus* and the account that Quinet had set out of human history as palingenesis, with the figure of Ahasvérus, or the Wandering Jew, symbolizing the

---

3. "Et, à ce propos, félicitons l'art actuel d'avoir compris, enfin, que les ouvrages dits, fort improprement jusqu'à cette heure, d'*imagination*, doivent être composés dans la vue de plaire à l'imagination. Cet heureux changement dans l'art date des premières années du xixe siècle. A la suite des grandes commotions sociales qui ont ébranlé l'Europe, de 1792 à 1816, nous avons fini par nous apercevoir que l'homme, même sous notre ciel tempéré, n'est pas seulement doué de raison et de sensibilité; qu'il y a encore en lui une autre faculté tout à fait distincte de ses deux compagnes, une faculté dont l'analyse a été à peu près oublié par la philosophie écossaise et kantienne; faculté plus énergique assurément et plus exigeante sous d'autres climats, mais qui, même sous le nôtre, a besoin d'exercice et d'aliments." Charles Magnin, *Causeries et méditations historiques et littéraires*, 2 vols. (Paris, 1843), 1:94 (reprinting his review of Edgar Quinet's *Ahasvérus* originally published in the *Revue des Deux Mondes* in 1833).

4. Ibid., p. 97.

course of history in the way that was to become the basis of Chenavard's never-to-be-accomplished redecoration of the Panthéon. To Magnin, however, what mattered was not so much the historical content of the epic as its imaginative and poetic power.

A parallel description of Quinet's thought was made a generation later by a nineteenth-century Genevan diarist and philosophy professor named Henri Frédéric Amiel. "This evening," he wrote in his diary on 23 January 1861, "I read almost the whole of the first volume of *Merlin.*" This was one of several epic poems that Quinet published, beginning with *Ahasvérus* and followed by four further epics, on Prometheus, Napoleon, Merlin, and the Creation. *Merlin* left Amiel unimpressed. The poem, he wrote, "is less a legend of the human soul than a legend of its author, a fantastic apotheosis of his inner life, a colossal autobiography." Quinet, he complained, "is constantly oracular (*pythonise constamment*)," "mercilessly and relentlessly dithyrambic," and, even more damningly, someone who "collapses into triviality as soon as he tries to be simple." "At bottom," Amiel concluded, "his mind belongs to another country (*c'est un esprit dépaysé*)."

> He may well mock Germany and curse England, but this does not make him any the more French. His thought is from the North but his imagination is from the South. The marriage is not a success. He has a compulsion for unremitting exultation and the inveterate sublime. He personifies his abstractions as colossal beings who invariably talk and act in ways that have no proportion. He is drunk on infinity.

He was a French version of Herder, whose *Ideas on the History of Humanity* Quinet had translated a generation earlier. Amiel was still, however, willing to be forgiving. Quinet's self-absorption, he wrote, was a recognizable failing. It "was because the heart is generous that the mind is egocentric," and "because Quinet really believes that he is French that he really is so little like the French." He was, as Amiel put it, a kind of *Görres franc-comtois*, meaning a Burgundian version of the German Catholic philosopher Joseph Görres, a follower of Schelling and a student of mythology who, as Amiel probably knew, Quinet had described sardonically as a hopelessly quixotic fighter for lost causes, a revolutionary papist, and a fanatical exponent of Schelling's *Naturphilosophie*.[5] Quinet, as Amiel described him, was like a republican mirror image of his own portrait of Görres, but with the Catholicism left out. Although he was French, he had no home or place in French culture. His "real superiority,"

---

5. Edgar Quinet, "Allemagne et Italie," in his *Œuvres complètes*, 12 vols. (Paris, 1857), 6:194–99.

Amiel concluded, "is apparent in his historical work (*Marnix, Italy, The Roma-nians*), especially in his studies of nationalities. He is someone who was made to understand souls that are more vast and sublime than individual souls."[6] In the Anglophone world, his nearest equivalent was the American transcen-dentalist Ralph Waldo Emerson, whom Quinet read and admired.

Amiel's assessment is plausible but was also incomplete. If it gets the mea-sure of Quinet's achievement as a historian, it does not really entertain the possibility that the quality of his history was indebted to the grander and more philosophical ambition of his poetry. By highlighting Quinet's singularity, it also failed to pay enough attention to the intense intellectual interaction among the cohort of writers, poets, dramatists, and historians to which he belonged. Quinet (who was born in 1803) was the youngest of a remarkable constellation of writers, including Lamartine (born in 1790), Vigny (born in 1797), Michelet (born in 1798), and Victor Hugo (born in 1802). Together, the five members of this group were the contemporaries of Guizot, Cousin, and Sainte-Beuve. Between 1815 and 1830, their ideas and political allegiances began, haltingly, to converge, but by 1840 the two groups of public intellectuals were enemies. In this context, the two sets of political trajectories were as much a matter of recurrent argument and cumulative choice as of individual ability or original insight. Both the discussions and the choices centred on a number of subjects with a long-standing presence in German thought, including the re-lationship between enthusiasm and the imagination, on the one hand, and, on the other, the part played by the symbolic, the metaphorical, and the allegori-cal in forming a bridge between the real and the ideal. From the early nineteenth century onwards, positive evaluations of both enthusiasm and the symbolic had been features of the thought of the Coppet group and its various European intellectual outposts. Quinet and his generation, however, made these subjects their own.

They did so by taking the subjects of enthusiasm, the imagination, and the symbolic in a new direction in the years preceding and following the revolu-tion of 1830. In part, this involved transferring the concept of a symbol from a largely theological to a largely legal context as a way of explaining how the idea of the rule of law could have the ability and authority to work. In part it also

6. Henri Frédéric Amiel, *Fragments d'un journal intime*, ed. Bernard Bouvier, 3 vols. (Paris, Stock, 1927),1:141–42. Earlier (p. 132), Amiel wrote of Quinet: "Il est trop protestant d'inclination et trop oriental de forme pour le monde français. C'est au fond un étranger, tandis que Prou-dhon, Michelet, Renan sont des nationaux. La naïveté tue dans la patrie de Voltaire. Le sublime fatigue dans le pays de calembours. L'esprit de chimère discrédite dans le siècle des faits ac-complis." For further assessments of Quinet, see *Edgar Quinet, une conscience européenne*, ed. Sophie Guermès and Brigitte Krulic (Brussels, Peter Lang, 2018).

involved developing a new and different type of aesthetics, with a focus on ugliness rather than on beauty or the sublime. This new type of aesthetic judgment did not displace its previous counterparts, but instead added an extra dimension of locality and particularity to earlier examinations of the interrelationship of beauty, the emotions, and morality, with the result that they could all be given a more historically bounded moral and social setting. Although the emotion of enthusiasm still mattered, as it had done for Germaine de Staël and Wilhelm von Humboldt, it was now integrated into a new and different type of cultural history that highlighted the causal power of the emotions, whether as sources of political stability or as agents of revolution. From this perspective, Quinet's achievement amounted to a synthesis of four distinct subjects, in which the concept of the symbol, the emotion of enthusiasm, the aesthetics of ugliness, and the idea of the rule of law were integrated into a radically different account of the origins and nature of the modern age. Focusing on these four subjects reveals how many aspects of Quinet's historical and political vision were bound up with the concurrent choices and achievements of his peers, and, at the same time, how much of his vision corroborates Amiel's 150-year-old assessment that, with Quinet, the values and culture of the North were reconceived under the aegis of the South. It did so too, it is also important to stress, in the context of the escalating spiral of incompatibilities that produced the sequence of switches of ideological allegiance running from romanticism to Hegelianism, and from Saint-Simonianism to humanitarianism and classicism, that were tracked so conscientiously by Sainte-Beuve. Quinet established an alternative to them all. The first steps, however, were supplied by the dramatist, poet, and novelist Victor Hugo.

The Limits of Rationality

Among Hugo's many achievements was the creation of a significant counter to the Hegelian concept of the impersonality of reason adopted by Cousin and Guizot. It was set out vividly in the famous preface that he published in 1827 as an introduction to his play *Cromwell*.[7] In it, Hugo began to show why the arts,

7. On Hugo and the preface to *Cromwell*, see, particularly, the contributions to Jan Miernowski, ed., *Le sublime et le grotesque* (Geneva, Droz, 2014); Bernard Franco, "La «Préface» de *Cromwell*, entre Friedrich Schlegel et Walter Scott," in *Victor Hugo ou les frontières effacées*, ed. Yann Jumelais and Dominique Peyrache-Leborgne (Nantes, 2002), pp. 285–302, Dominique Peyrache-Leborgne, "Hugo, le grotesque et l'arabesque," in *Romantismes: l'esthétisme en acte*, ed. Jean-Louis Cabanès (Paris, PU de Paris Ouest, 2009), pp. 109–22; as well as Siddhartha Bose, *Back and Forth: The Grotesque in the Play of Romantic Irony* (Newcastle, Cambridge Scholars, 2015). On the political side of the preface, see Yves Reboul, "Hugo, *Cromwell* et la Défection,"

and the dramatic arts in particular, contained many of the ingredients that ex-plained why certain types of emotion like melancholy or enthusiasm were the keys to understanding the relationship between moral authority and state power. Rather than something impersonal and rational, the arts and their prod-ucts had a power of affect that was social and collective as well as individual and personal. They could, therefore, form a bridge between the modern value of autonomy and the ancient value of democracy. A symbol, even one that was not religious, seemed to be able to produce and maintain the nexus of alle-giance, aspiration, and emotion that was standardly involved in patriotism, al-truism, or cosmopolitanism. This, as Hugo went on to show, meant that the two concepts of autonomy and democracy were not as distinct or as different as they had been described, notably by Kant and his followers, and consequently did not need to rely on as many of the complicated constitutional and institu-tional arrangements to keep them in place as Kant had claimed because both types of capacity were connected to the feeling—and the concept—of enthu-siasm. Enthusiasm could be seen as something personal and individual, as might be required for autonomy. But it could also be seen as something social and collective, as might be required for democracy. Combining both types of capability appeared to offer the prospect of a new type of politics, with room for both autonomy and democracy, but with less room for the old mixture of sovereignty, states, and governments. It was a synthesis that, with Hugo's close familiarity with the religious motivation involved in the Spanish *guerrilla* against Napoleon and his own early leanings towards the Catholic and legiti-mist side of Restoration politics, was one that he was well placed to make. The novelty of the insight was that it showed that it was possible to use aesthetics to explain collective action and, by doing so, to produce a philosophy of history that could look outside—or beyond—the idea of the state.

Hugo's preface to *Cromwell* was organized around a stadial history of aes-thetics with a focus on the properties of the grotesque as the key, not only to the relationship between popular culture and modern art, but also to a more comprehensive philosophy of history. The first of the three stages that Hugo identified was redolent of a tradition of Christian moral theory that, in the eighteenth century, was frequently associated with ancient Cynic philoso-phy.[8] "In primitive times," Hugo wrote, "when man is just awakening in a world

in *Voix de l'écrivain: Mélanges offerts à Guy Sagnes*, ed. Jean-Louis Cabanes (Toulouse, PU du Mirail, 1996), pp. 53–64. For helpful earlier studies, see Maurice Souriau, *La «Préface» de Cromwell: Introduction, textes et notes* (Paris, 1897); Eunice Morgan Schenck, *La part de Charles Nodier dans la formation des idées de Victor Hugo jusqu'à la* Préface *de* Cromwell (Paris, Cham-pion, 1914), and Jean Mallion, *Victor Hugo et l'art architectural* (Paris, PUF, 1962).

8. On this tradition, see Sonenscher, *Sans-Culottes*.

which is just born, poetry awakes with him. In presence of the marvellous sights which dazzle and intoxicate him, his first words are naught but a hymn."[9] Then, he continued, the earth was barely cultivated. "There are families, but no nations; fathers, but no kings. Each race exists as it pleases; no property, no law, no clashing, no wars. Everything belongs to each and to all. Society is a community." Its cultural archetype was the lyric poem. "This poem, this ode of primitive times," Hugo announced, "is Genesis."[10]

Subsequently, as families became tribes and tribes became nations, "the nomad instinct" gave way to "the social instinct." Animals began to be tamed and flocks began to be formed. "The camp gives place to the city, the tent to the palace, the ark to the temple." These early societies were still shepherd societies, but their rulers were now kings and priests. As Quinet's admirer, the French literary critic Charles Magnin, was later to put it, "the age of singing" began to give way to the "age of reading."[11] Nations began to press against one another. "Their interests conflict: hence the crash of empires meeting, which we call war." Poetry registered these great events, and as it did, the lyric turned into the epic, crowned by the works of Homer. The great cultural transformation that accompanied these developments gave ancient civilization its character. The epic housed its historical memory, while its moral compass was supplied by tragedy. "The same fables, the same catastrophes, the same heroes. All of them," Hugo wrote, "draw their inspiration from the Homeric stream."[12]

The third turning point began with Christianity. Against the materialism of the Greeks and Romans, Christianity's most significant quality was its dualism, meaning its abidingly perplexed and intermittently prurient concern with the complex relationship between the physical and the spiritual that was one of the most durable and deep-seated effects of the discovery of the soul. With it, "a new

9. "Aux temps primitifs, quand l'homme s'éveille dans un monde qui vient de naitre, la poésie s'éveille avec lui. En présence des merveilles qui l'éblouissent et qui l'enivrent, sa première parole n'est qu'un hymne." Victor Hugo, Cromwell [1827], ed. Annie Ubersfeld (Paris, Garnier Flammarion, 1968), p. 63. Translations are from Victor Hugo, Dramas: Oliver Cromwell, trans I. G. Burnham (London, 1896), here p. 9.

10. "Il y a des familles, et pas de peuples; des pères et pas de rois. Chaque race existe à l'aise; point de propriété, point de loi, point de froissements, point de guerre. Tout est à chacun et à tous. La société est une communauté." Hugo, Cromwell, p. 63; Hugo, Oliver Cromwell, p. 9.

11. On Magnin's distinction (made in 1843), see Michel Espagne, "Les élèves de Claude Fauriel," in Claude Fauriel et l'Allemagne. Idées pour une philologie des cultures, ed. Geneviève Espagne and Udo Schöning (Paris, Champion, 2014), pp. 405–22 (p. 417). On Fauriel, see also Sandrine Maufroy, Le philhellénisme franco-allemand (Paris, Belin, 2011).

12. "Mêmes fables, mêmes catastrophes, mêmes héros. Tous puisent au fleuve homérique." Hugo, Cromwell, p. 65; Oliver Cromwell, p. 10.

sentiment found its way into the popular mind—a sentiment unknown to the ancients, but developed to a remarkable degree among the moderns—a sentiment which is something more than solemnity, something less than sadness: melancholy."[13] The emotion, Hugo wrote, was a sentiment that had arisen at the confluence of three, originally unrelated, developments. The first was the Christian reappraisal of poverty and its bearing on the moral quality of both this life and the next. The second was an event-driven awareness of the inescapable scale and unavoidable impact on ordinary lives of the decline and fall of empires. The third was the spirit of investigation and curiosity produced by— but partly as a bewildered response to—the huge social catastrophe triggered by the collapse of the Roman Empire. Together these three developments gave rise to a radically new and modern evaluation of beauty, which, as Hugo put it, was envisaged at one pole by the Roman rhetorician Cassius Longinus, the author of a highly influential treatise on the sublime that had been rediscovered in the seventeenth century, and, at the other, by Saint Augustine. Juxtaposing the two names, as Hugo did here, was designed to indicate that Christian dualism not only enhanced the positive qualities of the spiritual, but also magnified the negative properties of the physical.

The combination, Hugo argued, meant that alongside the ideal beauty of ancient culture, modern culture also had room for what was ugly, dark, misshapen, or evil. It had room, in short, for the grotesque as well as the sublime, and, as with the character of Quasimodo in *Notre Dame de Paris*, for levels of insight whose particularity and specificity went beyond the generalities of the purely ideal. This addition, Hugo went on to argue, was what separated "modern art from ancient art" or "*romantic* literature from *classical* literature."[14] It did so because the combination of the sublime and the grotesque opened up a space for comedy alongside tragedy and gave modern art the means to rise to a level that could not be reached by the sublime alone. "The beautiful," Hugo wrote, "has but one type; the ugly has a thousand. The reason is that the beautiful, humanly speaking, is form considered in its simplest aspect, in its most perfect symmetry, in its most absolute harmony with our organization. And so, taken as a whole, though complete in its way, it is restricted as we

---

13. "A cette époque . . . nous ferons remarquer qu'avec le christianisme et par lui, s'introduisait dans l'esprit des peuples un sentiment nouveau, inconnu des anciens et singulièrement développé chez les modernes, un sentiment qui est plus que la gravité et moins que la tristesse: la mélancolie." Hugo, *Cromwell*, p. 67; *Oliver Cromwell*, p. 11. On Quasimodo and his relationship to the grotesque, see Elizabeth K. Menon, "Victor Hugo and the Hunchbacks of the July Monarchy," *Studies in the Humanities* 21 (1994): 60–71, and her "The Utopian Mayeux: Henri de Saint-Simon meets the *Bossu à la mode*," *Canadian Journal of History* 33 (1998): 249–77.

14. Hugo, *Cromwell*, p. 69; *Oliver Cromwell*, p. 13.

ourselves are restricted. What we call ugly, on the other hand, is one detail of a great whole, which passes our comprehension and which is in perfect harmony, not with man, but with all creation. That is why it constantly presents itself in new, but incomplete shapes."[15]

The grotesque, not the sublime, was therefore the dynamic component of modern culture. Its variety and multiplicity allowed the otherwise more stable attributes of beauty to acquire a wider range of qualities because the endless variations that could be produced by adding the diversity of the grotesque to the uniformity of the sublime made modern conceptions of beauty both more elastic and richer. The particularity of the grotesque was analogous to the particularity of irrationality. It was, Hugo argued, picking up a phrase used by the historian Augustin Thierry, what gave history and historical writing the "local colour" that could be found in the novels of Walter Scott.[16] The medium most suited to this new combination, Hugo argued, was the drama and the mixture of "the grotesque and the sublime, the terrible and the absurd, tragedy and comedy" that had been typified, above all, by Shakespeare's dramatic works. With the drama, but because it also shared the same qualities with the novel, Hugo's stadial history was complete, because the drama was the art form that allowed culture to capture nature in both its outward and inward forms.[17] "Primitive times," Hugo wrote somewhat formulaically, "are lyric, ancient times are epic, modern times are dramatic. The ode sings of eternity; the epic imparts solemnity to history; the drama depicts life. The characteristic of the first form

15. "C'est que le beau, à parler humainement, n'est que la forme considérée dans son rapport le plus simple, dans sa symétrie la plus absolue, dans son harmonie la plus intime avec notre organisation. Aussi nous offre-t-il toujours un ensemble complet, mais restreint comme nous. Ce que nous appelons le laid, au contraire, est un détail d'un grand ensemble qui nous échappe, et qui s'harmonise, non pas avec l'homme, mais avec la création tout entière. Voilà pourquoi il nous présente sans cesse des aspects nouveaux, mais incomplets." Hugo, *Cromwell*, pp. 73–74; *Oliver Cromwell*, p. 16. For contemporary discussion of the subject, including Hugo's evaluation of ugliness, see Karl Rosenkranz, *Esthétique du laid* [1853] (Paris, Editions Circé, 2004).

16. On the concept of local colour in both Hugo and Thierry, see Odile Parsis-Barubé, "La notion de couleur locale dans l'œuvre d'Augustin Thierry," in *Augustin Thierry: L'histoire pour mémoire*, ed. Aude Déruelle and Yann Potin (Rennes, PU de Rennes, 2018), pp. 63–82. On the conceptual context, see Paule Petitier, "Entre concept et hypotypose: l'histoire au xixe siècle," *Romantisme* 144 (2009): 69–80. See too Barzun, *Romanticism and the Modern Ego*, pp. 270–71.

17. On the parallel between the drama and the novel, see Franz Norbert Mennemeier, "Les premiers romantiques allemands et la 'Préface' de *Cromwell* de Victor Hugo: un exemple du rapport littéraire franco-allemand," *Francofonia* 14 (1988): 75–86.

is innocence, of the second simplicity, of the third truth."[18] Or, as he put it a little later, "society begins by singing of what it dreams, then tells of what it does, and lastly undertakes to paint what it thinks."[19] This, Hugo continued, was what the drama could do. Its distinctive feature was its ability to present "the real" or "the natural combination of the two types, the sublime and the grotesque, which meet in the drama as they meet in life and in the creation. For true poetry, complete poetry, consists in the harmony of contraries."[20] In modern art what mattered was the grotesque as much as the sublime, the physical as much as the spiritual, comedy as well as tragedy, and the popular, vernacular, and demotic as much as the patrician, exclusive, and refined.

With Hugo and his preface to *Cromwell* of 1827, romanticism became political. Hugo himself underlined the point three years later in the preface to his play *Hernani*, the play that precipitated the riot that heralded the end of the reign of Charles X. "Romanticism," he wrote there, "which has been so often badly defined, is nothing else than *liberalism* in literature—and this is its real definition when seen solely in campaigning terms. This truth has already been understood by almost everyone of good sense—and their number is considerable—and soon, because the process is already far advanced, literary liberalism will be no less popular than political liberalism."[21] The claim matched the more general approach to historical and cultural change followed in the wake of the Coppet group by a broader body of political opinion. It was visible, for example, in a letter written in 1825 by Prosper Enfantin, the founder of the Saint-Simonian movement's eponymous religion.

18. "Les temps primitifs sont lyriques, les temps antiques sont épiques, les temps modernes sont dramatiques. L'ode chante l'éternité, l'épopée solennise l'histoire, le drame peint la vie. Le caractère de la première poésie est la naïveté, le caractère de la seconde est la simplicité, le caractère de la troisième, la vérité." Hugo, *Cromwell*, pp. 75–76; *Oliver Cromwell*, p. 17.

19. "La société, en effet, commence par chanter ce qu'elle rêve, puis raconte ce qu'elle fait, et enfin se met à peindre ce qu'elle pense." Hugo, *Cromwell*, p. 76; *Oliver Cromwell*, p. 18.

20. "La poésie née du christianisme, la poésie de notre temps est donc le drame; le caractère du drame est le réel; le réel résulte de la combinaison toute naturelle de deux types, le sublime et le grotesque, qui se croisent dans le drame, comme ils se croisent dans la vie et dans la création. Car la poésie vraie, la poésie complète, est dans l'harmonie des contraires." Hugo, *Cromwell*, p. 79; *Oliver Cromwell*, pp. 19–20.

21. "Le romantisme, tant de fois mal défini, n'est, à tout prendre, et c'est sa définition réelle, si l'on ne l'envisage que sous son côté militante, que le *libéralisme* en littérature. Cette vérité est déjà comprise à peu près de tous les bons esprits, et le nombre en est grand; et bientôt, car l'œuvre est déjà bien avancé, le libéralisme littéraire ne sera pas moins populaire que le libéralisme politique." Victor Hugo, *Hernani* [1830], ed. Yves Gohin (Paris, Gallimard, 1995), p. 32.

Poussin and Claude Lorrain, he wrote there, would be unlikely to recognize themselves in modern painting. But, Enfantin continued, although it had turned away from antiquity, modern painting had continued to follow what he called the road that leads forwards because it sought its models in the future, not the past, and took inventiveness, not imitation, as its watchwords. "To pass from this," Enfantin commented, "to philosophical considerations on the classical and the romantic, and on the politics of the ultras or the liberals properly described, and on our own, is a matter of no more than a single step (because we are the romantics of the politics of the Greeks and the Romans, or the English and the Americans, or the immobile and retrograde politics of the ultras)."[22] A decade or so later, the claim was given a popular content. "There is a whole new literature to be created, based on those genuinely popular mores that are so little known by the other classes," wrote the novelist George Sand in her *Le Compagnon du tour de France* in 1840. "That literature will begin among the people themselves and it will come out shining in a very short space of time. This is what will refresh (*retrempera*) that eminently revolutionary muse, the romantic muse, that has been trying to find its way and the family to which it belongs ever since its first appearance in literature.[23]

The effects of these developments were crystallized initially in the phenomenon of Béranger. Populism, at least in France, began with Pierre-Jean Béranger. He was the first in a line of nineteenth-century French poet-singers, from Gustave Nadaud and Pierre Dupont to Loïsa Puget and Aristide Bruant, whose songs were both popular and political, with a durable bearing on subsequent

22. "Pour passer de ceci à des considérations philosophiques sur le classique et le romantisme, et sur la politique des ultras ou des libéraux proprement dits et la nôtre (nous sommes les romantiques de la politique des Grecs et des Romains, des Anglais et des Américains, ou de la politique immobile ou rétrograde des ultras) il n'y a qu'un pas à faire." Bibliothèque de l'Arsenal, Fonds Enfantin, 7676/2, Prosper Enfantin to Aglaé Saint-Hilaire, 26 August 1825. A slightly garbled version of the letter is cited by Philippe Régnier, "Les Saint-Simoniens et le mouvement romantique," in *Romantismes et socialismes en Europe (1800–1848)*, ed. André Billaz and Ulrich Ricken (Paris, Didier Erudition, 1989), pp. 207–23 (p. 208). Thanks to Graham Clure for supplying a photograph of the letter.

23. "Il y aurait toute une littérature nouvelle à créer avec les véritables mœurs populaires, si peu connues des autres classes. Cette littérature commence au sein même du peuple; elle en sortira brillante avant qu'il soit peu de temps. C'est là que se retrempera la muse romantique, muse éminemment révolutionnaire, et qui, depuis son apparition dans les lettres, cherche sa voie et sa famille." George Sand, *Le Compagnon du tour de France* [1840], ed. Jean Louis Cabanès, (Paris, Editions de Poche, 2004), p. 47.

conceptions of the relationship between music and politics.[24] "Among the illustrious poets of our age," wrote the socialist Louis Blanc, "how many would anyone dare to place above Béranger?"[25] For Jules Michelet in *Le Peuple* of 1846, Béranger was "the nation's singer" (*le chansonnier national*). For others, including Sainte-Beuve's friend Hippolyte Fortoul, he, more than Ronsard, Racine, or Rousseau, was "the national poet" (*le poète national*).[26] For Sainte-Beuve himself, writing soon after the July Revolution of 1830, Béranger had "made his mark in the ranks of pure democracy." His songs "dramatized a whole political economy of impotence, a whole system of crushing taxation," going, according to Sainte-Beuve, to the heart of the "question of real equality, the right to work, to own, to live, in a word, to the whole question of the proletarian."[27] Others, however, were less impressed. For Ernest Renan, writing a decade after the national poet's death, Béranger was a "fake drunk" (*faux ivrogne*) and a "fake libertine" (*faux libertin*), looking out for the means to win popularity by way of "philanthropic songs and sentimental socialism." He was "the god of the *guinguette* and of plain folk at table," the kind of person who would slap you on the shoulder and treat you as his fellow but who could soon be seen to be as much of a fraud as any usurper of a noble title. He was, in short, a bourgeois populist, free with his convictions, but careful with his money, whose way of dealing with religion was like his way of dealing with women. They both lacked discretion, subtlety, and tact. His one real target was "the devout" side of the Restoration with its fixation on the alliance of throne and altar. France, Renan

24. On this lineage, see Daniel Fabre, "Proverbes, contes et chansons," in *Les lieux de mémoire*, ed. Pierre Nora, 7 vols. (Paris, Gallimard, 1992), pt. 3, *Les France 2: Traditions*, pp. 613–39 (p. 635 for the list of *chansonniers*). See too Roger Bonniot, *Pierre Dupont, poète et chansonnier du peuple* (Paris, Nizet, 1991), and, on political songs in mid-nineteenth-century France, Edward Berenson, *Populist Religion and Left-Wing Politics in France, 1830–1852* (Princeton, NJ, Princeton UP, 1984), pp. 127–68.

25. "Parmi les plus illustres poètes de notre époque, combien en est-il qu'on osât placer audessus de Béranger?" Louis Blanc, *Organisation du travail* [1840], 9th ed. (Paris, 1850), p. 126. The passage is not in the first (1840) edition.

26. For the best and fullest studies, see Jean Touchard, *La gloire de Béranger*, 2 vols. (Paris, Armand Colin, 1968), and, with generous recognition of the range and quality of that earlier work, together with a modern CD of some of Béranger's most famous songs, Sophie Anne Leterrier, *Béranger: des chansons pour un peuple citoyen* (Rennes, PU de Rennes, 2013), together, more broadly, with Philippe Darriulat, *La muse du peuple. Chansons politiques et sociales en France 1815–1871* (Rennes, PU de Rennes, 2010). On Michelet's characterization, see Jules Michelet, *Le peuple*, 2nd ed. (Paris, 1846), p. 195.

27. The passages are quoted by Prendergast, *The Classic*, p. 229.

wrote, loved vulgar impiety but could not tolerate genuine disinterest. "If a thinker were to invoke the sacred rights of science and free inquiry, he would soon be denounced as an innovator and, if he actually had any readers, would be said to be someone dangerous. But if, instead, he was to sing of Lisette and mock what was sacred, glass in hand, then any cleric who dared to oppose him would be branded immediately as odious, backward, and an enemy of enlightenment with the shade of the national poet rising up to warn every honest French toper of the threat to liberty and the principles of '89."[28]

Renan's hostility was as much testimony to Beranger's popularity as, earlier, was Michelet's enthusiasm. Whether either or both of their assessments were also testimony to what Sainte-Beuve called a "political economy of impotence" raises a more complicated set of questions. This, in the first instance, is because Béranger's songs were a compound of the old and the new in several related senses. The music, which he did not compose, was either the work of one of his composer-collaborators or, more frequently, a recycled version of an established tune. The words, however, were more fully his own. Béranger's songs were about ordinary people and their moral entitlements. They centred largely on Napoleon Bonaparte and the great events of the First Empire, either, as with "Le roi d'Yvetot," in a hostile and satirical sense, or, during the period of the Restoration, as an image of a common past made up of ordinary memories, now set—nostalgically, collectively, and patriotically—against a more offensively individualistic and less just, communal, or fraternal present. These were the messages of songs like "The Old Flag" ("Le vieux drapeau"), "The Old Corporal" ("Le vieux caporal"), "People's Memories" ("Les souvenirs du peuple"), or "The Elysian Field" ("Le champ d'asyle"). Alongside this sentimental image of the past was a more satirically abrasive evaluation of the present and, as Béranger presented them, the mixture of monetary influence, religious hypocrisy, and titled pedigrees that he associated with the Restoration and its divisive legacy. In an assessment made in 1853 by the author of a book on the influence of French literature between 1830 and 1850 on public opinion and manners, Béranger had become a socialist after 1830, but it was not clear how his socialism could be defined. It was not hard, however, to notice his reaction

---

28. "Que le penseur réclame les droits imprescriptibles de la science et du libre examen, c'est un novateur, et, s'il a des lecteurs, un homme dangereux. Mais s'il voulait bien, au lieu de cela, chanter Lisette et rire des choses saintes le verre à la main, le clergé serait odieux, rétrograde, ennemi des lumières en s'opposant à lui, et l'ombre du poète national se lèverait pour montrer à tous les joyeux convives de France la liberté menacée et les principes de 1789 en danger." Ernest Renan, "La théologie de Béranger," in his *Questions contemporaines* [Paris, 1868], 5th ed. (Paris,1912), pp. 461–77. For a later endorsement of Renan's attack, see Edouard Berth, *La fin d'une culture* (Paris, 1927), pp. 34–35, 98–99.

to the pitiless quality of modern society towards the poor or to recognize an emblem of a more just world in his song "Les fous" ("The Lunatics"), with its vivid, Lamennais-inspired image of a madman, drenching a cross with his blood, who was in fact to bequeath us a God. It was, according to a biography of the socialist Charles Fourier published in 1839, "a masterpiece of reason as much as poetry."[29] Together, the combination of moralism and populism meant that the songs could be described as the starting point of the cult of the war veteran, whether as the hero of Jena and Waterloo, the unknown soldier of Versailles, or the forgotten victim of Vietnam. From Afghanistan to Zimbabwe, the tradition that Béranger inaugurated turned the human aftermath of war into one of the key components of modern politics. For George Sand, in a review of Béranger's published correspondence, his songs had been what had kept France alive in the years of occupation and austerity after the defeat at Waterloo.[30]

At its best, the outcome of this mixture of adaptability and creativity was a highly successful popular song, with the message and topicality of the lyrics wrapped in a recognizably familiar melody. The combination itself was not new. Nor, in a sense, was its popularity. But both earlier types of song were associated more usually with a number of more discrete settings, like the land, with its multiple seasonal activities and its many different types of work; or the urban trades, with their guilds, corporations, and *compagnonnages*, and their episodically striking public presence both in municipal life and in the complicated life cycles and life chances of young migrant men; or, in the broadest and most durable setting of all, in the organized activities of Europe's armies and navies, and the discipline and drilling that, in the seventeenth and eighteenth centuries, provided a long-drawn-out musical accompaniment to the militarization of European life. From this perspective, even the almost immediate success of the "Marseillaise" during the period of the French Revolution owed as much to an established martial and musical tradition as it did both to the new scale of popular mobilization and to the new claims upon patriotic sacrifice generated by the American and French revolutions.

The Béranger phenomenon was the starting point of the modern association between popular music and popular politics. To Hugo, the new

29. Charles Menche de Loisne, *Influence de la littérature française de 1830 à 1850 sur l'esprit public et les mœurs* (Brussels, 1853), pp. 32–35, quoting (p. 35) the punch line—"Un fou qui meurt nous lègue un Dieu"—of Béranger's song "Les fous." On the association of the song with Fourier, see Charles Pellarin, *Notice biographique sur Charles Fourier* (Paris, 1839), p. 11.

30. George Sand, "Voyez-le dans son œuvre, dans sa pensée jeune et fraiche, épurée par le travail et enflammée par ces grands instincts de la liberté qui ont empêché la France de mourir après l'invasion": in her *Autour de la table* (Paris, 1879), pp. 215–27 (here p. 227).

association meant that there was no aesthetic need for the unities of time, place, and action of classical theory because the various parts of modern drama could cater to them all. They could create enough of an illusion of reality to make it unnecessary to insist on the further constraints of the unities themselves. In this sense, as Hugo put it, "far from demolishing art, the new ideas simply seek to reconstruct it on a more substantial foundation." Reality "from the standpoint of art" would certainly be different from "reality from the standpoint of nature," but it would also be more complete because "the magic wand of art" could bring together a whole society and a whole age and give them "that life and sparkle which give birth to illusion, that prestige of reality which arouses the enthusiasm of the spectator and, first of all, the poet."[31] The power and emotional impact of drama also had a strongly historical dimension because the progression from lyric to epic to drama meant that there was now a growing body of linguistic and conceptual resources available to capture the endless amalgamations of the grotesque and the sublime that, on Hugo's terms, not only made the drama the archetype of modern art, but also cast a retrospective and melancholy aura over the residual legacies of the lyric and epic forms that modern art had absorbed.[32] In this sense, both historicity and veracity were built into modern art.

As Hugo emphasized in a letter published in the *Journal des débats* in July 1824 during an earlier round of the argument between the supporters of the classics and the romantics, the real world was the key to the ideal world. "It is no more possible for the romantics than for the classics," he wrote, "to conceive of an ideal world by abstracting from the real world." Images, he continued, "are the basis of every human language, and it is as impossible to speak without images as to paint without colours. We can conceive of something only in terms of what we have seen and invent imaginary forms only as a result of some combination of real forms."[33] The preface to *Cromwell*, published three years later, took the argu-

---

31. "Et ici, afin de montrer que, loin de démolir l'art les idées nouvelles ne veulent que le reconstruire plus solide et mieux fondé." Hugo, *Cromwell*, p. 89; *Oliver Cromwell*, p. 27. "Le théâtre est un point d'optique. Tout ce qui existe dans le monde, dans l'histoire, dans la vie, dans l'homme, tout doit et peut s'y réfléchir, mais sous la baguette magique de l'art." *Cromwell*, p. 90; *Oliver Cromwell*, p. 27.

32. Hugo, *Cromwell*, p. 97; *Oliver Cromwell*, pp. 32–33

33. "Il n'est pas plus donné aux *romantiques* qu'aux classiques de concevoir le monde idéal, abstraction faite du monde réel. . . . Les images sont le fondement de tout langage humain et il serait aussi impossible de parler sans images que de peindre sans couleurs. Nous ne pouvons concevoir que selon que nous avons vu et nous ne saurions inventer des formes imaginaires qui ne fussent le résultat de quelque combinaison des formes réelles." *Journal des débats*, 26 July 1824. On the context in which Hugo wrote the letter, see Gabriel Lanyi, "Debates on the Definition

ment one step further by claiming not only that the tension between the grotesque and the sublime was the fundamental ingredient of modern art, but also that it was the grotesque, not the sublime, that gave modern art its purchase on the ideal. The move brought the reevaluation of the imagination that began in the second half of the eighteenth century to a kind of conclusion.[34]

It was a move that paralleled (and possibly also owed an intellectual debt to) a short essay entitled "Réflexions sur la vérité dans l'art" (Reflections on truth in art) that Hugo's friend Alfred de Vigny published in 1826 as an introduction to his historical novel Cinq-Mars. There, the conceptual bridge between democracy and autonomy began to come more fully into view. "France above all," Vigny wrote there, "simultaneously loves history and the drama because the one describes the vast destinies of *humanity* and the other the particular fate of *man*." Although, he continued, this seemed to indicate that the two genres were quite distinct, there was, in fact, a substantial measure of similarity in their treatment of their respective subject matters. This was because a successful drama and a successful work of history both needed a form that could accommodate but also identify and convey meaning in the array of relevant facts. This addition, Vigny argued, was what gave a drama its power and injected coherence into a work of history. In both cases, he claimed, the addition was something produced by the imagination because it was the imagination that could add the truth of art to what was true in fact (or *la vérité de l'art* to *le vrai du fait*) and, by doing so, make either a work of history or the ingredients of a drama seem real. "That purely beautiful, purely intellectual, truth (*vérité*) that I feel, that I see and seek to define," Vigny wrote, "and whose name, to make myself better understood, I dare to distinguish from that of the true (*vrai*) is like the soul of all the arts."

> It is the choice of a sign that is characteristic of every type of beauty and of all the grandeurs of the visibly true, but is still different, because the truth is better than what is simply true. It is an ideal whole made up of its principal forms, a luminous hue made up of its most lively colours, a dizzying balm of its purest aromas, a delicious elixir of its most savoury nectars, a perfect harmony of its most melodious sounds; in short, it is the total sum of all its values.

This, Vigny concluded, was why the subject matter of history and the drama were not as far apart as they seemed, and why too, as he went on to put it

---

of Romanticism in Literary France (1820–1830)," *Journal of the History of Ideas* 41 (1980): 141–50 (especially pp. 145–46).

34. See Sonenscher, *Jean-Jacques Rousseau*, pp. 86–114.

memorably, "history is a novel whose author is the people (*l'histoire est un roman dont le peuple est l'auteur*)."[35]

In the most immediate sense, the imaginative link between history and drama identified by Vigny allowed Hugo to add a new dimension to the concept of the grotesque. In earlier usage, that concept was used mainly to refer to what was decorative or nonrepresentational and nonmimetic. This usage was not entirely absent from Hugo's procedure, but in his usage the concept of the grotesque could, for example, be applied to "the Christian hell" housing "those hideous forms evoked by the harsh genius of Dante and Milton," as well as to "those absurd figures in whose midst would play Jacques Callot, that Michelangelo of the burlesque." As with the earlier usage, there was nothing functional or utilitarian in this version of the grotesque, but there was also nothing simply decorative, as in the parallel concept of the arabesque.[36] Instead, the grotesque was intended to be a window onto the sublime. As Hugo put it, "a very new and interesting book could be written upon the employment of the grotesque in art. It would show what powerful effects modern artists have obtained from this fruitful type, which is the favourite target for narrow-minded criticism even in our own day. . . . We will simply say here that as a glass through which to examine the sublime, as a means of contrast, the grotesque is, in our judgment, the richest source of inspiration that nature can throw open to art."[37]

The stadial theory underlying the claim also implied a more elaborate way of thinking about history. If, as Hugo claimed, modern drama was a synthesis of the sublime and the grotesque, with the variety of the latter reinforcing the splendour of the former, then, as Vigny had indicated, something like the same combination could also be applied to thinking about history. The resulting combination of unity and diversity seemed to indicate that human history

---

35. "Cette *vérité* toute belle, toute intellectuelle, que je sens, que je vois et que je voudrais définir, dont j'ose ici distinguer le nom de celui du *vrai* pour me mieux faire entendre, est comme l'âme de tous les arts. C'est un choix de signe caractéristique dans toutes les beautés et toutes les grandeurs du *vrai* visible; mais ce n'est pas lui-même, c'est mieux que lui; c'est un ensemble idéal de ses principales formes, une teinte lumineuse qui comprend ses plus vives couleurs, un baume enivrant de ses parfums les plus purs, un élixir délicieux de ses sucs les meilleurs, un harmonie parfaite de ses sons les plus mélodieux; enfin c'est une somme complète de toutes ses valeurs." The addition of imaginative truth to the truthfulness of historical facts was why "*l'histoire est un roman dont le peuple est l'auteur*." Alfred de Vigny, "Réflexions sur la vérité dans l'art," in *Cinq-Mars* (Paris, 1826), pp. 1–9.

36. On this, see Alain Muzelle, *L'arabesque: la théorie romantique de Friedrich Schlegel à l'époque de l'Athenäum* (Paris, 2006).

37. Hugo, *Cromwell*, pp. 71–72; *Oliver Cromwell*, pp. 14–15.

could be seen as a process accentuating both convergence and divergence as more of the range of possibilities of both nature and human nature came, over time, to be uncovered and understood. The interplay between unity and diversity pointed towards a more erratic, but causally self-contained—or dialectical—theory of historical development, with those parts of human culture that could be described as grotesque making a positive contribution to those parts of human culture that could be described as sublime and, inversely, with the intermittent uniformity of the sublime leading in turn to the proliferating multiplicity of the grotesque. In one guise, the resulting template for thinking about historical causation lent itself to the Europe-wide discovery of Vico. In another guise, the same interest in the oscillating patterns of historical development that could be associated with Vico's concepts of *corso* and *ricorso* overlapped with the parallel concepts of organic and critical periods of history laid out, under the aegis of the comte de Saint-Simon, in the competing philosophies of history developed by Auguste Comte on the one side and by the Catholic socialist Philippe Buchez on the other. For a time, mainly before 1830, but still before 1848, the thought of Vico, Hugo, and Saint-Simon appeared to suggest that much the same subject matter was involved in thinking about politics, culture, and history.[38] However discrete the three subjects might once have seemed, they now appeared to be linked by their common connection to the further subjects of autonomy and democracy.

Cyprien Desmarais and the Dilemmas of the Modern Age

The scale of the transformation involved in adding the popular and cultural to the political and constitutional can be followed conveniently in a series of publications by a minor French royalist writer named Cyprien Desmarais. The first of these appeared in 1824 under the title *Essai sur les classiques et romantiques* (Essay on the classics and the romantics). In this essay, Desmarais set out to show that the romantic could be reconciled with the classic because, he argued, both could be set against the scepticism and materialism of the eighteenth century. There was, he argued, a spiritual side to both classical formality and romantic sensibility that was absent from the culture of the eighteenth century. In this sense, Chateaubriand and Germaine de Staël shared enough

38. As the baron d'Eckstein noted dismissively in 1854, "les Saint-Simoniens et les Fouriéristes ont emprunté à Vico sa combinaison de symboles et de formules. Ils ont substitué à la réflexion et à la raison de Vico leur fantaisie, leur arbitraire, sans prendre garde que le système de Vico allait contre leurs doctrines, contre la théorie du progrès qu'ils doivent à Condorcet." Eckstein, "Essai d'une philosophie de l'histoire," p. 10.

common moral and religious ground with Racine and Fénelon for their values to trump the values of Voltaire, Diderot, and the baron d'Holbach in the eighteenth century and those of the nineteenth-century French Ideologues and their *Doctrinaire* allies. As Desmarais presented them, the real enemies of romantics like Chateaubriand, Staël, and their followers were not the supporters of the classics, represented by figures like Racine or Bossuet, but the religious sceptics of the eighteenth century, because, he asserted, the social disintegration produced by their morally corrosive thought had, ultimately, been responsible for Robespierre and the Terror. The real antidote to romanticism was, therefore, to be found in a regime that could combine romantic enthusiasm with classic authority.

By 1826, however, Desmarais had modified his views. He did so mainly because of the new alignment between romanticism and liberalism that began to emerge in the wake of Hugo's preface to his play *Cromwell* and the questions that it raised about the apparently fundamental similarity between romanticism and classicism that Desmarais himself had described only two years earlier. As Desmarais now recognized in 1826 in a book entitled *Le temps présent, ou essais sur l'histoire de la civilisation du dix-neuvième siècle* (The present age, or essays on the history of the civilization of the nineteenth century), the classic-romantic split was not the same as the royalist-liberal split. Taking his cue as much from Germaine de Staël as from Louis de Bonald, he began by emphasizing the close relationship between literature and society. This, in the context of postrevolutionary and post-Napoleonic France, meant that literature was especially attuned to politics and, in particular, to the problems of reconciling political legitimacy with the economic and social divisions left by the legacy of the revolution and the empire. This was the context in which what Desmarais called "the quarrel" between supporters of the classics and the romantics had occurred. "Those," he wrote, "who took this to be an argument over words failed to understand it. Those who took it to be an argument over things were unable to solve it. In fact, it became more and more insoluble because everything became involved in it. Among the subjects brought into the debate were liberalism, royalism, religion, and politics, and, instead of lying on the sidelines, all these subjects became involved."[39] This made matters more complicated because some of the partisans of both the classics and the romantics were now to be found on the same political sides.

39. Cyprien Desmarais, *Le temps présent, ou essais sur l'histoire de la civilisation au dix-neuvième siècle* (Paris, 1826), p. 111. It is worth noting that Desmarais published a second, considerably modified, edition of the same book a year later, under the title of *Voyage pittoresque dans l'intérieur de la chambre des députés, suivi du temps présent* (Paris, 1827).

This, Desmarais explained, was because each side of the classic-romantic divide could house supporters of either liberalism or royalism. If romanticism set itself against classicism as the means to escape from the established rules of literary decorum and tradition, and if it was also inclined to look down on everything existing before 1789, then romanticism really was "an entirely liberal entity." If, however, romanticism was, as Desmarais put it, more a matter of endorsing religious feeling and the elements of primitive poetry, then "you will find, with good reason, that romanticism is entirely royalist."[40] The same divisions within divisions applied to the supporters of the classics. In one guise, a supporter of the classics could be a republican, like the painter Jacques-Louis David. In another, however, the same allegiance to the classics could be the basis of the moral and aesthetic choices of a royalist like Louis de Bonald.

Despite these divisions, Desmarais now asserted, the outcome of the romantic-classic argument was most likely to be a victory for the supporters of the romantics. This, he explained, had less to do with how romanticism had been defended than with how it had been attacked. Ever since the Académie française had come down against romanticism, "everyone" had become more or less romantic. In addition, Desmarais now argued—contradicting what he had written two years earlier—there was no real common ground between the supporters of the classics and the romantics because the argument between them was, fundamentally, an argument over two distinct forms of poetics. Classicism was, above all, a matter of memory and tradition, while romanticism was a matter of feeling and the future. Since this was the case, and since the future was inescapable, the romantics would win. But the inevitability of this outcome meant that the real question was now whether the remnants of the defeated, pro-classic side would go to liberalism or to royalism. Here, Desmarais argued, the supporters of the classics faced a choice. Romanticism, he argued, was not an innovation but a result. It was a result of the excesses of the French Revolution, and this, ultimately, meant that romanticism would be royalist. "From the moment," he argued, "that it is accepted that the poetics of romanticism are legitimate, then religious inspiration also has to be recognized as the most fertile source of *all* literary beauty." This set romanticism against liberalism and aligned it with royalism. "But how," Desmarais continued, implicitly answering his own questions, "can this type of inspiration be reconciled with systems of pure liberalism? Who can be made to believe that it is possible to make materialist, positive, and industrial civilization march in step to the sounds of melancholy, religious, romantic poetry?" From this perspective, the concept of a "romantic liberalism" was an oxymoron. Any fusion of

40. Desmarais, *Le temps présent*, p. 112.

the two would have to be either a "disguised royalism" or "liberalism dreaming of its own suicide."[41] Religion could be the basis of a new alignment between the supporters of the romantics and the classics under the aegis of a more highly spiritualized royalism. Desmarais had, in fact, repeated his earlier argument but with a different justification.

Desmarais continued to rehearse the argument after the revolution of 1830. This time, however, his target was the putative affinity of liberalism, civilization, and progress. In reality, Desmarais now argued in a third book—published in 1833 and entitled *De la littérature française au dix-neuvième siècle considérée dans ses rapports avec le progrès de la civilisation et de l'esprit national* (On French literature in the nineteenth century and its relation to the progress of civilization and the national spirit)—the affinity was largely spurious. This, he claimed, was because the concept of civilization on which liberalism relied was too narrowly material and industrial to produce anything amounting to genuine moral progress. "There is," he wrote, "something astonishing at the sight of a people dominated by both a deep and lively sensibility and an almost barbarous egoism; a people whose literature is becoming more religious by the day, while its society is given over to scepticism and unbelief; where luxury has been carried to so great an excess that it seems not only to gild opulence but even to hide the rags of misery; a people who, over thirty years, have done nothing except make laws and revolutions to reach morality and raise up civilization, but among whom morality and civilization still resemble two travellers who have lost their way."[42] The mixture, he argued, was an effect of what he called "the complex state of our civilization." While "our industry improves, our moral state goes backwards and a sort of intellectual anarchy that seems to presage barbarism becomes ever more visible."[43]

Desmarais's three books capture the moral and political ambiguities and uncertainties quite well. By the third decade of the nineteenth century what

41. Ibid., p. 118.

42. "N'est-ce pas, en effet, une chose étonnante, de voir un peuple dominé à la fois de toutes parts par une sensibilité vive et profonde et par un égoïsme presque barbare; un peuple chez lequel la littérature devient de jour en jour plus religieuse, tandis que la société est livrée au scepticisme et à l'incrédulité; ou le luxe est porté à un excès si grand qu'il sert non seulement à parer à l'opulence, mais même à cacher les haillons de la misère; enfin un peuple qui depuis trente ans ne fait autre que des révolutions et des lois pour conquérir la morale et pour agrandir la civilisation, et chez lequel la morale et la civilisation sont encore comme deux voyageurs égarés dans leur route." Cyprien Desmarais, *De la littérature française au dix-neuvième siècle considérée dans ses rapports avec le progrès de la civilisation et de l'esprit national* (Paris, 1833), pp. 8–9.

43. "Car tandis que notre industrie se perfectionne, notre état moral va se dégradant; et une sorte d'anarchie intellectuelle se montre parmi nous comme le funeste avant-coureur de la barbarie." Ibid., p. 18.

was ancient could well be classic, but could also be described as either royal or republican and could be symbolized by any one among Brutus, Caesar, or Louis XIV. In a parallel sense, what was modern could well be romantic, but could also be described as royal or republican, with different conceptions of religion or history now supplying the main underlying sources of divergence. The same ambiguity applied to the idea of empire. In one guise, imperial rule could be described as ancient and militaristic, while monarchy could be described as modern and legalistic. In another guise, however, the same system of imperial rule could be associated with a modern plebiscitary democracy and a range of financial and social resources that were unavailable in the ancient past. A Bonaparte, on these terms, was a caesar or kaiser, but with a new layer of national, social, and democratic resources added to the earlier, largely military and martial, sources of legitimacy.[44] For Desmarais, the problem was that the distinctions represented by the proliferating array of labels did not seem to have any ability to reinforce one another and produce the kind of legitimacy that heralded social and political stability.

Jules Michelet and Edgar Quinet

A generation later, many of these uncertainties and ambiguities had disappeared. One result was the modern concept of the Renaissance.[45] Another was the array of different objects of ideological allegiance that still forms the terrain on which modern political divisions have come to be based. For someone like Desmarais, writing mainly before 1830, the Romans and Germans still stood in opposition to one another—with the former standing for what was classic, ancient, pagan, republican, or imperial, and the latter standing for what was romantic, modern, Christian, royal, or federal. In the course of the nineteenth century, however, all these antitheses began to dissolve. What began to take shape in their place was a new fusion—both of the classic and the

44. On these ambiguities, see Peter Baehr, "An 'Ancient Sense of Politics'? Weber, Caesarism and the Republican Tradition," *Archives européennes de sociologie* 40 (1999): 333–50. See, more recently, Peter Baehr and Melvyn Richter, eds., *Dictatorship in History and Theory* (Cambridge, CUP, 2004), and Peter Baehr, *Caesarism, Charisma and Fate: Historical Sources and Modern Resonances in the Work of Max Weber* (New Brunswick, NJ, Transaction Books, 2008).

45. On the concept of the Renaissance, see, classically, Lucien Febvre, *Michelet et la Renaissance* (Paris, Flammarion, 1992), and, more fully, Rubini, *The Other Renaissance*, and, particularly, Ruehl, *The Italian Renaissance in the German Historical Imagination*. See too J. B. Bullen, *The Myth of the Renaissance in Nineteenth-Century Writing* (Oxford, OUP, 1994), and Yannick Portebois and Nicholas Terpstra, eds., *The Renaissance in the Nineteenth Century/Le xixe siècle renaissant* (Toronto, Victoria University of Toronto, Centre for Reformation and Renaissance Studies, 2003).

romantic and of the Roman and the German—that pushed the original ancient-modern opposition out of the political and historiographical picture (it had to wait until the late twentieth century and the related concepts of civic humanism and neo-Roman liberty to come back). The process was more protracted and complicated than what has been described recently as "the shock of the ancient."[46] In this interpretation, the final outcome of the seventeenth-century *querelle des anciens et des modernes* was a victory for the apologists of the ancients and an endorsement of the range of moral, cultural, and aesthetic differences on which justifications of the ancients had, putatively, been based. In fact, the real outcome was more complicated because the victors in this iteration of the argument were not, in fact, the apologists of the ancients but the apologists of the moderns.

The twist, however, was that the qualities of the moderns had turned into the qualities of the ancients, but in a romantic rather than a classic guise. From this perspective, the original ancient-modern parallel of the reign of Louis XIV, which was singled out by Quinet as a prime example of the dangers of misplaced comparisons, had come full circle. Then, the apologists of the moderns had highlighted the similarities between the culture and the arts of the ancients and their modern counterparts. A hundred years later, the apologists of the moderns—now known as romantics—had highlighted the differences. "What applies to classic tragedies also applies to the paintings of David," noted Ludovic Vitet, one of the great French painter's obituarists after his death in 1825. To Vitet, the purity of his forms could not offset the poverty of their human affects. For all their order and symmetry, they had all the life of a frieze. "Once," Vitet continued, "you agree to turn your eyes away from nature as it is and, like David, dream of beings animated by a colder, more severe, less passionate life than our own . . . then, but only then, will you come to admire those beauties that the absence of other beauties has concealed from your gaze." As was the case with his classically oriented near contemporaries, the dramatist Vittorio Alfieri and the composer Christoph Willibald Gluck, Jacques-Louis David was to be admired for "qualities that were, in a sense, foreign to the arts that they cultivated."[47] Here, the romantic was sharply

46. Norman, *The Shock of the Ancient*.
47. "On peut ne pas sympathiser avec ces figures dont aucune affection humaine ne semble altérer les traits; on peut trouver dans la manière dont elles sont disposées quelque chose de trop symétrique, de trop analogue à l'ordonnance d'un bas-relief, mais il est impossible, à moins qu'on ne soit pas prévenu par le système contraire, de ne pas être frappé de cette harmonie de toutes les parties entre elles, de cette unité de conception qui se reconnaît dans les moindres détails, et de ces formes idéales, il est vrai, mais d'un type si pur et si parfait. A la vérité c'est là un plaisir tout rationnel, tout réfléchi: il en est des tableaux de David comme des tragédies

distinct from the classic. A generation later, however, by the time that Saint-Beuve published his definition of a classic, the romantic had become the classic, just as the German had become Roman. Rome, in short, was back.

The point was underlined two decades later by the great historian of the ancient city Numa Denis Fustel de Coulanges. "It is usually customary," he wrote in 1872 in an article entitled "L'invasion Germanique au cinquième siècle: son caractère et ses effets" (The character and effects of the Germanic invasion of the fifth century), "to conceive of the history of France as beginning with a great Germanic invasion."

> It is assumed that Gaul was vanquished, conquered, and enslaved. The event has assumed an enormous proportion in books and in our imaginations. It seems to have changed the face of the whole country and given it a destiny that it would never have had without it. To many historians and much of the public, it became the source of the entire old regime, with the sons of the Germans turning into feudal lords and the sons of the Gauls turning into serfs of the glebe.[48]

None of this, Fustel insisted, was true. There had been no Germanic invasion because the Germanic peoples were in fact clients or allies of Rome. There had, certainly, been a Germanic immigration, but its effect had been to maintain and consolidate the broad array of Roman institutions and Roman law that remained in France long after the decline and fall of the Roman Empire. The details of the argument are not particularly important. For Fustel, what was important was the continuity, from Rome to France and from the ancients to

---

classiques. . . . Alfieri, Gluck et David, trois grands artistes, trois esprits puissants, mais qu'il faut admirer pour des qualités en quelque sorte étrangères aux arts qu'ils ont cultivés." Anon. [Ludovic Vitet], "J. L. David," *Le Globe* 3, no. 10 (14 January 1826): 52, reprinted in Ludovic Vitet, *Etudes sur les beaux-arts*, 2 vols. (Paris, 1846), 1:181–88 (p. 186 for the passage quoted).

48. "On se représente ordinairement, au début de l'histoire de la France, une grande invasion des Germains. On se figure la Gaule vaincue, conquise, asservie. Cet évènement a pris, dans les livres et dans les imaginations, des proportions énormes. Il semble qu'il ait changé la face du pays et donné à ses destinées une direction qu'elles n'auraient pas eue sans lui. Il est, pour beaucoup d'historiens et pour la foule, la source d'où est venu tout l'ancien régime. Les seigneurs féodaux passent pour être les fils des Germains, et les serfs de la glèbe pour être les fils des Gaulois. Une conquête, c'est-à-dire un acte brutal, se place ainsi comme l'origine unique de l'ancienne société française." Numa Denis Fustel de Coulanges, "L'invasion Germanique au cinquième siècle: son caractère et ses effets," *Revue des Deux Mondes* 99 (1872): 241–68 (p. 241 for this passage). On Fustel, see especially François Hartog, *Le xixe siècle et l'histoire. Le cas Fustel de Coulanges* (Paris, PUF, 1988), along with L. de Gérin-Ricard, *L'Histoire des Institutions Politiques de Fustel de Coulanges* (Paris, Société française d'Editions Littéraires et Techniques, 1936).

the moderns. As Fustel's disciple Camille Jullian put it, looking back at the first French Empire from the end of the nineteenth century, "a new France was born and, in her, Rome lived again."[49] The idea that the modern world had had two starting points, one Roman, but the other German, as Sismondi had claimed much earlier in the nineteenth century, was simply a recently invented historical tradition.

It is tempting to assign the argument to the context of the Franco-Prussian War of 1870–71 and the more deep-seated eclipse of French power that the war underlined. But the Roman revival in nineteenth-century moral and political thought was a more protracted and complicated affair, with origins that went back before the Franco-Prussian War to the time that preceded the two French revolutions of 1830 and 1848. It began with the great Vico revival of the 1820s and was developed most prominently in the work of the two French historians and philosophers of history Jules Michelet and Edgar Quinet. What both Michelet and Quinet found in Vico was a philosophy of history that lent itself not only to legal history but also to the more difficult problem of explaining why Roman law and Roman institutions had outlived the Roman Empire. The starting point was Vico's distinction between creating and making.[50] God, according to Vico, created because God existed beyond space and time and, with the help of the other divine attributes, could simply create what was right and true. Humans, however, inhabited both space and time and were, therefore, obliged to make. Making was as likely to be wrong as right, but what was

49. "Une France nouvelle était née, et c'était Rome qui revivait en elle." Camille Jullian, *Extraits des historiens français du xix siècle* (Paris, 1897), p. v. For helpful ways in to the subject of Rome and Roman law in nineteenth-century French thought, see Henri Tronchon, "Une concurrence à la philosophie de l'histoire en France: la philosophie du droit," in *Mélanges offerts à M. Charles Andler par ses amis et ses élèves*, [ed. Anon.] (Strasbourg, 1924), pp. 371–81; Claude Nicolet, "Rome et les conceptions de l'état en France et en Allemagne au xixe siècle," in *Visions sur le développement des états européens*, ed. Wim Blockmans and Jean-Philippe Genet (Rome, Collection de l'Ecole Française de Rome, 171, 1993), pp. 17–44, and, particularly, Nicolet, *La fabrique d'une nation*. See too Ando, "A Dwelling beyond Violence," and Käthe Panick, *La Race Latine. Politischer Romanismus im Frankreich des 19. Jahrhunderts* (Bonn, Ludwig Röhrscheid Verlag, 1978).

50. See, still helpfully, Robert Flint, *Vico* (London, 1884), and, for a brilliant summary, Isaiah Berlin, "Corsi e Ricorsi," *Journal of Modern History* 50 (1978): 480–89. On the interrelationship of Vico's thought, legal history, and the background to the nineteenth-century Vico revival, see Elio Gianturco, "Vico et les débuts de l'historiographie du droit français," *Archives de philosophie* 40 (1977): 87–105; Steinberg, "The Twelve Tables," and, especially, Mouza Raskolnikoff, "Vico, l'histoire romaine et les érudits français des lumières," *Mélanges de l'école française de Rome* 96 (1984): 1051–77.

made and what could last would also be something more like the products of divine creation. This initial difference between creating and making was the key to understanding human history and the recurrent switches between creation and preservation, innovation and tradition, and the ebbs and flows (*corsi e ricorsi*) that history housed. It could explain continuity as much as discontinuity, just as it could deal with particularity as well as generality. The resulting elasticity made it possible to deal with historical causation in ways that were neither too weak nor too strong, with rather less providential guidance than was usual in universal history, but with rather more than the undifferentiated sequence of events of ordinary chronologies. The rediscovery of Vico dovetailed neatly with the concept of palingenesis.

As one of Michelet's early reviewers, the German philosopher Eduard Gans, commented, Michelet's approach brought providential history down to earth but could still show that there was a pattern and direction in human affairs independently of either the authority of scripture or the many arbitrary and discordant interpretations imposed by historians on the flow of events. This, according to Gans, was because Michelet's history was predicated on a real philosophy of history. It could accommodate regress as well as progress, decline as well as development, and this made it different from the types of history produced by his French contemporary François-Auguste Mignet, the author of a successful recent history of the French Revolution, as well as those by Auguste Comte and the followers of Saint-Simon. They, Gans wrote, had been too inclined to project the idea of progress, "the principal demand of today's world," back onto past times.[51] Michelet's use of Vico made it easier to avoid this type of teleology and the mixture of ambiguity and circularity built into the Saint-Simonian distinction between critical and organic periods of history. Instead of the circularity involved in trying, independently of conflict or stability, to explain what made a period critical or organic, and the ambiguity involved in deciding whether the one or the other was an effect or cause, Michelet's history was simpler. It began with conflict, but dropped the initial Bonaldian and Saint-Simonian typological concern with different types

51. Edouard Gans, review of Jules Michelet, *Introduction à l'histoire universelle, Jahrbücher für wissenschaftliche Kritik* 1 (1832): 141–57 (see pp. 141–42 for the passages summarized here). Thanks to Diana Siclovan of the British Library for her help in translating the review. On Michelet's historical thought, see Paul Viallaneix, *La 'voie royale': essai sur l'idée du peuple dans l'oeuvre de Michelet* [1959] (Paris, Flammarion, 1971); Nelly S. Hoyt, "Michelet: A Historian Paints French History," in *Thomas Couture and the Painting of History*, Springfield Museum of Fine Arts 1980 exhibition, curated by Albert Boime and Robert Henning Jr. (Springfield, MA, 1980); and, recently, Michèle Hannoosh, *Jules Michelet: Writing Art and History in Nineteenth-Century France* (University Park, Pennsylvania State UP, 2019).

of period and different forms of conflict. Conflicts could happen for many
reasons, but they usually gave way to stability under the aegis of the law and
legality. The nature of both the law and legality could vary immensely in terms
of concepts, procedures, and institutions. But adding the law and legality to
the subjects of conflict and stability made it easier to identify and examine a
middle ground lying somewhere between historical contingency and historical inevitability and between historical particularity and historical generality.[52] This, for Michelet, was Vico's real significance.

Michelet first highlighted the salience of Vico to the new historiography in
the preface that he wrote for his *Histoire romaine* (Roman history) of 1831. "The
key," he wrote, "to the *Scienza Nuova* (Vico's great alternative to the natural
jurisprudence of Grotius, Hobbes and Locke) is this: *humanity is its own work.*
God acts on humanity, but through humanity. Humanity is divine but no
single individual is divine. Those mythical heroes, a Hercules whose arms part
mountains; those swift legislators who, like Romulus or Lycurgus, accomplish
the work of ages in a single lifetime are the creations of the thought of
nations."[53] Humanity and palingenesis were two sides of the same coin. Echoing the earlier claim by the German philologist and classicist Friedrich August
Wolf that Homer was the personification of a society and a culture rather than
a real individual, Michelet applied the same idea to the figures of a legislator
or a founder. Like Homer, they were symbols, or signs, of those abstract ideas
and moral qualities that humanity had been able to envisage, but not name.
They were personifications of whole generations, allowing "one hero" to combine "the conceptions of a whole poetic cycle."[54] Wolf's move, published in
1795 in his *Prolegomena to Homer*, was repeated by a generation of German or
German-language scholars, including Johann Gottfried Herder, Barthold
Georg Niebuhr, Friedrich Wilhelm Joseph Schelling, Joseph Görres, Friedrich

52. On legal thought in nineteenth-century France, see Kelley, *Historians and the Law in
Post-revolutionary France*, pp. 41–55, 72–84, and, helpfully, Alfons Bürge, *Das französische Privatrecht im 19. Jahrhundert. Zwischen Tradition und Pandektenwissenschaft, Liberalismus und Etatismus* (Frankfurt am Main, Vittorio Klostermann, 1991). Thanks to Peter Garnsey for this latter
reference.

53. Jules Michelet, *Histoire romaine* [1831], ed. Paule Petitier (Paris, Belles Lettres, 2003), p. 11.
I have followed, with minor modifications, the translation in Jules Michelet, *History of the
Roman Republic*, trans. William Hazlitt (London, 1847), p. 4. On Michelet, legal history, and
Rome, see Paule Petitier, "Les *Origines du droit français* de Michelet," *Littérature et Nation*,
2nd ser., 9 (1992): 31–61; Olivier Remaud, *Michelet. Le magistrature de l'histoire* (Paris, Michalon,
1998), especially pp. 21–35.

54. Ibid. On Wolf, see Anthony Grafton, "Prolegomena to Friedrich August Wolf," *Journal
of the Warburg and Courtauld Institutes* 44 (1981): 101–29.

Creuzer, and Eduard Gans, whose publications supplied much of the conceptual architecture of Michelet's history. Theirs, Michelet noted, was the work that formed the context for the Vico revival of the early nineteenth century and the European-wide interest in historical personification that it brought in its wake.

Vico's originality, Michelet wrote, was to have "proved" that "these historical fictions were a necessity of our nature. Humanity, at first gross and material, was unable, in languages that were still entirely concrete, to express abstract thought unless it gave thought reality by giving it a body, a human personality and a proper name." This was why what had actually been the morally and causally complicated product of a collection of individuals was given a human name. Romulus, for example, stood for strength and for a people that was strong, while the name Judea stood for divine election and an elect people. "Thus," Michelet announced, "humanity began with the symbolic—in history, law and religion." This was the insight that was the basis of the philosophy of history that, after Vico, had been developed in Germany by Herder, Wolf, Görres, Schelling, and Creuzer. Humanity might have begun with "the materialised, individualised idea," but had proceeded towards "the pure and general idea," or, as Michelet put it, "in the motionless chrysalis of the symbol is operated the mystery of the transformation of the mind."[55] Symbols were physical, while minds were spiritual. Symbols could carry the mind only so far before it was able to cast them off, either in favour of a more apposite symbol or, ultimately, by producing the more abstract terminology that surrounded the concept of liberty.

The idea of history as a protracted, and ongoing, transition from symbols to concepts was particularly salient to the subject of law, the subject that supplied Michelet both with his introduction to Vico and, five years after the appearance of his *Histoire romaine*, with the title of his first major historical publication, *Origines du droit français cherchées dans les symboles et formules du droit universel* (An inquiry into the origins of French law in the symbols and formulae of universal law). Laws, clearly, could have authors. But even where authorship was unequivocal, something more was required to explain the mixture of general assent, spatial dissemination, effective implementation, and temporal durability that played a part in turning inscribed tablets—or, later, black font—into rules governing people's behaviour. From this perspective, outcomes were as interesting as authors because both seemed to be required to explain how laws came to have legitimacy and authority as well as consistency and legality. As Michelet went to some lengths to show in his *Histoire*

55. Michelet, *History of the Roman Republic*, p. 5; Michelet, *Histoire romaine*, pp. 11–12.

romaine, the key to understanding this extra aspect of law was conflict. This was because, to be legitimate as well as legal, laws had to add a further level of intelligibility, utility, or morality to human agency and, by doing so, make it easier to bring disputes to an end. Making sense of laws was, therefore, not only a matter of tracking the protracted transition from symbols to concepts, but was also a process of reconstructing the dynamics of the underlying conflicts in which the law supervened to provide a more peaceful and stable range of solutions to earlier disputes.

These were the insights that gave Michelet's *Histoire romaine* its shape and direction. Together, they meant that Roman history was no longer mainly a matter of the rise and decline of republican values or republican social arrangements. The increasingly broad cycles of conflict in which the republic was involved—whether they were within Rome itself and took place among its assorted patrician, plebeian, and other social components, or were between Rome and its assorted Etruscan, Latin, Italian, and Transalpine neighbours—meant that the scale and scope of Roman expansion was matched by the scale and scope of legal arbitration under the increasingly capacious aegis of Roman law. As Michelet put it in his *History of France*, "the Gallic world is the world of the tribe, the Etrusco-Roman world that of the *cité*," meaning a *civitas* or state.[56] From this perspective, what mattered about Rome was that it combined the attributes of a city and an empire within a single system, and that it was the dynamic development of this combination that favoured the switch from symbols to concepts. As Michelet put it in his *Introduction à l'histoire universelle*, published in the same year as his Roman history, Rome "housed in its walls two cities, two races, the Etruscan and the Latin, the sacerdotal and the *heroic*, eastern and western, patrician and plebeian, landed property and movable property, stability and progress, nature and liberty."[57] Ultimately, it was the law that was able to resolve the conflicts between these multiple binaries, just as it also set the seal on Rome's victory over Carthage in the Punic Wars. These wars, Michelet wrote, "not only determined the fate of two cities or two empires, but also determined to which of the two races—Indo-Germanic or Semitic—should belong the dominion of the world." One side, he continued, stood for "heroic genius, meaning that of art and legislation," while the other embodied

56. The passage is cited in the review of Michelet's *Histoire de France*, by Ferdinand, baron d'Eckstein, reprinted in Jules Michelet, *Œuvres complètes*, ed. Paul Viallaneix, 21 vols. (Paris, Flammarion, 1971–87), 4:775.

57. Jules Michelet, *Introduction à l'histoire universelle* [1831], in Michelet, *Œuvres complètes*, 2:232–33.

"the spirit of industry, navigation and commerce." In this version of multi-cultural history, Rome's victory marked not only the triumph of "heroic genius" over "industry, navigation and commerce," but also the triumph of the West over the East.[58]

In legal terms, Roman expansion meant that the transition from the Roman republic to the Roman Empire was almost seamless. Regime change amounted to little more than an adjustment to the new scale and scope of the Roman legal system. It meant too that it was the empire rather than the republic that was the setting that most favoured legal and social equality. This was why it was Caesar, not Cato, who, as Michelet put it, was "the man of humanity."[59] Here, Michelet had no inhibition about displaying his Bonapartist sympathies. Just as the legal equality promoted by the Caesars had prepared a favourable ground for the spiritual equality of Christianity, so the civil code that was the work of their modern equivalents had now prepared an equally favourable ground for the industry and individuality that were in the process of becoming the hallmarks of the modern age. In the hands of the young Michelet, Rome came back under Caesarist and Bonapartist auspices because both relied on Roman law as the medium of their power. Although, as Michelet's ideological allegiances changed, the French Revolution was soon to displace Napoleon as the heroic symbol of the modern age, he continued to maintain the parallel between Rome and France. Just as Roman law had replaced the symbols of earlier systems, so the civil code held out the same promise to supersede feudal systems. "France," Michelet wrote in 1837, "is the true continuator of Rome. She continues the work of interpretation. It is logical, prosaic, and antisymbolic."[60] It would also, he went on to claim, be social, democratic, and republican.

58. Michelet, *History of the Roman Republic*, p. 137.

59. Michelet, *History of the Roman Republic*, p. 326, and also pp. 332, 374.

60. "La France est le vrai continuateur de Rome. Elle poursuit l'œuvre de l'interprétation. Travail logique, prosaïque, anti-symbolique." Jules Michelet, *Origines du droit français cherchées dans les symboles et formules du droit universel* [1837], in Michelet, *Œuvres complètes*, 3:646. As Michelet put it later in a letter to his friend Adam Mickiewicz, "Le dernier héros qui ait paru, ce n'est pas Napoléon, comme ils disent, c'est la Révolution." Michelet to Mickiewicz, as cited in Hartog, *Anciens, modernes, sauvages*, p. 169. On this aspect of Michelet's thought and his aversion to the label "imaginative," see Paule Petitier, "L'imagination dans l'histoire: Michelet et les critiques du Second Empire," in *Ecrire/Savoir: littérature et connaissances à l'époque moderne*, ed. Alain Vaillant (Saint-Etienne, Editions Printer, 1996), pp. 121–38.

The Romantic Renaissance

The fusion of autonomy with democracy was taken a step further by Edgar Quinet. "M. Quinet belongs to the same school in poetry as M. Michelet does in history, to the symbolic school," noted a reviewer in 1838 echoing an earlier description of their common intellectual debt to Vico and his so-called symbolic school.[61] The point applied not only to Quinet's poetry, but also, more substantively, to the underlying philosophy of history that gave his poetry its direction and shape. It was this philosophy of history, visible in his inaugural lecture in 1839 as a literature professor in Lyon and in his later, extraordinary, *Révolutions d'Italie* of 1848, that supplied a new and different answer to the social question. While a rather conventional legitimist like Cyprien Desmarais could make a point about the underlying moral and political character of the social question by highlighting the tension between "melancholy, religious, romantic poetry" and "materialist, positive, industrial civilization," Quinet made a point of highlighting their compatibility.

He did so by means of what is now called "history from below."[62] As with later iterations of the genre, this was not simply a matter of trying to describe

61. "M. Edgard Quinet appartient en poésie à la même école que M. Michelet en histoire, à l'école symbolique." Athénaïs Mourier, "Le Prométhée de M. Edgard Quinet," *Revue française et étrangère* 6 (1838): 93–110 (p. 94 for the passage cited). For the term "école symbolique," see Antoine de Latour, *Essai sur l'étude de l'histoire en France au dix-neuvième siècle* (Paris, 1835), pp. 58–76. On Quinet and Chenavard, see Guernsey, *The Artist and the State*, p. 161; and Sloane, *Paul Marc Joseph Chenavard*, pp. 101–10.

62. For a parallel claim, this time about the historical work of one of Quinet's German intellectual mentors, Karl Friedrich Eichhorn (whose work Quinet referred to in his translation of Herder), see Small, *Origins of Sociology*, p. 65: "Indeed, before he was through he had ranged alongside of legal and political elements so many other elements which he found on different occasions to have been related to the legal and the political, that, whether by intention or not, in effect he had presented a sort of outline scheme of what has since been known as 'social history.'" See too the earlier description of the same process by the Russian and British medievalist Paul Vinogradoff in the introduction to his *Villainage in England* (Oxford, OUP, 1892), p. 17: "The Germanist school had to fight its way not only against Romanism but against diverse tenets of the Romantic school as represented by Savigny and Eichhorn, of which the Romanists had availed themselves. The whole doctrine was to be reconsidered in the light of two fundamental assumptions. The foundations of social life were sought not in aristocracy, but in the common freedom of the majority of the people: the German middle class, the 'Burgers', who form the strength of contemporary Germany, looked to the past history of their race as vouching for their liberty; the destinies of that particular class became the test of social development." For later discussion of the subject, see Maurice Agulhon, "Le problème de la culture populaire en France autour de 1848," *Romantisme* 9 (1975): 50–64.

ordinary lives, everyday activity, and popular culture, although it certainly included all these subjects. It was also a matter of trying to explain popular agency and, more comprehensively, of trying to understand what, for Quinet, was the fundamentally popular character of historical causation. As with Michelet, laws were the outcome of conflict and were couched in terms that, on the one hand, could settle the initial causes of conflict while, on the other hand, forming the basis of further conflictual cycles and increasingly extensive legal arrangements. Conflict and its causes were, therefore, the keys to historical and political understanding. It was this emphasis on conflict and its popular dynamics that governed Quinet's fierce hostility towards Hegel and, as he saw them, Hegel's eclectic and Saint-Simonian counterparts. On his terms, their politics were bound up with a philosophy of history that presupposed a predetermined goal and, as a result, an abdication of individual responsibility for collective agency. The result was either "nihilism" or "fatalism" (Quinet applied both terms to Hegel's philosophy), as God, humanity, or the absolute struggled towards self-consciousness over the course of time. "Put simply, and according to the doctrine of the absolute," Quinet wrote, taking aim at both Hegel and Schleiermacher, "God slumbered in a half-vegetable, half-animal dream for billions of years, without showing the least sign of life. Moses and Christ did cause him to stir once or twice from this eternal slumber, but he soon fell back to sleep and this time more deeply than ever."

> Things stayed mainly like this until the year 1804, with the exception of a few intervals of not very significant dreaming. At the beginning of that year, God had not yet acquired the least awareness of who he was and what he could be. Only towards the middle of the autumn was he definitively introduced to himself in the person and consciousness of Doctor Hegel. This important episode in the life of God took place on 23 October, on the road to Bayreuth, at 3:30 in the afternoon. From this moment, the Eternal felt himself to be alive and was no longer in any doubt about his own existence. A little later, he was appointed to be an ordinary professor and director of the Academy of Berlin, and his career was henceforth assured.[63]

63. "Suivant la doctrine de l'absolu, réduite à son expression la plus simple, Dieu sommeillait dans un rêve, moitié végétal, moitié animal, depuis des milliards d'années; il ne se donnait d'ailleurs pas le moindre signe de vie. Moïse et le Christ le tirèrent de cet engourdissement éternel. Mais il y retomba bien vite, et cette fois plus profondément que jamais. Les choses durèrent ainsi jusqu'à l'an 1804, avec quelque mélange de rêves insignifiants. Au commencement de cette même année, Dieu n'avait pas encore la moindre conscience de ce qu'il était ou pouvait être. Ce ne fut que vers le milieu de l'automne qu'il fit définitivement connaissance de lui-même dans la personne et la conscience de M. le docteur Hegel. Cet épisode important dans la vie de

Real history was not like this. It was less a matter of purposes, goals, and intentions than of unintended outcomes and unforeseen consequences, with no pregiven end point. This was why history from below was not like political history and still less like Hegelian history. Its agents were multiple and composite; their actions were complicated and various; and their outcomes were unexpected and unsynchronized. If this way of thinking about history owed something to scripture and theology, it also owed something to the eighteenth-century interest in the imagination and its ability to turn multiplicity into unity and general ideas into particular emotions. Here, much of the initial conceptual impetus came from Herder, whose *Ideen* Quinet had translated two decades earlier. "Popular songs," Herder had written, "are the archive of a people, the treasure house of its knowledge, its religion, its theogony, its cosmology, of the life of its forefathers and the splendours of its history. They are the outpouring of its heart, the image of what lies within, both in joy and in sorrow, by the bedside or the graveside."[64] With this type of starting point, history from below began as history as aesthetics because something more than what was purely physical was required to explain both the power of symbols and their transformation into the type of concept required to identify states, laws, or governments. In Quinet's version, history as aesthetics provided real interpretative and hermeneutical purchase on the assortment of signs, symbols, and songs that—on his terms—formed the nexus of popular culture, popular action, and historical change.

History as aesthetics was also national history. Civilization, Quinet wrote in an essay on the people of Romania that he published in 1857, was predicated on a multiplicity of nationalities (the assertion also had a biographical point because Quinet's first wife was German while his second wife was Romanian). "Every day," he claimed, "people admire the mechanisms of a machine, particularly if it has been discovered recently." The same attitude applied to nationality. "What is a nationality if it is not a kind of divine machine made by

<hr />

Dieu se passa le 23 octobre, sur le chemin de Bayreuth, à trois heures et demie de l'après-dinée. Depuis ce moment l'Eternel se sentit vivre, et ne garda plus le moindre doute sur sa propre existence. Un peu plus tard, il fut nommé professeur ordinaire et directeur de l'Académie de Berlin. Aussi sa carrière fut assurée." Quinet, *Allemagne et Italie*, pp. 121–22. See pp. 63 and 121 for the descriptions of Hegelianism as nihilism or fatalism. For commentary, see Guy Lavorel and Laurence Richer, eds., *Quinet en Question* (Lyon, C.E.D.I.C., 2004). See also Bernard Peloille, "A propos de la question des origines dans la pensée de Quinet," *Littérature et Nation*, 2nd ser., 9 (1992): 71–86.

64. The passage, from the introduction to Herder's *Volkslieder*, was quoted by Quinet's contemporary Xavier Marmier, in the introduction to his *Chants populaires du Nord* (Paris, 1842), p. ii.

the hands of a divine worker? What is nationality if it is not a system of aptitudes, of purely moral mechanisms, intellectual functions, and vital forces that
can only be seen there?" The hallmark of barbarism was to destroy—or to
accept the destruction of—one of these systems, just as the hallmark of civilization was to preserve and promote as many of them as possible.[65] Barbarism
was uniformity; civilization was diversity. History as aesthetics was, therefore,
the historiography of Hugo's preface to *Cromwell* or the novels of Alessandro
Manzoni and Sir Walter Scott, and, above all, of the Europe-wide rediscovery
of Vico in the first quarter of the nineteenth century. In Quinet's case it was
informed as well by the overlapping intellectual legacies of Herder, Görres,
and Creuzer, just as, with Michelet, it was informed by those of Vico, Pagano,
and Romagnosi. For both Quinet and Michelet, however, history as aesthetics
was popular history and historiography, as against Hegelian history and *its*
historiography.

The results began to appear in Quinet's inaugural lecture as professor of
literature at the Collège de France in 1842. The lecture was entitled "De la renaissance dans l'Europe méridionale" (On the Renaissance in southern Europe). The title was partly a gesture towards the name of the chair to which
Quinet had been appointed: his chair at the Collège de France was in southern
literature, while the chair of northern literature was held by another member
of the college, named Philarèthe Chasles. But the title of the lecture also had
a more immediate historical and political purpose, which we can identify
by setting Quinet's inaugural lecture against the inaugural lecture given by
Chasles a few weeks earlier. Chasles began his lecture course on northern literature by rehearsing and developing some of the familiar themes of romantic
historiography, as these had been established by Sismondi, Constant, and
Germaine de Staël. Modern civilization, he asserted, "is the particular fruit of
two influences: the influence of the South, which came first, and that of the
North, which came later, but was regenerative and fertilizing. The influence of
the North renewed the vital forces of the whole civilized world after the fall
of Rome. The servility of minds, worse even than the servility of bodies, was
overwhelming a dying society when the genius of liberty, barbarous but alive

---

65. "Tous les jours les hommes admirent le mécanisme d'une machine, surtout si elle est
nouvellement découverte. . . . Qu'est-ce donc qu'une nationalité si ce n'est une mécanique divine sortie des mains du grand ouvrier? Qu'est-ce encore, sinon un système d'aptitudes, de
ressorts tout moraux, de fonctions intellectuelles, de forces vives qui ne peuvent se montrer que
là?" Edgar Quinet, *Les Roumains*, in Edgar Quinet, *Œuvres complètes*, vol. 6 (Paris, 1857), pp. 122–
23. For the intellectual background to this type of claim, see Timothy Baycroft and David Hopkin, eds., *Folklore and Nationalism in Europe during the Long Nineteenth Century* (Leiden, Brill,
2012), especially pp. 1–10, 11–26, 371–401.

and active, reappeared in the form of the northern races." These two influences, Chasles explained, were typical of the broader process underlying "human civilizations" whose progress, he asserted, was the outcome of two opposing movements or, as he put it, "two principles that give one another a mutual impulse by struggling with, without destroying, one another," like love and knowledge, faith and examination, heat and light, belief and doubt. In Europe's case, the North had affected the South on five separate occasions, starting with the early migrations of the Scythian peoples into Scandinavia, continuing with the Gothic descent on imperial Rome, and culminating at the moment when Luther "opened the door to every modern reform and modern negation" as the first act of a northern trilogy that was to continue, first with the transformation of England into "a representative and constitutional country," and then with the age of the French Revolution, "on which," Chasles commented, "the curtain has yet to fall."[66]

There is no reason to think that Quinet set out deliberately to contradict Chasles's historical examination of the modern age, and, given their personal relations, it is entirely possible that the discrepancy between their two lectures was planned. Quinet, nonetheless, made it clear that it was the South, not the North, that was the real source of what mattered culturally and politically in the modern world. "I find it difficult to understand," he said in his lecture, "how, ever since Madame de Staël, what is called romantic art is most often attributed to the peoples of the North, to the exclusion of those of the South."

If this is taken to mean the immediate inspiration of feelings, customs, and modern beliefs, whose theatre is not more fully clad, not only in a national costume but also in a national genius? Is there a single example of a theatre, not even Shakespeare's, which owes less to the study or imitation of antiq-

66. "Je crois que la civilisation moderne est le fruit particulier de deux influences: l'influence du Midi, influence antérieure, et l'influence du Nord, venue la dernière, mais régénératrice et fécondante. L'influence du Nord a renouvelé toute la sève du monde civilisé, à dater de la chute de Rome. La servitude des esprits, pire que la servitude des corps, accablait une société qui se mourait, lorsque le génie de la liberté reparut, barbare, mais vivant et active, dans les races du Nord.... Il me parait indubitable que les civilisations humaines suivent un progrès permanent, et que ce progrès résulte de deux mouvements contraires, de deux principes qui se prêtent une impulsion mutuelle, qui luttent sans s'anéantir, et qui font marcher le monde: l'*amour* et le *savoir*; en d'autres termes, la *foi* et l'*examen*; la *chaleur* et la *lumière*; la *croyance* et le doute.... Je regarde comme un seul drame et comme un drame qui n'est pas achevé, comme un drame septentrional, la réforme de Luther, premier acte de cette trilogie; puis la transformation de l'Angleterre en un pays constitutionnel et représentatif, deuxième acte; enfin... la révolution française... sur lequel le rideau n'est pas tombé." Philarèthe Chasles, "Cours de littérature du nord," *Revue de Paris*, n.s., 2 (1842): 116–32 (pp. 118, 119, 120 for the passages quoted).

uity? If you would like to see what can be done by a modern people, left to itself as if the Greeks and Romans had never existed, and achieved by a race of people given over entirely to the inspiration of art and entirely independent of the rules and opinions accredited by the rest of the human race, then study the Spanish theatre. You will sometimes be shocked, but you will often be charmed, and you will always be astonished by these prodigies of novelty and audacity. I would be surprised to learn if anyone, like the character in Pascal abandoned on a desert island, was better able to preserve the original quality of his thought, fully protected from every type of servile imitation.[67]

Quinet's claim about the originality of the South was based on several earlier developments in his thought. The first was an increasingly hostile attitude towards German philosophy, particularly towards Hegel and Hegelianism. The second was a parallel hostility towards French philosophy, particularly towards Victor Cousin and eclecticism. In both these respects, Quinet's intellectual trajectory paralleled the one followed by the socialist political philosopher Pierre Leroux (the two, it is worth mentioning, were personal friends and, according to Quinet, planned to spend the year 1838 together in Heidelberg).[68] Like Leroux, Quinet was also initially sympathetic towards,

67. "Aussi ai-je peine à comprendre que, depuis Mme de Staël, ce que l'on a appelé l'art romantique soit les plus souvent attribué au génie des peuples du Nord, à l'exclusion de ceux du Midi. Si l'on entend par là l'inspiration immédiate des sentiments, des coutumes, des croyances modernes, quel théâtre s'est plus revêtu, non seulement du costume, mais aussi du génie national? En est-il un seul, non pas même celui de Shakespeare, qui doive moins à l'étude, à l'imitation de l'antiquité? Voulez-vous voir tout ce que peut faire un peuple moderne, renfermé en lui-même, comme si jamais ni Grecs ni Romains n'eussent existé, une race d'hommes qui se livre à l'inspiration de l'art, indépendamment de l'opinion et des règles accréditées dans le reste du genre humain: étudiez le théâtre espagnol. Vous serez quelquefois heurtés, souvent charmés, toujours étonnés, par ces prodiges de nouveauté et d'audace. Je doute qu'un homme abandonné, comme cet homme de Pascal, dans une ile déserte, eut mieux conservé le type original de sa pensée à l'abri de toute espèce d'imitation servile." Edgar Quinet, "De la Renaissance dans l'Europe Méridionale," *Bibliothèque choisie des meilleures productions de la littérature française contemporaine*, 1st ser., 2 (1842): 678–90 (p. 686 for this passage). On Quinet's thought, see too Claude Lefort, *Lectures politiques. De Dante à Soljenitsyne* (Paris, PUF, 2021), pp. 75–100.

68. On their friendship, see Jean-Pierre Lacassagne, "Quinet et Leroux," in *Edgar Quinet, ce juif errant*, ed. Simone Bernard-Griffiths and Paul Viallaneix (Clermont-Ferrand, 1978), pp. 191–206. In a note that he added to a review of David Strauss's *Life of Jesus* published in the December 1838 issue of the *Revue des Deux Mondes*, Quinet announced that Leroux and his *Encyclopédie nouvelle* collaborator Paul Reynaud were about to take the subject of religion further and in a post-Hegelian direction.

but then highly critical of, the French Saint-Simonians. After 1830, both came to the view that Saint-Simonianism was simply a French version of Hegelianism. In this sense, the real French equivalents of the German Young Hegelians were not, as has been suggested, the French Saint-Simonians, but their critics, like Leroux and Quinet.[69]

These biographical and intellectual details have a bearing on Quinet's approach to romanticism. As he indicated, romanticism was usually associated with Madame de Staël and the sequence of steps that, as she wrote, enabled the North to rescue the South by supplying the ingredients of the process that had brought Europe back to life after Rome's decline and fall. This, summarily, had been the story that Philarèthe Chasles described in his earlier Collège de France lecture. Here, the key initial component of the story was the culture of the Germanic peoples responsible for the downfall of imperial Rome, particularly their attenuated system of private property, their admiration of physical courage, and their strong respect for women. According to the story, it was a culture that favoured chivalry but was also receptive to Christianity because its emphasis on individual virtue and spiritual equality made it a guilt culture, rather than a shame culture. This, in turn, meant that morality was as much a matter of free choice and individual accountability as of shared values and a common way of life. From this perspective, religion, romanticism, and the Reformation were different facets of the same subject or, as Philarèthe Chasles put it, different parts of the dramatic trilogy underlying the history of the modern world.

Quinet's version of the story was different. He began his lecture by saying that the Renaissance (which he made a proper noun) had what he called a "double character." This feature of the Renaissance, he continued, could be seen more clearly in Italy than anywhere else because it was in Italy that the character of the Renaissance came to be symbolized by the opposition between two names, Ariosto and Tasso. Ariosto stood for scepticism, love of the fine arts, and sympathy towards the humanist critics of dogmatic religion, including the dogmatic reformed religion of Martin Luther. He was, in short, rather like Erasmus or Voltaire. Tasso was different. As Quinet put it, "what Chateaubriand did in France after the revolution, Tasso did in Italy after the Reformation."[70] His *Jerusalem Delivered* symbolized the new spiritual power of the Catholicism of

69. Compare to Espagne, "Le saint-simonisme est-il jeune hégélien?" On Quinet and Leroux (as well as their common friend Jean Reynaud), see Edgar Quinet, *Lettres à sa mère*, ed. Simone Bernard Griffiths and Gérard Peylet, 4 vols. (Paris, 1995–2008), 4:264, 268. On Reynaud, see Guillaume Cughet, "Utopie et religion au xixe siècle: l'oeuvre de Jean Reynaud (1806–1863), théologien et saint-simonien," *Revue historique* 306 (2004): 577–99.

70. "[C]e que Chateaubriand a fait en France après la révolution, le Tasse l'a fait en Italie après la reforme." Quinet, "De la Renaissance dans l'Europe Méridionale," p. 680.

the Counter-Reformation and the new route taken by the arts, notably in the music of Palestrina and in the "ascetic paintings" of Fra Angelico (Quinet called him "Le Guide"). The revival of religion provoked a revival of philosophy and, often, a fierce and deadly conflict between the two, as illustrated by the trials of Giordano Bruno and Galileo. And, although the process began in Italy, both the religious-philosophical revival and the conflicts between them reached an even higher level of intensity in sixteenth-century Spain. "Where," Quinet asked rhetorically, "do we find original Spanish philosophy at the time of the Renaissance? In its theology.... Its deepest, most eloquent and most captivating thinkers are those who made a profession of not thinking, namely, Saint John of the Cross, Saint Theresa, or that accomplished poet and essayist Luis de Léon.... Enthusiasm, inebriation of divine love, magnificence of those invisible heavens, who has ever made them more alive, present, or palpable than Saint Theresa?... What are all the school psychologies besides the revelations of the inner life released by a heroic heart?"[71]

The real Renaissance was southern, not northern, and had all the features of what was romantic, not classic. It had, however, all gone. Despite this, its occurrence still revealed something significant. Although, Quinet said, it was often asserted that it was wrong to apply the lessons of yesterday to the choices of tomorrow, the southern European Renaissance still represented something exemplary. This was that it was important to prevent the mind from going to sleep because the sleep of the mind was a hundred times more difficult to wake up from than the sleep of the body. "Do not believe," Quinet concluded, "(because this is one of the ideas by which it begins to happen), do not believe, along with our age, that money makes everything, or can do or be everything. Who, once, had more money than Spain and who, now, has hands that are emptier than Spain? Never give up, in the name of tradition, that freedom of discussion and the sacred independence of the human mind. Who gave them up more than Spain and who, in the Christian family, has been more harshly punished than Spain?"[72]

71. "Où chercherons-nous la philosophie originale de l'Espagne au moment de la renaissance? Dans sa théologie.... Ses penseurs les plus profonds, les plus éloquents, les plus entrainants, ce sont ceux qui font profession de ne pas penser, c'est saint Jean–de-la-Croix, c'est sainte Thérèse, c'est ce poète et ce prosateur accompli, frère Luis de Léon.... Enthousiasme, ivresse de l'amour divin, magnificence de ce ciel invisible, qui jamais les a rendus présents, vivants, palpables, si ce n'est sainte Thérèse?... Que sont toutes les psychologies de l'école à côté des révélations de la vie intérieure qui s'échappent d'un cœur héroïque?" Ibid., p. 688.

72. "Vous savez si ce tableau est véritable; et bien que l'on m'assure que dans les choses humaines la leçon de la veille ne doit jamais servir au lendemain, je vous dirai, comme le résultat de l'enseignement qui ressort de ce spectacle du Midi: Préservez-vous, défendez-vous, gardez-

The problem was to find a way to keep the mind awake by separating money and property from creativity and industry. This, as Quinet went on to argue in one of his most historically and philosophically ambitious books, *Les révolutions d'Italie* (The Italian revolutions), which recycled much of the text of his 1842 lecture into one of its chapters, was why the history of Italy mattered.[73] It was the key to understanding what modern history had made available to modern politics. "Anyone wishing to learn how a Christian nation can die and be reborn several times," he announced in his introduction, dated significantly Paris 20 February 1848, "needs to look towards Italy. It is the broken vase thrown by the prophet in the path of modern peoples."[74]

Italian history was modern history at its most stark. It was a window on the broader forces underlying modern states and the unpredictable dynamics of modern politics because, as Quinet presented them, Italy and its history were where modern politics began. "I came to be convinced," he wrote in a revised introduction that he added to his book in 1857, "that the key to modern things was to be found at the very beginning of the Middle Ages."[75] Superficially, this made his approach to Italian history look similar to Sismondi's. Quinet, however, made it clear that this was not the case. "Instead of the liberalism that has been attributed to the republics of the Middle Ages," he announced, "I found the continuous principle of government to be terror." In addition, "the arts, which seemed to have no connection to the real constitution of Italy, were in fact tightly connected to it, just as were poetry and philosophy."[76] Modern

---

vous du sommeil de l'esprit; il est trompeur; il pénètre par toutes les voies, cent fois plus difficile à rompre que le sommeil du corps. Ne croyez pas (car c'est là une des idées par lesquelles il commence à insinuer), ne croyez pas, avec votre siècle, que l'or peut tout, fait tout, est tout. Qui donc a possédé plus d'or que l'Espagne, et qui a les mains plus vides que l'Espagne? Ne reniez pas, au nom de la tradition, la liberté de discussion, l'indépendance sainte de l'esprit humain. Qui donc les a reniées plus que l'Espagne, et qui est aujourd'hui plus durement châtiée que l'Espagne dans la famille chrétienne?" Ibid., p. 690.

73. Edgar Quinet, *Les révolutions d'Italie* [1848], 5th ed., 2 vols. (Paris, 1874), vol. 2, bk. 3, ch. 3. Unless otherwise indicated, all citations will be from this edition. On the broader context, see Martin Thom, "City, Region and Nation: Carlo Cattaneo and the Making of Italy," *Citizenship Studies* 3 (1999): 187–201, and the introduction by Michele Campopiano to his recent edition of Carlo Cattaneo, *La città considerata come principio ideale delle istorie italiane* (Pisa, Scuola Normale de Pisa, 2021).

74. "Quiconque veut apprendre comment une nation chrétienne peut mourir et renaitre plusieurs fois, qu'il regarde du côté de l'Italie: c'est le vase brisé que le prophète jette sur le chemin des peuples modernes." Quinet, *Les révolutions d'Italie*, 1:xix.

75. "Je venais de me convaincre que c'est à l'origine même du moyen âge que se trouve le nœud des choses modernes." Ibid., 1:xiii.

76. "A la place du libéralisme que l'on attribuait aux républiques du moyen âge, je retrouvai la terreur comme principe continu du gouvernement. Les arts qui paraissaient ne se rattacher

politics, he went on to claim, were the product of this unusual nexus of terror and the arts, poetry, and philosophy.

Where Sismondi's *History of the Italian Republics of the Middle Ages* looked back to the Middle Ages to establish a political pedigree, Quinet's *Révolutions d'Italie* looked forward from the Middle Ages to identify a range of future political possibilities. These were as likely to include catastrophe as liberty. This, however, was not because of the age-old unpredictability of revolution but, more fundamentally, because of the myriads of actors now involved in modern politics. In Quinet's rendition, modern politics began in Italy because the nexus of terror, poetry, the arts, and philosophy that arose in Italy was popular in both its nature and its causal dynamics. His *Révolutions d'Italie* was an examination of the origins and present implications of this unstable nexus, and, in particular, of what it could mean, for both individuals and political societies, to think about politics under the threat of catastrophe.

His starting point was the decline and fall of the Roman Empire. It had, Quinet argued, been far more complete than any other imperial collapse. "The day the Roman world ended," he wrote (it was the very first sentence of his book), "was the day when Cassiodorus wrote these lines in the consular annals: 'In this year, Theodoric, king of the Goths, *summoned by the will of all,* invaded Rome; he treated the Senate with kindness and distributed largesse to the people.'"[77] The phrase, Quinet commented, indicated that the barbarians had become masters not only of Rome's towns and fields but also of the Romans' minds. No society existed after the conquest because no society had actually existed before the conquest occurred. While Roman Gaul had turned into France, Roman Brittany into England, and Roman Iberia into Spain, there was no underlying residual entity to form the basis of a postimperial Italy, or even a postimperial Lombardy. Postimperial Rome had no name, no institutions, and nothing to counter the endlessly warring Lombards, Franks, and Goths in the Italian Peninsula because even the authority of the invaders was tied, loosely and treacherously, to what lay beyond the Alps. There was no sovereignty, not even the surrogate of sovereignty formed by the slow consolidation of feudalism that took place in the northern reaches of the former empire. While the secular remains of imperial Rome had moved haphazardly east, such institutional continuity as there was in Italy was now represented by the Catholic Church and a spiritually oriented pope, and their prime concern

---

par aucun lien à la constitution réelle de l'Italie, s'y rattachèrent étroitement, aussi bien que la poésie et la philosophie." Ibid., 1:xiv.

77. "Le jour où finit le monde romain fut celui où Cassiodore écrivit ces lignes dans les fastes consulaires: 'Dans cette année, le roi des Goths, Théodoric, *appelé par les vœux de tous,* envahit Rome; il traita le sénat avec douceur et fit des largesses au peuple.'" Ibid., 1:25.

was to maintain their joint independence by playing off the invaders against one another. Since no one possessed sovereignty, there was a void where Italy could have been.[78]

The aftershocks of this catastrophic collapse took their toll on the communes of medieval Italy. They turned into fortified asylums, clinging to their customs and traditions as the last bulwarks of a precarious existence. In northern Europe, the communes were emancipated; in Italy, they were simply preserved. Only those on the coast—Venice, Pisa, and Amalfi—were able to break free. Those inland turned to antiquity, legal precedent, and half-remembered tradition to resist baronial power. The problematic character of this medieval revival of the past was compounded by the fact that there were now two incarnations of Rome. Both, in addition, were absent geographically and morally. The empire was German with a head located beyond the Alps. The church, in principle, was universal, with *its* head being neither fully Italian nor completely cosmopolitan. The resulting competition for the legacy of Rome formed the context of the protracted Guelf-Ghibelline conflict of the following centuries. Since each side claimed universal allegiance, but since there was also a void where sovereignty should have been, some communes gave their loyalty to the church and others to the empire. "This," Quinet wrote, "was the original grandeur of the disputes between Guelfs and Ghibellines. It was a world always looking outside itself for its right to exist, always looking towards a foreign authority. It was an Italy that was reborn, but could not believe that it belonged to itself, a nation that had conquered its liberty, but had renounced its independence, for fear of usurping itself."[79]

The result was endless interstate feuding, compounded by what came to be called the right of reprisal, or the right of a citizen of one republic who had been harmed by a member of another republic to take back what had been lost from any other citizen of that second republic (Shakespeare's *Romeo and Juliet* made its consequences lastingly memorable). It was, Quinet commented, a kind of "barbarous solidarity" that amounted to a rough sketch of that "cosmopolitan right by which human society would one day answer to all for the crimes of each."[80] The same embryonic significance attached to the papal practice of excommunicating whole peoples as punishment for the behaviour of

78. Ibid., 1:28–29.

79. "Voilà la grandeur originale de ces disputes des Guelfes et des Gibelins: un monde qui toujours cherche son droit de subsister en dehors de soi dans une autorité étrangère; l'Italie qui renait et ne peut croire qu'elle s'appartient; le phénomène d'une nation qui conquiert la liberté, et renonce à son indépendance, par la crainte d'usurper." Ibid., 1:37.

80. "[S]olidarité barbare, qui n'est peut-être, au reste que l'ébauche entrevue d'un droit cosmopolite par lequel la société humaine répondrait des crimes de tous." Ibid., 1:59.

their prince or podesta. It was, Quinet noted, an early version of the principle that "each people is responsible towards every other for the government that it tolerates."[81] Both, in the short term, fed into the endless competition for Rome's mantel that dominated Italian politics during the Middle Ages. "Ordinary people, bourgeois, nobles, Guelfs, Ghibellines, poets, lawyers, priests, and popes could all agree only on one thing: idolatry of the old Roman Empire. This renaissance of antiquity that, for every other people, was to be no more than an amusement of the imagination, a literary performance, or an artistic occupation was taken more seriously on the other side of the Alps. Instead of being a mental relaxation, it was a belief, a political creed. Born in a tomb, modern Italy was never to leave it. A living people died in an attempt to resuscitate one that was dead."[82]

Each side claimed legitimacy, but neither the pope nor the emperor could restore the unity that had been Rome. Trying, as Quinet put it, to establish "liberty" without "nationality" was like putting up a building without a foundation. It collapsed as fast as it rose. The first to go were the Ghibellines, followed by the Guelfs and then by the vestiges of chivalric society. "Neither the German Caesar, nor the Caesar of the Vatican; neither the spiritual nor the temporal power could revive the Holy Pagan Empire."[83] In their place emerged a grand commercial bourgeoisie and further schisms among the previously united pro-imperial or pro-papal alliances. Only trade and industry, notably under the aegis of the Medici in Florence, could supply a new foundation for social stability. This was the context in which the Renaissance began. "When the real world went missing, there remained another universe, the Ideal. Italy rushed into it. Divested of her soil, wandering from republic to republic, from illusion to illusion, without any capacity to grasp itself anywhere, Italy built a city of light in the clouds, a city of sounds, colours, and harmony that she called art, which the barbarian could not overturn, nor the foreigner invade, and which, eternally invincible, would rise above the wreckage

81. "C'était enseigner que chaque peuple est responsable envers tous les autres du gouvernement qu'il tolère." Ibid., 1:50.

82. "Peuples, bourgeois, nobles, Guelfes, Gibelins, poètes, jurisconsultes, prêtres, papes, s'entendaient dans une seule chose, l'idolâtrie du vieil empire romain. Cette renaissance de l'antiquité qui, pour tous les autres peuples ne devait être qu'un amusement d'imagination, une fête littéraire, une occupation d'artistes est prise au sérieux de l'autre côté des Alpes. Au lieu d'un divertissement d'esprit, c'est une croyance, une foi politique. Née dans un tombeau, l'Italie moderne ne veut pas en sortir; un peuple vivant périt pour s'obstiner à ressusciter un peuple mort." Ibid., 1:78–79.

83. "Ni le César allemand, ni le César du Vatican, ni la puissance spirituelle, ni la temporelle, n'avaient ressuscite le saint empire païen." Ibid., 1:82.

of all the rest, never tied to any party, nor limited by any municipal boundary."[84] Art became the Italian homeland and a surrogate for the homeland that both the emperor and the pope had withheld.

Art was given its initial expression in demotic terms. This, in the first instance, was not a particularity of Italy but a generic feature of Christianity. Unlike the culture of Asia, with its focus on nature, or that of ancient Greece and Rome, with their emphasis on humanity, Christian culture was divided profoundly between the physical and the spiritual. This, as Quinet put it, meant that the church and the poet used different languages. Latin was the language of religion and the church, while local languages were the languages of life and, then, the languages of the arts. Since the language of the church remained the language of the ancients, the language of life became the language of the moderns. In Italy, it was shaped not only by the legacies of Rome's pagan past and Christian present, but also by the proximity of Islam and the ever-recurrent possibility of war. Religion in Italy was a religion of battle as much as a religion of love.[85] Modern culture, from this perspective, was the work of "slaves, workers, ordinary people, provincial peasants, all with their idioms that were so different from those of the patricians. In emancipating themselves, they emancipated their dialects, which became the underlying principle of the language of Dante."[86] Modern culture was paganism transformed by a combination of Christianity and Islam into Provençal poetry and the music of the troubadours. It made Italy the home of "the popular song, the heroic lament, the feudal romance, the poetry of a people who were gentlemen."[87] In the South, no philosophy could be rejected by the people because the people themselves were oblivious to philosophy. "One ideal succeeded another, without affecting the real world. Among the unbridled liberties of art, there was always a forbidden fruit, something that no one called seriously into question, and that forbidden question was the mystery of soci-

84. "Quand tout le monde réel lui manquait, il lui restait un autre univers, l'idéal; elle s'y précipita. Dépouillé de son sol, errante, de républiques en républiques, d'illusions en illusions, sans pouvoir se saisir nulle part, elle se bâtit sur les nues une cité de lumière, de son, de couleurs, d'harmonie qu'elle appelle l'art, que le barbare ne peut renverser ni l'étranger envahir, qui, éternellement invincible, surnage dans la ruine de tout le reste, sans se laisser enchaîner jamais par aucun parti ni limiter dans aucune circonscription municipale." Ibid., 1:86.

85. Ibid., 1:92.

86. "Les esclaves, les ouvriers, le petit peuple, les paysans des provinces avaient leur idiome distinct de celui des patriciens; en s'émancipant, ils émancipent leur dialectes qui deviennent le principe de la langue de Dante." Ibid., 1:107–8.

87. "A l'Italie . . . je trouve le chant populaire, la complainte héroïque, la romance féodale, poème d'un peuple gentilhomme." Ibid., 1:96.

ety, of belief, of life." Life coexisted with religion without either of the two calling the other into question. Only in France, and only with the Reformation, did the "internal war between the soul and itself" break out.[88]

The Renaissance made both the Reformation and Counter-Reformation democratic. This was because it was the Renaissance that was the true source of chivalry and the real starting point of the human capacity for autonomous love. "When," Quinet wrote, "Rousseau made love the source of the first stammerings of pagan language, he was Romanesque, because he had mistaken the period. He would have written the literal truth if, instead of humanity in general, he had spoken of modern humanity."[89] Chivalry gave rise to modern humanity because it relied on individual consciousness and was based on the power of women, whereas the ancient agora relied on collective consciousness and was based on a strong demarcation between differently gendered social spheres. "Ancient society," as Quinet put it, "began with the accord of a nation; modern society began with the accord of two voices, through the marriage of a man and a woman in chivalrous love."[90] This kind of accord had no equivalent in the ancient world because it reversed the old hierarchical relationship between gender and power and, at the same time, broke with the established boundaries of feudal society. "The distinctive trait of the troubadours was that almost all of them were the sons of serfs who, because of the hazards of talent and the elevation of the heart, found themselves in a relationship of artificial equality with the feudal aristocracy."[91] With the troubadours, women had the position of power, while men were the powerless supplicants. This made the troubadours the mediators between different social conditions and the first agents of modern equality. "The beginning of modern society," Quinet announced, "was

88. "Un idéal succède à un autre idéal, mais sans jamais porter atteinte au monde réel. Au milieu des libertés effrénées de l'art, j'aperçois toujours un fruit défendu, une chose que personne ne met jamais sérieusement en délibération avec soi-même; et cette question interdite, c'est le mystère de la société, de la croyance ou, pour mieux dire, de la vie. . . . En France, au contraire, la religion et la poésie, la croyance et la science se sont bientôt nettement divisées et niées. . . . C'est dans la Réforme, au cœur même des races germaniques qu'a éclaté cette guerre intestine de l'âme avec elle-même." Ibid., 1:100–101.

89. "Quand J-J Rousseau attribuait à l'amour le premier bégayement des langues païennes, il était romanesque, puisqu'il se trompait d'époque. Il eût été littéralement vrai si, au lieu de l'humanité en général, il eut parlé de l'humanité moderne." Ibid., 1:111.

90. "La société antique débute par l'accord d'une nation, la société moderne par l'accord de deux voix, par le mariage de l'homme et de la femme dans l'amour chevaleresque." Ibid., 1:109.

91. "Le trait distinctif des troubadours, c'est que presque tous sont des fils de serfs qui, par le hasard du génie, par l'élévation du cœur, se trouvent un moment dans une relation d'égalité factice avec l'aristocratie féodale." Ibid., 1:111.

this alliance between a chatelaine and a son of the people from the fringes of barbarism. In this chimerical tie, in this moment of ecstasy bringing together the two extremes of humanity, and marrying together two conditions that were divided over the ages, is truly to be found the civil birth of the modern world."[92] In this historically orgasmic moment, the love of the Lady and the Troubadour not only implied the emancipation of the slave, but also symbolized an explicit acknowledgement of social fraternity and joint recognition of real equality. In historical and cultural terms, the languages of both the emotion and the relationship were, necessarily, popular. Latin, Quinet wrote, was "a patrician idiom," but the Romance languages were the product of "the genius of every class."[93]

It was, Quinet commented, perplexing to see scholars still claiming to have discovered "the principle of love" in the "peculiar genius of the northern peoples" even though nothing comparable to the troubadours could be found in any Germanic epic. But the principle was still not the substance. Years of revolution had stripped Italy of everything required for more than a purely nominal existence. "Italy's destiny by the fifteenth century," Quinet wrote, "was to arrive at irreligion by means of Catholicism and the negation of law by means of the law schools themselves." In the endlessly shifting switches of allegiance produced by the conflict between the Guelfs and Ghibellines, neither papal authority nor imperial power could escape the effects of partiality, weakness, or both. The legacy of Saint Peter turned into the achievements of Alessandro Borgia, just as the great traditions of the medieval jurists culminated in the works of Machiavelli. In a culture dominated by religious superstition and empty legal formalism, the only effect of clear thinking was to give a green light to power politics. "Someone was required to give expression to so strange and new a situation in history," and this, Quinet concluded, "is where we come to Machiavelli."[94]

---

92. "Le commencement de la société moderne, c'est cette alliance de la châtelaine et de l'enfant du peuple sur les confins de la barbarie; dans ce lien chimérique, dans ce moment d'extase qui rapproche des deux extrémités de l'humanité, et marie deux conditions que toute l'étendue des siècles avait tenue divisées, est vraiment renfermée la naissance civile du monde modern." Ibid., 1:118.

93. "La différence essentielle du latin et des langues romanes, c'est que le premier, dans son origine, est surtout un idiome des patriciens, et que les secondes, au contraire, sont formées du génie de toutes les classes." Ibid., 1:120.

94. "La destinée d'Italie a voulu qu'elle arrivât, dans le quinzième siècle, à l'irréligion par le catholicisme, à la négation du droit par les écoles des jurisconsultes. . . . En même temps que les traditions de Saint-Pierre, réduites à des superstitions extérieures, se perdaient dans Alexandre Borgia, les traditions des grands jurisconsultes allaient se perdre dans Machiavel. . . . Il fallait

As a young man, Quinet wrote, Machiavelli had been a follower of the reforming Florentine monk Savonarola, and Savonarola's failure was Machiavelli's starting point. "Thus, for the first time in history, was born the theory of
a politics without God, without providence, and without Christian or pagan
religion. Mankind, abandoned by God in the Middle Ages, abandoned God
in turn." All that Machiavelli kept of Christianity was the doctrine of original
sin. "This debris of a decapitated Christianity, this vision of a humanity wicked
by nature, with no mediator and no redeemer, with its own destiny and its own
providence, such was the citizen of the new society."[95] This, ultimately, was
Italy's legacy to the modern world. Alongside it, however, was the cosmopolitanism of the original church and the doctrine of collective solidarity implied
by the idea of excommunication. Together, Quinet argued, these were the
moral resources that could have prevented the Protestant North from following the trajectory of the Catholic South. In the short term, however, Machiavelli turned into Machiavellianism and mutated again into the poisonous
doctrine of reason of state that was used to justify the imperial ambitions of
the princes and potentates of Renaissance Europe.

But no society, Quinet argued, could find stability in a religion without faith
or a legal system without legitimacy. Well before he published his *Révolutions
d'Italie* with its hyperbolic account of the southern origins of modern political
societies, he had already gestured towards the possible outcome of the whole
historical process. This was the message of his *Le christianisme et la révolution
française* (Christianity and the French Revolution), published in 1845 after his
lecture course on the literature of the South had been suspended because,
according to the authorities, its subject matter strayed far too far from its title.
Quinet dedicated the work to Michelet and, like Michelet, made no attempt
to disguise his muted Bonapartist sympathies. As with Michelet too, the
Bonapartist orientation was more moral than political because it implied admiration of authority rather than an endorsement of power. Leadership was
exemplary, not coercive, because real human motivation was a product of individual and collective choice. This was why the American transcendentalist
Ralph Waldo Emerson was as significant a figure as Bonaparte in Quinet's

---

un homme pour exprimer hautement une situation si étrange, si nouvelle dans l'histoire; ici
nous touchons à Machiavel." Ibid., 1:346–47, 354.

95. "Ainsi nait pour la première fois dans le monde, la théorie d'une politique sans Dieu, sans
providence, sans religion, ni païenne, ni chrétienne. L'homme abandonné par le Dieu du moyen
âge, l'abandonne à son tour. . . . Débris de ce christianisme décapité, l'homme mauvais par sa
nature, sans médiateur, sans rédempteur, devenu à lui-même son destin et sa providence, tel est
le citoyen de la société nouvelle." Ibid., 2:6.

examination of the French Revolution.[96] Just as, Quinet wrote, Bossuet had claimed that the whole of ancient history led towards the Crucifixion at Golgotha, so, for similar reasons, the same could be said of modern history and the French Revolution. "It inherited what preceded it," he asserted (in a passage that could have been made for Paul Chenavard); "the spirit of every people is contained in this living pantheon. Rousseau who was its legislator gave it the spirit of Protestantism, so that the germ of each earlier revolution was also present in it: the Reformation by way of the sovereignty of the people; Catholicism by way of unity, and philosophy by way of abstraction and the qualities of the mind that it injects into everything."[97]

The French Revolution was, in short, an immense historical palimpsest of every preceding revolution. It brought together an array of essentially reflective, northern qualities alongside an array of popular, demotic, and southern qualities to produce an outcome that would be a mixture of both. Ancient law, Quinet wrote, was predicated upon a fundamental distinction between free individuals and slaves. This, he explained, was why in Roman law only a slave could be tortured. Among the Romans, he noted, torture could be inflicted only on slaves because they were taken to be without personality. In modern law, with its starting point in the Christian doctrine of the equality of souls, everyone could be tortured, at least under the aegis of the papal Inquisition. But the Reformation and the French Revolution had brought back the doctrine of the equality of souls in combination with the modern concept of democratic political sovereignty.[98] Modern law was, therefore, fundamentally egalitarian. "The ideal of the future," Quinet wrote, "which will develop over the centuries, is one that should contain and bring together the moral breadth of

96. Emerson, Quinet wrote, was "l'écrivain le plus idéaliste de notre temps." Edgar Quinet, *Le christianisme et la révolution française* (Paris, 1845), pp. 294–95. On Quinet and Emerson, see Maurice Chazin, "Quinet: An Early Discoverer of Emerson," *PMLA* 48 (1933): 147–63, and Edmund Ordon, "Mickiewicz and Emerson," in *Mickiewicz and the West*, ed. B. R. Bugelski (Buffalo, NY, U of Buffalo Press, 1956), pp. 31–54. For a helpful selection of passages on the more political aspects of Quinet's thought, see Bernard Peloille, "Nation, formes d'état, classes, dans la pensée politique d'Edgar Quinet," *Cahiers Pour l'Analyse Concrète* 10 (1981): 3–23.

97. "Elle hérite de ce qui l'a précédée; l'esprit de tous les peuples est renfermé dans ce panthéon vivant. Rousseau qui en est le législateur y verse l'âme du protestantisme; en sorte que le germe de chaque révolution précédente y est représenté: la réforme par la souveraineté du peuple, le catholicisme par l'unité, la philosophie par l'abstraction et l'âme qu'elle mêle à tout." Quinet, *Le christianisme et la révolution française*, p. 356.

98. Edgar Quinet, "L'ultramontanisme, ou l'église romaine et la société moderne" [1844], in Edgar Quinet, *Œuvres*, vol. 2 (Paris, 1857), pp. 223–28 (particularly p. 227 n. 1, for the claim summarized here).

the Constituent Assembly, without its illusions, the energy of the Convention, without its cruelty, and the splendour of Napoleon, without his despotism."[99] The Revolution symbolized the future just as, according to Quinet, the dual legacies of the North and the South had been symbolized earlier by the individualism of Daniel Defoe's Robinson Crusoe and the communitarianism of the sixteenth-century Spanish monk Tommaso Campanella's theological and political treatise *The City of the Sun*. "The world," Quinet ended, "is still trying to find its way between these two dreams."[100] If it could do so, and if it could find a way between Robinson Crusoe and the City of the Sun, it would become a home for both autonomy and democracy.

99. "L'idéal de l'avenir, qui se développera par les siècles, doit renferme et concilier tout ensemble l'essor moral de la Constituante sans ses illusions, l'énergie de la Convention sans la cruauté, la splendeur de Napoléon sans le despotisme." Quinet, *Le christianisme et la révolution française*, p. 385.

100. "Entre ces deux rêves, le monde cherche son chemin." Ibid., p. 406.

10

Civil Society and the State

INITIALLY, THE ROMAN REVIVAL was not well received. Sismondi was horrified by the neo-Roman turn in history and historiography made by Michelet and Quinet (as too, but for different reasons, was the attentive baron d'Eckstein).[1] Despite Michelet's many tributes ("you have done better than make books, you have made men—as if you were the father of that generation of young historians now seen to be rising up. *Felix proles virum*—happy lineage of men"), Sismondi made it increasingly clear that, on his terms, he belonged to another moral and political world.[2] "I feel a sort of fear, as if you had shown me something at my feet that I had not noticed, and feel that fear too because I cannot accept that fatality of race and locality that apparently dominates human existence and seems to destroy free will," he informed Michelet early in 1834 after reading the first two volumes of the latter's history of France.[3] Although the point of the two volumes was to provide a historical explanation of how human creativity had found ways to overcome these two physically given obstacles, Sismondi was unwilling to accept the strong initial opposition between nature and culture underlying Michelet's philosophy of history. By 1840, the feeling of vertigo had turned into outright hostility. "You are," he informed Michelet in April of

---

1. For Eckstein's assessment of Michelet, see his five-part review, beginning in the February 1834 issue of the *Revue Européenne*, of Michelet's *Histoire de France*, conveniently reprinted in Jules Michelet, *Œuvres complètes*, ed. Paul Viallaneix, 4:756–844.

2. "C'est vous qui avez donné en France l'essor aux études historiques; vous avez fait mieux que des livres, vous avez fait des hommes, vous êtes comme le père de cette génération de jeunes historiens que nous voyons s'élever. *Felix proles virum.*" Michelet to Sismondi, 16 September 1825, in Jules Michelet, *Correspondance générale*, 12 vols. (Paris, Champion, 1994–2001), 1:215. See too 1:215 n. 2, 272, 500; 2:144; and, with qualifications, 3:799, for later examples.

3. "J'en éprouve une sorte d'effroi, comme si vous me révéliez ce qui était inaperçu sous mes pieds; d'effroi encore parce que je me refuse à cette fatalité de race et de localité qui dominerait l'existence humaine et détruirait son libre arbitre." Sismondi to Michelet, 17 January 1834, in Michelet, *Correspondance*, 2:153–54.

that year, "very French. You wish to excite enthusiasm for France. Desirous of power, you take conquests, unions, aggrandizement to be goods and goals worthy of the efforts of the French. As for me, I am not French. . . . and I still belong to the Middle Ages by dint of a preference for resistance rather than force, for local powers in opposition to centralization, and for individual existences. This is the same view (*sentiment*) that can be found underlying my political economy and my politics; it is one that makes me reject great factories, great farms, and great railways just as much as great armies, great treasuries, great ministries, and great empires. My hopes and affections no longer belong to our age."[4]

Towards a New Synthesis

It was a powerful valediction. But, by the end of the nineteenth century, the view had changed. "M. de Sismondi's great *Histoire des républiques italiennes du moyen age* is still the most complete and readable work on its subject," noted a late nineteenth-century legal historian. "It is more interesting than ever to compare its almost despairing conclusion with the rapid progress now being made."[5] The judgment echoed Sismondi's assessment of his own historical thought, but it was less explicit about the content of the "rapid progress" that, apparently, had begun to occur. Somehow, it seems, a solution had been found to the problem of finding a way between the arrangements symbolized, as Quinet had put it, by Crusoe and Campanella. It now seemed to be possible, both theoretically and practically, to establish a position somewhere between the competing claims of individualism (Crusoe) and socialism (Campanella). The claim became one of the major themes of the political thought of the second half of the nineteenth century because it appeared to address the full range of subjects earlier associated with the rival legacies of

4. "Très français vous-même, vous voulez exciter l'enthousiasme pour la France. Désireux de puissance, vous regardez les conquêtes, les réunions, l'agrandissement comme un bien, comme un but suffisant aux efforts des Français. Pour moi, je ne suis pas français . . . et j'appartiens encore au moyen-âge par une préférence pour la résistance plutôt que de la force, pour les pouvoirs locaux opposes à la centralisation, pour les existences individuelles. C'est le même sentiment qui se retrouve au fond de mon économie politique, comme de ma politique, et qui me fait repousser les grandes manufactures, les grandes fermes, et les grands chemins de fer, comme les grandes armées, les grands trésors, les grands ministres et les grands empires. Mes affections et me vœux ne sont plus de notre temps." Sismondi to Michelet, 5 April 1840, in Michelet, *Correspondance*, 2:221–22.

5. William Hastie, translator's introduction to Diodato Lioy, *The Philosophy of Right, with special reference to the Principles and Development of Law*, 2 vols. (London, 1891), 1:xv n. 1.

the Romans and the Germans. Its most significant feature, however, was that the differences between the two legacies now seemed to be more apparent than real, and that the boundary dividing them was more porous than it had earlier appeared. If this was the case, then the type of claim about the double origin of modern civilization made in the early nineteenth century by Sismondi and the Coppet group also began to look less tenable. Instead of a sequence of historically explicable turning points, in which the legacy of the German woods displaced that of the Roman forum, the relationship between history and politics in Europe turned into a story of continuity rather than discontinuity, and, more substantively, a new and different version of the part that Rome had played in the making of the modern world. In this context, the concept of palingenesis turned either into the modern concept of revolution, or, more gradually, into the more recognizable concept of the Renaissance, and, under the aegis of both these changes, the Montesquieu-inspired idea of the Germanic origins of modern political societies slowly faded from view.[6] But, as with the transformation of the romantic into the classic, which was exemplified by Sainte-Beuve's political trajectory, the new emphasis on continuity relied upon a number of discreet, but considerable, evaluative switches. These not only had the effect of eroding the earlier emphasis on discontinuity, but also added a new set of concerns and connotations to the early nineteenth-century concepts of autonomy and civil society. The Roman revival was matched by a transformation of both concepts, with autonomy reverting to its older meaning of self-government, and civil society recovering its earlier association with the state.

One initial example of what these switches involved was formed by the subject of property. In the seventeenth and eighteenth centuries, the idea of applying the concept of distributive justice to the ownership of land was associated as readily with ancient Sparta and the original Hebrew republic as with ancient Rome. The idea was given a strongly Roman inflection during the period of the French Revolution when the subject of property came to be associated with a combination of popular insurrection and landed redistribution. When, in 1793, François-Noel Babeuf decided to change his name to Gracchus, his decision was a deliberate gesture towards a symbol that, for many hundreds of years, was associated with the idea of an agrarian law as a solution to the problem of economic and social inequality.[7] Gracchus Babeuf first used his new name on the eve of an aborted Parisian insurrection on the night of 9–10 May 1793, when some of the leaders of the Paris Commune and

6. On revolution, see Dunn, *Modern Revolutions*.
7. On Babeuf, see Sonenscher, "Property, Community and Citizenship."

its forty-eight sections started, then abandoned, an armed attempt to force the French Convention to include the principle of "real equality," as its advocates called it, in the articles dealing with the right to private property in the new, republican, Declaration of the Rights of Man. According to Babeuf, the correct principles had been presented to the Convention by the Jacobin leader Maximilien Robespierre in a draft Declaration of Rights that specified that property was a right to dispose of those goods that were guaranteed to each citizen by law, a right that could not be exercised in ways that were prejudicial to the security, liberty, existence, or property of others without being deemed unlawful and immoral. From this perspective, Robespierre's additions to the Declaration of Rights meant that the old Roman republican maxim *Salus populi suprema lex esto* (Public safety should be the highest law) was rightfully entitled to trump the right of individuals to dispose of their property as they chose. When, after the revolution of July 1830, the subjects of inequality, reform, and the distribution of property returned to the agenda of European politics, they did so largely under the shadow of Robespierre and Rome. The association was particularly pronounced in France, not only in Filippo Buonarotti's very positive history of Babeuf and the conspiracy for equality published in 1828 and in the cluster of sympathetic biographies of Robespierre published around the time of the July Revolution, but also in the multivolume parliamentary history of the French Revolution that began to appear after 1830 under the aegis of Pierre-Joseph-Benjamin Buchez and Prosper-Charles Roux. Together, they made the subject of agrarian laws Roman rather than Spartan, Hebrew, or Germanic.

Outside of France, however, much the same interest in Rome and the Gracchi came to motivate the Danish and German historian Barthold Georg Niebuhr's early nineteenth-century research into Rome's agrarian laws. Properly understood, Niebuhr argued, the agrarian laws were capable of becoming the basis of a more peaceful process of economic and social reform.[8] Here, the key to the move was the concept of possession because, as Niebuhr described it, it formed a bridge between land that was public and land that was private. Something about possession as it was understood in Roman law, he argued, was compatible with both public and private ownership, but was also radically incompatible with the hybrid character of feudal ownership and the

8. On Niebuhr, see Arnaldo Momigliano, "New Paths of Classicism in the Nineteenth Century" [1982], reprinted in A. D. Momigliano, *Studies in Modern Scholarship*, ed. G. E. Bowerstock and T. J. Cornell (Berkeley, U of California Press, 1994), pp. 223–85 (especially pp. 229–36), and, more recently, Oded Y. Steinberg, *Race, Nation, History: Anglo-German Thought in the Nineteenth Century* (Philadelphia, U of Pennsylvania Press, 2019), pp. 52–58.

two interlocking domains of direct and useful ownership that were the hallmark of feudal property. In this context, the legal concept of possession had the power to act as a solvent of feudal property and the means to use the law to promote the gradual redistribution of property. "Niebuhr," wrote his friend and admirer, the founder of the German historical school of law, Friedrich Carl von Savigny, "has explained the origin of possession in a very satisfactory manner. Land, under the republic, was of two kinds, *ager publicus* and *ager privatus*, in the latter of which only could property be acquired. But possession and enjoyment of the *ager publicus* also, according to the old constitution, were for the most part made over to individual Roman citizens, under the condition of being reclaimable at will by the republic."[9] In showing how this had been possible, Savigny had in fact shown the way and Niebuhr had been his follower. As Savigny went to great lengths to show in his 1803 treatise on the right of possession, this was because Roman law contained a number of technical concepts (like usucaption and interdiction) that, under feudal conditions of land tenure, enabled private individuals to turn the fact of possession into rights of property protected by the full force of the law.[10] The most important feature of this aspect of Roman law was that its provisions applied directly to individuals. Unlike the old German law, with its codes of honour and trials by ordeal, Roman law bypassed the tension between community and society by giving an individually applicable content to rules held in common. On these terms, possession was primary and, in Roman law, the basis of the Roman system of rights. Although a twentieth-century French law professor named Michel Villey was once famous for claiming that Roman law and society had no concept of a subjective right, Savigny simply took the concept for granted.[11] For the German historical school, subjective rights began with

9. Friedrich Carl von Savigny, *On Possession, or the Ius Possessionis of the Civil Law* [1803], trans. Sir Erskine Perry (London, 1848), p. 136. On Niebuhr and Savigny, see Luigi Capogrossi Colognesi, *Dalla storia di Roma alle origini della società civile* (Bologna, Il Mulino, 2008), pp. 15–76, and his earlier *Modelli di stato e di famiglia nella storiografia dell' 800* (Rome, La Sapienza, 1994), pp. 303–13. See too Giovanni Bonacina, *Hegel, il mondo romano e la storiografia* (Rome, La Nuova Italia, 1991), pp. 6–7, 31–38, 40–46.

10. For a clear summary, see Whitman, *The Legacy of Roman Law in the German Romantic Era*, pp. 181–90.

11. See Sylvain Piron, "Congé à Villey," *L'Atelier du Centre de recherches historiques* 1 (2008): 1–16, and Peter Garnsey, *Thinking about Property* (Cambridge, CUP, 2007), pp. 177–203. See too Yan Thomas, "Michel Villey, la romanistique et le droit romain," in his *Droit, nature, histoire* (Aix-Marseille, 1985), pp. 31–41, and Dario Mantovani, "Le détour incontournable. Le droit romain dans la réflexion de Yan Thomas," in *Aux origines des cultures juridiques européennes. Yan Thomas entre droit et sciences sociales*, ed. Paolo Napoli (Rome, Ecole Française de Rome, 2013),

Roman law and were a product of the fact of possession. Roman law, as Savigny proceeded to claim, was the means to bridge the gap between the real and the ideal because it had a built-in capacity to make rights available to those beyond the boundary of existing legal entitlement.

A generation later, however, the evaluations had changed. From this perspective, Sismondi's reproachful dialogue with Michelet was part of a broader sequence of switches in which the subjects of property, inequality, and reform lost much of their earlier association with Rome and agrarian laws and, instead, were given a more Germanic set of connotations. "Law in its initial formation," wrote the German jurist Georg Beseler in 1845, "is not the product of chance or human discretion, deliberation or wisdom; it is created neither by legislation nor by philosophical abstraction. Rather, it develops directly in the life of the people, like morals and language, on the broad basis of general human relations; it lives in the common consciousness of the people, from whose individual constitution it receives its special character."[12] This was a different version of Karl Ludwig von Haller's Germanism because of its emphasis on popular culture and, by extension, on customarily regulated property. One example of the change was a book published in 1853 by a German lawyer named Carl Adolf Schmidt on the principal difference between Roman and German law (*Der principielle Unterschied zwischen dem römischen und germanischen Recht*).[13] For Schmidt, the difference in question gave rise to two different conceptions of property. In Roman law, property was something subject to someone's will. In Germanic law, however, property was limited by common custom and functional use. As with Beseler, property was not created by legislation or philosophical

---

pp. 26–27. For a relatively recent follower of Villey's view, see Tuck, *Natural Rights Theories*, pp. 7–8, 12–13.

12. Georg Beseler, *Volksrecht und Juristenrecht* (Leipzig, 1843), p. 59. Cited in Emanuele Conte, "The Order and the *Volk*: Romantic Roots and Enduring Fascination of the German Constitutional History," in *De rebus divini et humanis: Essays in Honour of Jan Hallebeek*, ed. Harry Dondorp, Martin Schermaier, and Boudewijn Sirks (Göttingen, V&R Unipress, 2019), pp. 37–53 (pp. 41–42 for this passage).

13. On Schmidt, Röder, and the broader Roman-German debate, see Klaus Luig, "Römische und germanischen Rechtsanschauung, individualistische und soziale Ordnung," in *Die Deutsche Rechtsgeschichte in der NS-Zeit: ihr Vorgeschichte und ihr Nachwirkungen*, ed. Joachim Rückert and Dietmar Willoweit (Tübingen, J.C.B. Mohr, 1995), pp. 95–137. More generally, see Michael John, *Politics and the Law in Late Nineteenth-Century Germany: The Origins of the Civil Code* (Oxford, OUP, 1989), pp. 18–31; Otto von Gierke, *Die historische Rechtsschule und die Germanisten* (Berlin, 1903); and Frederick William Maitland, introduction to Otto von Gierke, *Political Theories of the Middle Age* (Cambridge, CUP, 1900), pp. vii–xlv.

abstraction, but was part of a common way of life and of what, in other contexts, has been called a moral economy.

"From these points of view," Schmidt wrote, "it follows, first, for Roman law that the variant nature of *things* cannot influence the concept of ownership at all." But in ancient Germanic law, he emphasized, "the individual character of particular things exercises an essential influence upon the ambit and content of proprietary rights—in other words, the ownership of things of varying nature is itself variable." Against what Schmidt described as the absolutism and abstraction of Roman law, Germanic law turned ownership into "no more than the right and the duty to control and use a thing in keeping with socially approved purposes."[14] Although the claim seemed to make Germanic law look somewhat similar to the clauses on property in Robespierre's draft Declaration of the Rights of Man (in reality, the similarity went both ways), the idea underlying what Schmidt called "socially approved purposes" was intended to evoke the common values and traditional system of collective decision making of early Germanic society. Here, property was subordinate to the claims of kinship and, more broadly, to the customary rules surrounding the uses of land and livestock. In this context, the key institution was the feud or trial by combat, an institution that had its basis in the initial idea of an ordeal as the price that an individual was willing to pay to earn the respect of the whole community. The counterpart of an ordeal was the concept of a *Genossenschaft*, meaning a fellowship, guild, corporation, or community, which, it could be said, was the Germanic equivalent of the *civitas* although it was one dominated by custom rather than the law. The *Genossenschaft* formed the setting in which trials took place, respect was won or lost, and guilt or innocence was vindicated. In this context, what mattered was authority rather than the power, and trust rather than the law. Together, Schmidt claimed, echoing the claims of Karl August Rögge and the Grimm brothers a generation earlier, they made morality, rather than legality, the cement of society.

Schmidt's comparison of Roman and Germanic law soon became the principal target of a wide-ranging examination of the growing body of literature on the two systems. This was a pamphlet entitled *On the Basic Conceptions and Meaning of Roman and Germanic Law* (*Grundgedanken und Bedeutung des römischen und germanischen Rechts*) that was published in 1855 by another German law professor, this time from the University of Heidelberg, named Karl David

---

14. Karl Adolf Schmidt, *Der principielle Unterschied zwischen dem römischen und germanischen Recht* (1853), pp. 223–24, 225, cited by Francis S. Philbrick, "Changing Conceptions of Property in Law," *University of Pennsylvania Law Review* 86 (1937–38): 691–732.

August Röder.[15] Röder, whose speciality at the university was criminal law, took strong exception to Schmidt's willingness to conflate law with morality and use this as the basis of his very positive evaluation of Germanic law. Without a distinction between law and morality, Röder argued, it would be impossible to have a clear concept of a crime, and this in turn would allow states and their governments to assert an unlimited right to interfere in anything that they happened at one time or another to dislike. Dropping the distinction between morality and the law amounted to building a direct road to despotism, and this, Röder emphasized, had certainly not been the aim of either Schmidt or the Germanists in general. The problem, he wrote, had arisen because neither the Romanists nor the Germanists were able to fill the void created by the combined effects of modern natural jurisprudence and, more comprehensively, Rousseau's "pernicious" doctrine of a social contract and the irretrievably nebulous quality of Kant's concept of a categorical imperative.[16] Initially, Röder wrote, Savigny and his followers in the German historical school had tried to show how the long afterlife of Roman law could fill the void that Rousseau and Kant had opened up by providing a time-based bridge between history and politics or, more broadly, between causation and normativity. But the content of Roman law was too abstract and inflexible to be able to prevent the idea of a legal system from having to rely on state power. This, according to Röder, was why much the same type of claim about continuity and connectivity had been made by the Germanists about the attributes of customary law. But as Schmidt's comparison helped to show, neither side had been able to combine legality with morality in a way that still left room for both.

For Röder the two sides were mirror images of each other, with the result that their respective positions simply cancelled one another out. This was most apparent in their respective treatments of the concepts of subjective and objective rights. The terminology was usually associated with Hegel, but both the Romanists and the Germanists made use of it in radically incompatible ways. For Germanists like Schmidt, Roman law enshrined rights that were purely subjective, which was why it was the basis of individualism and liberalism, with their socially divisive effects. For Röder, Germanism was no better because a system based solely on objective rights amounted to socialism. On

---

15. This and the following paragraphs summarize Karl David August Röder, *Grundgedanken und Bedeutung des römischen und germanischen Rechts* (Leipzig, 1855). On the discussion, see too Friedrich von Hahn, *Die materielle Übereinstimmung der römischen und germanischen Rechstprincipien* (Jena, 1856).

16. Röder, *Grundgedanken und Bedeutung*, p. 56.

these terms, individualism and socialism were simply different names for Romanism and Germanism, which, in turn, were products of two, exaggerated, conceptions of subjective and objective rights. The need now was to find a synthesis that was neither individualist nor socialist because it recognized the merits of each side of the argument.

This, Röder wrote, meant coming to terms in the first instance with some of the genuine benefits of Roman law by recognizing that Roman law was responsible for "the consistent legal treatment of the individual as a person." Although it was often said that this was not the case because, as was also said, Roman law had eliminated the concept of the individual as such, leaving only the German Reformation as the source of the modern significance attached to the concept of personality, neither assertion, Röder claimed, was correct. The Reformation had given a new value to individuality, not personality, and from this perspective its legacy had as much in common with the individualism of Adam Smith as with the more morally attractive assertion of individual self-worth of Germanic custom. The same need for a synthesis applied to the broader idea of a political society. Although, as Montesquieu had been the first to show, the idea of representation was Germanic in origin, it had been the Roman distinctions between public and private law and between human law and divine law (*ius* as against *fas*) that made it possible for the idea of the rule of law to apply even to individuals who played no part in the making of law. These distinctions, Röder emphasized, were particularly salient to the great imperial city that Rome had become because they enabled plebeian immigrants to benefit from Roman law despite the fact that they were not Roman citizens.[17] Subsequently, the Roman concept of personality coupled with the Germanic concept of individuality meant that the modern world now housed the conditions for a new synthesis of the two traditions.

This possibility, Röder argued, was already visible in the way that Roman law had incorporated a concept of the rights of others to go alongside individual rights just as, on the Germanic side, it had become usual to recognize a concept of sole ownership alongside common possessions. This meant that although the Romans had no legal concept of a corporate body, the Germanic concept of a *Genossenschaft* made it possible to attribute the ownership of common property to something that was distinguishable from the individual members of a collective association. The combination meant that the old Roman concept of the law as will, a concept that Hegel had picked up and used as the foundation of his own concept of property, could now be

17. Ibid., p. 39.

dropped because it could be replaced by the idea of the law as a system that was designed to keep a community together. As Röder presented it, this concept of the law as a system had two important features. The first was that it favoured the existence of the many different associations that were a hallmark of modern economic and social life. The second was that the existence of these associations was essentially voluntary. Together, these two features of modern associations meant that they could play a part in the life of states that did not have to rely on the individualism of the political economy of Adam Smith. In making the argument, Röder made it clear that he was drawing upon the thought of two other individuals. One was a philosopher named Karl Christian Friedrich Krause, while the other was one of Krause's most consistent followers, a law professor named Heinrich Ahrens who, by 1855, held a chair at the Austrian University of Graz. As Röder emphasized throughout his comparison of Roman and Germanic law, his own concept of modern economic and social arrangements was largely designed to rehearse what Krause and, particularly, Ahrens had written. On the basis of Röder's description of their work, it could be said that what, in the twentieth century, came to be called pluralism began with the now-forgotten thought of Krause and Ahrens. Once, however, it was more widely known. "Ever since its publication," wrote one mid-nineteenth-century Italian commentator, "the Course on Natural Law (*Corso di Diritto naturale*) by Professor Ahrens has rapidly had the good fortune bestowed on no more than a tiny number of books, even among the best, of traversing the globe and of making a profound impact in Europe and America."[18] Although the comment could have had a certain edge because it repeated, perhaps ironically, Ahrens's own, rather self-congratulatory, description of the various editions and translations of his book, it was still an accurate description of what was once a very successful textbook.

18. For the comment see the first (unnumbered) page of the introduction to Alessandro de Giorgi, *Esamine del Diritto Filosofico, ossia del Sistema e delle Dottrine esposte nella Terza Edizione Francese del* Cours de Droit Naturel ou de Philosophie du Droit *del Prof H. Ahrens* (Padua, 1853). For a similar, but more sincere, encomium, see Rupert Emerson, *State and Sovereignty in Modern Germany* (New Haven, CT, Yale UP, 1928), p. 40: "Heinrich Ahrens, a follower of Krause, was the first to give the pluralist view an expression adequate to its importance." Emerson's assessment has not been echoed in more recent studies of pluralism: see David Runciman, *Pluralism and the Personality of the State* (Cambridge, CUP, 1997); Cécile Laborde, *Pluralist Thought and the State in Britain and France, 1900–25* (Basingstoke, Macmillan, 2000); Marc Stears, *Progressives, Pluralists, and the Problems of the State* (Oxford, OUP, 2002).

Heinrich Ahrens and Karl Christian Friedrich Krause

By most assessments, whether by his contemporaries or by posterity, Heinrich Ahrens was a fairly ordinary nineteenth-century law professor. Because of his familiarity with both French and German, he seems, however, to have been the first to have turned the German word *Rechtsstaat* into the French phrase *état de droit*, meaning approximately the English term, the rule of law.[19] He was born in 1808 in Kniestedt, now a suburb of the small German town of Salzgitter in Hanover, and began his academic career in 1827 when he matriculated at the nearby University of Göttingen. In the years that followed he never became as famous in the German-speaking parts of Europe as, for example, Friedrich Carl von Savigny, Johann Kaspar Bluntschli, Paul Laband, Karl Friedrich Wilhelm Gerber, or Rudolf von Jhering. Nor did he establish much more of an intellectual presence in the academic life of Francophone Europe when, after the revolutionary upheavals of 1830, he was forced to leave Göttingen. His departure was a result of a student insurrection precipitated by a decision by the University of Göttingen to prevent his dissertation on the confederation of German states from being printed.[20] The dissertation itself (which seems to have survived in only a single copy with two missing, unprinted, pages) was a call to turn the German confederation established by the Vienna peace settlement into a federal German state. In this respect at least, it was a dissertation that chimed with a theme that was to inform both German history and Ahrens's own academic career for much of the rest of the century.

The contents and footnotes of the dissertation already foreshadowed much of the subject matter of Ahrens's later publications. Kant's concept of liberty was "merely negative" and needed to be matched by a concept that contained a clearer idea of freedom's goal. Karl Ludwig von Haller's *Restoration of Political*

19. See, for example, Heinrich Ahrens, *Cours de droit naturel ou de philosophie du droit fait d'après l'état de cette science en Allemagne*, 3rd ed. (Brussels, 1850), p. 153, §X, headed "De l'établissement et de l'organisation du droit dans la société, ou de l'Etat": "Car comme le droit comprend les conditions essentielles de l'existence humaine et du développement social, aucun état de vie n'est concevable sans un état correspondant de droit. Or c'est cet *état de droit*, réglé d'une manière plus ou moins parfaite par un *pouvoir social*, que nous devons appeler *l'Etat* dans le sens ordinaire du mot, ou que nous devons considérer du moins comme son origine." See, but with a later example, Luc Heuschling, *Etat de droit, Rechtsstaat, Rule of Law* (Paris, Dalloz, 2002), p. 326 and his "Etat de droit. Etude de linguistique, de théorie et de dogmatique juridiques comparées," in *Verfassungsprinzipien in Europa/Constitutional Principles in Europe*, ed. Hartmut Bauer and Christian Calliess (Berlin, Berliner Wissenschafts Verlag, 2008), pp. 103–55.

20. See Adolf Bock and Heinrich Albert Oppermann, *Die Universität Göttingen* (Leipzig, 1842), pp. 97–98.

Science wrongly conflated the historical origins of states with their moral ends and purposes. Sieyès (available in the 1796 German translation of his publications) had shown the difference between "a true republic" and democracy, or between democracy and "representative rule." The concept of law that was the basis of the whole dissertation was taken, Ahrens emphasized, from two books on natural law and the philosophy of law by an obscure German philosopher named Karl Christian Friedrich Krause that were published in 1803 and 1828.[21] After the dissertation was rejected by its examiner, the legal historian and translator of the famous chapter 44 of Gibbon's *Decline and Fall of the Roman Empire*, Gustav Hugo, the insurrection began. For a week, between 8 and 16 January 1831, Göttingen was ruled by an insurrectionary council (Ahrens was its secretary) before it was taken back by the Hanoverian army. Ahrens, along with two other Göttingen academics, Johann Ernst Arminius von Rauschenplatt and Carl Wilhelm Theodor Schuster, left both the university and the principality of Hanover soon afterwards. Ahrens himself moved first to Paris and then to Brussels, where he taught for nearly fifteen years between 1833 and 1848 at the newly established Free University of Brussels (Université libre de Bruxelles.[22] In 1848, however, he returned to Germany as one of the 649 members of the Frankfurt Parliament, the constituent assembly elected in May 1848 to draft a new constitution for the whole German nation. As the Frankfurt Parliament began to disintegrate, Ahrens resumed his career as a law professor in 1849, this time at the University of Graz in Austria, where he taught for a further fifteen years until, in 1863, he moved to the University of Leipzig. He retired on the grounds of ill-health from his Leipzig chair in 1873 and died a year later at the age of sixty-seven at his birthplace of Salzgitter. It was an academic career that had spanned nearly forty years.

21. Heinrich Ahrens, *De Confoederatione Germanicarum Civitatum* (Göttingen, 1830). An incomplete printed copy of the dissertation was located in the archives of the University of Göttingen under the callmark UAG: Kur. 6. a. 64/3. The callmark is now Kur. 8141.

22. On the Göttingen insurrection of January 1831, see Jörg H. Lampe, "Die Schüler Karl Christian Friedrich Krause und die Göttinger Unruhen von 1831. Legenden und Tatsachen," *Göttinger Jahrbuch* 46 (1998): 47–70; Johannes Tütken, *Privatdozenten im Schatten der Georgia Augusta*, 2 vols. (Göttingen, Universitätsverlag, Göttingen, 2005), 1:292; and Sabine Freitag, Peter Wende, and Markus Mösslang, eds., *British Envoys to Germany*, 4 vols. (Cambridge, CUP, 2000–2006), 2:10. On Ahrens, see initially Max Klüver, "Sozialkritik und Sozialreform bei Heinrich Ahrens" (doctoral diss., University of Hamburg, 1967); Gerhard Dilcher and Bernhard Diestelkamp, eds., *Recht, Gericht, Genossenschaft und Policey* (Berlin, Erich Schmidt Verlag, 1986), pp. 157–67; Peter Goller, *Naturrecht, Rechtsphilosophie oder Rechtstheorie? Zur Geschichte der Rechtsphilosophie an Osterreichs Universitäten (1848–1945)* (Frankfurt, Peter Lang, 1997), pp. 46–55.

In at least one respect, however, it was a rather unusual academic career. Although his time in Paris and Brussels belonged entirely to his early years, Ahrens continued to write and publish in French right up to the end of his life. His first two books were actually written in French and were published in Paris, accompanied by a generous acknowledgement of the local assistance that he had relied upon to bring his prose up to the requisite grammatical and syntactic standards. The first to appear (in 1836) was not actually about the law at all, although it still throws considerable light on the broader moral and philosophical concerns involved in Ahrens's legal and political thought. It was the first volume of a *Cours de psychologie*, or a lecture course on psychology, although it did not actually have very much to do with the concept of psychology, at least as that concept was usually understood in early nineteenth-century France. There, the focus fell mainly on *idéologie*—meaning the study of the origin of ideas and the workings of the mind—or on the criticism of ideology developed by Victor Cousin and his eclectic followers. In both cases and despite their otherwise considerable differences, the focus fell on the analytical merits of starting with conceptual simplicity (like sense perception) in order to develop a better understanding of synthetic complexity (like the concept of a person, a state, or a law). For Ahrens, on the other hand, the focus fell mainly on the substantive reality of synthetic concepts themselves and on the benefits to human culture and its improvement produced by a better understanding how they originated and worked. The claim applied not only to fundamental concepts like space, time, or individual personality but also to almost every aspect of modern life, from the idea of a people, a nation, or a deity to the institution of marriage, the ownership of property, or the capacity to vote. Ahrens signalled this difference in emphasis by giving his book a pair of conceptually capacious subtitles, announcing that the first of its two volumes, the one published in 1836, would contain "a general anthropology," while only the second, published two years later, would deal with "psychology properly speaking, as well as the general part of metaphysics." As the two subtitles were intended to indicate, this meant that the whole course was designed to be a wide-ranging examination of the long-drawn-out, largely German-language, discussion of the origin, nature, and development of human knowledge from Leibniz to Hegel, with an emphasis, as Ahrens went to some lengths to show, on the relationship of unconscious to conscious thought and their joint bearing on the emergence and development of human language, rationality, aesthetics, culture, and spirituality. In more concrete terms, Ahrens's treatment of psychology was designed to show how human development could lead to the emergence of a multitude of differentiated, but interdependent, associations. As he pointed out in the preface to the second volume of the course, the whole work should really have been called a course of philosophy rather than a course of psychology.

The broad range of subjects covered by the lecture course was connected to a second, equally unusual, aspect of Ahrens's academic career. This was his abiding and very open allegiance to the thought of Karl Christian Friedrich Krause and his long involvement in the work of the small and loosely associated network of lawyers, philosophers, and political activists who were committed to the publication and promotion of Krause's ideas. Over time, Krause's thought turned into the movement that came to be known as Krausism, or, more accurately, *Krausismo* because it was in Spain and South America in the second half of the nineteenth century that Krausism became a real movement.[23] Before 1848, however, it acquired a significant early following in Belgium and France, notably among the students and academics associated with the recently founded Université libre de Bruxelles where Krause's thought was publicized energetically by the philosophy professor Guillaume Tiberghien, and in France in the circles associated with the socialist Pierre Leroux, the novelist George Sand, the political radical Pierre-Joseph Proudhon, his secretary Alfred Darimon (who dedicated a book that he published in 1848 on Krause's thought to Ahrens), and the future promoter of the Statue of Liberty, Edouard Laboulaye.[24] In Germany Krause's thought was publicly endorsed by Karl David August Röder and Hermann Karl von Leonhardi at Heidelberg University, the university that became the main conduit from which Krausism spread to Spain and Italy. Here, the most influential intermediary was a young Spanish philosopher named Julián Sanz del Rio who travelled to Heidelberg from the University of Madrid in 1843, stopping along the way to meet Cousin in Paris and Ahrens in Brussels, possibly because Ahrens had been recommended by Cousin or, more probably, because Ahrens's book on natural law had already been translated into Spanish in 1842. Sanz del Rio was responsible for a Spanish translation of a number of articles that Krause had written when

23. On Krause and Krausism (or *Krausismo*), see, initially, Oscar Ferreira, ed., *Krausisme juridique et politique en Europe* (Paris, Classiques Garnier, 2021); Emerson, *State and Sovereignty in Modern Germany*; George Gurvitch, *L'idée du droit social* (Paris, 1932), pp. 442–70; Pierre Jobit, *Les éducateurs de l'Espagne contemporaine, I, les Krausistes*, 2 vols. (Paris, 1936); Michael Dreyer, "German Roots of the Theory of Pluralism," *Constitutional Political Economy* 4 (1993): 7–39; Pierre Bidart, "L'influence du philosophe allemand F. Krause dans la formation des sciences sociales en Espagne," *Revue Germanique Internationale* 21 (2004): 133–48; Juan López-Morillas, *The Krausist Movement and Ideological Change in Spain, 1854–1874* [1956] (Cambridge, CUP, 1981); Christian Rubio, *Krausism and the Spanish Avant-Garde* (New York, Cambria Press, 2017).

24. On these circles, see Klüver, "Sozialkritik und Sozialreform bei Heinrich Ahrens," and Dilcher and Diestelkamp, *Recht, Gericht, Genossenschaft und Policey*. On Sand and Leroux, see Sand, *Le Compagnon du Tour de France*, pp. 7–32.

he had been at the University of Göttingen at about the same time that Ahrens had been a student there (Ahrens could, therefore, have proposed or provided the material for the translation). The translation appeared under the title of Krause's only relatively well-known work, a pamphlet entitled *Das Urbild der Menschheit* (The ideal of humanity), which Krause had published in 1811 and which, with the somewhat different content that Sanz del Rio gave to it, became the manifesto text of *Krausismo*.

By the time that Sanz del Rio visited Heidelberg in 1843, the embryonic movement had become better known partly because Ahrens was involved in a fairly protracted and very heated public dispute with a Belgian theologian named Joseph Tits over the subject of Krausism's putative pantheism. The dispute and the interest in Krausism, particularly in France, that it began to generate made the period between 1840 and 1848 the movement's European high-water mark. After 1848, however, its following in northern Europe began to decline, although it continued grow in Spain and, subsequently, in many parts of South America. The combination of decline in Europe and expansion outside of Europe was, at least in part, an effect of positivism and the fact that Krausist moral theory had nothing to match the preoccupation with altruism that was one of the hallmarks of the moral and political thought of Auguste Comte. It was also an effect of the fact that positivism was better able than Krausism to keep up with developments in natural science, and to accommodate the gradual eclipse of early nineteenth-century German *Naturphilosophie* by the sciences of electricity, magnetism, chemistry, and biology. Together this new range of scientific subjects pushed the more generic concepts of vital forces, natural powers, and organic life largely off the analytical and scientific map. Finally, however, it was also, as Röder's pamphlet indicates, an effect of the way that Krause's thought became increasingly entangled with the long-drawn-out argument over the rival legacies of the Romans and the Germans, and, as that argument played out, Krausism was gradually displaced by two new and different attempts to find a position midway between the two sides. One was the effort made by one of Röder's colleagues at the University of Heidelberg, the Swiss-German law professor Johann Kaspar Bluntschli who moved to Heidelberg in 1861, to produce a new synthesis of Romanist and Germanist theories of the origins and nature of political society. The other was the transformation by the legal historian Otto von Gierke of the concept of a *Genossenschaft* into something that was as compatible with the legacy of the Romans as with that of the Germans. Cumulatively, the combination of these developments pushed Krausism into obscurity.

When, however, Ahrens came to Paris early in 1831, its prospects looked more positive. France had a new, Orleanist, dynasty with a commitment to constitutional government, while Belgium had seceded from the Netherlands to become an independent state with a new, self-consciously secular, university in the Université libre de Bruxelles. As Ahrens announced in 1836 in his preface to the published version of his psychology lectures, he had been invited to give them in Paris by the two best-known and most influential figures in the political and intellectual life of the new French regime, François Guizot and Victor Cousin. It is not clear how either Cousin or Guizot came to know of Ahrens, or what their motivation might have been in allowing him to say publicly that they had authorized his lectures. Ahrens was, however, already known as the author of an article entitled "The Social and Religious Tendencies of German Philosophy" published in the *Revue Encyclopédique* in 1831 by the heterodox Saint-Simonian philosopher Pierre Leroux, and the titles of both the article and the periodical can be taken as an initial clue as to why Guizot and Cousin were willing to take an interest in what Ahrens was likely to say.[25] At that time, both the periodical and its editor could be readily associated with Saint-Simonianism. So too could Krausism. But, while Saint-Simonianism could also be associated with Hegel, the same did not apply to Krausism. From this perspective, Cousin's interest in Ahrens and his lecture course could have been designed to generate an interest in explaining why it was desirable to open up a distance between the French Hegelians and the French Saint-Simonians.

Alternatively, however, Cousin could have seen Ahrens's lecture course as an opportunity to use Krause's thought to build a bridge between the French Saint-Simonians and their critics as well as between the French Hegelians and their critics. In this case, Ahrens was supported because he seemed to be able to establish a middle ground between the Scylla of Hegelianism on the one side and the Charybdis of Saint-Simonianism on the other. Ahrens himself had been quick to see the similarity between Krause and Saint-Simon. In several of the letters that he sent to Krause from Paris in 1831 and 1832, he made a point of highlighting the convergence between Krause's vision of an economically differentiated but institutionally integrated society and the parallel social and political reform programme of the French Saint-Simonians. But there was still a real divergence. It had, however, less to do with industry, trade, and finance than with the role of the state and centralized decision making and uniform policy in promoting social reform. Here, both Krause and Ahrens had less in common with the Saint-Simonians and more in common with their

25. Ahrens, "Tendance sociale et religieuse de la philosophie allemande," p. 687, and his "Uber den Saint-Simonismus." See also Bartier, *Naissance du socialisme en Belgique*, pp. 124–31. On Ahrens's publications, see Wolfgang Forster, "Belgian Origins of Krausism–Heinrich Ahrens in Brussels," in *Les Professeurs Allemands en Belgique*, ed. Raphaël Cahen et al. (Antwerp and Brussels, ASP, 2022), pp. 93–120.

French critics who, after 1830, included the former Saint-Simonian Pierre Leroux, the publisher of Ahrens's first article on German philosophy.

If this was the role that Ahrens was expected to play, it was one that was not entirely consonant with his own approach to his lectures. As he indicated in his preface to the version that he published, he had not been very happy with the term "psychology." He had in fact spent some time thinking about what he was going to say because a letter that he sent in 1832 from a Parisian address to the French socialist Constantin Pecqueur indicates that he was beginning to contemplate a course of lectures on the subject of German philosophy almost a year before he began to give them in the autumn and winter of 1833–34. In the lectures themselves, Ahrens immediately began to highlight the importance of Krause and his philosophy, and, at the same time, to attack Hegel and Hegelianism. As a notice in the January 1834 issue of the Parisian *Nouvelle Revue Germanique* reported, he had begun to give "a lecture course on the history of German philosophy" on Friday evenings at 7:00 p.m. at a venue on the rue Taranne, and that "MM Ballanche, Cousin, Mignet, and, generally, the principal representatives of the various French philosophical schools had been present at the inaugural lecture." A second notice, this time in the January 1834 issue of the *Revue du progrès social* published by another dissident French follower of Saint-Simon, Jules Lechevalier, mentioned the same names among the audience but also gave a fuller account of the content of the lectures themselves. According to it, Ahrens had set out an impressive overview of the thought of Kant, Fichte, Schelling, and Hegel, but had also begun to explain why, in his view, the philosophy of the almost entirely unknown Krause amounted to a real alternative to Hegel's philosophy. Although Lechevalier made it clear that he had yet to be persuaded by Ahrens either of Hegel's limitations or of Krause's merits, he ended his report by writing that any philosopher who had acquired "so enlightened and conscientious a disciple as Monsieur Ahrens" had to have more than a limited range. "No one in France," he ended, "had yet to say anything about a system that, even in Germany, had not made much of a noise."[26]

As Lechevalier intimated, Ahrens's attempt to publicize Krause's philosophy was met with largely baffled silence. Ahrens, however, continued to maintain his allegiance to Krause and Krausism for the rest of his life and, having used his psychology lectures to lay the conceptual foundations of his treatment of law and politics, went on to publish the book that was to occupy the rest of his career as a law professor. It was entitled *Cours de droit nature* (Course on natural law) and was published in Paris in 1838, the same year of publication as the second part of his psychology course. By then, Ahrens had moved from Paris to Brussels, which

26. For this description of Ahrens's lectures, see *Revue du progrès social* 1 (1834): 108–9.

meant that the natural law course was based not on a course of public lectures, as had been the case with the psychology lectures, but upon the lecture course that Ahrens now gave at the Free University of Brussels. In his preface to the book's first edition Ahrens made a point of highlighting its pedagogic and didactic character, and emphasized too that it was aimed primarily at university students in Belgium and France. It was, he wrote, designed to make developments in German-language works on philosophy and jurisprudence over the past forty years better known in France and Belgium. As things stood, he pointed out, the absence of a modern guide meant that students in the Francophone world still had to rely on "the almost hundred-year-old" work of Jean-Jacques Burlamaqui for something like a textbook on natural law.

Ahrens had spotted a real gap in the market. Over the following thirty years, he proceeded to fill it with a sequence of revised editions of his natural law lecture course. A second edition was published in 1844, followed by four further French-language editions in 1848, 1853, 1860, and 1868. By the time of the second edition, translations into Italian, Portuguese, and Spanish had already appeared, followed by two German translations in 1846 and 1852, which were then incorporated into a German-language *Juristische Enzyklopädie* published in Vienna in 1855. This encyclopaedia was subsequently translated into French in 1880 and was followed soon afterwards by a full-scale intellectual biography of its author written by the book's translator, an obscure magistrate in the southern French town of Albi named Anatole Chauffard, who went on to publish a number of strikingly bigoted contributions to an already-crowded list of conspiracy-theory-based approaches to modern politics in the years that straddled the Boulanger and Dreyfus affairs during the long, precarious, consolidation of the French Third Republic. Further printings of the natural law book occurred in Mexico and Spain, while an English-language summary of its first part was added to a collection of texts on the science of jurisprudence published in Edinburgh in 1887. By then, a seventh edition of the course on natural law had been published in 1875, incorporating several small additions that Ahrens had made shortly before his death. There had, he noted in 1860 in the preface to the fifth edition of his course, been sixteen original editions or translations of the book. In the sixth edition, in 1868, he carefully revised the number up to nineteen.

Ahrens's very last publication helps to throw some light on how his legal encyclopaedia came to be translated by the conspiratorially minded Catholic Anatole Chauffard. It was a long article entitled "Die Abwege in der neuern deutschen Geistesentwicklung" (Wrong turnings in the development of the modern German mind) that was published in Prague in 1873 in a periodical named *Die Neue Zeit* (Modern times) edited and largely written by another of Krause's followers, the former Heidelberg University professor Hermann Karl von Leonhardi, who had moved subsequently to the University of Prague. As the title of the article indicates, it was a forthright attack on modern German intellectual and political life in the aftermath of the Franco-Prussian War of 1871. Here, Ahrens's hostility was aimed at both the militarization of politics and the centralization of policy under Prussian domination of Germany. To- gether, he argued, they pointed towards a world of religious conformity, her- alded by the beginnings of the *Kulturkampf*; social inequality, symbolized by Bismarck and Prussian Junkers; mindless materialism, typified by the vogue for Charles Darwin and his theory of evolution; and state power, underpinned by the new enthusiasm for what Prussia's admirers called *Machtpolitik*, or power politics. France under Napoleon III had been no better (here Ahrens made a point of singling out for special opprobrium the onetime Saint- Simonian Hippolyte Fortoul who, as minister of public instruction during the Second Empire had been responsible, he claimed, for promoting all the same failings). The outcome, Ahrens warned, was likely to be military despotism rather than peaceful progress and, ultimately, political turmoil rather than so- cial harmony. It would, in short, be exactly the opposite of what in 1811, towards the end of the Napoleonic Wars, Karl Christian Friedrich Krause had de- scribed as the ideal of humanity.

Ahrens's broadly negative evaluation of recent developments in history and politics was based, however, on one, more specific but equally unwel- come, feature of the modern age. This was the part that Roman law had come to play in the economic, social, and political life of modern states. For Ahrens, it was this development that was the basis of the combination of *Machtpolitik*, materialism, and centralization that, in his view, now threat- ened to dominate modern economic and political life. Substantial passages of the later editions of his natural law course were, accordingly, informed by his growing hostility towards Roman law. Initially, however, he voiced his anxieties in a largely technical way, as he did in the introduction to the legal encyclopaedia (*Juristische Enzyklopädie*) that was published in 1855 and was translated almost simultaneously into French in a periodical published in Brussels by Pascal Duprat, another of Krause's earlier, now exiled, French admirers. In this introduction, Ahrens noted that divergences in what he called "synthetic conceptions" in law had generated "a new liveliness in the dispute between the Romanists and Germanists." The dispute had arisen, he claimed, because there was no substantive theoretical link between pri- vate law (*droit personnel*) and public law (*droit public*) in contemporary legal science, causing both subjects to become conceptually impoverished and mutually exclusive. His aim, he wrote, at least in relation to what he called the "the fundamental principles of civil law" (*droit civil*) was to bring "greater philosophical depth to the notions of possession, property, and obligations" in order to help to reconcile the theory of Roman law with that of its Germanic counterpart.[27]

By the time that Ahrens published the preface to the sixth, 1868, edition of his natural law course, these technical reservations had become more straightforwardly political. In this preface, Ahrens called upon his readers to pay particular attention to the historical overview that he had added to his text, and to think about its bearing on what he described as "the grave political situation in which almost all the civilized countries now find themselves." "We are," he wrote at the beginning of the historical overview itself, "living in an age that seems, once again, to be displaying a recrudescence of those elements, tendencies, and passions that will only divert peoples and humanity from their noble destiny." This, he continued, was because "it could be said that the spirit of ancient Rome, with its propensities to absolutism, unification, and centralization in politics, and to cupidity and self-enrichment in private life, has been reborn."[28] These propensities, he went on to claim, were deep-seated features of Roman law because Roman law was radically individualistic in both form and substance. It was an aspect of Roman law that had positive as well as negative implications. "The Roman people," Ahrens wrote, "in taking the individual and the will of a person as the starting point of their conceptions of right and of the state, was, more than any other people, able to disentangle private law (*droit privé*) from public law (*droit public*) and was, therefore, the first to found the former on the great principle of personality and free will that, being equal for all citizens, called for equal rights without distinctions of class, orders, or castes."[29]

In this sense, it was the Roman law principle of "liberty and equality" that, in the longer term, had sapped "feudal organization" and favoured the establishment of a system of civil law that applied to every social condition and

27. Heinrich Ahrens, *Juristische Enzyklopädie* (Vienna, 1855), pp. v–vi. The French translation of Ahrens's introduction was published in *La Libre Recherche* (ed. Pascal Duprat) 1, no. 1 (1855): 302–5.

28. "La grave situation politique dans laquelle se trouvent presque tous les pays civilisés." "Cependant nous vivons à une époque qui présente encore une fois dans son mouvement une recrudescence d'éléments, de tendances et de passions qui ne peuvent que détourner l'humanité et les peuples de leur noble destination." "On dirait que l'ancien esprit romain renaît encore une fois avec ses tendances d'absolutisme, d'unification et de centralisation dans la politique, de cupidité et d'enrichissement dans la vie privée." Ahrens, *Cours de droit naturel* [1838], 6th ed. (Leipzig, 1868), pp. v and 273–74.

29. "Le peuple romain, il est vrai, en partant dans sa conception du droit et de l'état, de l'individu, de la volonté de la personne, a dégagé plus qu'aucun autre peuple, le droit privé du droit public, et a fondé le premier sur le grand principe de la personnalité et de la volonté libre, qui, étant égal, sans distinction de classes, d'ordres et de castes." Ibid., p. 258.

social state. But the same principle also favoured "monarchical absolutism in the most pernicious way" because it was part of a political system that promoted the "principles of imperialist law." This, somewhat paradoxically, was because of the very same primacy of private law in the Roman legal system. It meant that there was no surrounding framework of public law to offset the individualism of Roman private law. Since, Ahrens argued, the Roman state was not "constituted for labour, or for production in an order of human culture, but for domination and the extension of empire (so that even agricultural labour itself was transferred into the hands of slaves)," private law consisted largely of those forms that were centred on the acquisition, transfer, or extinction of power over men and things. "Neither the state nor the individual had any higher goal. Egoism taken to the highest degree dominated the nation in the sphere of public law and the individual in that of private law."[30] To reinforce the point, Ahrens quoted a parallel description from his colleague at the University of Graz Rudolf von Jhering's *The Spirit of Roman Law* which emphasized that "the Roman character, with its virtues and vices, can be defined as a system of rational egoism. Its fundamental principle is that the inferior should be sacrificed to the superior, the individual to the state, the particular case to the general, or abstract, rule, and the accidental to the permanent." Rome's greatness had no independent source of morality. Greatness itself was, accordingly, Rome's only justification and, at the same time, also the ultimate source of its own downfall.[31] Rome had a state, but no public law.

On Ahrens's terms, therefore, Roman liberty was not modern liberty, and neo-Roman liberty would simply open a door to imperialism, just as it had

---

30. "C'est par ce principe de liberté et d'égalité que le droit romain, depuis sa réception dans l'empire germanique, a contribué, pour une grande part, à miner l'organisation féodale, à fonder un droit civil commun pour les états sociaux, en favorisant cependant d'un autre côté, de la manière la plus pernicieuse, par ses principes du droit impérialiste (*quod principi placuit, legis habet vigorem*), l'absolutisme monarchique. Mais on méconnaît complètement l'idée du droit, quand on la croit réalisée d'une manière éminente dans le droit romain. D'abord, comme le principe du droit embrasse à la fois le droit public et privé, dont le premier est le cadre, le fondement et le régulateur de l'autre, le droit privé sera toujours le reflet de l'esprit que anime un peuple dans toute la constitution de son état. Or, l'état romain n'était pas constitué pour le travail, pour la production dans un ordre de culture humaine (car le travail agricole même passa de plus en plus dans la main des esclaves), mais pour la domination, pour l'extension de l'empire sur les peuples." Ibid., p. 258.

31. "Le caractère romain avec ses vertus et ses vices peut être défini le système d'égoïsme raisonné. Le principe fondamental de ce système, c'est que l'inferieur doit être sacrifié au supérieur, l'individu à l'état, le cas particulier à la règle générale ou abstraite, l'accidentel au permanent." Ibid., p. 259 n. 1.

done to Rome itself. He made it clear, however, that Roman law had certainly had beneficial effects. It had been "an important agent of the destruction of the feudal order; it favoured those just tendencies towards constituting man as the free master of his strength and property." In this respect, Ahrens pointed out, it was "a good ally of those schools of political economy that, like those of Adam Smith and the physiocrats, called for freedom of human labour and the emancipation of the land from all those feudal burdens that were so harmful to good cultivation."[32] But its limitations had become ever more apparent in the modern age, "where great questions concerning various types of association and better regulation of every type of economic, industrial, commercial, and agricultural labour need to be resolved, not according to the narrow principles of a partnership (*societas*) as in Roman law, or according to a number of abstract principles of obligation, but in full knowledge of the nature of the whole of social labour and the laws governing it. Roman law can well go on for a long time as an important element in the historical study of law, but modern society needs a form of law that is more complete and more human." Taken as a whole, Ahrens wrote, Roman law had had "the pernicious effect of detaching the state and the law from its living sources within the nation, making the state an affair—and almost the patrimony—of princes and their officials, and the law an affair of lawyers."[33] The need now, Ahrens argued, was to look towards England, where "the German spirit of *self-government* had promoted the representative system and the institution of the jury," and to use these as models for establishing a new political edifice on

32. "Pour le droit privé, la réception du droit civil romain n'a eu également qu'une valeur relative; il a été un important levier de destruction de l'ordre féodal, il a favorisé les justes tendances à constituer l'homme le maitre libre de ses forces et de sa propriété, il est devenu un bon allié des écoles d'économie politique, qui, comme celles d'Adam Smith et des physiocrates, demandaient la liberté du travail humain et l'affranchissement du sol des charges féodales, si nuisibles à une bonne culture." Ibid., p. 271.

33. "[D]e même l'insuffisance du droit romain se montre de plus en plus aujourd'hui, où de grandes questions concernant divers genres d'associations et un meilleur règlement de tout travail économique, industriel, commercial, agricole, doivent être résolues, non d'après les principes étroites de société (*societas*) du droit romain, ou d'après quelques principes abstraits d'obligation, mais en pleine connaissance de la nature de tout le travail social et des lois qui le régissent. Le droit romain peut bien encore rester longtemps un élément important dans l'étude historique du droit; mais la société moderne a besoin d'un droit plus complet et plus humain. . . . Envisagé dans son ensemble, le droit romain a eu l'effet pernicieux de détacher l'état et le droit de ses sources vives dans la nation, de faire de l'état une affaire et presque un patrimoine des princes et de leurs fonctionnaires, et du droit une affaire des juristes et des légistes." Ibid., pp. 271–72.

analogous lines. The age of Roman law had passed, both politically and legally, and a new, post-Roman, legal system now had to modify "the narrow spirit of individualism and egoism of Roman law, in developing, always in keeping with the German spirit and the true principles of the philosophy of law, a law of association (*droit d'association*) in which the private interest is not destroyed, but harmonized with the common interest of both the associates and the public order."[34]

This political vision was based on a philosophy of history that, as Ahrens acknowledged, was common to the Hegelians, Saint-Simonians, and the followers of Krause. It was also similar to the philosophy of history described by August Cieszkowski (who, along with Ahrens, Röder, and Dietzel, was a member of an International Welfare Congress, or Congrès international de bienfaisance, that met periodically in several different European cities around the middle of the nineteenth century).[35] In broad terms, Ahrens wrote, it amounted to a claim that history was a progression from unity to variety to harmony. This threefold typology was applicable to a range of different subjects, including political societies and the growing range of components of culture that they housed. Thus Rome and Roman law could be situated in the first, unitary, category. Christianity, particularly when coupled with the legacy of Roman law, could be associated with the second, while philosophy, particularly German philosophy after Kant, not only provided the resources that enabled harmony to emerge from variety, but also made it possible to understand the type of moral and historical progress involved in the transition from the former to the latter. The same schematic typology could be applied to the economy and the idea of the division of labour, just as it could also encompass the many different types of association established in almost every sphere of life, from dining clubs and women's institutes to musical societies and football clubs. In earlier times, when there had been guilds and professional corporations, associations were simply the other side of the division of labour. But with the rise of individual liberty and the gradual erosion of restrictions on individual choice, associations could now become entirely voluntary, with no necessary connection to any prior occupation or activity. For Krause, the model of this trajectory was Freemasonry, which was one

34. "[M]ais le droit civil doit encore plus profondément modifier l'esprit étroit d'individualisme et d'égoïsme du droit romain, en développant, toujours d'accord avec l'esprit Germanique et les vrais principes de la philosophie du droit, un droit d'association dans lequel l'intérêt privé n'est pas détruit, mais harmonisé avec l'intérêt commun des associés et de l'ordre public." Ibid., p. 273.

35. See the list of members printed in [Anon]. *Congres international de bienfaisance de Francfort-sur-le-Main. Session de 1857*, 2 vols. (Frankfurt and Brussels, 1858), 1:32–39.

reason why he had had no inhibition about publicizing many of its most secret arrangements and institutions.

The increasingly voluntary character of human association was, according
to Ahrens, the promise of the modern age. It housed the possibility of a new
federal system made up of a multiplicity of interlocking associations held together by a system of law and government that would be compatible with
social harmony, rather than simple social variety. This was the prospect that
lay at the heart of Krause's moral and political philosophy and, from Ahrens's
point of view, was now under threat from the revived politics of Rome and
Rome's imperial legacy. Philosophy, as Ahrens presented it, was a synthesis of
the ancient and pagan on the one side and the modern and Christian on the
other. The former had been oriented too strongly towards the physical and
material, while the latter had lurched too far towards the intellectual and the
spiritual. Philosophy was the bridge between the two. Its emancipation from
subordination to both church and state meant, Ahrens wrote, that "the whole
of life took a new direction towards the cultivation of those elements that the
church had called human, worldly, or earthly. There is a deep significance in
the fact that this new tendency was called *humanism* because it began in effect
by linking a notable portion of humanity and Greek and Latin culture to the
new age."[36] Once it had acquired an identity of its own, philosophy could
rise above "the dualism of church and state" that had been the hallmark of the
Middle Ages and establish new foundations for both. In this sense it was philosophy, "with its new doctrines of the state and society, that paved the way
towards the renewal of the social order. It could even develop the great principles of Christianity—personality, liberty, and equality in all that is human—as
the governing principles of the whole social order. Without knowing it, and
despite the deviations that it has experienced, it has been more Christian than
the churches with their limited views of the need for human progress in this
life. In the end, it is philosophy that has been summoned to prepare the third
age of an organic and harmonic synthesis of everything human and divine."[37]
It was, in all but name, civic humanism.

36. "Toute la vie prend une nouvelle direction vers la culture des éléments que l'église avait
appelés humains, mondains, terrestre. Ce n'est pas sans une profonde signification que cette tendance s'appelle *humanisme*, qui commence en effet par relier une portion notable de l'humanité,
la culture grecque et latine, à l'ère nouvelle." Ahrens, *Cours de droit naturel*, 6th ed., p. 262.

37. "C'est elle [la philosophie] qui a préparé, par les nouvelles doctrines de l'état et de la
société, le renouvellement de l'ordre social; ce sont même les grands principes du christianisme,
la personnalité, la liberté, l'égalité dans tout ce qui est humain, que la philosophie a développés
comme les principes régulateurs de tout l'ordre social; elle a été, sans le savoir elle-même, et
malgré les déviations qu'elle a éprouvées, plus chrétienne que les églises avec leurs vues trop

Ultimately, of course, the philosophy in question was that of Krause. "In the theory of the state," Ahrens wrote, "Krause was really able to harmonize clashes between established doctrines on the subject. He considers the state to be an institution with a special responsibility for the law that, therefore, does not absorb man or society into the state. He calls, instead, for distinct social organizations for morality, religion, the sciences, the arts, industry, and commerce, but he sets political organization, or the state, in an intimate relationship to all human activity and with all the institutions of society."[38] At first sight, the description could have equally fitted Hegel's concept of political society or that promoted by the French Saint-Simonians. But Ahrens went to some lengths to emphasize the differences between Krause and Hegel and, at the same time, the continuities from Kant to Krause. "The God Progress had his school in Hegelianism and his temple in Saint-Simonianism," Ahrens wrote dismissively.[39] The real breakthrough had, instead, come from Kant, because it had been Kant who had shown how to reconcile the spiritual and the social within a single conceptual system.

Kant, Ahrens wrote, had been "the first to introduce the important and precise term of a condition into the notion of a law." He had done so by way of his concept of the categorical imperative and the recognition of "subjective liberty" that, according to Ahrens, the concept implied. Although he had abstracted from the related subjects of human well-being and culture by taking law's purpose to be no more than maintaining subjective liberty, Kant had identified a real principle.[40] Acting according to the maxim that an act could be willed as a universal law meant unconditional abstention from doing harm and, by extension, unconditional recognition that others had the ability to act in the same way. Kant, Ahrens wrote in the first edition of his treatise, had

---

peu ouvertes aux besoins du progrès humain dans la vie actuelle; c'est enfin la philosophie qui est appelée à préparer la troisième ère de synthèse harmonique et organique de tous les éléments divins et humains." Ibid., p. 263.

38. "Dans la théorie de l'état, Krause harmonise encore les doctrines opposées qui ont été établies sur cette matière; il considère l'état comme l'institution spéciale du droit, et n'absorbe dans l'état l'homme et la société; il demande des organisations sociales distinctes pour la morale, la religion, les sciences, les arts, l'industrie et le commerce; mais il met l'organisation politique ou l'état dans un rapport intime avec toute l'activité humaine, avec toutes les institutions de la société." Ibid., p. 79.

39. "Le Dieu-progrès a eu son école dans le hégélianisme et son temple dans le saint-simonisme." Ibid., p. 75.

40. "C'est Kant qui le premier introduisit le terme important et précis de condition dans la notion du droit. . . . Kant lui-même avait d'ailleurs fait abstraction de l'ordre de bien et de culture, et placé le but du droit dans le maintien de la liberté subjective." Ibid., p. 136.

rejected "the useless hypothesis of the state of nature" on the one side and "the old doctrine of Grotius, who derived right from the instinct of sociability," on the other.[41] In place of these two starting points, he had begun with the old scholastic distinction between internal and external actions. The former were governed by moral laws, or the laws of conscience, while the latter were governed by external laws, or the positive laws of society. Only the latter were truly binding. Since people had to live in society, there had, as Kant himself had put it, "to be a general law by which the freedom of action of each individual could coexist with the freedom of all." By basing the law on what Ahrens called "the external conditionality of human life," he could identify "a *criterion* for justice that would be recognized by everyone and could be adopted in all legislation."[42] It meant, he claimed, that the law could be defined as "the totality of conditions under which the external liberty of each can coexist with the liberty of all."[43] This definition, Ahrens wrote, which Krause had also followed, "can be regarded as the true scientific formulation of modern political liberalism" because its aim was to establish "a political system in which individual liberty was guaranteed and, at the same time, was compatible with the liberty of all." It was because of "this liberal principle, in the true sense of the word, that Kant's system has had so great and happy an influence on every branch of public and private law."[44]

The association between Kant and Krause now looks rather odd. Expressing admiration for Krause was not, however, always as unusual as it has become.

41. "Kant, en rejetant d'un côté l'hypothèse inutile d'un état de nature, et d'un autre côté l'ancienne doctrine de Grotius, qui faisait dériver le droit de l'instinct de sociabilité, sans en préciser davantage les principes, fonda le premier le droit naturel sur des principes rationnels résultant de l'étude de la nature et de la société humaine." Ahrens, *Cours de droit naturel*, 1st ed. (Brussels, 1838), p. 69.

42. "En fondant ainsi le droit dans la conditionnalité extérieure de la vie humaine, on arrive à un *criterium* de justice qui peut être reconnu de tout le monde, et par conséquent adopté dans toute législation." Ibid., p. 59.

43. For this version of Kant's definition, see the notes on Immanuel Kant, *Metaphysics of Morals*, in Immanuel Kant, *Lectures on Ethics*, ed. Peter Heath and Jerome B. Schneewind, (Cambridge, CUP, 1997), p. 287. The published version was cited by Ahrens in the first edition of his *Cours*, pp. 69–70.

44. "Cette définition renferme une grande vérité. On peut la regarder comme une véritable formule scientifique du libéralisme politique moderne, qui cherche à fonder un système politique où la liberté de chacun soit garantie et conciliée avec la liberté de tous. Et c'est par ce principe libéral dans le vrai sens du mot que le système de Kant a exercé une grande et heureuse influence sur toutes les branches du droit privé et publique." Ahrens, *Cours de droit naturel*, 1st ed., p. 70.

"Read Krause's *Philosophy of History*," noted the Genevan academic Henri Frédéric Amiel in his diary some time before 1848. "It is a complete philosophy: God, the world, humanity, liberty, evil, religion, law, science, art, virtue, morality, life, death, peoples, ages, marriage, nations, time, eternity, the future and the past, the present state of the world and the other planets, the role of philosophy— all these subjects are dealt with and settled."[45] Nor was his philosophy always disassociated from Kant's. As an early twentieth-century American survey of German jurisprudence put it, "Krause is now recognized as the definite founder of the organic and positive school of natural law, and brings to its fullest effect the philosophy of Kant."[46] From this perspective, Krause had shown how to develop and extend Kant's moral and political philosophy. More than Kant, he had shown that liberty was not static, and, by extension, had explained why the definition and content of the law had, correspondingly, to respond to the various ways in which liberty had developed in time and space. Kant's definition of the law, Ahrens wrote, paralleling the assessment made by Georges Frédéric Schützenberger, was "negative and restrictive," whereas a "correct definition" had to be "affirmative," with "a positive content" that would match the development of liberty.[47]

> Liberty is generally understood in negative fashion, as the absence of constraint. But this is simply a minor aspect of the concept. Man is truly free when, once emancipated from partial impulses that might constrain or make him lose his balance, he can dominate and master things by the use of his own central powers and can guide his own actions according to the one principle of the good. Then, he has a capacity for self-determination and for autonomy in his actions. It is really *he* who acts. It is his higher self, lifted to its highest power by the principle of the good, which judges calmly, with no partiality or egoistical interest, in choosing what conforms most to the totality of relationships to which an action applies.[48]

45. Henri Frédéric Amiel, *Essais critiques*, ed. Bernard Bouvier (Paris, Stock, 1932), p. 131.

46. Edwin M. Borchard, "Jurisprudence in Germany," *Columbia Law Review* 12 (1912): 301–20 (p. 310 for the passage cited here).

47. Ahrens, *Cours de droit naturel*, 1st ed., pp. 70–71. On Schützenberger's assessement, see the introduction, above.

48. "La liberté est généralement comprise d'une manière négative, comme l'absence de contrainte; mais ce n'est là qu'une face subordonnée; l'homme est vraiment libre quand, affranchi des impulsions partielles qui l'entraineraient et lui feraient perdre son équilibre, il sait tout dominer et maitriser par sa force centrale, en se guidant dans ses actions d'après le principe unique du bien. Alors il acquiert la détermination propre, l'autonomie dans ses actes; c'est réellement *lui* qui agit, c'est son moi supérieur, élevé par le principe du bien à sa plus haute puissance, qui juge avec calme, sans être préoccupé d'une vue exclusive ou d'un intérêt égoïste, en

This capacity was, ultimately, rational. For Ahrens, this was why Krause's philosophy mattered.

As Ahrens put it, Krause had shown that reason was the distinguishing feature of humanity. It was "a special higher force or faculty that imprints a higher character on all those other faculties which are more analogous to animal spirits."[49] It was the reflexive faculty, or the one faculty that enabled other faculties to be aware of their own activity. Without it, as Krause, Schelling, and the natural philosopher Carl Gustav Carus had shown, the line dividing consciousness from the unconscious would be hard to identify.[50] It was reason, not feeling, that was responsible for the human ability to feel feeling, just as it was reason that was responsible for the human ability to be aware of reason reasoning. Without reason, human life would be either an eternal present or an infinite regress, with nothing to distinguish the one from the other. The real circuit breaker was the mind's ability to conceive of itself as itself, as an entity endowed with a personality. The rational human mind, as Ahrens put it, "in conceiving of itself as an I, detaches itself from the infinite totality of things and sets itself against the entire universe by an act of absolute spontaneity."[51] In this way, reason was the bridge between sensibility (or the ability to register what came from the outside) and reflexion (or the ability

---

choisissant ce qui est le plus conforme à l'ensemble des rapports auxquels l'action s'applique." Ahrens, *Cours de droit naturel*, 6th ed., p. 117.

49. "Cette capacité de l'esprit humain présuppose en lui une force ou faculté supérieure spéciale, qui imprime à toutes les autres facultés dont l'esprit animal présente les analogies, un caractère supérieur, et les dirige, en les ordonnant et en les harmonisant vers des buts plus élevés." Ibid., pp. 110–11.

50. Ahrens, *Cours de droit naturel*, 4th ed. (Brussels, 1853), p. 125 n. 1. On Carus, see Nicolas Jardine, "*Naturphilosophie* and the Kingdoms of Nature," in *Cultures of Natural History*, ed. James A. Secord and Emma C. Spary (Cambridge, CUP, 1996), pp. 230–45, as well as his earlier "The Significance of Schelling's 'Epoch of a Wholly New Natural History': An Essay on the Realization of Questions," in *Metaphysics and Philosophy of Science in the Seventeenth and Eighteenth Centuries*, ed. R. S. Woolhouse (Dordrecht, Kluwer, 1988), pp. 327–50; Matthew Bell, "Carl Gustav Carus and the Science of the Unconscious," in *Thinking the Unconscious. Nineteenth-Century German Thought*, ed. Angus Nicholls and Martin Liebscher (Cambridge, CUP, 2010), pp. 156–72; and Desző Gurka, "The Role of 'Dream' and 'Unconscious' in Carl Gustav Carus' Image of Man," in *Changes in the Image of Man from the Enlightenment to the Age of Romanticism*, ed. Desző Gurka (Budapest, Gondolat Publishers, 2019), pp. 172–88.

51. "D'abord l'esprit humain résume par cette force supérieure son être et son activité dans l'unité du *moi*, en se concevant comme une personnalité. Dans la conscience propre du moi se révèle de prime abord la force de l'infini, parce que, ce qui n'a guère été remarqué, l'esprit en se concevant comme un moi, se détache du tout infini des choses et s'oppose à l'univers entier par un acte de spontanéité absolue." Ahrens, *Cours de droit naturel*, 6th ed., p. 112.

to compare and generalize what was on the inside). Without reason, there was either an endless stream of sense-data or an interminable maze of reflection. Reason set limits, formed concepts, and could test its own rationality. It was, therefore, what gave humanity its synthetic, creative, capacity, and this in turn was the ultimate source of humanity's ability to turn synthetic insight into social harmony.

Reason, Ahrens wrote, was both the source of the higher unity and equality of mankind and the basis of "the infinite perfectibility of all the faculties of the mind." It could differentiate and it could integrate, and, since it could do both, it could supply a potentially infinite number of variations on the idea of human association and its relationship to the development of the division of labour. "The faculties of thinking, feeling, and willing are," Ahrens asserted "inexhaustible because, given the infinite principle of human rationality, they tend continuously to embrace the entire domain of finite things and their relationships." Although he did not use the word, life on the basis of this type of conceptual foundation was a continuous process of *oikeiosis*, the old Stoic word used to describe the human ability to turn something strange, unfamiliar, or unknown—like an experience, an idea, a language, a habitat, or even a world—into something that had become one's own. "This," Ahrens concluded, "is how the individual, who is merely an organ of humanity, seeks successively to complete and fulfil itself by means of the increasingly capacious organisms formed by the family, the city, the state, and national confederations. Individuals tend, in completing and fulfilling their own personalities, to constitute associations for all the rational purposes of life, and, in these associations, the link that gives them their strength and cohesion always then becomes a further moral goal established by reason."[52]

There was no conceptual room in Roman law for these widening circles of human association. In this respect, modern natural jurisprudence was simply a recycled and radically streamlined version of Roman law. Its starting point

52. "Enfin la raison qui constitue l'*unité* et l'*égalité* supérieure de tous les hommes, étant tous capables de comprendre les principes rationnels et d'ordonner, d'après eux, leur vie, est aussi la cause de la *perfectibilité* infinie de toutes les facultés de l'esprit. Les facultés de penser, de sentir et de vouloir sont inépuisables, parce qu'elles tendent sans cesse à embrasser, par les principes infinis, tout le domaine fini des choses et de leurs rapports. . . . C'est ainsi que l'individu, qui n'est qu'un organe de l'humanité, cherche à se compléter successivement dans les organismes toujours plus vastes de la famille, de la cité, de l'état et des confédérations nationales. Partout il tend à constituer, en complétant de plus en plus sa personnalité propre, des associations pour tous les buts rationnels de la vie, et dans ces associations, le lien qui leur donne la force de la cohésion, est toujours un but moral établi par la raison." Ibid., pp. 118–19.

was the morally and historically untenable concept of the state of nature, just as its culmination was the equally untenable concept of the unitary sovereign state. For Ahrens, both conceptual deviations had been given their most unequivocal expression by Jean-Jacques Rousseau. "Rousseau's theory, with its atomistic individualism, a consequence of the fiction of an isolated life in the state of nature, became," he complained, "the principal instrument used, first in France and then in almost every European state, to break up the natural groups of peoples, the provincial divisions, and, above all, the corporations and corporate bodies that were the great obstacles to the free movement of individuals." But this negative capability had no positive countercapability. From Grotius and Hobbes to Rousseau and Sieyès, it relied solely on numbers, whether they divided minorities from majorities or, more crudely, individual vulnerability from armed might. Without some prepolitical social bond, the politics of contractualism was bound to default into power politics. "The doctrine of a political or social contract," Ahrens warned, "presupposes an initial ethical and anthropological doctrine of the good of both man and society. Once separated from these regulatory principles, it turns into no more than a theory of what is arbitrary and a means for perpetual agitation, revolution, anarchy, and despotism."[53]

Johann Kaspar Bluntschli and the Theory of the Modern State

Krausism acquired a significant French follower in the person of modern socialism's self-proclaimed founder, Pierre Leroux. "I cannot prevent myself from stating," he wrote in the coruscating attack on Victor Cousin that he published in 1839 as a *Réfutation de l'éclectisme* (Refutation of eclecticism), "that all the recent philosophical work in Germany has reached the conclusions that I have reached. If Monsieur Cousin had really understood the meaning of Kant, Schelling, and Hegel, he would not have introduced the

53. "La théorie de Rousseau, par son individualisme atomistique, suite de la fiction de la vie d'isolement dans l'état de nature, est devenu le principal instrument dont on s'est servi, pour briser d'abord en France et ensuite dans presque tous les états européens les groupes naturels des peuples, les divisions provinciales et surtout les corps et les corporations devenus en effet de grandes entraves au libre mouvement des individus. . . . La doctrine du contrat politique ou social, présuppose donc une doctrine anthropologique et éthique du bien de l'homme et de la société; quand elle se détache de ces principes régulateurs, elle ne devient qu'une théorie de l'arbitraire, un moyen d'agitation perpétuelle, de révolution, d'anarchie, et de despotisme." Ahrens, *Cours de droit naturel*, 7th ed. (Leipzig, 1875), pp. 33–34, 35.

false psychology that presently reigns in France."[54] The most significant of the individuals whom Leroux associated with "recent philosophical work in Germany" was, however, Krause. It had, Leroux wrote in 1840 in his *De l'humanité*, been "Kant, Fichte, Schelling, and above all Krause" who had developed the concept of perfectibility in the wake of Leibniz, Turgot, and Condorcet. Here, it was Krause's examination of the concept, with its emphasis on perfectibility as a "yearning of every being to be independent and perfect in its kind" and as a drive that took precedence over social stability, that had made the difference.[55] With this version of the concept it was possible to see how to combine individuality with humanity, variety with unity, and particularity with generality within a single historical narrative. As a result, it was also possible to think of human history in terms of divergence as well as convergence and of separation as much as integration. As Leroux described it, Krause's philosophy of history had established a way to reconcile the diversity of the division of labour with the unity of humanity. Leroux called it socialism.

This version of socialism had a strong appeal in the United States of America where Leroux's publications were reviewed very favourably before 1848 by the pugnacious American transcendentalist Orestes Augustus Brownson.[56] In Europe itself, however, the reaction was less positive. In 1857, the whole subject of the interrelationship of civil society, politics, and the state was given an extensive and critical review by one of Karl August Röder's colleagues at the University of Heidelberg, the jurist Johann Kaspar Bluntschli, already the author of one of the standard textbooks on the idea of the state (*The Theory of the State*) that came to be used in university teaching all over late nineteenth-century Europe.[57] The title

54. Pierre Leroux, *Réfutation de l'éclecticisme* (Paris, 1839), p. 187. By the time that he produced his own intellectual autobiography, the *Lettre au Docteur Deville*, published in the periodical *L'Espérance* in 1859 when he was in exile on Jersey, Leroux had dropped all references to German philosophy and political thought. For a modern edition of the text, see Miguel Abensour, *Le procès des maitres rêveurs* suivi de *Pierre Leroux et l'utopie* (Arles, Sulliver, 2000), pp. 119–67.

55. Pierre Leroux, *De l'humanité*, 2 vols. (Paris, 1840), 1:141 n. 1 (in this edition, the name Krause was misprinted as Kranze, but it was corrected in later editions; it is printed as Krauze in the Paris, Fayard, 1985 edition, p. 118, n. 1).

56. On Brownson, see recently Naomi Wulf, *Une autre démocratie en Amérique: Orestes Brownson, un regard politique (1824–1845)* (Paris, PUPS, 2017); Richard M. Reinsch, *Seeking the Truth: An Orestes Brownson Anthology* (Washington, DC, Catholic University of America Press, 2016), and, earlier, Arthur M. Schlesinger, *A Pilgrim's Progress: Orestes A. Brownson* [1939] (Boston, Little Brown, 1966).

57. Johann Kaspar Bluntschli, "Uber die neuen Begründungen der Gesellschaft und des Gesellschaftsrechts: Saint-Simon, Cabet, Hegel, Ahrens, Robert von Mohl," *Kritische Überschau*

of the review—"On the New Foundations of Society and Social Right"—and, more particularly, its subtitle—"Saint-Simon, Cabet, Hegel, Ahrens, Robert von Mohl"—help to throw more light on both the broader conceptual context to which Ahrens's thought belonged and on the reasons for Bluntschli's critical assessment of the concept of civil society. Two of the names that Bluntschli listed (Hegel and Saint-Simon) are still well known. Of the other three, one (Etienne Cabet) was French and an admirer of the early nineteenth-century French moral and political thinker Charles Fourier, while the two others (Heinrich Ahrens and Robert von Mohl) were both German jurists. All five, however, were on the wrong side of the argument of Bluntschli's review because, as its title was intended to indicate, the review itself was an examination of the merits and demerits of the concept of civil society, the putative source of the new foundations of social right.

Bluntschli had been a student of Savigny and, despite some reservations about the narrowness of Savigny's approach to the law (the concept of humanity, he argued, rather than any particular nation—even Rome—was the most appropriate setting for the historical study of the law), he was, like Savigny, resolutely hostile to the concept of civil society. Once, Bluntschli argued, there had been a clear distinction between public and private law. This, he claimed, was what the Romans had first established. "Already," he wrote, "nearly two thousand years ago, the Roman jurists instructed the world that *public law* presupposes and encompasses the *state of the Roman nation* (statum res Romanae), while *private law* presupposes and encompasses *individual utility* (singulorum utilatatem)." Although, he continued, there would always be arguments about where to draw a line between the two types of law, the distinction itself was what mattered. Public law was "indispensable for the welfare and majesty of the modern state," just as private law was "irremissible for the protection of individual freedom and legal security." Together, they had once formed the foundations of political society. Recently, Bluntschli complained, the two concepts had turned into three. A new doctrine, he announced, had emerged that, "in place of the two major concepts, aims to set up three, and talks of a third sphere of *social life* midway between individual lives and the collective life of the nation." It had originated, Bluntschli claimed, with the socialists and Saint-Simon,

---

der deutschen Gesetzgebung und Rechtswissenschaft 3 (1856): 229–66. I am grateful to Samuel Garrett Zeitlin for translating the text. All the passages cited in the following paragraphs are from this article. For the textbook, see Johann Kaspar Bluntschli, *The Theory of the State*, 3rd English ed. (Oxford, Clarendon Press, 1895). On Bluntschli's political thought, but without his allegiance to Savigny and animus towards Hegel, see Duncan Kelly, "Popular Sovereignty as State Theory in the Nineteenth Century," in *Popular Sovereignty in Historical Perspective*, ed. Richard Bourke and Quentin Skinner (Cambridge, CUP, 2016), pp. 270–96.

and had become more pronounced and crude in the thought of the communists and Cabet, but its most elaborate and, ultimately, contentless formulation had been made by Hegel. Everything in Hegel's thought, Bluntschli wrote, came in threes. First there were individuals, families, and property; then civil society, morality, and corporate life; finally, religion, rationality, and the state. The difficulty was to see how they were connected, or to understand why Hegel had jettisoned the old binary distinction between the family and the state in favour of the strange new triad of individuals, civil society, and the state.

Hegel's critics, Bluntschli continued, were no better. Although, he wrote, Ahrens (whose *Juristische Encyclopädie* [Legal encyclopaedia] was the target of this part of the review) was a very different type of thinker from Hegel, he too distinguished civil society from the state. Unlike Hegel, however, he saw civil society as "the *fulfilment* of human relations" rather than a preliminary and subordinate sphere of largely instrumental economic activity. But, Bluntschli argued, adding corporate diversity to state uniformity was still incompatible with the original Roman distinction between public law and private law because, he claimed, it meant that the unity of the state "would then be broken from the ground up," leaving no more than "a plurality of different independent organisms" with as much potential for conflict as for cooperation, to find a way to coexist under the aegis of a state that now had no clear public function or distinctive identity. The same problems, Bluntschli went on to claim, applied to the more scholarly *Geschichte und Litteratur der Staatswissenschaften* (The history and literature of state theory) that was published in 1855 by the legal theorist and Heidelberg University professor Robert von Mohl. Here the key term was a *Genossenschaft* and the multiplicity of collective associations or group personalities located between individuals and states. These collective entities could be classes, occupations, mutual societies, religious communities, or cultural associations, but they all shared the common characteristic of being different from either private life or the life of the state. Together, they formed "a third sphere of life and of law" that, as Bluntschli presented it, housed all the attractions, and all the dangers, of Hegel's system. "Hegel's state," he wrote later in his widely translated textbook *The Theory of the State*, "is ... only a logical abstraction, not a living organism, a mere logical notion, not a person. Hegel, by founding the state and law merely upon will, overlooks the fact that in the state not only is the collective human will operative, but so too are all the powers of human spirit and feeling together."[58] For Bluntschli, Ahrens's theory of the state was something like a travesty of a genuinely organic

58. Bluntschli, *The Theory of the State*, p. 73.

theory of the state because, he wrote dismissively, "by the organism of the state, he does not so much understand a personal and collective being as an organic arrangement for community in law."[59] It was, in short, Hegel's concept of civil society without Hegel's theory of the state.

Bluntschli's own political thought was something like a counterpart to his future Heidelberg colleague Karl August Röder's call to find a compromise between Romanist and Germanist state theories. Unlike Röder, however, Bluntschli's starting point was firmly on the side of Roman law. "It is the special merit of the German school of historical jurists," he wrote early in his book, "to have recognised the organic nature of the nation and the state. This conception refutes both the mathematical and mechanical view of the state and the atomistic way of treating it, which forgets the whole in the individuals."[60] This idea of an organism, he emphasized, had nothing to do with any natural capacity for production and reproduction (still less, it could be added, with the concept of palingenesis) and very much more to do with the related ideas of coordinated action, internal development, and external growth. Together, Bluntschli explained, all three required something that was able to ensure that these different attributes of a nation and a state could coexist and work together effectively. This, he claimed, was what the law, and particularly Roman law, could do. It had this ability, Bluntschli argued, because it was the creation of a state. This, in the first instance, meant that the law was radically different from morality. In this respect, Bluntschli's argument joined up with Röder's. But where Röder had argued that the difference between law and morality made it possible to define a crime and, by extension, to develop a system of criminal law, Bluntschli argued that the real implication of the difference was that it made it possible to establish a viable concept of the state. If the law was the medium that could bring together collective action, internal development, and external growth, its existence called, first, for the prior existence of a state and, second, for the type of state that could establish and maintain laws that met these three requirements.

It would, therefore, be a state with something like the attributes of a person because it would have to have a capacity to distinguish action that was lawful from action as such. This reflexive capacity would have to be met by a constitution and, more importantly, by a constitution with a broad capacity for active citizenship. Without both, Bluntschli argued, the concept of the personality of the state would be vitiated because the person in question would be private, not public. But, to ensure that both the constitution and the concept of active

59. Ibid., p. 76.
60. Ibid., p. 18.

citizenship could have a stable and durable existence, the state itself would have to make provision for the welfare of its members. This too had been a Roman achievement, making "the welfare of the state the highest law (*salus populi suprema lex*)." It was, Bluntschli acknowledged, "a formula" that had been "used too often to excuse the arbitrary despotism either of princes or of majorities, and it has been completely discredited by the horrors of the Parisian Committee of Public Safety." But despite its abuse he was still willing to accept that the Romans saw "the real function of the state in the *public welfare*." On these terms, he concluded, "the expression is really above criticism if one regards the natural limits of the state and especially the judicial order and administration, and if one avoids trespassing upon matters outside those limits such as the free life of the individual and of religious communities."[61]

Heinrich von Treitschke and the Liberal Foundations of *Realpolitik*

Bluntschli's theory of the state was one of a range of Roman-inspired state theories that came to form the intellectual and political mainstream of German political thought after 1848. In them, the strong emphasis on the technicalities of Roman law that was the hallmark of the German historical school was matched by an equally strong emphasis on the personality of the state. Here, the key figures were the jurists Wilhelm Eduard Albrecht, Karl Friedrich Wilhelm Gerber, and Paul Laband. Albrecht had been the first to articulate this position in a review of a book on the state by the Germanist, and follower of Karl Ludwig Haller, Romeo Maurenbrecher in which Maurenbrecher, echoing Haller, had emphasized the identity of the sovereign with the ruler. Albrecht disagreed, asserting, in opposition to Maurenbrecher's claim about ruler sovereignty and the concept of a patrimonial state, that what was required was "nothing less" than "an essentially different fundamental idea of the juridical nature of the state." This meant thinking of the state "not as an association of men which is designed solely and immediately for the individual ends and interests of those men, be they all, or many, or even individuals, notably the ruler, but as a commonwealth, as an institution, standing above individuals, which is dedicated to ends which are by no means merely the sum of the individual interests of the ruler and his subjects, but constitute a higher general collective interest."[62]

---

61. Ibid., pp. 39, 319

62. Albrecht in *Göttingische gelehrte Anzeigen* 3 (1837): 1491–92, cited by Emerson, *State and Sovereignty in Modern Germany*, p. 52. On Gerber, see Olivier Jouanjan, *Une histoire de la pensée*

As Ahrens registered, the pressure to create a German state after 1848 and, more urgently, after Napoleon III's seizure of power in France in 1851, accentuated this new emphasis on the state as a person. Gerber went on to amplify on Albrecht's identification of the state as a *res publica*, with laws that were commensurate with its public, rather than private, character. It was this public quality, he emphasized, that gave it the right to rule and made its will binding in a way that could not occur with a private will. On these terms a state was first and foremost a legal entity and, in the language made famous by the British political philosopher Michael Oakeshott, a *universitas* rather than a *societas*, meaning that the whole had an existence that was separate from its constituent parts. It was an entity that could be identified not only by its possession of territory or its responsibility for certain types of institution like a fiscal system, a currency, or a law (which, almost by definition, could not be privately owned or private goods), but also by the fact that it could be distinguished entirely from all of its members, including its monarch if it had one. On these terms, the existence of the state was predicated on the existence of the law, making the rule of law, or, in Rousseau's language, the general will, synonymous with the rule of the state. From this perspective, Gerber's concept of the state was the exact opposite of Ahrens's concept. If, as Bluntschli described it, Ahrens's concept was Hegel's concept of civil society minus Hegel's concept of the state, Gerber's concept was Hegel's concept of the state minus Hegel's concept of civil society. Gerber went on to widen the gap with an article on the concept of autonomy.[63] In it, he made it clear that autonomy was a legal rather than a moral concept and had more to do with the older idea of a self-governing corporation, town, or province than with Kantian moral and political theory. On Gerber's terms, autonomy was connected to decentralization rather than individuality.

The move was reinforced in the aftermath of the Franco-Prussian War by the historian Heinrich von Treitschke in a collection of three articles entitled "Socialism and Its Patrons," which he published in 1874. Where Gerber had set out to neutralize the moral and political connotations of the concept of autonomy by restoring its association with the subjects of administration and government, Treitschke did something similar to the concept of civil society by restoring *its* association with the eighteenth-century concepts of civility,

---

juridique en Allemagne (1800–1918) (Paris, PUF, 2005), pp. 187–281, and his "Carl Friedrich Gerber et la constitution d'une science du droit public allemand," in *La science juridique française et la science juridique allemande de 1870 à 1918*, ed. Olivier Beaud and Patrick Wachsmann (Strasbourg, Annales de la Faculté de Droit de Strasbourg, 1, 1997), pp. 11–63.

63. Karl Friedrich Wilhelm Gerber, "Uber den Begriff der Autonomie," *Archiv für die Civilistische Praxis* 73 (1854): 35–62.

396 CHAPTER 10

decorum, and culture. He had already, in a critical examination of the subject of social science published in 1859, signalled his hostility both to the more ago- nistic and class-oriented connotations of the concept of civil society that had been given to it by Hegel and his followers (including Karl Marx) and to the more pluralistic and association-oriented connotations given to it by Robert von Mohl and Heinrich Ahrens.[64] Although Treitschke, like Bluntschli two years earlier, singled out both Ahrens and von Mohl for their reluctance to combine the concept of a *Genossenschaft* with a theory of the state, his own state theory had more in common with Gerber than with Hegel because, like Gerber (whose article on autonomy Treitschke cited), he took the idea of an association to be no more than a branch of the administration. From this per- spective, the idea of a social science was redundant.

The same applied to Hegel's insistence on the tension between civil society and the state. Thinking about both could be subsumed under the rubric of *Realpolitik*, the new term coined, to liberal acclaim, by Ludwig August von Rochau in 1853 to fit the real parameters of modern economic and social life (later, in 1888, the Austro-German jurist Rudolf von Jhering, taking his cue from "the great masters of *Realpolitik*," announced that his aim was to move juris- prudence "from the formalistic to the realistic").[65] In this context, civil society was associated with culture rather than conflict, and with talent and ability rather than lineage and inheritance. This, as Treitschke went on to argue in his later work on socialism and its patrons, was why it was a mistake to think of civil society as no more than a battleground of warring class interests. There were, certainly, deep-seated economic and social divisions in every society. But civil society was also a sphere of work and culture, innovation and oppor- tunity. "The dogma of the exploitation of man by man," Treitschke thundered in reply to the socialist economist Gustav Schmoller (the target of his attack on socialism and its patrons), "breaks the complex unity of society roughly into pieces. Strong peoples have always lived in the belief that the first com- mandment of folk-thrift is: *labour! Much; very much; and well!* Only in the second rank came the question about the distribution of the fruits of the com- mon labour."[66] Civil society, he wrote in the first of the three parts of his book,

64. Heinrich von Treitschke, *Gesellschaftswissenschaft, ein kritische Versuch* (Leipzig, 1859), pp. 1–2, 4, 36, 40, 58, 63, 74, for comments on Ahrens or von Mohl.

65. On Treitschke and *Realpolitik*, see Paul Bew, *Realpolitik: A History* (Oxford, OUP, 2016), pp. 68–76, 97–98, and Karl H. Metz, "The Politics of Conflict: Heinrich von Treitschke and the Idea of *Realpolitik*," *History of Political Thought* 3 (1982): 269–84. On Jhering's announcement (in a letter to Bismarck), see François Gény, *Méthode d'interprétation et sources en droit privé positif* [1919], 2 vols. (Paris, LDGJ, 2016), vol. 1, p. 6 n. 21.

66. Heinrich von Treitschke, *Der Socialismus und seine Gönner* (Berlin, 1875), p. 46.

a section entitled "Die Grundlagen der bürgerlichen Gesellschaft" (The fundamentals of civil society), housed work, with its repetition and rewards, its perseverance and productivity. These were the qualities that had been celebrated in Henry Wadsworth Longfellow's poem "Nuremberg," with its "cobbler-bard," Hans Sachs, and its last line—"The nobility of labor, the long pedigree of toil"—which Treitschke proceeded to quote. Work, in this rendition, was the substance of human history just as civil society was its human setting. "Man alone," Treitschke wrote, "is an historical existence and hence the one true societary being. He receives in language and morality, in law and industry, the works of the fathers. They live with him and he is effective by means of them."

> He lives only in and through submitting himself to the aggregate culture of his people. What occasionally oppresses a genius by appearing to be a narrowing fetter is, for the inert majority, a wholesome spur to activity and progress. The generations of a people's lives are joined together and limited by a community of views about life, from which even the strong man cannot break away. How eloquently did Niebuhr champion against Fichte, the glorifier of the unlimited power of the will, the noble theorem that the richest poetic gifts could not have produced a complete work of art in the days of Alexander the Great. The strong as well as the weak feel this dependence. The businessman loses money and trouble when he offers goods for sale which no longer satisfy the wants of his time. The most talented inventor starves if his creative idea outruns the intelligence of the time. Ten years later, perhaps, the same idea brings new well-being to thousands and the name of the dead lives in all mouths.[67]

Work, on Treitschke's terms, was the solution to the problem that Kant had unleashed. If its emblem was the shoemaker Hans Sachs, its home was civil society. Its activities, values, and beliefs (Treitschke was notoriously anti-Semitic) were the engine underlying both the power of culture and the culture of power.[68]

The drift from culture to power in Treitschke's thought formed the subject of the penultimate chapter of the great study of the doctrine of *raison d'état*, and its place in modern history, that was published by the German historian

---

67. Ibid., p. 14. I have relied here on the translation of the passage in Small, *Origins of Sociology*, pp. 277–78. This aspect of Treitschke's evaluation of work is not discussed in the otherwise helpful monograph by Joan Campbell, *Joy in Work, German Work: The National Debate, 1800–1945* (Princeton, NJ, Princeton UP, 1989), pp. 49–50.

68. The phrase has been applied to the eighteenth century by Blanning, *The Culture of Power and the Power of Culture.*

Friedrich Meinecke in 1925. Meinecke's explanation of Treitschke's political trajectory hovered between a relatively predictable rehearsal of the argument between the Romanists and the Germanists and a more insightful assessment of the moral and political problems built into Kantian and post-Kantian philosophies of history. "How did it really come about," he asked rhetorically, "that the ideas of Machiavelli which arose on Latin territory and developed within the realm of Latin states, were minted afresh after the beginning of the nineteenth century and this precisely on German soil?" It was a question that presupposed too many received ideas to give rise to much of an original answer. But the other part of Meinecke's answer captured rather more of the reasons for Treitschke's conflation of culture with power. "The ideas of identity and individuality," Meinecke wrote, "constituted the new ferments. . . . Both ideas (but particularly the idea of individuality) also permeated the thought of other nations, and linked with analogous needs there too. It was these nations most of all, which now on all sides began to become conscious of their individuality, and now, each in its own way, entered upon the great question of deciding between the ideals of life as universal or national, as general or individual, between world citizenship or the national state."[69] Although he made no reference to Kant, it was Kant's concept of unsocial sociability played out in real historical time. On Treitschke's terms, it was played out without any awareness of the distinctions between civil society and the state, or between market competition and power politics. Bluntschli's criticisms of Hegel, von Mohl, Saint-Simon, and Ahrens had, clearly, left a mark.

Ferdinand Lassalle and the Politics of Reform

The overlap between the concepts of the state and civil society was taken a step further from a different, socialist, direction in a large, two-volume legal treatise entitled *A Systematic Theory of Acquired Rights* (*Der System der erworbenen Rechte*) published in 1861 by the heterodox German socialist Ferdinand Lassalle. Its immediate purpose was, as, two generations earlier, Savigny's had been, to address the subject of feudal property and entitlements with the aim, also like Savigny, of finding a way to eliminate them peacefully. Lassalle described the problem bound up with the subject by quoting a passage from a speech given by Benjamin Constant in 1828 on the subject of the retroactive application of the law. "Retroactivity," Constant had said, "is the greatest outrage that the law can commit. It amounts to tearing up the social pact and the

---

69. Friedrich Meinecke, *Machiavellism: The Doctrine of Raison d'état and Its Place in Modern History* [1925] (London and New Brunswick, NJ, Transaction Publishers, 1998), pp. 392–93.

cancellation of the conditions under which society has the right to demand individual obedience by stripping that individual of the guarantees promised by society in return for that obedience and the sacrifices that it can involve. Retroactivity robs the law of its character. A retroactive law is not a law."[70] Constant's speech was made in the context of the legacy of the French Revolution and, in particular, of the huge transfers of property that had taken place between 1789 and 1799, with the confiscation not only of the land belonging to the church but also of the land and buildings belonging to emigrant opponents of the new regime that had been confiscated mainly between 1791 and 1795. After the Restoration, and particularly after the accession to the throne of Charles X in 1824, there had been an intense campaign by royalists and clerics to legislate to bring this property back into the possession of its original owners or, failing that, to compensate them for their losses. Constant's speech was part of the opposition to this campaign, which had a significant, and still largely unrecognized, bearing on the revolution of July 1830. After it took place, this particular form of retroactive legislation was ruled out.

But, as Lassalle pointed out, there were still circumstances in which there did seem to be a case for retroactive legislation. Slavery, after all, was part of Europe's recent past, and the legislation that had abolished it had not been designed to apply only to future slave ownership because it had, retroactively, abolished slavery itself. A similar, potentially comprehensive programme of legislation also seemed possible for feudal property and entitlements. The problem was to identify a set of criteria that could be used to distinguish legitimate from illegitimate retroactive legislation by establishing an initial distinction between legitimately and illegitimately acquired rights. Here, Lassalle had no hesitation in endorsing Savigny's treatment of the subject of possession and the way that, using the technicalities of Roman law, he had shown how the law could be used as a medium that could turn possession into property. But, to Lassalle, something more was needed if Savigny's treatment of the Roman law of possession was to be more broadly applicable. For Savigny, at least as Lassalle described his thought, the key to the continuing salience of Roman law long after the decline and fall of the Roman Empire was the concept of a tradition. A tradition was something different from a record because it housed something that was living. In this Burke-, Schelling-, or Schlegel-inspired version of the idea of a tradition, with its connotations of a national culture or a *Volksgeist*, Savigny had shown that there was the basis of a distinction between what was living and dead in the law, and, by extension, why some provisions of the law were still applicable while others were not. But, as Savigny's Hegelian critics,

---

70. Ferdinand Lassalle, *Théorie systématique des droits acquis*, 2 vols. (Paris, 1904), 1:19–20.

notably Hegel's follower Edouard Gans, had pointed out, the concept of a tradition could be described more accurately as the present consciousness of a tradition. From this perspective, the present would always trump the past. To Lassalle, both positions would, in fact, turn out to be arbitrary because neither seemed to be based on any initial explanation of why either a tradition or a decision had any rightful force. There had, he argued, to be a general set of underlying principles that would make it possible to distinguish legitimate from illegitimate acquisition, because, with this in place, retroactive legislation could then be used to arm the state with real redistributive authority. To identify these principles, Lassalle devoted his book to the Roman law of inheritance. Properly understood, he argued, it contained all the component parts of the various instruments that were needed to make the correct distinctions.

Lassalle set out to show that the distinction between legitimate and illegitimate retroactive laws could not be the basis of a simple binary choice. Although this was how it looked, Lassalle argued that either side of the choice would turn out to be self-defeating because what actually made the distinction significant was the fact that the existence of the difference was the exception rather than the norm. Under most systems of rule, he pointed out, retroactive legislation was the norm because, under these systems, individuals were usually subject to the power of an existing government, and this meant that rights inherited from the past were usually subordinated to the needs of the present. If this despotic principle was the norm in most times and places, the alternative was equally arbitrary because it amounted to endorsing the type of claim made by Karl Ludwig von Haller that every acquired right was inviolate.[71] Ultimately, Lassalle argued, there had to be a way to overcome either the potential for paralysis caused by clinging blindly to the legacy of the past or the potential for chaos caused by making a precipitate and purely present-centred endorsement of communism. Roman law, Lassalle claimed, provided a way out because it supplied a criterion for discrimination that varied over time. This was because Roman law was, fundamentally, a compound of two heterogeneous things, human will and physical goods.

Initially, Lassalle argued, these two attributes of Roman law were entirely distinct, as could be seen in the original Roman inheritance laws. These centred on the patriarchal character of the Roman household and the corresponding idea of a single patriarchal will that was transmitted continuously from one generation to the next. Inheritance, in this system, was not a matter of choice and, at least in this respect, was based on a principle that was carried over into the phrase *le mort saisit le vif* (the dead command the living) that had come to

71. Ibid., 1:223–24.

be used to describe the principle of representative succession underlying the inheritance of the French throne. In a corresponding sense, inheritance in the same original system was not a matter of goods because these could have been mortgaged, donated, or given away before the patriarch died. As Lassalle's French editor, a specialist of German thought named Charles Andler, pointed out, this distinction between a will and a bequest, or between an inheritance and a patrimony, had its origins in a tradition of scholarship that was centred on early Roman religion and the difference between the ancestor worship associated with the Roman god Manes and the cult of the household and its land associated with the Etruscan god Lares.[72] Roman law, Lassalle argued, was the outcome of a fusion of these two sources of value. It occurred, he claimed, because inheritance under purely Roman conditions could be more of a curse than a blessing if the heir to a will did not inherit any goods but, as his father's representative, was still saddled with duties and burdens that did not apply to other members of the family. Gradually space had to be made to make it possible either to repudiate a will or to inherit real goods. The space that was gradually created, Lassalle explained, gave Roman law its enduring significance because it was a space that had been created for free will. The legal capacity to repudiate a will, or to accept or reject an inheritance, gave human freedom its original and uniquely Roman setting. On Lassalle's terms, subjective rights began with Rome.

Lassalle took the argument a step further by showing how the principle of a subjective right could be used both to establish a viable distinction between legitimate and illegitimate retroactive legislation and, by extension, to show why the line dividing the one from the other would change over time. As human freedom became more entrenched in human life, there would be less and less room for retroactive legislation. The existence of a subjective right, Lassalle argued, presupposed the prior existence of both a choice and a capacity for choice, and it was the real or even apparent violation of that choice that made retroactive legislation illegitimate. But many aspects of human life do not initially involve choice. This applied most obviously to slavery, but could also apply to occupations and education, as well as to the claims of kinship and marriage. It could apply too to aspects of economic and political life, like insurance, pensions, or health care on the one hand or the voting age, the size of electoral units, or the nature of numerical majorities on the other, because they would not be likely to survive on a purely voluntary basis. There were, in short, large swathes of human life in which retroactive legislation was unlikely to be

72. Ibid., 1:xxi–xxiv. See also the summary of Lassalle's argument in George Brandes, *Ferdinand Lassalle* (London, Heinemann, 1911), pp. 66–84.

controversial because these were the areas of life that fell outside the sphere of subjective rights. There was, therefore, a principle that could be used to guide state policy and enable governments to strike a balance between the legacy of the past and the prospects for the future. However paradoxical it might seem, Lassalle wrote in a long and famous footnote, "it was no less true that the *evolution of law over the course of history* amounts to an *ever-greater limitation on private property*." Roman law had the paradoxical power to generate its opposite.[73] This was because its real foundation was not property, but a free and inalienable human will. Initially, Lassalle argued, property helped to shield individual wills from the ancestral will. But as property became more extensive, particularly under feudal or corporate conditions, the imposition of limits on property favoured the emancipation of individual wills. From this perspective, the legacy of Roman law supplied the guidance required for discrimination between legitimate and illegitimate retroactive legislation and, at the same time, provided the means to bring the state and civil society into closer alignment. This was Lassalle's aim. There is good reason to think that when Michel Villey set out to show that the concept of subjective rights had nothing to do with ancient Rome, he had more than Roman law in his sights. His real target had as much to do with Lassalle and socialism as with Rome and rights.

Otto von Gierke and the Concept of the *Genossenschaft*

As Lassalle presented it, Roman law supplied the means to overcome the tension between the state and civil society because it housed the conceptual resources that could guide the policies to be followed by a reforming government. To his critics, however, the conceptual resources built into Roman law were no real obstacle or barrier to centralized state power and the spectre of state socialism. One of the most prominent of these critics was the legal historian Otto von Gierke. As one of his contemporaries and critics, the Heidelberg jurist Georg Jellinek, noticed, Gierke's political thought was very similar to the—by then—virtually extinct political thought of Krause and his follower Heinrich Ahrens.[74] Like Krause and Ahrens, Gierke, in his political thought, focused on civil society rather than the state. Where, for Bluntschli or Lassalle,

73. Lassalle, *Théorie*, 1:274–81 (fn. 2).

74. Jellinek, *L'état moderne et son droit*, 1:156 (erroneously numbered p. 165 in the text). On Krause, Ahrens, and Krausism, see Michael Sonenscher, "Krausism and Its Legacy," *Global Intellectual History* 5 (2020): 20–40. See too the dismissive comments about them by the twentieth-century jurist Hermann Heller, *La crise de la théorie de l'état* [1926], ed. Olivier Jouanjan (Paris, Dalloz, 2012), pp. 12–13. For a similar identification of Gierke with Krause and Ahrens, see

the significant part of the state–civil society pairing was the state, for Ahrens and Gierke, the significant part of the pairing was the concept of civil society. The result of this switch of emphasis was, ultimately, a full-fledged theory of society that, Jellinek claimed, was increasingly hard to distinguish from the sociology of Auguste Comte in France and that of Herbert Spencer in Britain. "In this sociological doctrine," Jellinek concluded, "society and the state were not set against one another, as had been the case in the theories just described. Instead, the state now appears to be no more than one of the forms of society."[75] This was the position that he associated with the thought of Otto von Gierke.

Its best-known product was Gierke's version of the concept of a *Genossenschaft*. The term was a staple of early nineteenth-century Germanist thought, where it was used by Germanists like Karl August Rögge to describe the common values and institutions underlying the trials by ordeal and the oaths of allegiance of the early Germanic peoples. In this rendition, these ancient institutions were the key to understanding the origins and nature of the modern jury, meaning, in some interpretations, that the jury was entitled to decide on matters of law as well as matters of fact. As a later historian put it, "the judge himself had no voice; his business was merely to receive and to pronounce the verdict."[76] The idea of a *Genossenschaft* was used in something like this legal and political sense by the Germanist jurist Georg Beseler (who was one of Gierke's law professors) and then by the Heidelberg law professor Robert von Mohl. According to a later historian, von Mohl was also the first to point out, in the course of making a critical assessment of the uses to which the concept of civil society had been put, that "a mass of groupings, schools, churches, economic associations, etc." still did not add up to "any general conception of society in contradistinction to the state."[77] Gierke, however, used the concept of a *Genossenschaft* in both senses. His most important move was

---

Ralph H. Bowen, *German Theories of the Corporative State* (New York, Whittlesey House, 1947), pp. 66–69.

75. Jellinek, *L'état moderne et son droit*, 1:158.

76. Johannes Janssen, *History of the German People at the Close of the Middle Ages*, 16 vols. (London, 1905–25), 2:143. On this aspect of the history of the jury, see Antonio Padoa Schioppa, ed., *The Trial Jury in England, France, Germany 1700–1900* (Berlin, Duncker & Humblot, 1987), p. 272, and the comments on it by Guizot described in ch. 8 above. On later developments, see Markus Dirk Dubber, "The German Jury and the Metaphysical Volk: From Romantic Idealism to Nazi Ideology," *American Journal of Comparative Law* 43 (1995): 227–71.

77. Nikolaï Mikhaïlovitch Korkounov, *General Theory of Law* [1903] (New York, Macmillan, 1922), p. 334. On Beseler and von Mohl, see Dreyer, "German Roots of the Theory of Pluralism."

to change the sense of the Roman law concepts of a *universitas* and a *societas*. Before the nineteenth century, the two concepts were usually associated with the medieval idea of a legal fiction. That idea made it possible to explain why an entity like a corporation, a university, or a commercial partnership could be endowed with a legal existence that was distinct from the legal existence of its real human members. In Gierke's version of the concept of a *Genossenschaft*, the idea of a legal fiction was turned into a collective agent with a real personality, and what was earlier taken to be no more than a setting for a fictive personality now began to take on a life of its own. "Take away our relationship to a nation and a state," Gierke wrote, "to religious bodies or churches, to profession and family and all kinds of unions and guilds, and we would not be able to recognise ourselves in the miserable remnant that would remain."[78] From this perspective, the association was as real as its members, with the same type of holistic unity as a real individual. As a later commentator put it, this implied that the idea of a "moral person" was "in no way a fictitious being devised by lawyers in order to facilitate certain business operations" but was, instead, "a real union" able to ensure that "a craft-guild, a city, a state" would be "real beings, who live in the life of their members and possess a distinct consciousness and a common will." They would, in short, "be subjected to all the consequences of the notion of real personality."[79]

Gierke used the concept of a *Genossenschaft* as a way to try, in a manner that paralleled the thought of the jurist and novelist Felix Dahn, to reconcile the rival camps of Romanists and Germanists in nineteenth-century German legal and political thought. Just as Dahn, in his best-selling historical novel *The Struggle for Rome*, made the Germanic Goths the principal protagonists of the struggle to keep Rome's legacy alive, so Gierke tried to show that the concept of the *Genossenschaft* was both Roman and German.[80] Although, he ar-

---

78. Paul Vinogradoff, *Outlines of Historical Jurisprudence*, 2 vols. (Oxford, OUP, 1920), 1:132 n. 2, citing Otto von Gierke, *Das Wesen der menschlichen Verbände* [1902], p. 22. The same idea, relying explicitly on Gierke, was applied to the concept of an association by the French jurist Raymond Saleilles, *De la personnalité juridique, histoire et théories* [1910], 2nd ed. (Paris, 1922), pp. 57–67. See also H. S. Jones, *The French State in Question: Public Law and Political Argument in the Third Republic* (Cambridge, CUP, 1993), pp. 71–78.

79. Vinogradoff, *Outlines*, 1:133–34. Interestingly, the chapter in which Vinogradoff made this description of Gierke's thought was entitled "Nationalists." On the broader subject of holism and individualism, see Susan James, *The Content of Social Explanation* (Cambridge, CUP, 1984).

80. On Dahn, see, helpfully, Hinnerk Bruhns, "Grecs, Romains et Germains au xixe siècle: quelle Antiquité pour l'état national allemand?" *Anabases* 1 (2005): 17–43, and his "La fondation de l'état national allemand et la question des origines," in *Le corps, la famille et l'état*, ed. Myriam Cottias, Laura Downs, and Christiane Klapisch-Zuber (Rennes, PU de Rennes, 2010), pp. 207–19.

gued, the name was German, its more remote origins and real content were, in fact, generic because the attributes of the concept were as applicable to the Roman *comitiae* or *centuriae* as they were to medieval guilds or modern corporations. What had prevented the formation of a real Roman equivalent of a *Genossenschaft* was the purely negative content of the Roman concept of freedom. "The single Roman individuality," he wrote, "was posited purely in itself and essentially for its own purpose. Its freedom was recognised by the state as an objective concept endowed with an unchangeable content and protected from all incursions. However, a Roman individual did not receive that kind of autonomy which was required for the genesis of the communal will, for he was not granted the autonomy to form a union of individual wills. Roman law therefore did not cede a specific legal essence to any association derived from private law. It knew no associations that were based upon private law nor did it have the potential to do so."[81] This purely individualistic concept of freedom was, Gierke argued, the basis of the binary quality of Roman life and the sharp distinction between the public and private that was built into Roman law.[82] It meant that subjectivity and a capacity for purposeful or accountable action were qualities that could be found only among individuals or in the whole Roman state. Nothing with the attributes of personality could be found in any of the intermediate institutions or associations located between the individual and the state.

The idea of a *Genossenschaft* was, therefore, equally salient to both the ancients and the moderns because its corporate and communal orientation made the combined legacies of the Romans and the Germans a genuine social and legal antidote to the atomism of modern individualism and the centralized power of the modern state. As Gierke emphasized, without this type of antidote, political power would be entirely in the hands of a sovereign defined on Hobbist specifications. "Hobbes's account of the similarity and difference between the monarchical and republican sovereign," he argued, "illustrates particularly how much he identifies the 'personality' of the Ruler with the physical substance of a man or a body of men. The republican sovereign only really exists for him as long as it is actually in session; in the interval it sleeps, and this sleep becomes death if the right of meeting at its own discretion is

---

On Gierke, see the penetrating examination of his thought in Frederick Hallis, *Corporate Personality* (Oxford, OUP, 1930), beginning with the passage on pp. 152–53: "To appreciate Gierke's thought we must note carefully just how much he is a revolutionary in the orthodox Roman camp and how much he still accepts of its juristic theory."

81. Otto von Gierke, *Associations and Law: The Classical and Early Christian Stages*, ed. George Heiman (Toronto, U of Toronto Press, 1977), p. 100.

82. Ibid., pp. 102–3.

lost."[83] From this perspective, active citizenship, this time in the guise of the *Genossenschaft*, was the real alternative to the concept of a sleeping sovereign that Gierke associated with both Hobbes and Rousseau.

Some years after the publication of the first volume of his huge *Deutsche Genossenschaftsrecht* (German corporate law) in 1868, Gierke also discovered a real precedent for applying the concept to modern political societies in the thought of an early seventeenth-century German-Dutch Calvinist named Johannes Althusius. Althusius was a monarchomach. His most famous work was a treatise on politics published in 1603 under the title *Politica methodice digesta atque exemplis sacris et profanis illustrata*, or *Politics Methodically Set Forth and Illustrated from Sacred and Secular Examples*, as it has been entitled in a more recent abridged translation. For Althusius, human societies were based upon expanding networks of social ties. They began with families, kin, and clans. They grew to become communities, peoples, and nations. In early modern European thought, the mechanism underlying these widening circles of association was usually said to be the ancient Greek Stoic concept of *oikeiosis*, or the human ability to make something one's own. The thing in question could be property, but it could also be a language, a craft, a skill, or, in the case of a sexual relationship, a person. For Gierke, the significance of this aspect of Althusius's thought was its striking compatibility with the concept of a *Genossenschaft* and its equally striking difference from the concept of a state. Together, he claimed, these two features of Althusius's thought meant that there was an acceptable alternative to the legacy of Roman law that Gierke associated not only with Hobbes and Rousseau but also with the state socialism of Ferdinand Lassalle. In the early twentieth century, the combination came to be called pluralism.

Gierke's political thought was a mirror image of Lassalle's. Where Lassalle set out to show how the legacy of Roman law could be used to emancipate individuals from the collective character of Germanic custom, Gierke set out to show how the legacy of Germanic law could be used to add a collective character to the individualism of Roman law. For Lassalle, Roman law supplied the criteria required to guide state policy. For Gierke, Germanic law enabled collective associations to escape state power. But just as, for Lassalle, the promise of reform lay in the hands of the state, so, for Gierke, the entitlements of association drew the state more deeply into the life of civil society. He emphasized

---

83. Otto von Gierke, *Natural Law and the Theory of Society 1500–1800* (Cambridge, CUP, 1934), p. 267 n. 153, cited by Miguel Vatter, "Liberal Governmentality and the Political Theology of Constitutionalism," in *Sovereignty in Action*, ed. Bas Leijssenaar and Neil Walker (Cambridge, CUP, 2019), pp. 115–43 (p. 121).

the complementarity by calling for the introduction of a third type of law, which he called social law, to go alongside private law and public law. Juxtaposing Gierke's thought alongside Lassalle's suggests a kind of inadvertent pincer move in which both sides combined to erode the distinctions between sovereignty and government, the state and civil society, and autonomy and democracy that had been taken, a generation or two earlier, to be the hallmark of modern politics. By 1939, in an article entitled "The German Doctrine of Natural Right," an exiled German sociologist named Paul Honigsheim, who was a contributor to the Frankfurt School's *Zeitschrift für Sozialforschung*, reported that "it would be interesting" to show how far "those doctrines that tended to highlight and preserve the value of the individual in the law" had been "isolated, misunderstood, or were alien in Germany." Only two, he continued, could still be mentioned. One was "the philosophy of Krause and his disciples Ahrens and Röder in the age of romanticism," while the other was "the sociology of Max Weber in the present age."[84] It is quite a surprising juxtaposition but was also not an entirely inaccurate assessment.

84. Paul Honigsheim, "La doctrine allemande du droit naturel aux xvii et xviii siècles," *Archives de Philosophie du Droit et de Sociologie Juridique* 9 (1939): 216–37 (pp. 236–37 for the passages cited). See too his *The Unknown Max Weber* (New Brunswick, NJ, Transaction Publishers, 2000), pp. 198–99. For a helpful examination of Gierke's British reception, see James Kirby, "History, Law and Freedom: F. W. Maitland in Context," *Modern Intellectual History* 16 (2019): 127–54.

11

From Autonomy to Democracy

BY THE THIRD QUARTER of the nineteenth century, only one European state appeared to conform to the combination of political and institutional continuity at the level of the state and of economic and social change at the level of civil society that were the hallmarks of the body of political thought associated with Kant and Hegel. The state in question was Great Britain. The difference between Britain and the rest of Europe became the starting point of a durable historiographical tradition, with its overlapping preoccupations with the social origins of dictatorship and democracy, the nature of American exceptionalism, the causes of the putative German *Sonderweg*, and, most famously, the Whig Interpretation of History. It was matched, in the nineteenth century, by a growing number of French-, German-, and Italian-language publications centred on the distinctive properties and the unusual capacity for stability and reform of what, variously, was called the English, Anglo-Saxon, or British constitution.[1] From either side of this type of comparison, it was hard to avoid a framework formed by the difference between an exception and a norm.

The aim of this chapter is to try to bypass this framework by describing the work of a number of individuals whose approach to the difference was informed as much by the legacy of Kant and Hegel, and by the questions that they had raised about the interrelationship of economics, politics, and the law both within and between states. The first, Felix Esquirou de Parieu, was French, but with a strong interest in the British political system. The next two, Henry Halford Vaughan and James Reddie, were British, but their approach to the British political system was mediated very strongly by the thought of Kant, Savigny, and, surprisingly, Adam Smith. The fourth, Henry Sumner Maine, is by far the best known. His comparison of British and other European political systems was also by far the most wide-ranging. It was, in fact, so wide-ranging that his

---

1. See, recently, Tanguy Pasquiet-Briand, *La réception de la constitution anglaise au xixe siècle* (Paris, Institut Universitaire Varenne, 2017).

treatment of modern political societies was, in a sense, generic. But the conceptual foundations of that treatment were formed very strongly by a combination of Roman law, the German historical school, and an ingenious use of Hegel. With Maine, the question of whether the British constitution was an exception or the norm fell by the wayside because it was pushed out of the analytical framework by the broader subject of the relationship between status and contract. Maine's work became the basis of a new set of binaries, formed notably by the opposition between a *Gemeinschaft* and a *Gesellschaft* in the work of Ferdinand Tönnies, or between mechanical and organic solidarity in the work of Emile Durkheim, and, finally, between idealism and utilitarianism in the history of political thought. Focusing on Maine, however, makes it possible to get behind these later binaries and begin to piece together the conceptual context in which they were given their content and shape.

Felix Esquirou de Parieu and the Principles of Political Science

The French counterpart of the arguments over the relationship between civil society and the state that took place among the assorted groups of Hegelians, Young Hegelians, former Hegelians, and anti-Hegelians in the German-speaking parts of Europe took much of its cue from the textbook on natural law by Heinrich Ahrens. In the last years of the French Second Empire his version of natural jurisprudence became the starting point of one of the first full-blown and wide-ranging treatises on political science. This was the work of Félix Esquirou de Parieu, a minor but still highly placed minister in Napoleon III's Second Empire, who is now best known as an early advocate of a single European currency (to be called "The European") and a broadly federal system of European government (to be headed by a Council of Europe, and which actually began with what was called a Latin Union).[2] Parieu's proposals

---

2. On this aspect of Parieu's thought, see the fascinating studies by Luca Einaudi, "From the Franc to the 'Europe': The Attempted Transformation of the Latin Monetary Union into a European Monetary Union," *Economic History Review* 53 (2000): 284–308, and, more fully, *Money and Politics: European Monetary Union and the International Gold Standard (1865–1873)* (Oxford, OUP, 2001). More recently, see Lucien Gillard, *L'Union latine, une expérience de souverainetés monétaires partagées (1865–1926)* (Paris, Garnier, 2017). On the subject of Latinity, now visible mainly in the concept of Latin America, see John L. Phelan, "Pan-Latinism, French Intervention in Mexico (1861–1867) and the Genesis of the Idea of Latin America," in *Conciencia y Autenticidad Históricas*, [ed. Anon.] (Mexico City, UNAM, 1968), pp. 279–98; Arturo Ardao, *Genesis de la Idea y el Nombre de America Latina* (Caracas, Centro de Estudios LatinoAmericanos Romulo Gallegos, 1980), and Walter D. Mignolo, *The Idea of Latin America* (Oxford, Blackwell, 2005). On the

were made in the 1860s, in the aftermath of Italian unification and the Austro-Prussian War, and with the looming possibility of what was to become the Franco-Prussian War supplying the vision and motivation for the *Principes de la science politique* (Principles of political science) that he published in 1870 and reissued in 1875 once the shattering effects of the war had become clear. By then, Parieu also had some reason to feel vindicated because many of his chapters on the dangers of war and the fragility of the Second Empire had first been presented as papers to the French Academy of Moral and Political Sciences several years before the war began. As the name of the Latin Union was intended to signal, the counterpart to Prussian hegemony in the North would be French hegemony in the South with a stable balance of power underpinning their respective spheres of influence.

Parieu took his definition of political science from Ahrens. It was, he wrote, quoting Ahrens, something that lay midway between "the philosophy and the history of law (*droit*)" because it was concerned on the one hand with "the goal and general principles of the organization of civil society" and, on the other, with "the precedents, character, and *moeurs*" of a people, together with its institutions and "the present state of its culture" as well as its "external relations with other peoples." Together, these amounted to the basis of "the reforms for which its previous state had prepared it, and which its present state was now able to allow."[3] This, Parieu emphasized, meant that political science was a relatively recent intellectual development. First, there had been the political art, or the many different skills involved in acquiring and holding on to power, status, and wealth. Then there was political science, with its more considered awareness of political forms and the relatively circumscribed range of possibilities that any individual form could accommodate. If the art of politics was blatantly self-interested, this was not necessarily the case with political science.

Parieu also followed Ahrens in his definition of the state. "The true doctrine," he wrote, again quoting Ahrens, "is to make the goal of the state consist of the social realization of the principle of justice, so that the activity of the state extends to every domain of the social order, but in such a way that it provides no more than the external conditions for its development by giving assistance to each domain without intervening in their internal activity and without surrendering the principles of their organization to the political

---

broader subject of a European common market, see Jacob Viner, *The Customs Union Issue* (London, Carnegie Endowment for International Peace, 1950).

3. Félix Esquirou de Parieu, *Principes de la science politique* [1870], 2nd ed. (Paris, 1875), p. viii, citing Ahrens, *Cours de droit naturel* (1838), p. 30.

principle."[4] The same applied to systems of government. As Ahrens had also shown, governments were usually mixed, which meant that the "relative value of political forms" had to consist of "a combination that, to be appropriate, should be one that provides for a growing presence of the democratic element as civilization extends itself over the greater part of the nation." This, Parieu continued, still citing Ahrens, meant that "the weighting or value of different forms of government and their various combinations should, first and foremost, be historical and in proportion to the various levels of culture of a people. The best form will always be that which, at a given time, most fits general interests by placing power in the hands of those who can, with the most intelligence and independence, make the principle of justice prevail over ignorance and partial interest."[5] In some cases, this would make monarchical or different types of aristocratic government necessary because democratic politics at the wrong time or place was a ready formula for conflict or stagnation or—as was the case in the most democratic Swiss cantons—both. But the *telos* of political science was still democracy. It would, however, be a plural, rather than a unitary, version of democracy, underpinned by a proliferating array of professional, confessional, and social organizations. This, Parieu emphasized, was why fiscal policy mattered. It could be used to set a ceiling on luxury or, inversely, to raise the threshold at which taxes on certain levels of income, rents, or certain types of consumer good would begin to apply or, more broadly, could be calibrated progressively to claw back the cumulative effects of hereditary wealth, as Ahrens himself had recommended.[6]

---

4. "La vraie doctrine fait, suivant l'auteur [meaning Ahrens], consister le but de l'état 'dans la réalisation sociale du principe de justice d'après lequel l'activité de l'état s'étend à tous les domaines de l'ordre social, mais de manière à former seulement les conditions extérieures de développement, en venant à leur secours sans intervenir cependant dans leur mouvement intérieur, et sans abandonner les principes de leur organisation au principe politique.'" Parieu, *Principes*, p. 379, citing Ahrens, *Cours*, p. 361.

5. "Les conclusions d'Ahrens sur la valeur relative des formes politiques méritent d'être citées: 'La combinaison', dit-il, 'pour être juste, doit être telle qu'elle permette un agrandissement successif de l'élément démocratique, a mesure que la civilisation s'étend sur une plus grande partie de la nation.

"La valeur des différentes formes et de gouvernement et de leurs combinaisons est avant tout historique, et proportionnée aux différents degrés de culture d'un peuple. La meilleure forme est toujours celle qui, a une époque donnée, satisfait le mieux les intérêts généraux, en plaçant le pouvoir dans les mains de ceux qui peuvent faire triompher avec le plus d'indépendance et d'intelligence le principe de justice, sur l'ignorance et l'intérêt particulier.'" Parieu, *Principes*, pp. 392–93, citing Ahrens, *Cours*, p. 386.

6. Parieu, *Principes*, p. 160 n. 1, referring to Ahrens, *Cours*, p. 221.

As Parieu recognized, the problem with political science was not so much its comparative approach as its frequently unspoken endorsement of a particular regime form. Although he recognized that democracy was certainly the underlying *telos* of political society, he also made it clear that democracy still belonged to a relatively remote, and not particularly welcome, future. As with Alexis de Tocqueville (whose work Parieu cited frequently and, usually, favourably), this disenchanted acceptance of democracy meant it was the comparative side of political science that was given more conceptual and analytical prominence than its unavoidably democratic goal.[7] The result was an unusually wide-ranging examination of different regime forms under the broader aegis of the conceptual framework that Ahrens had supplied, an examination that was supplemented by reference to scores of relevant books and articles, in English, German, Italian, and Spanish, as well as French. Although Parieu has sometimes been described as a "highly placed, ultra-conservative civil-servant," he made it clear at various points of his *Principes* that his prime political guides were Kant and Constant, while the title of his book was a deliberate echo of Macaulay's phrase "that noble science of politics."[8] The choice, together with his frequent citations from the works of Adam Ferguson, George Cornewall Lewis, John Stuart Mill, Herbert Spencer, and Henry Brougham, chimed readily with his obvious fascination with British politics. The initial source of that fascination, however, was supplied by the thought of the seventeenth-century English republican James Harrington.

Civil government, Parieu wrote—here quoting Harrington—was "the art by which a people guides itself or is guided by someone else."[9] The definition helped to capture the binary character of almost all political societies because, Parieu argued, most political societies were based essentially on subordination or association, inequality or equality, and on authority or liberty. In addition,

7. Parieu's only substantive objection to Tocqueville was, interestingly, occasioned by what he described as the latter's endorsement of stronger royal or presidential power than he himself was willing to accept: see Parieu, *Principes*, pp. 168–69.

8. On Parieu as an "ultra-conservative," see Pierre Favre, *Naissances de la science politique en France 1870–1914* (Paris, Fayard, 1989), p. 54. On Macaulay, see Parieu, *Principes*, pp. xxii–xxiii, and, on Kant and Constant, pp. xix–xxi n. 2. For further endorsement of Constant (on religion and on his hostility towards capital cities and the desirability of decentralization), see Parieu, *Principes*, p. 268. On the "noble science of politics," see John Burrow, Stefan Collini, and Donald Winch, *That Noble Science of Politics* (Cambridge, CUP, 1983), and, on Macaulay, see Aude Attuel-Hallade, *T. B. Macaulay et la révolution française: la pensée libérale whig en débat* (Paris, Michel Houdiard, 2018).

9. Parieu, *Principes*, p. 4, citing Harrington's *Political Aphorisms* (which had been published in French translation in 1795).

each of the two sides of these three binaries complemented one another, not only in substance, but also in time. Subordination not only went together with inequality and authority, but also with the assorted legacies of the nomadic and pastoral peoples responsible for Europe's feudal past, just as association was the product of the many different types of liberty and equality that were the outcomes of Europe's urban and Christian past. From this perspective, the emancipation of political science from the art of politics matched the broader direction of historical travel involved in giving political power a variety of more highly differentiated political forms. Here, as Harrington had shown, the balance of power (*imperium*) followed the balance of property (*dominium*), and, as property became more varied, so too did the forms of government.[10] Of these, Parieu argued, mixed governments (again echoing Harrington) brought together more of the advantages and fewer of the disadvantages than pure versions of either monarchy, aristocracy, or democracy. Some, he noted, had tried to define a polyarchy as a fourth type, but, he argued, its most salient feature, namely, a multiple elected executive, was something that could be incorporated into a system of mixed government.[11] The same type of addition, he wrote, also applied to the idea of the separation of powers. As with an elected executive, separate legislative, executive, and judicial functions could be incorporated into a mixed system under the aegis of party politics and ministerial accountability.

These additions, Parieu claimed, were one of the main sources of political stability. Party politics ruled out court politics. Party politics injected electoral competition into all levels of the political system, and this in turn meant that regional or municipal politics were less likely to be overshadowed by the centralized politics and centralized political complexion of capital cities than was presently the case in most European states. Party politics also meant that ministers were not only responsible but also replaceable, and this in turn meant that domestic political intrigues and manoeuvres, as well as some of the dramas involved in ministerial responsibility, could be offset either by a simple cabinet reshuffle or, ultimately, by the verdict of the ballot box. Finally, party politics made it easier to promote radically different policies under the aegis of the same political labels, as had been shown by the English Tories over the Corn Laws under the leadership of Sir Robert Peel and, more recently, by the American Democrats and their Whig (or Hamiltonian) competitors over the related subjects of western expansion and free trade (here, it seems that the underlying interest in the subject was shaped by the transition from the

10. Parieu, *Principes*, p. 12, citing (in English) Harrington's *Oceana*.
11. Parieu, *Principes*, p. 22.

authoritarian to the liberal empire under Napoleon III). Parieu was fascinated
by an article on political parties in the United States that had been published
two decades earlier in in the *Revue des Deux Mondes*. The chameleon-like capacity for reinventing themselves that was exhibited by modern political parties amounted, the article noted, "perhaps to a universal trait that has come to
characterize the development of free states." It meant that the type of "metamorphosis that is capable of rubbing out old political distinctions under the
growing empire of a set of common interests born in a new setting" could
be considered to be "a constitutional law of their nature."[12] Free states and party
politics were, from this perspective, mutually supportive if only because
party politics had a built-in propensity to endorse novelty and alter the image
of the past, including most particularly their own.

The subject of political parties as vehicles of both innovation and stability
had an obvious relevance to politics in both France and the United States in
the aftermath of the Commune and the Civil War. But the Harringtonian side
of Parieu's investigations also pointed to a further source of political stability.
Britain, as almost every political commentator noted, was highly inegalitarian,
but also highly stable. For Parieu, this apparent paradox had a great deal to do
with the way that the trusts and settlements that were so prominent a feature
of English landed society had the effect of building an array of interests into
the system of marriage and inheritance that was broader and deeper than it
seemed. The elaborate legal provisions and the extended membership of the
trusts responsible for managing the inheritance of property and the rights of
married women meant that a far more extensive array of interests was tied up
with economic and social stability than appearances seemed to suggest. This
was particularly the case because of the nexus generated by the management
of trusts and settlements and the scale of investment in the British national
debt.[13] If property was held in trust and could not be alienated, income from

12. "Peut-être même, à bien réfléchir, serait-ce là comme un trait universel qui viendrait
aujourd'hui caractériser le développement des états libres; peut-être est-ce une loi constitutionnelle de leur nature que cette métamorphose qui efface les veilles distinctions politiques sous
l'empire croissant des intérêts communs nés dans un milieu nouveau. Il s'opère ainsi une concili-
ations favorable à tous les progrès, le meilleur moyen de débattre avec fruit les questions
d'avenir, c'est assurément de pacifier l'arène où l'on débattait les questions du passé." [Anon.],
"Situation des partis aux Etats-Unis," *Revue des Deux Mondes*, n.s. 16 (1846): 1127–32 (p. 1128 for
this passage). For a similar, possibly related, examination of party politics, see the fascinating
discussion by Johann Kaspar Bluntschli, *La Politique* [1879], 2nd ed. (Paris, 1883), especially
pp. 318–405.

13. Parieu, *Principes*, pp. 226–32. On trusts and their relationship to modern political societies, see notably Alan Macfarlane, *The Making of the Modern World* (London, Palgrave, 2002).

that property could still be used to cover the costs of loans invested in the public funds. This meant that gilts could be sold even if land could not, and rental income could be used to offset the interest payments required to service mortgages. In this setting, the more divisive effects of party politics could be offset by the more general commitment to property and public debt that trusts and settlements maintained.

Parieu's interest in a Council of Europe and a European currency was an extension of the same logic. "Money," he wrote, "seems to be one of the most suitable institutions for bringing people together because it is already the most irradiative element of each nationality, with as much to do with people as with business and with travel as with trade."[14] Just as the multiple interests involved in trusts and settlements helped to counteract the more divisive effects of property and inequality, so the multiple functions of a single currency could offset the more damaging potential of economic competition and interstate rivalry. Although, like Kant, Parieu indicated that he expected Europe's future to be federal (the Germans, he wrote, had developed the most sophisticated array of concepts for describing the different types of federal arrangement that were now potentially available for Europe), a common currency did not initially have to depend on a political union. The range of possibilities indicated by the concepts of a league of states (*Bündniss*), a federation of states (*Staatenbund*), and a federal state (*Bundesstaat*), coupled with the growing range of nongovernmental organizations like postal unions or copyright agencies, meant, first, that monetary union and political union could be treated separately, and, second, that full convergence would at most be gradual and, probably, more durable than the Achaean or Panbeotic Leagues of ancient Greece.[15]

It remains to be seen whether monetary unions and political unions can really be as separate as Parieu imagined. What was clearer—perhaps more so in France in 1870 than in more recent times—was his concurrent insistence upon the death of the old political categories. The old preoccupation, Parieu wrote, with monarchies and republics was over. This, he emphasized, was the real legacy of Bonapartism and the Second Empire. Napoleon III had been the first to apply "the principle of nationalities" to Italy but had then found the same principle applied by Bismarck to France, just as the first Napoleon had paid a price for being the first to revive the old Roman plebiscite under modern economic and social conditions. Modern France would now have to live with a world of nation-states and find a way to deal with democracy without

14. Parieu, *Principes*, p. 351.
15. Ibid., pp. 339, 346.

Bonapartism. The situation, Parieu commented with relish, would have led the "theosophist Ballanche" to say that "the initiator was killed by the initiated."[16] Where once it had been possible to hope that "Rome will always be free and Cesar all-powerful"—as Racine had put it in his play *Britannicus*—aspirations like this were now simply "tragic."[17] But the end of the old royal and republican divide did not mean the end of ideology. Instead it meant something like its opposite. In place of the old opposition between royalism and republicanism, or between the various forms of government associated with either liberty or authority, equality or inequality, and association or sub-ordination, there was now simply politics. Politics in this sense, however, now meant party politics and electoral competition, not only for government, but also for the leadership of every party, potentially all the way up or down, from the lowest to the highest offices of the state. Politics, Parieu wrote, now filled the space between a republic and "a monarchy that was truly free and stable at the same time," because, as he put it, "we are now at a certain distance from both the one and the other."[18] The earlier binaries between different forms of government had, in other words, become party politics and, and under the aegis of the electoral system, had turned the many different objects of allegiance of party politics into either majorities and minorities or into government and opposition. In these guises, however, the binaries were partial and temporary, not general and permanent. Yet, despite their limited and transitory qualities, these were now the hallmarks of a political system that a patriot could admire, because it was now politics that supplied most of the ingredients of a common memory and a common future or, it could be added, the constituent parts of sociability. This, Parieu noted, had been the view of the seventeenth-century French moralist Jean de la Bruyère and the eighteenth-century Scots philosopher Adam Ferguson, as well, on some accounts, as the Dutch pantheist Benedict Spinoza.[19] From this perspective, what had once been one of the more complex and contentious aspects of discussions of the natural state had become one of the chief components of examinations of the political state. The concept of unsocial sociability, it could be said, had turned into political science.

16. Ibid., pp. 423, 466.

17. Ibid., p. 403.

18. "S'il faillait dire toute ma pensée sur l'éloignement qui nous sépare, soit d'une monarchie vraiment libre et stable à la fois, soit d'une république, je trouverais peut-être que nous sommes à une certaine distance et de l'une et de l'autre." Ibid., p. 404.

19. Ibid., p. 405 n. 1, and, on the connection between party politics and patriotism, pp. 468–69.

The Origins of the Whig Interpretation of History

Parieu's interest in the origins and nature of British political stability belonged to what, from the time of the French Revolution, but particularly after 1848, had become a recognizable and self-standing historical genre. Its best-known—and most widely dismissed—product was what came to be known as the Whig Interpretation of History. Tracking its emergence, however, makes it possible to see that the Whig Interpretation of History was the unintended outcome of the broader European attempt to establish a philosophy of history that could accommodate Kant's insistence on the gap between the length of an individual life and the putatively progressive character of human history. One indication of what this involved can be found in two general lectures on modern history delivered early in the autumn of 1849 by Henry Halford Vaughan, recently appointed as Regius Professor of Modern History at the University of Oxford, to mark his inauguration to the chair. Although he was later to produce a three-volume study of Shakespeare's tragedies, the two lectures that Vaughan delivered in October 1849 turned out to be his only published historical work.[20] They were, however, based on an ambitious philosophy of history that complemented Parieu's interest in the causes of British political stability and, more importantly, addressed the subject in the immediate aftermath of the 1848 revolutions. As with many post-Kantian philosophies of history, Vaughan's philosophy of history had a *telos*, meaning something more than a simple historical pattern, but also something less than a determinate historical goal. In Vaughan's case, the *telos* had something to do with Europe, although his concept of Europe was deliberately vague. One effect of this vagueness (and one reason, perhaps, for Vaughan's later historiographical sterility) was that it helped to turn the *telos* from a goal into a question. As Vaughan presented it, Europe was certainly not a state or a nation like Britain or France—or even Germany or Italy—but it was still enough of a society for some institutions, events, or arrangements to make more sense in a European than in a purely national context. Religious institutions were one, but so too was the recent cycle of revolution that had covered most of Europe in 1848 (Vaughan was more sympathetic to what they had stood for than many other Oxford academics, which was one reason why, despite his formal position, he never moved to Oxford from London and, finally, resigned his chair when he was officially required to reside in the university town). However indeterminate it was, the existence of Europe as a kind of society formed, Vaughan

---

20. On Vaughan's life, see E.G.W. Bill, *University Reform in Nineteenth-Century Oxford: A Study of Henry Halford Vaughan, 1811–1885* (Oxford, OUP, 1973).

claimed, a line separating ancient from modern history. It also, however, gave rise to a range of questions about what had brought it into existence, and, if it was ever to materialize fully, what it was likely to be.

The indeterminate quality of the type of society that Europe might be—and the equally indeterminate character of the kind of line that, putatively, had been crossed to bring that type of society into being—meant that the focus of Vaughan's lectures fell not so much on what Europe was, or would become, as on a range of causal processes and imaginative projections that, he went on to suggest, had given Europe a kind of virtual existence, somewhere between the ideal and the real. Some centred on the relationship between the ancients and the moderns, and the similarities and differences between the empires and republics of the ancient past and the constitutional monarchies and representative governments of more recent times. Others centred on the parts played by economic development, the division of labour, occupational specialization, and institutional differentiation in the emergence of modern political societies and the assortment of states and governments that they had come to house. Others highlighted the protracted cultural and intellectual mutations that had given rise to the range of partly moral and partly aesthetic concerns of the rival supporters of the classics and the romantics. Others consisted of the many different reactions and responses to the question of reform—some positive and others negative—and, by the time of the revolutions of 1848, their gradual crystallization into a more recognizable array of competing political ideologies, from liberalism and socialism to communism, conservatism, and nationalism. Others, finally, focused on the law and legal history, and the respective legacies of the Romans and Germans in the emergence of the mixture of individual entitlements and political arrangements that, from the time of the American and French Revolutions, had come to be symbolized by the idea of a Declaration of Rights.

Vaughan's lectures amounted to a concise examination of this overlapping array of subjects. They were followed a year later, in 1850, by a prize essay, clearly written with Vaughan's two lectures in mind, on the subject of "The Ancients and Moderns Compared in Regard to the Administration of Justice" that was read out in the University Theatre in Oxford by a member of Worcester College named George Osborne Morgan, who later went on to become a successful lawyer and a prominent Liberal Party politician. Three years later, Morgan published a further pamphlet, this time on the different political trajectories followed by Britain and France before and after 1848, and, by extension, on the underlying reasons for the glaring difference in outcomes that the events of that year had produced. In one sense, the later publication was a straightforward celebration of how, unlike France and most of the rest of Europe, Britain had weathered the storm. In another sense, however, it was also a register of a number of more durable comparative questions, not only about British political stability and European instability, and the reasons for the difference between revolution and reform, but also about the kind of conceptual vocabulary that was needed to bring together the historical and analytical dimensions of this type of comparison into one synthetic view. Set alongside one another, the three publications amount to quite a comprehensive overview of the range of subjects and questions that, by the middle of the nineteenth century, had come to be associated with both the subject of revolution and the politics of reform. Three subjects, in particular, stand out. The first was the subject of centralization, in all its various constitutional, institutional, cultural, or geographical forms. The second was the subject of inequality, also in all its various economic, social, or political forms. The third was the subject of politics and, more specifically, the question of the type of political system that could accommodate the first two subjects and still find room for change.

The three publications by Henry Halford Vaughan and George Osborne Morgan provide an initial set of answers to the question. Vaughan's underlying aim in his two lectures on modern history was to distance his own assessment of the relationship between history and politics from that of his predecessor as Regius Professor at Oxford and his earlier teacher at Rugby School, Thomas Arnold. Arnold had been one of the many historically minded political thinkers, in Italy, France, and Germany as well as Britain, who had been responsible for the early nineteenth-century rediscovery of the thought of the seventeenth-century Neapolitan theologian Giambattista Vico. For Arnold, echoing Vico, nations were the fundamental units of the obscure historical processes involved in the formation and transmission of human culture over time and space.[21] Nations had a symbolic, poetic, or linguistic inner life, or culture, that bound their members together. What was less clear, however, was how an entity like a nation could escape from this bounded condition to become part of something broader and more continuous, like history. This, for Vaughan, was why the fundamental units of historical investigation were not nations and nationality, but individuals and society. History, he announced, could be defined "*as a disclosure of the critical changes in the condition of society*" (the italics were his).[22] The definition was designed initially to capture the ambiguity of the

21. See, particularly, his essay "On the Social Progress of States" [1830], originally published as an appendix to his edition of Thucydides and reprinted in Thomas Arnold, *Miscellaneous Works* (London, 1845), pp. 79–111. On Vico and the broader Vico revival, see, still helpfully, Flint, *Vico*, and, for a brilliant summary, Berlin, "Corsi e Ricorsi."

22. Henry Halford Vaughan, *Two General Lectures on Modern History delivered on Inauguration, October 1849* (Oxford, 1849), p. 5. Vaughan's lectures, and their claim about society as the fundamental unit of historical inquiry, are examined concisely, but without comment on their

English-language word "history" and the fact that it could refer both to events and arrangements in the past and to knowledge of those same events and arrangements, but this time in the present. In this sense, history was both a closure and a disclosure, and this, Vaughan continued, meant that keeping the two points of view in focus called for studying things that were not limited entirely to the past or restricted solely to the present. Something more than the concept of a nation was needed to bring together both perspectives into a single view because only something whose conceptual existence could straddle both perspectives and the combination of continuity and change that they implied could be a real foundation for the study of history.

This, Vaughan explained, was why the study of history had to begin with "the conception of *society*" on the one hand and "the idea of the *individual*" on the other.[23] States, nations, and empires, he argued, were certainly important historical subjects, as too were their rulers, governments, and members, but their relatively transient quality meant that they did not exhibit the same combination of continuity and change that made individuals and society, along with the relationship between the two, the most suitable starting points for historical inquiry. The generic character of the relationship between individuals and society provided a vantage point that could encompass the two perspectives involved in the compound made up of history and the knowledge of history. The "mortality of nations," Vaughan pointed out, "has been hitherto a general fact; it has been the general lot of nations as such to perish."[24] Individuals and societies also died, but the structural quality of their relationship, sometimes shaped by the creative energies of a small number of exceptional individuals, but more usually shaped by the everyday routines of the many more ordinary members of society, made the relationship between individuals and societies foundational for the study of history.

Vaughan was also careful to indicate that the study of history had to begin with both a *concept* of society and an *idea* of the individual, rather than simply with individuals and society. This difference made it possible for him to make a sharper distinction between history in general and modern history in particular because, he went on to claim, adding this further, more reflexive, component to both history and the study of history meant that modern history "presents itself as a most various, complicated and manifold fact."

European orientation, in the still-unsurpassed study by Duncan Forbes, *The Liberal Anglican Idea of History* (Cambridge, CUP, 1952), pp. 121, 182. See also Joshua Bennett, *God and Progress: Religion and History in British Intellectual Culture, 1845–1914* (Oxford, OUP, 2019).

23. Vaughan, *Two General Lectures*, p. 6 (here too the italics are Vaughan's).

24. Ibid., p. 15.

We see without difficulty that there are principles at work which tend to give it greater complexity and a larger sphere of existence as society moves forward. Institutions are multiplied, professions and arts are separated and increased, the grades in society become more numerous. At the earliest periods of modern history in our own country, the king and his council *executed* the laws as well as *framed* them. By continual separation of functions this Council has developed itself into three Courts of Common Law, two Houses of Parliament, many Courts of Equity, a grand Chamber of Appeal, a Privy Council, and a Cabinet. Each of these branches again has divided itself into distinct functions and been assigned to separate persons. This fact in the progress of social life is seen to be the natural result of increased numbers, accumulated experience, necessities more urgent, desires more numerous, enjoyments multiplied, faculties discriminated, capabilities evoked and multiplied. It may be called somewhat vaguely, a principle of development.[25]

It was, it could be said, modernization theory in all but name. But its most important feature was more historical and reflexive than either modernization theory or its twin, differentiation theory, has come to be.[26] As Vaughan emphasized, the principle of development informing his own historical vision was something that could be identified only retrospectively. It was, he wrote, the peculiarity of modern history that it was able to disclose "society in its rudimentary state" and reveal "the elements out of which it is formed." Only with hindsight, Vaughan wrote somewhat ponderously, was it possible to see the course of modern history as a passage "from the heterogeneous to the complex, and from the complex to the manifold; from aggregation to envelopment, and from envelopment to development."[27] This, historically generated insight explained why modern history could be the basis of considered policy, and why, in the modern age, the politics of reform had come to have a built-in historical dimension.

Importantly, the principle of development that Vaughan described was not based on a concept of history consisting of a straightforward switch from original simplicity to modern complexity. The early condition of society, he emphasized, was not simple in any general or uniform sense. "A small tract of country, and a scanty population, contained many languages, distinct systems

25. Ibid., p. 11 (the passage was later cited by George Osborne Morgan in his essay described below).

26. For one, well-known version, see Douglass C. North and Robert Paul Thomas, *The Rise of the Western World: A New Economic History* (Cambridge, CUP, 1973).

27. Vaughan, *Two General Lectures*, p. 11

of law, several magistracies: it would exhibit the vital operation of distinct political ideas, religious beliefs, domestic and social institutions." The difference between the earlier and later conditions was, therefore, not one between the simple and the complex, but was instead between two distinct forms of complexity. One, the putatively simple, housed "the complexity of disintegration and intermixture," while the other displayed "the complexity of division, distribution and development." Where the latter was "the complexity of different ends and different functions assigned to separate organs," the former was "the complexity of similar or identical effects accomplished by different instruments." Thus, in "the earlier society, three or four languages were doing the work of one. Two or three systems of law were controlling the devolution of the same kind of property upon different principles." Similarly, the principle of authority was sometimes embodied in a "general and leader," but also sometimes found expression "in allegiance" to a "ruler as civil magistrate." Thus, Vaughan concluded, "the ruder age has its natural simplicity balanced by its heterogeneous character, as the more advanced age has its uniformity qualified by its prolific spirit of discrimination. The first is introductory to the second."[28]

The pattern that Vaughan identified had two clear dimensions. One was spatial and the other was temporal. "The order of events," he wrote, "has worked with accumulated effect through centuries to form a European as distinct from a French, English, German or Italian character, and to elicit from these separate and heterogeneous compounds an identity which, however vague and partial, still serves to present them occasionally to the eye in a single group."[29] The same change of scale applied to time. If modern history showed that it was possible to combine "national progress and national duration in a manner and on a scale unknown to ancient history," this was because there were "institutions, laws, customs, tastes, traditions, beliefs, convictions, magistracies, festivals, pastimes and ceremonies, and other such elements of social organization" that, over time, could be detached from the largely local or national context in which they had first emerged, and integrated into a new and different set of social arrangements. This, Vaughan pointed out, was why "while nations perish, society lives on."[30] Modern history was, therefore, "the coalition of two systems of society, which had subsisted for ages and for ages had been held apart."[31] One system was simple, but heterogeneous; the other was more differentiated, but also more uniform. One system was ancient while

---

28. Ibid., pp. 10–11.
29. Ibid., p. 13.
30. Ibid., pp. 16–17.
31. Ibid., p. 17.

the other was modern. Although what Vaughan called the coalition—or fusion—of the two types of system applied to all three of the great nations of Europe, meaning France, Britain, and Germany, it had happened in different ways. In France, he claimed, the fusion was primarily physical, as depopulation and agricultural decline produced a void that was, literally, filled by the Germanic invaders from the North, but which did not alter the institutional superstructure of Roman law and Roman administration. In England, on the other hand, the fusion was largely moral, with Christianity forming a bridge between the Romans and the Germans. "As," Vaughan wrote rhapsodically, "the old Roman society had the physical strength to survive in France, so did it possess spiritual energy to migrate into England. A monk, a hymn, a crucifix and a sermon, brought two worlds together in a village of Kent." In Germany, in the third place, the fusion was more piecemeal and protracted. Here, the binding element was also more imperial than material or spiritual, with the names of Charlemagne and Caesar symbolizing the nature of the fusion. "Last of all," Vaughan concluded, "was imbibed the very soul of Roman society, the civil law, which seized upon all personal rights, controlled all domestic relations and carried Roman principles into the public and private conscience of the Teutonic people."[32]

Vaughan, it is clear, was a kind of post-Kantian idealist, rather like the type of scholar who came to be satirized by George Eliot in the figure of Mr Casaubon (he was later accused of trying to Germanize the University of Oxford; his accuser was Edward Pusey, one of the leaders of the Anglo-Catholic Oxford Movement and another of the reasons for Vaughan's preference for living in London rather than Oxford).[33] He did not refer to any of the sources of his ideas or add any footnotes to the published version of his lecture. But his follower George Osborne Morgan inserted a great many in his essay entitled "The Ancients and Moderns Compared in Regard to the Administration of Justice." The theme of the essay was a development of Vaughan's and was centred on the gradual process of differentiation involved both in the separation of powers and in the more varied functional separation of different types of legal and judicial institution. As Morgan presented them, these legal institutions had, over time, passed through three different phases. Initially, in the very earliest societies, they had been patriarchal or theocratic, with a special class of elders, priests, or druids responsible for the administration of justice. Later, in ancient Greece or republican and imperial Rome, justice had been in the hands of the

32. Ibid., pp. 18–19.

33. On Casaubon and Eliot, see, recently, Colin Kidd's marvellous *The World of Mr Casaubon: Britain's Wars of Mythography 1700–1870* (Cambridge, CUP, 2016).

whole community or had been delegated to tribunals selected or, as Morgan put it, elected to represent the whole state. In a third and later setting, however, the administration of justice was performed by a jury, with individuals of the same rank and locality chosen, not to represent the community or the state, but to represent and adjudicate between the contending parties. The line separating institutions of the third type from the other two was the line dividing the ancients from the moderns. It was also the line separating the Romans from the Germans. "While the Roman empire was approaching its dissolution," Morgan wrote, "a new germ of life was struggling into existence—the life of the Teutonic nations of the north."

> In the conflict which ensued between the Roman and German character, we have the commencement of a struggle, which was destined to agitate the world for centuries after the phases under which it originally presented itself had disappeared. Roman civilization organised the social system, German barbarism developed individual freedom.[34]

Modern European legal and political arrangements, Morgan went on to claim, were a synthesis of both individual freedom and the social system. "Of," he announced, "the three systems of judicature which we originally described, it is clearly the third which had never appeared in ancient times which is here denoted. The judges are no longer the representatives of the sovereign or of the state; they are the representatives of the individual whom they try."[35] This peculiarly modern system of representation, he went on to explain, had originated under the feudal regime. It had begun with the invading Germanic peoples of the North and had originally been part of the procedure used for settling disputes within the jurisdictions of the baronial and manorial courts of feudal times. Although Morgan did not use the name, the institutional prototype of this form of dispute settlement was something called a *Genossenschaft*, or a fellowship, which relied on the idea that all of its members were jointly and severally responsible for each other's conduct. To some, it was the prototype of the jury. As with Rome and Roman law, the idea of a *Genossenschaft* was to have considerable significance in the history of nineteenth-century political thought, mainly in the work of Otto von Gierke. As Morgan presented it, this collective form of dispute settlement had also undergone a mutation during the Middle Ages, caused by the rise of royal government and "the long struggle which for so many years convulsed west-

34. George Osborne Morgan, *The Ancients and Moderns Compared in Regard to the Administration of Justice* (Oxford, 1850), p. 23.
35. Ibid., p. 28.

ern Europe, the struggle between the kings and the barons, between feudalism and monarchy."[36] Royal courts were established alongside feudal courts, and royal law officers took over much of the administration of justice from manorial or feudal legal officials.

The outcome, Morgan argued, was the combination of professional magistrates and civil juries that had become the distinctive feature of the English judicial system. Unusually, however, it was one that turned out to be durable. Thus, Morgan wrote, "was gradually accomplished the partition of the judicial functions between the king's judges, the remnant of the Roman system, and the local juries, the offspring of the feudal organization."

> On the continent the Roman law had been everywhere revived. Its tendency was to check the growth of the old national institutions, to crush and paralyse, in particular, the jury system, to impede the separation of the judicial functions, the only true guarantee of its efficacy. The great monarchs of Europe found it a convenient instrument for the acquisition of absolute power. Aided by the servile temper of the crown lawyers, they everywhere encouraged its ascendancy.[37]

Roman law, in this rendition, was the other face of centralized power. Trial by jury, on the other hand, embodied the principle of differentiation that Morgan took over from Vaughan. In keeping with this principle, the emergence of the jury established a relationship between citizens and magistrates that had no equivalent in the ancient world. There, an Athenian or Roman was both a citizen and a magistrate. In the modern world, however, the two roles were distinct, with professional magistrates and citizen jurors. The distinction also had a further effect. Although the members of a jury deliberated and decided as individuals, they were also taken to be collectively responsible for representing the accused. Since they were required to find for the accused in the light of evidence presented to a judge by legal officials or by the original plaintiff, the representative character of the jury was taken to be best maintained by the requirement that its verdicts had to be unanimous, and this in turn meant that its decisions were best limited to matters of fact. Judges and magistrates, on the other hand, deliberated and decided as representatives of the state and based their decisions on matters of law. "Thus," Morgan commented, "a twofold change has taken place in the judicial administration. Freed from external control, its internal workings have grown more complicated and more regular."[38] From this perspective, complexity and

36. Ibid., p. 29.
37. Ibid., p. 31.
38. Ibid., p. 47.

regularity went together because they had the combined effect of giving individual freedom a new layer of protection from state power.

The combination, Morgan claimed, was a measure of the gulf that now existed between the ancients and the moderns. "All those countless phenomena which we sum up under the abstract term civilization," he concluded, "are, as it were, set in the framework of the law. In proportion as they embody these different phenomena, the laws of a nation become a living picture of the whole national existence."

> Thus, ancient jurisprudence was the reflex of ancient civilization. Simple and uniform, it was the development of a few principles, the expression of a few leading ideas. To the genius of modern society, such uniformity is absolutely foreign. Its features are as varied as its growth has been uncontrolled. A thousand conflicting impulses agitating and convulsing the social frame—a thousand conflicting wants struggling to find a vent and an expression—these are what constitute its energy and its life.[39]

Authority in the modern world was decentralized and differentiated, with, at most, no more than a remotely centralized source. Morgan drove home the point about the relationship between institutional complexity and individual freedom by ending his essay with a quotation from the *Laws of Ecclesiastical Polity* by the sixteenth-century Anglican divine Richard Hooker. "Even one and the self-same thing," Hooker had written, "may, under diverse considerations, by conveyed through many laws, and that to measure by any one kind of law all the actions of men were to confound the admirable order wherein God has disposed all laws, each, as in nature so in degree, distinct from one another."[40] It was a passage that could almost have come from *The Spirit of Laws*, the huge, almost epigrammatic, examination of laws and their manifold purposes that had been published in 1748 by the French magistrate, philosopher, and legal historian Charles-Louis de Secondat, baron de Montesquieu.

Although the subject matter of Morgan's essay was largely English, Montesquieu's intellectual presence was visible not only in Morgan's treatment of the interrelationship of the Romans, the Germans, and the modern age but also in the bearing of Montesquieu's thought on the range of authorities on which Morgan's essay was based. Its epigraph—"A people who takes no part in judgments may be calm, contented and well-governed, but it does not belong to itself; it is not free; it is under the sword"—was taken from François Guizot's *History of Civilization in France*. Alongside Guizot, and his two multivolume

39. Ibid., pp. 47–48.
40. Ibid., p. 48, quoting Hooker, *Laws of Ecclesiastical Polity* [1594], bk. 1, ch. 16.

histories of civilization, first in Europe and then in France, Morgan also re-
ferred to works by the Franco-Swiss historian of France and, earlier, of the
Italian republics of the Middle Ages Jean-Charles-Léonard Simonde de Sismondi; the Danish-German historian of ancient Rome Barthold Georg
Niebuhr; the founder of the German historical school of legal theory Friedrich
Carl von Savigny; the German historian of dramatic literature August Wilhelm
Schlegel; and two early nineteenth-century French-language legal histories,
one by Jean-Daniel Meyer and the other by Joseph Bernardi, together with an
assortment of books on political institutions, legal history, or ancient and
modern history by such well-known figures as William Blackstone, David
Hume, Henry Hallam, George Grote, and Montesquieu himself.

The impressive scholarly lineup that Morgan drew upon for his essay raises
an intriguing question about the relationship between the relatively narrow
focus of its subject matter and the broad range of its conceptual sources. Morgan's essay, far more than Vaughan's earlier lectures, was about one aspect of
what, at the time, was usually called the English constitution. At the same
time, however, it was also about the relationship between what Morgan called
Roman civilization and German barbarism, and their joint bearing on what
he presented as the modern relationship between the social system and individual freedom. The usual way of describing how these subjects were treated
over the course of the nineteenth century has come to be known as the Whig
Interpretation of History, and Morgan, in one of his later publications, went
on to produce a particularly egregious example of why that interpretation of
history has acquired so bad a name.[41] "Unlike any other state, either of ancient or modern times," he announced in a lecture in 1852 (given, didactically,
to the friends and supporters of a group of church schools), "this country has
at no times been the seat of a pure despotism, or of an exclusive oligarchy, or
of an unbridled democracy." It had, instead, been the seat of a mixed or balanced government, and, Morgan explained, it had been this combination of
monarchy, aristocracy, and democracy, sealed over the centuries, that had
formed the "bulwarks" and "foundations" of "our national constitution."[42]
As should be clear, the lecture was a straightforward panegyric of the English constitution with no room at all for the putatively European dimension
of modern history that had been visible both in Vaughan's earlier lectures

41. See, classically, Herbert Butterfield, *The Whig Interpretation of History* (London, Bell,
1931), and, on his book, C. T. McIntire, *Herbert Butterfield: Historian as Dissenter* (New Haven,
CT, Yale UP, 2004), pp. 56–77, 95–97, 117–22.

42. George Osborne Morgan, *Great Britain and France: Why is Their Present Condition So
Different?* (Carnarvon, 1853), p. 5.

and in Morgan's own earlier essay. After 1848 and, a fortiori, after 1851 and Napoleon III's rise to power, the content of the later lecture now seemed, at least to the lecturer, to be so self-evident that it was no longer necessary to explain how the English constitution had come into being, or what, ultimately, something called a national constitution was supposed to be. Both Roman civilization and German barbarism, as well as their combined bearing on individual freedom and the modern social system, had all disappeared from Morgan's later, more pedagogically streamlined, version of the relationship between history and politics.

Vaughan's two lectures were something like an echo of the philosophy of history that Kant had set out in his essay answering the question "What is Enlightenment?" If, as Kant had argued, the private use of reason favoured the development of the public use of reason, but not the other way around, then the first step in generating the right sequence would be the gradual proliferation of government institutions and, put crudely, the growth of a bureaucratic state. There would be a growing body of legal, economic, fiscal, financial, military, educational, industrial, agricultural, commercial, and welfare-oriented institutions, each with a specialized function and each with a core of trained or skilled personnel. Some institutions might be local, while others might be regional or national, and this geographical and administrative variety would add to the aggregate number of institutions and activities in which the private use of reason preceded its public counterpart. Specialization would be both institutional and occupational, with both favouring the higher productivity and economies of scale associated with the development of the division of labour. The whole incremental process of institutional differentiation would mean that the private use of reason would extend over a growing range of individual and social activities, and as their number and variety grew, so too would the need for their many component parts and specialized functions to become more connected and accountable to one another. This, then, would be the stage of the sequence when the public use of reason really would come into play. But, with the proliferation of governing institutions and the multiplication of their many different functions, the public use of reason would be refracted into a constantly changing kaleidoscope of competing political claims. The many-sided array of institutions would turn the subjects of centralization and inequality into as many different causes of contention as the proliferating number of units that, over time, would turn into the new locations of the original problems. The public use of reason would, consequently, follow on from its private use. Common, however, to all these dimensions of possibility and choice was the idea of a divided self, or a self that was autonomous because it was both the subject and object of its own decisions and choices. In this sense, the sequence that

Kant set out in 1784 amounted to a more elegant version of what Henry Halford Vaughan was, more ponderously, to call the switch "from the heterogeneous to the complex, and from the complex to the manifold; from aggregation to envelopment, and from envelopment to development" in his 1849 lectures on modern history.

The nexus of overlapping distinctions was described more clearly and crisply some six years later in 1857 by the English political theorist Herbert Spencer. As he put it in the essay entitled "Progress: Its Law and Cause" that both made his name and formed the analytical core of many of his subsequent publications, "the transformation of the homogenous into the heterogenous is that in which progress essentially occurs."[43] The most salient and durable feature of this transformation was a double process of differentiation. The first part centred on authority, while the second part centred on freedom. "Very early," Spencer wrote, "in the process of social evolution we find an incipient differentiation between the governing and the governed." It was matched "by a second differentiation of a still more familiar kind; that, namely, by which the mass of the community has become segregated into distinct classes and orders of workers." The outcome was "that minute division of labour characterizing advanced nations" which, Spencer argued, would give rise in the long term to the erosion of states and their cumbersome systems of laws and government.[44] Differentiation theory, in short, long predated the work of Niklas Luhmann, and, with Spencer and his strongly organic theory of how social differentiation could be combined with social integration, the concepts of autonomy and democracy began to merge.[45]

Even at the time that Vaughan gave his lectures and Morgan published his two pamphlets, the difference between the politics of autonomy and the politics of democracy had begun to fade. As the horizons of political possibility began to narrow, particularly after 1848, much of the political significance of the causal sequence that Kant had set out in his two essays on the idea of history and on the question of enlightenment began to disappear from historical view. But, as it did, what was left of the sequence resurfaced, paradoxically, as

43. Herbert Spencer, "Progress: Its Law and Cause," *Westminster Review* 67 (1857): 445–85 (here p. 447).

44. Ibid., 453, 456. On Spencer, see Michael W. Taylor, *The Philosophy of Herbert Spencer* (London, Continuum, 2007), and Mark Francis, *Herbert Spencer and the Invention of Modern Life* (Stocksfield, Acumen, 2007). See too Daniel Becquemont and Laurent Mucchielli, *Le cas Spencer* (Paris, PUF, 1998), pp. 86–92.

45. On Luhmann and differentiation theory, see Niklas Luhmann, *The Differentiation of Society* (New York, Columbia UP, 1982), and his *Law as a Social System* [1993] (Oxford, OUP, 2004).

the Whig Interpretation of History. In one sense, this is not surprising. By the time that Henry Halford Vaughan gave his lectures on modern history in 1849, the only actual historical example of the type of reforming sequence that Kant had described was, in fact, to be found in the United Kingdom of Great Britain and Ireland. The point was underlined some six years later in an essay on Hegel's *Philosophy of Right*. "The picture given of what a state must be, according to the necessities of man's nature, and the exigencies of his position on this earth," its author wrote, "is nothing less than a closely copied sketch of the British Constitution. England is not mentioned, or is only mentioned in the most cursory way. But King, Lords, and Commons are there: a sovereign who is to have no power, but who shall express the highest personality, who is to pardon criminals, and sign his name when he is told; one assembly, which shall reflect what is permanent in property, and another which shall give vent to what is fluctuating in popular opinion." It was, as Hegel's expositor put it, "rather startling to find the minutiae of English constitutional law delivered as the dictates of the highest philosophical reason, and invested with the grandeur of eternal and indisputable truth."[46] But if, as has sometimes been said, Kant's concept of enlightenment was part of something grand called the Enlightenment Project, then the real paradox of Kant's essay seems to be that the Enlightenment Project was actually realized in Great Britain. Put like this, the claim seems far-fetched. It does, however, have a more meaningful point. The parallel between the initial idea of a state-based reforming sequence and the reality of British history makes it easier to explain how most of the historical details and causal subtleties of Vaughan's lectures could have collapsed so readily and easily into Morgan's later rendition of the Whig Interpretation of History. Whatever else it was, the Whig Interpretation of History was an effortlessly self-confident version of Kant's more careful examination of the politics of reform, and an endlessly repeated celebration of its apparently immutable English location. In a real sense, its existence is what makes it interesting.[47]

46. Sandars, "Hegel's Philosophy of Right," p. 215.

47. On its later mutations and ramifications, see Charles Kingsley, *The Roman and the Teuton: A Series of Lectures Delivered Before the University of Cambridge* [1861], new edition with a preface by Max Muller (London, 1889), and the memorably vicious review of it by Edward A. Freeman, "Mr Kingsley's Roman and Teuton," *Saturday Review* 17 (9 April 1864): 446–48. For more recent commentary, see Jonathan Conlin, "An Illiberal Descent: Natural and National History in the Work of Charles Kingsley," *History* 96 (2011): 167–87, and Oded Y. Steinberg, "'Contesting Teutomania': Robert Gordon Latham, 'Race', Ethnology and Historical Migrations," *History of European Ideas* 47 (2021): 1331–47.

James Reddie and the Adam Smith Problem

The rise of the Whig Interpretation of History was connected to a second, more specialized historiographical development that followed on, chronologically and analytically, from the celebration of stability and reform that gave the Whig Interpretation of History its thematic content. This was the Adam Smith Problem. The Adam Smith Problem was first identified by the Swiss historian August Oncken in an article entitled "The Consistency of Adam Smith" that was published in 1897. It was followed by the article that gave the problem its official name as "Das Adam Smith-Problem," which Oncken published in 1898.[48] As Oncken explained in his 1897 article, it had not been his aim to create the problem because it had already been given an existence, if not a name, in a number of earlier, largely German-language, commentaries on Smith's work. The problem in question was a problem about the relationship between the moral theory that Smith set out in his *Theory of Moral Sentiments* of 1759 and the market theory of the *Inquiry into the Nature and Progress of the Wealth of Nations* that Smith published in 1776. According to Smith's later critics, the basis of the moral theory was sympathy, while the basis of the market theory was self-interest. The Adam Smith Problem was whether the one could be reconciled with the other.

As Oncken described it in 1897, the problem had been highlighted in a number of publications by the German *Kathedersozialisten* (socialist academics) Bruno Hildebrand, Karl Knies, and Lujo Brentano that had been produced after 1848 with the aim of giving political economy the kind of moral and social foundations that, they asserted, Smith had once known but had since abandoned. In this sense, their publications were a continuation of the earlier, initially Francophone, discussions of socialism, the division of labour, the social question, and the role of the state in either correcting market failures or in promoting economic and social reform. Oncken's own position was different. In 1877 he published a book entitled *Adam Smith und Immanuel Kant* with the aim of showing the proximity between their respective moral theories and, by extension, the consistency between Smith's investigation of the nature of moral sentiments and his later examination of the origins of the wealth of nations. "If Smith is studied without prejudice," he wrote in 1897, "many passages will be found that prove him to have been a forerunner of Kant, the idealistic philosopher."[49]

---

48. August Oncken, "The Consistency of Adam Smith," *Economic Journal* 7 (1897): 443–50; and "Das Adam Smith-Problem," *Zeitschrift für Sozialwissenschaft* 1 (1898): 25–33, 101–8, 276–87.

49. Oncken, "The Consistency of Adam Smith," p. 445.

By 1897, however, Oncken also had a new resource at his disposal in the form of the recently discovered set of student notes on Smith's lectures on jurisprudence that had been published by Edwin Canaan in 1896. These notes, Oncken wrote, underlined the significance of the preface that Smith had added to the sixth and final edition of the *Theory of Moral Sentiments* that was published shortly before his death in 1790. In this preface, Smith referred back to the announcement that he had made at the end of the first edition of his book, where he had written that he planned to follow it up with "an account of the general principles of law and government and of the different revolutions that they had undergone in the different ages and periods of society, not only in what concerns justice, but in what concerns police, revenue and arms and whatever is the object of the law." Setting Smith's statement of 1790 alongside the newly discovered student notes, Oncken now wrote, underlined how important it was for scholars "to set themselves the task of inquiring fully into the Adam Smith problem." Reconstructing Smith's theory of justice to fill the space between his moral theory and his political economy meant, Oncken wrote, "that we are at last in a position to do full justice to the noble structure of ideas in the mind of the great Scotchman" by revealing "his teaching in its entirety as a system of moral philosophy in which political economy forms but a part."[50]

Over the years, Oncken's formulation of the Adam Smith Problem has become more blurred, mainly because the significance that he attached to Smith's missing theory of jurisprudence has usually taken second place to a broader cluster of related questions.[51] The first is a question about the level of conceptual continuity or discontinuity between the two books. The second is whether the answer to the question about continuity is best found by focusing on the moral theory or on the relationship between the state and the market. The third is whether the moral theory of the original edition of the *Theory of Moral Sentiments* is the same as—or different from—that of the final, sixth, edition of the book published in 1790, shortly before Smith's death in July of that year. The fourth has less to do with the putative variations in

50. Ibid., pp. 448–49.

51. These are set out very clearly in Laurence Dickey, "Historicizing the 'Adam Smith Problem': Conceptual, Historiographical and Textual Issues," *Journal of Modern History* 58 (1986): 579–609. For further discussion, see Keith Tribe, *The Economy of the Word: Language, History and Economics* (Oxford, OUP, 2015), pp. 139–62, and his "'Das Adam Smith Problem' and the Origins of Modern Smith Scholarship," *History of European Ideas* 34 (2008): 514–25, and, more recently, "The 'System of Natural Liberty': Natural Order in the *Wealth of Nations*," *History of European Ideas* 47, no. 3 (2020): 1–11, as well as Leonidas Montes, *Adam Smith in Context* (Basingstoke, Macmillan, 2004), pp. 15–56.

the content of Smith's books because it is a question about the broader subject of Smith's concept of justice and the extent to which it was either an anticipation of a Rawlsian theory of distributive justice, an echo of an earlier, Grotian, distinction between strict justice and moral virtue, or, possibly, part of a dual system designed to house them both.[52] Curiously, none of these approaches to Smith's thought have taken their cue from Oncken's original intuition that there was significant common ground between Smith and Kant. Oncken's reason for making the claim was to rescue Smith from his critics within the historical school of German political economy by showing that Smith's moral theory had more in common with Kant's than his critics assumed. Oncken did not know, however, that he was even more correct than he had guessed because Smith's concept of justice and its relationship to morality on the one side and to political economy on the other was surprisingly similar to Kant's. In this respect, Smith's concept of justice, with its emphasis on justice as a virtue and justice as utility, cleared the ground for a theory of justice that was more compatible with Hegel's distinction between the state and civil society than with the concept of justice as fairness produced in the twentieth century by John Rawls.

The idea of a dual theory of justice, with justice described either as a virtue or as utility, was in fact how Smith's theory of justice was described before the Adam Smith Problem became a problem. The description was a feature of a book by a Scottish lawyer named James Reddie entitled *Inquiries Elementary and Historical in the Science of Law* that was first published in 1840 and then in an enlarged second edition in 1847. The other feature of the book was Reddie's claim that Smith's theory of justice was the same as Immanuel Kant's. The reasons that he gave to support the claim not only help to answer the fourth question, but also indicate much of the substance of the answers to the first three.

Reddie's description singled out two aspects of Smith's theory of justice. The first was the difference between justice and all the other virtues. While the other virtues were usually recognized as virtues because of their freely chosen

---

52. See Istvan Hont and Michael Ignatieff, "Needs and Justice in the *Wealth of Nations*: An Introductory Essay," in *Wealth and Virtue: The Shaping of Political Economy in the Scottish Enlightenment*, ed. Istvan Hont and Michael Ignatieff (Cambridge, CUP, 1983), pp. 1–44; Samuel Fleischacker, *On Adam Smith's Wealth of Nations: A Philosophical Companion* (Princeton, NJ, Princeton UP, 2004), pp. 200–202, 209–26; Samuel Fleischacker, *A Short History of Distributive Justice* (Cambridge, MA, Harvard UP, 2004), pp. 17–18, 26–40; J. R. Otteson, "The Recurring 'Adam Smith Problem,'" *History of Philosophy Quarterly* 17 (2000): 51–74; and Knud Haakonssen and Donald Winch, "The Legacy of Adam Smith," in *The Cambridge Companion to Adam Smith*, ed. Knud Haakonssen (Cambridge, CUP, 2006), pp. 366–94.

and voluntary character (liberality at gunpoint is more usually described as robbery), the same voluntary character did not apply to justice. Justice, Smith emphasized, was the only virtue that would retain its character even when it was backed up by force, usually in the form of the power and authority of the state. This was why justice was not quite the same as the other virtues. If it was an attribute of a person or the quality of an individual, it could also be described equally readily as a quality of a relationship or a property of a system. Justice, in short, had as much to do with the rule of law and the concept of a legal system as with the actions and behaviour of individuals, peoples, or nations. This, in the second place, meant that justice could be associated with two, radically different, types of evaluation. One set of evaluations applied to human actions and the feelings of approbation or disapprobation involved in assessments of their various possible causes, motives, and effects. But another set of evaluations applied to human behaviour and the more rational range of assessments of the various possible consequences of different types of behaviour. Smith's use of the distinction, one that Reddie echoed, was a variation on the old Roman and Ciceronian distinction between the *honestum*, or honourable, and the *utile*, or useful.[53] Human actions could be subject to either type of evaluation, and this in turn meant that the evaluations themselves would differ. One would centre on justice itself, but the other would centre on expediency or utility. The most obvious example of how in practice the distinction could work was in a market society. Here, face-to-face transactions did not have to occur. But there would still be rules and procedures, and their violation could still have consequences. In this case, however, the consequences would not necessarily be backed up by legal sanctions because questions of utility could apply to commercial relationships that stretched beyond the boundaries of any single state or legal system. The concept of justice was, in short, something that was likely to exist in several different ways. It could exist with or without a state, and could be associated with what was either honourable or useful. It was a product of rules but was also a product of judgment.

Reddie made it clear that he had adopted this dual approach to the subject of justice from a book entitled *A General View of the Progress of Ethical Philosophy* published by Sir James Mackintosh in 1831. Mackintosh (who died the following year) was associated quite closely with the Coppet group. He had known Benjamin Constant when both were students at the University of Edinburgh during the 1780s, and also became Sismondi's brother-in-law when they each married one of the three Allen sisters (the third sister married one

---

53. James Reddie, *Inquiries Elementary and Historical in the Science of Law* (London, 1840), p. 16. Unless otherwise stated, reference will always be to the first edition.

of Josiah Wedgwood's sons) towards the end of the eighteenth century. In his book, Mackintosh made it clear that previous moral theorists had not been sufficiently clear in differentiating between what he said were "two perfectly distinct subjects: 1. The nature of the distinction between right and wrong in human conduct, and 2. The nature of those feelings with which right and wrong are contemplated by human beings."[54] The latter, he continued, gesturing towards Smith, had been called *The Theory of Moral Sentiments*, while the former amounted to investigating the criteria of morality itself. It was easy, Mackintosh acknowledged, to conflate the two subjects by asserting, as William Paley had done, that the principle of a moral sense was opposed to the principle of utility, as if the two principles referred to the same object of moral theory. A moral sense, however, was something that approved of what was right and condemned what was wrong because it could identify something about the qualities of an action. Utility, on the other hand, was a claim about the consequences of an action rather than whether the action itself was right or wrong. "As these affirmations relate to different subjects," Mackintosh concluded (in a passage that Reddie quoted), "they cannot be opposed to each other any more than the solidity of earth is inconsistent with the fluidity of water and a very little reflection will show it to be easily conceivable that they may both be true."[55] People could, spontaneously, approve or disapprove of certain actions on the basis of their feelings, but they could also use their reason to claim that the consequences of those actions were compatible or incompatible with general happiness or well-being.

In pointing out the difference, Mackintosh had, in a sense, dispelled the Adam Smith Problem before it existed. Reddie was not slow to point out its implications. "Indeed, in one vast department of human affairs," he wrote, "the principle of general expediency is the chief and almost the only moral criterion to which recourse can be had. In the complex details of political arrangement, in the intercourse of nations, the moral feeling which serves as a rule of conduct to the individual, although not silent, speaks with a comparatively feeble voice. We are led by a sort of moral impulse to perform the various duties of private life, but this guide in a great measure deserts us when we investigate the legislative, executive, judicial and economical establishments of civil society or the reciprocal transactions of independent states."[56] The theory of utility (or expediency) was not an alternative to a virtue-oriented theory of justice. They were different

---

54. James Mackintosh, *A General View of the Progress of Ethical Philosophy* [1831] (Philadelphia, 1834), p. 12.

55. Ibid., p. 13.

56. Reddie, *Inquiries*, p. 10.

aspects of the same thing, and, as Reddie pointed out, both, in their different ways and in their different settings, were true. "While," he wrote, "with an Epicurus, a Hume or a Bentham," we can calculate pains and pleasures, we could also "with a Plato, a Marcus Aurelius, or a Seneca, with a Fénelon, a Shaftesbury, a Smith or a Brown" show "an ardent love and admiration of that incorruptible integrity, that disinterested and generous beneficence, that devoted and enlightened patriotism which are maintained and pursued solely as the right and becoming exercise by man of the powers delegated to him by his all-perfect creator."[57] The two were complementary, not incompatible.

Law, Reddie wrote in the second edition of his book, could be considered as a branch of morality that was centred on the virtue of justice. But if this was the case, law was a rather special branch of morality because its precepts operated "under the marked distinction (which Dr Adam Smith, it is believed, first pointed out in this country) that its rules are susceptible of enforcement, whereas compulsion is quite inconsistent with and even repugnant to the nature of the other virtues and would be destructive of their moral value."[58] In this respect, the law was concerned with mankind not as rational or moral beings, but rather "as sentient beings, dependent for their subsistence, clothing and shelter on their labour and on the produce of the earth, natural and industrial." In this context, the law was a body of rules arising from "circumstances, necessity or urgent general expediency" and for "the safety, security and welfare of each individual and for the prosperity of the whole of these individuals united into one community." It relied for its enforcement on "the united strength of the community concentrated in the state or government," and this collective capacity was, in turn, put into effect "not so much by appealing to moral sentiment and the benevolent feelings of our nature as by operating, directly or indirectly, corporeally and mentally, upon the selfish feelings and the regard which every individual has for his own safety and welfare."[59] Here, alongside Smith, Reddie now signalled Immanuel Kant as the prime source of this identification of the law with expediency. This view of law "as separate and distinct from, and independent of, morality," he wrote, "seems in modern times to have been first prominently brought forward by the German philosopher Kant, though perhaps it is only a more full development of the *necessitas* or *ratio juris* of the Roman Law."[60]

57. Ibid., p. 14.
58. Reddie, *Inquiries* (2nd ed.), p. 223.
59. Ibid., p. 224.
60. Ibid., pp. 224–25. The same point about Kant as the first to make a sharp distinction between morality and the law was made by the French law professor William Bélime in his *Philosophie du droit, ou cours d'introduction à la science du droit*, 2 vols. (Paris, 1855), 1:10: "C'est

Reddie's identification of Kant with Roman law had the effect of bringing Kant's moral and political thought into alignment with the thought of Friedrich Carl von Savigny and the German historical school of law (and, as August Oncken was later to point out, of setting the German historical school of economics against both Kant and Smith). As Reddie emphasized, particularly in the second edition of his book, much of his own legal thinking owed a great deal to Savigny. This applied as much to Savigny's use of Kant as to the substance of Savigny's own legal thought. To explain what they had in common, Reddie quoted a long passage from the first volume of Savigny's *System of Modern Roman Law* in which the German law professor had described the law as something that established "an invisible line of demarcation" that enabled all individuals to enjoy "a secure and free space" as the basis of their dealings with others. The image revealed both the connection and the difference between the law and morality. "Law," Savigny wrote, "is subservient to morality, not because it accomplishes its precepts, but because its power secures to every individual the exercise and exhibition of his free will."[61] It was, therefore, a kind of carapace that allowed morality to function in much the same sense as in Kant's concept of autonomy. This, Savigny continued, meant that there was no contradiction if the continued existence of the law maintained "the immoral exercise" of a right that had been previously recognized as an actual right because, he explained, "the existence of law is a consequence of the imperfection of our condition: not an accidental historical imperfection, but such an one as is inseparably connected with the present stage of our existence." This idea too was very compatible with Kant's historical vision.

From this perspective, the law functioned as a protective shield covering the development of humanity. It was, in this sense, more than a simple remedy for injustice and more than a weapon to be used to right a wrong. As Savigny had emphasized, those who adopted this latter approach to the law and its functions "hazard a negative" because the implication of their claim was that if wrongs were righted and injustice was eliminated, then the state and its laws would no longer be necessary. "To them," Savigny wrote, "the state appears as a necessary weapon of defence which might itself disappear or be dispensed with as superfluous under the presupposition of an extended or enlarged sense or feeling of right, or justice, or moral duty. Instead of that, the state, according to our view, would in that case, exhibit itself only

au surplus un des principaux services de Kant que d'avoir le premier tracé d'une main ferme cette importante distinction,"

61. Reddie, *Inquiries* (2nd ed.), p. 225. The passage was taken from Savigny's *System des Heutigen Römischen Rechts*, which began to appear in 1840. See Friedrich Carl von Savigny, *System des Heutigen Römischen Rechts* (Berlin 1840), §52.

the more noble and powerful."[62] It was, particularly coming from Savigny, a surprisingly Hegelian extrapolation from Kant's initial description of the relationship between the law and freedom. Reddie endorsed them both not only because, on either interpretation, the two characterizations of the law underpinned the difference between the law and morality, but also because both of the characterizations made by Savigny and Kant made it clear that there was no further form of human association lying somewhere beyond the state. There was, therefore, no reason or need to expect the law to be replaced by morality itself or even, as Savigny had written, to reinforce the law by providing moral instruction. Here, despite his admiration for Savigny, Reddie hesitated. On this basis, it now seemed possible that even Savigny was ultimately willing to collapse the law into morality or morality into the law. Reddie made it clear that he preferred to cleave to the more consistent distinctions made by Smith and Kant. As Smith had shown, Reddie wrote, the law was "a branch of the moral virtue of justice which admits of compulsory regulation."[63] This meant that the law had two types of responsibility and two types of goal: one act-based and the other rule-based; one concerned with justice, the other with utility. From this perspective, Oncken's intuition was right, provided that the two different ways of thinking about the law were not collapsed into one. In reality, and as was the case with Kant, Smith's theory of justice straddled them both. In the original German and Swiss context in which the Adam Smith Problem took shape, collapsing the one into the other—or merging legality with morality—meant signing up either to the German historical school of law, with its emphasis on Roman law and the entitlements of ownership, or to the German historical school of economics, with its emphasis on Germanic law and the morality of the *Genossenschaft*.

The dual quality of Smith's theory of justice, with its emphasis on both sides of the Ciceronian categories of the *honestum* and the *utile*, makes it possible to avoid a choice between the two best-known recent interpretations of the relationship between needs and justice in Smith's moral and political theory. The first, made by Istvan Hont and Michael Ignatieff, emphasized the distinction between the compulsory quality of justice and the voluntary character of virtue in the thought of the tradition of modern natural jurisprudence associated with both Grotius and Smith. The second, made by Samuel Fleischacker (with Hont and Ignatieff very much in his sights), emphasized the similarity between Grotian and non-Grotian versions of

62. Reddie, *Inquiries* (2nd ed.), p. 226.
63. Ibid., p. 228.

natural law, at least in terms of their common endorsement of the kind of action required to ensure that needs and justice were kept in the right moral alignment (this was one reason why Grotius and his followers were sometimes known as "socialists" until well into the nineteenth century).[64] For Hont and Ignatieff, conditions of scarcity of basic food supplies were an exceptional occurrence that, unusually, allowed human survival needs to trump property rights. For Fleischacker, the distinction between norms and exceptions where food supplies were concerned was a standard feature of early modern European jurisprudence, which meant that there was nothing unusual in Smith's treatment of the subordination of property rights to the right to life. To Fleischacker, Smith's real achievement was to develop a self-standing theory of distributive justice that, by definition, superseded the earlier opposition between norms and exceptions. For Smith, at least on Mackintosh's interpretation, what was at issue was not a concept of distributive justice, nor a distinction between justice and virtue, but a judgment about when and where to apply a rule-based or an act-based concept of justice. According to Dugald Stewart, quoting Smith's former student John Millar, Smith in his lectures on moral philosophy at Glasgow University "followed the plan that seems to be suggested by Montesquieu; endeavouring to trace the gradual progress of jurisprudence, both public and private, from the rudest to the most refined ages, and to point out the effects of those arts which contribute to subsistence and to the accumulation of property, in producing correspondent improvements or alterations in law and government." He had planned to publish this account of the development of laws and government, but it was instead no more than the final part of his lectures, centred on "those political regulations which are founded not upon the principle of *justice*, but that of *expediency*," which turned out to be the only part of Smith's lecture course that became available for public inspection.[65] From this perspective, Smith took justice and expediency to entail two distinct set of political regulations. Those based on the principle of expediency formed the subject matter of the *Wealth of Nations*, while the only traces of the unpublished examination of laws and government based on the principle of justice were to be found in the final edition of the *Theory of Moral Sentiments*. As Reddie recognized, justice sometimes had to trump expediency, but most of the time, expediency would be enough.

64. For one, relatively late example, see Bélime, *Philosophie du droit*, vol. 1, p. 11 n. 1.

65. Dugald Stewart, *An Account of the Life and Writings of Adam Smith* [1793], in *Biographical Memoirs of Adam Smith, William Robertson and Thomas Reid*, ed. Sir William Hamilton (Edinburgh, 1858), p. 12.

Henry Sumner Maine and the Properties of Roman Law

Reddie's strikingly positive endorsement of Roman law and his unhesitating acceptance of the compatibility between Roman law and Kant's system were echoed a generation later in the work of the British historian and law professor Henry Sumner Maine (1822–1888). There are several noticeable parallels between Savigny's thought and Maine's.[66] Where Savigny's thought owed some of its content and direction to an extended intellectual dialogue with Georg Wilhelm Friedrich Hegel and, more directly, with Hegel's follower Edouard Gans, Maine's thought owed some of *its* content and direction to an extended intellectual dialogue with Jeremy Bentham and, more directly, with Bentham's follower John Austin. The parallel is most apparent on the subject of legal codification, with Hegel and Bentham (and, a fortiori, Gans and Austin) favouring the existence of a comprehensive legal code, and with Savigny and Maine objecting to anything like this type of codification. In this sense, Bentham was to Maine as Hegel was to Savigny with, in each case, the former serving as an intellectual foil to the latter. The parallel on codification can be extended, by a further step, to the subject of sovereignty and, consequently, to each pair's assessments of the nature of a state. For Hegel, as for Bentham, sovereignty was unitary and indivisible, with commensurate implications for thinking about the nature and institutional structure of a state, while for Maine, as for Savigny, neither of these descriptions of either sovereignty or the state had to apply, at least axiomatically. The parallel could also, equally logically, encompass the subject of the law, with both Savigny and Maine highlighting the importance of Roman law and its continuing salience to modern European economic and social arrangements, but with Bentham and Hegel emphasizing the need for a different and distinctively modern legal system to fit the same economic and social arrangements.

Here, however, the symmetrical pattern of opposing positions begins to break down because both Savigny and Maine were as committed to a progressive conception of history as were Bentham and Hegel. Maine in fact gave the idea of historical progress a significant twist by introducing a distinction between what he called "stationary and progressive societies" as the basis of his own version of the idea. He set out this version most fully in his best-known

66. On Maine, see M. E. Grant Duff, *The Life and Speeches of Sir Henry Maine* (London, 1892); George Feaver, *From Status to Contract: A Biography of Sir Henry Maine 1822–1888* (London, Longmans, 1969); Stefan Collini, *Public Moralists* (Oxford, OUP, 1991), pp. 251–80; Michael Lobban, "Was There a Nineteenth-Century 'English School of Jurisprudence'?" *Legal History* 16 (1995): 39–62, and his "The Varieties of Legal History," *Clio@Thémis* 5 (2012): 1–29; together with Alan Diamond, ed., *The Victorian Achievement of Sir Henry Maine* (Cambridge, CUP, 1991).

book, *Ancient Law*, in 1861. The most "remarkable" feature of progressive societies, he wrote there, was "their extreme fewness," a fact, he commented, that had barely been noticed by modern students of different societies. In spite of overwhelming evidence to support the proposition, Maine continued, "it is most difficult for a citizen of western Europe to bring thoroughly home to himself the truth that the civilization that surrounds him is a rare exception in the history of the world."[67] The claim echoed the provocative assertion made over a century earlier in 1748 by Montesquieu in *The Spirit of Laws*, and endorsed in 1762 by Jean-Jacques Rousseau in his *Social Contract*, that "liberty, not being the fruit of every climate, is not accessible to all peoples." The "more we consider this principle established by Montesquieu," Rousseau wrote, "the more we perceive its truth."[68] Liberty is not, of course, civilization, but for Maine, as for Montesquieu and Rousseau a century earlier, both conditions were historical outliers. For Maine, writing long after Montesquieu and Rousseau, and in the wake of Hegel and Savigny, the basis of this assessment of the exceptional character of civilization was quite similar to those available from Montesquieu and Rousseau. For them, liberty in its several different guises was the product of a complex interrelationship of political institutions, private property, and direct taxation. For Maine, civilization was the product of a more deep-seated set of legal preconditions underlying much the same combination of political institutions, private property, and direct taxation. These preconditions were in fact the basis of the process that Maine, famously, summed up as "a movement *from Status to Contract*."[69] As he went on to show, it was this movement from status to contract that was the hallmark of progressive societies. Oddly, however, both the beginning and end of the movement were supplied by Roman law.

The significance that Maine attached to Roman law meant that his examination of the movement from status to contract was not really based upon a story about the formation of private property, the growth of individualism, and the emergence of unitary sovereign states. These developments were, certainly, part of the story and, equally certainly, had played a major part in both Europe's rise to global power and the modern competition for empire. But the real story was a story about the peculiar properties of Roman law and the prospects for domestic and international stability that it housed. This focus on law and

67. Henry Sumner Maine, *Ancient Law* [1861], ed. Lawrence Rosen (Tucson, U of Arizona Press, 1986), p. 21. Henceforth Maine, *AL*, followed by the page number(s).

68. "La liberté n'étant pas un fruit de tous les climats n'est pas à la portée de tous les peuples. Plus on médite ce principe établi par Montesquieu, plus on en sent la vérité." Rousseau, *Social Contract*, bk. 3, ch. 8, in Rousseau, *Collected Writings*, 4:181.

69. Maine, *AL*, p. 165.

legality meant that if Maine was an imperialist, he was an imperialist in much the same sense that David Hume was a Whig. Just as Hume's account of the origins of justice, private property, and civil liberty paid almost no attention to the standard components of Whig historiography, so Maine's analysis of the properties of progressive societies dispensed with almost all the standard components of imperial entitlement. Empire could be dropped, but the properties of progressive societies would remain.[70] "The western world," Maine wrote in his *Lectures on the Early History of Institutions* in 1874, "must be conceived as having undergone two sets of changes. The states of modern Europe must be conceived as having been formed in a manner different from the great empires of antiquity (save one), and from the modern empires and kingdoms of the East, and a new order of ideas on the subject of *legislation* must be conceived as having been introduced into the world through the empire of the Romans."[71] A few paragraphs later, he amplified on the point about the Roman Empire (which was the referent of the phrase "save one") by way of a vivid analogy. "There is much reason to believe," he wrote, "that the Roman Empire was the source of the influences which have led, immediately or ultimately, to the formation of highly-centralised, actively legislating, states. It was the first great dominion which did not merely tax, but legislated also." In doing so, it not only established law; it also destroyed custom. As a result, Maine concluded, "a vast and miscellaneous mass of customary law was broken up and replaced by new institutions. Seen in this light, the Roman empire is accurately described in the Prophecy of Daniel. It devoured, broke in pieces, and stamped the residue with its feet."[72]

Superficially, Maine's version of the part played by Roman law in the movement from status to contract was quite similar to Savigny's and, although he did not refer to Savigny's publications very frequently, he made no secret of his admiration for his work. In one respect, however, Maine introduced an entirely new element into their otherwise similar treatment of the relationship between Roman law and modern economic and social arrangements. This was the natural jurisprudence of the seventeenth-century Dutch humanist Hugo Grotius. For Maine, Grotian natural law was a continuation of Roman law

70. For a range of well-balanced assessments of Maine's thought, see the contributions by Sandra den Otter, Karuna Mantena, Casper Sylvest, and Gareth Stedman Jones to Duncan Bell, ed., *Victorian Visions of Global Order: Empire and International Relations in Nineteenth-Century Political Thought* (Cambridge, CUP, 2007). None, however, quite succeeds in specifying the unusual quality of the connection that Maine made between Roman law and international law.

71. Henry Sumner Maine, *Lectures on the Early History of Institutions* [1874]. 7th ed. (London, 1905), pp. 385–86.

72. Ibid., pp. 390–91.

because, like Roman law when Rome was simply a city-state, it had a set of qualities and properties that allowed it to adapt to an unusually wide variety of social and economic conditions and circumstances. This combination of legal authority and internal adaptability was, fundamentally, why Roman law had survived the fall of the Roman Empire, and why its revival as Grotian natural law had made it the basis of modern international law. In this respect, Maine's approach to the combination of legal history and political theory was redolent of Hume and Smith.

The peculiar property of Roman law and Grotian natural law was that, while both were lawful, neither seemed, at least at some fundamental level, to require the legitimating authority and the coercive power of a sovereign state. The effects of this initial quality were most striking in the case of international law, and, as Maine went to some lengths to show, international law could be taken to be a paradigmatic case of how the distinctive properties of Roman law made it a comprehensive legal system that, somehow, could straddle the boundary separating private or municipal law from international law. At first sight, the idea of international law seems to presuppose the existence of a world state because, in its absence, sovereignty would necessarily be an attribute of more than one state, and states, together with their statute laws, are bounded and particular. In this sense, the idea of international law would have to be an oxymoron, but in another sense it still seems to be binding. It was this paradoxical combination of legality without sovereignty, Maine claimed, that was the real source of the movement from status to contract in progressive societies. Roman law was not purely customary because it relied on something more than precedent, memory, and forensic skill. Nor, however, was it purely statutory because it owed its authority as much to its internally organized conceptual architecture as it did to any externally generated, but unavoidably particular, imperative mandate. The distinctive attribute of Roman law was that it seemed to have been able to overcome, or to avoid, these divisive particularities. It was lawful because it was legal, irrespective of whether it was customary or statutory.

Maine introduced the subject of the relationship between Roman law and Grotian natural law in his very first publication, an essay entitled "Roman Law and Legal Education" published in 1856 in a volume entitled *Cambridge Essays contributed by Members of the University.* He did so in far more than a technical sense. "If," he wrote,

> international law be not studied historically—if we fail to comprehend, first the influence of certain theories of the Roman jurisconsults on the mind of Hugo Grotius and, next, the influence of the great book of Grotius on international jurisprudence—we lose at once all chance of comprehending

that body of rules which alone protects the European commonwealth from permanent anarchy, we blind ourselves to the principles by conforming to which it coheres, we can understand neither its strength nor its weakness, nor can we separate those arrangements which can be safely modified from those which cannot be touched without shaking the whole fabric to pieces.[73]

Maine's prime concern was with rules, rather than empire, and with the rule of law rather than the power of states. The subjects were closely connected but, as Maine set out to show, this was why it was important to understand how they could be distinguished. This, it could be said, was his life's work, beginning with "Roman Law and Legal Education" in 1856 and ending with the posthumous publication of *International Law* in 1888.

Maine began his examination of the mutation of Roman law into Grotian natural law in "Roman Law and Legal Education." He picked up and developed its argument five years later in the penultimate chapter of *Ancient Law*. Most of the leading ideas of *Ancient Law* were, however, already visible in the earlier essay, including the conceptual framework underpinning the claim about the relationship between progressive societies and the movement from status to contract that is now associated largely with the later work. The whole process, Maine emphasized in the essay, was connected to the distinctive attributes of Roman law and the way that these attributes had been carried over into the Grotian version of natural law. Roman law itself, Maine wrote, was "distinguished before all others by its symmetry and its close correspondence with fundamental rules." Almost from the beginning, he claimed, it was to law what mathematics had become to thinking about relations of space.[74] This seemed to imply that the revival of Roman law in the hands of Grotius and his followers was more of a reversion to first principles than a genuine novelty. But, Maine emphasized, the Grotian revival of Roman law had also established a real and durable division in moral and legal thought. With the consolidation of Christianity after the fall of the Roman Empire, both law and moral theory had been part of theology and had been subsumed under the broader authority of the teachings of the church. But, with the Reformation of the sixteenth century, things began to change. "Shortly after the Reformation," Maine wrote, "we find

73. Henry Sumner Maine, "Roman Law and Legal Education," in *Cambridge Essays contributed by Members of the University* (London, 1856), pp. 1–29 (here p. 12). It was reprinted in the third and subsequent editions of Maine's *Village Communities in the East and West* (London, 1876), pp. 330–83. Much of its content was earlier reproduced, more or less verbatim, in the fourth and ninth chapters of *Ancient Law*.

74. Maine, "Roman Law and Legal Education," pp. 2, 4.

two great schools of thought dividing this class of subjects between them."[75] One was casuistry; the other was natural jurisprudence. Modern law was essentially a product of the gradual displacement of the former by the latter and, by extension, a product of the Grotian transformation of Roman law.

Casuistry, Maine wrote, was a legacy of the great theological treatises of the Middle Ages. Although these treatises did not exclude the idea of natural law from their brief, their prime concern was with the relationship between this life and the next and, more immediately, with the related subjects of sin, salvation, and damnation. In this context, Roman law took second place to theological discussion of the philosophy of right and wrong and, in particular, to discussions of the distinction between mortal and venial sin.[76] The increasingly elaborate body of discussion of how, when, and where to draw a line between the two formed the core of casuistry, especially in the centuries after the Reformation. Casuistry flourished, Maine wrote, mainly in response to the rigidity and narrowness of Protestantism, but gradually, between the early sixteenth and the late seventeenth centuries, it overreached itself, and when it did, it was abruptly discredited by satire, most famously by Blaise Pascal's memorable *Provincial Letters*. "The whole field of ethical science," Maine commented, "was thus left at the exclusive command of the writers who followed Grotius; and it still exhibits, in an extraordinary degree, the traces of that entanglement with Roman law which is sometimes imputed as a fault and sometimes as the highest of its recommendations to the Grotian theory."[77] On Maine's terms, the overlap between Roman law and Grotian natural jurisprudence was the key both to the continued development of progressive societies and, given the multiplicity of even a small number of progressive societies, to the potential for stability of international relations.

The synthesis between Roman law and Grotian natural law, Maine argued, was peculiarly compatible with the property-based, market-oriented, and individualistic features of the modern world. This, in part, was an effect of the clarity and conceptual consistency of Roman law, and these qualities were, in turn, an effect of its unusually precocious development. In contradistinction to Elizabethan England, for example, where, Maine asserted, the arts, literature, science, and politics had all claimed their share of "the national intellect," the law had been almost unchallenged as a career open to talent and ability in the centuries that began with Rome's Augustan Age. It had, therefore, acquired a level of sophistication that had no modern equivalent. This, Maine argued,

75. Maine, *AL*, p. 338.
76. Maine, "Roman Law and Legal Education," p. 5.
77. Ibid, p. 6.

was why, despite the massive presence of the common law in English economic and social life, Roman law was still relevant to an English legal education. Studying Roman law alongside the common law was a requirement not because "they were *once* alike" but "because they *will be* alike."[78] This, at least in part, was because Roman law was a compact and integrated system of "express written rules," while the common law was a ramifying system of cases and precedents. The "wonderful terminology" of the former, with its precise conceptual renditions of terms like "obligation," "convention," "contract," "consent," "possession," or "prescription," made it a kind of "short-hand of jurisprudence" with no real equivalence in the common law lexicon.[79] But the main reason for studying Roman law was that, right from the start, it was already international law. This, Maine claimed, was because it had a modular and flexible quality that lent itself readily to the normative requirements of a divided world. It had acquired this quality during the first epoch of the Roman Empire, between the triumph of Augustus and about AD 300, when, as Maine put it in his *International Law*, Roman law had been transformed "from a technical to a plastic system."[80] It was this plasticity that made it possible for something like international law to exist in a world of sovereign states.

The mechanism underlying the transformation of Roman law from something technical into something plastic was the gradual substitution of contracts for commands and the changes in the obligations produced by the switch from a top-down to a more reciprocal type of relationship. In the beginning, Maine argued, and in very simple societies, laws were commands. The model of this type of relationship was scripture and the imperatives of the Decalogue that it contained. God, in this rendition, was the Father, just as in early social arrangements the rulers of households, clans, or groups of kin were patriarchs. The distinctive feature of this type of command-based authority was that it was personal. It applied primarily to people and, by extension, to their possessions, but could apply only with much greater difficulty to inanimate objects like a river, a tree, or the land. This, Maine argued, was why authority over inanimate objects relied more usually on a mixture of force, ritual, and custom. Force secured their possession; ritual identified their owners; and custom supplied continuity from one generation to the next. Together, the combination of force, ritual, and custom formed the basis of stationary societies. They were stationary, Maine claimed, because force, ritual, and custom not only left little room for individual decision making and choice but also provided very few resources

78. Ibid., p. 2.

79. Ibid., pp. 11, 20.

80. Henry Sumner Maine, *International Law* (London 1888), pp. 28–29.

for any positive engagements with the outside world. In this sense, the internal life of a world made up of stationary societies was rather like the internal life of a world made up of sovereign states. It was a world made up of very rigid vertical divisions between its various components because nothing that it contained could supply a durable link interconnecting the many different social units scattered across what might otherwise be a densely populated human environment. Stationary societies were more like aggregations than associations and, since this was the case, their underlying principle was autarchy.

On Maine's terms, all the apparently distinctive features and problems of international law were already visible in stationary societies. Common to both was the absence of any mechanism able to transmit authority beyond a boundary. Just as it was hard to see how to reconcile the idea of international law with the existence of sovereign states, so it was equally hard to see how to reconcile the comprehensive idea of a law with the particular authority of a specific command. Commands, like sovereignty, applied locally. International law, however, applied globally. But, without international sovereignty, it was hard to see how it could be applied, just as, without something beyond patriarchal authority, it was hard to identify something general beyond a command-based system of law. The boundaries of the household, clan, or community seemed to set the boundaries of the law. "Ancient jurisprudence," Maine wrote, "if a perhaps deceptive comparison may be employed, may be likened to international law, filling nothing as it were except the interstices between the great groups which are the atoms of society."[81] But Roman law had somehow managed to become legal beyond its own boundaries. The origins of this mysterious capacity were more than a product of empire because, Maine argued, Roman law had acquired the special property of being legal even though it was not the work of a legislator, and despite the fact that its provisions coexisted with local custom. From this perspective, it was a real-world example of how to think about the origins and development of a system of international law. And, since international law began as a bridge between self-sufficient households and autarchic communities, it also meant that Roman law was the prime example of a legal system that was compatible with a progressive society.

Maine supplied the fullest explanation of why Roman law was the key to the switch from status to contract in the ninth chapter of *Ancient Law*, the chapter dealing with the early history of contract. The explanation centred on property and the transition, as Maine put it, from "viewing the rights of property as exclusively sacred to looking upon the rights growing out of the mere unilateral repose of confidence as entitled to the protection of the penal

81. Maine, *AL*, p. 161.

law."[82] Property, he explained, began as something sacred but turned into a simple belief. In its first guise, it belonged to the ceremonial life of a people, but in its second guise it belonged to a system based mainly on trust backed up by the penal law. The process that involved the substitution of property in its second guise for property in its first began, Maine explained, on the frontiers of households or communities, and the command-based systems of law that they housed. In this sense, as he put it in *International Law*, the law of nations began as "mere market law."[83] It arose when the existence of separate households or different communities meant that the law had no purchase in disputes over matters that straddled their respective boundaries. Roman law, unusually, was able to bridge the gap. It could do so, Maine argued, because it had available a concept called "a contract of the law of nations" (*ius gentium*) that had developed alongside the purely local content of the original Roman version of natural law. Initially, the concept had nothing to do with relations between states or international law in the modern senses of the terms. It was instead a product of disputes over the types of market- or property-related arrangements like credit, debt, sale, lease, hiring, or inheritance that arose among the members of different households or communities. It was the outcome of efforts to reconcile Roman law with those of the many other Italian communities that came to be involved with Rome and the activities of its people by identifying a *ius gentium*, or a body of law that could encompass several different local legal arrangements.

Roman law, Maine argued, had acquired this capacity and, with it, an unusual ability to exercise authority in disputes straddling different legal jurisdictions. It had done so because it housed the component parts of what had once been an integrated ceremonial nexus that governed the performance of property-based transactions. Over time, these components had become increasingly differentiated from one another, and, as they did, each component acquired a more general and abstract quality. The original nexus was formed by a combination of conveyance and contract. The combination of these two types of legal act meant that there was almost no difference between them because transfers of property, or conveyances, required a cluster of ceremonial procedures before they could be legal. The contractual side of the transfer was therefore subordinate to the ceremonial side of the conveyance because conveyance itself required a number of variously verbal, literal, real, and consensual ceremonial steps before the whole, implicitly contractual transactional nexus was completed. Gradually, Maine claimed, this nexus began to break down and "a

82. Ibid., p. 298.
83. Maine, *International Law*, p. 28.

change from the general to the special" began to take place as "ancient conceptions" and "ancient terms" were "subjected to a process of gradual specialisation," and as "the subordinate conceptions" that were originally part of the conveyance-contract nexus "gradually disengaged themselves" and "the old general terms" gave way to "special appellations."[84] The process meant that over time the concept of a contract was severed from that of a conveyance.[85] The sequential quality of the process of differentiation was easiest to see in the fourth, consensual, stage of a transaction. Since a consensual transaction minimally required an agreement of wills, this part of the transaction could be differentiated readily from the other components of the whole nexus. Here, the key concept—and the key to the process of differentiation—was the Roman-law concept of a quasi-contract.[86] This was the name given to a transaction that straddled two or more different jurisdictions. Since the jurisdictions were different, a quasi-contract could not be a contract. But since it still looked like a contract, it was possible to identify something about the attribute responsible for the apparent similarity by singling out the final, consensual, step of the nexus made up of conveyances and contracts. Whatever else it was, a quasi-contract was formed by a consensual will, and it was this aspect of the nexus that could be taken to be the evidence of something legally binding despite the absence of anything like a common legal authority.

With this established, Maine wrote, "the motion of the will which constitutes agreement was now completely insulated and became the subject of separate contemplation. Forms were entirely separated from the notion of contract and external acts were only regarded as symbols of the internal act of volition." The result, as he put it in his lectures on international law, was that "the old law of nations" gradually became "an ideal system especially distinguished by simplicity and symmetry and became a standard for the legal institutions of all systems of jurisprudence."[87] As the process unfolded, it was the sign of an internal act rather than the observance of an external form that could be taken to be the real hallmark of a transaction, and, since the combination of a will and an act did not call for authorization or prohibition by an initial command, something like a contract could be recognized among members of different communities, societies, or nations. Although there is no reason to think that Maine or Lassalle had any knowledge of one another, the arguments of their respective publications relied heavily on the concept of a

84. Maine, *AL*, pp. 305–6.
85. Ibid., p. 312.
86. Ibid., pp. 332–36.
87. Maine, *International Law*, p. 30.

subjective right. Ultimately, Maine claimed, it was a thought like this that allowed legal thought to become distinguished from poetry and history or philosophy and science in the thought of the West. "I can only express my surprise," he wrote somewhat hyperbolically, "at the scantiness of the attention that has been given to the difference between Western ideas and Eastern, between Western theology and Eastern, caused by the presence of a new ingredient." The ingredient in question was the law, and, in this respect, Roman law was "the one intellectual result of Roman civilization."[88]

The same idea, Maine argued, applied to international law in the proper sense. Just as Roman law supplied a framework for thinking about legality independently of custom or statute, so it had also supplied a foundation for a system of international law despite the existence of a world made up of separate sovereign states. International law, like Roman law itself, did not work solely by way of commands, but also by way of an organized system of rules. This, Maine explained, was why, contrary to the claims of Bentham and Austin, the phrase "the rule of law" had a real meaning not only within, but also beyond, the boundaries of sovereign states.[89] The combination of territory and sovereignty, he argued, was relatively recent in origin because territorial sovereignty itself was derivative rather than foundational. The mechanism responsible for its development had, in fact, been supplied by feudalism and by the gradual disintegration of the collective character of the village community as a system of government, first into a system of common ownership of landed property, and then into a multitude of privately owned individual units. As Maine put it succinctly, "the feudalization of Europe" had the effect of "converting the Mark into the Manor and the Village-Community into the Fief."[90] In this process, Roman law had again played the key part. As Maine explained in a lecture on the process of feudalization, it contained a number of different terms that, initially, referred to goods that could be commonly enjoyed, like *res nullius, res publici usus, res omnium* or *universorum*.[91] Their existence made it easier to distinguish goods that could be commonly owned from those that belonged to individual households, and, in a further step, to refer to the owners of the first type of goods as having a special status, including, ultimately, the status of sovereign.

As the process unfolded, sovereignty turned from something purely personal into something more fully territorial. Originally, Maine argued, the concept of sovereignty applied solely to individuals in positions of authority

88. Maine, *AL*, pp. 331–32.
89. Maine, *International Law*, pp. 48–49.
90. Maine, *Lectures on the Early History of Institutions*, p. 85.
91. Maine, *Village Communities*, p. 142.

and power. A sovereign was a king, a queen, an emperor, or a leader, and since sovereignty was personal, it was not a concept that was readily applicable to territory or to the authority of something impersonal, like a state. "Territorial sovereignty," Maine wrote in a famous passage in *Ancient Law* "—the view which connects sovereignty with the possession of a limited portion of the earth's surface—was distinctly an offshoot of *feudalism*. This might have been expected *a priori*, for it was feudalism which for the first time linked personal duties, and by consequence personal rights, to the ownership of land."[92] The association between sovereignty and territory developed quite slowly. But, in an analysis that was redolent of Montesquieu, Maine showed that it first occurred with the advent of the Capetian dynasty in France. "Hugues Capet and his descendants were kings in quite a new sense," he wrote, "sovereigns standing in the same relation to the soil of France as the baron to his estate, the tenant to his freehold." They were kings of France, rather than kings of the French.

It was this development, reinforced by the effect of the Reformation in causing both the papacy and the Holy Roman emperor to align together against the Protestant Reformation, that allowed Roman law to become natural law and made it possible for Grotius to describe the content of natural law in terms of Roman law itself. "It is obvious," Maine concluded, "that the speculative perfection of the Grotian system is intimately connected with that conception of territorial sovereignty which we have been discussing."

> The theory of international law assumes that commonwealths are, relative to each other, in a state of nature; but the component atoms of natural society must, by the fundamental assumption, be insulated and independent of each other. If there be a higher power connecting them, however slightly and occasionally, by the claim of a common supremacy, the very conception of a common superior introduces the notion of positive law and excludes the idea of a law natural. It follows, therefore, that if the universal suzerainty of an imperial head had been admitted even in bare theory, the labours of Grotius would have been idle.... What then is the inference? It is that if there had been no such change as I have described in the estimate of sovereignty—if sovereignty had not been associated with the proprietorship of a limited portion of the earth, had not, in other words, become territorial—three parts of the Grotian theory would have been incapable of application.[93]

On Maine's terms, it was not a theory of subjective rights that was missing from Roman law or ancient Roman culture but a theory of sovereignty that

92. Maine, *AL*, p. 102.
93. Ibid., pp. 107–8.

could encompass both a ruler and all the members of the state. In addition, and in his version of the origins of the modern concept of sovereignty, what mattered was not so much its contractual as its feudal origins, just as what mattered about sovereignty itself was not so much its association with people as with territory. With Maine, there was no need for social contract theory or the combined intellectual legacies of Hobbes and Rousseau to arrive at a modern theory of a representative sovereign state. As with Montesquieu and Savigny, the legacy of Roman law was enough.

"At bottom," wrote Roscoe Pound, a once-famous Harvard University legal historian and law professor, in 1923, "Maine's theory is Hegelian."

> The idea which is realizing is liberty—free individual self-assertion. The way in which it is realized is a progress from status to contract. It is a progress away from legal institutions and legal rules and legal doctrines in which one's legally recognised claims and legally enforced duties flow from a condition in which he is put or in which he finds himself without reference to his will or of which he cannot divest himself by any manifestation of his will It is a progress toward legal institutions and rules and doctrines in which legally recognized claims flow from personality, from being a conscious free-willing human individual, and legally enforceable duties with respect to others are consequences of willed action, either in assuming the duties by some legally recognized form of undertaking or by willed culpable action or by willed action culpably carried on.[94]

It was a capacious description and one that applied an unusual label to someone who had begun his intellectual career as a champion of Roman law. It suggests something of the transformation that had taken place since the early nineteenth century. Then, in the publications of Staël, Sismondi, and the Coppet group, it had been the legacy of the Germans that had been the foundation of the institutions of the moderns. With Maine, the story turned full circle because its analytical and historical core was formed by the legacy of the Romans. But adding the legacy of the Romans to the legacy of the Germans brought back the problem of unsocial sociability that, as Kant had showed, was one of the effects of trying to use a historical starting point to establish a normative goal. From this perspective, it seemed that modern politics were both Roman and German and, as a result, that modern politics were, in fact, the politics of unsocial sociability.

94. Roscoe Pound, *Interpretations of Legal History* (New York, Macmillan, 1923), p. 89 (there is also a CUP edition of the book, also published in 1923, in which this passage appears on p. 54.

12

The Politics of Unsocial Sociability

History and Normativity

The period between the Franco-Prussian War of 1870 and the Nazi seizure of power in 1933 led to a gradual erosion of much of the content of the long-drawn-out discussion of the legacies of the Romans and the Germans, and turned those legacies into a more politically and racially charged set of dichotomies. Some of the racial stereotypes continued to be redolent of early nineteenth-century royalist and legitimist criticism. "Wherever universalism establishes its abstractions instead of, and in place of, concrete givens," wrote the Swiss music critic Robert Godet in 1913 in his introduction to his own translation of *The Foundations of the Nineteenth Century* by the racist historian Houston Stewart Chamberlain, "the crime of *lèse-réalité* begins to be perpetrated, soon followed by *lèse-humanité*, with the humanity thus lesioned being the one that is real: not man, but real human beings."[1] This was the true legacy of the Roman Empire—with its uniform legal code, its centralized system of rule, and its sustained indifference towards community. Where Rome was synonymous with imperialism, the Germans were synonymous with particularism and what Chamberlain called "the law of limitation" that was the distinguishing feature of modern, postimperial, social and institutional arrangements.[2]

By 1933 it was possible to claim, as Alfred Rosenberg and Adolf Hitler claimed, that the Greeks and the Romans were, fundamentally, Germanic peoples, and, by extension, that the real content of Roman law, here associated with the Germanic concept of the *Genossenschaft*, had been corrupted by an Etruscan and Semitic interest in individualism, materialism, and private

---

1. Houston Stewart Chamberlain, *La genèse du xixe siècle*, 2 vols. (Paris, 1913), 1:xxxviii. On Robert Godet, see Clára Móricz, *Jewish Identities: Nationalism, Racism, and Utopianism in Twentieth-Century Music* (Berkeley, U of California Press, 2008), pp. 105–13.

2. Chamberlain, *La genèse du xixe siècle*, 1:lix

property. As Article 19 of the National Socialist Party programme of 1920 put it, "We demand the substitution of German common law for Roman law. Roman law serves a materialistic world order."[3] Curiously, much the same type of evaluation was made by at least some of their opponents. "The analogy between the systems of Hitler and of ancient Rome is so striking that one might believe that Hitler alone, after two thousand years, has understood how to copy the Romans," wrote the French political thinker Simone Weil in 1939. Inversely, however, Romanists like Fustel de Coulanges came to be seen as French patriots, against the Germanism of the Nazis.[4] The different kinds of historical blindness involved in the assertions, together with the later horror generated by what the long-drawn-out argument between the Romanists and Germanists appeared to have produced, meant that much of the content and purposes of those earlier arguments have largely disappeared from the history and historiography of the nineteenth century. One effect of this loss of historical memory has been that much of the more recent history and historiography of political thought has begun, at least in analytical terms, with the problematic relationship between historical origins and normative outcomes that the original arguments were intended to supersede, and, consequently, have gone on inadvertently to repeat parts of the content of those now largely forgotten nineteenth-century discussions without knowing why they began or what they were intended to achieve. The problem is most apparent in the

3. See Johann Chapoutot, *Greeks, Romans, Germans: How the Nazis Usurped Europe's Classical Past* [2008] (Berkeley, U of California Press, 2016), especially pp. 51–97, and his "The Denaturalization of Nordic Law: Germanic Law and the Reception of Roman Law," in *Roman Law and the Idea of Europe*, ed. Kaius Tuori and Heta Björklund (London, Bloomsbury, 2019), pp. 113–25, together with his *The Law of Blood: Thinking and Acting as a Nazi* (Cambridge, MA, Belknap Press of Harvard UP, 2018). See also Julia Hell, *The Conquest of Ruins: The Third Reich and the Fall of Rome* (Chicago, U of Chicago Press, 2019) and her earlier "Imperial Ruin Gazers, or Why Did Scipio Weep," in *Ruins of Modernity*, ed. Julia Hell and Andreas Schönle (Durham, NC, Duke UP, 2010), pp. 169–92; Lucien Calvié, "Philosophie, littérature et politique: le romantisme allemand et sa critique hégélienne," *Romantisme* 182 (2018): 15–25. On the Etruscans in twentieth-century thought, see particularly the three collections edited by Marie Laurence Haack and Martin Miller: *La construction de l'étruscologie au xxe siècle* (Bordeaux, Ausonius, 2015); *Les Etrusques au temps du fascisme et du nazisme* (Bordeaux, Ausonius, 2016); and *L'étruscologie dans l'Europe d'après-guerre* (Bordeaux, Ausonius, 2017). See too Philippe Foro, ed., *L'Italie et l'antiquité du siècle des lumières à la chute du fascisme* (Toulouse, PU du Midi, 2017), and, for more on the intellectual background, see Patrick McGuiness, *Poetry and Radical Politics in Fin-de-Siècle France* (Oxford, OUP, 2015), pp. 182–232.

4. Simone Weil, "The Great Beast" [1939], in Simone Weil, *Selected Essays 1939–1943* [1962], ed. Richard Rees (Eugene, OR, WIPF and Stock, 2015), p. 101. On Fustel as a symbol of anti-Nazi Romanism, see Gérin-Ricard, *L'Histoire des Institutions Politiques de Fustel de Coulanges*, pp. 25–29.

interest in the assorted legacies of the Romans, the Greeks, the Christians, or the Hebrews and their putative bearing on modern political institutions and arrangements. But it is also visible in the range of more bleakly teleological studies of modern politics, with their stronger orientation towards one or other of the many putative political pathologies of the modern age—from democratic political sovereignty to social atomization, unaccountable bureaucracy, the tyranny of the majority, the crisis of the nation-state, and downhill, apparently, all the way from there on in.

The aim of this book has been to tell a different type of story or, rather, two different types of story. Both, however, were the largely unforeseen outcomes of chance and choice. The first is a contextually oriented story about the unintended consequences of Kant's "Idea for a Universal History with a Cosmopolitan Aim." The second is a story about creativity and opportunity that began as a reaction against the criticisms of Kant. Both were stories about human freedom and the relationship between states and human freedom. The first story began with Kant's essay and the gap that it exposed between the spatial and temporal limitations of any determinate set of human achievements and the scale and scope of the comparatively small number of rational concepts that appeared to have broken free of the boundaries of time and place. The second story began with Herder's criticism of Kant and Rousseau and the unexpected convergence between these narrowly technical philosophical and theological arguments and the broader body of moral and political debate generated by the events of the French Revolution. In this context, a significant link between the two was supplied by the concept of palingenesis and its compatibility with the idea that modern Europe had had two starting points, one with the Romans and the other with the Germans. In the hands of Herder, the German romantics, and their later French followers, the concept of palingenesis began to be used to refer to a broader range of subjects than the natural philosophy with which it had earlier been associated, and, for a time, it turned into a significant counterconcept to the disquieting teleology of Kant's *Idea of Universal History*. Something similar happened to the transformation of the old idea of a romance into the new concept of romanticism. Usually, romanticism is taken to be a reaction against the Enlightenment. In this broad sense, the assertion is mistaken. But if romanticism is taken to be a reaction against Kant's philosophy of history, the assertion is more plausible. In this more narrowly contextual interpretation romanticism was, as its authors envisaged, an effort to protect the concept of enlightenment from Kant's bleak philosophy of history, and there is a great deal of evidence, from Herder and Mendelssohn to Novalis and the Schlegel brothers, to support the claim. In this context, as Sismondi and, later, Guizot reported, the significance attached to the Romance languages, the culture of the troubadours, and their medieval ramifications as a bridge between both the North and the South and the ancients and the moderns made the content of what was romantic a further counter to Kant's philosophy of history. Where one story centred on the concept of palingenesis and its later mutation into the modern ideas of renaissance and revolution, the other story centred on the concept of metamorphosis and its later mutation, under the aegis of money, the law, and public debt, into the modern idea of reform.

By the early twentieth century, however, the reaction against Kant had turned into a more intransigent defence of community. The change can be measured by the radically different interpretations of the concepts of a *Gemeinschaft* and a *Gesellschaft* first set out by Ferdinand Tönnies in his *Gemeinschaft und Gesellschaft* (*Community and Civil Society*) in 1887. To Tönnies, "the adoption of the ready-made system of *global Roman law* has served, and still serves, to further the development of mass commercial society in a large part of the Christian-Germanic World." Its availability, he continued, "favoured all those with wealth and power, enabling them to make their wealth and power absolute and unconditional."[5] But Tönnies was also careful to emphasize that Roman law was not, in itself, an independent agent. "It was only a serviceable tool, ready to hand, employed not as a rule with deliberate calculation, but in the honest belief that it was right and appropriate."[6] The same switch from community to civil society, he pointed out, had happened in England without the presence of Roman law. A generation later, however, in the first year of the First World War, the perspective had been reversed. According to the German philosopher Max Scheler, in his *Der Genius des Krieges und der Deutsche Krieg* (The spirit of war and the German war), British capitalism and British utilitarianism had made Britain an authentic *Gesellschaft*. Germany, however, had been able to keep the communitarian attributes of a *Gemeinschaft*.[7] In this rendition, Scheler (who later disowned this nationalistic work but remained a sophisticated anti-Kantian) turned Tönnies's historical concepts into moral

5. Ferdinand Tönnies, *Community and Civil Society* [1887], ed. Jose Harris (Cambridge, CUP, 2001), p. 219.

6. Ibid.

7. On Scheler, and for this example, see Shane Weller, *The Idea of Europe: A Critical History* (Cambridge, CUP, 2021), p. 144. On Scheler's use of the *Gemeinschaft/Gesellschaft* opposition, see Max Scheler, *Trois essais sur l'esprit du capitalisme* [1914], ed. Patrick Lang (Nantes, Editions Nouvelles Cécile Defaut, 2016), pp. 149–53. For commentary, see Stephen Frederick Schneck, *Persons and Polis: Max Scheler's Personalism as Political Theory* (Albany, State U of New York Press, 1987), pp. 58–66. On its place in Scheler's thought, see the editorial introduction by Werner Stark to Max Scheler, *The Nature of Sympathy* [1913] (London, Routledge, 1954), and, more generally, Gurvitch, *Les tendances actuelles de la philosophie allemande*, pp. 117–25.

concepts and made the two different types of social arrangement that Tönnies had described the basis of a more highly charged moral choice between two rival objects of political allegiance.

The examples can be multiplied, and the broader contextual point can be amplified still further.[8] In the early nineteenth century, for example, the opposite of "national" was not necessarily "international" or "global," or even "local." Instead, it was just as likely to be "classical" because it was this opposition that had the most salience to contemporary evaluations of modern national languages like French, English, German, or Italian—as against ancient transnational languages like Latin or Greek—and assessments of their respective abilities to bring culture and morality to life.[9] The same slight shifts of meaning applied to many other apparently anodyne terms, like "original," "individual," or even "modern." Once restored to their original conceptual settings, quite a large number of apparently modern political terms—from liberalism to socialism and from conservatism to communism—begin to look considerably less familiar than they now seem because their original meanings belonged to arguments that either are over or have since been forgotten. According to the German law professor Heinrich Ahrens writing in 1838, the seventeenth-century natural jurist Samuel Pufendorf "had simply developed the principles of Grotius in a more scholarly and rigorous manner. The school of natural law founded by these two famous men was the *social school*, whose supporters were called socialists."[10] The same, now somewhat unexpected origin once applied to liberalism. It too, according to its first historian, a German philosophy professor named Wilhelm Traugott Krug, had a long-established pedigree. As Krug wrote in 1823 in his *Geschichtlichen Darstellung des Liberalismus alter und neuer Zeit* (A historical description of liberalism in ancient and modern times), many of the values associated with what he took liberalism to be (like the idea of a social contract, or freedom of artistic expression, or the emancipation of women) were often attributed solely (and, he emphasized, wrongly) to

8. For further examples, see Keith Tribe, "Capitalism and Its Critics," in *The Cambridge Companion to Nineteenth-Century Thought*, ed. Gregory Claeys (Cambridge, CUP, 2019), pp. 123–40.

9. For a helpful collection of essays on the subject, see Michel Espagne and Michael Werner, eds., *Qu'est-ce qu'une littérature nationale? Approches pour une théorie interculturelle du champ littéraire*, Philologiques, 3 (Paris, Editions de la Maison des Sciences de l'Homme, 1994), and, for a fascinating account of the life and afterlife of one ancient language, see Françoise Waquet, *Latin, or the Empire of a Sign* [1998] (London, Verso, 2001).

10. "Pufendorf n'a fait que développer le principe de Grotius d'une manière plus savante et plus rigoureuse. L'école que ces deux hommes célèbres fondèrent en droit naturel, était *l'école sociale*, dont les partisans furent appelés socialistes." Ahrens, *Cours de droit naturel*, 1st ed., p. 67.

the period of the French Revolution and its aftermath. But they were, he claimed, already to be found either in ancient Greece or in some of the modern European monarchies (including those of Frederick the Great of Prussia and Catherine of Russia, as well as those currently leagued together in the more recently established Holy Alliance).[11] There was, of course, a polemical point to the claim. But, Krug argued, it could be justified by focusing on the idea of free will or moral autonomy as the substantive source of the continuity. He drove home the claim in a periodical article entitled "Fénelon's Liberalismus" that appeared immediately after the publication of his *Historical Description*. In it, the early eighteenth-century French archbishop and critic of Louis XIV's system of absolute government was associated unambiguously with religious toleration, the rule of law, and free trade—all, Krug stressed, core liberal values.[12] In an echo of Kant, Krug also went to some lengths to emphasize that they were values that cut across earlier divisions between royal and republican forms of government.

The contextual point helps to highlight the part played by chance and choice in the way that the two stories unfolded. It also, however, helps to highlight the problematic quality of the apparently self-evident concept of continuity and the way that some discoveries, creations, or achievements had the power to live longer than the original settings in which they had first been made. Here, as Hegel emphasized, hindsight was the real guide to what mattered because only hindsight could distinguish what had come through from the past from what had been left behind, and, consequently, could also try to explain how and why the differences had arisen. But how it could do so and how it could establish a clear line separating continuity from discontinuity was a further source of discussion and debate. Gradually, however, and in the line of intellectual descent that ran from Hegel to Stein, Jellinek, Simmel, and Weber, the two ways of thinking about the relationship between the past and the present crystallized into a more durable version of dualism. On one side of this dualism were durable values and apparently timeless norms; on the other there were local circumstances and bounded beliefs. The outcome was a recognition that there was no need to set the Romans against the Germans and no need even to subscribe to the idea that modern Europe had two starting points rather than one. To the young Max Weber, the long-established association between Roman law and modern capitalism was an easy target.

11. Wilhelm Traugott Krug, *Geschichtlichen Darstellung des Liberalismus alter und neuer Zeit* (Leipzig, 1823).

12. Wilhelm Traugott Krug, "Fénelon's Liberalismus," *Literarisches Konversation Blatt* 53 (4 March 1823): 209–10.

As he set out to show in his doctoral thesis, the joint responsibility and shared accountability of the modern business organization was better understood not as a continuation of the possessive individualism of Roman law but as an unintended outcome of the ancient Germanic institution of the *Genossenschaft*. Behind the apparent continuities, there were more complicated transvaluations of values.[13] This chapter is an account of what lay behind this type of insight, and how, particularly in Switzerland with its double orientation towards both Francophone and Germanic intellectual life, the problematic relationship between historicity and normativity began to be given a more historically considered treatment, and the rival legacies of the Romans and the Germans began to be described as components of a dual system. With this combination available, it began to be possible to think more fully and imaginatively about the properties and attributes of those institutions and arrangements that, like industry, money, sovereignty, and the law, looked most likely to be able to bridge the moral and historical divide that Kant had opened up.

The most significant of these institutions and arrangements was the rise of modern electoral—or democratic—politics. This, it should be emphasized, was not because modern electoral politics were themselves taken to be, somehow, more compatible with industry, money, sovereignty, and the law than any other form of rule. Instead, it was the obvious *incompatibility* between the vagaries of electoral politics and the continuities of industry, money, sovereignty, and the law that helped to raise a more pressing set of questions about how both sides of this mixture of continuity and change could coexist. As the French law professor Maurice Hauriou put in an article entitled "Le régime d'état" (The state regime) published in 1904, it was "paradoxical or almost mad" for laws, meaning "the foundation itself of the state regime," to be the product of the "electoral game." But this, in fact, was what they were. Everything in modern politics seemed to be up for grabs. To Hauriou, however, the fact that everything, in principle, really was up for grabs helped to highlight the gap between the dizzying possibilities of an election and the underlying continuities of everyday life. Majority rule still, apparently, called for the sanction of ordinary life. This, Hauriou argued, was why it was vital to separate the political regime from the property regime and start to work out the reasons that enabled the two to coexist. The question that he raised was a twentieth-century version of the question underlying Sieyès's concept of *science sociale*.

13. See Max Weber, *The History of Commercial Partnerships in the Middle Ages* [1889], trans. and ed. Lutz Kaelber (New York, Rowman and Littlefield, 2003).

Hauriou's question has a further, more recent, historiographical implication. For several generations, the history of political thought has appeared to consist of two rival traditions, one liberal, the other republican; one state-centred, the other community-oriented; one individualistic, the other civic.[14] The differences between these two traditions have turned, in part, on two rival concepts of freedom, one negative, the other positive. As has been shown, however, both these concepts of freedom began to be used in the late eighteenth century and were both connected to a concurrent interest in the concept of autonomy.[15] Curiously, the more recent historiographical emphasis has fallen on the idea that the positive preceded the negative because it is usually assumed that positive liberty—as, following Isaiah Berlin, it is usually called— was ancient while negative liberty is modern, or, in a somewhat different idiom, that there was once liberty before liberalism because liberty first meant nondomination before it fell under the aegis of the representative sovereign state.[16] The same sequence also seems to apply to the relationship between republicanism and rights. First, there was a civic tradition, stretching back from the American Founders to James Harrington, Machiavelli, and Aristotle, and then there were rights, starting with Hugo Grotius, Thomas Hobbes, and John Locke and running forwards to Jean-Jacques Rousseau and the Declaration of the Rights of Man.[17]

Starting with the early nineteenth-century claim that there were two turning points, not one, involved in the making of modern political societies and modern political thought—and that the second was a response to the first— makes it possible to revise this historical sequence and, in the light of this, to reassess the relationship between the various concepts of freedom involved in the rivalry between republicanism and rights. From this perspective, the key difference between the two foundational moments in the making of modern politics—one in the sixteenth and seventeen centuries, the other in the late

14. For Hauriou's question, see Maurice Hauriou, "Le régime d'état," *La Revue socialiste* 39 (1904): 564–81 (especially pp. 578–79). More generally, see Maurice Hauriou, *Ecrits sociologiques*, ed. Frédéric Audren and Marc Milet (Paris, Dalloz, 2008). For a recent overview of the republicanism-liberalism divide, but without Kant or the concept of autonomy, see Rachel Hammersley, *Republicanism: An Introduction* (Cambridge, Polity, 2020).

15. See, to begin with, Berlin, "Two Concepts of Liberty," pp. 166–217, and, for a helpful recent collection of articles, Kari Palonen, Tuija Pulkkinen, and José María Rosales, eds., *The Ashgate Research Companion to the Politics of Democratization in Europe: Concepts and Histories* (Farnham, Surrey, 2008).

16. Skinner, *Liberty before Liberalism*.

17. Pocock, *The Machiavellian Moment* (1975, 2003); see too the further, 2016, Princeton edition, with an illuminating introduction by Richard Whatmore.

eighteenth and nineteenth centuries—was supplied by Kant's concept of autonomy.[18] Although the concept came into existence only in the second of these two foundational moments, it has been projected backwards onto the first. In this light, a great deal of what now seems to be ancient and republican was, chronologically and conceptually, unambiguously modern.[19] Beginning with the idea that there were two turning points rather than one in the history and historiography of political thought makes it possible to avoid this conflation and, by doing so, to begin to put the sequence back into the right historical and analytical order. Liberty might well have preceded liberalism, but autonomy came later, and came too. The modern concept of autonomy grew out of the problem of finding a way to combine political sovereignty with limited state power and to reconcile personal qualities with general equality. In this combination, the more room there was for autonomy, the less need there was for a state. Inversely, however, the more room there was for domination— by age, industry, wealth, education, talent, gender, caste, religion, race, or even sport—the more need there was for a state. The problem of domination versus nondomination was, in this light, not something that could be treated in binary terms. The solution, instead, was to see whether it was possible to keep both sides of the binary alive.

Joseph Marc Hornung and Roman History

Recognition of the need to do so coincided with the rehabilitation of Rome and its legacy that was already visible in the work of Michelet and Quinet well before 1848. One example of what it entailed can be seen in an essay submitted to the law faculty of the University of Geneva in 1847 on the subject of why the Romans had been what its author called "the juridical people" of the ancient world. Its author was an individual named Joseph Marc Hornung who went on subsequently to become a law professor at the Academy of Lausanne and, later, the University of Geneva.[20] Hornung was a political and religious thinker who was rather similar to Guizot (he dedicated one of his books to the

18. On autonomy, see initially Schneewind, *The Invention of Autonomy* and his earlier "The Use of Autonomy in Ethical Theory," in *Reconstructing Individualism: Autonomy, Individuality and the Self in Western Thought*, ed. Thomas C. Heller, Morton Sosna, and David E. Wellbery (Stanford, Stanford UP, 1986), pp. 64–75.

19. For an examination of the historiographical consequences, see Sonenscher, "Liberty, Autonomy and Republican Historiography."

20. For a biography, see André Oltramare, "Notice biographique sur Joseph Hornung," *Bulletin de l'Institut National Genevois* 27 (1885): 295–375. A self-standing version with the addition of a new appendix containing extracts from some of Hornung's unpublished works was

French politician). He was probably even better acquainted with German-language publications in history, philosophy, and law than Guizot had been (in two of his later publications he even referred to the work of Schmidt and Röder on Germanic and Roman law), and he was also more receptive to the work of some of Guizot's historical and political critics, like Quinet and Michelet.[21] But his political thought was nearer to Guizot's (and Hegel's) than to theirs. According to one of his obituarists, his real heroes were Rousseau and Germaine de Staël, both because they were Genevan and because of their ability to bring together previously separate bodies of thought. Where Rousseau "had the glory of bringing to completion the work of emancipation begun by English writers," Mme de Staël "embodied the European mission of Switzerland" in a "powerful synthesis" that brought together "Germanic idealism and Latin individualism."[22] Although Hornung repeatedly announced his intention to publish a book on the history of theories of the state, this was something that he never did. The subject, however, was the basis of his 1847 essay because it was the unusual concept of the Roman state that he described in the essay that, he argued, made it a prototype of a modern political society. Although Hornung did not say so, the concept of the Roman state that he went on to describe was not only rather like a *Rechtsstaat* but was also surprisingly Swiss in character.

Hornung set out the answer to his initial question at the very beginning of his essay. "In Rome," he wrote, "two peoples compressed within the same state were able to transact with one another in the same forum. There, for a long time, words were their only weapons or, at the very least, one order never exiled the other or plotted its extermination. In Rome, therefore, a true juridical and political contract was born because of the coexistence, under the same government, of two perfectly distinct and separate peoples."[23] The peoples in question were Rome's two orders of patricians and plebeians, but behind them were the many different peoples drawn from the Etruscans, Umbrians, Sabines, Latins, Samnites, Campagnians, and Lucanians who made up the mem-

---

published in 1886. See also the list of his publications in the obituary published in *Annuaire de l'Institut de Droit International* 8 (1886): 45–53.

21. Joseph Hornung, "Quelques vues sur le droit romain en lui-même et dans son action dans le monde moderne, à propos d'une histoire récente de ce droit," *Revue de droit internationale et de législation comparée* 5 (1873): 194–202 (here, p. 197 n. 5); and his "Les races de la Suisse au point de vue historique et juridique," in *Actes du Congrès des Sociétés suisses de géographie* (Geneva, 1882), pp. 1–21 (here p. 6 n. 2)

22. Oltramare, "Notice biographique sur Joseph Hornung," p. 317.

23. Joseph Hornung, *Essai historique sur cette question: Pourquoi les Romains ont-ils été le peuple juridique de l'ancien monde?* (Geneva, 1847), p. 3.

bership of the two classes underlying Rome's legal and political system. It was a system that, Hornung explained, was a product of several connected facts, which he went on to list. "The existence in the Roman state of two peoples, one of which was dominant, but by virtue of acquired rights, while the other had to conquer equality by legal means; the formation of fundamental law by means of a transaction; and the establishment of that law by way of a legislative assembly, not by an individual or a caste. These facts explain why the Romans had been the juridical people of the ancient world."[24]

Together, Hornung wrote, the facts in question explained why the Roman republic had become "the common motherland of the West," while "the castes of the Orient, based initially on differences of objective capacity," and the states of Greece, "based on the principle of race," had either been impenetrable to renewal from without or were impervious to change from within. These differences in internal structure and capability helped to explain why it was appropriate to contrast the full-blown wars between Athens and Sparta to the more peaceful transactions between the patrician Senate and the plebeian tribunes of the Roman republic. Where the wars in Greece centred on questions of nationality, the transactions in Rome centred on civic rights (*droit de bourgeoisie*), as had been the case in Geneva in more recent times.[25] "In Italy, there was no single nationality whose tendencies came out freely into the open. There were peoples who were very different from one another and who came together only within the boundaries of Rome's seven hills. In Greece, the nation was made up of several states, but in Rome, the state was made up of several nations. The idea of race was, therefore, subordinated to that of the state, just as, with Greece, the idea of race had, earlier, destroyed the primacy of the castes of the Orient." Where, once, race neutralized caste, states, now, neutralized race. In Italy, there was no underlying unity. If unity had been achieved, it had been achieved by something that was able to bring together Italy's diverse elements into what Hornung called a common life. "That unity," he wrote, "had to be a state because there was no Italian nation."[26] It was a real republican state that, Hornung emphasized, continued to retain many of its republican features long after the seizure of power by Augustus Caesar and the transition from the Roman republic to the Roman Empire.

The subject of the differences distinguishing the Roman republic, the Roman Empire, and the many Italian and non-Italian nations incorporated into both had a growing and increasingly obvious salience in the period that

24. Ibid., p. 4.
25. Ibid., pp. 62–63.
26. Ibid., pp. 67–68.

preceded Napoleon III's seizure of power in France in 1851. Hornung began to address the subject in 1850 in a large pamphlet entitled *Idées sur l'évolution juridique des nations chrétiennes et en particulier sur celle du peuple français* (Ideas on the juridical evolution of the Christian nations and, particularly, that of the French people). The pamphlet was intended to be a companion piece to his earlier examination of the significance of Roman law in the ancient world, but this time the focus was on France and its place in the political and legal life of the modern world. It was organized around a framework that was supplied in part by Alexis de Tocqueville's *Democracy in America* and, possibly, by a long review of its first volume that had been published in 1836 by the energetic baron d'Eckstein very soon after Tocqueville's book appeared. In the review, Eckstein had criticized Tocqueville for his failure to place enough causal stress on the connection between American Puritanism and American democracy. It meant, Eckstein claimed, that Tocqueville had conflated too many aspects of Protestant Europe, or the Europe of the Anglo-Saxons and the North, with the different attributes of Catholic Europe, or the Europe of France, Italy, Spain, and the South, and had turned them all into a single, highly predictive examination of democracy as the system of government of the future.[27] Hornung endorsed the same idea, but turned it back upon itself to produce an argument that anticipated much of the analytical content of Tocqueville's posthumously published *The Old Regime and the French Revolution*.

The basis of Hornung's argument was supplied by the concept of dualism. This was the concept that, in his earlier examination of Roman law, he had used to explain why it was a product of the transactional relationship between the patricians and plebeians of republican Rome. In the later pamphlet, he gave it a more generic quality. "The idea of law," he wrote, "always has its source in a duality, an opposition."[28] The patrician-plebeian opposition had played this part in ancient Rome, but its most fully realized modern counterpart was, as Hornung put it, a product of the superimposition of a powerful feudal monarchy on the Anglo-Saxon nation. The source of this idea was the book first published in 1770 by the eighteenth-century Genevan political exile Jean-Louis Delolme, *The Constitution of England*, but Hornung now turned it into a modern equivalent of republican Rome. "Political life," he wrote, "again took the Anglo-Saxon organism as its basis and endowed it with value by means of

27. Ferdinand, baron d'Eckstein, *"De la Démocratie en Amérique* par Alexis de Tocqueville," *Le Polonais* 6 (1836): 235–63, 408–29. For Hornung's use of Tocqueville, see Hornung, *Essai*, p. 69 n. 1.

28. Joseph Hornung, *Idées sur l'évolution juridique des nations chrétiennes et en particulier sur celle du peuple français* (Geneva, 1850), p. 45.

the *county* and the *borough*, which became the centres of life and legal resistance. The representative system became a reality because it was based on a nation whose parts were all alive but could not pretend to power and, instead, only to the preservation and development of the rule of law. Thus, the archetype of the *citizen* that once seemed to have disappeared into the night along with the Roman plebs was reproduced in England. Just as Roman plebeians joined a feeling of their rights to the rights of patricians, so the English nation, guided by its nobility, set its rights against the rights of Norman royalty."[29] This, Hornung claimed, was the culture that had been reinforced by the individualism of the Protestant Reformation and had been transported to the United States by the American Puritans. Its real origins, however, were Roman and legal, just as its real prospects were tied to the dualism that, since the time of the Roman republic, had given European social and political life its distinctive legal foundation.

Although the word "duality" made it look as if a modern political and legal system had to have two parts, Hornung made it clear that it actually had to have three. The rule of law, he explained, was a product of the opposition between two entities, principles, interests, or nations that, but for the law, would usually give rise to naked class conflict and a straightforward struggle for power. In England, Hornung wrote, "*Germanic organization*, combined with *feudal royalty*, became the site and basis of a profoundly national *political life*, and the idea of the *right of the nation* was formed within the struggles resulting from this fundamental duality."[30] The content of that political life subsequently became more juridical than political after the English revolution of 1688, which, in this respect, was a modern equivalent of the Roman law of the Twelve Tables and whose theoretical content was captured most fully and powerfully in the political thought of John Locke.[31] Although Hornung called both the British and Roman systems of government a mixed system, their most important feature was supplied by the idea of the rule of law and, as Michelet had argued earlier, by the way that the various agencies responsible for establishing and maintaining the rule of law were able to provide a medium that could be used to reconcile, neutralize, or defuse otherwise directly antagonistic forces.

Elsewhere, however, developments followed a different course. In France, Hornung claimed, anticipating much of the argument of Tocqueville's later examination of the old regime, the action of the state had dissolved society,

29. Ibid., p. 47.
30. Ibid., pp. 48–49.
31. Ibid., p. 68.

leaving nothing to form the other side of a duality formed either by the state and the nation or by individuals and the state. Since both the nation and individuals were now subsumed within the state, individual rights were defenceless. Something analogous had happened in the German-speaking world, although there, in the aftermath of the events of 1848, the dissolution of both the nation and individual rights was more the work of speculative philosophy than of state power. In both countries, Horning wrote, "nationality and individuality have been almost annihilated, and people now seem to have become no more than *instruments*" of either the state or philosophical speculation.[32] The problem, however, was most pronounced in France. "Elsewhere the nation preexisted and gave the state its form; in France, the state *preexisted*, and, far from being a product of national life, it was the state that constituted the nation, piece by piece."[33]

Hornung amplified on his assessment fifteen years later in 1865 in a long and critical review of a history of Julius Caesar written by France's Emperor Napoleon III. "Rome," Hornung began, "created a form of state that continues to impose itself upon us. The empire is still a reality. Caesar and Augustus Caesar inaugurated a new kind of monarchy that, although it undoubtedly destroyed all political life, also guaranteed private rights and, in general, showed itself to be neutral and tolerant. The empire was the age of jurists, whose equity was absolute and who saw mankind in the terms that are most general and abstract, as the man of nature, and not as the man of any particular religion or nationality."[34] Although it lacked a real substantive moral and national content, the combination of legal rights and state power that was the legacy of imperial Rome was now visible again in modern France. Like Rome, France was a multinational empire. Its constituent peoples had neutralized one another to produce individual identities that were no longer purely occupational, confessional, or national but were "more abstract" and were, consequently, the basis of "a new, larger, and more human civilization." What France still lacked was "a determinate ideal" or "an organized nationality, like that of England." It meant that when the revolution "came to consummate the work of centralization that began with the monarchy, there was nothing left other than the state and individuals."[35] There was no French nation that could be differentiated from the French state.

To Hornung, the mixture of unity and differentiation that was the basis of the formation of a nation-state had almost happened in Rome. Since, he argued,

32. Ibid., p. 77.
33. Hornung, *Essai*, p. 121.
34. Joseph Hornung, *L'Histoire romaine et Napoléon III* (Lausanne, 1865), p. 5.
35. Ibid., p. 6.

the Roman state contained an increasingly large and diverse range of social elements, and had instituted what, in principle, was a purely legal relationship among them, it had to pay attention to the private interests that fell under the jurisdiction of its various legal institutions. The combination of a unitary state, many competing interests, and legal conflict among them made the law a force in its own right for much of the life of the republic and well into the early years of the empire. Problems had begun, however, with the growth of the state and the difficulty of establishing a viable relationship between Rome's central government and the growing number of Roman provinces. The Roman solution had been administrative, and, for a time, it had worked because the inhabitants of Rome's provinces also enjoyed many of the same legal rights as those of the metropolis. But as the administration took on more of a life of its own, an overlapping series of gaps—between administrators and inhabitants, lawyers and citizens, the state and civil society—began to undermine the uniquely Roman distinction between legal and political conflict, and between the rule of law and the brutality of power politics. Gradually, the latter overrode the former, and, as they did, any capacity to equip the Roman republic with a viable system of representative government receded gradually from possibility.

France, clearly, was at a comparable turning point. It could go the way of Rome or become more like modern Britain. This, Hornung commented, was what, in his *History of Julius Caesar*, Napoleon III had not seen. He had not made use of the insights into the Roman constitution that were available in Polybius, or been able to recognize the parallel that could be drawn between Polybius on Rome and what Montesquieu had written about the English constitution. He had not taken advantage of the thought of "that great patriot Machiavelli" who, like Polybius, had compared, not Rome to Greece, but the Florentine republic to its Roman counterpart, and had highlighted the part played by legal argument and rule-governed conflict in the political life of both.[36] He had also failed to register the one great change that had happened to historical thinking in the eighteenth century. This was the emergence of the concept of the nationality. It was a product of "the renovation of historical studies that had its principal cause in the reaction against Greek and Roman ideas and the return to Germanic origins. It was the antithesis between Romanism and Germanism that when it at last began to be clearly perceived gave the mind the sense of nationality in its most intimate principle." If the antithesis between "Germanic origins and the Roman spirit" had already been apparent in sixteenth-century France (in, for example, the work of individuals like François Hotman), it was only in the second half of the

36. Ibid., pp. 20, 28.

eighteenth century that "this duality appeared in all its precision." German literature then began to revert to its origins, "and Zurich was the first centre of that renovation that took the name of *Romanticism*" (the allusion here was probably to the late eighteenth-century Swiss writer Jean-Jacques Bodmer).[37] From Bodmer's time onwards, Hornung continued, "the ancient liberalism of Germanic institutions was brought back to light by men like Justus Möser, and since then the movement has been unstoppable. In France at the same time the problem of the two national origins became the great preoccupation of historians. Some favoured the Roman spirit; others, like Montesquieu, the feudal and Germanic spirit. But, as a result of this preoccupation with races in themselves, the originality of Rome, which united races within a common form, was not yet fully understood. Thus, Montesquieu could not see the true causes of the grandeur of Rome; his famous book is full of no more than detailed and particular observations. He understood the Middle Ages and England far better."[38]

Current French historiography, with the single exception of the work of Amédée Thierry (far superior, Hornung emphasized, to the work of his better-known brother Augustin), was still mired in the subject of race and had failed to build on Michelet's earlier insight into the true nature of Rome's originality. German-language historiography of either the Germans or the Romans was also overly preoccupied with origins and focused too heavily either on early Germanic institutions or on the many different races, like the Etruscans, who were absorbed by Rome. "What they have understood well and brought into light are the races of Italy," Hornung commented. "But the union of these races in Rome, and the new, derivative, formal, juridical state, is what has eluded them."[39] In general, the idealism of German philosophers like Hegel and his most able follower, Edouard Gans, meant that they were less fair-minded towards both the Romans and the English and more partial towards the Greeks. The best things about Rome and, by extension, the best anatomies of the real attributes of modern states had been written by "simple jurists, meaning Savigny, Jhering, and authors who have compared Roman law with Germanic law." Jhering in particular stood out. He had risen to the level of being able to produce "some very just general considerations on the purely juridical and abstract character of the Roman state." He was, however, an exception. No German scholar had been able to do what Michelet and Quinet had done to Rome. But, Hornung pointed out, the Germans understood France infinitely

37. Ibid., p. 29.
38. Ibid., p. 29.
39. Ibid., p. 32.

better than Rome. "No one" he concluded, "has explained France better than Stein, whose ideas, moreover, are perfectly unknown in Paris."[40]

Apart from the gestures towards Stein and Jhering, Hornung's review could be mistaken for an early anticipation of civic humanist or neo-Roman historiography. But his acknowledgement of Stein and Jhering suggests a different story, one centred on the idea of a union of opposites and the many different ways in which what Hornung called "dualities" could be given a genuinely stable, durable, and productive relationship. Although the initial components of these dualities could be very different, the stabilizing mechanism was supplied, as Hornung put it, by the idea of the state as something abstract and purely juridical. It was, in short, an idea that was similar to the idea of the state that, a generation later, the German lawyer Georg Jellinek began to call a two-sided idea of the state. In one guise, a state would consist of all those institutions, resources, and agencies that were responsible for adding power to political authority. In another guise, however, a state would also have an ability to ensure that all these institutions, resources, and agencies could act independently and, in a sense, autonomously. The state would be sovereign, but its sovereignty would consist largely of its capacity to preserve the independence, or autonomy, of both its members and its government by relying on the rule of law to prevent them from coming into more direct physical conflict. As with Hegel, the resulting system would have three parts: a state, a civil society, and a government that straddled them both. The binding mechanism, however, had to come from conflict, but from conflict expressed as argument and ideas rather than as real material and physical force.

Hornung made this description of the interrelationship of the state, civil society, and government the basis of a comparison between the respective civilizations of the ancients and the moderns in a later article, published in 1873.[41] Modern civilization, he wrote, had one particular difference from the civilizations of antiquity. Modern civilization was "eminently derivative and *secondary*" because "it made use of and brought together elements prepared by other peoples." The civilizations of antiquity on the other hand were "original and *primary*." Modern civilization was more unified because, as Hornung went on to explain, it was a synthesis of the primary elements of Christianity, Hellenic culture, and Roman law. Later it had also absorbed Germanic culture, or what Hornung called Germanism. The outcome of this protracted process of historical osmosis was "a vast whole, an immense society, that dominates individual states, and, because of its substantive character, it differs profoundly

40. Ibid., p. 34.
41. Hornung, "Quelques vues."

from the very sharply delimited national forms of the ancient world."[42] The integrated character of modern civilization meant that it had come to change as a single entity and to encompass phases of historical development that, in antiquity, were confined to separate peoples. Its evolution took place in time, while the evolution of the ancient world took place in space, when one state succeeded another from age to age. Even Rome continued to retain many of its original institutions and forms long after its empire and laws had become far more cosmopolitan. The modern world, by contrast, had no determinate form. In it, what was predominant was "its social matter and the movement of the whole."[43]

The difference between the primary and original qualities of the ancients and the secondary and derivative qualities of the moderns, Hornung argued, was based on a broader range of distinctions between the real and the ideal. Ancient civilizations were self-contained because their constituent elements were generated entirely from their own physical and cultural resources. Modern civilization had an extra level of imaginative and historical creation that had spilled over from the immediate settings in which they originated. Being ideal, Hornung claimed, the constituent elements of modern civilization had a greater significance among the moderns than was the case with their counterparts among the ancients. Christianity, Hellenism, Roman law, and Germanic culture had all come to matter far more among the moderns than any of the more specific local attributes that had once given each nation and state its particular form. Since, among the ancients, each nation and state was genuinely autochthonous, they carried their particular pasts within themselves without needing much historical reflection. Among the moderns, however, progress was measured more usually in terms of how far they had maintained and preserved their original primary elements. The resulting more acute historical sensibility had given rise to a correspondingly more intense quest for origins, and by extension to "a series of *renaissances* and *reformations*" that would have astounded the ancients. "The scholastics went back to Greek philosophy; the glossators to Roman law; the Albigensians and Waldensians to primitive Christianity; and all this was followed by the great Renaissance of classical learning; the religious Reformation of the sixteenth century, and, finally, by the scientific and literary reappearance of Celticism, Slavism, and Germanism." Only in the seventeenth and, above all, in the eighteenth century had this long interrogation of the past begun to end. "Only after a long subjection to others' thoughts," Hornung concluded,

42. Ibid., p. 194.
43. Ibid., p. 195.

in Kantian and Hegelian vein, "did we rediscover nature and recover the autonomy of the self."[44]

The key to this process of intellectual and moral emancipation was comparison. Comparison could occur either in space or in time, with either approach sometimes generating strong feelings of approval or disapproval. But comparison could also give rise to new information, and this addition could turn initial evaluations into more neutral historical concepts. This was what had happened to Christianity. Historical criticism had now made it possible to see that what Protestant orthodoxy had taken to be an absolute value could now be appreciated as just another religion (although Hornung did not say so, the allusion here was probably to the work of David Strauss and Ernest Renan). The same switch from an absolute value to an abstract concept had also occurred to the idea of a classic in literature (here the allusion was probably to Sainte-Beuve) and was also now well underway with Roman law. Here too, comparison was the key. It could be found in François Hotman and his *Franco-Gallia*. It could also be found in Machiavelli and his comparisons between the Florentine republic and republican Rome. Above all, however, it could be found in the Germanist legal tradition, starting with the jurist Heineccius in the early eighteenth century and continuing into the nineteenth century with the comparison between Roman law as lawyers' law (*Juristenrecht*) and Germanic custom as national law (*Volksrecht*) that had come to dominate the protracted argument between the Romanists and the Germanists (here Hornung referred to the discussions between Schmidt and Röder on Roman and Germanic law).[45] The need now was to generate a new synthesis out of the underlying comparisons involved in that long-drawn-out argument and do to law what had already been done to religion and the dispute between the supporters of the classics and the romantics.

Hornung's approach to the relationship between history and politics was echoed in a law thesis published in 1867, some two decades after Hornung had submitted his own thesis on Roman law in the life of the Roman republic. It was entitled *De l'enseignement du droit romain* (On the teaching of Roman law) and was submitted to the Academy of Lausanne, where Hornung then taught, by an individual named Henri Brocher de la Fléchère, who went on to become a law professor at the Free University of Brussels where Heinrich Ahrens once taught. In most respects, Brocher followed Hornung's endorsement of Roman law and echoed his favourable assessment of the compatibility between ancient Roman institutions and modern British economic and social arrangements. But,

44. Ibid.
45. Ibid., p. 197.

as Brocher pointed out, Roman law itself had no place in English legal life, which meant that there was an obvious need for a more deep-seated explanation of the apparent compatibility. To Brocher, the explanation in question could be found in the underlying properties of Roman law. If, as many of its critics emphasized, its most conspicuous feature was its concern with utility, then, Brocher argued, something about utility had to be what set Roman law apart from every other system of law. This, he continued, could not be utility itself because it was no more than a generic motivation and goal. Instead it had to be the awareness of both the individual and the common self underlying the concept of utility. Anyone, in short, could recognize utility. Only a Roman, however, could be a utilitarian.

As Brocher recognized, the distinction matched Hornung's preoccupation with duality. If, on the one hand, utility amounted to naked self-interest, it still presupposed something of value in both the individual and collective self. That prior source of value was, simply, the concept of a self, and it was this additional level of awareness that was the basis of the distinction between ordinary utility and self-conscious utilitarianism. If the first was purely self-centred, the second called for consideration of a further level of discrimination and self-determination. To Brocher the two sets of considerations were nicely illustrated by the devices on the escutcheons of the British monarchy and its Order of the Garter. One, *Dieu et mon droit*, was utility writ large; while the other, *Honi soit qui mal y pense*, was an acknowledgement of the claims of conscience.[46] The two devices matched the distinction between legality and morality that had been signalled earlier in the nineteenth century by Mackintosh and Savigny as one of the more conspicuous common features of the thought of Immanuel Kant and Adam Smith. Brocher had no hesitation (his essay was part of his job application for the chair of Roman law at the Academy of Lausanne) in driving home the significance of its implications. It meant that Roman law itself was the source of a very significant dualism. This one, he claimed, promised to put an end to the earlier dualisms dividing Germanists from Romanists, socialists from individualists, and moralists from legalists, provided, however, that both sides of the duality could be maintained.

Brocher was one of the first political commentators to give the names of utilitarianism and idealism to the difference between legality and morality that Smith and Kant had highlighted. But, where earlier commentators had aligned Smith with Kant, Brocher stressed that the relationship between utilitarianism and idealism was antagonistic. "Vilified by its enemies, betrayed by its friends, distorted on all sides," he wrote in his 1867 dissertation, "utilitarianism has on its opposite side another tendency that we will call idealism, although

---

46. Henri Brocher, *De l'enseignement du droit romain* (Lausanne, 1867), pp. 72–73.

the name is possibly not well chosen."[47] The antagonism was not, however, a product of the distinction between legality and morality, but was an effect of how they had been conflated with one another in the thought of Jeremy Bentham. Bentham's version of utilitarianism, Brocher claimed, was a form of monism. It placed too much emphasis on the dynamics of pleasure and pain and did not give enough recognition to the concept of duty.[48] The really important aspect of Roman law, Brocher claimed, was that its version of utilitarianism was, as both Bluntschli and Jhering had seen, compatible with both types of motivation. If, as the utilitarians rightly claimed, the self was the only motivator of our actions, it could not also be their only rule. "We live in a milieu made up of forces that are independent of ourselves," he wrote, "and these have to be taken into consideration."[49] This had also been Jhering's point. Roman law was a product of conflict but had the ability to turn one type of conflict into conflict of a different kind. It could accommodate utilitarianism and idealism just as, for Smith and Kant, it could reconcile legality with morality.

Henry Maine and *The History of the Troglodytes*

A comparable claim was made at about the same time by Henry Maine. He too was both an admirer and a critic of utilitarianism.[50] He explained how it was possible to be both in an extended set of comments on the thought of Jeremy Bentham and, in particular, on what Bentham had written about Montesquieu's story about the Troglodytes. "The importance which the observance of promises is to the happiness of society," Bentham had written in his *Fragment on Government* in 1776, "is placed in a very striking and satisfactory point of view in a little apologue of Montesquieu entitled *The History of the Troglodytes*."

> The Troglodytes are a people who pay no regard to promises. By the natural consequences of this disposition, they fall from one scene of misery into another and are at last exterminated. The same philosopher in his *Spirit of Laws*, copying and refining upon the current jargon, feigns a law for this and other purposes, after defining a law to be a *relation*. How much more instructive on this head is the fable of the Troglodytes than the pseudo-metaphysical sophistry of the *Esprit des Loix*![51]

47. Ibid., p. 69.

48. Ibid., p. 70.

49. Ibid., p. 98.

50. On Maine, see Grant Duff, *The Life and Speeches of Sir Henry Maine*; Feaver, *From Status to Contract*.

51. Jeremy Bentham, *A Fragment on Government* [1776], 2nd ed. (London, 1823), note k, pp. 41–42 (ch. 1, §§42–43).

For Bentham, the correct approach to the subjects of promises, duty, and political obligation was supplied by the concept of utility and, more specifically, by the relationship between the locally specific and temporally sequential nature of crimes and misdemeanours and the more comprehensive and durable quality of the scale and scope of general happiness or welfare. The lack of fit between the two sides of the relationship meant that crimes and misdemeanours would be punished seriatim while the general and durable quality of happiness or welfare would offset the particular and local pain associated with crime and punishment. From Bentham's perspective, the Troglodyte tale made it clear why general utility had to override particular advantage. In the calculus of pleasures and pains, utility won hands down.

Bentham's assessment of *the History of the Troglodytes* chimed with his broader anticontractualism. Utilitarianism, he argued, either presupposed contractualism or supplied a yardstick for deciding whether any particular contract really was compatible with the principle of the greatest happiness of the greatest number. With utility as a criterion, Bentham's system could rely either on evaluations of rules or on assessments of acts to be able to measure how far one or the other could be relied upon to bridge the gap between morality and legality. But, as some of Bentham's critics pointed out, relying solely on the concept of utility to close the gap between morality and legality simply amounted to giving a new name to the power and authority of a sovereign state. In this sense, it was simply another attempt to find a way to produce a real reconciliation between long-standing moral or social asymmetries, like those between wealth and virtue or, more generally, the plethora of assorted asymmetries associated with gender, age, race, or religion. Ultimately, as both Bentham and his most influential nineteenth-century follower, John Austin, argued, getting out of the potentially infinite regress involved in promising to keep promises called for a combination of governmental authority and the gradual generalization of what Bentham had called the habit of obedience. This, as Austin went on to claim, was why legislation mattered, and why the figure of the legislator was the real architect of the scale and scope of the province of jurisprudence. To Savigny's Scottish admirer James Reddie, however, "Mr Bentham, although he avoids the error of Montesquieu and Rousseau, and so many older jurists, in imagining an ideal state of nature, antecedent to civil society, falls into a similar error in imagining a legislator, contemplating human actions, and by his fiat creating crimes or offences, positive or negative, thereby imposing obligations and services and conferring rights and then distributing these rights and obligations among the members of the community." To Reddie, the idea of the legislator as a kind of ex nihilo lawgiver began with Bentham. The problem, he argued, was that unless the legislator was God, the idea of a legislator had to be "a mere fictitious personage, having no real existence and unable either to impose obligations or to confer rights."[52] It simply failed to explain the real origin and foundation of rights and obligations

Maine made the same assessment of Bentham's endorsement of Montesquieu's *History of the Troglodytes*. Although he applied it to Montesquieu, it is clear from its content that the real targets of his criticism were Bentham and his follower John Austin. "The mistake of judging the men of other periods by the morality of our own day," he wrote towards the end of his *Ancient Law* in 1861, "has its parallel in the mistake of supposing that every wheel or bolt in the modern social machine had its counterpart in more rudimentary societies."[53] This was what Montesquieu had done in his Troglodyte history, and was the underlying defect of utilitarianism. "If the story bears the moral which its author intended," Maine explained, "it is most unexceptionable; but if the inference be obtained from it that society could not possibly be held together without attaching a sacredness to promises and agreements which should be on something like a par with the respect that is paid to them by a mature civilization, it involves an error so grave as to be fatal to all sound understanding of legal history."[54] As Maine went on to argue, the type of society to which a people like the Troglodytes belonged did not rely on reciprocity and recognition of rights for its stability and continuity, but on authority and imperative command. In ancient law, status, not rights, was what mattered. Such rights as did matter were supplied from above, not created from below, because they belonged to economic and social arrangements based on the power to command.

For Maine, the significance of Montesquieu's Troglodyte tale had less to do with the principle that it was supposed to illustrate than with the unusual historical process that it helped to reveal. Maine was as much of an anti–social contract theorist as Bentham and Austin, but his anticontractualism was based on a higher level of historical curiosity and a stronger measure of forensic scepticism. He was, in a sense, a nineteenth-century version of David Hume. If he did not have quite as much of the eighteenth-century Scot's analytical precision, he made up for it with the flair and creativity of his historical imagination. For Maine, the Troglodyte story was an allegory of something like the whole history of modern European political thought. This, he argued, was because its most fundamental message—about keeping promises, honouring obligations, and recognizing contracts—was based on a conflation of two

52. Reddie, *Inquiries*, pp. 139–40..
53. Sumner Maine, *Ancient Law*, p. 301.
54. Ibid., p. 302.

quite different types of human relationship. One presupposed equality, reciprocity, and rights, while the other presupposed inequality, authority, and obedience. Importantly, however, Maine's concern was not with trying to unravel or eliminate this conflation, but with trying instead to explain how both types of relationship had arisen, and how they could both be used for thinking about politics. From Maine's perspective, *The History of the Troglodytes* was a cryptic summary of the sequence of switches that ran from scriptural beginnings to modern conceptions of politics. The first switch was the transformation by François Hotman of a biblical story about the Jewish people, the Hebrew republic, and the kingdom of Israel into a historical story about the Germanic peoples, monarchomach politics, and the limits of sovereign power. In the second switch, by Montesquieu, the biblical and the historical stories became a fictional story about the Troglodyte people and, by extension, about the political implications of their gradual incorporation into a fiscal nexus of private property and royal power. There were also significant variations in where the emphasis fell in the three versions of the story. In the first, Hebrew, version of the story, the emphasis fell upon the characteristics of a republic. In the second, Germanic, version, it fell upon the rights of resistance. In its third, Troglodyte, incarnation, it fell upon the problem of state power.

In Montesquieu's hands, the whole sequence of switches became a more comprehensive story that ran discretely all the way through *The Spirit of Laws* to form a sustained analysis of different types of law and the interrelationship of the Roman republic, the Roman Empire, and the legacy of the Germanic peoples who were responsible for both the decline and fall of imperial Rome and the long process of European revival and renewal that was its aftermath. As Montesquieu emphasized, it was a story with two sides. One looked backwards to the original arrangements of the Germanic peoples with their trials by ordeal, mixed system of government, and common oversight of private property. From this vantage point the modern English system of government, with its trials by jury, its common law, and its tripartite structure of monarch, lords, and commons, was a real echo of the earlier institutions of the Germanic peoples. But there was also another side to the story that had less to do with the original arrangements of the Germanic peoples and more instead to do with those that they had acquired after the conquest of Roman Gaul. Although it was still a Germanic story, it was now a story about the inheritance of property and the inheritance of thrones as both came under the aegis of Roman law. On Montesquieu's terms, Roman law turned the legacy of the Germans into the institutions of the moderns. With Maine, the story turned full circle because its analytical core was made up of the legacy of the Romans. In this version of the story, Montesquieu's interest in the feudal and postfeudal legacy of the Germans was effaced by Maine's interest in the original qualities of the Romans and, more particularly, by the peculiar Roman legal ability to establish contractual relationships without having to rely either on an initial social contract or on the power of a centralized imperial authority. As Maine presented it, Roman law had a unique capacity to fill the space between a contract and an empire, and it was this that made it the key to the switch from status to contract that was the real foundation of modern politics.

Words That End in -ism

The verdict went with the grain of the two parallel Swiss assessments of the relationship between utilitarianism and idealism that Henri Brocher had highlighted. As Brocher also indicated, the two terms were really new names for what had earlier been known as Romanism and Germanism.[55] Both, he argued, could coexist under the aegis of a state that was more like a Swiss or a British state than one that was French. Conflict under its aegis would be conflict between competing interests, parties, or ideologies. Its most salient feature, however, would be that it was conflict that was compatible with reform rather than revolution and, as Hornung had shown, conflict between ideals and interests rather than between forces and weapons. It would, in short, be ideological conflict or conflict between things whose names end in -ism.[56]

55. For later and rather different versions of Germanism, see Stern, *The Politics of Cultural Despair.*

56. One of the few monographs to have paid much attention to the "-ism" phenomenon is Richard Koebner and Helmut Dan Schmidt, *Imperialism: The Story and Significance of a Political Word, 1840–1960* (Cambridge, CUP, 1964), especially pp. xiii–xxv. More recently, see Cesare Cuttica, "To Use or Not to Use . . . The Intellectual Historian and the *Isms*: A Survey and a Proposal," *Etudes Epistémè* 13 (2013): Varia, http://episteme.revues.org/268; Jussi Kurunmäki and Jani Marjanen, "A Rhetorical View of Isms: An Introduction," *Journal of Political Ideologies* 23 (2018): 241–55, and their "Ism, Ideologies and Setting the Agenda for Public Debate," in the same issue, pp. 256–82, as well as Jani Marjanen, "Ism Concepts in Science and Politics," *Contributions to the History of Concepts* 13 (2018): v–ix, together with the further bibliography supplied there. For a more ideologically focused approach, see Terry Eagleton, *Ideology: An Introduction* (London, Verso, 1991), and, for a recent collection of texts, see Matthew Festenstein and Michael Kenny, *Political Ideologies* (Oxford, OUP, 2005). See too Andrew Vincent, *Modern Political Ideologies* [1992], 2nd ed. (Oxford, Blackwell, 1995), and, for a wide-ranging overview, see Michael Freeden, Lyman Tower Sargent, and Marc Stears, eds., *The Oxford Handbook of Political Ideologies* (Oxford, OUP, 2013).

Usually the context in which many of the most familiar modern political ideologies took shape has been taken to be a context informed by the legacy of the French Revolution and the impact of European industrialization before and after 1848. Although this is certainly true, the facts of their emergence still have to be combined with an explanation of how and why this proliferating range of political ideologies has been able to coexist. In one sense, this calls for something like the type of explanation of whatever has been involved in enabling, for example, Catholicism to coexist with Calvinism or Lutheranism because they too are words that end in -ism. In another sense, however, it also calls for something broader because, in the last analysis, it is likely that almost any noun or adjective can turn into a word ending in -ism. This, it could be said, was the real message of the concept of unsocial sociability.

Some ideologies, like liberalism, conservatism, socialism, or nationalism, are still well known. Others, like Chartism, Boulangism, autonomism, or panpolism (the opposite of monopolism), are either long forgotten or never really got off the ground.[57] All of them, however, began with the form of a name that was already in existence long before any particular political ideology took hold. The form in question was, as it still is, a word ending in -ism, as is now the case with, for example, feminism, environmentalism, or republicanism. The same applies in almost every modern European language with, for instance, a range of words ending in *-isme*, *-ismo*, or *-ismus* forming the French, Italian, or German versions of their more or less similar Anglophone counterparts. This generic quality means that a single, originally Greek, form preceded a multitude of names, and, too, that discussions of the properties of the form began well before it had any stable association with a political ideology or its name. As a journalist writing at the time of the French Revolution reported, the French political economist André Roubaud had shown in his *Nouveaux synonymes françaises* (New French synonyms) of 1785 that "endings in *-ism* are the sign of a *doctrine*, of a *systematic opinion* or the opinion of a *sect*, often even of a *schism*." It was for this reason, the journalist continued, "that when party hatred creates a word to designate its adversaries, the word in question always ends in *-ism*, as in *alarmism*, *federalism*, *moderatism*, or *royalism*." As had been the case a century earlier with *Jansenism*, the journalist wrote, the point of the ending was to

---

57. "Panpolism" was a term coined by the nineteenth-century socialist Karl Marlo (1810–65; his original name was Karl Georg Winkelblech); see G.D.H. Cole, *A History of Socialist Thought*, 5 vols. (London, Macmillan, 1953–54), 2:26–27, and Edgard Allix, *L'Oeuvre économique de Karl Marlo* (Paris, Giard, 1898).

blacken the designated target because this, he added, was what *vocabulism* was able to do.[58]

Words ending in -ism, noted a later dictionary entry, this time referring to the word *atheism*, were "systemative," meaning that they indicated "a system, a doctrine, a way of acting, thinking, or doing things."[59] Although, as another authority noted in the course of discussing the word *realism*, the ending made the words "excessively vacuous," they would still "be used by the public as markers or milestones" in order to label or classify people or doctrines.[60] This, remarkably, was what the ending itself could do. "Words ending in -ism," wrote the author of a lecture on individualism, helpfully entitled "Being Oneself," "refer readily to systems, while words ending in -ty refer to their corresponding substantives or the object of these systems." Thus, the lecture continued, "spiritualism refers to that system whose object is the spirituality of the soul, materialism refers to its *materiality*; *utilitarianism* has the principle of *utility* as its object, just as individualism has *individuality* as its object."[61] The names, in short, were systematic, bringing together, classifying, and evaluating individuals, doctrines, and actions under a single synthetic term.

Importantly, however, the terms themselves were usually quite distinct from both the individuals and their doctrines and actions. Like maps or milestones, their synthetic power meant that words ending in -ism usually began by referring to things that were almost entirely different from their constituent parts until, for further reasons, the word itself became a name of choice. Something like this actually happened to ideology itself. It began as the French word *idéologie*, or the study of the origin of ideas. It then turned into "ideologism" (as in "separating the truth from the dark and scholarly impenetrabilities of

58. "Roubaud a observé dans ses *Synonymes français*, ouvrage d'un grand mérite, que les terminaisons en *isme* sont le signe d'une *doctrine*, d'une *opinion systématique*, d'une opinion de *secte*, souvent même d'un *schisme*. C'est par cette raison que quand les haines de parti créent un mot pour désigner des adversaires, ce mot se termine toujours en *isme*; de là l'*alarmisme*, le *fédéralisme*, le *modérantisme*, le *royalisme*, etc." Louis XIV's confessor, continued the article, had described attacking Jansenism as "c'est mon noir à noircir." "Cette anecdote," it concluded, "est l'histoire du *vocabulisme*, du barbarisme, du barbarrer-isme moderne." [Anon.], *L'Esprit des journaux, français et étranger*, 480 vols., but with no annual volume numbers (Liège, Brussels, and Paris, 1772–1814), May–June 1795 (or vol. 3, 1795), p. 347.

59. Joseph Benoit, *Belgicismes ou les vices de langage et de prononciation les plus communs en Belgique corrigés d'après l'Académie et les meilleurs écrivains* (Antwerp, 1857), p. 12.

60. "Ce sont des mots excessivement creux, mais qui servent de jalons au public." Jules Husson (aka Champfleury), *Contes d'automne* (Paris, 1854), p. 99.

61. Antoine-François Arbousse-Bastide, "Etre soi. Conférence sur l'individualisme," *Revue Chrétienne* 17 (5 January 1870): 28 n. 1.

ideologism," as an early nineteenth-century French periodical put it).[62] Finally, the original name came to be conflated with its pejorative product, and, as was shown by Granier de Cassagnac, a new subject, centred on identifying the realities behind the abstractions, was born. Behind the names, therefore, there was initially likely to be no more than a loosely bounded assortment of individuals, doctrines, and actions that, when taken severally, had little intrinsic to do with the putatively systematic properties of the terms themselves. This is why starting with an ideology is to begin at the end. It is also why this is a book that has been about somewhat more than a number of different objects of ideological allegiance, like conservatism or communism, and why, instead, it has tried to deal as much with the modern age as with modern politics, and as much with the adjective as the nouns. In more fashionable terms, its aim has been to be a genealogy, not a teleology, with as much room for choice and chance as for causes and consequences.[63] It has, certainly, set out to try to describe something of the content of liberalism, nationalism, or socialism as well as conservatism or communism. But it has also, more substantively, been a book about what was going on politically and intellectually when these terms took shape. Its main concern, however, has been to try to identify some of the concepts and moves involved in turning masses of initially heterogeneous doctrines and actions, arguments and debates into the endlessly changing, but still identifiable, cluster of -isms and ideologies that informs modern politics. The results were laid out towards the end of the nineteenth century by a French political scientist named Henry Michel in a book on the idea of the state.[64] There, just as Constant had done by turning the parallel between the ancients and moderns into an argument between the classics and romantics and, finally,

62. "Legislation," the periodical announced, had to be based on facts: "seule marche indiquée par la saine philosophie, qui en dégageant la vérité des savantes ténèbres de l'idéologisme et des abstractions d'une métaphysique contentieuse, conduit, en cette matière comme en toute autre, à la véritable science du droit public." *Archives françaises, ou recueil authentique d'actions honorables pour servir à l'histoire depuis le 1er janvier 1789 jusqu'au 1er janvier 1818* 1 (1818): 177–78. For a thought-provoking examination of the concept of ideology in the thought of Marx and Engels, see Etienne Balibar, *Masses, Classes, Ideas* (London, 1994), pp. 87–124.

63. For a concise and careful overview of a large subject, see Melissa Lane, "Doing Our Own Thinking for Ourselves: On Quentin Skinner's Genealogical Turn," *Journal of the History of Ideas* 73 (2012): 71–82.

64. Henry Michel, *L'idée de l'état* [1895], 3rd ed. [1898] (reprinted Paris, Fayard, 2003). Henceforth reference will be made to the 2003 edition. On Michel (not to be confused with his near contemporary, the German political sociologist Robert Michels), see Serge Audier, ed., *Henry Michel: l'individu et l'état, Corpus: revue de philosophie* 48 (2005), and Jean-Fabien Spitz, *Le moment républicain en France* (Paris, Gallimard, 2005), pp. 63–110.

into a synthesis of what he associated with both ancient and modern liberty, Michel now set out to show that there was no way back from the combination of autonomy and democracy that, he claimed, had become the key to modern politics. Where, for Constant, the politics of autonomy was the alternative to the politics of democracy, for Michel the politics of democracy was, instead, the precondition of the politics of autonomy.

The starting point of Michel's examination of the idea of the state was the view that modern politics and modern political science were in a state of crisis. There were many variations on this theme. For some, it was connected to the eclipse of representative government by democratic accountability. In this version, an elected representative was taken to be something other than a representative of the nation, the sovereign, or any comparable single source of legitimate political authority. A representative was, instead, a delegate of a constituency, a primary assembly, or a district, and the multiplicity of these different, and potentially discordant, units threatened to create a void rather than a union. For others, the source of the crisis was the rise of the politics of distribution at the expense of the politics of legislation. Here, as questions of welfare and taxation began to take precedence over constitutional and legal questions, the old quest for formal equality under the rule of law gave way to a new emphasis on social equality under the aegis of justice or fairness. For yet others, the source of the crisis was the rise of organized party politics and the corresponding eclipse of political leadership or voter involvement in public life. In this version of the condition, the growing unaccountability of the political elite was matched by the apathy of the electorate. In all these variations on the theme of crisis, the emphasis fell on the difficulties of decision making and, more immediately, on the increasingly acute problem of making legitimate decisions in the face of the putatively growing disaggregation and disintegration of modern political societies. To some, the crisis raised a further question about the line separating the legitimate from the illegitimate. The prevailing tendency of domestic politics, they argued, was to favour welfare more than warfare. But in a divided world, warfare might have to take precedence over welfare. In these conditions, ordinary politics would have to give way to power politics, and constitutional proprieties would be forced to take second place to executive action.

All these problems were highlighted in a book entitled, somewhat blandly, *The Development of Parliament in the Nineteenth Century* that was published in 1895 by a British academic named Goldsworthy Lowes Dickinson. Dickinson's solution was to advocate the adoption of the referendum as a means to check the cluster of threats represented by these modern political developments and neutralize their capacity to increase executive power. A referendum, he argued, could prevent divisive issues from becoming entangled in party-political manoeuvres by making the whole electorate responsible for a single decision on a single issue. "So essential, indeed," he wrote, "is the referendum to the complete theory of democracy, that when we find a hesitation on the part of democrats to apply it, it is difficult to avoid the conclusion, so forcibly suggested by history, that after all, a democrat, as a rule, is only a Jacobin in disguise."[65] Much, however, would depend on the initial question. This, Dickinson also argued, was why it was also necessary to reform the British House of Lords both by turning its existing hereditary peerage into a life peerage and by giving it responsibility for drafting the provisions of future referendums. As he recognized, introducing the Swiss-inspired principle of the referendum would lower the status of Parliament, but reforming the House of Lords would give Parliament a better chance to survive.

Dickinson's initial diagnosis of the crisis of modern politics was matched by a series of articles by a French law professor named Maurice Deslandres that were subsequently published in 1902 as a single book entitled *La crise de la science politique et le problème de la méthode* (The crisis of political science and the problem of method). Deslandres's examination of the causes of the crisis was remarkably similar to Dickinson's, so much so that Deslandres subsequently went on to write a fifty-page introduction to his own translation of the book.[66] He did so partly because of the small stream of replies that his original series of articles helped to provoke. But he did so too because his own solution to the putative crisis of modern politics was designed to parallel what he called *historisme*, or "the intellectual tendency that can result from the use of historical methods," that he singled out as the main feature of Dickinson's examination of the British system of government.[67] Since France's history was not

65. Goldsworthy Lowes Dickinson, *The Development of Parliament in the Nineteenth Century* (London, 1895), p. 172.

66. Maurice Deslandres, *La crise de la science politique et le problème de la méthode* (Paris, 1902) and his own introduction to Goldsworthy Lowes Dickinson, *Le développement du parlement pendant le dix-neuvième siècle* (Paris, 1906). On Deslandres, see Stéphane Pinon, *Maurice Deslandres et le droit constitutionnel. Un itinéraire* (Dijon, Editions Universitaires de Dijon, 2012), and Guillaume Sacriste, *La république des constitutionnalistes. Professeurs de droit et légitimation de l'état en France (1870–1914)* (Paris, Presses de Sciences Po, 2011), pp. 357–58, 451–68, 502–10. See too Jones, *The French State in Question*, pp. 39–45.

67. On "historisme," see Deslandres's introduction to Dickinson, *Le développement du parlement pendant le dix-neuvième siècle*, pp. xx, xxii. On the publications provoked by Deslandres's *La crise de la science politique*, see Raymond Saleilles, *Y a-t-il une crise de la science politique?*, ed. Carlos Miguel Herrera (Paris, Dalloz, 2012), p. 1 n. 1, notably the review of the book by François Gény, "L'histoire et la science politique: à propos d'un ouvrage récent," *Revue de synthèse historique* 5 (1902): 186–99.

British history, the solution to the modern political crisis was, for Deslandres, both more democratic, by extending the franchise to women, and less democratic, by adding proportional representation to the electoral system, an upper chamber based on professional associations to the legislative system, and an electoral college to a more strongly presidential system of government. The outcome was something like a historically updated version of Sieyès's original draft of the French Constitution of the Year VIII (1800). The same emphasis on *historisme* lay behind the large, three-volume constitutional history of France that Deslandres began to publish in 1932, long after his initial diagnosis of the crisis of modern political science had passed. Even the Owl of Minerva, it could be said, had to make judgments and choices about when to take flight.

Henry Michel and the Politics of Unsocial Sociability

Michel's approach to the subject was very different. He was, to begin with, unfazed by political ideologies. "A foreigner who is unfamiliar with our affairs," he wrote in a short essay entitled "On Some Words Ending in -*Ism*" published at the beginning of the twentieth century, "might think that Paris is a very fertile ground for factions. By turn autonomist, Boulangist, and nationalist, it seems to produce a proliferating abundance of the most varied crops." But, Michel continued, appearances were deceptive. Over time, it was almost always the "same" electors who would vote for one or other of these different -*isms*. In this sense, the apparently substantial shifts of allegiance were more like passing clouds. Sometimes they would look like a palace, sometimes an animal, but, at bottom, they were still simply clouds, just as Paris was still Paris even if it was also "sometimes autonomist and sometimes nationalist." The parts, in short, still belonged to a whole, however antagonistic they sometimes seemed to be. Behind the divisions, there was still politics; and behind politics there were still governments, states, and power.[68]

68. "Un étranger, qui ne serait pas au courant de nos affaires, pourrait croire que Paris est un sol merveilleux pour les factions. Tour à tour autonomiste, boulangiste et nationaliste, il semble produire avec une fécondité débordante les moissons les plus variées. Mais, nous autres, qui connaissons Paris, nous ne devons pas nous laisser prendre à ces apparences. Nous savons très bien que ce sont presque toujours «les mêmes» électeurs qui votent pour ces différents *ismes*, selon la caprice du jour. Regardez les nuages qui fuient: ils affectent tantôt la forme d'un palais, et tantôt celle d'un animal. Mais, au fond, c'est toujours le nuage, un peu de brouillard en suspension dans l'atmosphère. Tel Paris: il se proclame tantôt autonomiste et tantôt nationaliste." Henry Michel, "De quelques mots en *isme*," in his *Propos de morale*, 2nd ser. (Paris, 1904), pp. 19–21.

On Michel's terms, politics was the new sociability. Or, it could be said, politics was Kant's concept of unsocial sociability in practice. Where sociability had once meant something prepolitical, because it was a noun that referred mainly to the question of whether, for example, it was love, need, language, or law that originally formed the first bonds of society, the sequence was now reversed. Instead of sociability preceding politics, politics now preceded sociability because politics had become the force driving the range and variety of overlapping allegiances that societies had now come to house. In this sense, the end of history was not, as has sometimes been said, the end of ideology, however much it has sometimes been easy to conflate the two terms. On Michel's terms, history's end was where ideologies began. In place of the ancients and the moderns, the Romans and the Germans, and the classics and the romantics, there was now a proliferating and endlessly changing cluster of words ending in -ism. The earlier antitheses had given way to modern political ideologies, and these, in the first instance, could be differentiated quickly and comprehensively solely on the basis of the synthetic properties of their names. Moreover, just as the content of modern politics could be reduced to a cluster of synthetic terms, so the assortment of choices that these terms had come to stand for was now the real key not only to party government and electoral politics but also to the curious social cohesion that was sometimes the other side of political divisions and party-political conflict.

Politics here were democratic and, in a muted sense, also federal. The broader theory on which the claim was based was an outcome of Michel's earlier examination of the idea of the state. That examination (in what is probably still the best history of nineteenth-century French political thought in existence) took the form of a detailed history of the origins and implications of what Michel took to be a mistaken, but deeply entrenched, conceptual opposition between individuals and the state. This opposition—which has continued into the twentieth century as a further series of oppositions between markets and states, atomism and collectivism, individualism and socialism, negative liberty and positive liberty, *Gemeinschaft* and *Gesellschaft*, or, more recently, between communitarianism and liberalism or between liberalism and republicanism—was, Michel argued, a product of the nineteenth-century erosion of the earlier, eighteenth-century, concept of individualism that had first been established by Rousseau and Kant (as one early reviewer commented, the correct title of Michel's book should have been "Individualism: Its Friends and Enemies from the Eighteenth Century to the Present").[69] In this account, both Rousseau and Kant were critics of what Michel was one of the first to call

69. Emile Faguet, *Propos littéraires* (Paris, 1902), pp. 53–70.

"enlightened despotism," or the idea that the politics of reform were best managed by, as Bentham and Austin had insisted, a sovereign legislator, a sovereign ruler, or, finally, a centralized absolute government.[70] For Rousseau and Kant, Michel argued, there was no opposition between individuals and the state because, Michel claimed, they had both taken the individual-state relationship to be one of ends and means. Individuality for both was synonymous with liberty, while states, laws, and governments were simply the means to that end. As Michel put it, "the true character of the type of individualism that does not annihilate the state is nowhere better seen than in the thought of Rousseau and Kant." It was, he wrote, a position that had been captured neatly by Rousseau in his assertion, in book 2, chapter 12, of the *Social Contract* that "it was only the power of that state that can make for the liberty of its members."[71]

According to Michel, the formulation was designed to show that the opposition between the individual and the state that "was to become the essential characteristic of the individualist orthodoxy" was not "an integral part of eighteenth-century individualism."[72] This was because eighteenth-century individualism was the individualism of autonomy and personality, not the individualism of interest and utility. The former was an individualism of ends; the latter was an individualism of means. The two could coexist for as long as the distinction between means and ends remained clear, but they were also likely to clash as soon as their different attributes began to be blurred or conflated. The aim of Michel's history was to show, first, how Rousseau and Kant had established the initial difference between the two types of individualism; second, to explain why that difference had been lost or denied by a range of nineteenth-century political thinkers, from Bentham, Bonald, and de Maistre to Spencer, Comte, and Benoît Malon; and, finally, to show how the original compatibility between individualism and the state could be revived in the light of the thought of Alexis de Tocqueville and, in particular, of the neo-Kantian French philosopher Charles Renouvier.

Michel made a strong connection between Rousseau and Tocqueville. The link was supplied by a line of thinkers who had explained why democratic sovereignty had to be matched by a democratically elected system of government. Somewhat surprisingly, the first was Montesquieu, not so much because of what he had written about government and sovereignty, or about

70. Michel, *L'idée de l'état*, pp. 22, 23–41.

71. "Le vrai caractère de cet individualisme qui n'annihile pas l'état, ne se marque nulle part mieux que chez Rousseau et chez Kant." Ibid., p. 97 and, p. 98, citing Rousseau, "Il n'y a que la force de l'état qui fasse la liberté de ses membres." Rousseau, *Social Contract*, bk. 2, ch. 12.

72. Michel, *L'idée de l'état*, p. 104.

the separation of powers, but because of what he had written about welfare. "The state," he had written (in a passage that Michel quoted), "owes to all its citizens an assured subsistence, food, and suitable clothing and a way of life that is not at odds with health."[73] Rousseau, Michel continued, had endorsed the same idea in calling for the establishment of public granaries to store cereals for distribution to individuals and households in conditions of scarcity. Condorcet had substituted insurance and "a democratization of credit" for Rousseau's public granaries, while both Kant and Sieyès had accepted that "the notion of a democratic state" had to be "constituted essentially on these two principles: the provision of the means to exist and the opportunity for moral and intellectual cultivation to every individual."[74] This, Michel asserted, was the conception of the state that had been passed down to Tocqueville. "It is a contradiction," Tocqueville had written in a passage that Michel quoted, "for the people to be both destitute and sovereign."[75] The main difference separating modern from both ancient and Christian morality, Tocqueville also wrote in a letter to Arthur de Gobineau in 1843, was the idea that a political society was responsible for the welfare of all its members. In early drafts of his book on the Old Regime and the French Revolution, he singled out Guizot's claim about the atomization of social life in the wake of the barbarian invasions as the underlying cause of the decline and fall of the Roman Empire and applied it to modern political societies.[76] Without welfare, life under conditions of economic and social interdependence would produce the same process of social dissolution that it had done to imperial Rome.

Michel made it clear that he accepted the claim. It was this recognition of the state's responsibilities, he wrote, that separated a democrat like Tocqueville

73. "L'état doit à tous les citoyens une subsistance assurée, la nourriture, un vêtement convenable et un genre de vie qui ne soit point contraire à la santé." Ibid., p. 94, citing Montesquieu, *De l'esprit des lois*, bk. 23, ch. 29 (see, for example, the two-volume Paris, 1979, Garnier-Flammarion edition, ed. Victor Goldschmidt, 2:134).

74. Michel, *L'idée de l'état*, pp. 98 (Rousseau), 100–104 (Condorcet and Kant), 107–8 (Sieyès).

75. "Il est contradictoire que le peuple soit à la fois misérable et souverain." Ibid., p. 299 (citing Tocqueville).

76. On Tocqueville's use of Guizot, see Robert T. Gannett Jr, *Tocqueville Unveiled: The Historian and His Sources for* The Old Regime and the Revolution (Chicago, U of Chicago Press, 2003), pp. 1–2. On Tocqueville's endorsement of the idea of public welfare as the distinctive feature of modern morality, see the exchange of letters between Tocqueville and Gobineau of 8 August and 5 and 8 September 1843, in Alexis de Tocqueville, *Oeuvres complètes*, ed. J. P. Mayer et al., 17 vols. (Paris, 1951–2021), 9:43–56. See too, in the same volume, pp. 309–28 for Gobineau's "Coup d'œil général sur l'histoire de la morale." For Guizot's original historical claim, see above, ch. 8.

from liberals like Benjamin Constant or Germaine de Staël. But, while Tocqueville diverged from the Coppet group in his endorsement of welfare provisions, his assessment of the parts played by the law and the administration in the government of modern states was very similar to those made by Constant's two political allies, Etienne Aignan and Jean-Pierre Pagès. "If we study what has passed in the world since men began to preserve the remembrance of events," Tocqueville wrote in an essay entitled "Political and Social Condition of France" published in the *London and Westminster Review* in 1836, "we soon discover that, in civilized countries, by the side of a despot who governs, there is almost always a lawyer who regularizes and strives to render consistent with one another the arbitrary and incoherent decrees of the monarch."

> The general and indefinite love of power which animates kings is, by the lawyers, tempered with a love of method and with the skill which they naturally possess in the management of business. Kings can constrain, for the time being, the obedience of men; lawyers can bend them almost voluntarily to a durable obedience. Kings furnish the power; lawyers invest that power with the form and semblance of a right. Kings seize upon absolute power by force; lawyers give it the sanction of legality. When the two are united, the result is a despotism which scarcely allows a breathing place to human nature.
>
> He who conceives the idea of the prince without that of the lawyer sees only one of the aspects of tyranny; to conceive it as a whole it is necessary to contemplate them both at once.[77]

As with Aignan and Pagès, the problem was connected to the codified version of Roman law established under Napoleon. It was an assessment that Tocqueville, who started in life as a magistrate, maintained throughout his life. "Roman law," he wrote in a letter to his godson shortly before he died, "has played a very important part in the history of almost every modern nation. It has done them much good and, in my view, even more harm. It perfected their civil law and perverted their political law." This, Tocqueville went on to explain, was because Roman law had two faces. One dealt with relations between individuals, and in this respect it was one of the "most admirable products of civilization." The other face, however, dealt with relations between subjects and sovereigns, and in this respect it was redolent of the spirit of the age and the system of servitude in which it was formed. "It was with the help of Roman law and its interpreters," Tocqueville concluded, echoing a familiar theme,

---

77. Alexis de Tocqueville, "Political and Social Condition of France," *London and Westminster Review* 3 (1836): 137–69 (here, p. 161).

"that kings founded absolute power on the ruins of the free institutions of the Middle Ages. Only the English refused to receive it and they alone have preserved their independence."[78] Among the most important of these free institutions was the jury, although Tocqueville was careful to avoid describing it as a purely Germanic institution. Juries, he emphasized, belonged as much to the history of the Roman republic as to the Normans or Germans because, with variations, they were the spontaneous creation of every free people.[79] The problem, however, was whether they could hold rulers and governments to account as readily as ordinary private individuals.

Tocqueville described the nature of the problem more fully in 1846 in a review of a textbook on administrative law. The author of the book, a law professor named Louis-Antoine Macarel, whom Tocqueville knew personally, had written that France, like other modern societies, housed two types of law. One was the civil code whose provisions applied to disputes and infringements among private individuals or communities. The other was the code of administrative law that applied to disputes in which the state was an interested party. As Macarel presented it, this latter type of law allowed the state and its officials to avoid the type of accountability that applied to individuals. Tocqueville took strong exception to Macarel's assumption that the civil law and administrative law were simply two complementary systems of justice, with two sets of rules and procedures. "These," he wrote, "are axioms of law that no free people and, I would add, no civilized people could ever accept." Macarel's endorsement of the equivalence between civil and administrative law amounted to saying that "where the adversary is weak and the partiality of the judge little to be feared," a citizen could choose to go to court. But "where the adversary is strong and the partiality of the judge is to be feared," a citizen was condemned to rely on a comparatively dependent judge, with one of the parties also having the right to judge. There was, in short, no equivalence between civil and administrative law. To assume that the only distinction between the one and the other was that, in matters of administrative law, the state was an interested party was tantamount to claiming that the principles of administrative law should apply to cases of political crimes and

78. Alexis de Tocqueville to Alexis Stöffels, 4 January 1856, in Alexis de Tocqueville, Œuvres complètes, ed. Françoise Mélonio and Anne Vibert, Tome xvii, vol. 3 (Paris, Gallimard, 2021), p. 229. The letter is signalled in the thorough study by Michael Drolet, Tocqueville, Democracy and Social Reform (Basingstoke, Macmillan, 2003), p. 83.

79. See his report of 1842 to the Académie des sciences morales et politiques on I. Labastard Delisle, De l'administration de la justice criminelle chez les Romains, and Joseph-Laurent Couppey, De l'administration de la justice criminelle en Normandie dans le Moyen Age, in Alexis de Tocqueville, Œuvres complètes, vol. 16, ed. Françoise Mélonio (Paris, Gallimard, 1989), pp. 170–84.

political offenses. After all, Tocqueville wrote, "the state's interest is even more engaged in cases like these than in cases involving no more than the execution or nonexecution of a transaction."[80]

The problem was the more acute, Tocqueville wrote, because the French system of administration was the one genuine innovation of the French Revolution. As he was to point out repeatedly, most of what seemed new in the French Revolution, from its principles to its institutions, was already in place or in the process of being established well before 1789. The one exception was the administrative system, which, he argued, was a genuine novelty. Although, he continued, it was now usual to associate the French administration and French administrative law with Napoleon and the First Empire, both were in fact the one great achievement of the French National and Constituent Assembly of 1789. All that Napoleon had done was to transform the elected administrative system established by the Constituent Assembly into a system whose officials were not elected but appointed from above. In this sense, a system that was designed to preserve liberty had become an instrument of despotism. But, Tocqueville asserted, it would be imitated all over Europe. Every country would see the formation of something like French administrative law because that system of administrative law was itself no more than "one of the forms of the new state of the world." "We call it the *French* system but we should say the *modern* system."

The problem was, therefore, a modern problem, not simply a French problem. It was a modern problem because it was not clear what could or should be done to reconcile modern administrative institutions with representative government. We should never forget, Tocqueville wrote in the same review, "that if our administrative system was conceived in liberty, it was realized by despotism, leaving unresolved the problem of reconciling its consecration of extreme centralization with the reality and morality of representative government." The question remained an open one. It meant, Tocqueville continued, that the question of how "to establish agreement between the principles of administrative law and political laws, between the needs of government and the necessary existence of centralization with the spirit and rules of representative government, is a subject that awaits a book." It would, he concluded, "be one of the greatest works that our generation could undertake."[81]

Michel's extensive examination of the idea of the state was, substantively, a long commentary on Tocqueville's observation. The problem that Tocqueville

---

80. Alexis de Tocqueville, "Rapport sur le cours de droit administratif de M. Macarel," *Séances et travaux de l'Académie des sciences morales et politiques* 9 (1846): 105–20 (here p. 118).
81. Ibid., p. 120.

had identified meant, Michel wrote, that the conceptual antagonism between individuals and the state had begun with the liberals of the nineteenth century rather than with absolute government's enlightened critics of the eighteenth century. It also meant that modern politics called for the revival of the eighteenth century's conception of the complementary character of the relationship between individuals and the state. Although this did not mean jettisoning all aspects of the liberal legacy, since Constant's famous distinction between the liberty of the ancients and the liberty of moderns continued to apply, it still meant that modern liberty was autonomy, not nondomination. Michel, accordingly, had no hesitation in aligning Tocqueville with Heinrich Ahrens on the grounds that both were critics of Roman law, and of the way that Roman law had been revived in the thought of Savigny and the German historical school. As Michel noted, the British legal historian Sir Frederick Pollock had described Savigny as "a Darwinist before Darwin," while, Michel added approvingly, Heinrich Ahrens had written that "the historical school came to consider the Roman people as the elect people, bringing forth law, and raising up Roman law into a universal code."[82] As many other late nineteenth-century commentators also argued, the German historical school had, inadvertently, superimposed Roman law upon German realities.[83]

With Michel, the argument over legal codification had come full circle, adding a further inflection to the overlapping dialogues between the ancients and moderns, the classics and the romantics, and the critics and supporters of Smith and Kant. Where Savigny and his followers had accused the German codifiers of riding roughshod over history, morality, and politics, the same charge of standardization and centralization could now be applied to the historical school itself. Something similar, Michel claimed, had happened to the broader argument between the ancients and the moderns. In this case, what had begun as an assertion of the salience of what was ancient and Roman had

82. Michel, *L'idée de l'état*, p. 171 and n. 1.

83. See, for example, Frederick William Maitland, *English Law and the Renaissance* (Cambridge, CUP, 1901), pp. 7–8 and 46–47 n. 13: "This [the early sixteenth century] was the time when Roman law was driving German law out of Germany or forcing it to conceal itself in humble forms and obscure corners. If this was the age of the Renaissance and the age of the Reformation, it was also the age of the 'Reception'. I need not say that this Reception—the reception of Roman law—plays a large part in modern versions of German history, and by no means only in such as are written by lawyers. I need not say that it has been judged from many different points of view, that it has been connected by some with political, by others with religious and by yet others with economic changes. Nor need I say that of late years few writers have had a hearty good word for the Reception. We have all of us been nationalists of late. Cosmopolitanism can afford to wait its turn."

turned once again into an endorsement of what was modern and German. But, unlike earlier generations of like-minded political thinkers, including Sismondi, Ahrens, Tocqueville, and Laboulaye, Michel did not take the further step of associating modern political societies with a federal system of government. He made this clear in the course of a discussion of the concept of law in the thought of one of his contemporaries, a French philosophy professor named Alfred Fouillée.

Fouillée's conception of the law was loosely Kantian. There were, he had written in his *L'idée moderne de droit* (The modern idea of law) three main, partly correct, ways of talking about the law. Law could be identified with force, or could be seen as an interest that was more powerful than any other, or could be taken to be an expression of the inner freedom of the human soul.[84] The problem was that these three conceptions of law did not seem to be compatible. Force, Fouillée argued, was simply another way of talking about causation, and if this was the case, a higher version of the idea of force would be to redescribe the rule of law as a self-perpetuating causal system. The same idea applied to the concept of interest. An interest could be immediate and self-centred, but a higher version of the same concept would come out as general utility. Force, in other words, could be aligned with liberalism, just as interest could be aligned with utilitarianism. But these two higher versions of self-centred systems still needed something disinterested to bridge the gap between the particular and the general or the individual and the state. This, it seemed, would be where the feeling of inner freedom came in. But to do so, there would have to be some sort of criterion to justify freedom's choices. This criterion, Fouillée argued, could not be found in any actual choice because any actual choice could always be redescribed either as something arbitrary or as something caused. It followed, Fouillée claimed, that the feeling of freedom had to be seen as something outside the natural world, because it could not be tied down by causation or by any particular type of utility. In this sense, the feeling of freedom was a kind of known unknown, or, as Fouillée put it, a feeling produced by "the certainty of the unknown and the possibility of the unknowable."[85] Its existence, however, supplied the emotional and practical bridge between the particular and the general that was missing from both liberalism and utilitarianism. It made it possible to envisage a federal system, with a state that was responsible for preserving the feeling of individual freedom, and, below it, a multiplicity of subordinate institutions working as either markets or governments on liberal or utilitarian principles. Simply because the

84. Michel, *L'idée de l'état*, p. 617.
85. Ibid., p. 620.

state would be different from its subordinate parts, it would be an object of allegiance that would be an alternative to those other objects of allegiance represented by its liberal or utilitarian components.

The difficulty was to see how something unknown could still be known by the members of a political society in ways that could be verified (one answer might have involved symbols or metaphors). But, to Michel, any claim about the existence of this type of common knowledge would have to imply a kind of collective consciousness, and if it did, it was not clear how this collective consciousness could be reconciled with individual agency and choice. "If," Michel wrote, quoting another of Fouillée's critics, "the *I* is an *us*, then the *us* is an *I* for the same reasons."[86] However negative Fouillée's concept of liberty appeared to be, it was not clear that it actually supplied a working concept of liberty at all. Michel, accordingly, was unpersuaded. "More than one philosopher or jurist, in Germany and in France," he wrote, "has tried using similar means to appease the quarrel between the state and the individual by bringing together what Bluntschli has called the historical and philosophical methods." The best known, he continued, were now Karl Christian Friedrich Krause and Heinrich Ahrens. Fouillée, he claimed, belonged to the same camp. The "only difference," he wrote, distinguishing "the 'ideal organism' of Krause, the 'moral organism' of Ahrens, and the 'contractual organism' of Fouillée" was a difference in names. The similarity, he added, was quite easy to explain because it was Schelling who had been the common intellectual source from which Krause and Ahrens on the one side, and Fouillée on the other, had taken their metaphysical principles and, by extension, the principles of their political and social theories.[87] The problem was that there was no way of identifying what Fouillée himself had called "the just limit" of the rights of the state over the individual or, inversely, those of the individual over the state. The state of the future might well be federal, or, as Fouillée had put it, "an association of associations."[88] It might also consist, as Fouillée had also put it, of "freely agreed centralization arising from decentralization itself." But it would still be unable to escape the problem of political obligation. If a state was the supreme

86. "Si le moi est un nous, le nous est un moi pour les mêmes raisons." Ibid., p. 629 (citing a comment by Alfred Espinas, one of Fouillée's better-known critics).

87. "Sans remonter jusqu'à Krause, il faut citer Ahrens, l'un des représentants les plus qualifies de l'école éthico-organique. Entre 'l'organisme idéale' de Krause, 'l'organisme moral' d'Ahrens, et 'l'organisme contractuel' de M. Fouillée, il n y a guère d'autre différence que celle des mots. . . . On s'explique, d'ailleurs, ces analogies puisque Schelling est la source commune ou Krause, Ahrens d'une part, M. Fouillée, de l'autre, ont puisé les principes de leur métaphysique et, par suite, ceux de leurs théories politiques et sociales." Ibid., pp. 629–30.

88. Ibid., p. 622.

judge of its duties, it was also the supreme judge of its rights.[89] There was, in short, no way out of politics and no way of avoiding individual decision making and choice.

Michel's discussion of Fouillée was part of a section headed "The Present Crisis of Social and Political Ideas" that ended the final, historical, part of *L'idée de l'état*. The title, together with the later, tiny essay on words ending in -ism, can be taken as a kind of climacteric. As Michel himself put it, the particular idea of the state that had supplied the subject matter of his thesis now seemed to be over. "Indicated by Rousseau, fortified by Condorcet, the individualist philosophy of law and right (*droit*) found precise and, it would seem, complete expression first in Kant and then in Fichte. Everything is there: law reconciled with liberty, the equality of moral persons, the autonomy of the members of the state, tying and untying at will the contract that binds them."[90] The point of Michel's historical research, however, was to show that the real history of both the state and the idea of the state had been quite different. "Everything" might well have been there, but everything now seemed to have gone. After following the idea of the state from the beginning to the end of the nineteenth century, he found that there appeared to be nowhere further to go. The need, once again, was for a new start.[91] By the late nineteenth century, however, the starting point had moved nearer. Once, modern political thought had begun with the fall of the Roman Empire and the rise of Christianity. Later, the starting point moved forward to the pietism of the Reformation and, again, to the humanism of the Renaissance. Later still, as the long-drawn-out argument between the ancients and the moderns turned into a further argument between the respective supporters of the classics and the romantics, the starting point moved forwards again, this time away from the legacy of the Romans towards the legacy of the Germans, and then, finally, towards a fusion of both. In this increasingly compressed temporal setting, the many dimensions of the old arguments began to disappear from politics, leaving behind an endlessly changing kaleidoscope of words ending in -ism.

89. Ibid., pp. 623–24.

90. "Indiquée par Rousseau, fortifiée par Condorcet, la philosophie individualiste du droit a trouvé chez Kant d'abord, puis chez Fichte une expression précise et, à ce qu'il semble, achevée. Tout y est: le droit ramené à la liberté; l'égalité des personnes morales; l'autonomie des membres de la Cité, nouant ou dénouant à leur gré le contrat qui les lie." Ibid., pp. 69–70.

91. For Michel, that new start began with the philosophy of Charles Renouvier, but there is no reason here to follow his lead. On this aspect of Renouvier's thought, see Laurent Fedi, "Philosopher et républicaniser: la *Critique philosophique* de Renouvier et Pillon, 1872–1889," *Romantisme* 115 (2002): 65–82.

Behind the synthetic terms there have usually been more complicated stories with less predictable outcomes. Part of the point of this book has been to try to show how a number of overlapping stories—first about the idea of progress and Kant's idiosyncratic assessment of its implications, then about the ancients and the moderns, then about the classics and the romantics, and then about autonomy and democracy—lay behind the emergence of the synthetic terms themselves. Many of the protagonists in this group of stories published their thought in French either because this was their own language or, as was the case with some of Krause's German and Belgian followers, because this was the language that they found in exile. Behind them lay the abiding problem of the relationship between the time-bound and the timeless, the particular and the general, the creative and the causal, the historical and the historicist, or, unavoidably, the fact and the norm. The problem was registered by the gifted neo-Kantian philosopher Emil Lask in 1905, at about the same time that Henry Michel published his short essay on words that end in -ism. "Historism is the exact opposite of natural law," Lask wrote, "and this constitutes its basic meaning. Natural law seeks to extract the empirical substratum from the absoluteness of value; historism seeks to extract the absoluteness of value from the empirical substratum. It is true that by its hypostatization of value natural law destroys the independence and autonomy of the empirical and in this way ends up with the error of anti-historicity. But its basic belief in supra-historical, timeless values has not been, as many think, an error refuted by the historical enlightenment of the present, but this rather has been its immortal merit. Historism, on the other hand—not history itself nor the historical view of the law—destroys all philosophy and representation of the world. It is the most modern, most widespread and most dangerous form of relativism and entails the levelling of all values. Natural law and historism are the twin dangers that the philosophy of law must avoid."[92] The point applies as much to political thought as to the philosophy of law and there is no reason to think that the small set of stories presented here can have come close to exhausting the range. Another set of stories, this time centred mainly on protagonists from the German-speaking parts of Europe, will certainly modify the whole picture considerably. This is because, alongside the distinctions between sovereignty and government and between the public and the private, a further set of distinctions also came to play a conspicuous part in the history of political thought.

92. Lask, "Legal Philosophy," in Patterson and Wilk, *The Legal Philosophies of Lask, Radbruch, and Dabin*. Here, I have preferred the translation in Enrique Martine Paz, "Lask and the Doctrine of the Science of Law," in *Interpretations of Modern Legal Philosophies: Essays in Honor of Roscoe Pound*, ed. Paul Sayre (New York, OUP, 1947), pp. 574–77 (see p. 576).

The most significant of these distinctions was identified by a German, but still in a French context. This was the distinction between the constitution and the administration of a state that supplied the underlying conceptual architecture of the *History of the Social Movement in France, 1789–1850* published in 1850 by the Danish-German-Austrian legal theorist Lorenz von Stein. As Stein presented it, this distinction added a further dualism to those that could already be found in the sovereignty-government and public-private distinctions. It did so, he argued, because modern constitutional principles applied essentially to individuals, while modern administrative principles applied essentially to groups. As with the other distinctions, the problem was to find a way to ensure that both sets of principles could be accommodated within a single state. Constitutional principles applied to individuals, regardless of their various circumstances, endowments, and life chances. Administrative principles applied to groups, precisely because of their various circumstances, endowments, and life chances. The first existed to secure formal equality, while the second existed to establish real social cohesion. As Stein recognized, combining the two sets of principles amounted to an embryonic theory of social democracy. "The transition from democracy towards this new configuration," he wrote, "is already apparent in the idea of social democracy. At present, the content of that idea is still obscure, and if it does not emerge from that obscurity, it will disappear. But if it does emerge, it will have to become a *theory of society*, and then *the future will belong to it*."[93]

The story of how that future came to be conceived, from Lorenz von Stein to Rudolf von Jhering or Max Weber, and from Max Weber to Martin Heidegger, Carl Schmitt, Carl Joachim Friedrich, Leo Strauss, Karl Löwith, Reinhart Koselleck, and Ernst-Wolfgang Böckenförde, does not belong here.[94] Here, it is enough to note the continuity from the initial insight into the dualism of modern political societies that was first articulated in the eighteenth century by Jean-Jacques Rousseau and was then developed by Immanuel Kant and his followers or critics. With this insight, sovereignty could be democratic,

93. Stein, *Geschichte*, pt. 3, pp. 218–19, cited in Ernst-Wolfgang Böckenförde, "Lorenz von Stein, théoricien du mouvement de l'état et de la société vers l'état social," in his *Le droit, l'état et la constitution démocratique* (Paris, L.G.D.J.; Brussels, Bruylant, 2000), p. 149. See too Stein, *Le concept de société*. For English-language versions of some of Böckenförde's publications, see his *State, Society and Liberty: Studies in Political Theory and Constitutional Law* (Oxford, Berg, 1991) and his *Constitutional and Political Theory*, ed. Mirjam Künkler and Tine Stein (Oxford, OUP, 2017).

94. For indications of its possible content, see, notably, Kelly, *The State of the Political* and, more directly, his "Revisiting the Rights of Man" and "Max Weber and the Rights of Citizens," *Max Weber Studies* 4 (2004): 23–49.

while government could be representative or, sometimes, autocratic. Public law could become private law, while private law could become public law, particularly under federal conditions. The same types of switch could be made to constitutional and administrative principles and the individuals or groups they were taken to concern. The effects of these arguments, claims, and insights have not always been benign, nor have they been studied particularly thoroughly. It is now clear, however, that the turning points that they once promised—from the Romans to the Germans; from the Gothic and feudal to the Roman and republican; from the classics to the romantics; from the ancients to the moderns; and from democracy to autonomy—have never been quite as final as they once seemed. Instead, their effects have been cumulative rather than transformative, so that what were taken initially to be alternatives have turned subsequently and more fitfully into syntheses. In the German-speaking parts of Europe, this type of combination of continuity and change was once given the name *Aufhebung*, mainly by Hegel and his followers, meaning a mixture of looking back and looking forward, particularly in the light of what looking back had been able to bring more fully into view. Although the word has acquired a more technical sense, its looser meaning still continues to apply here. The moderns did not displace the ancients any more than the romantics displaced the classics or than autonomy was able to displace democracy. Instead of what was once hoped or feared, they are all still there, ready, for better or worse, to add to the endless stream of words ending in -ism on which politics has come to rely. This is why it is still worth trying to find out not only where they came from and what they were intended to do, but also what their cumulative effects have come to mean for thinking about the mixture of the imaginative and the intractable or the possible and the causal that politics continues to be.

Appendix

Lord Acton on the Romans, the Germans, and the Moderns

THE ORIGINAL VERSION of this letter of 26 November 1861 from Lord Acton to Richard Simpson, his colleague and collaborator in the production of the Catholic periodical *The Rambler*, was published in *The Correspondence of Lord Acton and Richard Simpson*, 3 vols. [1971–78], ed. Josef Lewis Altholz, Damian McElrath, and James C. Holland (Cambridge, CUP, 2008), 2:207–9. In this version, I have omitted the first two paragraphs plus a line from the postscript because they are about other subjects. I have also modernized spelling and punctuation. It is not clear whether the terse remaining line of the postscript— "Read the 27*th* Book of Montesquieu"—was a report on Acton's own reading or a recommendation by Acton to Simpson about what to read. In either case, however, it was a significant statement. The book in question (in Montesquieu's *The Spirit of Laws* of 1748) was entitled *Of the Origin and Revolutions of the Roman Laws of Successions*, and its subject matter was, indeed, central to many nineteenth-century discussions of the Romans, the Germans, and the moderns.[1]

ACTON TO SIMPSON: 26 NOVEMBER 1861

Tuesday

My dear Simpson,

Your notion about an article on liberty is worth developing. But we must distinguish nations, or at least civilizations. Antiquity is not involved in the process to which we belong; it influences it,

---

1. On the intellectual ramifications of the succession problem, see Sonenscher, *Before the Deluge.*

but is itself quite separate. Our state begins with Conquest, at the Great Migration. (Feudalism is the common type of states founded on conquest—even in India, though there it is crossed by Castes, which represent permanence in opposition to progress, that is to say, the Pantheistic notion of the state, which is without history.) No European polity has been able to stand without feudalism. Poland never got ordered; Russia is called for this reason an Asiatic state. Hungary was founded on conquest, by a people not Teutonic, but yet Indo-Germanic, which therefore at once adopted Teutonic forms (S. Stephen).

The state is only ideally the original form of social life. Each particular state only gradually grew to be a power over the people. At first society was broken into pieces, self sufficient, every group—not every man—for itself, and only God for all. There was no notion of sovereignty. The feudal lord was the highest authority. Hence *feuds* between them—the token of feudal life—the assumption of functions now devolved on the state, then discharged by every man for himself. This is one instance of the state not existing above society. It is the same in taxation, all local, none imperial &c. Consider the Crusades. In the first Crusade you would suppose there is no such thing as a state in Europe—no authority above all these noble lords. What we now call the King was, in those days, a noble among other nobles—not interfering in their sphere and domain, except by feud, not by authority, possessing power, like each of them, only over his own dependents. (France in 11th century best instance). The Arragonese said to their King: 'We, each of whom is as good as you, all together better than you'. Of course all this was obnoxious to the church, for she had no room for her grand institutions in a society so broken up. Besides the development of the State is the business of profane history. But stick to this, that in that society out of which modern European states have grown, the corporation was the first thing, the sovereign state the second. But the state gradually gained ground, and took into its hands what was common to all. The Church accomplished this first by borrowing from the Jews the notion of an anointed King, thus elevating by a divine sanction a power which the then society could not develop out of itself.

Afterwards came Roman law (about the time of Frederick I) in which the state is the first thing, law comes downwards, from the sovereign, does not grow upwards from the people, as in the

Teutonic state. This difference not however in the original principle of the two legislations, but in this that the Roman law which began to be studied was that of a finished state, of a mature, yea an old people, of an empire which had developed the most extreme absolutism on the ruins of the *Populus*.

The political ideas of the Theodosian or Justinian Code are those of a society ground to atoms by the wheel of revolution, consisting no longer of parts, but like sand or water, in which all life and all power are in the sovereign. This is the very opposite extreme of that society to which this system was introduced. Hence Frederic found men at Bologna who told him that all the property of the people was his; and that he might take what he liked—that what he left was a concession on his part. As with property, so with liberty. The Germans were slow in realizing the state, so the legists clapped a pair of spectacles on their young noses, taught them to lean on a stick, and to have the ills of age. So they grievously overshot the mark, and introduced a dualism into European politics which went on increasing till now we stand alone on Teutonic ground. Italy follows Celto-Roman France, and 1789, and in Austria the two principles are at war.

Now the Church was at once attacked by this new power, under Frederic I and II, and especially under Philip the Fair, & *Nogaret*. This was no longer a war against feudal absolutism, as with Hildebrand, Anselm, Becket, but against the pagan state. 'Quod principi placuit legis habet vigorem.' To this enemy the church gradually succumbed, after Boniface VIII, himself a lawyer, until she fell prostrate in the Concordat of Leo X. She had invoked the same absolutism for herself, (*Unam Sanctam*). So completely had she become estranged from the Teutonic system that all scholastic writers from S. Thomas to Suarez, or even to Taparelli, entirely ignore it. All their ideas are either from Roman law, or from Aristotle, or from the Jewish Theocracy. So they did unspeakable harm. The evil was that the learned education in the Middle Ages was turned away from actual life to books written in a very different society. See John Salisbury's account of his studies, and his dreadful doctrines. The scholar did not drink of the ideas of the lay society of his time. Later on the Jesuits showed the same estrangement from the state in which they lived.

I don't know what you mean by freedom of the State. All liberty is conditional, limited and therefore unequal.

The state never can do what it likes in its own sphere. It is bound by all kinds of law. But I must stop my unintelligible rhapsody till you provoke it again.

Yours ever truly
J D Acton

Read the 27*th* book of Montesquieu

BIBLIOGRAPHY

[Anon.]. *L'Esprit des journaux, français et étranger*. 480 vols. [but with no annual volume numbers]. Liège, Brussels, and Paris, 1772–1814.

[Anon.]. *Archives françaises, ou recueil authentique d'actions honorables pour servir à l'histoire depuis le 1er janvier 1789 jusqu'au 1er janvier 1818*. 1 vol. [the only one published]. Paris, 1818–21.

[Anon.]. *Du Classique et du Romantique. Recueil de discours pour et contre, lus à l'Académie royale des sciences, belles lettres et des arts de Rouen, pendant l'année 1824*. Rouen, 1826.

[Anon.]. "Jean Paul Richter." *New Monthly Magazine and Literary Journal* 38 (1833): 154–60.

[Anon.]. "Quelques réflexions sur le plan total de la création et sur la palingénésie humaine de M. Nodier." *Annales de philosophie chrétienne* 7 (1833): 48–66.

[Anon.]. "Chrestomathy: or Analects and Apologues." *Fraser's Magazine for Town and Country* 10 (1834): 439–42.

[Anon.]. "Situation des partis aux Etats-Unis." *Revue des Deux Mondes*, n.s., 16 (1846): 1127–32.

[Anon.]. Review of Vito d'Ondes Reggio, *Introduzione ai principi delle umane società*. *La Libre Recherche* 7 (Brussels, 1857): 492–94.

[Anon]. *Congres international de Bienfaisance de Francfort-sur-le-Main. Session de 1857*. 2 vols. Frankfurt and Brussels, 1858.

[Anon.]. "Le mouvement philosophique en Belgique apprécié par l'Allemagne." *La Libre Recherche* 9 (1858): 132–37.

[Anon.]. "Sur la philosophie de Herbert Spencer." *Bulletin de la société historique d'Auteuil et de Passy* 1 (1892–94): 39–40.

Abrams, M. H. "Kant and the Theology of Art." *Notre Dame English Journal* 13 (1981): 75–106.

Aeschimann, Willy. *La pensée d'Edgar Quinet: étude sur la formation de ses idées avec essais de jeunesse et documents inédits*. Paris, Anthropos, 1986.

Agamben, Giorgio. *The Kingdom and the Glory: For a Theological Genealogy of Economy and Government*. Stanford, Stanford UP, 2011.

Agulhon, Maurice. "Le problème de la culture populaire en France autour de 1848." *Romantisme* 9 (1975): 50–64.

Ahnert, Thomas. "The Soul, Natural Religion, and Moral Philosophy in the Scottish Enlightenment." In *Eighteenth-Century Thought*, ed. James G. Buickerood, 2:233–53. New York, AMS Press, 2004.

Ahrens, Heinrich. *De Confoederatione Germanicarum Civitatum*. Göttingen, 1830. Archives of the University of Göttingen, callmark Kur. 8141.

———. "Tendance sociale et religieuse de la philosophie allemande." *Revue Encyclopédique* 52 (1831): 686–95.

———. "Uber den Saint-Simonismus in seiner letsten religiosen, moralischen und politischen Entwicklung." *Das Ausland* 190 (8 July 1832): 757–58; 191 (9 July 1832): 761–62; 192 (10 July 1832): 766–67.

———. *Cours de droit naturel ou de philosophie du droit fait d'après l'état de cette science en Allemagne.* 1st ed., Brussels, 1838; 3rd ed., Brussels, 1850; 4th ed., Brussels, 1853; 6th ed., Leipzig, 1868; 7th ed., Leipzig, 1875.

———. *Juristische Enzyklopädie.* Vienna, 1855.

———. Translation of the introduction to his *Juristische Enzyklopädie. La Libre Recherche* (ed. Pascal Duprat) 1, no. 1 (1855): 302–5.

Aignan, Etienne. *Histoire du jury.* Paris, 1822.

Ajouri, Philip. "'The Vocation of Man'—'Die Bestimmung des Menschen': A Teleological Concept of the German Enlightenment and Its Aftermath in the Nineteenth Century." In *Historical Teleologies in the Modern World,* ed. Henning Trüper, Dipesh Chakrabarty, and Sanjay Subrahmanyan, pp. 49–70. London, Bloomsbury, 2015.

Allix, Edgard. *L'Oeuvre économique de Karl Marlo.* Paris, Giard, 1898.

Altmann, Alexander. *Moses Mendelssohn: A Biographical Study.* London, Routledge and Kegan Paul, 1973.

Altmeyer, Jean-Jacques. *Cours de philosophie de l'histoire.* Brussels, 1840.

Amend-Sochting, Anne. *Zwischen 'Implosion' und 'Explosion': zur Dynamik der Melancholie im Werk der Germaine de Staël.* Trier, Wissenschaftlicher Verlag Trier, 1991.

Ameriks, Karl. *Kant and the Historical Turn.* Oxford, Clarendon Press, 2006.

Amiel, Henri Frédéric. *Fragments d'un journal intime.* Ed. Bernard Bouvier. 3 vols. Paris, Stock, 1927.

———. *Essais critiques.* Ed. Bernard Bouvier. Paris, Stock, 1932.

Ampère, Jean-Jacques. *Mélanges d'histoire littéraire et de la littérature.* 2 vols. Paris, 1867.

Amstutz, Nina. "Caspar David Friedrich and the Anatomy of Nature." *Art History* 37 (2014): 454–81.

———. *Caspar David Friedrich: Nature and the Self.* New Haven, CT, Yale UP, 2020.

Ancillon, Frédéric. *De la souveraineté et des formes du gouvernement.* Paris, 1816.

Ando, Clifford. "A Dwelling beyond Violence: On the Uses and Disadvantages of History for Contemporary Republicans." *History of Political Thought* 31 (2010): 183–220.

———. *Law, Language and Empire in the Roman Tradition.* Philadelphia, U of Pennsylvania Press, 2011.

———, ed. *Citizenship and Empire in Europe 200–1900.* Potsdam, Franz Steiner Verlag, 2016.

Andrews, Naomi J. "The Romantic Socialist Origins of Humanitarianism." *Modern Intellectual History* 17 (2019): 737–68.

Ankersmit, Frank. *Sublime Historical Experience.* Stanford, Stanford UP, 2005.

———. *Meaning, Truth and Reference in Historical Representation.* Leuven, Leuven UP; Ithaca, NY, Cornell UP, 2012.

———. "History as the Science of the Individual." *Journal of the Philosophy of History* 7 (2013): 396–425.

———. "Representationalist Logic." In *Other Logics: Alternatives to Formal Logic in the History of Thought and Contemporary Philosophy,* ed. Admir Skodo, pp. 101–22. Leiden, Brill, 2014.

———. "Sovereignty and Political Representation." *Redescriptions* 17 (2014): 10–43.

Arbousse-Bastide, Antoine-François. "Etre soi. Conférence sur l'individualisme." *Revue Chrétienne* 17 (5 January 1870).

Ardao, Arturo. *Genesis de la Idea y el Nombre de América Latina*. Caracas, Centro de Estudios LatinoAmericanos Romulo Gallegos, 1980.

Arendt, Hannah. *The Origins of Totalitarianism* [1951]. 2nd ed. Cleveland and New York, Meridian Books, 1958.

———. *The Human Condition* [1958]. 2nd ed. Chicago, U of Chicago Press, 1998.

———. *On Violence*. New York, Harcourt Brace Jovanovich, 1970.

———. *Crises of the Republic*. New York, Harcourt, Brace & Company, 1972.

———. *Lectures on Kant's Political Philosophy*. Ed. Ronald Beinerweltan. Chicago, U of Chicago Press, 1975.

———. "The Concept of History: Ancient and Modern." In her *Between Past and Future* [1961], ed. Jerome Kohn. London, Penguin, 2006.

———. *Il n'y a qu'un seul droit de l'homme*. Ed. Emmanuel Alloa. Paris, Payot, 2021.

Arkush, Allan. *Moses Mendelssohn and the Enlightenment*. Albany, State U of New York Press, 1994.

Arnold, Thomas. "On the Social Progress of States" [1830]. In Thomas Arnold, *Miscellaneous Works*, pp. 79–111. London, 1845.

Ashton, Rosemary. *The German Idea: Four English Writers and the Reception of German Thought 1800–1860*. Cambridge, CUP, 1980.

Attuel-Hallade, Aude. *T. B. Macaulay et la révolution française: la pensée libérale whig en débat*. Paris, Michel Houdiard, 2018.

Aucuy, Marc. *Les systèmes socialistes d'échange*. Paris, 1908.

Audier, Serge, ed. *Henry Michel: l'individu et l'état. Corpus: revue de philosophie* 48 (2005).

———. *La société écologique et ses ennemis*. Paris, La Découverte, 2017.

———. *L'âge productiviste*. Paris, La Découverte, 2019.

Avineri, Shlomo. "The Problem of War in Hegel's Thought." *Journal of the History of Ideas* 22 (1961): 463–74.

———. "Hegel and Nationalism." *Review of Politics* 24 (1962): 461–84.

———. *Hegel's Theory of the Modern State*. Cambridge, CUP, 1972.

Baader, François. "Sur la liberté négative et positive." *Revue Européenne* 2 (1831): 192–94.

Babbitt, Irving. *Rousseau and Romanticism*. New York. 1919.

Baehr, Peter. "An 'Ancient Sense of Politics'? Weber, Caesarism and the Republican Tradition." *Archives européennes de sociologie* 40 (1999): 333–50.

———. *Caesarism, Charisma and Fate: Historical Sources and Modern Resonances in the Work of Max Weber*. New Brunswick, NJ, Transaction Books, 2008)

Baehr, Peter, and Melvyn Richter, eds. *Dictatorship in History and Theory*. Cambridge, CUP, 2004.

Balanda, Flavien Bertran de. "Contre-révolution ou contre-subversion? Le sens rétabli selon Louis de Bonald, une métaphysique sémantique de la régénération sociale." In *Les mots du politique 1815–1848*, ed. Aude Déruelle and Corinne Legoy, pp. 31–46. Paris, Classiques Garnier, 2021.

Baldensperger, Fernand. "Le songe de Jean Paul dans le romantisme français." *Revue universitaire* 18 (1909): 132–39.

———. "Les théories de Lavater dans la littérature française." In his *Etudes d'histoire littéraire*, 4 vols., 2:51–91. Paris, 1907–39.

———. *Alfred de Vigny: Contribution à sa biographie intellectuelle*. Paris, 1912.

Balibar, Etienne. *Masses, Classes, Ideas*. London, 1994.

Ball, Terence. "The Incoherence of Intergenerational Justice." *Inquiry* 28 (1985): 321–37.

———. "'The Earth Belongs to the Living': Thomas Jefferson and the Problem of Intergenerational Relations." *Environmental Politics* 19 (2000): 61–77.

Ballanche, Pierre-Simon. *Essais de palingénésie sociale* [1827–29]. Reprinted in Pierre-Simon-Ballanche, *Œuvres*, 6 vols., vol. 4. Paris, 1833.

———. *Première sécession de la plèbe*. Ed. Jacques Rancière. Rennes, Editions Pontcerq, 2017.

Baranowski, Anne-Marie. *Conquête du mouvement et recherche de soi. L'imaginaire de Karl Philipp Moritz*. Bern, Peter Lang, 1996.

Barante, Prosper de. *De la littérature française pendant le dix-huitième siècle*. 2nd ed. London, 1813.

———. *A Tableau of French Literature during the Eighteenth Century*. London, 1833.

———. "Vie de Schiller." In Frédéric Schiller, *Œuvres dramatiques*. Paris, 1834.

Baraquin, Noëlla, and Jacqueline Laffitte, eds. *Kant. Idée d'une histoire universelle au point de vue cosmopolitique. Réponse à la question 'Qu'est-ce que les lumières?'* Paris, Editions Nathan, 1994.

Barash, Jeffrey Andrew, and Servanne Jollivet, eds. Issue on "Reinhart Koselleck." *Revue Germanique Internationale* 25 (2017).

Barnard, F. M. *Herder on Social and Political Culture*. Cambridge, CUP, 1969.

Baron, Hans. *The Crisis of the Early Italian Renaissance: Civic Humanism and Republican Liberty in an Age of Classicism and Tyranny*. 2 vols. Princeton, NJ, Princeton UP, 1955.

Bartier, John. *Naissance du socialisme en Belgique. Les Saint-Simoniens*. Brussels, Présence et Action Culturelles, 1985.

Barzun, Jacques. *Romanticism and the Modern Ego*. Boston, Little, Brown & Co., 1944.

Bautain, Louis. *De l'enseignement de la philosophie en France au xixe siècle*. Strasbourg, 1833.

Baycroft, Timothy, and David Hopkin, eds. *Folklore and Nationalism in Europe during the Long Nineteenth Century*. Leiden, Brill, 2012.

Bayly, Christopher A. *The Birth of the Modern World, 1780–1914*. Oxford, Blackwell, 2004.

Beaud, Olivier. *Théorie de la fédération*. Paris, PUF, 2007.

Beaud, Olivier, Catherine Colliot-Thélène, and Jean-François Kervégan, eds. *Droits subjectifs et citoyenneté*. Paris, Classiques Garnier, 2019.

Becquemont, Daniel, and Laurent Mucchielli. *Le cas Spencer*. Paris, PUF, 1998.

Behler, Ernst. *Irony and the Discourse of Modernity*. Seattle, U of Washington Press, 1990.

Behrent, Michael C. "Liberalism without Humanism: Michel Foucault and the Free-Market Creed, 1976–1979." *Modern Intellectual History* 6 (2009): 539–68.

———. "Pluralism's Political Conditions: Social Realism and the Revolutionary Tradition in Pierre Leroux, P-J Proudhon and Alfred Fouillée." In *Pluralism and the Idea of the Republic in France*, ed. Julian Wright and H. S. Jones, pp. 99–121. Basingstoke, Palgrave, 2012.

———. "Foucault and France's Liberal Moment." In *In Search of the Liberal Moment: Democracy, Anti-Totalitarianism and Intellectual Politics in France since 1950*, ed. Stephen W. Sawyer and Iain Stewart, pp. 155–65. London, Palgrave, 2016.

Behrent Michael C., and Daniel Zamora, eds. *Foucault's Neo-Liberalism*. Cambridge, Polity, 2016.

Beiser, Frederick C. *Schiller as Philosopher: A Re-Examination*. Oxford, OUP, 2005.

———. "Schleiermacher's Ethics." In *The Cambridge Companion to Friedrich Schleiermacher*, ed. Jacqueline Mariña, pp. 53–71. Cambridge, CUP, 2005.

———. "Historicism and Neo-Kantianism." *Studies in History and Philosophy of Science* 39 (2008): 554–64.

———. *Diotima's Children. German Aesthetic Rationalism from Leibniz to Lessing*. Oxford, OUP, 2009.

———. "Normativity in Neo-Kantianism: Its Rise and Fall." *International Journal of Philosophical Studies* 17 (2009): 9–27.

———. "Mendelssohn versus Herder on the Vocation of Man." In *Moses Mendelssohn's Metaphysics and Aesthetics*, ed. Reiner Munk. *Studies in German Idealism* 13 (2011): 235–44.

———. *Late German Idealism: Trendelenburg & Lotze*. Oxford, OUP, 2013.

———. *The German Historicist Tradition*. Oxford, OUP, 2015.

———. "Historicization and Historicism. Some Nineteenth-Century Perspectives." In *Historisierung: Begriff-Geschichte-Praxisfelder*, ed. Moritz Baumstark and Robert Forkel, pp. 42–54. Stuttgart, J. B. Metzler Verlag, 2016.

———. "Neo-Kantianism as Neo-Fichteanism." *Fichte-Studien* 45 (2018): 307–27.

Bélime, William. *Philosophie du droit, ou cours d'introduction à la science du droit*. 2 vols. Paris, 1855.

Bell, Duncan, ed. *Victorian Visions of Global Order: Empire and International Relations in Nineteenth-Century Political Thought*. Cambridge, CUP, 2007.

Bell, Matthew. "Carl Gustav Carus and the Science of the Unconscious." In *Thinking the Unconscious: Nineteenth-Century German Thought*, ed. Angus Nicholls and Martin Liebscher, pp. 156–72. Cambridge, CUP, 2010.

Bellantone, Andrea. *Hegel en France*. 2 vols. Paris, Hermann, 2011.

———. "L'expérience de l'ego dans le spiritualisme français: de l'objet à l'œuvre." In *Le renouveau de l'idéalisme*, ed. Giovanni Dotoli and Louis Ucciani, pp. 149–63. Paris, L'Harmattan, 2018.

———. "De la persévérance à la donation: la décision métaphysique de Ravaisson." *Revue philosophique de la France et de l'étranger* 144 (2019): 49–62.

Bennett, Joshua. *God and Progress: Religion and History in British Intellectual Culture, 1845–1914*. Oxford, OUP, 2019.

Benoit, Joseph. *Belgicismes ou les vices de langage et de prononciation les plus communs en Belgique corrigés d'après l'Académie et les meilleurs écrivains*. Antwerp, 1857.

Bentham, Jeremy. *A Fragment on Government* [1776]. 2nd ed. London, 1823.

Berenson, Edward. *Populist Religion and Left-Wing Politics in France, 1830–1852*. Princeton, NJ, Princeton UP, 1984.

Berlin, Isaiah. "Two Concepts of Liberty" [1958]. In Isaiah Berlin, *Four Essays on Liberty*. Oxford, OUP, 1969.

———. "Two Concepts of Liberty" [1958]. In his *Liberty*, ed. Henry Hardy, pp. 166–217. Oxford, OUP, 2009.

———. Introduction to Franco Venturi, *Roots of Revolution*. New York, Knopf, 1960.

———. "Corsi e Ricorsi." *Journal of Modern History* 50 (1978): 480–89.

———. *Russian Thinkers*. Harmondsworth, Penguin Books, 1994.

Bernard-Griffiths, Simone. "Lectures d'*Ahasvérus* d'Edgar Quinet: regards sur une palingénésie romantique du mythe du Juif errant." *Romantisme* 45 (1984): 79–104.

Bertauld, Alfred. *La liberté civile. Nouvelle étude critique sur les publicistes contemporains.* 2nd ed. Paris, 1864.

Berth, Edouard. *La fin d'une culture.* Paris, 1927.

Berthiot, François. *Le baron d'Eckstein, journaliste et critique littéraire.* Paris, Editions des Ecrivains, 1998.

Bertrand, Alexis. "Art et sociologie d'après les lettres inédites de Paul Chenavard." *Archives d'anthropologie criminelle, de médecine légale et de psychologie normale et pathologique* 26 (1911): 525–49.

Beseler, Georg. *Volksrecht und Juristenrecht.* Leipzig, 1843.

Bessi, Laura. "Palingénésies: de Charles Bonnet à Chenavard." In *Romantisme et révolution(s),* ed. Daniel Couty and Robert Kopp, pp. 375–94. Paris, Gallimard, 2008.

Bew, Paul. *Realpolitik: A History.* Oxford, OUP, 2016.

Bidart, Pierre. "L'influence du philosophe allemand F. Krause dans la formation des sciences sociales en Espagne." *Revue Germanique Internationale* 21 (2004): 133–48.

Bienenstock, Myriam, ed. "Trieb: Tendance, instinct, pulsion." *Revue germanique internationale* 18 (2002).

Bill, E.G.W. *University Reform in Nineteenth-Century Oxford: A Study of Henry Halford Vaughan, 1811–1885.* Oxford, OUP, 1973.

Bindman, David. *Ape to Apollo: Aesthetics and the Idea of Race in the Eighteenth Century.* London, Reaktion Books, 2002.

Binoche, Bertrand. *Les trois sources des philosophies de l'histoire (1764–1798).* Paris, PUF, 1994.

———, ed. *L'homme perfectible.* Seyssel, Champ Vallon, 2004.

———, ed. *Les équivoques de la civilisation.* Seyssel, Champ Vallon, 2005.

———. *La raison sans l'histoire.* Paris, PUF, 2007.

Blackstone, William. *Commentaries on the Laws of England* [4 vols., 1765–1769]. Ed. Thomas M. Cooley. Chicago, 1884.

Blaeschke, Axel. "Uber Individual- und Nationalcharakter, Zeitgeist und Poesie." In *Germaine de Staël und ihr erstes deutsches Publikum,* ed. Gerhard R. Kaiser and Olaf Müller, pp. 145–61. Heidelberg, Universitätsverlag Winter, 2008.

Blanc, Louis. *Organisation du travail* [1840]. 9th ed. Paris, 1850.

Blanning, T.C.W. *The Culture of Power and the Power of Culture: Old Regime Europe 1660–1789.* Oxford, OUP, 2003.

———. *The Romantic Revolution.* London, Weidenfeld, 2010.

Blanqui, Adolphe. *Histoire de l'économie politique en Europe depuis les anciens jusqu'à nos jours.* 2 vols. Paris, 1837.

Blix, Göran. "La palingénésie romantique: histoire et immortalité de Charles Bonnet à Pierre Leroux." In *Les formes du temps. Rythme, histoire, temporalité,* ed. Paule Petitier and Gisèle Séginger, pp. 225–40. Strasbourg, PU de Strasbourg, 2007.

———. *From Paris to Pompeii: French Romanticism and the Cultural Politics of Archaeology.* Philadelphia, U of Pennsylvania Press, 2009.

Block, Maurice. *Les progrès de la science économique depuis Adam Smith.* 2 vols. Paris, Guillaumin, 1890.

Bluntschli, Johann Kaspar. "Uber die neuen Begründungen der Gesellschaft und des Gesell-
schaftsrechts: Saint-Simon, Cabet, Hegel, Ahrens, Robert von Mohl." *Kritische Überschau
der deutschen Gesetzgebung und Rechtswissenschaft* 3 (1856): 229–66.
————. *La Politique* [1879]. 2nd ed. Paris, 1883.
————. *The Theory of the State.* 3rd English ed. Oxford, Clarendon Press, 1895.
Bobbio, Norberto. *Democracy and Dictatorship: The Nature and Limits of State Power.* Cam-
bridge, Polity Press, 1989.
Bock, Adolf, and Heinrich Albert Oppermann. *Die Universität Göttingen.* Leipzig, 1842.
Böckenförde, Ernst-Wolfgang. *State, Society and Liberty: Studies in Political Theory and Consti-
tutional Law.* Oxford, Berg, 1991.
————. "Lorenz von Stein, théoricien du mouvement de l'état et de la société vers l'état social."
In his *Le droit, l'état et la constitution démocratique.* Paris, L.G.D.J.; Brussels, Bruylant, 2000.
————. *Constitutional and Political Theory.* Ed. Mirjam Künkler and Tine Stein. Oxford, OUP,
2017.
————. "Political Theory and Political Theology: Comments on Their Reciprocal Relationship"
[1981]. In Ernst-Wolfgang Böckenförde, *Religion, Law, and Democracy: Selected Writings,* ed.
Mirjam Künkler and Tine Stein, pp. 248–58. Oxford, OUP, 2020.
Bonacina, Giovanni. *Hegel, il mondo romano e la storiografia.* Rome, La Nuova Italia, 1991.
————. "Hegel, il barone d'Eckstein e 'L'ala erudite della Congrégation.'" *Rivista di Storia della
Filosofia* 60 (2005): 409–41.
Bonald, Louis de. *Théorie du pouvoir politique et religieux dans la société civile* [1796]. 2 vols. Paris
1843.
————. *Œuvres choisies. Ecrits sur la littérature.* Ed. Gérard Gengembre and Jean-Yves Pranchère.
Paris, Classiques Garnier, 2010.
Bond, Donald F. "The Neo-Classical Psychology of the Imagination." *ELH: A Journal of English
Literary History* 4 (1937): 245–64.
Bond, Niall. "'Gemeinschaft und Gesellschaft': The Reception of a Conceptual Dichotomy."
Contributions to the History of Concepts 5 (2009): 162–86.
Bonnet, Jean. *Dékantations. Fonctions idéologiques du kantisme dans le xixe siècle française.* Berne,
Peter Lang, 2011.
Bonniot, Roger. *Pierre Dupont, poète et chansonnier du peuple.* Paris, Nizet, 1991.
Boralevi, Lea Campos. Introduction to Petrus Cunaeus, *De republica Hebraerorum libri tres.*
Florence, Centro Editoriale Toscano, 1996.
Borchard, Edwin M. "Jurisprudence in Germany." *Columbia Law Review* 12 (1912): 301–20.
Bösch, Sarah. *Wilhelm von Humboldt in Frankreich. Studien zur Rezeption (1797–2005).* Pader-
born, Ferdinand Schöningh, 2006.
Bose, Siddhartha. *Back and Forth: The Grotesque in the Play of Romantic Irony.* Newcastle, Cam-
bridge Scholars, 2015.
Bouglé, Célestin. "Revue générale des théories récentes sur la division du travail." *L'année soci-
ologique* 6 (1901–2): 73–122.
Bouillier, Francisque. *Théorie de la raison impersonnelle.* Paris, 1844.
————. "Raison." In *Dictionnaire des sciences philosophiques,* 5 vols., pp. 344–45. Paris, 1844–51.
Boulby, Mark. *Karl Philipp Moritz: At the Fringe of Genius.* Toronto, U of Toronto Press, 1979.
Bournique, Gladys. *La Philosophie de Josiah Royce.* Paris, Vrin, 1988.

Bouton, Christophe. "L'histoire de l'avenir. Cieszkowski lecteur de Hegel." *Revue Germanique Internationale* 8 (2008): 77–92.

Boutroux, Emile. *Historical Studies in Philosophy*. London, Macmillan, 1912.

Bowen, Ralph H. *German Theories of the Corporative State*. New York, Whittlesey House, 1947.

Bowman, Frank Paul. "Religion, Politics and Utopia in French Romanticism." *Australian Journal of French Studies* 11 (1974): 307–24.

———. *French Romanticism: Intertextual and Interdisciplinary Readings*. Baltimore, Johns Hopkins UP, 1990.

Brandes, George. *Ferdinand Lassalle*. London, Heinemann, 1911.

Bravard-Veyrières, Pierre-Claude-Jean-Baptiste. *De l'étude et de l'enseignement du droit romain et des résultats qu'on peut en attendre*. Paris, 1836.

Breaugh, Martin. *L'expérience plébéienne. Une histoire discontinue de la liberté politique*. Paris, Payot, 2006.

Breckman, Warren. *Marx, the Young Hegelians and the Origins of Radical Social Theory*. Cambridge, CUP, 1990.

———. *The Adventures of the Symbolic: Post-Marxism and Radical Democracy*. New York, Columbia UP, 2013.

Bremer, Thomas, Wolfgang Fink, Françoise Knopper, and Thomas Nicklas, eds. *La question sociale du Vormärz/Vormärz und soziale Frage 1830–1848*. Reims, Epure, 2018.

Bresky, Dushan. "Schiller's Debt to Montesquieu and Adam Ferguson." *Comparative Literature* 13 (1961): 239–53.

Brie, S. "Der Volksgeist bei Hegel und in der historischen Rechtsschule." *Archiv für Rechts- und Wirtschaftsphilosophie* 2 (1908/1909): 1–10.

Brocher, Henri. *De l'enseignement du droit romain*. Lausanne, 1867.

Bruhns, Hinnerk. "Grecs, Romains et Germains au xixe siècle: quelle Antiquité pour l'état national allemand?" *Anabases* 1 (2005): 17–43.

———. "La fondation de l'état national allemand et la question des origines." In *Le corps, la famille et l'état*, ed. Myriam Cottias, Laura Downs, and Christiane Klapisch-Zuber, pp. 207–19. Rennes, PU de Rennes, 2010.

Bruno, G. Anthony. "*Hiatus Irrationalis*: Lask's Fateful Misreading of Fichte." *European Journal of Philosophy*, 2021, 1–19. DOI: 10.1111/ejop.12719.

Bullard, Paddy, and Alexis Tadié, eds. *Ancients and Moderns in Europe: Comparative Perspectives*. Oxford, Voltaire Foundation, 2016.

Bullen, J. B. *The Myth of the Renaissance in Nineteenth-Century Writing*. Oxford, OUP, 1994.

Buonarroti, Filippo Michele. *Conspiration pour l'égalité dite de Babeuf*. 2 vols. Brussels, 1828.

Bürge, Alfons. *Das französische Privatrecht im 19. Jahrhundert. Zwischen Tradition und Pandektenwissenschaft, Liberalismus und Etatismus*. Frankfurt am Main, Vittorio Klostermann, 1991.

Burrow, John, Stefan Collini, and Donald Winch. *That Noble Science of Politics*. Cambridge, CUP, 1983.

Burtin, Nicolas. *Le baron d'Eckstein. Un semeur d'idées au temps de la Restauration*. Paris, 1931.

Burton, Richard. "The Death of Politics: The Significance of Dambreuse's Funeral in *L'éducation sentimentale*." *French Studies* 50 (1996): 157–60.

Burwick, Frederick. "Nexus in De Quincey's Theory of Language." In *Thomas De Quincey: Bicentenary Studies*, ed. Robert Lance Snyder, pp. 263–78. Norman and London, U of Oklahoma Press, 1985.

————. "Art for Art's Sake and the Politics of Prescinding: 1790s, 1890s, 1990s." *Pacific Coast Philology* 34 (1999): 117–26.

Busst, Alan. J. L. "Ballanche and Saint-Simonism." *Australian Journal of French Studies* 9 (1972): 290–307.

————. *La théorie du langage de Pierre-Simon Ballanche.* Lewiston, NY, Edwin Mellen Press, 2000.

Butler, Eliza Marian. *The Tyranny of Greece over Germany.* Cambridge, CUP, 1935.

Butterfield, Herbert. *The Whig Interpretation of History.* London, Bell, 1931.

Calaresu, Melissa. "Images of Ancient Rome in Late Eighteenth-Century Neapolitan Historiography." *Journal of the History of Ideas* 58 (1997): 641–61.

Calder, William M., III, and Renate Schlesier, eds. *Zwischen Rationalismus and Romantik. Karl Otfried Müller und die Antike Kultur.* Hildesheim, Weidmann, 1998.

Calvié, Lucien. "Philosophie, littérature et politique: le romantisme allemand et sa critique hégélienne." *Romantisme* 182 (2018): 15–25.

Campbell, Joan. *Joy in Work, German Work: The National Debate, 1800–1945.* Princeton, NJ, Princeton UP, 1989.

Campopiano, Michele. Introduction to Carlo Cattaneo, *La città considerata come principio ideale delle istorie italiane.* Pisa, Scuola Normale de Pisa, 2021.

Canale, Damiano, Paolo Grossi, and Hasso Hofmann, eds. *A History of the Philosophy of Law in the Civil Law World, 1600–1900.* Heidelberg, Springer, 2009.

Canfora, Luciano. "Dans la France des lumières: liberté des anciens, liberté des modernes." *Annales ESC* 38 (1983): 1075–83.

Capogrossi Colognesi, Luigi. *Modelli di stato e di famiglia nella storiografia dell' 800.* Rome, La Sapienza, 1994.

————. *Dalla storia di Roma alle origini della società civile.* Bologna, Il Mulino, 2008.

Carné, Louis de. *Souvenirs de ma jeunesse au temps de la Restauration.* Paris, 1872.

Carové, Friedrich Wilhelm. *Der Saint-Simonismus und die Philosophie des 19ten Jahrhunderts in Frankreich.* 1831.

Carrino, Agostino. "Law and Social Theory in Emil Lask." In *Rechtsnorm und Rechtswirklichkeit. Festschrift für Werner Krawietz zum 60. Geburtstag,* ed. Aulis Aarnio, Stanley L. Paulson, Ota Weinberger, Georg Henrik von Wright, and Dieter Wyducke, pp. 209–31. Berlin, Duncker & Humblot, 1993.

Casalena, Maria-Pia. "L'histoire à l'ombre de Coppet et de la Toscane: la découverte de l'individu et la marche des nations d'après Sismondi." *Cahiers Staëliens* 63 (2013): 157–79.

Case, Holly. "The 'Social Question,' 1820–1920." *Modern Intellectual History* 13 (2016): 747–55.

————. *The Age of Questions.* Princeton, NJ, Princeton UP, 2018.

Cassagnac, Adolphe Granier de. *Histoire des classes ouvrières et des classes bourgeoises.* Brussels, 1838.

————. *History of the Working and Burgher Classes.* Trans. Ben E. Green. Philadelphia, 1871.

Cassirer, Ernst. *Le problème de la connaissance dans la philosophie et la science des temps modernes* [1911–23]. 4 vols. Paris, Editions du Cerf, 1999–2005.

Castel, Robert. *Les métamorphoses de la question sociale* [1995]. Paris, Gallimard, 2013.

Catel, Amaury. *Le traducteur et le demiurge. Hermann Ewerbeck, un communiste allemand à Paris (1841–1860).* Nancy, Editions de l'Arbre Bleu, 2019.

Cavel, H. *Epitaphe des partis; celui dit du juste-milieu, son avenir.* Paris, 1833.

Cazzetta, Giovanni, ed. *Autonomia: Per un'Archeologia del Sapere Giuridico fra Otto e Novecento.* Milan, Giuffrè, 2014.

Cerutti, Patrick, ed.. "FWJ Schelling, 'Notice sur les tentatives de Monsieur Villers pour introduire la philosophie kantienne en France.'" *Revue Germanique Internationale* 18 (2013): pp. 7–26.

———. *La philosophie de Schelling: Repères.* Paris, Vrin, 2019.

Chaïbi, Olivier. "Entre credit public et credit mutuel: un aperçu des théories du crédit au xix siècle." *Romantisme* 151 (2011): 53–66.

Chamberlain, Houston Stewart. *La genèse du xixe siècle.* 2 vols. Paris, 1913.

Chamley, Paul. "Les origines de la pensée économique de Hegel." *Hegel Studien* 3 (1965): 225–61.

———. "Notes de lectures relatives à Smith, Steuart et Hegel." *Revue d'économie politique* 77 (1967): 857–78.

Chapoutot, Johann. *Greeks, Romans, Germans: How the Nazis Usurped Europe's Classical Past* [2008]. Berkeley, U of California Press, 2016.

———. *The Law of Blood: Thinking and Acting as a Nazi.* Cambridge, MA, Belknap Press of Harvard UP, 2018.

———. "The Denaturalization of Nordic Law: Germanic Law and the Reception of Roman Law." In *Roman Law and the Idea of Europe*, ed. Kaius Tuori and Heta Björklund, pp. 113–25. London, Bloomsbury, 2019.

Chasles, Philarèthe. "Cours de littérature du nord." *Revue de Paris*, n.s., 2 (1842): 116–32.

Chaudonneret, Marie-Claude, ed. *Paul Chenavard, 1807–1895: le peintre et le prophète.* Lyon, Musée des Beaux-Arts, 2000.

Chazin, Maurice. "Quinet: An Early Discoverer of Emerson." *PMLA* 48 (1933): 147–63.

Chêne, Christian. "L'histoire du droit par la biographie selon Charles Guillaume Hello et sa *Philosophie de l'histoire de France.*" In *Histoire de l'histoire du droit*, ed. Jacques Poumarède, pp. 133–43. Toulouse, Presses de l'Université des Sciences Sociales de Toulouse, 2006.

Cheney, Paul. "Istvan Hont, the Cosmopolitan Theory of Commercial Globalization, and Twenty-First Century Capitalism." *Modern Intellectual History*, 2021, pp. 1–29.

Chickering, Roger. *Karl Lamprecht. A German Academic Life.* Atlantic Highlands, NJ, Humanities Press, 1993.

Chollet, Antoine, ed. *La liberté des Anciens et des Modernes, deux cents ans après Benjamin Constant. Annales Benjamin Constant* 45 (2020).

Christin, Olivier, ed. *Demain La République.* Lormont, Le Bord de l'Eau, 2018.

———, ed. *Républiques et Républicanismes: Les Cheminements de la Liberté.* Lormont, Le Bord de l'Eau, 2019.

Christov, Theodore. *Before Anarchy: Hobbes and His Critics in Modern International Thought.* Cambridge, CUP, 2015.

Chytry, Josef. *The Aesthetic State: A Quest in Modern German Thought.* Berkeley, U of California Press, 1989.

Cieszkowski, August. *Du crédit et de la circulation.* Paris, 1839.

———. *Gott und Palingenesie.* Berlin, 1842.

———. *Prolégomènes à l'historiosophie.* Trans. Michel Jacob. Paris, Editions Champ Libre, 1973.

———. *Selected Writings.* Ed. André Liebich. Cambridge, CUP, 1979.

Claeys, Gregory. "'Individualism', 'Socialism' and 'Social Science.'" *Journal of the History of Ideas* 47 (1986): 81–93.

————, ed. *The Cambridge Companion to Nineteenth-Century Thought*. Cambridge, CUP, 2019.

Cleugh, M. F. *Time and Its Importance in Modern Thought*. London, Methuen, 1937.

Cognets, Jean des. "Lamartine et le comte de Carné d'après des documents inédits." *Le Correspondant* 273 (1925): 830–52.

————. "Autour du vieux roi Lamartine." *Le Correspondant* 275 (1927): 481–517.

Cole, G.D.H. *A History of Socialist Thought*. 5 vols. London, Macmillan, 1953–54.

Colebrook, Claire, and Jason Maxwell. *Agamben*. Cambridge, Polity, 2016.

Coleridge, Samuel Taylor. *The Friend* [1809]. London, Pickering, 1844.

————. *Biographia Literaria* [1817]. Ed. James Engell and W. Jackson Bate. 2 vols. Princeton, NJ, Princeton UP, 1983.

Colins, Jean-Guillaume-César-Alexandre Hippolyte, baron de. *De la souveraineté*. 2 vols. Paris, 1857.

Collingwood, R. G. *The Idea of History*. Oxford, OUP, 1946.

Collini, Stefan. *Public Moralists*. Oxford, OUP, 1991.

Commons, John R. *Legal Foundations of Capitalism*. New York, Macmillan, 1924.

————. *Institutional Economics: Its Place in Political Economy*. New York, Macmillan, 1934.

Comte, Auguste. "Matériaux pour server à la biographie d'Auguste Comte: correspondance d'Auguste Comte et Gustave d'Eichtal." *Revue Occidentale*, 2nd ser., 12 (1896).

Condorcet, Jean-Antoine-Nicolas de Caritat, marquis de. *Vie de M. Turgot*. London, 1786 and 1787.

Conlin, Jonathan. "An Illiberal Descent: Natural and National History in the Work of Charles Kingsley." *History* 96 (2011): 167–87.

Constant, Benjamin. "The Liberty of the Ancients Compared with That of the Moderns" [1819]. In Benjamin Constant, *Political Writings*, ed. Biancamaria Fontana. Cambridge, CUP, 1988.

————. *Commentary on Filangieri's Work* [1822–24]. Ed. Alan S. Kahan. Indianapolis, IN, Liberty Fund, 2015.

————*De la religion* [1824–31]. Ed. Tzvetan Todorov and Etienne Hofmann. Arles, Actes Sud, 1999.

————. *De la perfectibilité de l'espèce humaine* [1829]. Ed. Pierre Deguise. Lausanne, Age d'Homme, 1967.

————. "Of the Spirit of Conquest and Usurpation and Their Relation to European Civilization." In Benjamin Constant, *Political Writings*, ed. Biancamaria Fontana. Cambridge, CUP, 1988.

————. *Ecrits politiques*. Ed. Marcel Gauchet. Paris, Gallimard, 1997.

Conte, Emanuele. "The Order and the *Volk*: Romantic Roots and Enduring Fascination of the German Constitutional History." In *De rebus divini et humanis: Essays in Honour of Jan Hallebeek*, ed. Harry Dondorp, Martin Schermaier, and Boudewijn Sirks, pp. 37–53. Göttingen, V&R Unipress, 2019.

Coste, Clément. "L'économique contre le politique: la dette, son amortissement et son financement chez les jeunes et les vieux Saint-Simoniens (1825–1880)." *Cahiers d'économie politique* 70 (2016): 7–44.

Costelloe, Timothy M., ed. *The Sublime: From Antiquity to the Present*. Cambridge, CUP, 2012.

Cousin, Victor. *Philosophie de Kant* [1820]. 4th ed. Paris, 1864.

————, trans. *Œuvres de Platon*. Paris, 1826.

————. *Cours de l'histoire de la philosophie: philosophie du xviiie siècle*. 2 vols. Paris, 1829.

————. *Fragments philosophiques*. Paris, 1833.

————. "Avant-Propos" to Karl Ludwig Michelet, *Examen critique de l'ouvrage d'Aristote intitulé* Métaphysique. Paris, 1836.

————. *Cours de philosophie, professé à la faculté des lettres pendant l'année 1818 sur le fondement des idées du vrais, du beau, du bien.* Paris, 1836.

————. "Philosophy of Enthusiasm." In *Specimens of Foreign Standard Literature*, George Ripley, 2 vols., 1:213–22. Boston, 1838.

————. *Fragments et souvenirs.* Paris, 1857.

Coussin, Jean Antoine. *Du génie de l'architecture.* Paris, 1822.

Craiutu, Aurelian. *Liberalism under Siege: The Political Thought of the French Doctrinaires.* Lanham, MD, Lexington Books, 2003.

Crissafuli, Alessandro S. "Montesquieu's Story of the Troglodytes: Its Background, Meaning and Significance." *PMLA* 58 (1943): 372–92.

Crossley, Ceri. "Edgar Quinet: conscience de soi et mal du siècle." *Romantisme* 27 (1980): 47–58.

————. "Some Attitudes towards Architecture during the July Monarchy." *French Forum* 8 (1983): 134–46.

————. "Edgar Quinet et le monde animal: *La Création* et *l'Esprit Nouveau.*" In *Histoire(s) et enchantements: Hommages offerts à Simone Bernard-Griffiths*, ed. Pascale Auraix-Jonchière et al., pp. 403–13. Clermont-Ferrand, CELIS, 2009.

Croxton, Derek. "The Peace of Westphalia of 1648 and the Origins of Sovereignty." *International History Review* 21 (1999): 569–91.

Cubitt, Geoffrey, ed. *Imagining Nations.* Manchester, Manchester UP, 1998.

Cughet, Guillaume. "Utopie et religion au xixe siècle: l'oeuvre de Jean Reynaud (1806–1863), théologien et saint-simonien." *Revue historique* 306 (2004): 577–99.

Cunliffe, John. "Intergenerational Justice and Productive Resources: A Nineteenth-Century Socialist Debate." *History of European Ideas* 12 (1990): 227–38.

Cunliffe, John, and Guido Erreygers. *The Origins of Universal Grants: An Anthology of Historical Writings on Basic Capital and Basic Income.* Basingstoke, Macmillan, 2004.

Cuttica, Cesare. "*To Use or Not to Use* . . . The Intellectual Historian and the *Isms*: A Survey and a Proposal." *Etudes Epistémè* 13 (2013). Varia, http://episteme.revues.org/268.

Cuvier, Georges. *Histoire des sciences naturelles depuis leur origine jusqu'à nos jours.* 5 vols. Paris, 1845.

D'Agoult, Marie de Flavigny, comtesse. *Correspondance générale.* 12 vols. Paris, Champion, 2003–22.

D'Auria, Matthew. *The Shaping of French National Identity: Narrating the Nation's Past, 1715–1830.* Cambridge, CUP, 2020.

Darriulat, Philippe. *La muse du peuple. Chansons politiques et sociales en France 1815–1871.* Rennes, PU de Rennes, 2010.

Davies, J. K. "On the Non-usability of the Concept of Sovereignty in an Ancient Greek Context." In *Federazioni e federalismo nell' Europa antica*, ed. L. A. Foresti et al., pp. 51–65. Milan, Università Cattolico del Sacro Cuoro, 1994.

Dawson, Hannah, and Annelien De Dijn, eds. *Rethinking Liberty before Liberalism.* Cambridge, CUP, 2022.

De Francisco, Antonino. *The Antiquity of the Italian Nation: The Cultural Origins of a Political Myth in Modern Italy, 1796–1943.* Oxford, OUP, 2013.

De Quincey, Thomas. "Letters to a Young Man." In Thomas de Quincey, *Essays.* London, Ward, Lock and Co., no date, but c. 1870.

DeGooyer, Stephanie, Samuel Moyn, et al. *The Right to Have Rights*. London, Verso, 2018.

Deligiorgi, Katerina. *Kant and the Culture of Enlightenment*. New York, SUNY Press, 2005.

———. "The Convergence of Ethics and Aesthetics: Schiller's Concept of the 'Naive' and Objects of Distant Antiquity." In *Critical Exchange: Art Criticism of the Eighteenth and Nineteenth Centuries in Russia and Western Europe*, ed. Carol Adlam and Juliet Simpson, pp. 63–78. Bern, Peter Lang, 2009.

———. *The Scope of Autonomy: Kant and the Morality of Freedom*. Oxford, OUP, 2012.

Denis, Lara, ed. Kant's *Metaphysics of Morals: A Critical Guide*. Cambridge, CUP, 2010.

Derathé, Robert. "Quelques documents sur Chateaubriand, Napoléon et les Idéologues." *Revue européenne des sciences sociales* 17 (1979): 179–84.

Deslandres, Maurice. *La crise de la science politique et le problème de la méthode*. Paris, 1902.

Desmarais, Cyprien. *Le temps présent, ou essais sur l'histoire de la civilisation au dix-neuvième siècle*. Paris, 1826.

———. *Voyage pittoresque dans l'intérieur de la chambre des députés, suivi du temps présent*. Paris, 1827.

———. *De la littérature française au dix-neuvième siècle considérée dans ses rapports avec le progrès de la civilisation et de l'esprit national*. Paris, 1833.

Despland, Michel. *L'émergence des sciences de la religion. La monarchie de juillet: un moment fondateur*. Paris, L'Harmattan, 1999.

Di Giovanni, George. *Freedom and Religion in Kant and His Immediate Successors: The Vocation of Humankind, 1774–1800*. Cambridge, CUP, 2005.

———. "The Year 1786 and *Die Bestimmung des Menschen*, or *Popularphilosophie* in Crisis." In *Moses Mendelssohn's Metaphysics and Aesthetics*, ed. Reiner Munk, *Studies in German Idealism* 13 (2011): 217–34.

———. *Hegel and the Challenge of Spinoza: A Study in German Idealism, 1801–1831*. Cambridge, CUP, 2021.

Diamond, Alan, ed. *The Victorian Achievement of Sir Henry Maine*. Cambridge, CUP, 1991.

Dickey, Laurence. "Historicizing the 'Adam Smith Problem': Conceptual, Historiographical and Textual Issues." *Journal of Modern History* 58 (1986): 579–609.

———. "Saint-Simonian Industrialism as the End of History: August Cieszkowski and the Teleology of Universal History." In *Apocalypse Theory and the Ends of the World*, ed. Malcolm Bull, pp. 159–99. Oxford, Blackwell, 1995.

Dickinson, Goldsworthy Lowes. *The Development of Parliament in the Nineteenth Century*. London, 1895.

———. *Le développement du parlement pendant le dix-neuvième siècle*. Paris, 1906.

Dietzel, Carl. *Das System der Staatsanleihen im Zusammenhang der Volkswirtschaft Betrachtet*. Heidelberg, 1855.

Dilcher, Gerhard, and Bernhard Diestelkamp, eds. *Recht, Gericht, Genossenschaft und Policey*. Berlin, Erich Schmidt Verlag, 1986.

Dimova-Cookson, Maria, ed. "Benjamin Constant: 200 Years of Ancient and Modern Liberty." *History of European Ideas* 48 (2022): 193–307.

Dixon, Thomas. *The Invention of Altruism: Making Moral Meanings in Victorian Britain*. Oxford, OUP, 2008.

Dolens, Noel. *Le socialisme fédéral*. Paris, 1904.

Donaldson, John William. *The Theatre of the Greeks: A Series of Papers Relating to the History and Criticism of the Greek Drama*. 4th ed. Cambridge, 1836.

Doria, Corinne. *Pierre Paul Royer-Collard (1763–1845). Un philosophe entre deux révolutions.* Rennes, PU de Rennes, 2018.

Dreyer, Michael. "German Roots of the Theory of Pluralism." *Constitutional Political Economy* 4 (1993): 7–39.

Drolet, Michael. *Tocqueville, Democracy and Social Reform.* Basingstoke, Macmillan, 2003.

Dubber, Markus Dirk. "The German Jury and the Metaphysical Volk: From Romantic Idealism to Nazi Ideology." *American Journal of Comparative Law* 43 (1995): 227–71.

Dunn, John. *Modern Revolutions* [1972]. 2nd ed. Cambridge, CUP, 1989.

———. *Setting the People Free: The Story of Democracy.* London, Atlantic Books, 2005.

Dupin, Claude. "Dissertation sur Pothier." In Robert-Joseph Pothier, *Œuvres* [1824], rev. ed., 11 vols., vol. 1. Paris, 1827.

Duprat, Pascal. "Les philosophes socialistes contemporains." *Revue Indépendante* 12 (1844): 35–55; 13 (1844): 465–500; 14 (1844): 5–35.

Duroselle, Jean-Baptiste. *Les débuts du catholicisme social en France (1822–1870).* Paris, PUF, 1951.

Eagleton, Terry. *Ideology: An Introduction.* London, Verso, 1991.

———. *Culture and the Death of God.* New Haven, CT, Yale UP, 2014.

Eckstein, Ferdinand, baron d'. "Introduction." *Le Catholique* 1 (1826): 6–8.

———. "De ma carrière politique et littéraire en France et dans les Pays-Bas." *Le Catholique* 14 (1829): 308–38.

———. "Jugement ou examen de l'ouvrage de M. de Lamennais." *La France Catholique* 2 (1834). Reprinted in Félicité de Lamennais, *Paroles d'un croyant* [1834], ed. Louis Le Guillou. Paris, Flammarion, 1973.

———. "*De la Démocratie en Amérique* par Alexis de Tocqueville." *Le Polonais* 6 (1836): 235–63, 408–29.

———. "Essai d'une philosophie de l'histoire." *Le Correspondant* 33 (25 February, 25 April, 25 July, 25 November 1854; 25 August 1857, 25 November 1858 and 25 June 1860).

———. Review of Jules Michelet, *Histoire de France.* Reprinted in Jules Michelet, *Œuvres complètes,* ed. Paul Viallaneix, 21 vols., 4:756–844. Paris, Flammarion, 1971–87.

Edelstein, Dan. *The Enlightenment: A Genealogy.* Chicago, U of Chicago Press, 2011.

———. "The Birth of Ideology from the Spirit of Myth: Georges Sorel among the Idéologues." In *The Re-Enchantment of the World,* ed. Joshua Landy and Michael Saler, pp. 201–24. Stanford, Stanford UP, 2021.

Edwards, Stewart, and Elizabeth Fraser, eds. *Selected Writings of Pierre-Joseph Proudhon.* London, Macmillan, 1969.

Eggli, Edmond. *Schiller et le romantisme français.* 2 vols. Paris, 1928.

———. *Le débat romantique en France 1813–1816.* Paris, Les belles lettres, 1933.

Eich, Stefan. "The Theodicy of Growth: John Rawls, Political Economy and Reasonable Faith." *Modern Intellectual History* 18 (2021): 984–1009.

———. *The Currency of Politics: The Political Theory of Money from Aristotle to Keynes.* Princeton, NJ, Princeton UP, 2022.

Eichner, Hans, ed. *"Romantic" and Its Cognates: The European History of a Word.* Manchester, Manchester UP, 1972.

Einaudi, Luca. "From the Franc to the 'Europe': The Attempted Transformation of the Latin Monetary Union into a European Monetary Union." *Economic History Review* 53 (2000): 284–308.

————. *Money and Politics: European Monetary Union and the International Gold Standard (1865–1873)*. Oxford, OUP, 2001.

Elazar, Yiftah, and Geneviève Rousselière, eds. *Republicanism and the Future of Democracy*. Cambridge, CUP, 2019.

Emerson, Rupert. *State and Sovereignty in Modern Germany*. New Haven, CT, Yale UP, 1928.

Engell, James. *The Creative Imagination: Enlightenment to Romanticism*. Cambridge, MA, Harvard UP, 1981.

Erlin, Matt. "Reluctant Modernism: Moses Mendelssohn's Philosophy of History." *Journal of the History of Ideas* 63 (2002): 83–104.

Espagne, Geneviève. *Les années de voyage de Jean Paul Richter*. Paris, Editions du Cerf, 2002.

Espagne, Michel. "Le saint-simonisme est-il jeune hégélien?" In *Regards sur le saint-simonisme et les saint-simoniens*, ed. Jean-René Derré, pp. 45–71. Lyon, 1986.

————. "Humboldt à Paris, lecteur de Goethe." *Revue Germanique Internationale* 12 (1999): 195–209.

————. *En deçà du Rhin: l'Allemagne des philosophes français au xixe siècle*. Paris, Cerf, 2004.

————. "Les élèves de Claude Fauriel." In *Claude Fauriel et l'Allemagne. Idées pour une philologie des cultures*, ed. Geneviève Espagne and Udo Schöning, pp. 405–22. Paris, Champion, 2014.

Espagne, Michel, and Michaël Werner. "La construction d'une référence culturelle allemande en France: genèse et histoire (1750–1914)." *Annales. Histoire, Sciences Sociales* 42 (1987): 969–92.

————, eds. *Transferts. Relations interculturelles entre la France et l'Allemagne (18e et 19e siècles)* (Paris, 1988), pp. 447–64.

————, eds. *Contribution à l'histoire des disciplines littéraires en France et en Allemagne au xixe siècle*. Philologiques, 1. Paris, Editions de la Maisons des Sciences de L'Homme, 1990.

————. *Lettres d'Allemagne. Victor Cousin et les hégéliens*. Tusson, Charente, Du Lérot, 1990.

————, eds. *Qu'est-ce qu'une littérature nationale? Approches pour une théorie interculturelle du champ littéraire*. Philologiques, 3. Paris, Editions de la Maison des Sciences de l'Homme, 1994.

Esposito, Roberto. *Third Person* [2007]. Cambridge, Polity Press, 2012.

————. "The *Dispositif* of the Person." *Law, Culture and the Humanities* 81 (2012): 17–30.

————. "Totalitarianism or Biopolitics? Concerning a Philosophical Interpretation of the Twentieth Century." In *Biopower: Foucault and Beyond*, ed. Vernon W. Cisney and Nicolae Morar, pp. 348–59. Chicago, U of Chicago Press, 2016.

————. *Instituting Thought. Three Paradigms of Political Ontology*. Cambridge, Polity, 2021.

Evans, Richard J. *The Pursuit of Power: Europe 1815–1914*. London, Allen Lane, 2016.

Fabre, Daniel. "Proverbes, contes et chansons." In *Les lieux de mémoire*, ed. Pierre Nora, 7 vols., Part III. *Les France 2: Traditions*, pp. 613–39. Paris, Gallimard, 1992.

Faguet, Emile. *Propos littéraires*. Paris, 1902.

Fauché-Prunelle, Alexandre. *Essai sur les anciennes institutions autonomes ou populaires des Alpes Cottiennes-Briançonnaises*. 2 vols. Grenoble and Paris, 1856.

Fauré, Christine, Jacques Guilhaumou, and Jacques Vallier, eds. *Des manuscrits de Sieyès*. 2 vols. Paris, Champion, 1999–2007.

Favre, Pierre. *Naissances de la science politique en France 1870–1914*. Paris, Fayard, 1989.

Fazy, Jean-Jacques (James). *Principes d'organisation industrielle pour le développement des richesses en France*. Paris, 1830.

Feaver, George. *From Status to Contract: A Biography of Sir Henry Maine 1822–1888*. London, Longmans, 1969.

Febvre, Lucien. *Michelet et la Renaissance*. Paris, Flammarion, 1992.

Fedi, Laurent. "Philosopher et républicaniser: la *Critique philosophique* de Renouvier et Pillon, 1872–1889." *Romantisme* 115 (2002): 65–82.

———. *Kant, une passion française 1795–1940*. Hildesheim, Georg Olms, 2018.

Ferreira. Oscar, ed. *Krausisme juridique et politique en Europe*. Paris, Classiques Garnier, 2021.

Ferry, Luc. *Political Philosophy* [1984]. 3 vols. Chicago, U of Chicago Press, 1990–92.

Festenstein, Matthew, and Michael Kenny. *Political Ideologies*. Oxford, OUP, 2005.

Feuerbach, Ludwig. *The Essence of Christianity* [1841]. Trans. Marian Evans. New York, 1855.

Fichte, Johann Gottlieb. *Attempt at a Critique of All Revelation* [1792]. Ed. Garrett Green. Cambridge, CUP, 1978.

———. *Essai d'une critique de toute révélation (1792–1793)*. Ed. Jean-Christophe Godard. Paris, Vrin, 1988.

———. *Foundations of Natural Right* [1796–97]. Cambridge, CUP, 2000.

———. *La doctrine de l'état* [1813]. Ed. Jean-Christophe Goddard and Grégoire Lacaze. Paris, Vrin, 2006.

Fleischacker, Samuel. *A Short History of Distributive Justice*. Cambridge, MA, Harvard UP, 2004.

———. *On Adam Smith's* Wealth of Nations: *A Philosophical Companion*. Princeton, NJ, Princeton UP, 2004.

———. *What Is Enlightenment?* London, Routledge, 2013.

Flint, Robert. *The Philosophy of History in France and Germany*. Edinburgh, 1874.

———. *Vico*. London, 1884.

Forbes, Duncan. *The Liberal Anglican Idea of History*. Cambridge, CUP, 1952.

Foro, Philippe, ed. *L'Italie et l'antiquité du siècle des lumières à la chute du fascisme*. Toulouse, PU du Midi, 2017.

Forster, Michael N. *Hegel and Skepticism*. Cambridge, MA, Harvard UP, 1989.

———. *Kant and Skepticism*. Princeton, NJ, Princeton UP, 2008.

———. "The History of Philosophy." In *The Cambridge History of Philosophy in the Nineteenth Century*, ed. Allen W. Wood and Songsuk Susan Hahn, pp. 866–904. Cambridge, CUP, 2012.

———. "Friedrich Schlegel and Hegel." In *Idealismus und Romantik in Jena. Figuren und Konzepte zwischen 1794 und 1807*, ed. Michael N. Forster, Johannes Korngiebel, and Klaus Vieweg, pp. 139–80. Jena, Wilhelm Fink, 2018.

———. "Philosophy, History of Philosophy, and Historicism." In *Doing Humanities in Nineteenth-Century Germany*, ed. Efraim Podoksik, pp. 19–39. Leiden, Brill, 2020.

Forster, Wolfgang. "Belgian Origins of Krausism—Heinrich Ahrens in Brussels." In *Les Professeurs Allemands en Belgique*, ed. Raphaël Cahen et al., pp. 93–120. Antwerp and Brussels, ASP, 2022.

Forsyth, Murray. *Unions of States: The Theory and Practice of Confederation*. Leicester, Leicester UP, 1981.

Fortoul, Hippolyte. "De l'art actuel." *Revue Encyclopédique* 59 (1833): 151–52.

Francis, Mark. *Herbert Spencer and the Invention of Modern Life*. Stocksfield, Acumen, 2007.

Franco, Bernard. "La «Préface» de *Cromwell*, entre Friedrich Schlegel et Walter Scott." In *Victor Hugo ou les frontières effacées*, ed. Yann Jumelais and Dominique Peyrache-Leborgne, pp. 285–302. Nantes, 2002.

Franks, Paul. "'Nothing Comes from Nothing': Judaism, the Orient, and Kabbalah in Hegel's Reception of Spinoza." In *The Oxford Handbook of Spinoza*, ed. Michael Della Rocca, pp. 512–42. Oxford, OUP, 2017.

Freeden, Michael, Lyman Tower Sargent, and Marc Stears, eds. *The Oxford Handbook of Political Ideologies*. Oxford, OUP, 2013.

Freedman, Jeffrey. *A Poisoned Chalice*. Princeton, NJ, Princeton UP, 2002.

Freeman, Edward A. "Mr Kingsley's Roman and Teuton." *Saturday Review* 17 (9 April 1864): 446–48.

Freitag, Sabine, Peter Wende, and Markus Mösslang, eds. *British Envoys to Germany*. 4 vols. Cambridge, CUP, 2000–2006.

Freuler, Leo. "L'origine et la fonction de la metaphysica naturalis chez Kant." *Revue de métaphysique et de morale* 96 (1991): 371–94.

Friedman, Michael. *A Parting of the Ways: Carnap, Cassirer, and Heidegger*. Chicago, Open Court, 2000.

Frobert, Ludovic. "Pierre Edouard Lemontey et la critique de la division du travail." *Economies et sociétés* 35 (2001): 1735–57.

Frobert, Ludovic, and Michael Drolet, eds. *Jules Leroux. D'une philosophie économique barbare*. Lormont, Le Bord de l'Eau, 2022.

Früchtl, Josef. *The Impertinent Self: A Heroic History of Modernity*. Stanford, Stanford UP, 2009.

Fulda, Daniel. "Sattelzeit, Karriere und Problematik eines kulturwissenschaftlichen Zentralbegriffs." In *Sattelzeit. Historiographiegeschichtliche Revisionen*, ed. Elisabeth Décultot and Daniel Fulda, pp. 1–16. Berlin, De Gruyter, 2016.

Fustel de Coulanges, Numa Denis. "L'invasion Germanique au cinquième siècle: son caractère et ses effets." *Revue des Deux Mondes* 99 (1872): 241–68.

Gadamer, Hans-Georg. *Truth and Method*. London, Continuum, 2004.

Gallagher, Catherine. "What Would Napoleon Do? Historical, Fictional, and Counterfactual Characters." *New Literary History* 42 (2011): 315–36.

———. *Telling It Like It Wasn't: The Counterfactual Imagination in History and Fiction*. Chicago, U of Chicago Press, 2018.

Galston, William A. *Kant and the Problem of History*. Chicago, U of Chicago Press, 1975.

Gannett, Robert T., Jr. *Tocqueville Unveiled: The Historian and His Sources for* The Old Regime and the Revolution. Chicago, U of Chicago Press, 2003.

Gans, Edouard. Review of Jules Michelet, *Introduction à l'histoire universelle*. *Jahrbücher für wissenschaftliche Kritik* 1 (1832): 141–57.

Garnsey, Peter. *Thinking about Property*. Cambridge, CUP, 2007.

Gauchet, Marcel. *Philosophie des sciences historiques. Le moment romantique*. Paris, Seuil, 2002.

Gautier, Théophile. *L'art moderne* [1856]. Ed. Corinne Bayle and Olivier Schefer. Lyon, Editions Fage, 2011.

Geddes, Alexander, ed. *The Holy Bible*. 2 vols. London, 1797.

Genet-Delacroix, Marie-Claude. "Académisme et avant-garde dans la peinture française du xix siècle." In *Avenirs et avant-gardes en France: xix–xx siècles*, ed. Vincent Duclert, Rémi Fabre, and Patrick Fridenson, pp. 115–27. Paris, La Découverte, 1999.

Gengembre, Gérard. "Entre archaïsme et modernité: Bonald, la contre-révolution et la littérature." *Revue d'histoire littéraire de la France* 90 (1990): 705–14.

———. "De la perfectibilité en Amérique." *Littératures* 50 (2004): 39–54.

———. "Bonald ou l'esthétique sociale de la littérature." In *Romantismes: l'esthétisme en acte*, ed. Jean-Louis Cabanès, pp. 143–54. Paris, PU de Paris Ouest, 2009.

———. "Le romantisme de Madame de Staël, ou enthousiasme et politique." *Revue d'histoire littéraire de la France* 116 (2016): 69–78.

Gény, François. *Méthode d'interprétation et sources en droit privé positif* [1919]. 2 vols. Paris, LDGJ, 2016.

Georgel, Chantal, ed. *1848, La République et l'Art Vivant*. Paris, Fayard, 1998.

Gerber, Karl Friedrich Wilhelm. "Uber den Begriff der Autonomie." *Archiv für die Civilistische Praxis* 73 (1854): 35–62.

Gérin-Ricard, L. de. *L'Histoire des Institutions Politiques de Fustel de Coulanges*. Paris, Société française d'Editions Littéraires et Techniques, 1936.

Gervinus, Georg Gottfried. *Introduction to the History of the Nineteenth Century*. London, 1853.

Ghosh, Peter. "Max Weber and Georg Jellinek: Two Divergent Conceptions of Law." *Saeculum* 59 (2008): 299–347.

Gianturco, Elio. "Vico et les débuts de l'historiographie du droit français." *Archives de philosophie* 40 (1977): 87–105.

Gibbon, Edward. *The History of the Decline and Fall of the Roman Empire* [1776–88]. Ed. David Womersley. 3 vols. London, Allen Lane, 1994.

Gibbons, Sarah L. *Kant's Theory of Imagination: Bridging Gaps in Judgment and Experience*. Oxford, Clarendon Press, 1994.

Gierke, Otto von. *Die historische Rechtsschule und die Germanisten*. Berlin, 1903.

———. *Natural Law and the Theory of Society 1500–1800*. Cambridge, CUP, 1934.

———. *Associations and Law: The Classical and Early Christian Stages*. Ed. George Heiman. Toronto, U of Toronto Press, 1977.

Gilbert, Felix. *History: Choice and Commitment*. Cambridge, MA, Harvard UP, 1977.

Gillard, Lucien. *L'Union latine, une expérience de souverainetés monétaires partagées (1865–1926)*. Paris, Garnier, 2017.

Gillespie, Michael. *Nihilism before Nietzsche*. Chicago, U of Chicago Press, 1995.

———. "Nihilism in the Nineteenth Century: From Absolute Subjectivity to Superhumanity." In *The Edinburgh Critical History of Nineteenth-Century Philosophy*, ed. Alison Stone, pp. 278–93. Edinburgh, Edinburgh UP, 2011.

Giorgi, Alessandro de. *Esamine del Diritto Filosofico, ossia del Sistema e delle Dottrine esposte nella Terza Edizione Francese del* Cours de Droit Naturel ou de Philosophie du Droit *del Prof H. Ahrens*. Padua, 1853.

Gjesdal, Kristin. *Herder's Hermeneutics: History, Poetry, Enlightenment*. Cambridge, CUP, 2017.

———. "Literature, Prejudice and Historicity: The Philosophical Importance of Herder's Shakespeare Studies." In *The Insistence of Art*, ed. Paul A. Kottman, pp. 91–115. New York, Fordham UP, 2017.

Glaeser, Rolf. "Carl Dietzel (1829–1884): A Pioneering and Unorthodox Thinker on Public Debt and Fiscal Policy." In *European Economists of the Early 20th Century*, ed. Warren J. Samuels, 2 vols., 2:81–103. Cheltenham, Edward Elgar, 2003.

Gobineau, Arthur de. "Coup d'œil général sur l'histoire de la morale." In Alexis de Tocqueville, *Oeuvres complètes*, ed. J. P. Mayer et al., 17 vols., 9:43–56. Paris, 1951–2021.

Goetschel, Willi. *Spinoza's Modernity: Mendelssohn, Lessing, and Heine*. Madison, U of Wisconsin Press, 2004.

Goldhill, Simon. *The Christian Invention of Time: Temporality and the Literature of Late Antiquity*. Cambridge, CUP, 2022.

Goller, Peter. *Naturrecht, Rechtsphilosophie oder Rechtstheorie? Zur Geschichte der Rechtsphilosophie an Österreichs Universitäten (1848–1945)*. Frankfurt, Peter Lang, 1997.

Goodman, Dena. "Public Sphere and Private Life: Toward a Synthesis of Current Historiographical Approaches to the Old Regime." *History and Theory* 31 (1992): 1–20.

Gordon, Peter Eli. *Rosenzweig and Heidegger: Between Judaism and German Philosophy*. Berkeley, U of California Press, 2003.

———. *Continental Divide: Heidegger, Cassirer, Davos*. Cambridge, MA, Harvard UP, 2010.

Gossman, Lionel. *Between History and Literature*, Cambridge, MA, Harvard UP, 1990.

Gotlieb, Marc J. *The Plight of Emulation: Ernest Meissonier and French Salon Painting*. Princeton, NJ, Princeton UP, 1996.

Gottlieb, Gabriel, ed. *Fichte's Foundations of Natural Right: A Critical Guide*. Cambridge, CUP, 2016.

Grafton, Anthony. "Prolegomena to Friedrich August Wolf." *Journal of the Warburg and Courtauld Institutes* 44 (1981): 101–29.

Grandjonc, Jacques. *Marx et les communistes allemands à Paris*. Paris, Maspero, 1974.

Grant Duff, M. E. *The Life and Speeches of Sir Henry Maine*. London, 1892.

Gray, Richard T., et al., eds. *Inventions of the Imagination: Romanticism and Beyond*. Seattle, U of Washington Press, 2012.

Green, Thomas Hill. *Philosophical Works*. Ed. Richard Lewis Nettleship. 3 vols. London, Longmans, Green, and Co., 1885–88.

Grewe, Cordula. "Beyond Hegel's End of Art: Schadow's *Mignon* and the Religious Project of Late Romanticism." *Modern Intellectual History* 1 (2004): 185–217.

Griffin, Roger. *The Nature of Fascism* [1991]. Abingdon, Routledge, 2006.

Grün, Karl. *Die soziale Bewegung in Frankreich und Belgien*. Darmstadt, 1845.

Grünewald, Marie-Antoinette, ed. *Paul Chenavard et la décoration du Panthéon de Paris en 1848*. Lyon, Musée des Beaux-Arts, 1977.

———. "La théologie de Paul Chenavard: palingénésie et régénération." In *Romantisme et religion: théologie des théologiens et théologie des écrivains*, ed. Michel Baude and Marc-Mathieu Münch, pp. 141–52. Paris, 1980.

Guerci, Luciano. *Libertà degli antichi e libertà dei moderni: Sparta, Atene e i «philosophes» nella Francia dei Settecento*. Naples, Guido, 1979.

Guermès, Sophie, and Brigitte Krulic, eds. *Edgar Quinet, une conscience européenne*. Brussels, Peter Lang, 2018.

Guernsey, Daniel. *The Artist and the State, 1777–1855: The Politics of Universal History in British and French Painting*. Aldershot, Ashgate, 2007.

Guillemin, Henri. *Le Jocelyn de Lamartine*. Paris, 1936.

Guizot, François. *Essais sur l'histoire de France*. Paris, 1823.

———. *Histoire générale de la civilisation en Europe*. Paris, 1828.

———. *The History of Civilization in France* [1828–30]. In François Guizot, *Historical Essays and Lectures*, ed. Stanley Mellon. Chicago, U of Chicago Press, 1972.

————. *Cours d'histoire moderne. Histoire de la civilisation en France depuis la chute de l'empire romain jusqu' en 1789.* Paris 1829.

————. "De la démocratie dans les sociétés modernes." *Revue française* 3 (1837): 193–225.

————. *Histoire de la civilisation en France depuis la chute de l'empire romain.* 3rd ed., Paris, 1840. 6th ed., Paris, 1851.

————. *Allgemeine Geschichte der europäischen Civilisation in vierzehn akademischen Vorlesungen.* Trans. Karl Sachs. Stuttgart, 1844.

————. *Histoire des origines du gouvernement représentatif en Europe.* 2 vols. Paris, 1851.

————. *Historical Essays and Lectures.* Ed. Stanley Mellon. Chicago, U of Chicago Press, 1972.

————. "De la souveraineté." In François Guizot, *Histoire de la civilisation en Europe,* ed. Pierre Rosanvallon, pp. 307–89. Paris, Hachette, 1985.

————. *The History of the Origins of Representative Government in Europe.* Trans. Andrew R. Scoble. Introduced by Aurelian Craiutu. Indianapolis, IN, Liberty Fund, 2002.

Gumbrecht, Hans Ulrich. "A History of the Concept 'Modern.'" In his *Making Sense of Life and Literature,* pp. 79–110. Minneapolis, U of Minnesota Press, 1992.

Gurka, Deszõ. "The Role of 'Dream' and 'Unconscious' in Carl Gustav Carus' Image of Man." In *Changes in the Image of Man from the Enlightenment to the Age of Romanticism,* ed. Deszõ Gurka, pp. 172–88. Budapest, Gondolat Publishers, 2019.

Gurvitch, Georges. *Les tendances actuelles de la philosophie allemande: E. Husserl, M. Scheler, E. Lask, M. Heidegger* [1930]. Paris, Vrin, 1949.

————. *L'idée du droit social.* Paris, 1932.

Haack, Marie Laurence, and Martin Miller. *La construction de l'étruscologie au xxe siècle.* Bordeaux, Ausonius, 2015.

————. *Les Etrusques au temps du fascisme et du nazisme.* Bordeaux, Ausonius, 2016.

————. *L'étruscologie dans l'Europe d'après-guerre.* Bordeaux, Ausonius, 2017.

Haakonssen, Knud, and Donald Winch, "The Legacy of Adam Smith." In *The Cambridge Companion to Adam Smith,* ed. Knud Haakonssen, pp. 366–94. Cambridge, CUP, 2006.

Habermas, Jürgen. *The Structural Transformation of the Public Sphere* [1962]. Cambridge, MA, MIT Press, 1989.

————. "Dialectical Idealism in Transition to Materialism: Schelling's Idea of a Contraction of God and Its Consequences for the Philosophy of History" [1969]. In *The New Schelling,* ed. Judith Norman and Alistair Welchmann, pp. 49–89. London, Continuum, 2004.

Hahn, Friedrich von. *Die materielle Übereinstimmung der römischen und germanischen Rechstprincipien.* Jena, 1856.

Halévy, Daniel. *Proudhon d'après ses carnets inédits.* Paris, Sequana, 1944.

————. *Essai sur l'accélération de l'histoire.* 2nd ed. Paris, 1948.

Haller, Karl Ludwig von. *Restauration de la science politique, ou théorie de l'état social naturel opposée à la fiction de l'état civil factice* [1816–20]. 6 vols. Lyon and Paris, 1824–65.

Hallis, Frederick. *Corporate Personality.* Oxford, OUP, 1930.

Hammer, Dean. *Roman Political Thought: From Cicero to Augustine.* Cambridge, CUP, 2014.

Hammersley, Rachel. *Republicanism: An Introduction.* Cambridge, Polity, 2020.

Hannoosh, Michèle. *Jules Michelet: Writing Art and History in Nineteenth-Century France.* University Park, Pennsylvania State UP, 2019.

Harder, Marie-Pierre. "Les anciens contre-attaquent, ou la querelle revisitée." *Acta fabula* 13 (2012): 1–11.

Hare, Thomas. *The Machinery of Representation.* London, 1857.

———. *A Treatise on the Election of Representatives, Parliamentary and Municipal.* New ed. London, 1861.

Hartog, François. *Le xixe siècle et l'histoire. Le cas Fustel de Coulanges.* Paris, PUF, 1988.

———. *Régimes d'historicité. Présentisme et expériences du temps.* Paris, Le Seuil, 2003.

———. *Anciens, modernes, sauvages.* Paris, Galaade Editions, 2005.

———. *Chronos. L'Occident aux prises avec le temps.* Paris, Gallimard, 2020.

Hastie, William. Translator's introduction to Diodato Lioy, *The Philosophy of Right, with special reference to the Principles and Development of Law.* 2 vols. London, 1891.

Hauriou, Maurice. "L'alternance des moyen-âges et des renaissances et ses conséquences sociales." *Revue de métaphysique et morale* 3 (1895): 527–49.

———. "Le régime d'état." *La Revue socialiste* 39 (1904): 564–81.

———. *Ecrits sociologiques.* Ed. Frédéric Audren and Marc Milet. Paris, Dalloz, 2008.

Heath, Richard. *Edgar Quinet: His Early Life and Writings.* London, 1881.

Hegel, Georg Wilhelm Friedrich. *Elements of the Philosophy of Right* [1820]. Ed. Allen W. Wood. Cambridge, CUP, 1991.

———. *Lectures on the History of Philosophy* [1840]. 3 vols. Oxford, 1892–96. Special Combined Edition. Lector House, 2020.

———. *Philosophie de religion de Hegel.* Trans. Augusto Véra. 2 vols. Paris, 1878.

———. *The Philosophy of History.* Trans. J. Sibree. Introduced by Carl J. Friedrich. New York, Dover Publications, 1956.

———. *Leçons sur Platon.* Ed. Jean-Louis Vieillard-Baron. Paris, Aubier-Montaigne, 1976.

Heidegger, Martin. *Kant and the Problem of Metaphysics* [1927]. Ed. and trans. Richard Taft. Bloomington, Indiana UP, 1997.

———. *Chemins qui ne mènent nulle part* [1949 and 1962]. Paris, Gallimard, 1980.

Hell, Julia. "Imperial Ruin Gazers, or Why did Scipio Weep." In *Ruins of Modernity,* ed. Julia Hell and Andreas Schönle, pp. 169–92. Durham NC, Duke UP, 2010.

———. *The Conquest of Ruins: The Third Reich and the Fall of Rome.* Chicago, U of Chicago Press, 2019.

Heller, Agnes. "Freedom, Equality and Fraternity in Kant's *Critique of Judgment.*" *Critical Horizons* 19 (2018): 187–97.

Heller, Hermann. *La crise de la théorie de l'état* [1926]. Ed. Olivier Jouanjan. Paris, Dalloz, 2012.

Hello, Charles Guillaume. *Philosophie de l'histoire de France.* Paris, 1840.

Henning, Ian Allan. *L'Allemagne de Mme de Staël et la polémique romantique.* Paris, Champion, 1929.

Herder, Johann Gottfried. "Journal meiner Reise im Jahr 1769." In Johann Gottfried Herder, *Werke,* ed. Wolfgang Pross, 3 vols., 1:355–465. Munich and Vienna, 1984–2002.

———. *Essay on the Origin of Language* [1772]. In *Jean-Jacques Rousseau and Johann Gottfried Herder: Two Essays on the Origin of Language,* ed. Alexander Gode and John H. Moran. Chicago, U of Chicago Press, 1966.

———. "Némésis, symbole moral des anciens." In *Recueil de pièces intéressantes concernant les antiquités, les beaux-arts, les belles-lettres et la philosophie,* 6 vols., 6:404–24. Paris, 1796.

———. *Ideas on the Philosophy of History of Mankind* [1784]. Trans. T. Churchill. London, 1800.

Herskowitz, Daniel M. *Heidegger and His Jewish Reception*. Cambridge, CUP, 2021.

Hess, Jonathan. *Reconstituting the Body Politic: Enlightenment, Public Culture and the Invention of Aesthetic Autonomy*. Detroit, Wayne State UP, 1999.

Heuschling, Luc. *Etat de droit, Rechtsstaat, Rule of Law*. Paris, Dalloz, 2002.

———. "Etat de droit. Etude de linguistique, de théorie et de dogmatique juridiques comparées." In *Verfassungsprinzipien in Europa/Constitutional Principles in Europe*, ed. Hartmut Bauer and Christian Calliess, pp. 103–55. Berlin, Berliner Wissenschafts Verlag, 2008.

Hiebel, Dominique. "Denis Serrigny, le droit administrative romain et la dénonciation du despotisme impérial." *Revue française d'histoire des idées politiques* 41 (2015): 123–60.

Hill, John Spencer, ed. *The Romantic Imagination*. London, Macmillan, 1977.

Hobbes, Thomas. *Leviathan* [1651]. Ed. Richard Tuck. Cambridge, CUP, 1991.

Hobsbawm, E. J. *The Age of Revolution: Europe 1789–1848*. London, Weidenfeld, 1972.

Holland, Ben. "Sovereignty as Dominium? Reconstructing the Constructivist Roman Law Thesis." *International Studies Quarterly* 54 (2010): 449–80.

Holtfrerich, Carl-Ludwig. "Government Debt in the Economic Thought of the Long 19th Century." Discussion Paper 2013/4. School of Business and Economics, Freie Universität, Berlin, 2013.

———. "Public Debt in Post-1850 German Economic Thought vis-à-vis the Pre-1850 British Classical School." *German Economic Review* 15 (2013): 62–83.

Honigsheim, Paul. "La doctrine allemande du droit naturel aux xvii et xviii siècles." *Archives de Philosophie du Droit et de Sociologie Juridique* 9 (1939): 216–37.

———. *The Unknown Max Weber*. New Brunswick, NJ, Transaction Publishers, 2000.

Honneth, Axel. *The Struggle for Recognition: The Moral Grammar of Social Conflicts*. Cambridge, MA, MIT Press, 1996.

———. *The Pathologies of Individual Freedom*. Princeton, NJ, Princeton UP, 2010.

———. *Ce que social veut dire*. 2 vols. Paris, Gallimard, 2013.

Hont, Istvan. *Jealousy of Trade: International Competition and the Nation-State in Historical Perspective*. Cambridge, MA, Harvard UP, 2005.

———. "The Rhapsody of Public Debt: David Hume and Voluntary State Bankruptcy." In his *Jealousy of Trade: International Competition and the Nation-State in Historical Perspective*, pp. 325–53. Cambridge, MA, Harvard UP, 2005.

———. "Adam Smith's History of Law and Government as Political Theory." In *Political Judgment: Essays for John Dunn*, ed. Richard Bourke and Raymond Geuss, pp. 131–71. Cambridge CUP, 2009.

———. *Politics in Commercial Society: Adam Smith and Jean-Jacques Rousseau*. Cambridge, MA, Harvard UP, 2015.

Hont, Istvan, and Michael Ignatieff. "Needs and Justice in the *Wealth of Nations*: An Introductory Essay." In *Wealth and Virtue: The Shaping of Political Economy in the Scottish Enlightenment*, ed. Istvan Hont and Michael Ignatieff, pp. 1–44. Cambridge, CUP, 1983.

Hopkins, Thomas. "Liberal Economists and Owenism: Blanqui and Reybaud." *History of European Ideas* (2020). DOI: 10.1080/01916599.2020.1798622.

Hornung, Joseph. *Essai historique sur cette question: Pourquoi les Romains ont-ils été le peuple juridique de l'ancien monde?* Geneva, 1847.

―――. *Idées sur l'évolution juridique des nations chrétiennes et en particulier sur celle du peuple français*. Geneva, 1850.

―――. *L'Histoire romaine et Napoléon III*. Lausanne, 1865.

―――. "Quelques vues sur le droit romain en lui-même et dans son action dans le monde moderne, à propos d'une histoire récente de ce droit." *Revue de droit internationale et de législation comparée* 5 (1873): 194–202.

―――. "Les races de la Suisse au point de vue historique et juridique." In *Actes du Congrès des Sociétés suisses de géographie*, pp. 1–21. Geneva, 1882.

Hotman, François. *Anti-Tribonian* [1567].

Hourcade, Emmanuel, Charlotte Morel, and Ayşe Yuva, eds. *La perfectibilité de l'homme. Les lumières allemandes contre Rousseau?* 2 vols. Paris, Classiques Garnier, 2022.

Hoyt, Nelly S. "Michelet: A Historian Paints French History." In *Thomas Couture and the Painting of History*, Springfield Museum of Fine Arts 1980 exhibition, curated by Albert Boime and Robert Henning Jr. Springfield, MA, 1980.

Hugo, Victor. Letter to the *Journal des débats*, 26 July 1824.

―――. *Cromwell* [1827]. Ed. Annie Ubersfeld. Paris, Garnier Flammarion, 1968.

―――. *Hernani* [1830]. Ed. Yves Gohin. Paris, Gallimard, 1995.

―――. *Dramas: Oliver Cromwell*. Trans. I. G. Burnham. London, 1896.

Humboldt, Wilhelm von. *Le dix-huitième siècle*. Ed. Jean Quillien. Trans. Christophe Losfeld. Lille, PU de Lille, 1995.

Hunt, Herbert J. *The Epic in Nineteenth-Century France*. Oxford, Blackwell, 1941.

Hunter, Ian. "Giorgio Agamben's *Form of Life*." *Politics, Religion and Ideology* 18 (2017): 135–56.

―――. "Giorgio Agamben's Genealogy of Office." *European Journal of Cultural and Political Sociology* 4 (2017): 166–99.

Husson, Jules (aka Champfleury). *Contes d'automne*. Paris, 1854.

Iggers, Georg G. "Historicism: The History and Meaning of the Term." *Journal of the History of Ideas* 56 (1995): 129–52.

―――. *The German Conception of History: The National Tradition of Historical Thought from Herder to the Present* [1968]. 2nd ed. Hanover, NH, University Presses of New England, 1983.

Isbell, John Clairborne. *The Birth of European Romanticism: Truth and Propaganda in Staël's De l'Allemagne*. Cambridge, CUP, 1994.

Israel, Jonathan. *The Radical Enlightenment*. Oxford, OUP, 2001.

Jackson Ravenscroft, Ruth. *The Veiled God: Friedrich Schleiermacher's Theology of Finitude*. Leiden, Brill, 2019.

Jacoby, Russell. *On Diversity: The Eclipse of the Individual in a Global Era*. New York, Seven Stories Press, 2020.

Jacoud, Gilles, ed. *Political Economy and Industrialism: Banks in Saint-Simonian Thought*. London, Routledge, 2010.

Jaeschke, Walter. "Early German Idealist Reinterpretations of the Quarrel of the Ancients and Moderns." *Clio* 12 (1982–83): 313–33.

James, David. *Fichte's Social and Political Philosophy: Property and Virtue*. Cambridge, CUP, 2011.

―――. *Fichte's Republic: Idealism, History and Nationalism*. Cambridge, CUP, 2015.

James, Susan. *The Content of Social Explanation*. Cambridge, CUP, 1984.

Janet, Paul. *Histoire de la science politique dans ses rapports avec la morale* [1858]. 3rd ed. 2 vols. Paris, 1887.

———. *La philosophie française contemporaine.* Paris,1879.

Janicaud, Dominique. *Une Généalogie du Spiritualisme Français.* The Hague, Martinus Nijhoff, 1969.

Janssen, Johannes. *History of the German People at the Close of the Middle Ages.* 16 vols. London, 1905–25.

Jardine, Nicolas. "The Significance of Schelling's 'Epoch of a Wholly New Natural History': An Essay on the Realization of Questions." In *Metaphysics and Philosophy of Science in the Seventeenth and Eighteenth Centuries*, ed. R. S. Woolhouse, pp. 327–50. Dordrecht, Kluwer, 1988.

———. "*Naturphilosophie* and the Kingdoms of Nature." In *Cultures of Natural History*, ed. James A. Secord and Emma C. Spary, pp. 230–245. Cambridge, CUP, 1996.

Jaume, Lucien. "Aux origines du libéralisme politique en France." *Esprit* 243 (1998): 37–60.

———. "The Unity, Diversity, and Paradoxes of French Liberalism." In *French Liberalism from Montesquieu to the Present Day*, ed. Raf Geenens and Helena Rosenblatt, pp. 36–54. Cambridge, CUP, 2012.

———. "Germaine de Staël, une source jamais tariée pour notre temps." *Cahiers Staëliens* 67 (2017): 81–100.

Jauss, Hans Robert. "Ästhetische Normen und geschichtliche Reflexion in der 'Querelle des Anciens et des Modernes.'" In Charles Perrault, *Parallèle des anciens et des modernes en ce qui regarde les arts et les sciences* [1688], pp. 8–64. Munich, Eidos Verlag, 1964.

———. "Fr. Schlegels und Fr. Schillers Replik auf die 'Querelle des Anciens et des Modernes.'" In *Europäische Aufklärung: Herbert Dieckmann zum 60 Geburtstag*, ed. Hugo Friedrich and Fritz Schalk, pp. 117–40. Munich, Wilhelm Fink Verlag, 1967.

———. "The Idealist Embarrassment: Observations on Marxist Aesthetics." *New Literary History* 7 (1975): 191–208.

———. *Pour une esthétique de la réception.* Paris, 1978.

———. "Tradition, Innovation and Aesthetic Experience." *Journal of Aesthetics and Art Criticism* 46 (1988): 375–88.

———. "The Literary Process of Modernism from Rousseau to Adorno." *Cultural Critique* 11 (1988–89): 27–61.

———. "The Theory of Reception: A Retrospective of Its Unrecognized Prehistory." In *Literary Theory Today*, ed. Peter Collier and Helger Geyer-Ryan, pp. 53–73. Ithaca, NY, Cornell UP, 1990.

Javary, Auguste. *De l'idée du progrès.* Paris, 1851.

Jellinek, Georg. *L'état moderne et son droit.* 2 vols. [Paris, 1904 and 2013]. Ed. Olivier Jouanjan. Paris, Editions Panthéon Assas, 2005.

Jhering, Rudolf von. *L'esprit du droit romain dans les diverses phases de son développement.* 3 vols. [1852–65]. Paris, 1886.

———. *La lutte pour le droit* [1872]. Ed. Olivier Jouanjan. Paris, Dalloz, 2006.

———. *Law as a Means to an End* [1877]. Boston, The Boston Book Company, 1913.

Jobit, Pierre. *Les éducateurs de l'Espagne contemporaine, I, les Krausistes.* 2 vols. Paris, 1936.

John, Michael. *Politics and the Law in Late Nineteenth-Century Germany: The Origins of the Civil Code.* Oxford, OUP, 1989.

Jollivet, Servanne. *L'historisme en questions. Généalogie, débats et réception (1800–1930)*. Paris, Champion, 2013.

Jolowicz, Herbert Felix. "Political Implications of Roman Law." *Tulane Law Review* 22 (1947–48): 62–81.

Jones, H. S. *The French State in Question: Public Law and Political Argument in the Third Republic*. Cambridge, CUP, 1993.

Jouanjan, Olivier. "Carl Friedrich Gerber et la constitution d'une science du droit public allemand." In *La science juridique française et la science juridique allemande de 1870 à 1918*, ed. Olivier Beaud and Patrick Wachsmann, pp. 11–63. Strasbourg, Annales de la Faculté de Droit de Strasbourg, 1, 1997.

———. "Lorenz von Stein et les contradictions du mouvement constitutionnel révolutionnaire (1789–1794)." *Annales historiques de la révolution française* 328 (2002): 171–91.

———. *Une histoire de la pensée juridique en Allemagne (1800–1918)*. Paris, PUF, 2005.

Jullian, Camille. *Extraits des historiens français du xix siècle*. Paris, 1897.

Kain, Philip J. *Schiller, Hegel and Marx*. Kingston and Montreal, McGill-Queen's UP, 1982.

Kant, Immanuel. *Observations on the Feeling of the Beautiful and Sublime* [1764]. In Immanuel Kant, *Essays and Treatises on Moral, Political, Religious and Various Philosophical Subjects*, 2 vols. London, 1799.

———. *Critique of Pure Reason* [1781]. Ed. and trans. Paul Guyer and Allen W. Wood. Cambridge, CUP, 1998.

———. "An Answer to the Question: 'What is Enlightenment'" [1784]. In Immanuel Kant, *Political Writings*, ed. Hans Reiss [1970], pp. 54–60. 2nd ed. Cambridge, CUP, 1991.

———. "Idea for a Universal History from a Cosmopolitan Perspective" [1784]. In Immanuel Kant, *Toward Perpetual Peace and Other Writings on Politics, Peace, and History*, ed. Pauline Kleingeld, trans. David L. Colclasure, pp. 3–16. New Haven, CT, Yale UP, 2006.

———. *Groundwork of the Metaphysics of Morals* [1785]. Ed. H. J. Paton. London, 1948.

———. "Reviews of Herder's *Ideas on the Philosophy of the History of Mankind* [1785]. In Immanuel Kant, *Political Writings*, ed. Hans Reiss [1970], pp. 208–9. 2nd ed. Cambridge, CUP, 1991.

———. *Critique of Practical Reason* [1788]. In Immanuel Kant, *Practical Philosophy*, ed. Mary Gregor. Cambridge, CUP, 1996.

———. "On the Use of Teleological Principles in Philosophy" [1788]. Trans. J. Tissot. In Emmanuel Kant, *Mélanges de logique*, pp. 373–419. Paris, 1862.

———. *Critique of Judgment* [1790]. Trans. Werner S. Pluhar. Indianapolis, IN, Hackett, 1987.

———. *The Metaphysics of Morals* [1797]. In Immanuel Kant, *Practical Philosophy*, ed. Mary J. Gregor. Cambridge, CUP, 1996.

———. "An Answer to the Question, What is Enlightening." In Immanuel Kant, *Essays and Treatises on Moral, Political and Various Philosophical Subjects*, trans. A.F.M. Willich. 2 vols. London, 1798.

———. *The Conflict of the Faculties* [1798]. In Immanuel Kant, *Political Writings*, ed. Hans Reiss. Cambridge, CUP, 1991.

———. "Conjectures on the Beginning of Human History." In Immanuel Kant, *Political Writings*, ed. Hans Reiss [1970], pp. 221–34. 2nd ed. Cambridge, CUP, 1991.

————. *On the Common Saying: 'This May be True in Theory, but it does not Apply in Practice'*. In Immanuel Kant, *Political Writings*, ed. Hans Reiss [1970], pp. 61–92. 2nd ed. Cambridge, CUP, 1991.

————. *Metaphysics of Morals*. In Immanuel Kant, *Lectures on Ethics*, ed. Peter Heath and Jerome B. Schneewind. Cambridge, CUP, 1997.

Kapossy, Béla. *Iselin contra Rousseau: Sociable Patriotism and the History of Mankind*. Basel, Schwabe, 2006.

————. "Karl Ludwig von Haller's Critique of Liberal Peace." In *Commerce and Peace in the Enlightenment*, ed. Béla Kapossy, Isaac Nakhimovsky, and Richard Whatmore, pp. 244–71. Cambridge, CUP, 2017.

————. "Words and Things: Languages of Reform in Wilhelm Traugott Krug and Karl Ludwig von Haller." In *Languages of Reform in the Eighteenth Century: When Europe Lost Its Fear of Change*, ed. Susan Richter, Thomas Maissen, and Manuela Albertone, pp. 384–404. London, Routledge, 2020.

Kelley, Donald R. *François Hotman: A Revolutionary's Ordeal*. Princeton, NJ, Princeton UP, 1973.

————. *Historians and the Law in Post-revolutionary France*. Princeton, NJ, Princeton UP, 1984.

Kelley, Theresa M. *Reinventing Allegory*. Cambridge, CUP, 1997.

Kelly, Duncan. *The State of the Political: Conceptions of Politics and the State in the Thought of Max Weber, Carl Schmitt and Franz Neumann*. Oxford, OUP, 2003.

————. "Max Weber and the Rights of Citizens." *Max Weber Studies* 4 (2004): 23–49.

————. "Revisiting the Rights of Man: Georg Jellinek on Rights and the State." *Law and History Review* 22 (2004): 493–529.

————. "Popular Sovereignty as State Theory in the Nineteenth Century." In *Popular Sovereignty in Historical Perspective*, ed. Richard Bourke and Quentin Skinner, pp. 270–96. Cambridge, CUP, 2016.

Kelly, George Armstrong. "Notes on Hegel's 'Lordship and Bondage.'" *Review of Metaphysics* 19 (1966): 780–802.

————. *Hegel's Retreat from Eleusis: Studies in Political Thought*. Princeton, NJ, Princeton UP, 1978.

Kervégan, Jean-François, and Heinz Mohnhaupt, eds. *Influences et réceptions mutuelles du droit et de la philosophie en France et en Allemagne*. Frankfurt, Vittorio Klostermann, 2001.

————. "Is There Any Philosophy of History?" In *Concepts of Normativity: Kant or Hegel?*, ed. Christian Krijnen, pp. 216–34. Leiden, Brill, 2019.

Kidd, Colin. *The World of Mr Casaubon: Britain's Wars of Mythography 1700–1870*. Cambridge, CUP, 2016.

Kingsley, Charles. *The Roman and the Teuton: A Series of Lectures Delivered Before the University of Cambridge* [1861]. New ed. with a preface by Max Muller. London, 1889.

Kirby, James. "History, Law and Freedom: F. W. Maitland in Context." *Modern Intellectual History* 16 (2019): 127–54.

Kisiel, Theodore. "Das Entstehen des Begriffsfeldes 'Faktizität' im Frühwerk Heideggers." *Dilthey Jahrbuch* 4 (1986–87): 91–120.

————. "Heidegger, Lask, Fichte." In *Heidegger, German Idealism, and Neo-Kantianism*, ed. Tom Rockmore, pp. 239–70. New York, Humanity Books, 2000.

————. *Heidegger's Way of Thought*. New York and London, Continuum, 2002.

————. "On the Genesis of Heidegger's Formally Indicative Hermeneutics of Facticity." In *Rethinking Facticity*, ed. François Raffoul and Eric Sean Nelson, pp. 41–67. New York, State University of New York Press, 2008.

Kleist, Heinrich von. "On the Marionette Theatre" [1810]. Trans. Thomas G. Neumiller. *Drama Review* 16 (1972): 22–26.

————. *Essays on Dolls*. Ed. Indris Parry. London, Penguin Books, 1974.

Klimrath, Henri. "Essai sur l'étude historique du droit et son utilité pour l'interprétation du Code Civil" [1833]. Reprinted in his *Travaux sur l'histoire du droit français*, 2 vols. Paris, 1843.

Klüver, Max. "Sozialkritik und Sozialreform bei Heinrich Ahrens." Doctoral diss., University of Hamburg, 1967.

Kneller, Jane. *Kant and the Power of Imagination*. Cambridge, CUP, 2007.

Koebner, Richard, and Helmut Dan Schmidt. *Imperialism: The Story and Significance of a Political Word, 1840–1960*. Cambridge, CUP, 1964.

Kolakowski, Leszek. *Main Currents of Marxism*. 3 vols. Oxford, Clarendon Press, 1978.

Korkounov, Nikolaï Mikhaïlovitch. *General Theory of Law* [1903]. New York, Macmillan, 1922.

Körner, Axel. *Politics of Culture in Liberal Italy*. London, Routledge, 2009.

Korngiebel, Johannes. "Friedrich Schlegel's Sceptical Interpretation of Plato." In *Hegel and Scepticism: On Klaus Vieweg's Interpretation*, ed. Jannis Kotzatsas et al., pp. 165–84. Berlin, Walter de Gruyter, 2017.

Koselleck, Reinhart. *Critique and Crisis: Enlightenment and the Pathogenesis of Modern Society* [1959]. Cambridge, MA, MIT Press, 1988.

————. "Einleitung." In *Geschichtliche Grundbegriffe*, ed. Otto Brunner, Werner Conze and Reinhart Koselleck, 8 vols., 1: xiii–xxvii. Stuttgart, 1972–97.

————. *Sediments of Time: On Possible Histories*. Stanford, Stanford UP, 2018.

Koslowski, Peter, ed. *The Theory of Ethical Economy in the Historical School*. Berlin, Springer Verlag, 1995.

Krause, Karl Christian Friedrich. *Briefwechsel*. Ed. Paul Hohlfeld and Auguste Wünsche. 2 vols. Leipzig, 1903–7.

Kriegel, Blandine. *La politique de la raison*. Paris, Payot, 1994.

————. *The State and the Rule of Law* [1989]. Princeton, NJ, Princeton UP, 1995.

Krug, Wilhelm Traugott. "Fénelon's Liberalismus." *Literarisches Konversation Blatt* 53 (4 March 1823): 209–10.

————. *Geschichtlichen Darstellung des Liberalismus alter und neuer Zeit*. Leipzig, 1823.

Kuklick, Bruce. *Josiah Royce: An Intellectual Biography*. Indianapolis, IN, Hackett, 1985.

Kurunmäki, Jussi, and Jani Marjanen. "A Rhetorical View of Isms: An Introduction." *Journal of Political Ideologies* 23 (2018): 241–55.

————. "Ism, Ideologies and Setting the Agenda for Public Debate." *Journal of Political Ideologies* 23 (2018): 256–82.

Kusch, Martin, Katherina Kinzel, Johannes Steizinger, and Niels Wildschut, eds. *The Emergence of Relativism: German Thought from the Enlightenment to National Socialism*. London, Routledge, 2019.

Laborde, Cécile. *Pluralist Thought and the State in Britain and France, 1900–25*. Basingstoke, Macmillan, 2000.

Lacassagne, Jean-Pierre. *Histoire d'une amitié. Pierre Leroux et George Sand*. Paris, Klincksieck, 1973.

———. "Quinet et Leroux." In *Edgar Quinet, ce juif errant*, ed. Simone Bernard-Griffiths and Paul Viallaneix, pp. 191–206. Clermont-Ferrand, 1978.

———. "Un mage romantique: Pierre Leroux (1791–1871)." Thèse doctorale, Université de Paris IV, 1989.

Lacombe, Charles de. "Le comte de Serre." *Le Correspondant* 75 (1878): 257–60.

Lacordaire, Henri-Dominique. *Conférences de Notre Dame de Paris*. 4 vols. Paris, 1853.

———. *Conferences of the Rev. Père Lacordaire*. Trans. Henry Langdon. London, 1853.

Lacoste, Claudine. "*Grandeur de la vie privée* de H. Fortoul." In *Rousseau et Voltaire en 1978*, pp. 118–26. Geneva, Slatkine, 1981.

Lagi, Sara. *Georg Jellinek: storico del pensiero politico 1883–1905*. Florence, Centro Editoriale Toscano, 2009.

———, ed. *Georg Jellinek: 'Il Tutto' e 'l'Individuo'*. Rubbettino, Catanzaro, 2015.

———. "The Formation of a Liberal Thinker: Georg Jellinek and His Early Writings." *Res Publica* 19 (2016): 59–76.

Lamartine, Alphonse de. *Sur la politique rationnelle* [Paris, 1831]. Ed. Romain Jalabert. Paris, 2020.

———. *Voyage en Orient (1832–1833)*. In Alphonse de Lamartine, *Œuvres*. Brussels, 1836.

Lamennais. Félicité de. "Réponse à la lettre du Père Ventura." In Félicité de Lamennais, *Œuvres*, 10 vols., 10:249–68. Paris, 1836–37.

Lampe, Jörg H. "Die Schüler Karl Christian Friedrich Krause und die Göttinger Unruhen von 1831. Legenden und Tatsachen." *Göttinger Jahrbuch* 46 (1998): 47–70.

Lane, Melissa. "Doing Our Own Thinking for Ourselves: On Quentin Skinner's Genealogical Turn." *Journal of the History of Ideas* 73 (2012): 71–82.

Lanjuinais, Jean-Denis, comte. *Examen du Huitième Chapitre du Contrat Social de J. J. Rousseau.* Paris, 1825.

Lanyi, Gabriel. "Debates on the Definition of Romanticism in Literary France (1820–1830)." *Journal of the History of Ideas* 41 (1980): 141–50.

Lanzi, Andrea. "Démocratie et propriété chez les premiers socialistes républicains français: les enjeux politiques de l'organisation du crédit." *Histoire, Economie et Société* 30 (2011): 81–94.

Lask, Emil. *Fichtes Idealismus und die Geschichte*. Tübingen, J.C.B. Mohr, 1902.

———. "Legal Philosophy." In *The Legal Philosophies of Lask, Radbruch, and Dabin*, ed. Edwin W Patterson and Kurt Wilk. Cambridge, MA, Harvard UP, 1950.

———. *La logique de la philosophie et la doctrine des catégories: étude sur la forme logique et sa souveraineté* [1911]. Paris, Vrin, 2002.

Laski, Harold. *A Defence of Liberty against Tyrants: A Translation of the Vindiciae contra Tyrannos by Junius Brutus*. London, Bell, 1924.

Lassalle, Ferdinand. *Théorie systématique des droits acquis*. 2 vols. Paris, 1904.

Latour, Antoine de. *Essai sur l'étude de l'histoire en France au dix-neuvième siècle*. Paris, 1835.

Lavorel, Guy, and Laurence Richer, eds. *Quinet en Question*. Lyon, C.E.D.I.C., 2004.

Le Guillou, Louis, ed. *Lettres inédites du baron d'Eckstein: société et littérature à Paris en 1838–40*. Paris, PU de France, 1984.

———. *Le 'baron' d'Eckstein et ses contemporains: Lamennais, Lacordaire, Montalembert, Foisset, Michelet, Renan, Hugo, etc.: correspondances avec un choix de ses articles*. Paris, Champion, 2003.

Leary, David E. "German Idealism and the Development of Psychology in the Nineteenth Century." *Journal of the History of Ideas* 18 (1980): 299–317.

Lebow, Richard Ned. *The Politics and Ethics of Identity: In Search of Ourselves*. Cambridge, CUP, 2012.

Lecler, Joseph. "Montalembert et le baron d'Eckstein. En suivant leur correspondance inédite." *Revue d'histoire de l'Eglise de France* 56 (1970): 47–70.

Lecoq, Anne-Marie, ed. *La querelle des anciens et des modernes*. Paris, Gallimard, 2001.

Lednicki, Wacław. "Mickiewicz at the Collège de France." In *Polish Civilization: Essays and Studies*, ed. Mieczysław Giergelewicz, pp. 182–97. New York, New York UP, 1979.

Lefort, Claude. *Lectures politiques. De Dante à Soljenitsyne*. Paris, PUF, 2021.

Lehmann, A. G. *Sainte-Beuve: A Portrait of a Critic 1804–1842*. Oxford, Clarendon Press, 1962.

Leitzmann, Albert. "Wilhelm von Humboldt und Frau von Staël." *Deutsche Rundschau* 169 (1916): 95–112, 271–80, 431–42; 170 (1917): 95–108, 256–66, 425–35; 171 (1918): 82–95.

Lemontey, Pierre Edouard. *Raison, folie, petit cours de morale mis à la porté des vieux enfants* [1801]. 3rd ed. 2 vols. Paris, 1816.

Léon, Xavier. "Fichte contre Schelling." *Revue de Métaphysique et de Morale* 12 (1904): 949–76.

Lerminier, Eugène. *Lettres philosophiques adressées à un Berlinois* [1832]. Paris, Association Corpus/EUD, 2011.

Leroux, Pierre. *Réfutation de l'éclecticisme*. Paris, 1839.

———. *De l'humanité*. 2 vols. Paris, 1840.

———. *Lettre au Docteur Deville* [1859]. Reprinted in Miguel Abensour, *Le procès des maitres rêveurs suivi de Pierre Leroux et l'utopie*. Arles, Sulliver, 2000.

———. *La grève de Samarez: poème philosophique*. Ed. Jean-Pierre Lacassagne. Paris, Klincksieck, 1979.

Leroux, Pierre, and Jean Reynaud, eds. *Encyclopédie nouvelle*. 8 vols. 1839–43.

Leterrier, Sophie Anne. *Béranger: des chansons pour un peuple citoyen*. Rennes, PU de Rennes, 2013.

Lev, Amnon. *Sovereignty and Liberty: A Study of the Foundations of Power*. London, Routledge, 2014.

———. *Souveraineté et liberté. Etude sur les fondements du pouvoir*. Paris, Garnier, 2020.

Libhart, Byron R. "Madame de Staël, Charles de Villers, and the Death of God." *Comparative Literature Studies* 9 (1972): 141–51.

Lichtheim, George. *The Origins of Socialism* [1968]. London, Weidenfeld & Nicolson, 1969.

Liebich, André. *Between Ideology and Utopia*. Dordrecht, 1979.

Lilly, Reginald, ed. *The Ancients and the Moderns*. Bloomington, Indiana UP, 1996.

Lilti, Antoine. *The Invention of Celebrity* [2014]. Cambridge, Polity, 2017.

Lindberg, Susanna. "Les hantises de Clara." *Revue Germanique Internationale* 18 (2013): 235–53.

Lipovetsky, Gilles, and Jean Serroy. *L'esthétisation du monde. Vivre à l'âge du capitalisme artiste*. Paris, Gallimard, 2013.

Liszt, Franz, and Marie d'Agoult. *Correspondance*. Ed. Serge Gut and Jacqueline Bellas. Paris, Fayard, 2001.

Littré, Emile. *Auguste Comte et la philosophie positive* [1863]. 2nd ed. Paris, 1864.

Lloyd, Genevieve. *Providence Lost*. Cambridge, MA, Harvard UP, 2008.

Lobban, Michael. "Was there a Nineteenth-Century 'English School of Jurisprudence'?" *Legal History* 16 (1995): 39–62.

———. "The Varieties of Legal History." *Clio@Thémis* 5 (2012): 1–29.

Lockridge, Laurence S. *The Ethics of Romanticism*. Cambridge, CUP, 1989.

López-Morillas, Juan. *The Krausist Movement and Ideological Change in Spain, 1854–1874* [1956]. Cambridge, CUP, 1981.

Lossier, Jean-G. *Le rôle social de l'art selon Proudhon*. Paris, Vrin, 1937.

Lotterie, Florence. "Chateaubriand contre Madame de Staël: la lettre sur la perfectibilité, ou du progrès hors des limites de la simple raison." *Revue des sciences humaines* 247 (1997): 89–105.

———. "Les lumières contre le progrès? La naissance de l'idée de perfectibilité." *Dix-Huitième Siècle* 30 (1998): 383–96.

———. "L'année 1800—Perfectibilité, progrès et révolution dans *De la littérature* de Mme de Staël." *Romantisme* 108 (2000): 9–22.

———. "Madame de Staël. La littérature comme 'philosophie sensible.'" *Romantisme* 124 (2004): 19–30.

Luckscheiter, Roman, ed. *L'art pour l'art. Der Beginn der modernen Kunstdebatte in französischen Quellen der Jahre 1818 bis 1847*. Bielefeld, Aisthesis, 2003.

Luhmann, Niklas. *The Differentiation of Society*. New York, Columbia UP, 1982.

———. *Law as a Social System* [1993]. Oxford, OUP, 2004.

Luig, Klaus. "Römische und germanischen Rechtsanschauung, individualistische und soziale Ordnung." In *Die Deutsche Rechtsgeschichte in der NS-Zeit: ihr Vorgeschichte und ihr Nach-wirkungen*, ed. Joachim Rückert and Dietmar Willoweit, pp. 95–137. Tübingen, J.C.B. Mohr, 1995.

Lukács, Georg. *History and Class Consciousness* [1922]. Trans. Rodney Livingston. London, Merlin, 1971.

Lukes, Steven. "The Meanings of 'Individualism.'" *Journal of the History of Ideas* 32 (1971): 45–66.

Macfarlane, Alan. *The Making of the Modern World*. London, Palgrave, 2002.

Mackintosh, James. *A General View of the Progress of Ethical Philosophy* [1831]. Philadelphia, 1834.

Macpherson, C. B. *The Political Theory of Possessive Individualism*. Oxford, Clarendon Press, 1962.

Magnin, Charles. *Causeries et méditations historiques et littéraires*. 2 vols. Paris, 1843.

Maine, Henry Sumner. "Roman Law and Legal Education." In *Cambridge Essays contributed by Members of the University*, pp. 1–29. London, 1856.

———. *Ancient Law* [1861]. Ed. Lawrence Rosen. Tucson, U of Arizona Press, 1986.

———. *Lectures on the Early History of Institutions* [1874]. 7th ed. London, 1905.

———. *Village Communities in the East and West*. London, 1876.

———. *International Law*. London 1888.

Maissen, Thomas. "Reinhart Koselleck, historien allemand de la guerre civile européenne." In *Historiens d'Europe, historiens de l'Europe*, ed. Denis Crouzet, pp. 99–120. Ceyzérieu, Champ Vallon, 2017.

Maistre, Joseph de. *Essai sur le principe générateur des constitutions politiques* [Saint-Petersburg, 1814]. Lyon, 1833.

Maitland, Frederick William. *English Law and the Renaissance*. Cambridge, CUP, 1901.

———. Introduction to Otto von Gierke, *Political Theories of the Middle Age*. Cambridge, CUP, 1900.

Mallion, Jean. *Victor Hugo et l'art architectural*. Paris, PUF, 1962.

Malon, Benoît. *Le socialisme intégral*. Paris, 1890.

Malpas, Jeff, ed. *The Place of Landscape: Concepts, Contexts, Studies*. Cambridge, MA, MIT Press, 2011.

Manchester, Martin L. *The Philosophical Foundations of Humboldt's Linguistic Doctrines*. Amsterdam, J. Benjamins, 1985.

Mantoux, Paul. *La révolution industrielle au xviiie siècle* [1928]. 2nd ed. Paris, 1959.

Mantovani, Dario. "Le détour incontournable. Le droit romain dans la réflexion de Yan Thomas." In *Aux origines des cultures juridiques européennes. Yan Thomas entre droit et sciences sociales*, ed. Paolo Napoli. Rome, Ecole Française de Rome, 2013.

Maréchal, Christian. "L'abbé de La Mennais, le comte de Montlosier et le baron d'Eckstein: un problème d'influence." *Revue d'histoire littéraire de la France* 50 (1950): 16–26.

Maret, Henri. *Essai sur le panthéisme dans les sociétés modernes*. Paris, 1840.

Marjanen, Jani. "Ism Concepts in Science and Politics." *Contributions to the History of Concepts* 13 (2018): v–ix.

Marmier, Xavier. *Chants populaires du Nord*. Paris, 1842.

Martine, Jacques-Daniel. *Examen des tragiques anciens et modernes, dans lequel le système classique et le système romantique sont jugés et comparés*. 3 vols. Paris, 1834.

Marx, Karl. *The Eighteenth Brumaire of Louis Bonaparte* [1852]. In *Marx: Later Political Writings*, ed. Terrell Carver. Cambridge, CUP, 1996.

Matoré, Georges. *Le vocabulaire et la société sous Louis-Philippe*. Geneva, Slatkine, 1967.

Maufroy, Sandrine. *Le philhellénisme franco-allemand*. Paris, Belin, 2011.

Maza, Sara. *The Myth of the French Bourgeoisie: An Essay on the Social Imaginary*. Cambridge, MA, Harvard UP, 2003.

Mazlish, Bruce. "The Tragic Farce of Marx, Hegel and Engels: A Note." *History and Theory* 11 (1972): 335–37.

McCalla, Arthur. "*Palingénésie philosophique* to *Palingénésie sociale*: From a Scientific Ideology to a Historical Ideology." *Journal of the History of Ideas* 55 (1994): 421–39.

———. *A Romantic Historiosophy: The Philosophy of Pierre-Simon Ballanche*. Leiden, Brill, 1998.

———. "Paganism in Restoration France: Eckstein's Traditionalist Orientalism." *Journal of the History of Ideas* 76 (2015): 563–85.

McFarland, Thomas. *Originality and Imagination*. Baltimore, Johns Hopkins UP, 1985.

McGuiness, Patrick. *Poetry and Radical Politics in Fin-de-Siècle France*. Oxford, OUP, 2015.

McIntire, C. T. *Herbert Butterfield: Historian as Dissenter*. New Haven, CT, Yale UP, 2004.

McWilliam, Neil. *Dreams of Happiness: Social Art and the French Left, 1830–1850*. Princeton, NJ, Princeton UP, 1993.

———. "How to Change the World: Claude-Henri de Rouvroy, comte de Saint-Simon." In *Utopian Moments*, ed. Miguel A. Ramiro Avilés and J. C. Davis, pp. 106–12. London, Bloomsbury, 2012.

Meckstroth, Christopher. *The Struggle for Democracy: Paradoxes of Progress and the Politics of Change*. Oxford, OUP, 2015.

Mehigan, Tim. "The Scepticism of Heinrich von Kleist." In *The Oxford Handbook of European Romanticism*, ed. Paul Hamilton, pp. 256–74. Oxford, OUP, 2016.

Meinecke, Friedrich. *Machiavellism: The Doctrine of Raison d'état and Its Place in Modern History* [1925]. London and New Brunswick, NJ, Transaction Publishers, 1998.

Menche de Loisne, Charles. *Influence de la littérature française de 1830 à 1850 sur l'esprit public et les mœurs*. Brussels, 1853.

Mennemeier, Franz Norbert. "Les premiers romantiques allemands et la 'Préface' de *Cromwell* de Victor Hugo: un exemple du rapport littéraire franco-allemand." *Francofonia* 14 (1988): 75–86.

Menon, Elizabeth K. "Victor Hugo and the Hunchbacks of the July Monarchy." *Studies in the Humanities* 21 (1994): 60–71.

———. "The Utopian Mayeux: Henri de Saint-Simon meets the *Bossu à la mode*." *Canadian Journal of History* 33 (1998): 249–77.

Merle, Jean-Christophe. "The Principle of Equality Governing Actions and Reactions in Kant's Practical Philosophy." *Con-Textos Kantianos* 2 (2015): 62–71.

Merriam, Charles Edward. *History of the Theory of Sovereignty since Rousseau*. New York, Columbia UP, 1900.

———. *American Political Ideas*. New York, Macmillan, 1920.

Mestre, Achille. "La notion de personnalité morale chez Rousseau." *Revue du droit public et de la science politique* 18 (1902): 447–68.

Metz, Karl H. "The Politics of Conflict: Heinrich von Treitschke and the Idea of *Realpolitik*." *History of Political Thought* 3 (1982): 269–84.

Michel, Henry. "De quelques mots en *isme*." In his *Propos de morale*, 2nd ser. Paris, 1904.

———. *L'idée de l'état* [1895]. 3rd ed. [1898]. Reprinted, Paris, Fayard, 2003.

Michelet, Jules. *Histoire romaine* [1831]. Ed. Paule Petitier. Paris, Belles Lettres, 2003.

———. *Introduction à l'histoire universelle* [1831]. In Jules Michelet, *Œuvres complètes*, ed. Viallaneix, vol. 2.

———. *Origines du droit français cherchées dans les symboles et formules du droit universel* [1837]. In Jules Michelet, *Œuvres complètes*, ed. Viallaneix, vol. 3.

———. *Le peuple*. 2nd ed. Paris, 1846.

———. *History of the Roman Republic*. Trans. William Hazlitt. London, 1847.

———. *Œuvres complètes*. Ed. Paul Viallaneix. 21 vols. Paris, Flammarion, 1971–87.

———. *Correspondance générale*. 12 vols. Paris, Champion, 1994–2001.

Michelet, Karl Ludwig. *Geschichte des letzten System der Philosophie in Deutschland von Kant bis Hegel*. 2 vols. Berlin, 1837.

Michiels, Alfred. *Histoire des idées littéraires en France au dix-neuvième siècle et de leurs origines dans les siècles antérieurs*. 2 vols. [Paris, 1842]. 3rd ed. Brussels, 1848.

Michoud, Léon. *La théorie de la personnalité morale et son application au droit français*. Paris, LGDJ, 1906.

Miernowski, Jan, ed. *Le sublime et le grotesque*. Geneva, Droz, 2014.

Mignolo, Walter D. *The Idea of Latin America*. Oxford, Blackwell, 2005.

Miller, J. Hillis Miller. *The Disappearance of God: Five Nineteenth-Century Writers*. Cambridge, MA, Harvard UP, 1963.

Minter, Catherine J. *The Mind-Body Problem in German Literature 1770–1830: Wezel, Moritz and Jean Paul*. Oxford, Clarendon Press, 2002.

Moeglin, Jean-Marie. "François Guizot historien: à propos de la réfutation des thèses de Karl August Rögge dans l'*Histoire de la civilisation en France*." In *Des économies et des hommes. Mélanges offerts à Albert Broder*, ed. Florence Bourillon, Philippe Boutry, André Encrevé, and Béatrice Touchelay, pp. 475–86. Paris, Editions Bière, 2006.

———. "Le 'droit de vengeance' chez les historiens du droit au moyen âge (xix–xx siècles)." In *La Vengeance*, ed. Dominique Barthélemy, François Bougard, and Régine Le Jan, pp. 101–48. Rome, Ecole Française de Rome, 2006.

Moggach, Douglas, ed. *The New Hegelians: Politics and Philosophy in the Hegelian School*. Cambridge, CUP, 2006.

———. "Schiller's Aesthetic Republicanism." *History of Political Thought* 28 (2007): 520–41.

———. "Contextualising Fichte: Leibniz, Kant, and Perfectionist Ethics." *Fichte-Studien* 45 (2018): 133–53.

Moggach, Douglas, and Paul Leduc Browne, eds. *The Social Question and the Democratic Revolution: Marx and the Legacy of 1848*. Ottawa, U of Ottawa Press, 2000.

Moggach, Douglas, Nadine Mooren, and Michael Quante, eds. *Perfectionismus der Autonomie*. Paderborn, Wilhelm Fink/Brill, 2020.

Momigliano, Arnaldo. "Ancient History and the Antiquarian." *Journal of the Warburg and Courtauld Institutes* 13 (1950): 285–315.

———. "New Paths of Classicism in the Nineteenth Century" [1982]. In A. D. Momigliano, *Studies in Modern Scholarship*, ed. G. E. Bowerstock and T. J. Cornell, pp. 223–85. Berkeley, U of California Press, 1994.

Montes, Leonidas. *Adam Smith in Context*. Basingstoke, Macmillan, 2004.

Montesquieu, Charles-Louis de Secondat, baron de. *De l'esprit des lois* [1748]. Ed. Victor Goldschmidt. Paris, Garnier-Flammarion, 1979.

———. *The Spirit of Laws*. Trans. Thomas Nugent [London, 1751]. Ed. Franz Neumann. New York, Hafner Publishing Company, 1949.

———. *The History of the Troglodytes*. Chelmsford, 1766.

———. *The Persian Letters*. Trans. George R. Healy. Indianapolis, IN, Hackett, 1999.

———. *Lettres persanes*. In Charles Louis de Secondat, baron de Montesquieu, *Œuvres complètes*, vol. 1, ed. Jean Erhard and Catherine Volpilhac-Auger, letters 11–14, pp. 161–72. Oxford, Voltaire Foundation, 2004.

Morell, John Daniel. "German Philosophy in the Nineteenth Century." Originally published in *Manchester Papers* (1856), and reprinted in his *Philosophical Fragments Written during Intervals of Business*. London, Longmans, 1878.

Morgan, George Osborne. *The Ancients and Moderns Compared in Regard to the Administration of Justice*. Oxford, 1850.

———. *Great Britain and France: Why is Their Present Condition So Different?* Carnarvon, 1853.

Móricz, Clára. *Jewish Identities: Nationalism, Racism, and Utopianism in Twentieth-Century Music*. Berkeley, U of California Press, 2008.

Moritz, Karl Philipp. "Über die bildende Nachahmung des Schönen" [1788]. Translated as "Sur l'imitation formatrice du beau," in Karl Philipp Moritz, *Le concept d'achevé en soi et autres écrits (1785–1793)*, ed. Philippe Beck. Paris, PUF, 1995.

———. "An Attempt to Unify All the Fine Arts and Sciences under the Concept of That Which Is Complete in Itself." Ed. Elliott Schreiber. *PMLA* 27 (2012): 94–100.

Mourier, Athénaïs. "Le Prométhée de M. Edgard Quinet." *Revue française et étrangère* 6 (1838): 93–110.

Müller-Vollmer, Kurt. *Poesie und Einbildungskraft. Zur Dichtungstheorie Wilhelm von Humboldts, Mit der zweisprachigen Ausgabe eines Aufsatzes Humboldts für Frau von Staël.* Stuttgart, J. B. Metzlersche Verlagsbuchhandlung, 1967.

———. "Politique et esthétique: l'idéalisme concret de Constant, Humboldt et Madame de Staël." In *Benjamin Constant, Madame de Staël et le groupe de Coppet*, pp. 453–73. Oxford, Voltaire Foundation, 1982.

———. "Guillaume de Humboldt, interprète de Madame de Staël: distances et affinités." *Cahiers Staëliens* 37 (1985–86): 80–96.

———. "On Germany: Madame de Staël and the Internationalization of Romanticism." In *The Spirit of Poetry: Essays on Jewish and German Literature and Thought in Honor of Géza von Molnár*, ed. Richard Block and Peter Fenves, pp. 150–66. Evanston, IL, Northwestern UP, 2000.

Muzelle, Alain. *L'arabesque: la théorie romantique de Friedrich Schlegel à l'époque de l'Athenäum.* Paris, 2006.

Nakhimovsky, Isaac. "The Enlightened Epicureanism of Jacques Abbadie: *L'art de se connaître soi-même* and the Morality of Self-Interest." *History of European Ideas* 29 (2003): 1–14.

———. *The Closed Commercial State: Perpetual Peace and Commercial Society from Rousseau to Fichte.* Princeton, NJ, Princeton UP, 2011.

Nassar, Dalia. *The Romantic Absolute: Being and Knowing in Early German Romantic Philosophy.* Chicago, U of Chicago Press, 2014.

———, ed. *The Relevance of Romanticism: Essays on German Romantic Philosophy.* Oxford, OUP, 2014.

———. "Friedrich Schlegel (1772–1829)." In *The Oxford Handbook of German Philosophy in the Nineteenth Century*, ed. Michael N. Forster and Kristin Gjesdal, pp. 68–93. Oxford, OUP, 2015.

Naugle, David Keith. "A History and Theory of the Concept of Weltanschauung (Worldview)." PhD thesis, University of Texas at Arlington, 1998.

———. *Worldview: The History of a Concept.* Grand Rapids, MI, William B. Eerdmans, 2002.

Navet, Georges. *Pierre Leroux. Politique, socialisme et philosophie.* Besançon, Publications de la société P. J. Proudhon, 1994.

Nelson, Eric. *The Greek Tradition in Republican Thought.* Cambridge, CUP, 2004.

———. "Republican Visions." In *The Oxford Handbook of Political Theory*, ed. John S. Dryzek, Bonnie Honig, and Anne Phillips, pp. 193–210. Oxford, OUP, 2008.

———. *The Hebrew Republic: Jewish Sources and the Transformation of European Thought.* Cambridge, MA, Harvard UP, 2010.

———. *The Theology of Liberalism: Political Philosophy and the Justice of God.* Cambridge, MA, Belknap Press of Harvard UP, 2019.

Neuhouser, Frederick. *Rousseau's Theodicy of Self-Love: Evil, Rationality and the Drive for Recognition.* Oxford, OUP, 2008.

———. *Rousseau's Critique of Inequality: Reconstructing the Second Discourse.* Cambridge, CUP, 2014.

Nicholls, Angus, and Martin Liebscher, eds. *Thinking the Unconscious: Nineteenth-Century German Thought.* Cambridge, CUP, 2010.

Nichols, Robert. *The World of Freedom: Heidegger, Foucault, and the Politics of Historical Ontology.* Stanford, Stanford UP, 2014.

Nichols, Sophie. *Political Thought in the French Wars of Religion.* Cambridge, CUP, 2021.

Nicolet, Claude. "Rome et les conceptions de l'état en France et en Allemagne au xixe siècle." In *Visions sur le développement des états européens,* ed. Wim Blockmans and Jean-Philippe Genet, pp. 17–44. Rome, Collection de l'Ecole Française de Rome, 171, 1993.

———. *La fabrique d'une nation. La France entre Rome et les Germains.* Paris, Perrin, 2003.

Niebuhr, Barthold Georg. "Einleitung zu den Vorlesungen über die Römische Geschichte" [1810]. In his *Kleine historische und philologische Schriften.* Bonn, 1828.

Nitsch, Thomas O., Joseph M. Phillips Jr, and Edward L. Fitzsimmons, eds. *On the Condition of Labour and the Social Question One Hundred Years Later.* Lampeter, Edwin Mellen Press, 1994.

Nodier, Charles. Review of Germaine de Staël, *De l'Allemagne. Journal des débats politiques et littéraires* 16 (November 1818) [no pagination].

———. *Mélanges de littérature et de critique.* 2 vols. Paris, 1820.

———. "De la fin prochaine du genre humain." *Revue de Paris* 26 (1831): 224–40.

———. *Rêveries.* Ed. Hubert Juin. Paris, Editions Plasma, 1979.

Norman, Larry F. *The Shock of the Ancient: Literature and History in Early Modern France.* Chicago, U of Chicago Press, 2011.

———. "Ancients and Moderns." In *A History of Modern French Literature,* ed. Christopher Prendergast, pp. 269–90. Princeton, NJ, Princeton UP, 2017.

North, Douglass C., and Robert Paul Thomas. *The Rise of the Western World: A New Economic History.* Cambridge, CUP, 1973.

Norton, Robert E. *The Beautiful Soul: Aesthetic Morality in the Eighteenth Century.* Ithaca, NY, Cornell UP, 1995.

Oakes, Guy. "Weber and the Southwest German School: The Genesis of the Concept of the Historical Individual." In *Max Weber and His Contemporaries,* ed. Wolfgang Mommsen and Jürgen Osterhammel, pp. 434–46. London, Allen & Unwin, 1987.

Obitts, Stanley Ralph. "The Thought of Robert Flint." Unpublished Ph D. Thesis, Edinburgh University, 1962.

O'Brien, David. "Delacroix, Chenavard and the End of History." *Journal of Art Historiography* 9 (2013): 1–19.

———. *Exiled in Modernity: Delacroix, Civilization, and Barbarism.* University Park, Pennsylvania State UP, 2018.

Oltramare, André. "Notice biographique sur Joseph Hornung." *Bulletin de l'Institut National Genevois* 27 (1885): 295–375.

Oncken, August. "The Consistency of Adam Smith." *Economic Journal* 7 (1897): 443–50.

———. "Das Adam Smith-Problem." *Zeitschrift für Sozialwissenschaft* 1 (1898): 25–33, 101–8, 276–87.

Ordon, Edmund. "Mickiewicz and Emerson." In *Mickiewicz and the West,* ed. B. R. Bugelski, pp. 31–54. Buffalo, U of Buffalo Press, 1956.

Orr, Mary. *Flaubert's Tentation.* Oxford, OUP, 2008.

Ott, Auguste. *Hegel et la philosophie allemande.* Paris, 1844.

Otteson, J. R. "The Recurring 'Adam Smith Problem.'" *History of Philosophy Quarterly* 17 (2000): 51–74.

Oualid, William. "Proudhon banquier." In *Proudhon et notre temps*, ed. Célestin Bouglé et al., pp. 131–55. Paris, Chiron, 1920.

Oz-Salzberger, Fania. "Schiller, Ferguson, and the Politics of Play: An Exercise in Tracking the Itinerary of an Idea." In *In the Footsteps of Herodotus: Towards European Political Thought*, ed. Janet Coleman and Paschalis M. Kitromilides, pp. 117–39. Florence, Leo. S. Olschki, 2012.

Padoa Schioppa, Antonio, ed. *The Trial Jury in England, France, Germany 1700–1900*. Berlin, Duncker & Humblot, 1987.

Pagès, Jean-Pierre. *Principes généraux du droit politique dans leur rapport avec l'esprit de l'Europe et avec la Monarchie constitutionnelle*. Paris, 1817.

Palonen, Kari, Tuija Pulkkinen, and José María Rosales, eds. *The Ashgate Research Companion to the Politics of Democratization in Europe: Concepts and Histories*. Farnham, Surrey, 2008.

Panick, Käthe. *La Race Latine. Politischer Romanismus im Frankreich des 19. Jahrhunderts*. Bonn, Ludwig Röhrscheid Verlag, 1978.

Parieu, Félix Esquirou de. *Principes de la science politique* [1870]. 2nd ed. Paris, 1875.

Parsis-Barubé, Odile. "La notion de couleur locale dans l'œuvre d'Augustin Thierry." In *Augustin Thierry: L'histoire pour mémoire*, ed. Aude Déruelle and Yann Potin, pp. 63–82. Rennes, PU de Rennes, 2018.

Pascal, Blaise. *Pensées*. Ed. Léon Brunschvicg. Introduced by Charles Marc Des Granges. Paris, Garnier, 1958.

———. *Pensées*. Trans. John Warrington. Ed. H. T. Barnwell. London, Everyman, 1960.

Pascal, Roy. "'Bildung' and the Division of Labour." In *German Studies Presented to Walter Horace Bruford*, [ed. Anon.], pp. 14–28. London, Harrap, 1962.

Pasquiet-Briand, Tanguy. *La réception de la constitution anglaise au xixe siècle*. Paris, Institut Universitaire Varenne, 2017.

Pasquino, Pasquale. "Introduction to Lorenz von Stein." *Economy and Society* 10 (1981): 1–6.

Paul, Herman, and Adriaan Van Veldhuizen. "A Retrieval of Historicism: Frank Ankersmit's Philosophy of History and Politics." *History and Theory* 57 (2018): 33–55.

Paul, Jean-Marie. *Dieu est mort en Allemagne. Des Lumières à Nietzsche*. Paris, Payot, 1994.

Paz, Enrique Martine. "Lask and the Doctrine of the Science of Law." In *Interpretations of Modern Legal Philosophies: Essays in Honor of Roscoe Pound*, ed. Paul Sayre, pp. 574–77. New York, OUP, 1947.

Peden, Knox. *Spinoza contra Phenomenology*. Stanford, Stanford UP, 2014.

Pelczynski, Z. A., ed. *The State and Civil Society: Studies in Hegel's Political Philosophy*. Cambridge, CUP, 1984.

Pellarin, Charles. *Notice biographique sur Charles Fourier*. Paris, 1839.

Pelletier, Lucien. "L'influence d'Emil Lask sur le jeune Ernst Bloch." *Revue philosophique de Louvain* 110 (2012): 23–49.

———. "Les sources de la philosophie de l'histoire d'Ernst Bloch." *Revue internationale de philosophie* 3 (2019): 261–77.

Peloille, Bernard. "Nation, formes d'état, classes, dans la pensée politique d'Edgar Quinet." *Cahiers Pour l'Analyse Concrète* 10 (1981): 3–23.

———. "A propos de la question des origines dans la pensée de Quinet." *Littérature et Nation*, 2nd ser., 9 (1992): 71–86.

Pénisson, Pierre. "Kant et Herder: 'le recul d'effroi de la raison.'" *Revue Germanique Internationale* 6 (1996): 63–74.

Petitier, Paule. "Les *Origines du droit français* de Michelet." *Littérature et Nation,* 2nd ser., 9 (1992): 31–61.

———. "L'imagination dans l'histoire: Michelet et les critiques du Second Empire." In *Ecrire/ Savoir: littérature et connaissances à l'époque moderne,* ed. Alain Vaillant, pp. 121–38. Saint-Etienne, Editions Printer, 1996.

———. "Entre concept et hypotypose: l'histoire au xixe siècle." *Romantisme* 144 (2009): 69–80.

Pettit, Philip. *Republicanism: A Theory of Freedom and Government.* Oxford, OUP, 1997.

Peyrache-Leborgne, Dominique. "Hugo, le grotesque et l'arabesque." In *Romantismes: l'esthétisme en acte,* ed. Jean-Louis Cabanès, pp. 109–22. Paris, PU de Paris Ouest, 2009.

Peyre, Henri. *Louis Menard.* New Haven, CT, Yale UP, 1928.

Phelan, John L. "Pan-Latinism, French Intervention in Mexico (1861–1867) and the Genesis of the Idea of Latin America." In *Conciencia y Autenticidad Históricas,* [ed. Anon.], pp. 279–98. Mexico City, UNAM, 1968.

Philbrick, Francis S. "Changing Conceptions of Property in Law." *University of Pennsylvania Law Review* 86 (1937–38): 691–732.

Piché, Claude. "Rousseau et Kant: A propos de la genèse de la théorie kantienne des idees." *Revue philosophique de la France et de étranger* 180 (1990): 625–35.

———. "The Place of Aesthetics in Fichte's Early System." In, *New Essays on Fichte's Later Jena Wissenschaftslehre,* ed. Daniel Breazeale and Tom Rockmore, pp. 299–316. Evanston, IL, Northwestern U Press, 2002.

Pichois, Claude. *L'image de Jean Paul Richter dans les lettres françaises.* Paris, José Corti, 1963.

Pickering, Mary. "New Evidence of the Link between Comte and German Philosophy." *Journal of the History of Ideas* 50 (1989): 443–63.

———. *Auguste Comte: An Intellectual Biography.* 3 vols. Cambridge, CUP, 1993–2009.

Piguet, Marie-France. *Individualisme.* Paris, CNRS Editions, 2018.

Piirimäe, Eva. "State-Machines, Commerce and the Progress of *Humanität* in Europe: Herder's Response to Kant in *Ideas for the Philosophy of History of Mankind.*" In *Commerce and Peace in the Enlightenment,* ed. Béla Kapossy, Isaak Nakhimovsky, and Richard Whatmore, pp. 155–91. Cambridge, CUP, 2017.

———. "Human Rights and Their Realisation in the World: Herder's Debate with Kant." In *Passions, Politics, and the Limits of Society,* ed. Heikki Haara, Koen Stapelbroek, and Mikko Immanen, pp. 47–73. Berlin, Walter De Gruyter, 2020.

Pinkard, Terry. *Does History Make Sense? Hegel on the Historical Shapes of Justice.* Cambridge, MA, Harvard UP, 2017.

Pinon, Stéphane. *Maurice Deslandres et le droit constitutionnel. Un itinéraire.* Dijon, Editions Universitaires de Dijon, 2012.

Pippin, Robert B. *Philosophy by Other Means.* Chicago, U of Chicago Press, 2021.

Piron, Sylvain. "Congé à Villey." *L'Atelier du Centre de recherches historiques* 1 (2008): 1–16.

Pocock, J.G.A. *The Ancient Constitution and the Feudal Law* [1957]. Cambridge, CUP, 1987.

———. *The Machiavellian Moment: Florentine Political Thought and the Atlantic Republican Tradition.* Princeton, NJ, Princeton UP, 1975; 2nd ed., Princeton UP, 2003; 3rd ed., introduced by Richard Whatmore, Princeton, UP 2016.

———. *Barbarism and Religion*. 6 vols. Cambridge, CUP, 1999–2015.

Podoksik, Efraim. "Georg Simmel: Three Forms of Individualism and Historical Understanding." *New German Critique* 10 (2010): 119–45.

———, ed. *Doing Humanities in Nineteenth-Century Germany*. Brill, Leiden, 2020.

———. *Georg Simmel and German Culture: Unity, Variety and Modern Discontents*. Cambridge, CUP, 2021.

Polin, Raymond. *La création des valeurs: recherches sur le fondement de l'objectivité axiologique*. Paris, 1944.

———. *La politique de la solitude. Essai sur Jean-Jacques Rousseau*. Paris, Sirey, 1971.

Pons, Alain. "Charles Renouvier et l' *Uchronie*." *Commentaire* 47 (1989): 573–82.

Portalis, Jean-Etienne-Marie. *De l'usage et de l'abus de l'esprit philosophique durant le xviiie siècle* [1820]. 3rd ed. 2 vols. Paris, 1834.

Portebois, Yannick, and Nicholas Terpstra, eds. *The Renaissance in the Nineteenth Century/ Le xixe siècle renaissant*. Toronto, Victoria University of Toronto, Centre for Reformation and Renaissance Studies, 2003.

Postigliola, Alberto. "De Malebranche à Rousseau: les apories de la volonté générale et la revanche du 'raisonneur violent.'" *Annales de la société Jean-Jacques Rousseau* 39 (1972–77): 123–38.

Pound, Roscoe *Interpretations of Legal History*. New York, Macmillan, 1923.

Prendergast, Christopher. *The Classic: Sainte-Beuve and the Nineteenth-Century Culture Wars*. Oxford, OUP, 2007.

———, ed. *A History of Modern French Literature*. Princeton, NJ, Princeton UP, 2017.

Printy, Michael. "The Determination of Man: Johann Joachim Spalding and the Protestant Enlightenment." *Journal of the History of Ideas* 74 (2013): 189–212.

Proudhon, Pierre-Joseph. *Qu'est-ce que la propriété* [1840]. Ed. E. James. Paris, 1966.

———. *Système des contradictions économiques*. Paris, 1846.

———. *Solution du problème social et autres textes (mars–juillet 1848)*. Ed. Marc Lauder. Paris, Classiques Garnier, 2021.

———. *De la justice dans la révolution et dans l'église*. Paris, 1858.

———. *Du principe de l'art et de sa destination sociale*. Paris, 1867.

Quillien, Jean, ed. *La réception de la philosophie allemande en France aux xixe et xxe siècles*. Lille, PU de Lille, 1994.

Quinet, Edgar. *Ahasvérus* [1834]. Ed. Ceri Crossley. Geneva, Slatkine, 1982.

———. "Lettre sur *Ahasvérus*." *Revue du progrès social* 1 (1834): 616–19.

———. "De l'unité des littératures modernes." *Revue des Deux Mondes*, 4th ser., 15 (1838): 318–35.

———. *Allemagne et Italie. Philosophie et poésie* [1839]. Paris, 1846.

———. "Discours inaugural." *Revue du Lyonnais* 9 (1839): 445–71.

———. "De la Renaissance dans l'Europe Méridionale." *Bibliothèque choisie des meilleures productions de la littérature française contemporaine*, 1st ser., 2 (1842): 678–90.

———. "L'ultramontanisme, ou l'église romaine et la société moderne" [1844]. In Edgar Quinet, *Œuvres complètes*, 2:223–28. Paris, 1857.

———. *Le christianisme et la révolution française*. Paris, 1845.

———. *Les révolutions d'Italie* [1848]. 5th ed. 2 vols. Paris, 1874.

————. "Allemagne et Italie." In his *Œuvres complètes*, 12 vols., vol. 6. Paris, 1857.

————. *Les Roumains*. In Edgar Quinet, *Œuvres complètes*, vol. 6. Paris, 1857.

————. *La création*. 2 vols. Paris, 1870.

————. *Lettres à sa mère*. Ed. Simone Bernard Griffiths and Gérard Peylet. 4 vols. Paris, 1995–2008.

Rabban, David M. *Law's History: American Legal Thought and the Transatlantic Turn to History*. Cambridge, CUP, 2013.

Rahe, Paul A. *Montesquieu and the Logic of Liberty*. New Haven, CT, Yale UP, 2008.

Rancière, Jacques. *La mésentente. Politique et philosophie*. Paris, Galilée, 1995.

————. "The Aesthetic Revolution and Its Outcomes." *New Left Review* 14 (2002): 133–51.

Raskolnikoff, Mouza. "Volney et les Idéologues: le refus de Rome." *Revue Historique* 267 (1982): 357–73.

————. "Vico, l'histoire romaine et les érudits français des lumières." *Mélanges de l'école française de Rome* 96 (1984):1051–77.

Rawls, John. *A Theory of Justice*. Cambridge, MA, Harvard UP, 1971.

Reboul, Yves. "Hugo, *Cromwell* et la Défection." In *Voix de l'écrivain: Mélanges offerts à Guy Sagnes*, ed. Jean-Louis Cabanes, pp. 53–64. Toulouse, PU du Mirail, 1996.

Reddie, James. *Inquiries Elementary and Historical in the Science of Law*. London, 1840. 2nd ed. London, 1847.

Reedy, W. Jay. "Art for Society's Sake: Louis de Bonald's Sociology of Aesthetics and the Theocratic Ideology." *Proceedings of the American Philosophical Society* 130 (1986): 101–29.

Regier, Alexander. *Exorbitant Enlightenment: Blake, Hamann and Anglo-German Constellations*. Oxford, OUP, 2018.

Régnier, Philippe. "Les saint-simoniens et la philosophie allemande, ou la première alliance intellectuelle franco-allemande." *Revue de Synthèse* 109 (1988): 231–45.

————. "Les Saint-Simoniens et le mouvement romantique." In *Romantismes et socialismes en Europe (1800–1848)*, ed. André Billaz and Ulrich Ricken. Paris, Didier Erudition, 1989.

————. "La question romantique comme enjeu national: critique française et littérature allemande autour de 1830." *Romantisme* 73 (1991): 29–42.

————. "Michelet, les saint-simoniens et le saint-simonisme." In "Michelet et la «Question Sociale»," ed. Paule Petitier. *Littérature et Nation* 18 (1997): 49–73.

————. "Saint-Simon, les saint-simoniens et les siècles dits 'classiques.'" In *Les âges classiques du dix-neuvième siècle*, ed. Delphine Antoine-Mahut and Stéphane Zékian, pp. 215–39. Paris, Editions des archives contemporaines, 2018.

Reill, Peter Hanns. "Barthold Georg Niebuhr and the Enlightenment Tradition." *German Studies Review* 3 (1980): 9–26.

————. *Vitalizing Nature in the Enlightenment*. Berkeley, U of California Press, 2005.

Reimann, Mathias. "Historical Jurisprudence." In *The Oxford Handbook of Legal History*, ed. Markus D. Dubber and Christopher Tomlins. Oxford, OUP, 2018.

Reinsch, Richard M. *Seeking the Truth: An Orestes Brownson Anthology*. Washington, DC, Catholic University of America Press, 2016.

Remaud, Olivier. *Michelet. Le magistrature de l'histoire*. Paris, Michalon, 1998.

Renan, Ernest. "La théologie de Béranger." In his *Questions contemporaines* [Paris, 1868], 5th ed., pp. 461–77. Paris, 1912.

Rey, Lucie. *Les enjeux de l'histoire de la philosophie en France au XIXe siècle. Pierre Leroux contre Victor Cousin.* Paris, L'Harmattan, 2012.

———. "Leibniz à l'appui de la doctrine de perfectibilité de Pierre Leroux." *Corpus* 68 (2015): 119–38.

———. "Les lumières comme enjeu philosophique et politique: Pierre Leroux face à Victor Cousin." *Dix-Huitième Siècle* 47 (2015): 501–28.

———. "Le 'sphinx de la révolution.' Pierre Leroux et la promesse révolutionnaire." *Archives de Philosophie* 80 (2017): 55–74.

Richardson, Alan. *British Romanticism and the Science of the Mind.* Cambridge, CUP, 2001.

Richter, Jean Paul. *Siebenkäs* [1796]. 2 vols. Paris, Aubier, 1963.

———. "The Vision of a Godless World." *The Atheneum; or the Spirit of the English Magazines,* 3rd ser., 2 (Boston, 1829): 83–86.

———. "La dernière heure." *Revue de Paris* 16 (1830): 1–7.

———. *Une collaboration inconnue: la description du Panthéon de Paul Chenavard par Gautier et Nerval.* Paris, Lettres modernes, 1963.

Riedel, Wolfgang. *Der Spaziergang: Ästhetik der Landschaft und Geschichtsphilosophie der Natur bei Schiller.* Würzburg, Königshausen & Neumann, 1989.

Rieppel, Olivier. "The Reception of Leibniz's Philosophy in the Writings of Charles Bonnet." *Journal of the History of Biology* 21 (1988): 119–45.

Riley, Patrick. *The General Will before Rousseau: The Transformation of the Divine into the Civic.* Princeton, NJ, Princeton UP, 1986.

Ritchie, David George. "'Freedom'—Negative and Positive." In his *Principles of State Interference.* London, Swan Sonnenschein, 1891.

Ritter, Joachim. *Paysage. Fonction de l'esthétique dans la société moderne.* Paris, Editions de l'Imprimeur, 1997.

Rittiez, F. *Science des droits, ou idéologie politique.* Paris, 1844.

Roberts, Richard H. "God." In *The Oxford Handbook of Nineteenth-Century Christian Thought,* ed. Joel D. S. Rasmussen, Judith Wolfe, and Johannes Zachhuber, pp. 573–91. Oxford, OUP, 2019.

Robertson, John. *The Enlightenment: A Very Short Introduction.* Oxford, OUP, 2015.

Robinson, Henry Crabb. *Essays on Kant, Schelling and German Aesthetics.* Ed. James Vigus. London, Modern Humanities Research Association, 2010.

Rocker, Rudolf. *Nationalism and Culture.* Los Angeles, Rocker Publications Committee, 1937.

Rockmore, Tom. *Irrationalism: Lukács and the Marxist View of Reason.* Philadelphia, Temple UP, 1992.

Röder, Karl David August. *Grundgedanken und Bedeutung des römischen und germanischen Rechts.* Leipzig, 1855.

Roger, Jacques. "The Living World." In *The Ferment of Knowledge: Studies in the Historiography of Eighteenth-Century Science,* ed. G. S. Rousseau and Roy Porter, pp. 255–83. Cambridge, CUP, 1980.

Rogron, A. *Code politique.* Paris, 1838.

Rorty, Amélie Oksenberg, and James Schmidt, eds. *Kant's Idea for a Universal History with a Cosmopolitan Aim: A Critical Guide.* Cambridge, CUP, 2009.

Rosanvallon, Pierre. *Le moment Guizot*. Paris, Gallimard, 1985.

———. *Democracy Past and Future*. Ed. Samuel Moyn. New York, Columbia UP, 2006.

Rose, R. B. "*Prolétaires* and *Prolétariat*: Evolution of a Concept, 1789–1848." *Australian Journal of French Studies* 18 (1981): 282–99.

Rosen, Michael. *The Shadow of God: Kant, Hegel, and the Passage from Heaven to History*. Cambridge, MA, Harvard UP, 2022.

———. *Dignity: Its History and Meaning*. Cambridge, MA, Harvard UP, 2012.

Rosenblatt, Helena. *The Lost History of Liberalism: From Ancient Rome to the Twenty-First Century*. Princeton, NJ, Princeton UP, 2018.

Rosenkranz, Karl. *Esthétique du laid* [1853]. Paris, Editions Circé, 2004.

Rosenzweig, Franz. *Hegel et l'état* [1920]. Ed. and trans. Paul-Laurent Assoun and Gerard Bensussan. Paris, PUF, 1991.

Rosisch, Gerard. *The Contested History of Autonomy*. London, Bloomsbury, 2019.

Rossignol, Jean-Pierre. *Examen critique de l'histoire des classes ouvrières et des classes bourgeoise de M. Granier de Cassagnac*. Paris, 1839.

Roulin, Jean-Marie. "Alexandre Vinet lecteur de Madame de Staël." *Annales Benjamin Constant* 13 (1992): 129–41.

Rousseau, Jean-Jacques. *Discourse on the Origin and Foundations of Inequality among Men* [1755]. In Jean-Jacques Rousseau, *Collected Writings*, 14 vols., ed. Allan Bloom, Christopher Kelly, Roger D. Masters, Philip Stewart, et al., vol. 3. Hanover, NH, and London, University Presses of New England, 1987–2007.

———. *Emile* [1762]. In Jean-Jacques Rousseau, *Collected Writings*, vol. 13.

———. *Social Contract* [1762]. In Jean-Jacques Rousseau, *Collected Writings*, vol. 4.

———. *Emilius, or an Essay on Education*. 2 vols. London, 1763.

———. *Les pensées de J. J. Rousseau*. Amsterdam, 1763.

———. *Thoughts of Jean-Jacques Rousseau, translated by Miss Henrietta Colebrooke*. 2 vols. London, 1788.

———. *Discourse on Political Economy*. In Jean-Jacques Rousseau, *Collected Writings*, vol. 3.

———. *Oeuvres complètes*. 5 vols. Ed. Bernard Gagnebin and Marcel Raymond. Paris, Pléiade/Gallimard, 1959–95.

Roux, Alexandra, ed. *Schelling, philosophe de la mort et de l'immortalité: études sur Clara*. Rennes, PU de Rennes, 2014.

Rowe, Paul. *A Mirror on the Rhine? The Nouvelle Revue Germanique, Strasbourg 1829–1837*. Bern, Peter Lang, 2000.

Royce, Josiah. *The Spirit of Modern Philosophy* [1892]. Boston, 1901.

Rubinelli, Lucia. *Constituent Power: A History*. Cambridge, CUP, 2020.

Rubini, Rocco. *The Other Renaissance: Italian Humanism between Hegel and Heidegger*. Chicago, U of Chicago Press, 2014.

Rubio, Christian. *Krausism and the Spanish Avant-Garde*. New York, Cambria Press, 2017.

Ruehl, Martin A. *The Italian Renaissance in the German Historical Imagination, 1860–1930*. Cambridge, CUP, 2015.

Runciman, David. *Pluralism and the Personality of the State*. Cambridge, CUP, 1997.

———. *Confronting Leviathan*. London, Profile Books, 2021.

Ryan, Alan. "Isaiah Berlin: Contested Conceptions of Liberty and Liberalism." In *The Cambridge Companion to Isaiah Berlin*, ed. Joshua L. Cherniss and Steven B. Smith, pp. 212–28. Cambridge, CUP, 2018.

Sacriste, Guillaume. *La république des constitutionnalistes. Professeurs de droit et légitimation de l'état en France (1870–1914)*. Paris, Presses de Sciences Po, 2011.

Sainte-Beuve, Charles Augustin. *Portraits contemporains*. 2 vols. Paris, 1847.

———. "Qu'est-ce qu'un classique." In Sainte-Beuve, *Causeries de lundi*, 3rd ed., 16 vols., vol. 3. Paris, 1852–62.

———. *Causeries du lundi*. 16 vols. Paris, 1857–70.

———. *Nouveaux lundis*. 13 vols. Paris, 1875–78.

———. "What Is a Classic?" In Sainte-Beuve, *Essays*, trans. Elizabeth Lee. London, 1890.

Sakabe, Megumi. "Freedom as a Regulative Principle: On Some Aspects of the Kant-Herder Controversy on the Philosophy of History." In *Kant's Practical Philosophy Reconsidered*, ed. Yirimiyahu Yovel, pp. 183–95. Dordrecht, Kluwer, 1989.

Saleilles, Raymond. "L'histoire et la science politique: à propos d'un ouvrage récent." *Revue de synthèse historique* 5 (1902): 186–99.

———. *De la personnalité juridique, histoire et théories* [1910]. 2nd ed. Paris, 1922.

———. *Y a-t-il une crise de la science politique?* Ed. Carlos Miguel Herrera. Paris, Dalloz, 2012.

Salsman, Richard M. *The Political Economy of Public Debt: Three Centuries of Theory and Evidence*. Cheltenham, Edward Elgar, 2017.

Salzani, Carlo. "Foucault and Agamben: Taking Life, Letting Live, or Making Survive." In *Reading Texts on Sovereignty*, ed. Stella Achilleos and Antonis Balasopoulos, pp. 171–78. London, Bloomsbury, 2021.

Sand, George. *Le Compagnon du Tour de France* [1840]. Ed. Jean-Louis Cabanès. Paris, Livre de Poche, 2004.

———. *Autour de la table*. Paris, 1879.

Sandars, Thomas Collett. "Hegel's Philosophy of Right." In *Oxford Essays, Contributed by Members of the University, 1855*, pp. 213–50. London, 1855.

Sandel, Michael J. "The Procedural Republic and the Unencumbered Self." *Political Theory* 12 (1984): 81–96.

Sanseverino, Gaetano. *I principali sistemi della filosofia sul criterio discussi con le dottrine de' santi padri e de' dottori del medio evo* [1850]. 2nd ed. Naples, 1858.

Savigny, Friedrich Carl von. *On Possession, or the Ius Possessionis of the Civil Law* [1803]. Trans. Sir Erskine Perry. London, 1848.

———. *System des Heutigen Römischen Rechts*. Berlin, 1840.

Say, Jean-Baptiste. *Cours complet d'économie politique pratique*. 6 vols. Paris, 1826–28.

———. Review of James Fazy, *Principes d'organisation industrielle*. *Revue Encyclopédique* 46 (1830): 625–30.

Schaeffer, Jean-Marie. *Art of the Modern Age: Philosophy of Art from Kant to Heidegger* [1992]. Princeton, NJ, Princeton UP, 2000.

Scheler, Max. *Trois essais sur l'esprit du capitalisme* [1914]. Ed. Patrick Lang. Nantes, Editions Nouvelles Cécile Defaut, 2016.

Schelling, Friedrich Wilhelm Joseph. *Clara, or On Nature's Connection to the Spirit World* [1810]. Ed. and trans. Fiona Steinkamp. Albany, State U of New York Press, 2002.

———. *On the History of Modern Philosophy* [1856]. Trans. Andrew Bowie. Cambridge, CUP, 1994.

———. *Contribution à l'histoire de la philosophie moderne* [1856–61]. Trans. J. F. Marquet. Paris, PUF, 1983.

———. *Essais*. Trans. S. Jankélévitch. Paris, Aubier, 1946.

Schenck, Eunice Morgan. *La part de Charles Nodier dans la formation des idées de Victor Hugo jusqu'à la Préface de Cromwell*. Paris, Champion, 1914.

Schiller, Friedrich. *On the Aesthetic Education of Man* [1795]. Ed. Elizabeth M. Wilkinson and L. A. Willoughby. Oxford, Clarendon Press, 1967.

———. *The Minor Poems of Schiller*. Ed. John Herman Merivale. London, 1844.

———. *The Philosophical and Aesthetic Letters and Essays*. Ed. J. Weiss. London, 1845.

———. *Schiller's Poems and Plays*. Ed. Frederick Morley. London, Routledge, 1890.

———. *Poèmes philosophiques*. Ed. Robert d'Harcourt. Paris, Aubier, 1954.

———. "Über Bürger's Gedichte." In *Schillers Werke*, Nationalausgabe, 22, ed. Herbert Meyer. Weimar, 1958.

———. "On Naïve and Sentimental Poetry." In Friedrich Schiller, *Essays*, ed. Walter Hinderer and Daniel O. Dahlstrom. New York, Continuum, 1993.

———. *Grace et dignité et autres textes*. Ed. Nicolas Briand. Paris, Vrin, 1998.

———. *On the Aesthetic Education of Man*. Ed. Alexander Schmidt. Trans. Keith Tribe. London, Penguin, 2016.

Schlegel, Friedrich. *Athenaeum Fragments*. In *Friedrich Schlegel's* Lucinde *and the* Fragments, ed. Peter Firchow. Minneapolis and London, U of Minnesota Press, 1971.

Schleiermacher, Friedrich. *Soliloquies* [1800]. Ed. Horace Leland Friess. New York, Columbia UP, 1926.

———. *Der christliche Glaube* [1821–22]. In Friedrich Schleiermacher, *Kritische Gesamtausgabe*, ed. Hans-Joachim Birkner, Gerhard Ebeling, Hermann Fischer, Heinz Kimmerle, and Kurt-Victor Selge, vol. 7. Berlin and New York, Walter de Gruyter, 1980.

Schlesinger, Arthur M. *A Pilgrim's Progress: Orestes A. Brownson* [1939]. Boston, Little Brown, 1966.

Schlesser, Thomas. *Paul Chenavard: monuments de l'échec*. Dijon, Les Presses du Réel, 2009.

Schmidt, Alexander. "The Liberty of the Ancients? Friedrich Schiller and Aesthetic Republicanism." *History of Political Thought* 30 (2009): 286–314.

Schmidt, James. "The Question of Enlightenment: Kant, Mendelssohn, and the *Mittwochgesellschaft*." *Journal of the History of Ideas* 50 (1989): 269–91.

———. "What Enlightenment Was: How Moses Mendelssohn and Immanuel Kant Answered the *Berlinische Monatsschrift*." *Journal of the History of Philosophy* 30 (1992): 77–101.

———. *What Is Enlightenment? Eighteenth-Century Answers and Twentieth-Century Questions*. Berkeley, U of California Press, 1996.

Schmidt, Karl Adolf. *Der principielle Unterschied zwischen dem römischen und germanischen Recht*. Rostock und Schwerin, 1853.

Schmidt am Busch, Hans-Christoph. *Hegel et le saint-simonisme. Etudes de philosophie sociale*. Toulouse, PU du Mirail, 2012.

Schmidt am Busch, Hans-Christoph, Ludwig Siep, Hans Ulrich Thamer, and Norbert Waszek, eds. *Hegelianismus und Saint-Simonismus*. Paderborn, Mentis, 2007.

Schmitt, Carl. *The Value of the State and the Significance of the Individual* [1917]. In *Carl Schmitt's Early Legal-Theoretical Writings*, ed. Lars Vinx and Samuel Garrett Zeitlin. Cambridge, CUP, 2021.

———. *Political Romanticism* [1919]. Cambridge, MA, MIT Press, 1991.

———. *The Concept of the Political*. Trans. George Schwab. Forward by Tracy B. Strong. Notes by Leo Strauss. Chicago, U of Chicago Press, 2007.

Schmitz, Julia. "Hauriou versus Rousseau, Duguit et Kelsen." In *Mélanges en l'honneur du professeur Christian Lavialle*, ed. Nathalie Bettio et al., pp. 645–62. Toulouse, Presses de l'Université de Toulouse 1 Capitole, 2020).

Schneck, Stephen Frederick. *Persons and Polis: Max Scheler's Personalism as Political Theory*. Albany, State U of New York Press, 1987.

Schneewind, Jerome B. "The Use of Autonomy in Ethical Theory." In *Reconstructing Individualism: Autonomy, Individuality and the Self in Western Thought*, ed. Thomas C. Heller, Morton Sosna and David E. Wellbery, pp. 64–75. Stanford, Stanford UP, 1986.

———. *The Invention of Autonomy*. Cambridge, CUP, 1998.

Schochet, Gordon, Fania Oz-Salzberger, and Meirav Jones, eds. *Political Hebraism: Judaic Sources in Early Modern Political Thought*. Jerusalem and New York, Shalem Press, 2008.

Scholtz, Gunter. "Zum Historismusstreit in der Hermeneutik." In *Historismus am Ende des 20. Jahrhunderts*, ed. Gunter Scholtz, pp. 192–214. Berlin, Akademie Verlag, 1997.

Schreiber, Elliott. *The Topography of Modernity: Karl Philipp Moritz and the Space of Autonomy*. Ithaca, NY, Cornell UP, 2012.

Schulting, Dennis, and Jacco Verburgtt, eds. *Kant's Idealism: New Interpretations of a Controversial Doctrine*. Dordrecht, Springer, 2011.

Schützenberger, Georges Frédéric. *Etudes de droit public*. Paris and Strasbourg, 1839.

Seillière, Ernest. *Le mal romantique*. Paris, 1908.

———. *Alexandre Vinet, Historien de la Pensée Française*. Paris, Payot, 1925.

Seligman, Adam B. *The Idea of Civil Society*. Princeton, NJ, Princeton UP, 1992.

Selinger, William. *Parliamentarism: From Burke to Weber*. Cambridge, CUP, 2019.

Selinger, William, and Gregory Conti. "The Lost History of *Political* Liberalism." *History of European Ideas* 46 (2020): 341–54.

Sharp, Lynn L. *Secular Spirituality: Reincarnation and Spiritism in Nineteenth-Century France*. New York, Lexington Books, 2006.

———. "Reincarnation: The Path to Progress." *Handbook of Spiritualism and Channelling* 9 (2015): 219–47.

Shklar, Judith. *After Utopia: The Decline of Political Faith*. Princeton, NJ, Princeton UP, 1957.

Simmel, Georg. "Philosophie du paysage" [1913]. Trans. in his *La tragédie de la culture*, pp. 231–45. Paris, Rivages, 1988.

———. *Fundamental Problems of Sociology (Individual and Society)* [1917]. In *The Sociology of Georg Simmel*, ed. Kurt H. Wolff. New York, Free Press, 1950.

Sismondi, Jean-Charles-Léonard Simonde de. *Histoire des républiques italiennes du moyen âge*. 17 vols. Paris, 1809–19.

———. *De la littérature du Midi de l'Europe*. 4 vols. Paris, 1813.

———. *Historical View of the Literature of the South of Europe*. 4 vols. London, 1823.

———. *History of the Italian Republics, or The Origin, Progress, and Fall of Italian Freedom.* London, 1832.

———. *Etudes sur les constitutions des peuples libres* [Paris, 1836]. Brussels, 1839.

———. *Storia delle Repubbliche italiane.* Turin, Bollati Boringhieri, 1996.

Skinner, Quentin. *The Foundations of Modern Political Thought.* 2 vols. Cambridge, CUP, 1978.

———. *Liberty before Liberalism.* Cambridge, CUP, 1998.

———. "Conquest and Consent: Hobbes and the Engagement Controversy" [1972]. In his *Visions of Politics*, 3 vols., 3:287–307. Cambridge, CUP, 2002.

———. "On Neo-Roman Liberty: A Conclusion and Reassessment." In *Rethinking Liberty before Liberalism*, ed. Hannah Dawson and Annelien De Dijn, pp. 233–66. Cambridge, CUP, 2022.

Sloane, Joseph C. *Paul Marc Joseph Chenavard: Artist of 1848.* Chapel Hill, U of North Carolina Press, 1962.

Small, Albion. *Origins of Sociology.* Chicago, U of Chicago Press, 1924.

Smith, Bonnie G. "The Rise and Fall of Eugène Lerminier." *French Historical Studies* 12 (1982): 377–400.

Smith, Jonathan. "De Quincey's Revisions of the 'System of the Heavens.'" *Victorian Periodicals Review* 26 (1993): 203–12.

Snyder, Robert Lance. "'The Loom of *Palingenesis*': De Quincey's Cosmology in 'System of the Heavens.'" In *Thomas De Quincey: Bicentenary Studies*, ed. Robert Lance Snyder, pp. 338–59. Norman and London, U of Oklahoma Press, 1985.

Sonenscher, Michael. *Before the Deluge: Public Debt, Inequality, and the Intellectual Origins of the French Revolution.* Princeton, NJ, Princeton UP, 2005.

———. "Property, Community and Citizenship." In *The Cambridge History of Eighteenth-Century Political Thought*, ed. Mark Goldie and Robert Wokler, pp. 465–94. Cambridge, CUP, 2006.

———. *Sans-Culottes: An Eighteenth-Century Emblem in the French Revolution.* Princeton, NJ, Princeton UP, 2007.

———. "Revolution, Reform and the Political Thought of Emmanuel-Joseph Sieyès." In *Revolutionary Moments*, ed. Rachel Hammersley, pp. 69–76. London, Bloomsbury, 2014.

———. "Jean-Jacques Rousseau and the Foundations of Modern Political Thought." *Modern Intellectual History* 14 (2017): 311–37.

———. "Liberty, Autonomy, and Republican Historiography: Civic Humanism in Context." In *Markets, Moral, Politics: Jealousy of Trade and the History of Political Thought. Essays in Honor of Istvan Hont*, ed. Béla Kapossy, Isaac Nakhimovsky, Sophus Reinert, and Richard Whatmore, pp. 161–210. Cambridge, MA, Harvard UP, 2018.

———. *Jean-Jacques Rousseau: The Division of Labour, the Politics of the Imagination and the Concept of Federal Government.* Leiden, Brill, 2020.

———. "Krausism and Its Legacy." *Global Intellectual History* 5 (2020): 20–40.

———. *Capitalism: The Story behind the Word.* Princeton, NJ, Princeton UP, 2022.

Sorkin, David. *Moses Mendelssohn and the Religious Enlightenment.* London, Peter Halban, 1996.

Souriau, Maurice. *La «Préface» de Cromwell: Introduction, textes et notes.* Paris, 1897.

Spann, Othmar. *Types of Economic Theory* [1930]. Abingdon, Oxon, Routledge, 2000.

Spencer, Herbert. "Progress: Its Law and Cause." *Westminster Review* 67 (1857): 445–85.

Spinoza, Benedict. *Œuvres*. Ed. Emile Saisset [1842]. 3 vols. Paris, 1861.

Spitz, Jean-Fabien. *Le moment républicain en France*. Paris, Gallimard, 2005.

Staël, Germaine de. *De la littérature* [1800]. Ed. Gérard Gengembre and Jean Goldzink. Paris, Flammarion, 1991.

———. *The Influence of Literature upon Society*. London, 1812.

———. *Germany*. 3 vols. London, 1814.

———. *Considerations on the Principal Events of the French Revolution* [1818]. Ed. Aurelian Craiutu. Indianapolis, IN, Liberty Fund, 2008.

———. *De l'Allemagne*. Ed. Jeanne de Pange and Simone Balayé. 5 vols. Paris, Hachette, 1958–60.

———. *Correspondance générale*. Ed. Beatrice W. Jasinski et al. 9 vols. Paris, Pauvert; Geneva, Slatkine, 1962–2017.

Stahl, E. L. "Schiller on Poetry." In *German Studies Presented to Walter Horace Bruford*, pp. 140–52. London, Harrap, 1962.

Stark, Werner. Introduction to Max Scheler, *The Nature of Sympathy* [1913]. London, Routledge, 1954.

Starobinski, Jean. *Action and Reaction: The Life and Adventures of a Couple* [1999]. Trans. Sophie Hawkes. New York, Zone Books, 2003.

Stears, Marc. *Progressives, Pluralists, and the Problems of the State*. Oxford, OUP, 2002.

Stedman Jones, Gareth. "Engels and the Invention of the Catastrophist Conception of the Industrial Revolution." In *The New Hegelians: Politics and Philosophy in the Hegelian School*, ed. Douglas Moggach, pp. 200–219. Cambridge, CUP, 2006.

Steel, David, ed. *Lettres d'Emile Souvestre à Edouard Turquéty*. Rennes, PU de Rennes, 2012.

———. *Emile Souvestre: Un Breton des Lettres, 1806–1854*. Rennes, PU de Rennes, 2013.

Stein, Lorenz. *Geschichte der sozialen Bewegung in Frankreich von 1789 bis auf unsere Tage*. Leipzig, 1850.

———. *Le concept de société*. Trans. Marc Béghin. Ed. Norbert Waszek. Grenoble, Ellug, 2002.

Stein, Peter. *Legal Evolution: The Story of an Idea*. Cambridge, CUP, 1980.

———. *The Character and Influence of the Roman Civil Law*. London, Hambledon Press, 1988.

———. *Roman Law in European History*. Cambridge, CUP, 1999.

Steinberg, Michael. "The Twelve Tables and Their Origins: An Eighteenth-Century Debate." *Journal of the History of Ideas* 43 (1982): 379–96.

———. *Enlightenment Interrupted: The Lost Moment of German Idealism and the Reactionary Present*. Alresford, Hants. UK, John Hunt Publishing, 2014.

Steinberg, Oded Y. *Race, Nation, History: Anglo-German Thought in the Nineteenth Century*. Philadelphia, U of Pennsylvania Press, 2019.

———. "'Contesting Teutomania': Robert Gordon Latham, 'Race', Ethnology and Historical Migrations." *History of European Ideas* 47 (2021): 1331–47.

Stempel, Daniel. "Revelation on Mount Snowdon: Wordsworth, Coleridge and the Fichtean Imagination." *Journal of Aesthetics and Art Criticism* 29 (1971): 371–84.

Stepelevich, Lawrence S., ed. *The Young Hegelians: An Anthology*. Cambridge, CUP, 1983.

Stern, Fritz. *The Politics of Cultural Despair: A Study in the Rise of the Germanic Ideology*. Berkeley, U of California Press, 1961.

Sterrett, J. MacBride, ed. *The Ethics of Hegel: Translated Selections from his 'Rechtsphilosophie'.* Boston, 1893.

Stettner, Walter F. "Nineteenth-Century Public Debt Theories in Great Britain and Germany and Their Relevance for Modern Analysis." PhD thesis, Harvard University, 1944.

———. "Carl Dietzel, Public Expenditure and Public Debt." In *Income, Employment and Public Policy: Essays in Honor of Alvin H. Hansen,* ed. A. M. Lloyd, pp. 276–99. New York, Norton, 1948).

———. *Witness to a Changing World.* Huntingdon, WV, University Editions, 1999.

Stewart, Dugald. *An Account of the Life and Writings of Adam Smith* [1793]. In *Biographical Memoirs of Adam Smith, William Robertson and Thomas Reid,* ed. Sir William Hamilton. Edinburgh, 1858.

Straumann, Benjamin. *Roman Law in the State of Nature.* Cambridge, CUP, 2015.

———. *Crisis and Constitutionalism: Roman Political Thought from the Fall of the Republic to the Age of Revolution.* Oxford, OUP, 2016.

Strauss, Leo. *Natural Right and History.* Chicago, U of Chicago Press, 1953.

Strong, Tracy B. *Politics without Vision: Thinking without a Banister in the Twentieth Century.* Chicago, U of Chicago Press, 2012.

Sturn, Richard. "Public Credit, Capital and State Agency: Fiscal Responsibility in German-Language Finanzwissenschschaft." Graz Schumpeter Centre, Discussion Paper Series, Paper 19. Graz, 2019.

Sukiennicka, Marta. "La palingénésie philosophique de Charles Bonnet: le pouvoir heuristique d'un imaginaire matérialiste des lumières." *Studi Romanica Posnaniensa* 44 (2017): 25–34.

Swart, Koenraad W. "Individualism in the Mid-Nineteenth Century (1826–1860)." *Journal of the History of Ideas* 23 (1962): 77–90.

Sweet, Paul R. "Wilhelm von Humboldt, Fichte, and the Ideologues (1794–1805): A Re-Examination." *Historiographia Linguistica* 15 (1988): 349–75.

Taylor, Michael W. *The Philosophy of Herbert Spencer.* London, Continuum, 2007.

Texte, Joseph. *La jeunesse d'Edgar Quinet et son enseignement à Lyon.* Lyon, 1897.

Thériault, Patrick, and Jean-Jacques Hamm, eds. *Composer avec la mort de Dieu; littérature et athéisme au xixe siècle.* Paris, Hermann, 2014.

Thom, Martin. "City, Region and Nation: Carlo Cattaneo and the Making of Italy." *Citizenship Studies* 3 (1999): 187–201.

Thomas, Yan. "Michel Villey, la romanistique et le droit romain." In his *Droit, nature, histoire,* pp. 31–41. Aix-Marseille, 1985.

Thompson, E. P. "Disenchantment or Default? A Lay Sermon" [1969]. In his *The Romantics: England in a Revolutionary Age,* pp. 33–74. New York, The New Press, 1997.

Tocqueville, Alexis de. "Political and Social Condition of France." *London and Westminster Review* 3 (1836): 137–69.

———. Reports (1842) to the Académie des sciences morales et politiques on I. Labastard Delisle, *De l'administration de la justice criminelle chez les Romains,* and Joseph-Laurent Couppey, *De l'administration de la justice criminelle en Normandie dans le Moyen Age.* In Alexis de Tocqueville, *Œuvres complètes,* vol. 16, ed. Françoise Mélonio, pp. 170–84. Paris, Gallimard, 1989.

———. "Rapport sur le cours de droit administratif de M. Macarel." *Séances et travaux de l'Académie des sciences morales et politiques* 9 (1846): 105–20.

———. *Œuvres complètes*. Ed. Françoise Mélonio and Anne Vibert. 3 vols. Paris, Gallimard, 2021.

Toews, John Edward. "The Immanent Genesis and Transcendent Goal of Law: Savigny, Stahl and the Ideology of the Christian German State." *American Journal of Comparative Law* 37 (1989): 139–69.

———. *Becoming Historical: Cultural Reformation and Public Memory in Early Nineteenth-Century Berlin*. Cambridge, CUP, 2004.

Tomasello, Federico. "Il governo della storia. La dottrina delle capacita politiche nel pensiero di François Guizot." In *Libertà, uguaglianza, democrazia nel pensiero politico europea (xvi–xxi secolo)*, ed. Rossella Bufano, pp. 131–48. Milella, Lecce, 2018.

Tönnies, Ferdinand. *Community and Civil Society* [1887]. Ed. Jose Harris. Cambridge, CUP, 2001.

Tortajada, Ramón, ed. *The Economics of Sir James Steuart*. London, Routledge, 1999.

Tosel, André, Pierre-François Moreau, and Jean Salem, eds. *Spinoza au xixe siècle*. Paris, Publications de la Sorbonne, 2007.

Touchard, Jean. *La gloire de Béranger*. 2 vols. Paris, Armand Colin, 1968.

Trawny, Peter. "The Future of Time: Reflections on the Concept of Time in Hegel and Heidegger." *Research in Phenomenology* 30 (2000): 12–39.

Treitschke, Heinrich von. *Gesellschaftswissenschaft, ein kritische Versuch*. Leipzig, 1859.

———. *Der Socialismus und seine Gönner*. Berlin, 1875.

Trentman, Frank, ed. *Paradoxes of Civil Society: New Perspectives on Modern German and British History*. 2nd ed. New York, Berghahn Books, 2003.

Tresch, John. "The Order of the Prophets: Series in Early French Social Science and Socialism." *History of Science* 48 (2010): 315–42.

Tribe, Keith. "'Das Adam Smith Problem' and the Origins of Modern Smith Scholarship." *History of European Ideas* 34 (2008): 514–25.

———. "The Political Economy of Modernity: Foucault's Collège de France Lectures of 1978 and 1979." *Economy and Society* 38 (2009): 679–98.

———. *The Economy of the Word: Language, History and Economics*. Oxford, OUP, 2015.

———. "Capitalism and Its Critics." In *The Cambridge Companion to Nineteenth-Century Thought*, ed. Gregory Claeys, pp. 123–40. Cambridge, CUP, 2019.

———. "The 'System of Natural Liberty': Natural Order in the *Wealth of Nations*." *History of European Ideas* 47, no. 3 (2020): 1–11.

Tronchon, Henri. *La fortune intellectuelle de Herder en France: la préparation*. Paris, Rieder, 1920.

———. "Une concurrence à la philosophie de l'histoire en France: la philosophie du droit." In *Mélanges offerts à M. Charles Andler par ses amis et ses élèves*, pp. 371–81. Strasbourg, 1924.

———. *Allemagne-France-Angleterre. Le jeune Edgar Quinet ou l'aventure d'un enthousiaste*. Paris, Les Belles Lettres, 1937.

Truwant, Simon. *Cassirer and Heidegger in Davos: The Philosophical Arguments*. Cambridge, CUP, 2022.

Tuck, Richard. *Natural Rights Theories*. Cambridge, CUP, 1979.

———. "The 'Modern' Theory of Natural Law." In *The Languages of Political Theory in Early Modern Europe*, ed. Anthony Pagden, pp. 99–119. Cambridge, CUP, 1987.

———. *Philosophy and Government 1572–1651*. Cambridge, CUP, 1993.

———. *The Rights of War and Peace: Political Thought and the International Order from Grotius to Kant.* Oxford, OUP, 1999.

———. *Free Riding.* Cambridge, MA, Harvard UP, 2008.

———. *The Sleeping Sovereign: The Invention of Modern Democracy.* Cambridge, CUP, 2015.

Tuori, Kaius, and Heta Björklund, eds. *Roman Law and the Idea of Europe.* London, Bloomsbury, 2019.

Tuozzolo, Claudio. *Emil Lask e la Logica della Storia.* Milan, Franco Angeli, 2004.

Tütken, Johannes. *Privatdozenten im Schatten der Georgia Augusta.* 2 vols. Göttingen, Universitätsverlag, Göttingen, 2005.

Vacano, Otto Wilhelm von. *The Etruscans in the Ancient World.* London, Edward Arnold, 1960.

Van Caenegem, R. C. *European Law in the Past and the Future.* Cambridge, CUP, 2002.

Vatin, François. "Pierre-Edouard Lemontey, l'invention de la sociologie du travail et la question salariale." *Revue de MAUSS* 27 (2006): 398–420.

———. "Romantisme économique et philosophie de la misère en France dans les années 1820–1840." *Romantisme* 133 (2006): 35–47.

Vatter, Miguel. "Liberal Governmentality and the Political Theology of Constitutionalism." In *Sovereignty in Action,* ed. Bas Leijssenaar and Neil Walker, pp. 115–43. Cambridge, CUP, 2019.

Vaughan, Henry Halford. *Two General Lectures on Modern History delivered on Inauguration, October 1849.* Oxford, 1849.

Vergeot, Jean-Baptiste. *Le crédit comme stimulant et régulateur de l'industrie: la conception saint-simonienne.* Paris, 1918.

Vial, Eugene. *Chenavard et Soulary. Discours de Réception, Académie des Sciences, Belles-Lettres et Arts de Lyon, 20 mai 1919.* Lyon, 1919.

Viala, Alain. *La France galante.* Paris, PUF, 2008.

Viallaneix, Paul. *La 'voie royale': essai sur l'idée du peuple dans l'oeuvre de Michelet* [1959]. Paris, Flammarion, 1971.

Viaud, Pierre. *Une humanité affranchie de Dieu au xix siècle.* Paris, Cerf, 1994.

Vidal, François. "Economie sociale—Les économistes de l'Institut—Monsieur Rossi." *Revue Indépendante* 10 (1845): 307–48.

Viereck, Peter. *Metapolitics* [1941]. New Brunswick, NJ, Transaction Books, 2004.

Vieweg, Klaus. *The Idealism of Freedom: For a Hegelian Turn in Philosophy.* Leiden, Brill, 2020.

Vigny, Alfred de. "Réflexions sur la vérité dans l'art." In *Cinq-Mars,* pp. 1–9. Paris, 1826.

Vijn, J. P. *Carlyle and Jean Paul: Their Spiritual Optics.* Amsterdam, Utrecht Publications in General and Comparative Literature, 1982.

Villers, Charles. Introduction to Immanuel Kant, *Idée de ce que pourrait être une histoire universelle dans les vues d'un citoyen du monde.* Hamburg, 1798.

Vincent, Andrew. *Modern Political Ideologies* [1992]. 2nd ed. Oxford, Blackwell, 1995.

Viner, Jacob. *The Customs Union Issue.* London, Carnegie Endowment for International Peace, 1950.

Vinet, Alexandre. Review of Emile Souvestre, *Riche et Pauvre. Le Semeur* 5, no. 49 (7 December 1836).

———. Review of Lamartine, "Jocelyne." *Le Semeur,* 5, no. 12 (23 March 1836): 89–94.

———. *Etudes sur la littérature française au dix-neuvième siècle.* 3 vols. Paris, 1849–51.

Vinogradoff, Paul. *Villainage in England.* Oxford, OUP, 1892.

———. *Outlines of Historical Jurisprudence*. 2 vols. Oxford, OUP, 1920.

Visconti, Katia. "Italian Celticisms: A Second (Unpublished) Version of Giovanni Fabbroni's *Antichi Abitatori d'Italia* (1803)." In *In Search of Pre-Classical Antiquity: Rediscovering Ancient Peoples in Mediterranean Europe (19th and 20th Centuries)*, ed. Antonino De Francesco, pp. 19–40. Leiden, Brill, 2017.

Vitet, Ludovic. *Etudes sur les beaux-arts*. 2 vols. Paris, 1846.

Walicki, Andrej. *Philosophy and Romantic Nationalism: The Case of Poland*. Oxford, OUP, 1982.

———. *Russia, Poland, and Universal Regeneration*. Notre Dame, IN, U of Notre Dame Press, 1991.

Walter, François. *Les figures paysagères de la nation. Territoire et paysage en Europe (16–20e)*. Paris, Editions de l'EHESS, 2004.

Waquet, Françoise. *Latin, or the Empire of a Sign* [1998]. London, Verso, 2001.

Warnock, Mary. *Imagination*. London, Faber, 1976.

Waszek, Norbert. "L'état de droit social chez Lorenz von Stein." In *Figures de l'état de droit: Le Rechtsstaat dans l'histoire intellectuelle et constitutionnelle de l'Allemagne*, ed. Olivier Jouanjan, pp. 193–217. Strasbourg, PU de Strasbourg, 2001.

———. "Lorenz von Stein: Propagateur du droit français en Allemagne, 'ambassadeur' officieux de la recherche juridique allemande en France." In *Influences et réceptions mutuelles du droit et de la philosophie en France et en Allemagne*, ed. Jean-François Kervégan and Heinz Mohnhaupt, pp. 379–403. Frankfurt, Vittorio Klostermann, 2001.

Weber, Max. *The History of Commercial Partnerships in the Middle Ages* [1889]. Trans. and ed. Lutz Kaelber. New York, Rowman and Littlefield, 2003.

Weil, Simone. "The Great Beast" [1939]. In Simone Weil, *Selected Essays 1939–1943* [1962], ed. Richard Rees. Eugene, OR, WIPF and Stock, 2015.

———. "Human Personality" [1950]. In Simone Weil, *An Anthology*, ed. Sian Miles, pp. 81–82. London, Virago Press, 1985. Penguin Classics, 2005.

———. *La personne et le sacré*. Paris, Editions Allia, 2020.

Weinstein, David, and Avihu Zakai. *Jewish Exiles and European Thought in the Shadow of the Third Reich; Baron, Popper, Strauss, Auerbach*. Cambridge, CUP, 2017.

Weitz, Eric D. *A World Divided: The Global Struggle for Human Rights in the Age of Nation-States*. Princeton, NJ, Princeton UP, 2019.

Weller, Shane. *The Idea of Europe: A Critical History*. Cambridge, CUP, 2021.

Whistler, Daniel. "Schelling's Politics of Sympathy: Reflections on *Clara* and Related Texts." *International Yearbook of German Idealism* 15 (2017): 245–68.

White Beck, Lewis. *Kant on History*. New York, Macmillan, 1963.

Whitman, James Q. *The Legacy of Roman Law in the German Romantic Era*. Princeton, NJ, Princeton UP, 1990.

———. *The Origins of Reasonable Doubt*. New Haven, CT, Yale UP, 2008.

Wilcox, John. "The Beginnings of *L'art pour l'art*." *Journal of Aesthetics and Art Criticism* 11 (1953): 360–77.

Wilford, Paul T., and Samuel A. Stoner, eds. *Kant and the Possibility of Progress: From Modern Hopes to Postmodern Anxieties*. Philadelphia, U of Pennsylvania Press, 2021.

Williams, Elizabeth A. *The Physical and the Moral: Anthropology, Physiology and Philosophical Medicine in France, 1750–1850*. Cambridge, CUP, 1994.

Williams, Howard. *Kant's Political Philosophy*. Oxford, Blackwell, 1983.

———. "Metamorphosis or Palingenesis? Political Change in Kant." *Review of Politics* 63 (2001): 693–722.

———. "Liberty, Equality and Independence: Core Concepts in Kant's Political Philosophy." In *A Companion to Kant*, ed. Graham Bird, pp. 364–82. Oxford, Blackwell, 2006.

Willm, Joseph. *Histoire de la philosophie allemande depuis Kant jusqu'à Hegel*. 4 vols. Paris, 1846–49.

Windelband, Wilhelm. *A History of Philosophy* [2nd ed., Leipzig, 1899]. 2 vols. New York, Harper Torchbook, 1958.

Wokler, Robert. "The Influence of Diderot on the Political Theory of Rousseau." *Studies on Voltaire and the Eighteenth Century* 132 (1975): 55–111.

———. *Rousseau on Society, Politics, Music and Language*. New York, Garland Press, 1987.

Wolowski, Louis. *Cours de législation industrielle*. Paris, 1840.

Wood, Allen. "Herder and Kant on History: Their Enlightenment Faith." In *Metaphysics and the Good: Themes from the Philosophy of Robert Merrihew Adams*, ed. Samuel Newlands and Larry M. Jorgensen, pp. 313–42. Oxford, OUP, 2009.

Woodmansee, Martha. "The Interests in Disinterestedness: Karl Philipp Moritz and the Emergence of the Theory of Aesthetic Autonomy in Eighteenth-Century Germany." *Modern Language Quarterly* 45 (1984): 22–47.

———. *The Author, Art, and the Market: Rereading the History of Aesthetics*. New York, Columbia UP, 1994.

Woodward, William R. *Hermann Lotze: An Intellectual Biography*. Cambridge, CUP, 2015.

Wootton, David. "The True Origins of Republicanism: The Disciples of Baron and the Counter-Example of Venturi." In *Il repubblicanismo moderno: l'idea de Repubblica nella riflessione storica de Franco Venturi*, ed. Manuela Albertone, pp. 271–304. Naples, Bibliopolis, 2006.

Wright, Julian. *Socialism and the Experience of Time: Idealism and the Present in Modern France*. Oxford, OUP, 2017.

Wulf, Naomi. *Une autre démocratie en Amérique: Orestes Brownson, un regard politique (1824–1845)*. Paris, PUPS, 2017.

Xifaras, Mikhaïl. "Droit rationnel et droit romain chez Kant. Note sur le Conflit des Facultés." In *Généalogies des savoirs juridiques contemporains. Le Carrefour des lumières*, ed. Mikhaïl Xifaras, pp. 123–50. Brussels, Bruylant, 2007.

———. "La *Veritas Juris* selon Raymond Saleilles. Remarques sur un projet de restauration du juridisme." *Droits* 47 (2008): 77–148.

Yilmaz, Levent. *Le temps moderne. Variations sur les anciens et les contemporains*. Paris, Gallimard, 2004.

Yonnet, Franck. "De l'utopie politique à la pratique bancaire: les frères Pereire, le Crédit mobilier et la construction du système bancaire moderne sous le Second Empire." In *Les traditions économiques françaises 1848–1939*, ed. Pierre Dockès et al., pp. 203–16. Paris, CNRS Editions, 2000.

Yuva, Ayşe. "La raison pure peut-elle être pratique? La figure du philosophe allemand au début du xixe siècle en France." In *France-Allemagne: figures de l'intellectuel entre révolution et réaction, 1780–1848*, ed. Anne Baillot and Ayşe Yuva, pp. 115–33. Lille, PU du Septentrion, 2014.

————. *Transformer le monde? L'efficace de la philosophie en temps de révolution: France-Allemagne, 1794–1815.* Paris, Fondation Maison des Sciences de l'Homme 2016.

————. "Effets politiques et frontières culturelles de l'histoire de la philosophie au xixe siècle." In *Faire de l'histoire de la philosophie, ou les présents du passé,* ed. Chantal Jaquet, pp. 61–75. Paris, Garnier, 2020.

Zaleski, Z. L. "Edgar Quinet et Auguste Cieszkowski." In *Mélanges d'histoire littéraire générale et comparée offerts à Fernand Baldensperger,* 2 vols., 2:361–71. Paris, Champion, 1930.

Zammito, John H. "Stealing Herder's Thunder: Kant's Debunking of Herder on History in 'Conjectural Beginning of the Human Race.'" In *Immanuel Kant,* ed. Günther Lottes and Uwe Steiner, pp. 43–72. Saarbrücken, Wehrhahn, 2007.

————. "Philosophy of History: The German Tradition from Herder to Marx." In *The Cambridge History of Philosophy in the Nineteenth Century,* ed. Allen W. Wood and Songsuk Susan Hahn, pp. 817–65. Cambridge, CUP, 2012.

————. *The Gestation of German Biology: Philosophy and Physiology from Stahl to Schelling.* Chicago, U of Chicago Press, 2018.

Ziegler, Thomas. *La question sociale est une question morale.* Paris, 1893.

Zöller, Günter. "From Critique to Metacritique: Fichte's Transformation of Kant's Absolute Idealism." In *The Reception of Kant's Critical Philosophy,* ed. Sally Sedgwick, pp. 129–46. Cambridge, CUP, 2000.

INDEX

Abbt, Thomas, 183–84

Acton, John Emmerich Edward Dalberg, xv

administration, 244–45, 254–55, 495; and administrative law, 487–89; and constitution, 495. *See also* Hegel; Stein; Tocqueville

adunation, 195

aesthetics, 182, 200, 316, 344; and aesthetic education, 196–204; and aesthetic state, 180, 204; and history, 344

Agamben, Giorgio, 17–18

agrarian laws, 362–63, 364–65

Ahrens, Heinrich, 369, 370–89, 391–92, 395, 396, 398, 402, 407, 409, 410, 411, 457, 471, 490, 491, 492; Bluntschli on, 391–93; and International Welfare Congress, 382; on Kant, 384–86; on Roman law, 378–82; on Rousseau, 389

Aignan, Etienne, 100–104, 105, 106, 487

Albrecht, Wilhelm Eduard, 394, 395

Almain, Jacques, 109, 110

Althusius, Johannes, 406

altruism, 58

Amiel, Henri-Frédéric, 314–15; on Krause, 386

ancients, and moderns, ix, x, 22–23, 75–85, 106–11, 127, 137, 139, 200–204, 319, 322, 332, 334, 355–56, 362, 388–89, 405, 417–18, 424, 426, 469–71, 480–81, 484, 490, 496. *See also* classic; history; philosophy of history; romance

Ancillon, Friedrich, 279

Andler, Charles, 401

Arendt, Hannah, 9, 218, 229–33, 235

aristocracy, 427. *See also* Whig interpretation of history

Aristotle, 182, 232, 237, 275, 288, 460

Arnold, Thomas, 419

art, 123, 179–80, 187, 197, 204, 212, 224, 225, 226–28, 299–300, 313–14, 317, 319, 322, 326, 327–28, 353–55; for art's sake, 192. *See also* Constant; Hugo; Humboldt; Schelling; Schiller; Staël; Vigny

associations (voluntary), 369, 381–82, 383, 388, 403, 404, 406, 412

Athens, 425, 463

Augustine, Saint, 319

Austin, John, 440, 450, 474, 475, 485

authority, 330, 422, 426, 451; and liberty, 167, 175, 412; and sovereignty, 451

autonomy, xii, 1, 2–3, 27, 84, 119–20, 141, 158, 168, 174, 175–76, 177–80, 196, 198–99, 200, 214, 215–19, 226, 227, 229–36, 245–46, 247, 250, 251, 313, 317, 362, 395, 405, 407, 428–29, 437, 461, 471, 481, 490, 496; and autonomism, 478, 483; and imagination, 190–96

Baader, Franz, 98

Babeuf, François-Noel (Gracchus), 362

Babeuf, Louis-Pierre, 220

Ballanche, Pierre-Simon, 64–67, 71, 376, 416

Balzac, Honoré de, 171

Barante, Prosper de, 78, 290

barbarism, 281–84, 299, 332, 345, 427

Barbeyrac, Jean, 105

Barchou de Penhouen, Auguste, 272

Baron, Hans, 232–34

CPSIA information can be obtained
at www.ICGtesting.com
Printed in the USA
JSHW021212210523
42003JS00002B/3